Reading Our Histories, Understanding Our Cultures

Chapter Editors

KERRY BECKFORD
University of Hartford

SHERRY HORTON
University of Hartford

DONALD JONES
University of Hartford

EDWARD KLONOSKI
Charter Oak State College

CHARLES LIPKA
University of Hartford

LETA MARKS
University of Hartford

SUSHIL OSWAL
University of Hartford

CYNTHIA REIK
University of Hartford

ALAN G. SCHMIDT
Freelance writer and musician

SALLY TERRELL
Tunxis Community-Technical College

Reading Our Histories, Understanding Our Cultures:

A Sequenced Approach to Thinking, Reading, and Writing

General Editor
Kathleen McCormick
University of Hartford

Allyn and Bacon

Boston   London   Toronto   Sydney   Tokyo   Singapore

Vice President: Eben W. Ludlow
Editorial Assistant: Tania Sanchez/Linda D'Angelo
Markering Manager: Lisa Kimball
Production Admistrator: Mary Beth Finch
Editorial-Production Service: Modern Graphics, Inc.
Cover Administrator: Linda Knowles
Composition Buyer: Linda Cox
Manufacturing Buyer: Suzanne Lareau
Electronic Composition: Modern Graphics, Inc.

Library of Congress Cataloging-in-Publication Data
Reading our histories, understanding our cultures : a sequenced
    approach to thinking, reading, and writing / general editor,
    Kathleen McCormick; Charles Lipka . . . [et al .] .
        p.   cm.
    Includes bibliographical references and index.
    ISBN 0-205-26176-0 (pbk.)
    1. English language—Rhetoric   2. Critical thinking—Problems,
exercises, etc.   3. Report writing—Problems, exercises, etc.
4. College readers.   I. McCormick, Kathleen.   II. Lipka, Charles.
PE1408.R3827   1998
808' .0427—dc21
                                                            98-40539
                                                            CIP

Printed in the United States of America

10 9 8 7 6 5 4 3   RRDV   03 02 01 00

CONTENTS

2   Fashion: Selves and Surfaces   49
Sherry Horton and Kathleen McCormick

∿∿∿∿

PART II
Absorbing Stories, Creating Identities

3   Family Portraits: Changing Roles   119
Donald Jones and Kerry Beckford

4   Beauties and Beasts: The Tales Within Us   194
Leta Marks

5   Questioning U.S. High Schools: What to Teach and How to Learn   266
Sherry Horton and Donald Jones

6   Elvis Presley: Any Way You Want Me (That's How I Will Be)   338
Alan G. Schmidt

PART III
Contesting People, Contested Spaces

7   The American City: Dreams and Nightmares   403
Sally Terrell and Cynthia Reik

8   Galileo to Gates: Human Reactions to Technology   466
Edward Klonoski

9   Progress or Destruction? Developing the Environment   530
Sushil K. Oswal

LIST OF FIGURES

PREFACE

The United States is a country of conflicting perspectives. At almost any moment, we can open a newspaper or magazine or turn on the television or radio and witness people talking about different sides of an issue. But we do not always possess a wide spectrum of adequate ways of understanding or negotiating the complex positions people occupy and the often radically diverse practices and belief systems that underlie these differences. Students come to college familiar with popular representations of conflict that are often oversimplified and tend to extremes: They have seen differences discussed in terms of hierarchies, inferior and superior, absolute right and wrong, black and white. In such a context, the atmosphere of debate and discussion is often highly charged. Conflict is represented as titillating to witness, dangerous to engage in, and often insurmountable. Or conflict appears to have a "winner" and a "loser" when, in fact, differences exist and are perpetuated and people "win" and "lose" as a result of highly complex and often contradictory cultural and historical forces.

Because such oversimplified representations of conflict are so widespread, many students entering a university environment (regardless of their age) have had little experience with more detailed and subtle ways of analyzing competing perspectives—to ask *why* they exist, to inquire into their historical antecedents and implications, or to find out how they are connected to other perspectives and issues—in the present and in the past. Such inquiry is essential if students are to enter the intellectual worlds of colleges and universities and if they are to make interventions in the world, taking up positions of their own that they can understand, contextualize, and defend. This book offers students an accessible model for critically reading and analyzing the varied texts around them—whether these texts are written or visual—and for developing and critically evaluating their own perspectives in writing.

Historical and Cultural Analysis

The model we offer in this book falls under the rubric of cultural studies. But to help clarify the complexity of cultural studies methodology for first-year students, we divide this model into two parts: *historical analysis* and *cultural analysis*.

1. *Historical analysis* asks students to relate the values, practices, or beliefs of a text they are reading to those of a *different time period* from that in which the text was produced.

2. *Cultural analysis* asks students to relate the values, practices, or beliefs of a text they are reading to other ideas, beliefs, or practices from the *same time period* in which the text was produced.

Let us discuss each of these in turn, exploring their distinctions and complementarities.

Historical Analysis: Analysis Across Time

When we look at a subject *historically*, we come to see that perspectives on it have developed *over time*, as they come to be interpreted within different social and political or ideological frameworks. Historical analysis is more than pretending one is "back in time"; it is rather the active movement back and forth from the present to the past, or from the implied present to a comparison between two different points in the past. So, for example, Chapter 2 asks students to compare Amelia Bloomer's attitudes about female clothing in an article written in 1851 with attitudes they have today and attitudes presented by Marjorie Garber in 1995. This study of the ways in which values, attitudes, and beliefs develop across time is what we call historical analysis. See Figure 1.

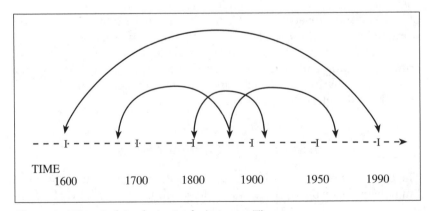

Figure 1: Historical Analysis: Analysis Across Time

Advantages of Historical Analysis

Using texts from the past to develop close reading strategies. In Chapter 2, we introduce students to the concept of *symptomatic reading.* They are asked to read texts not only for what they are literally saying but for symptoms of larger cultural tensions that the texts may only allude to indirectly but that are nonetheless underpinning the text's arguments. While this kind of close reading is sometimes difficult for students to perform on contemporary texts, it becomes much easier when students work with texts from the past whose underlying assumptions are more obvious because they are different from those of the present. After students gain practice developing symptomatic readings of older texts—and we have carefully chosen some in every chapter that lend themselves to this kind of reading—they can then use these close reading strategies on contemporary texts and on their own positions.

Discovering where present points of view may have had their origins. Finding *similarities* between past and contemporary perspectives leads students to discover where their present points of view had their origins. Many of the beliefs and assumptions that we think of as "ours" in the present have complex origins deep within our culture's past. This history influences our points of view without our being fully aware of it. In Chapter 5 on high school, for example, students discover that contemporary debates about what an "equal" education is are rooted in arguments that began over one hundred years ago. Does an equal high school education give all students the same college preparatory training, as was argued in 1893? Does it give students different training, depending on their abilities and interests, as was argued in 1918? In many respects, answers to this question have remained remarkably similar over the last hundred years, although social conditions have changed dramatically. By studying some of the historical antecedents of contemporary questions about high school education and by analyzing the implications of given answers for particular groups in the past, students can investigate more critically the implications of those same answers for people today.

Questioning the apparent universality of one's own points of view. Finding *differences* between the past and the present—for example, learning in Chapter 3 that the family of the seventeenth century was very different from the family of today—encourages students to question the apparent universality of their own points of view as they see that past perspectives can be rooted in very different assumptions from those they take for granted. This in turn leads students into cultural analysis in which they investigate the situatedness—the cultural embeddedness—of their own perspectives.

Cultural Analysis: Analysis of Issues within the Same Time Period

The other perspective we take is *cultural.* When we engage in cultural analysis, it is as if as we were social scientists taking a cross-section of a culture's development and examining the complex interrelationships of various attitudes and beliefs within a culture at a *single period of time.* While a historical analysis of Amelia Bloomer asks students to compare Bloomer's attitudes about female clothing from 1851 with attitudes from the present (see Figure P.1), a cultural analysis explores Bloomer's attitudes in relation to those of her peers, the ministers, newspaper editors, and fellow feminists of her day and in relation to the larger values of her particular cultural period. This study of the ways in which values, attitudes, and beliefs from any single time period complement, reinforce, contradict, or work against each other is what we call cultural analysis. See Figure 2.

Advantages of Cultural Analysis

Avoiding simplistic "right/wrong" arguments. Chapter 2 introduces students to the concept of *overdetermination*—that no one particular social factor in itself causes people to take up certain positions. Any situation is over-determined, that is, people encounter such a wealth of complex and con-tradictory ideological forces that they must continually negotiate among them. For example, the very diverse ideologies of democracy, work, and gender differentiation all interacted to create a general acceptance in the nineteenth century of men's wearing pants and less ornate clothing. (See Chapter 2.) No one of these alone can be said to have caused men's fashion to change. Discovering such connections among some of the forces of a cultural period gives students a sense of the complex interweaving of dif-ferent aspects of a culture and enables them to move away from simplistic right/wrong or cause and effect analyses.

One of the major goals of cultural analysis is to help students see any text they read or issue they address as part of an intricate prism or a tapestry, rather than, say, a tug of war between two sides. There are no

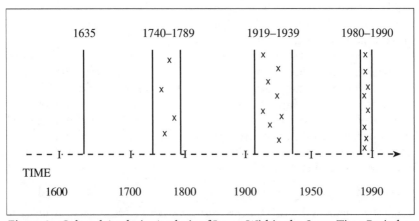

Figure 2: Cultural Analysis: Analysis of Issues Within the Same Time Period

simple answers to the questions of why Galileo was asked to recant by the Catholic church in 1633 (see Chapter 8) or why Elvis Presley became "the King of Rock and Roll" in the second half of the twentieth century (see Chapter 6). To understand phenomena as different as the fall of Galileo or the rise of Elvis Presley, one must inquire into the values, practices, and belief systems of the particular times in which these figures lived. This book contains interrelated readings and provides writing questions that encourage students to think about cultural periods in complex ways. If you or your students become particularly interested in the details of a certain period, we offer a bibliography at the end of each chapter and further references in the *Instructor's Manual.* It is from this model of cultural complexity that students learn to develop more complex argumentative skills in writing.

Moving from judgmental positions to analytical positions. The goal of the dominant ideology of any society is to encourage its members to accept certain differences and hierarchies within that culture as "natural" and "normal" rather than to see them as the product of complex power and ideological relations. This naturalizing of a dominant viewpoint—whether that one group is better than another, or one type of lifestyle is correct and all others are aberrations—encourages judgmental stances and can close off people's minds to perspectives other than their own. An important part of a liberal education is learning about a multiplicity of perspectives. Cultural analysis moves students away from dismissive, judgmental positions toward more reflective and analytical positions by asking them and giving them a way to understand *why* different perspectives exist.

Chapter 2 introduces students to Raymond Williams's concepts of dominant, residual, and emergent elements within a society's ideology, and we use these concepts throughout the book. Understanding these concepts gives students a rich and alternative way to grasp and analyze difference within a single cultural period—particularly the present, in which issues are often most contentious and about which students often find the most difficulty being open-minded and reflective. The book does not require that students take up one particular viewpoint on any subject but, rather, repeatedly asks them to take seriously a variety of beliefs, values, and expectations by trying to understand why each has been given a certain status within a certain time period.

This book is filled with examples of authors—from the dominant culture and from parallel cultures—analyzing some of the material consequences of the subject position they or others have been accorded by the dominant culture. Cornel West, an African American professor, writes of waiting for a taxi in New York City and repeatedly not being picked up while other white men and women were (Chapter 7). Richard Goldstein, senior editor of *The Village Voice,* explores the implications for lesbians and gay men of not being allowed legally to marry (Chapter 3). Cynthia

Riggs, writing for Exxon, argues in open distinction to environmentalists that she believes the U.S. government needs access to private lands to give the country greater access to raw materials, while Ted Trainer, a Green Activist, advocates a total rejection of affluence and growth (Chapter 9). Sherry Turkle, a professor of Sociology of Science at MIT and a former Woman of the Year, uses a variety of psychological models to illustrate how our thinking about artificial intelligence has influenced our thinking about human intelligence (Chapter 8). Angela Carter writes an alternative version to *Beauty and the Beast* in which Beauty, not the Beast, metamorphosizes (Chapter 4).

Visual texts from "Anatomy of a Shredder" to an 1850s cartoon of women in Bloomers (Chapter 2) to versions of American families (Chapter 3) to Elvis Presley show photos (Chapter 6) to Currier and Ives' "Across the Continent" (Chapter 9) challenge students to explore why particular attitudes and beliefs—and particular peoples—gain dominance at particular points in history.

Discovering differences across time. Recognizing conflicts and contradictions within the same time period. Connecting a particular issue to other issues. Tracing how it is woven into the larger cultural and social fabric. Making different connections at different points. This is where genuine critical inquiry begins. It is where this book begins.

ᘇ

Integrating Historical and Cultural Analysis

Within cultural studies, the distinction between what we are calling historical and cultural analysis would be more blurred than we present it. Clearly, the two forms of analysis are complementary: once one, say, has explored differences over time (what we call historical analysis), one will probably want to analyze a particular cultural period that helped to launch certain changes (what we call cultural analysis). Further, there comes a point where one of the forms of analysis could turn into the other: for example, the cultural cross-section one might decide to study could become so wide that it would come to involve historical analysis.

By the end of each chapter in various assignment sequences, we ask students to blend aspects of the two types of analyses. However, given students' relative lack of familiarity with cultural studies and given the need to teach a variety of quite distinct reading and writing skills in a freshman course, we find it more useful to break these down in our general model and in the post-reading questions so that students gain practice closely analyzing one particular area before they have to link it with another.

Redefining the Personal through Historical and Cultural Analysis

The nature of inquiry throughout this book is meant to engage students' personal interests, but, in the process, to reconceptualize "the personal" within larger social contexts. The place, in fact, where students may have developed the most complex understanding of the assumptions and beliefs underlying diverse perspectives is in their personal experiences, and it is there that we begin. We treat students' perspectives seriously, and we give students the option of writing about their perspectives in their reading of nearly every text. But we also ask students to critically analyze their own perspectives just as they would analyze those they read about. Thus students are asked to explore some of the historical antecedents of their positions. They are asked to determine how their perspectives relate to contemporary dominant or emergent culture in the United States. And they are asked to analyze how their relation to the dominant or the emergent affects their sense of themselves and others. In these ways, the personal becomes redefined as social.

Enabling Students to Develop Positions of their own after Analyzing the Complexity of Issues

We do not want to discourage students from taking a stand, from having an agenda, and from developing their own perspectives, but we want them to do so, finally, with an understanding of the complexity of the issues involved in any topic. While we ask students to write about their own perspectives at various stages in the historical and cultural questions throughout a chapter, our questions allow them room to grow, to change their mind, to interrogate their own positions. Once students have explored a topic from historical as well as cultural points of view, they are then ready to write essays that take up informed positions because they have begun to grasp the antecedents and the implications of the many perspectives that exist on the topic. The assignment sequences at the end of each chapter give students an opportunity to write complex position papers.

∾

The Texts Included and the Book's Organization

Reading Our Histories, Understanding Our Cultures includes texts from a wide variety of written and visual genres—essays, advertisements, music, poetry, photographs, paintings, biography, fiction—and we offer many suggestions for the use of video and audio texts. The critical skills taught by this book are applicable to texts of all kinds, and we want to give students the opportunity to experience analyzing as diverse a group of texts as possible. After the first chapter, every chapter contains a selection of texts spanning a significant historical spectrum up to the present, and students are given the opportunity to develop historical and cultural analyses of these texts individually and in various groupings.

Part I, "I and Ideology," introduces students to the methodology of the book. Chapter 1, "Locating Ourselves in History and Culture," does this in a sequence of assignments about personal conflict. Because one of the most important motivating factors for students to engage in critical thinking and writing is personal investment and interest, in this opening chapter we enable students to learn about historical and cultural analysis in the context of writing about their own personal experiences. Students are repeatedly asked not only what they think, but *why* they think something. "What are the effects on others of your positions?" "Why do other people think differently from you?" "What is the dominant view on your conflict within our society?" "Do you regard yourself as part of the dominant?" Questions such as these encourage students to begin to look more critically at the ways in which their own positioning in the world—their age, their gender, their religion, their race, and so on—encourage them to take up one perspective over another. The answers students develop to these questions can help them determine whether they want to maintain or resist certain positionings.

Chapter 2, "Fashion: Selves and Surfaces," provides a transition from Chapter 1 to the rest of the book: It explicitly introduces concepts of historical and cultural analysis and demonstrates ways of applying the critical skills taught in Chapter 1 to reading and writing about visual and printed texts. It walks students through the format that the rest of the chapters in the book follow, and it provides an in-depth discussion of some critical terminology—such as ideology, symptomatic reading, parallel cultures, and dominant, residual, and emergent cultural forces—that is used throughout the rest of the book. This chapter's strong focus on fashion and on the visual provides students with an area of study with which they will feel familiar and generally expert, but it contains some challenging readings as well. Fashion has an "ordinary" quality about it, and it can demonstrate that even the most everyday activity, such as getting dressed, has meanings and histories, enacts conflicts, and needs to be read critically. (Should the instructor not wish to teach the topic of fashion, the Instructor's Manual contains suggestions on alternative ways to introduce students to the critical concepts explained within it.)

The rest of the book relies on materials presented in Chapters 1 and 2. Following Part I, the book is divided into two other parts. While instructors will no doubt pick and choose among topics that interest them and their students, Parts II and III are organized to begin with subjects with which students are familiar but which they may not have thought about historically or culturally, and then to move gradually to subjects with which students may be less immediately connected.

In Part II, "Absorbing Stories, Creating Identities," *absorbing* is meant to have two meanings: an *absorbing* story is an interesting and captivating one, but *absorbing* also means taking in, both consciously and unconsciously, the values and beliefs of our surroundings. We learns stories about family, gender, about whether we will succeed in school, or in life, and these stories help to create our identities. Chapters in this section help students gain more control over the stories they absorb.

In Chapter 3, "Family Portraits: Changing Roles," we address a major arena in which most people have struggled to form their identity. The family is a topic that students know a lot about first hand, but which they may not have considered from a historical or cultural perspective. The chapter asks students to analyze some of the factors that underlie the variety of family portraits they discover both within a single historical period and across time.

Chapter 4, "Beauties and Beasts: The Tales within Us," looks at a familiar story—one that has been rewritten in virtually every culture—and asks students to explore the stories it tells us about gender, social class, and human sexuality. Chapter 5 explores what is taught and how students learn in high school, and encourages students to consider historical as well as current debates surrounding high school. It explores the various stories we have told ourselves about the purpose of high school and the impact those stories have had on individual lives.

Chapter 6, "Elvis Presley: Any Way You Want Me (That's How I Will Be)," focuses in on one individual life—that of a man who became a cultural icon. Whether readers are Elvis fans or not, the chapter provides startling accounts of how a man absorbed the many and often conflicting stories—of race, regionality, the American Dream, and masculinity—told to him by a constantly changing public. Offering numerous suggestions of audio and visual texts to accompany the written texts of the chapter, "Elvis" seeks to address the ways in which all of our identities are formed by absorbing the stories around us.

Part III of the book, "Contesting People, Contested Spaces," broadens the scope of inquiry further and asks students to explore the ways in which people construct and are constructed by the spaces in which we live, whether these are geographical, institutional, technological, or industrial. Chapter 7, "The American City: Dreams and Nightmares," looks at different views of U.S. urban living spaces. It explores why people live in cities and why the city is a source of both fear and excitement for so many people.

While technology may seem an especially contemporary topic, Chapter 8, "Galileo to Gates: Human Reactions to Technology," demonstrates that social and political uses of science and technology have complex histories. This chapter juxtaposes the responses to and the uses of Galileo's telescope with the responses to and uses of computers and networks today. It asks whether computers and networks may change the way we define ourselves, our world, and our place in it as dramatically as Galileo's telescope changed these ideas and concepts in the seventeenth century.

Chapter 9, "Progress or Destruction? Developing the Environment," asks students to analyze the varied relationships to the land we have had from Colonial America to the present. Why is the land frequently represented as female? As something that needs to be tamed? What did development mean in eighteenth-century Colonial America? What does it mean today? The chapter encourages students to inquire into the environmental implications of a variety of their current behaviors and practices—from shopping to showering—and to link these behaviors with larger values of capitalism, consumption, and development in our country.

The three parts of the book ask students questions that require them to think critically about different perspectives, to explore their antecedents and implications, and to discover how they are connected to other perspectives and issues in the present and in the past. But they do so in three somewhat different arenas: personal conflict, the larger social contexts in which identities are made, and the spaces in which we live. These arenas move back and forth from the personal to increasingly larger worlds.

∾

Editorial Apparatus

Every chapter begins with a brief *introduction* to the material that includes one or two *fastwrite questions* asking students to quickly put down on paper some of their personal experiences and ideas about the topic. Other fastwrite questions occur at various points throughout each chapter, both to alter the pacing and to make students more comfortable with communicating their ideas in writing. While personal response and the expression of personal feelings is not a good stopping point for a freshman composition class, it is still a good starting point, and the use of personal experience to launch historical and cultural analysis is a key feature of this book. There then follows a selection of texts spanning a significant historical spectrum. We have chosen texts that we think play off each other in interesting and exciting ways in their points of contrast and continuity and that will, therefore, encourage students' critical inquiry.

After each reading selection, there are two sets of questions: historical and cultural. The *Historical Questions* ask students to relate some aspect of the text they are reading to a value, practice, or belief of a different time period. The *Cultural Questions* ask students to relate the ideas of a text they are reading to other ideas or practices from the same time period. These questions ask students to do close readings for what the text explicitly says and for what it might be implying or assuming without directly articulating. They ask students to compare the text they are reading either with other texts included in the chapter or with the students' own experiences, and thus explicitly encourage students to make more and more connections with each selection they read. Finally, these questions encourage students to continue to articulate their own developing perspectives on the issue by using the texts to situate their perspective historically and culturally.

At the end of each chapter there are two *Assignment Sequences*. These sequences build on some of the links students will have developed in the historical and cultural questions of the chapter. Each sequence has three parts. It begins with a fairly detailed *Essay Question*, which is the primary question of the sequence. This question is new and integrates historical and cultural analysis, but it is drawn from a key set of issues that has been developing throughout the chapter. Then the sequence recommends *Review Questions* from a selection of the chapter's postreading questions that relate to the overarching question. Finally, it provides *Questions for Further Reflection*. These questions are meant to reinforce the points about revision made in Chapter 1—that genuine revision is not simply line-editing or piecing together previously written shorter pieces but rather the active rethinking and reconsideration of the work read and written thus far. The questions for further reflection guide students so that what they write in answer to the primary question will, in fact, be a genuine revision of what they have written previously. We also offer *For Further Research*, a bibliography, at the end of each chapter that includes visual as well as written texts.

The organization of the assignment sequences is helpful for students and teachers alike. While there is plenty of room for teachers to make up their own sequences or to choose a subset from the recommended questions, the list provides a possible starting point (particularly for new teachers) for selecting some of the postreading questions they might assign their students. We also provide further suggestions in the Instructor's Manual for teachers to build their own assignment sequences, depending on the needs and interests of students.

Requiring that students reflect on particular postreading questions within the sequence demonstrates the need to work gradually over a period of time to know enough about one's own position and those of others to

even begin to develop an answer to a larger question. The questions for
further reflection provide a space in which students can transform the
material they have read and studied—in which they can integrate it, synthesize it, and develop a particular take on it—for a rhetorical purpose of
their own.

We recognize the difficulty as well as the importance for most college
freshmen of taking this step of transforming information for a purpose of
their own. Indeed, it is the major goal of every chapter and of every assignment sequence. The careful combination of historical and cultural analysis,
the consistent integration of personal experience with analysis, culminating
in an assignment sequence that requires reflection, synthesis, and transformation of previous work—these, we believe, enable students to develop
positions of their own in dialogue with those of others whose antecedents
they understand and whose implications they can defend.

ᕰ

Our Creation and Your Use of
Reading Our Histories, Understanding Our Cultures

Like other cultural practices and texts, this book also has a distinctive
history and a distinctive cultural place. It grew from collaborative work
by a group of teachers of the University of Hartford's first-year reading
and writing courses mounted by the Department of Rhetoric, Language,
and Culture from 1994 onwards. Its distinctive history reflects struggles
and contradictions in defining what a freshman student needs in the last
decade of the twentieth century as he or she looks into the twenty-first.
Our students at the University of Hartford and at other institutions in
which some of the contributors have taught or currently teach are future-
oriented and need analysis of both the complex present in which they live
and the equally complex pasts that have produced and continued to influence them.

As a group, we came to the University of Hartford with our own
different histories—personal, institutional, and intellectual. We have
taught at a variety of colleges and universities—from community colleges,
to small liberal arts colleges, to state schools, to research institutions. Our
theoretical orientations run the gamut from classical rhetorical to expres-
sivist, to new rhetorical, to cultural studies, with a number of hybrids in
between. And yet we found that while our approaches vary, our goals are
quite consistent.

Like many composition teachers across America, we wanted our students to read, think, and write critically and analytically about their own
perspectives and those of others. We want them to connect texts studied

in class with other texts and contexts and to be able to transform these texts to create arguments of their own. And yet none of the books we were using and none of the approaches we were trying were as successful as we would have liked in helping students to achieve these goals. We developed the methodology in *Reading Our Histories, Understanding Our Cultures* to help us better meet the traditional intellectual goals of freshman composition courses. Every reading and writing assignment in this book has been user-tested in a number of different classrooms. The collaborative authors of the book argued, discussed, debated, tested, rethought, and reinterpreted all of the texts and the various assignments in this book, and the result is a book that is not merely conceptually, but also practically, distinctive and useful.

Because this book is written by a team of teachers, readers will find that, within the general framework, we have somewhat different emphases, assignments, and approaches. We think this is all to the good. We know that teachers using this book will want to interpret it and use it in a variety of ways, depending on their theoretical orientation, their institutional demands, and their students' capabilities and interests. The range of assignments we offer throughout the book and our more extended discussion of them in the Instructor's Manual suggest the flexibility of the general framework of the book, its capacity both to be shaped by a variety of different theoretical approaches and to provide a coherent strand of emphasis among them as we move back and forth between the present and the past.

Although we emphasize the importance of the past, we cannot keep our students solely in the historical where tensions, however powerful, are blunted because of temporal distance. Finally, we need to return with them to the contemporary, to the many debates on the radio shows, on television, in cities, on the Internet, and in the classroom—debates that may grip, amuse, challenge, or, at times, even frighten us. But we need to help our students return to these debates with a sense of difference, not to take a quick stand on them or to switch them off, but with a capacity to extend the context in which they conceptualize them and with an ability to connect them to other debates in other moments in our multiple and contradictory histories and cultures.

ACKNOWLEDGEMENTS

We would like to begin by thanking Lori Smith, the Allyn and Bacon book representative, who, in the fall of 1994, when we couldn't find a book to meet our needs, suggested that we write one of our own. Lori supported us through the early stages of the conception of the book and helped to introduce us to many of the people at Allyn and Bacon with whom we have worked so closely over the last few years.

The process of collaboration, of moving from a program to a book has taken us four years, and we are grateful for the help and support of many people. Our Rhetoric, Language, and Culture department chair, Bernard denOuden has offered endless support for this project and has understood the time and energy that it takes to work persistently on a large collaborative project. We want to thank our Dean, Ed Gray, who has endorsed our work across the university, and who has granted me the leaves necessary to complete the book in a timely fashion. Our Dean of Faculty, Catherine Stevenson, and our Associate Provost, Chuck Colarulli, have helped our writing program in our efforts to work collaboratively with faculty across our university. The feedback we have had from our colleagues in other programs has helped to shape this book in a number of ways.

Our librarians, Kitty Tynan, Jean Prescott, and Kim Farrington, have offered us much assistance in our research. Karen Attmore, our department secretary, has helped at every stage of this project—and we are extremely grateful to her. Cynthia Reik offers special thanks to Fred Pfeil for work on the City chapter. Kerry Beckford wants to thank Oswald and Gloria Beckford, Kimberly Beckford, Christopher and Leanne Beckford, and Nora Kirkland and Frances Grant for their continual support of her work. Robert Logan, of our English Department, has been supportive of our project and has consistently taught in the RLC program. We thank you, Bob, for your continued support.

Allyn and Bacon has been helpful to us at every stage of this project. We particularly want to thank Eben Ludlow, our editor, for his continued faith in and support of our work. Eben, you know when to step in and when to let us just get on with it, and we are grateful for your willingness to work with such a large collaborative group. Linda D'Angelo has been consistently available to help us with issues large and small, and we are all grateful to her. The production team Mary Beth Finch put together worked well, and we are indebted to the hard work and dedication of each member and, in particular, to Laurie Frankenthaler, our photo researcher.

We want to thank all of the reviewers of the book at its various stages.: Kathleen Shine Cain, Merrimack College; William A. Covino, Florida Atlantic University; Kathy Evertz, University of Wyoming; Joseph Harris, University of Pittsburgh; Lee Jacobus, University of Connecticut; Eileen I. Oliver, Washington State University; George Otte, Baruch College, CUNY; Hephzibah Roskelly, University of North Carolina; Irwin Weiser, Purdue University. Your positive and critical comments enabled us to see the book from new angles and aided tremendously in our revision process. In particular, we want to thank Hephzibah Roskelly, who identified herself to me as a reviewer, for her strong support and enthusiasm for the project.

Special thanks also go to Andrea Lunsford, Jerry Graff, and Lois Fowler for their continual support of my work, and to Ann Policelli, Mary Mackley, and the Connecticut Writing Project for giving me the opportunity to think about ways of adapting my work—and many of the ideas in this book—for students in the schools in all grade levels. Working with Connecticut teachers in the Writing Project has given me a space to try out many of the ideas we were developing for the book and to have them critiqued. In this process, I have learned much about ways of conceptualizing reading and writing from a variety of alternative approaches.

Special thanks go to Andrew Waller and all of his photo studio crew who came through in the final hour. I feel that my nine-year-old son, Philip Waller, has grown up during the process of my writing this book. No longer does he just ask me to stop working—though, luckily, he still suggests this regularly—but he also, perhaps because he has become a prolific reader and a good writer himself during the last three years, now asks me serious and engaging questions about the book. I am grateful, Philip, for your interest, for the patience you have learned to demonstrate during the writing of this book, and for your joyful and witty personality. You can always get me to lighten up.

I owe so much to my husband, Gary Waller, who has lived with this book every day for a very long time—and on a variety of continents—as I have taken it with me almost every place we have gone. Thank you for the love and support you have shown, when, even working 80 miles away, you help so often to organize our family time to give me space to work. My most productive work on this book has occurred with all of us together in Purchase. Thank you also for finding creative ways to help me to stop working—always the harder task. Sherry Horton and I are also very grateful for your extensive consultation with us on Chapter Two. Those discussions with you about the chapter enabled us to bring it to the conceptual level we wanted without losing its accessibility.

We are perhaps most deeply indebted to the many adjunct and full-time faculty who have used our material and the literally thousands of students who have gone through our program at Hartford—and countless other students that our adjuncts have taught at neighboring colleges—who have offered us feedback both about our readings and our assignments. You have helped us, at times to fine tune, at other times, to alter our assignments quite radically. The sense of community and support we have felt from our colleagues and students have helped us all to keep researching, rethinking, and writing—while we have been teaching.

CONTRIBUTORS

Kathleen McCormick is Professor of Rhetoric, Language, and Culture and Director of Freshman Reading and Writing at the University of Hartford, having previously directed the Freshman Reading Program at Carnegie Mellon University. She is the winner of the Modern Language Association's Mina Shaunessey Award (1995) for *The Culture of Reading and the Teaching of English* (1994), and the University of Hartford's Bent Award for Creativity (1998). She is also the author of *Reading Texts* (1987) and other books on rhetoric, theory, and modern literature.

Kerry Beckford teaches in the department of Rhetoric, Language, and Culture at the University of Hartford, where she also teaches communication. She has also worked as a communication consultant, in college admissions, and television production.

Sherry Horton is Director of the Center for Reading and Writing at the University of Hartford and teaches in the Department of Rhetoric, Language, and Culture.

Donald Jones is Assistant Professor of Rhetoric, Language, and Culture at the University of Hartford and is a former high school teacher. He has written on theories of writing in *College English* and other journals.

Edward Klonoski is Director of Information Technology at Charter Oak State College, Hartford. He previously taught in the English and Rhetoric, Language, and Culture departments at the University of Hartford, where he was Director of Advanced Educational Computing. He has published widely in the fields of information technology, writing, and pedagogy.

Charles Lipka teaches in the department of Rhetoric, Language, and Culture at the University of Hartford, where he has also taught literature. A prize-winning poet, he has also worked as an editor and tutor.

Leta Marks teaches in the Department of Rhetoric, Language, and Culture at the University of Hartford, where she has also taught literature. She has worked as a high school teacher and as an assessor for the Connecticut State Department of Education. Her first book, *Tales of Live Oaks: Four Generations of a New Orleans Family,* was published in 1997.

Sushil Oswal is Assistant Professor of Rhetoric, Language, and Culture at the University of Hartford, where he is Director of Professional and Technical Writing. He previously taught at the Universities of Cincinnati and Middle Tennessee State. He has been the winner of the C. R. Anderson Award (1997), was a Taft Foundation Research fellow (1991–92), and is the author of articles on portfolio writing, environmental problem solving, and technical writing.

Cynthia Reik teaches in the Department of Rhetoric, Language, and Culture at the University of Hartford and has also taught at St. Joseph College, the University of Connecticut, and Hartford High School. She is the author of articles and studies on Harriet Beecher Stowe, creative writing, and the changing roles of women.

Alan G. Schmidt is a freelance writer and musician currently living in Chico, California, where he works in public television. He has taught composition in the Department of Rhetoric, Language, and Culture at the University of Hartford.

Sally Terrell is on the English faculty at Tunxis Community-Technical College in Farmington, Connecticut. She has also taught composition at Norwalk Community-Technical College and in the Department of Rhetoric, Language, and Culture at the University of Hartford. In addition, she works as an editor and a writing consultant to industry.

INTRODUCTION

Kathleen McCormick

❧

Entering the Intellectual Worlds of College

The beginning of a new phase of your life can seem pretty overwhelming at times. But, in fact, you are better prepared than you may think to meet the academic challenges of college life. In this book, we ask you to draw consciously on the skills you already possess—from all aspects of your life—to develop better abilities to read and write. We ask you to read and write about a variety of different perspectives—from the past and the present, including your own—with understanding and conviction. At the heart of this book is the assumption that your own personal life and experiences are connected to the life of the larger culture, of which college is a part. This book provides you with four key entry points into the intellectual worlds of college:

1. *Accessing critical skills you already possess* but that you may not usually apply to academic situations through challenging and interesting issues to write about.
2. *A method for reading, writing, and thinking critically*—which we term *historical* analysis and *cultural* analysis—that builds on your everyday critical skills and extends them.
3. *A sequenced process for writing* that is manageable and realistic because it works in stages.
4. *A range of interesting topics and texts* from which to choose—beginning with subjects that most students know a lot about and moving gradually to more abstract topics—so that you can gain practice and expertise in applying your critical reading, writing, and thinking skills to academic work.

Let us discuss each of these in turn.

❧

1. Accessing Critical Skills You Already Possess

Throughout this book, we ask you questions that engage your personal interest, but also encourage you to go beyond it. This book helps you put

1

the reading and writing processes under a microscope, showing you the details of what really goes on, details that professors in other classes often expect you to know but that they often do not specifically teach you.

Writing Questions on a Personal Conflict

The place where you may have developed the most complex understanding of the assumptions and beliefs underlying diverse perspectives is in trying to understand and make decisions about your personal experiences. It is there that we begin in Chapter 1. Chapter 1 asks you to write about a past conflict (one that you feel comfortable discussing in class) about which you have now changed your mind. The chapter asks you not only to tell the story of the conflict but also to analyze why it occurred and why you feel differently about it today. In this process of moving from describing your conflict and how you feel about it to exploring *why* you took the particular actions you did, making certain decisions and not others, you will be drawing on your own often unstated or even unconscious analytical abilities, making them conscious and explicit. Further, you will begin writing about ways that your personal life—your beliefs and experiences—is connected with the larger life of the culture in which we live.

Fastwriting Assignments

We treat *your* perspectives seriously throughout the book. All the chapters have questions asking you to write about your own perspectives on the texts you are reading. Some of these questions are *fastwriting assignments*, assignments in which you time yourself for ten to fifteen minutes and write as much as you can, with no editing. These assignments are especially helpful for students who are not that comfortable with writing: They enable you to quickly break through that unpleasant stage of staring at a blank page or screen. But they also help all writers discover ideas that they did not realize they had in a fast and efficient way. Most of us find that when we talk about a subject, we discover all sorts of thoughts and feelings that we didn't consciously know we had. Fastwriting comes as close to talking through your ideas in writing as you can get.

Historical and Cultural Questions

In the historical and cultural questions that follow each reading (we describe these questions below), we frequently ask you to articulate your own perspectives and use them as a point of reference to compare with others whom you are reading—from the past or the present. We ask you time and again to critically analyze in writing *why* you feel or believe what you do. We might ask you to find places where your underlying assumptions differ radically from those of an author you are reading. Or we might ask you to explore the reasons why you agree with a particular author so strongly. We ask you to analyze the mixed reactions you have to particular texts as well, for it is in those places of ambiguity or maybe even confusion that you might have the most to discover about both yourself and how your views are formed by and within the larger culture.

2. A Method for Reading, Writing, and Thinking Critically

The United States is a country of conflicting perspectives. At almost any moment, we can open a newspaper or magazine or turn on the television or radio and witness people talking about different sides of an issue. But, as a country, we do not possess a wide spectrum of ways to adequately understand or negotiate the complex positions people occupy and the often radically diverse practices and belief systems that underlie these differences. The images of conflict from the popular culture with which we are all familiar are often oversimplified and tend to extremes: Differences are most often discussed on television and on the radio in terms of inferior and superior, absolute right and wrong, black and white; there is a clear "winner" and "loser." The media frequently does not engage in the more detailed and subtle types of analyses in which you may engage in your personal life and which are essential if you are to enter the intellectual worlds of college.

This book offers you an accessible model for critically reading and analyzing the varied texts around you—whether these are written or visual—and for developing and critically evaluating your own perspectives in writing. The model consists of two parts: *historical analysis* and *cultural analysis*.

1. *Historical analysis* asks you to relate the values, practices, or beliefs of a text you are reading to those of a *different time period* from that in which the text was produced.

2. *Cultural analysis* asks you to relate the values, practices, or beliefs of a text you are reading to other, often different or seemingly unrelated ideas, beliefs, or practices from the *same time period* in which the text was produced.

Let us discuss each of these in turn, exploring their distinctions and complementarities.

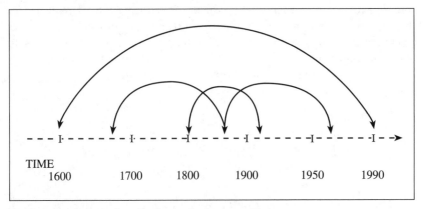

Figure I.1. Historical Analysis: Analysis across Time

Historical Analysis: Analysis across Time

When we look at a subject *historically*, we come to see that perspectives on it have developed *over time*, as they come to be interpreted within different social and political, or ideological, frameworks. Historical analysis, as used throughout this book, is more than just pretending that you are back in time; it is the active movement back and forth from the present to the past or between two different points in the past. So, for example, in Chapter 2, you are asked to compare Amelia Bloomer's attitudes about female clothing in an article written in 1851 with attiudes you have today and attitudes presented in 1995 by Marjorie Garber, a well-known expert on the subject. This study of the ways in which values, attitudes, and beliefs change or remain the same across time is what we call historical analysis. See Figure I.1.

What can we learn from historical analysis?

Discovering the belief systems underlying past and present practices. Most people take for granted that the assumptions and beliefs they hold—for example, that men and women can wear the same styles and brands of jeans—are just natural and normal. Doing historical analysis, however, you begin to recognize specific ways in which the past was different from the present. This recognition of historical difference helps us in the present to question the apparent naturalness or universality of our own points of view: We come to see that there are changing beliefs and assumptions behind even such everyday activities as wearing jeans to class. Why, for example, does our manner of dress differ so dramatically from the dress of only one hundred years ago? What larger values and beliefs are revealed by the clothing that we wear? Asking questions such as these is part of what historical analysis entails.

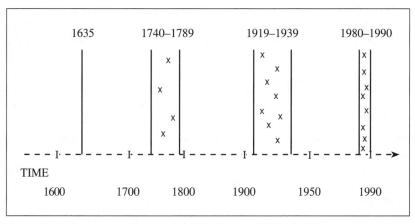

Figure I.2. Cultural Analysis: Analysis of Issues within the Same Time Period

Discovering where present points of view may have their origins. Historical analysis also leads us to find continuities between past and contemporary perspectives. Looking at the past results in our discovering some origins of our own points of view. Many of the beliefs and assumptions that we think of as "ours" have complex beginnings deep within our culture's pasts. This history influences our points of view without our being fully aware of it. By studying the past, we can come to understand why we hold the views we do today.

Cultural Analysis: Analysis of Issues within the Same Time Period

The other perspective we take we call *cultural.* When we engage in cultural analysis, we act as social scientists taking a cross-section of a culture's development and examining the complex interrelationships of various attitudes and beliefs within a culture at a *single period of time.* A historical analysis of Amelia Bloomer asks you to compare Bloomer's 1851 attitudes about female clothing with attitudes from the present. (See Figure I.1.) A cultural analysis, in contrast, explores Bloomer's attitudes in relation to those of her peers—the ministers, newspaper editors, and fellow feminists of her day—and in relation to the larger values of her particular cultural period. This study of the ways in which values, attitudes, and beliefs from any single time period complement, reinforce, contradict, or work against each other is what we call *cultural analysis.* See Figure I.2.

What can we learn from cultural analysis?

Avoiding simplistic right/wrong arguments. Discovering connections between a perspective, an issue, or a text and other aspects of its cultural period gives you a sense of the complex interweaving of different aspects of a culture. It also enables you to move away from simplistic right/wrong analyses. The reasons, for example, why most men and a large number of women joined together to fight Amelia Bloomer's wearing pants in the nineteenth century are intricate and complex. They involve attitudes about gender, health, work, domesticity, and even religion. Discovering how these attitudes interweave and support each other during a single period in time is part of what cultural analysis is about.

Moving from judgmental to analytical positions. Yet what about the disagreements, the places where attitudes clash and work against each other? Whether disagreements are among family members or members of different nations living in the same time period, we need to ask not so much who is right and who is wrong, but *why* such differences exist in the first place. Cultural analysis provides ways for you to ask and answer such questions.

Combining Historical and Cultural Analysis: Negotiating Conflict

Critical reading and writing are about finding points of connection as well as points of difference among ideas. Critical thinking involves a lot of knowledgeable speculation in which you move back and forth between discovering difference and finding points of connection. It involves a repeated inquiry into why particular perspectives exist and what their implications are. Critical reading, writing, and thinking are not simply about taking a stand or saying one side is right and one side is wrong. As we have suggested, our capacity to think critically is seriously limited by the stereotypical notion that "there are two sides to every story." Inevitably, there are far more than two. While often said in an attempt to be open-minded, the image of "two sides" debilitates our thinking, not because it makes us look tolerant but because it so oversimplifies.

Historical and cultural analysis enables us to replace the image of conflict as a two-sided tug of war with an image of a prism with many facets that are at once interconnected and distinct and that also change with the angle of the light and the angle of the viewer. Or we might think of different perspectives as tapestries—complex and tightly woven of many different colored threads. A particular thread looks different depending on the color of the threads it is woven next to. There are many more than two sides to any story, for within any apparent single side, there are many facets or many threads. We ultimately may want to choose one particular perspective on an issue, but we should do so knowing the complexity of the issue and not oversimplifying it just to make the choice seem straightforward.

Critical thinking involves discovering differences and connections across time, which is what occurs in historical analysis. It involves recognizing conflicts and continuities within the same time period, what occurs in cultural analysis. It is the capacity to explore the relationship of one perspective to other perspectives and to connect those perspectives to larger practices, systems of belief, and expectations, in the past and the present. It is (perhaps you now realize) what you have been doing in many daily activities. But as you progress through this book, you will also witness the gradual transformation of your everyday critical skills into more finely tuned, deeper, more academic skills.

∾

3. A Sequenced Process for Writing

You wouldn't expect to play a guitar solo at a concert after one lesson. You wouldn't expect to score that winning goal after one soccer practice. But often, students expect that in one attempt they should be able to put together a coherent, well-thought out, polished essay, often about a subject that they knew little about before they sat down to write.

For you to write well, you may have to lower your expectations. Yes, you read that correctly. It may seem unusual advice at first, but that's what we think. We've met too many students who say they hate to write or that they "can't write" because, in fact, their expectations of writing at this initial stage are way too high. Most published writers—whether they are writing essays, poems, a TV script, ad copy, or a novel—do not expect too much of a first draft. Experienced writers know that writing is a process of exploration in which an idea grows and develops and changes as it is probed and examined during many stages of writing. When people set themselves too difficult or impossible a task—like writing a finished paper in one sitting—they often fail, and rarely do they enjoy the process.

Writing is not always easy or pleasurable, but it can be easier, much more pleasurable, and often of a much better quality if it occurs in stages. At the end of each chapter in this book are two *assignment sequences*. An assignment sequence is a set of assignments that build on each other, eventually leading to a larger paper. The sequence provides a path towards, a way into, the larger paper. The larger paper topic is always central to the assignment sequence, and in many ways it may be similar to paper topics you are given in other classes. Our assumption, however, is that most entering college students need guidance in learning how to forge their own path through complex paper topics, and the sequence is meant to provide that guidance. It is meant to make a difficult task not only manageable but an exciting and enriching experience because you are going about it with appropriate expectations and at an appropriate pace. At the end of almost every assignment sequence that any of us has taught, we have found that a large number of our students are amazed at the quality of the work they were able to produce.

While each sequence provides you with a specific set of questions, the determination of the actual sequence for any paper will be made by you and your instructor. There is no magic formula. It depends a lot on the makeup of your class, on your particular areas of knowledge and interest, on your willingness to share ideas, on whether you find a particular text difficult or not. There is room for great deal of flexibility.

ᐧᐧ

4. A Range of Interesting Topics and Texts

Reading Our Histories, Understanding Our Cultures includes a great diversity of written and visual texts—essays, advertisements, music, poetry, photographs, paintings, biography, fiction—and we offer many suggestions for the use of video and audio texts. We want to give you the opportunity to experience analyzing as diverse a group of texts as possible.

Part I, "I and Ideology," introduces you to the methodology of the book. Chapter 1, "Locating Ourselves in History and Culture," asks you to write a sequence of assignments on a past conflict about which you have changed your mind.

In studying the various factors—the assumptions, beliefs, and expectations—that led you to change your mind over time, you will be performing historical analysis, but in a way that builds on your everyday critical skills and extends them. The changing perspectives that you will study will be your own.

In analyzing the conflict itself and the different perspectives of the individuals involved in the conflict, you will be doing cultural analysis, that is, examining the conflicting perspectives within a culture at a *single period* and how they interconnect with or contradict one another. But once again, this cultural analysis will be intimately connected with critical skills you already possess, and you will be writing about a subject on which only you in the class have expert knowledge.

Chapter 2, "Fashion: Selves and Surfaces," provides a transition from Chapter 1 to the rest of the book: It walks you through the format that the rest of the chapters in the book follow and provides an in-depth discussion of some critical terminology that is used throughout the book. It also demonstrates ways of applying the critical skills you learned in Chapter 1 to reading and writing about visual and printed texts. This chapter's strong focus on fashion and on the visual provides an area of study with which most students feel familiar and generally expert, but it contains some challenging readings as well. Fashion has an "ordinary" quality about it, and it can demonstrate that even the most everyday activity, such as getting dressed, has meanings and histories, enacts conflicts, and needs to be read critically.

The rest of the book relies on materials presented in Chapters 1 and 2. Following Part I are two other parts. Each of these parts contains a range of interesting topics and texts from which to choose—beginning with subjects that most students know a lot about and moving gradually to more abstract topics—so that you can gain practice and expertise in applying your critical reading, writing, and thinking skills to academic work.

In Part II, "Absorbing Stories, Creating Identities," *absorbing* is meant to have two meanings: An absorbing story is an interesting and captivating one; absorbing also means taking in—both consciously and unconsciously—the values and beliefs of our surroundings. We learn stories about family, gender, about whether we will succeed in school or in life, and these stories help to create our identities. Chapters in this section all work to help you gain more control over the stories you absorb.

Chapter 3, "Family Portraits: Changing Roles" addresses a major arena in which most people have struggled to form their identity. The family is a topic that you know a lot about firsthand but that you may not have considered from a historical or cultural perspective. The chapter asks you to analyze some of the factors that underlie the variety of family portraits you will discover, both within a single historical period and across time.

Chapter 4, "Beauties and Beasts: The Tales within Us," looks at a familiar story—one that has been rewritten in virtually every culture—and asks you to explore the stories it tells us about gender, social class, and human sexuality. Chapter 5, "Questioning U.S. High Schools: What to Teach and How to Learn," encourages you to consider historical as well as current debates surrounding high school. It explores the various stories we have told ourselves about the purpose of high school and the impact those stories have had on individual lives.

Chapter 6, "Elvis: Any Way You Want Me (That's How I Will Be)" focuses in on one individual life, that of a man who became a cultural icon. Whether you are an Elvis Presley fan or not, the chapter provides startling accounts of how a man absorbed the many and often conflicting stories—of race, regionality, the American Dream, and masculinity—told to him by a constantly changing public. Offering numerous suggestions of audio and visual texts to accompany the written texts of the chapter, "Elvis" seeks to address the ways in which all of our identities are formed by absorbing the stories around us.

Part III, "Contesting People, Contested Spaces," broadens the scope even further and asks you to explore the ways in which people construct and are constructed by the spaces in which we live—whether these are geographical, institutional, technological, or industrial. Are you from the city? From the suburbs? Do you like to go to the city? Do you live in a rural area, as far from the city as you can get? Chapter 7, "The American City: Dreams and Nightmares," looks at different views of American living spaces. It explores why people live where they do and why the city is a source of both fear and excitement for so many people.

While technology may seem an especially contemporary topic, Chapter 8, "Galileo to Gates: Human Reactions to Technology," demonstrates that social and political uses of science and technology have complex histories. This chapter juxtaposes the responses to and the uses of Galileo's telescope with the responses to and uses of computers and networks today. It asks whether computers and networks may change the way we define ourselves, our world, and our place in it as dramatically as Galileo's telescope changed these ideas and concepts in the seventeenth century.

Chapter 9, "Progress or Destruction? Developing the Environment," asks you to analyze the varied relationships to the land that we have had in the United States from the colonial times to the present. It encourages you to inquire into the environmental implications of a variety of your current behaviors and practices—from shopping to showering—and to link these behaviors with larger values of capitalism, consumption, and development in our country.

All three parts of the book, therefore, ask questions that require you to think critically about different perspectives, to explore their antecedents and implications, and to discover how they are connected to other per-spectives and issues in the present and in the past. But they do so in three somewhat different arenas: personal conflict, the larger social contexts in which identities are made, and the spaces in which we live. Throughout you are asked to move back and forth from the personal to gradually larger and larger worlds.

As you work through those parts of this book that your instructor chooses, we wish you all the pleasures that come from intellectual challenge, personal growth, and discovery. This book, of course, is just one contri-bution to your college education, and in the end, you are the one who will decide how committed you will be to different subjects, how much time you will invest, how many intellectual risks you will take. We hope, however, that our book helps you to recognize how much you already know and can do. For such a recognition can enable you to glimpse the extent to which you can grow and learn from others—voices from the past, images from the present, statements from your fellow students—and the extent to which you can enter and find your own voice in their debates. Whether the perspectives you encounter are comforting or disturbing to you, we hope that by connecting them to other debates within our complex histories and cultures, you are able to better understand and evaluate them and to then take up positions of your own whose antecedents and implications you understand, believe in, and can critically defend.

PART I
I and Ideology

❧ 1 ❧

LOCATING OURSELVES IN HISTORY AND CULTURE

Kathleen McCormick and Charles Lipka

This chapter systematically introduces you to the methods of critical reading, writing, and thinking discussed in the introduction. The "texts" you will study are extracts from an assignment sequence written by a student and then an assignment that you write. The assignment asks you to write about and then analyze some of your own experiences; it is meant to be relevant, interesting, and stimulating to you personally. It starts with the assumption that your personal life is intimately connected to your varied histories and to the larger life of the culture.

❧

Assignment Sequence

We are going to ask you in an *assignment sequence*—a series of manageable writing tasks that build on each other—to write a story about a conflict you have experienced in your life. You will then gradually develop this story further by analyzing it *historically* and *culturally*. The sequence of assignments about your conflict experience involves four to five parts:

1. personal conflict narrative;
2. analysis of multiple perspectives at the time of the conflict (cultural analysis);
3. analysis of your changing perspective on the conflict over time (historical analysis);
4. analysis of the conflict and your change over time in relation to other students in your class (optional synthetic analysis);
5. final paper—rethinking, revising, and putting it all together (combining cultural and historical analysis).

Why a *sequence* of assignments? A sequence suggests not just one unconnected or random assignment after another, but a series of *connected* assignments, one leading to the next. An assignment sequence slows down the different stages of writing and therefore gives you the time and the mental space to let your writing grow and develop—often, you will find, in unanticipated ways. At each stage in the sequence of assignments, you are also asked to write something new, but you are also asked to go back and—using insights from your instructors, your fellow students, and your own writing as you produce it—to rethink and revise an earlier part of your work.

Revision: Developing New Ideas through the Process of Writing

The kind of revision we encourage you to engage in for much of the sequence is not what many students coming to college are most familiar with—what is called *line editing*, that is, checking spelling, punctuation, and perhaps sentence structure. Nor will it be simply adding new material to a previous draft—a sentence here, a paragraph there. Rather, we encourage you to develop a sense of revision as literally reseeing and rethinking. As you write, you will develop new ideas and insights. Because you will often be writing quickly, we ask that you try to feel freer to cut some of what you have written in an earlier draft as you move from draft to draft, realizing that some of your writing was simply your own form of a warmup exercise, getting you ready for more important work and insights.

Watch Yourself

Perhaps the most important advice is to watch yourself. Watch yourself as you move gradually through these stages of writing and analysis. Pay attention to how your arguments develop, to how your positions strengthen and become more complex, and to how you learn about yourself and others through the process of writing. This gradual process of growth and discovery is one of the most exciting aspects of writing, and it is one that a number of students coming to college may not have yet experienced. If you are one of those people who says "I don't like to write" or "I'm not good at writing," it may be because you have never written in this way. Give this method, and give yourself, a chance.

Sample Student Essay

At each stage in this chapter's sequence, we include extracts from the work that one of our students, Matthew Link, wrote for this particular assignment sequence. We also give our analysis of his work and discuss a number of the comments of his classmates. Matt's essay is not meant to be a model essay. It is a sample for you to learn from, analyze, and critique. While his work exhibits growth from draft to draft, there is still a lot of room for improvement. At each stage of the sequence, you have the opportunity not only to read our analysis of Matt's writing, but also to develop an analysis of your own in which you assess his writing, his process of discovery, places where you think he genuinely revised, and places where he resisted. In learning to critique the work of others, you will gradually develop a more critical eye about your own work.

✑ Assignment 1: Personal Conflict Narrative

Write a *narrative* of a past *conflict* about which you have *changed* your mind. Give as much specific detail as you can (sights, sounds, smells, feelings, a description of the scene) so that you place yourself, as well as your reader, back in the moment of the conflict.

How do you start? Before you begin an assignment, it's always good to spend some time thinking about its *task definition*, that is, *what* it's actually asking you to do and *why* it's asking you to do it. Do not hesitate to ask your instructors for explanatory details about an assignment. It is much better to talk with them about what an assignment means than to waste time nervously speculating on your own, time that might usefully be spent thinking about your topic and doing some writing.

So far the assignment is pretty skimpy. It needs a clearer task definition. Before you start writing the paper, it is reasonable to want clarification in two areas:

1. definitions of the terms of the assignment;
2. a justification for the assignment.

Throughout this chapter, we define the terms of each assignment in the sequence and give you our justification for creating it. As well, at this first stage, we offer, you some suggestions for how to begin writing and how to work through a draft. These suggestions are applicable for all stages of writing.

Definitions

Narrative: A narrative is a story. It is a representation in words of an event. But because it is a representation, the particular words with which you choose to tell it, the tone, the descriptions of characters, and the order in which events are told all deeply affect how readers experience it. The same story can be told in a number of different ways. Many people have said that one of the fundamental human capacities is the ability to tell stories. People tell stories all the time. "Let me tell you what happened in Ms. Peters' class today." "Do you remember when we first met in Pittsburgh?" "Wait until you hear what James did!" These are all lead-ins to stories. Because most people tell stories all the time, writing narratives is often regarded by many as the easiest form of writing. And yet bear in mind that as you write your narrative, you will most likely want to revise it over the course of the sequence as you begin to realize some of implications of the different ways in which it can be told.

Conflict: A conflict does not necessarily denote an argument or a fight, but rather a set of differing—often *many* differing—perspectives or emotions. Recall the discussion in the introduction about replacing the oversimplified notion of conflict as "two-sided" or "black and white" with a much more complex image of a tapestry with many tightly woven threads. Whatever image you develop, real conflicts are complex, even if they might seem simple on the surface. A conflict can be within the self as well as between the self and others, but most often it is both. Conflicts often occur when a person's conscious or unconscious beliefs, expectations, or desires meet with opposition of some kind or when arguments may seem rational or logical, but somehow don't *feel* right.

Change: Changing your mind does not necessarily mean that your perspective has reversed itself, only that it has altered itself in some way. Perspectives can change by evolving: They may essentially stay the same, but they can still develop and become enriched. You learn something about yourself, about others, or about a situation and get a different, perhaps more complex, picture of it. You discover some things you weren't previously aware of. It is likely that the very process of writing about and analyzing this conflict will create some change in your perspective about it.

Justification
Why would we ask you to do this assignment?

Historical and cultural analysis. First, we believe that the foundation for successful critical reading, writing, and thinking in college is being able to perform complex historical and cultural analysis. This assignment sequence has both of these forms of analysis at its core. See Figures 1.1 and 1.2.

Personal investment. Assignment 1 asks *you* to write the story that will become the subject of your analysis in later assignments. Why? We want your first attempt at historical and cultural analysis using this book to be successful and interesting, and we want you to feel that you have really

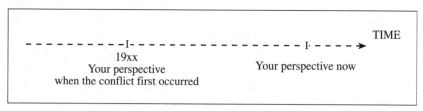

Figure 1.1. Historical Analysis: Why your perspective *changed over time*

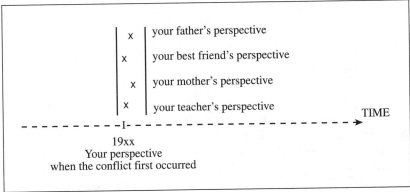

Figure 1.2. Cultural Analysis: Why *differing* perspectives can *exist at the same period of time* and cause conflict

learned something worthwhile by writing it. What better way to begin than with a subject of your own choice that means something to you and that you are the only expert on in the class?

∾

Beginning Writing

Brainstorming

You don't necessarily want to end up writing about the first topic that comes to mind, and yet you don't want to spend a lot of time staring at a blank piece of paper or a screen. *Brainstorming* can help. When you brainstorm, you simply write whatever comes into your mind on the subject—as fast as you can and without making any judgments about it. In this way, you accumulate a lot of details, ideas, and information that you can use in a variety of ways later.

So, make a list of conflicts you've been involved in. At this stage, don't be critical. There's time for that later. Any conflict that comes to mind is a possibility not to be overlooked. The more you think of, the more options you'll have. Just write or type out a list of about eight to ten as fast as you can. Here is a sample list of some of the conflicts that students in one of our classes initially came up with:

1. teaching disruptive child in day care
2. dog being put to sleep
3. playing in band
4. best friend
5. younger boyfriend

6. feeling unsafe in a new neighborhood
7. deciding to go back to school
8. "straight edge" lifestyle
9. caught between two friends
10. moving to a new city

These quick notes may not even make sense to you—although there are some you can probably relate to and speculate about—but they made sense to the people who wrote them down. And that's all you need at this stage of brainstorming—a list of options that makes sense to you.

After you make your initial list, stop for a while and just keep the assignment in the back of your mind. Let your process of writing interweave itself with the rest of your day. Thoughts might come to you while you're at dinner, talking with a friend, or while you're walking between classes. These may be thoughts for other possible topics or expansions of ones you've already jotted down. If you think about your writing on and off at other times in the day, you'll have more to say when you sit down the next time to write.

Timed Fastwriting

Read over the list you generated during your brainstorming. Which of your topics interests you the most? Choose the two or three conflicts in which you feel a personal investment. Remember to choose conflicts that you will feel comfortable discussing with your class. Then write nonstop for ten minutes on each of them. Time yourself beginning when you start writing and don't stop until the time is up. Don't correct your grammar or typing errors during the timed period. Just keep writing. This will take twenty or thirty minutes in total, perhaps more if you really get into one of them. Begin to bring a part of the conflict to life for yourself—you might focus at this stage on just one key event in it— anything that keeps you writing and helps to stimulate your memory about it.

If you have the time, get up and take a break. Do something else. Again, try to keep what you have written in the back of your mind. Which has the best detail? What could you have added to this story or to that one? Which one are you thinking most about? Which one might you want to talk about with your classmates? Which one would you be most interested in analyzing in depth? Often you'll get ideas from what other students are writing about. Listen to your peers carefully; they have a lot to teach you, as you do them. Their conflicts may remind you of conflicts of your own that you haven't thought of yet.

—It occured in the past
—You have changed your mind about it in the present
—It is of genuine interest to you, and you would like to analyze in detail
—You feel comfortable discussing it with your instructor and your classmates

Figure 1.3. Criteria for Choosing Your Conflict Story

Choosing the Conflict Story

The time has come to choose one conflict from among the two or three you wrote about. Perhaps you have an instinct about which one you think is the best. You should probably go with that because you are most interested in it. But before you make a final decision, it's a good idea to review some of the criteria for selecting a conflict. See Figure 1.3.

ॐ

Writing a First Draft

The discussion in this section applies to the writing of a first draft of any paper. It is a process you should attempt to use throughout this book. You and your instructor will most likely develop variations on it, but the main goal of this section is to give you some strategies to generate a lot of writing and to think in a disciplined and efficient manner. Writing well, like any skill, requires discipline and practice.

Untimed Fastwrite

Once you've chosen your topic, read through what you've written on it already. Continue to write some more about it in fast bursts for as long as you can. You are setting the scene, giving a sense of the people involved, telling the story in as much fullness as you can. Try not to edit or worry about word choice at this point. Just keep writing until you need to take a break. If you discover that your attention lags or your pace slows, you may find that you can write better and faster if you continue to time your fastwrites for a while. Do what works so long as you are generating a detailed story.

Details Draw Readers In

When you feel the need to stop writing, sit back and read the text you have created so far. You are trying to develop an account of what happened that will enable your readers to understand the conflict from your perspective. From what you've written so far, do you think someone could understand what happened, how you felt, and why you felt it? Are there points where you need to provide more details? More background information? An explanation of your feelings? A description of the setting? Do you need to change some of the language? Now is the time to add what you think your readers need. Using sensory details—that is, details that appeal to the five senses, like pictures, sounds, smells, sensations, tastes—helps bring your narrative to life. Trust your judgment about what's relevant to add, but don't immediately assume that certain details have no relevance. Vague and abstract papers are boring; it is the detail that draws readers in.

Reading Aloud: Moving from Writer-Based to Reader-Based Prose

At this point, you may want to read your paper out loud. This is a great strategy for seeing what's actually on the page rather than what was in your head while you were writing. Reading your paper aloud helps you to move from inside your head—where you know your story so intimately that you do not need to go over every aspect of it—to an understanding that your readers need more descriptive language, more details, more explanations for your experiences to become concrete and vivid to them. This is a move from *writer-based prose*—in which you stay inside your own head, saying things that make sense to you, the writer, but not necessarily to anyone else—to *reader-based prose*—in which you begin to write in anticipation of what your readers need to know to truly understand your narrative.

Have you assumed that your readers will understand relationships, experiences, beliefs, and feelings that you have not yet explained? Have your details kept your focus or do some lead readers away from the direction you want them to be moving in? Does your organization and your individual sentence structure make sense and flow? Do they make sense as a story? Remember, a narrative is told in parts—the pieces of the story. Does your paragraphing coincide with those pieces?

Line Editing

Now is the time to smooth out your style, to edit, and to proofread. Have you put all the periods in? Have you watched for any sentence fragments and joined them with the sentences they go with? Have you used apostrophes for possession? Have you checked your spelling? Have you checked for typographical errors?

Notice that we are suggesting that you leave all of this kind of mechanical line editing until the end of each draft. Although you want your papers to be well edited, many students begin this line editing too soon; some, in fact, initially try to edit each sentence immediately after they write it. Such editing breaks a writer's train of thought and prevents him or her from building any momentum.

While you certainly need to line edit your papers, you don't want to waste time editing something that may not be worth saving. All good writers realize that they need to cut a certain amount of what they initially wrote once they discover what it is they really want to be saying. And most writers aren't sure of what their major points are until they have written a fair bit. As we have suggested, writers learn in the very act of writing. You will be much more willing to cut or significantly rewrite a paragraph that doesn't work if you haven't spent a lot of time pouring over every word and punctuation mark in it.

Often when you figure out what it is you want to say, your writing quality improves markedly. This makes sense; muddled writing is usually an indication of muddled thought. So while you may notice and change incidental details as you revise, don't start line editing prematurely. Work on the substance before you worry about things like typographical errors. Focus on these only in the last stages before you hand in this draft to your instructor or classmates.

∞

Sample Student Assignment 1: Personal Conflict Narrative

What follows is an extract from our student Matthew Link's first assignment. Matt's is not the best paper ever written, nor (certainly) the worst. But it illustrates how a keen and conscientious student learned to improve his sense of himself as a writer by working through the questions shown in Figure 1.4.

In reading each draft of Matt's paper, you will not only get a sense of what you might like or not like to do in your own paper, but you will also learn how to analyze and critique the writing of someone who may be much like you or one of your fellow students. Learning to critically read the writing of others is a vital stage in learning to critically read your own writing. Peer review—in which students develop written critical analyses of their classmates' work—is a key component of this process.

Over the course of the discussion of Matt's paper, we use some of Figure 1.4's six questions to guide our analysis. We invite you to apply the

1. **What is the author's conflict?**
   For a reader to be able to answer this, the essay must contain *details* and be *reader-based*. This is also a *site of possible revision* from draft to draft.

2. **What is the author's perspective at the time of the conflict?**
   For a reader to be able to answer this, the essay must contain *details* and be *reader-based*. This is also a *site of possible revision* from draft to draft.

3. **Why did the author hold his or her initial perspective?**
   To answer this requires *cultural analysis*, a study of the larger factors—dominant beliefs, expectations, assumptions—helping to shape the author's subject position.

4. **Why do different perspectives exist in the same period of time?**
   To answer this requires *cultural analysis*, a study of the larger factors—dominant beliefs, expectations, assumptions—helping to shape the subject position of others who are involved in the conflict.

5. **What is the author's change in perspective over time?**
   For a reader to be able to answer this, the essay must contain *details* and be *reader-based*. This is also a *site of possible revision* from draft to draft.

6. **Why does the author's perspective change over time?**
   To answer this requires *historical analysis*, a comparison of the values, attitudes, and beliefs that affected the author at the time of the conflict with those that are affecting him or her at the present.

Figure 1.4. Six Critical Questions for the Conflict Essay Sequence

questions to your paper as well. These questions are also helpful when responding to one of your classmates' papers. In figure 1.4, we highlight the significance of each of them for the model of analysis we are developing.

Questions 1, 2, and 5 are more specifically about the story or narrative. If you cannot answer them about your own paper or someone else's, then crucial details are missing. These questions are less analytical than the other three. However, remember that we noted that there are many ways to tell a story. Questions 1, 2, and 5 need to be sufficiently detailed for you to develop the analysis required to answer questions 3, 4, and 6. A skimpy story leads to skimpy and uninteresting analysis. Further, writing a draft of your analysis may influence the story you have to tell, and you may decide to change the way you write that story quite significantly from draft to draft as you develop your historical and cultural analyses. Watch your own writing, Matt's, and your classmates for such changes.

Here is the paper Matt wrote for his first assignment. As you read it, pay attention to your first reaction to it. Write some comments in the margins, perhaps noting parts of the paper you like and parts that you have questions about.

Matthew Link
Professor McCormick
9/19

(1) In the sixth grade my life took a wild turn down the road of life. That year I knew what I had to do. After a few long months of coaxing, my parents agreed to let me take guitar lessons. The instrument was a part of me the first time that I played it. Day and night, the guitar never left my side. I had finally found something that I would live and die for. My only dream since the sixth grade was to be able to make a living playing music. In my opinion, that would be success.

(2) A few years later I started a band with some good friends. We called ourselves Good Morning Richard. At first it was only playing in the basement, but eventually I was able to make a few calls and book a show. The name of this venue was Club Blue. Before I stepped out on the stage, for the first time, I thought that I wanted to perform music for a living, but afterwards it was confirmed. I knew that was my "calling" and I could not be happy doing anything else. This was the first of many shows for Good Morning Richard.

(3) One year after our first show, we were asked to play this venue again. This time we made the demand of not selling a minimum of twenty-five tickets. This request was quickly shot down, but we compromised on only selling as many tickets as we could. That week we needed to use our replacement drummer because our regular drummer, Mike, was going away for a while. Needless to say, this replacement drummer did not sell any tickets. Ryan, my bass player did not sell any either. At this point I called the promoter to let him know what was going on. He quickly answered the phone and I told him that I had fourteen tickets sold, and only two days left before the show. He said, "No problem." and that is where the phone call ended. I thought everything was going to be just fine.

(4) The night of the show we loaded in all of our equipment and set it up on stage. Our set decided to hang out backstage for a while and discuss the show that night. I was very excited, as always, because I was on my way to living my dream. When our promoter called me over to discuss the ticket sales everything changed.

(5) He called me over to his office, which was the coat room, and asked about how many tickets we sold. When I told him the amount, he gave me a double-take. I asked what was wrong, and he said that he was not ready for that small an amount of tickets sold. At that point I started to get a little angry. When I reminded him of our phone conversation earlier in the week, he flat out denied that we even discussed ticket sales. After he was done calling me a liar, he proceeded to tell me that we owed him money for the tickets that we could not sell. That is where I put my foot down. We exchanged a few four letter words and after a few minutes he backed down and said we had to go on around seven-thirty. That was two hours before we were supposed to go on.

(6) We reluctantly began playing our set. Somewhere in the middle I was so caught up in playing, that I forgot about the incident. Playing music is a form of therapy for me. I just drift away into my own world where everything is less harsh. After the set we loaded our equipment into the cars. Then I had to wait outside of the club to tell anyone coming to see us that we had already played. That was one night that I will never forget.

(7) The reason that I will never forget that evening is because that was the first time my heart was broken. Up to that point in time all I did was anything to move my band closer to my goal. That night I learned that I could not trust anyone in the local music scene. I also realized that there were so many bands out there and the clubs did not care about any of them. All they wanted was their almighty dollar. To me it was about music, not money. From that point on I knew that my chances of becoming all that I dreamed of were as close to nothing as possible.

(8) To this very day it saddens me to think of never living my dream. I would do anything to have a chance. If by some miracle I do succeed, I would never work again. Music is never work, just an emotion that becomes as much a part of you as your heart. I just could not live without it. I guess that is why they are called dreams.

∾ Fastwrite 1

What is your first response to Matt's paper? Take a few minutes and jot down your initial answers to the first two questions in Figure 1.4: What is the author's conflict, and what is his perspective at the time of the conflict?

Critical Question 1. What Is the Author's Conflict?

A summary of Matt's conflict at this stage of the narrative goes something like this: Matt is having a dispute with his promoter (who doesn't have a name yet) about ticket sales for his band's show. The promoter expected the band to sell twenty-five tickets to perform; Matt thought they had agreed that the band would just sell as many tickets as they could. They argued and the result was that the band had to perform two hours earlier than it was supposed to. But is this enough?

We could tell you repeatedly about the need to include details in what you write, to articulate your position clearly, and to think about your audience, but often seeing a paper like Matt's can really help student writers understand what that means. When thinking about what Matt's conflict was, his fellow students offered a number of helpful comments and suggestions.

1. Most of Matt's classmates felt that he had chosen an interesting topic and that his paper had potential. Most also agreed, however, that his paper had not yet reached that potential.
2. From his first draft, the class could tell that Matt cares deeply about his music and that he was quite upset by the dispute he had with the promoter at Club Blue. Yet many of the students told Matt that they could not yet *feel* what he felt.
3. Some were not certain what exactly Matt's conflict was.
4. Many were not sure why he had reacted the way he did or whether his position about the conflict had actually changed over time.

At this stage of the narrative, the different perspectives are presented in black and white terms. Matt is good. He is idealistic: "It was about music." The promoter is bad. He is deceptive, calls Matt a liar, and is only concerned with money: "All they wanted was their almighty dollar." The picture Matt paints is uncomplicated, black and white. It fits with the dominant two-sided representations of conflict discussed in the introduction, but, as it turns out, it does not explain all of what was going on for Matt. Life is usually much more complex than good/bad representations allow for, but it is natural in a first draft to go for a simple and familiar plot line. Watch for some of the ways in which Matt's depiction of the conflict becomes increasingly complex and interesting as his essay develops.

Critical Question 2. What Is the Author's Perspective at the Time of the Conflict?

Matt tells us that his "only dream since the sixth grade was to be able to make a living playing music," but many students felt that for his position to be persuasive or vivid, they needed Matt to tell more about it—perhaps to *show*, not just tell, them how he felt at various points in the narrative, particularly about his perspective before the conflict. Students suggested that lines like "Before I stepped out on the stage, for the first time, I thought that I wanted to perform music for a living, but afterwards it was confirmed," cried out *Why? What happened on stage? How did you feel? What was it like?* Questions such as these ask Matt to move from writer-based prose in which he, the writer, can understand what he means to reader-based prose in which he describes his experiences in sufficient detail for his readers to understand as well.

Matt's first response to his fellow students' questions was that words could not explain his personal experience of playing the guitar. "It's just a feeling," he said. But one student pointed out how crucial it was to understand his feelings about his music to be able to relate to him and to sympathize with his reaction to the promoter. Simply saying that he felt good or felt disappointed wasn't enough. Students kept asking Matt to explain what playing music on stage felt like to him. Eventually, he began to talk about this and he began to find the words. The final section shows how Matt revised this discussion to include many more details and explanations, making his feelings come alive for his readers. Also note that the particular nature of his conflict is significantly changed from the first to the last draft.

∾   **Fastwrite 2**

Do you think that your paper exhibits some of the same strengths and weaknesses as Matt's? What different strengths and weaknesses does yours have? For example, are there places that are written in writer-based prose? Are there places that need more explanation and details for your readers to really understand your conflict and your perspective and to find it interesting? Have you, like Matt, represented your conflict in conventional black and white terms in which there appear to be only two sides? Have you done justice to the different perspectives involved?

Take a few minutes and think about how in your later drafts you might want to create a more detailed and complex picture of the conflict and your perspective, a picture that avoids the simplistic two sides image.

∾

The Limits of a First Draft and the Promise of Future Drafts

It is often not easy to articulate your own (or someone else's) position on a subject, even if it is something you feel strongly about. Why is this? Most writers, like Matt, write a first draft in a somewhat vague way either because the important details are so obvious to them that they fail to mention them or because they don't really understand what exactly it is that they're trying to say. The details may be so complex that the writer may not have fully thought them through.

In Matt's next stages of writing, he does not just become better at describing what he knew all along; in the very act of trying to articulate and analyze his conflict, Matt actually learns and discovers much more about it. Writing is not just a matter of finding the right words to describe something that you already understand; writing often helps you discover something new.

As you move your paper to the next stage in the sequence, remember that in a sequence you are continually building on your previous work, both by revising what you already wrote and by extending it with some new writing. When you return to your narrative after a day or two, you will inevitably see changes you would like to make; story lines that need clarification, motivations that need explaining, feelings that need articulation. Discovering that you left details and explanations out of your first draft does not mean that you failed. It demonstrates that a first draft can only do so much and that a first draft of a paper should not be a final draft.

∾ Assignment 2: Analysis of Perspectives at the Time of the Conflict

1. Revision: *Revise* the conflict narrative started in assignment 1, following your instructor's comments, your fellow students' comments, and your own emerging sense of what extra details you need to develop a substantive analysis of your narrative.
2. New work: Analyze the different *perspectives* at the time of the conflict, including your own, by exploring some of the larger cultural factors—the beliefs, expectations, and assumptions of the time—that may have influenced and helped to determine these perspectives (*cultural analysis*).

Definitions

Revising: Try to think about your revision in two stages.

1. *Changing or adding various details missing from your first draft.* Class discussion, comments from your instructor, or simply rereading your paper after letting it sit for a day or two can make you see areas that need changing or development. You may want to write those revisions before you begin your analysis. Or you may feel that some of the details in your first draft are extraneous to what you now see as your main points and you may want to delete them.
2. *Making changes in your narrative after you have begun writing your cultural analysis.* The very act of writing your cultural analysis may also make you want to revise your narrative. As you begin to think about some of the cultural reasons why you and others held the positions that you did, you may find the need to go back to add or change some other details—points that you've just remembered or that previously seemed insignificant that suddenly seem important because of the larger cultural factors you are describing in your analysis. This kind of reseeing can

Person #1: *Name*
Summary of Perspective:
Cultural Factors Underlying Perspective:

Person #2: *Name*
Summary of Perspective:
Cultural Factors Underlying Perspective:

Person #3: *Name*
Summary of Perspective:
Cultural Factors Underlying Perspective:

Figure 1.5. Perspectives Involved in Conflict

occur when you write in stages and give yourself the opportunity to think about what you've said.

Perspective: A *perspective* is a point of view from which a person or group of people looks at something at a given time. In this book, we argue that while each perspective seems "personal," it is also linked with the larger beliefs of the culture. Thus, it can only be understood and analyzed once it has been placed in those larger contexts.

To prepare yourself to analyze your conflict narrative, list each of the important players involved in the conflict. The list may look something like Figure 1.5. Your list may include more people than you wrote about in your first draft. When Matt did this, for example, he discovered that he did not want simply to list himself and his promoter as involved in the conflict. His family members and friends also became important players. The introduction of other people begins to change the nature of the conflict narrative.

∾ Fastwrite 3

After making your list, fastwrite for three to five minutes on each of the people involved in your conflict. Try to summarize, not judge, what you think their perspective was.

Cultural analysis: Most analysis works to answer the question *Why?* When you develop a cultural analysis of your conflict story, you explore why each person felt the way he or she did by looking at the relationship of their personal feelings to the larger systems of beliefs, expectations, and representations of their immediate culture. Although no cultural analysis can fully explain the development of a particular perspective, the attempt to link that perspective with a broad range of cultural influences—some of which initially might not even seem directly related to it—helps you begin to understand the issues surrounding the perspective, its rationale, and its apparent validity to the person or group who maintains it. So before you take a stand on a position, you need to have a sense of how it came to be developed. It doesn't just come naturally; it derives from a particular context, a particular set of values, beliefs, and assumptions. Figure 1.6 (p.30) lists some areas within the culture to explore that help to shape "personal" perspectives. When you look at these areas in relation to the issues involved in your conflict, try to think of as many *specific* examples as you can— specific ads and television shows, specific values from your family, church or temple, or school—that could have affected you and the others involved. Keep in mind that a variety of often contradictory values exist within any single cultural period and that these contradictory values can be simultaneously influencing you or someone else in your story. We discuss some of these below as we look at two paragraphs from Matt's paper.

Justification

Increasing the control you have over your beliefs. When and where we live affects us in profound ways. It does not determine specifically what we think, but it does both open up and constrain possible ranges of thoughts, beliefs, and expectations; it does so in ways that we are not always conscious of. Developing the ability to connect your own and others' perspectives with larger systems of belief, social practices, and common assumptions increases your understanding of yourself and others. But it does more than that; it also increases the control you have over your beliefs by allowing you to choose more actively what you believe and why you believe it. This knowledge also enables you to articulate your perspectives more clearly in writing.

Increasing your critical understand of others' perspectives. Instead of reacting to the different perspectives you uncover in your conflict story by taking sides—"I was right; he was wrong"—which, as suggested earlier, is so debilitating to serious critical understanding, this assignment asks you to first articulate what each of the important perspectives were in the conflict— that is, to put into words the points of view of the major participants. Then it asks you to explore why people would hold these perspectives, not whether you agree with them.

What you are being asked to do is not easy. We all often tend to dismiss views with which we disagree, often without even listening to them. And we often have difficulty articulating our own views because they seem so obvious or commonsensical to us.

Representations in the media and commercial displays: ads, magazines, newspapers, television, films, catalogues, and stores: The media and commercial sellers are major sources of values, particularly dominant values because they are so all pervasive. Some examples of media influences include:

1. images of what an "attractive" man or woman is;
2. representations of how one should act to be popular;
3. images of how one should dress to look wealthy;
4. depictions of the kind of car one should drive to look "cool" or "like a good parent";
5. representations of the number of possessions one "needs" to be happy.

Myths of the culture: The myths of a culture are the beliefs that are held unquestioningly about the society: for example, in American society that everyone has equal educational and job opportunities; that all Americans strive to achieve the American Dream; that the American Dream means having a well-paying job, owning a house, being in a heterosexual marriage, and having children; that any American could become president.

Values, beliefs, and practices learned in one's family, religious organization, school, and peer groups: While cultural representations and cultural myths are probably the most constant and pervasive throughout the country, we are also influenced by more local contexts and institutions whose values may coincide with or work against the values presented in cultural representations and myths.

Figure 1.6. Larger Cultural Factors Influencing Individual Perspectives

After you have spelled out the different perspectives, then try to determine where they came from and why the person or persons would maintain their particular point of view. This involves speculating about the diversity of factors that could have influenced each person in your conflict story to take up his or her perspective. Remember that you are doing this in an attempt to understand the perspective, not at this point to agree or disagree with it.

As you begin drafting assignment 2, remember to use the generative strategies—brainstorming, freewriting, drafting, and editing—discussed in assignment 1.

ॐ

Sample Student Assignment 2: Analysis of Perspectives at the Time of the Conflict

Here is an extract of Matt's assignment 2. The discussion of it follows the outline presented in Figure 1.5: person, summary of perspective, cultural factors underlying perspective. We will also address critical questions 3 and 4 from Figure 1.4 that are a necessary part of cultural analysis: Why did the author hold his or her initial perspective? Why do different perspectives exist in the same time period?

We focus on two paragraphs of Matt's analysis of the different perspectives involved in his conflict. As you read Matt's first paragraph, in which he discusses his own perspective and that of his friends and family, quickly jot down your reaction to it. What strikes you? What might you have said in Matt's position? Where might you expand the analysis? Consider it especially in relation to the analysis you are developing of your own conflict.

(1) I felt the way that I did because of my deep love of music. Music was what I put all my spare time into, and really cared about. My love of music came from a passion that lay inside of me from the moment I first played the guitar. The belief in my own ability to succeed stems from many places. As a youth, my parents, teachers, friends, and the rest of my family (except my sister) told me that I would never make it as a musician. That negative energy just made me want to show them that I could make it as a musician. These two things tied together were the fuel for my dream. . . .

Person #1: Matt

Summary of Perspective

Inner passion and conflict with family. Matt's depiction of his perspective has become more complex, and yet much more needs to be articulated. In the first draft, his perspective was simply that he had a dream of making a living playing music. In this draft, however, Matt's perspective is itself implicitly conflicted. Matt says that his dream to become a successful musician came from two places: "a passion that lay inside" himself from the moment he first played the guitar and the "negative energy" exerted by most of his family and friends who told him that he would never make it as a musician. Matt's revisions of his narrative in this draft (not quoted in the paragraph above) gives us more insight into the positive feelings he had about music. Matt wrote: "I knew that was my 'calling' and I could not be happy doing anything else. The feeling that I had on stage was like a drug induced high. The rush was so intense that I became a junkie of music. I had to play music in order to feel complete."

But Matt's discussion of the negative energy is something new. Because Matt's family and friends discouraged him from pursuing a career in music, he is somewhat defensive. He wants to "show them" that he can make it, even though they think he can't. The presence of this negative energy might put his conflict with the promoter in a new light.

Critical Question 3. Why did the author hold his or her initial perspective?

Cultural Factors Underlying Matt's Perspective

Representations in the media: Images associated with guitar players by young people: rich, sexually attractive, rebellious superstars.

Cultural myth: Anyone can become a star. Matt has wanted to play the guitar professionally since he was in the sixth grade. He believes his life would be a success if he could make his living in this way. While this belief is a "personal" belief of Matt's, it is also linked with the culture in which he lives. Why, for instance, might Matt want to play the guitar rather than, say, the harp or the flute? To answer such a question, we need to look at the larger contexts—particularly the cultural representations and myths attached to playing certain types of instruments within our culture, representations that can help to influence our inner passions and desires.

While Matt has expanded the discussion of his perspective, his analysis at this stage focuses solely on the personal. He has not yet attempted to put these feelings in a larger social context. Can you suggest any ways he might do this? Many students in Matt's class argued that to understand the sources of Matt's positive feelings about the guitar—and his family's negative feelings—he needed to look at the time period in which they occurred. These students suggested (perhaps you have already thought of this as well) that the images and values associated with rock stars who play guitars in our culture must have had an effect on the eleven-year-old Matt, even if he was not aware of it.

∞ Fastwrite 4

What kinds of images of guitar players could be influencing Matt? Spend a few minutes writing down a description of the images that come to your mind (and remember that this all started for Matt when he was in the sixth grade, so don't think only of the most contemporary examples). Which rock stars were around when you were in the sixth grade? What characteristics do you associate with them? Don't censor your reactions. Write down the first thing that comes to your mind for the next three minutes or so.

Thousands of songs played on the radio, on MTV, on tape and CD players throughout Matt's life and thousands of images of rich, sexually attractive, guitar-playing superstars obviously have played some role in making Matt become, in his own words, "a junkie of music." In fact, when Matt was in the sixth grade, Dire Straits's "Money for Nothing" was playing on every major radio station and was repeatedly shown on MTV. Our culture—and particularly our youth culture—loves rock stars. Many male rock stars are idolized. (See Chapter 6 on Elvis Presley.) Matt acknowledged in class that, of course, he had had many dreams of fame, of being a rock star. Thus, the cultural representations of sexually desirable, wealthy male guitar players combined with the cultural myth that anyone can become a star and the sense of rebellion against the older generation that music signified to him all contributed to Matt's personal pleasure in playing the guitar.

Person #2: Matt's Family and Friends

Summary of Perspective
While Matt's conflict story in assignment 1 was supposedly just about his argument with his promoter, we discover in assignment 2 that another conflict preceded it, one that is perhaps more profound because it has been ongoing in Matt's life, because it involves people he is close to—his parents, teachers, friends, and most of his family—and because, in many ways, it lay the foundation for his reaction to the promoter. No one, Matt tells us, except his sister, thinks that he will achieve his dream of becoming a musician, and Matt's desire to succeed is fueled by a desire to prove all of them wrong. How can we account for their negative reactions? If Matt is so obviously drawn to the guitar, why do others seems so bent on pushing him away from it? Are they just being perverse? Matt does not attempt any analysis here, but perhaps you can. What larger assumptions do you think might underlie the position of Matt's family and friends?

Critical Question 4. Why do different perspectives exist in the same period of time?

Cultural Factors Underlying Perspectives of Matt's Family and Friends
   Representations in the media: Negative image of rock stars. Looking to the conflicting representations, myths, and values of the larger culture can help us understand Matt's family's and friends' perspectives just as cultural analysis helped us to understand Matt's. The image of rock stars as idols discussed above is not the whole picture. For many people, rock stars symbolize degeneracy and immorality; many people regard rock stars as people who corrupt others and who are themselves corrupted—drinking too much, taking drugs, being sexually promiscuous. Who in our culture are more likely to hold these beliefs? Why? To what extent do you feel that these kinds of beliefs and values influenced some of the people in Matt's life?

Values within one's family: Generation gap. Many students—whether they are eighteen or fifty years old—suggested that their parents dislike the music they listen to. Differences of age seem to play a significant role in people's musical tastes. As younger people may be attracted to particular songs or artists because of their apparent rebellion, parents may be turned off to that music for just those reasons. Age is not the only factor affecting Matt's parents' reaction to him, but it is one possible factor that a number of students could identify.

Values of family and friends on the American Dream: Economic and psychological concerns. If a generational gap were the only factor involved in this conflict, why would some of Matt's friends be against his wanting a career in music? Some students suggested that economic and psychological concerns about Matt could have affected his friends and family. These students pointed out that while a few people "make it big" in music, most do not. Very few people in our society become "stars." In many careers, not being a star does not really affect one's capacity to earn a livelihood. Some students pointed out that one can be an "okay accountant" or an "okay doctor" and still earn a decent living and still feel relatively successful. But there are many fewer self-supporting jobs for someone who is only an "okay guitarist." So maybe Matt's friends and family were responding out of genuine concern that he would be terribly disappointed if he didn't become a star, and that he would not be able to support himself financially as a musician.

This one paragraph of Matt's analysis focused on thus far suggests so much: contradictory images of rock stars in our culture, economic factors for musicians in our country today, as well as the psychological effect of the cultural myth in America that one is either a big success or a failure. All may all be contributing to Matt's love of music and to his conflict with others about it. The picture is one of a complexity of factors interwoven to create a certain dynamic. Notice the difference from the first draft.

∞ **Fastwrite 5**

What do you think is the most important change so far in Matt's second draft from his first draft? What, at this point, is the most important change you want to make in your second draft? Fastwrite for five to ten minutes on each of these questions.

Matt's analysis of the promoter's perspective has also changed.

Perspective #3: Paul

Summary of Paul's Perspective
Of his promoter, Matt wrote:

(2) Paul wanted to make money off of the bands, so he did it any way that he could. Even if it meant stealing it. Many factors could have come into play. One being that he was not wealthy, to say the least. He could always use a couple extra dollars to make ends meet. Another reason could be that he was in the music scene so long, without getting a break, that he just wanted his dollar and did not care about the bands. I believe that the later is closer to the truth. A desperate man could sink to the level of ripping off young bands, just because most people would have fallen for it.

Cultural Factors Underlying Paul's Perspective

The myth of success/failure: desperation for recognition. Matt starts this paragraph with a fairly angry and accusatory tone, going so far as to say that what Paul was doing was actually "stealing" money from the bands. But as he begins to consider Paul's perspective from a cultural vantage point, exploring Paul through the myth of success or failure discussed above, Matt begins to paint Paul in a somewhat more sympathetic light. Paul goes from consciously being a thief to being a man himself rather hard up for money, a man who himself had never gotten a break, a man who is "desperate," not only for money, but also for recognition. Matt does not completely let him off the hook—he ends by repeating the accusation that Paul was "ripping off young bands"—but he suggests that in some way the members of the bands are letting him do this to them—"most people would have fallen for it." By qualifying his position on Paul, by looking at Paul from a different perspective, Matt is beginning to move away from the two-sides-only, right/wrong notion of conflict into a more complex understanding of the multiple sides involved for even one individual.

Further questions for cultural analysis

Why would most people have fallen for Paul's scam that to get to play, you need to sell twenty-five tickets? Matt doesn't say. What do you think? Matt could explore the relationship between Paul and the young bands. What might Paul symbolize to a young band wanting to get on stage in front of an audience? Why do they agree to sell the tickets? Why does Paul ask them to do this? What larger issues—some of which we may have discussed here, some of which we haven't yet—come into play here for both Paul and the bands? Finally, what do you make of Matt's apparent change in his depiction of Paul in just this one paragraph?

∞ Fastwrite 6

Now look back at your own paper and fastwrite on any of the following questions that seem relevant. Have you listed all of the key perspectives that you want to discuss? Have you summarized each of the perspectives fairly? What questions might you still want to ask about each perspective? What specific parts of your cultural analysis can you still expand on? Look back at Figure 1.6 to remind you of the diversity of cultural influences to take into account as you explore why you held your initial perspective and why different perspectives can exist in the same period of time.

❧   Assignment 3: Analysis of Change in Your Perspective over Time

1. **Revision**: Revise your analysis of the different perspective at the time of the conflict, including more detail and examples, following your instructor and fellow students' comments.
2. **New work**: Analyze the *changes* in your perspective over time, explaining why your perspective changed and where you stand today. You may still have conflicting perspectives. This is fine, and a discussion of these conflicting perspectives can help you develop a rich and subtle *historical analysis*. Avoid clichés and stereotypes ("I guess I just matured"). Explore the specific historical factors that might have influenced your thinking.

Definitions

   Change: In asking you to think about how your perspective has changed over time, we are asking you to engage in historical analysis. What you are analyzing, of course, is *your* history. Recall the discussion in assignment 1 about how your perspective can change in a variety of ways; it can evolve as you learn something about yourself, about others, or about a situation. You may develop a different, perhaps more complex picture of it for a variety of reasons.

   Historical Analysis: In Figure 1.7 are some possible historical factors that can influence individual perspectives over time. Bear in mind that while a large number of factors might influence an individual to change over time, only a few of these may relate to your narrative. With Matt, for example, it is his changing relationship to media representations of rock stars, to the cultural myth of success, and to the work world that most affected him.

Justification
Writing knowledgeably about why changes occur and internal conflicts exist.
While any society works to maintain continuity, it is, in fact, in constant flux as different groups vie for power and struggle to change dominant values. Flux in any one area may not be obvious to the society at large, however, until it has gone on for a number of years. And yet, it often affects individuals profoundly, even without their being aware of it. For example, most people do not have just one unified perspective on a given subject

but rather have a variety of feelings. These stem from their complex negotiation of competing influences on them and competing values, beliefs, and expectations within the culture.

Changing representations in the media and commercial displays: ads, magazines, newspapers, television, and stores:
1. increased images of women entering the workforce;
2. greater representations of gay characters on television.

Dominant myths of a society being challenged by alternatives:
1. two parent families are "normal"/greater acceptance of single parent families;
2. America is number one in everything/American students are not as well educated as students from many other countries;
3. "socialized medicine is un-American"/every American should have health care;
4. premarital sex is wrong/living together before marrying is sensible, given the divorce rate.

Changing history of a person in relation to the myths of the culture:
1. younger students may be more prone to conform to gender stereotypes;
2. people who have been working for a number of years may realize that hard work does not always bring success.

Changing history of a person in relation to one's position in one's family, religion, school, and peer group:
1. having to work and contribute financially to one's family;
2. becoming a parent or experiencing the death of a close relative or friend;
3. changing religions, losing or increasing one's faith;
4. moving to a school with a different set of values;
5. developing different sets of relationships with different friends over time.

Figure 1.7. Larger Historical Factors Influencing Individual Perspectives

That a person would have conflicting perspectives about something is no surprise to most of you. Yet despite experiencing and being able to talk about internal conflicts, many students are not used to *writing about* and *analyzing* conflicting perspectives within themselves or in others. Somehow, the notion that the self is unified—of one mind—is how most students represent themselves on paper, if they talk about themselves at all. Having conflicts or changing one's mind is often depicted in writing instruction as a sign of weakness, of not knowing what you think.

You have probably been told at one time or other that you have written an argument that seemed to contradict itself. And such contradictions may, in fact, show a weakness in your argument. But sometimes something more interesting is going on. Those contradictions may be parts of the "I" that is "you". But for them to be legitimated for your reader, you must write about them with self-awareness. You must be sure you *know* that these contradictions are part of your attitude toward the subject in question, and you must be able to account, at least in part, for *why* you think they exist.

The difference is vast between writing an argument that contradicts itself in which you seem unaware of those contradictions and writing one in which you openly discuss your internal contradictions or changes and attempt to analyze why you think they have occurred. Looking at the contradictions or conflicts in your own perspective can be a demonstration of subtle and careful analysis, and it is really a much more accurate reflection of almost anyone's position on anything.

Finally, don't forget that in analyzing your changes in perspective, there may be points when you return to your earlier thoughts on a topic. That is also a measure of change. You have rethought the issue from a changed perspective and decided that you were right all along. First thoughts are sometimes the best, but they still need to be tested over time.

∾

Sample Student Assignment 3: Analysis of Change in Your Perspective over Time

Here is an extract from Matt's paper.

My own perspective came from realizing that my dream was unattainable. This came from my experiences with Club Blue and Paul, my promoter. These experiences made me come to terms, so to speak, with my chances of having a successful music career. Up to that time, I thought that clubs would support bands, but I learned that I was alone. All the clubs wanted was money, and they did not care if they destroyed the bands that bring them this money in the process. I also realized that there were so many bands in the area, so it was impossible to change the system. There would always be one band that would sell tickets no matter what the circumstances were. Paul was just doing his job when he tried to scam me. He did not only try this with my band, but with every band. That is how the system worked in that area. The system is one of the reasons that I had a conflict within myself. Another reason is my desire to succeed as a musician. If that desire were not there I would not care so much about the system.

My perspective changed over time because I was able to see how the music scene really worked. This opened my eyes to the harsh realities of life. Before this incident I was rather naive about how everything worked. New bands starting out may not be supported to succeed at all. Now I am able to accept the truth for what it is, and to make the best out of what I have. My experience has a good side to it. The good side is I am no longer trusting of promoters and clubs. I also know how to better manage a band. These changes, good or bad, will influence my decisions in the future.

My perspective changed over time due to many reasons. At first I experienced similar symptoms that one goes through dealing with death. I went through denial, where I did not want to accept that I may not live my dream. Then I was angry at the club. I guess I was angry because the club pointed out what I should have known all along, and I blamed them for that. Realizing that it was something that I should have thought about beforehand, eventually made it a lot easier to accept.

Critical Question 5. What is the author's change in perspective over time? Critical Question 6. Why does his perspective change?

Matt's changing relationship to media representations: rock stars. Although he never comes right out and says it, it seems that Matt had really believed for six years that he would become a successful rock star, despite what everyone had told him. What he experienced the night of his conflict with Paul was the death of the fantasy begun when he was just eleven years old. At the beginning of his dream when all he knew about music careers was through the media, there seemed to be so many rock stars; now that he has begun to have experience with the music scene, he sees that there are so few.

Matt's conflict with the club displayed to him the differences between the dominant representations of musicians as stars and the material realities of most musicians. Matt recognizes that he has moved from being naively influenced by the popular culture's myths of successful rock stars—dreams with no experience—to the beginnings of an actual understanding of the music scene. It isn't about just playing and then succeeding; it's also about such more mundane realities as negotiating with clubs and managing a band.

Matt's changing relationship to a cultural myth: anyone can succeed. While Matt's conflict was intensely personal, it is also deeply imbedded in the fabric of our culture, and it extends well beyond the music scene. A major contradiction in American ideology is the dominant belief that anyone who works hard can achieve the American Dream of money, success, and status, juxtaposed with the realities that many in America will never achieve wealth and status, regardless of how hard they work. Seeing Matt's conflict in relation to this broader American context—or, as we could put it, within some of the *ideological* conflicts of American culture—helps to explain it and to give it significance and validity.

Revision through writing: moving away from two-sided analysis. Matt's perspective also seems to be changing in part as a result of having written this assignment sequence. Notice that while he recognizes the unlikelihood of his ever achieving superstar status, he no longer sees the whole incident in such black and white terms. No longer is Paul simply bad and Matt simply good. No longer are the alternatives simply total success or ultimate failure. Matt is moving away from that debilitating two-sided version of conflict. The situation is much more complex, and even Matt's band members' perspectives are brought in. Matt recognizes that he would now be a better band manager because of his experiences. Matt can talk about making a different commitment to music, one based on his love of playing, and although he does not want fully to divest himself of young fantasies of stardom, his position now attempts to accept the ambiguity of the future.

❧ Fastwrite 7

1. Is your historical analysis explicit? Are you moving away from two-sided analysis?
2. Despite the great potential of his paper, Matt has yet to explicitly articulate the relationship of his changing perspective to the larger culture. Before moving on, take one paragraph of Matt's and rewrite it in your own words, making this relationship much more explicit. Now go back to your own paper and check to see whether you have analyzed your own changing perspective within concrete historical contexts. Take one of your own paragraphs and do a ten-minute rewrite of it to make your own historical analysis more explicit and to suggest a more complex analysis than a two-sided one.

❧ Assignment 4 (Optional): Analysis in Relation to Other Students

Analyze your conflict and your change over time in relation to some of the other students in your class. Look for *historical and cultural patterns* and points of connection among the different stories and analyses in the class.

Definitions

Historical and cultural patterns: In analyzing your own conflict narrative from cultural and historical perspectives, you begin to move from the concrete detail of your own personal life to greater levels of abstraction and generalization as you link your own experiences with the values and material realities of the larger world. Asking you to look for connections with some of your classmates moves you to a further level of abstraction. At this stage, when you read other students' papers, you are not necessarily looking for thematic connections, that is, other students who have written about the same topic as you have. Rather, you are looking for patterns and connections in your analysis of why you had the experiences you did. Your work will be at the larger, more abstract level of cultural or historical values, beliefs, and practices. Try to find other students who have gone through similar processes of discovery or who seem to be having similar debates about different subjects and explore some of the cultural and historical factors that might be underlying those similarities.

Justification

A typical kind of assignment during your college career will ask you to look at a variety of approaches to analyzing a particular subject, whether it is the family, the environment, gender, television, and so on. Instructors will often give you a variety of essays on a subject and ask you to relate them in some way. To do that kind of assignment well, you need not only to understand the details of the different arguments made in each of the essays, but also to be able to move out of those details and see what larger issues or patterns of belief they have in common and what they disagree about. Every chapter in this book asks you to perform this kind of comparison and synthesis. But it is best to begin with the work you have produced yourself because you understand it well and because, in the process of writing the assignment sequence, you have probably already begun to notice various patterns and points of connection among the narratives of various students in your class.

∾

Sample Student Assignment 4: Analysis in Relation to Other Students

We will not discuss in detail the connections Matt found with other students' papers. But just to give you a sense of the range of topics with which you might find connections, here are three of the paper topics of the students Matt found relationships with:

1. conflict with a working class friend over his motivation to go to college;
2. conflict of a returning student working part time in an engineering firm who was concerned that he could not rise in his company because he was already viewed as a low-level worker;
3. conflict about whether to attend a private or public school.

Although each of these students had different personal experiences and wrote on different topics, Matt saw that they shared an underlying belief that anyone who works hard can achieve success and status in America today. They all tended early in their assignment sequence to equate success with having wealth. They also all share an experience of realizing that despite this belief, someone they know—or they themselves—may never achieve wealth and status, regardless of how hard they work.

That these students share this belief and these experiences is not all that unusual, for these experiences are part of the tension surrounding the American Dream—the myth that anyone in America can "make it big"—and the reality that there are different types of successes, that not everyone shares this dream, and that not everyone who wants it can achieve it. While each of these students' experiences was different, they found that looking for the underlying connections among their experiences allowed them to uncover some of the workings of the ideology within their own relationships.

This process potentially enables all of us to become more critical readers of ourselves and our world and more active agents in that world. By recognizing the connections between our own assumptions, our life experiences, and the larger culture, we are better able to actively determine the beliefs we want to maintain. When we engage in such critical work, we no longer accept beliefs simply because they are widespread views. We can actively choose them because we are capable of analyzing them.

∾ Assignment 5: Final Paper

Write a narrative of a past conflict that you have changed your mind about. Analyze the different perspectives at the time of the conflict, including your own, by exploring some of the larger cultural and historical factors that may have influenced and helped to determine them. Analyze the changes in your perspective over time, explaining why your perspective changed and where you stand today. Evaluate your conflict and your change over time in relation to the other students in the class. Look for patterns and points of connection among the different stories in the class, and end by making some general observations about conflicts.

Justification

You might be asking yourself why, if you have written all these drafts, we would ask you to write it again. The answer is that you have written a variety of pieces; now is your chance for genuine revision and synthesis. Now is the chance to articulate clearly points of analysis that you may have only been hinting at before. You may be more in control of this piece of writing than you've ever been of anything you've written. Go with it. Let yourself feel the details of your essay.

Watch the ways in which your narrative opens up possibilities as you revisit one final time those moments before, during, and after the conflict. Watch how you weave connections among different perspectives, subtly preparing your readers for your analysis. Watch the ways in which your analysis draws on and develops points you made earlier. But do not feel tied to all of the words you have written. Much of what you write for your final paper might be new (or at least you will surround what you have written with new ideas) with a clear thesis, with "point sentences" that say just what you might have wanted to say all along. You know where they go, and at this stage you probably know just how they need to be said.

For you have not only identified differences among various perspectives, you have traced how they may have evolved. You have come to understand some of the threads of different people's histories. The webs of our beliefs, experiences, and positions are tightly woven, and history and culture—both social and individual—are about interrelation. And you, in writing this history, contribute to creating those interrelations.

ॐ

Putting It All Together

As you read a large extract from Matt's final paper, notice in particular the change in Matt's analysis of Paul, the discussion of other band members, and the added detail about his encounters with his family. Look at the way in which his capacity to articulate his change over time has developed. But also keep in mind areas where you think Matt could have revised more, made a point more clearly, or sharpened an analysis.

Included are some teacher comments on the paper, but much of it is without comment, inviting you to make marginal notes as you read this paper. When you finish, do a fastwrite on your general impressions of how Matt wrote his paper, comparing it to how you plan to write yours.

(1) In the sixth grade I underwent a series of changes. That year I knew what I had to do. After a few long months of coaxing, my parents agreed to let me take guitar lessons. The instrument was a part of me the first time that I

played it. Day and night, the guitar never left my side. My only dream since the sixth grade was to be able to make a living playing music. In my opinion, that would be success.

Notice detailed explanation of feelings

(2) A few years later I started a band with some good friends. We called ourselves Good Morning Richard. At first it was only playing in the basement, but eventually I was able to make a few calls and book a show. The name of this venue was Club Blue. Before I stepped out on the stage, for the first time, I thought that I wanted to perform music for a living, but afterwards it was confirmed. I knew that was my "calling" and I could not be happy doing anything else. The feeling that I had on stage was like a drug induced high. The rush was so intense that I became a junkie of music. I had to play music in order to feel complete. The only way to describe playing music to me is the free flowing of my emotions at that time. Music is never about thinking what note to play next, but about feeling what note should be played.

Notice detailed explanation of situation

(3) When bands get a "gig" at any of the many clubs on the New Jersey coastline, they are required to sell tickets to that show. This is hated among bands, but welcomed by the clubs. The usual amount of tickets required to be sold prior to playing is twenty-five. That does not seem like much, but when you try selling twelve dollar tickets to your friends for the fourth time in two months, they are not as willing to buy. If a band cannot sell the ticket minimum, the club does not let them play. My friend's band sold forty-nine tickets out of fifty and the club kicked them out the night of the show before they went on. This is quite common, and there is no way around it.

Details about bass player now make sense

(4) Exactly one year after our first show at Club Blue, we were asked to play there again. This time we made the demand of not selling a minimum of twenty-five tickets. This request was quickly shot down by our promoter, but we came to a verbal agreement of only selling as many tickets as we could. That week we needed to use our replacement drummer because our regular drummer, Mike, was going away for a while. Needless to say, this replacement drummer did not sell any tickets. Ryan, my bass player did not sell any either. At this point I called the promoter to let him know what was going on. He quickly answered the phone and I told him that I had fourteen tickets sold, and only two days left before the show. He said, "No problem" and that is where the phone call ended. I thought everything was going to be just fine.

(5) The night of the show we loaded in all of our equipment and set it up on stage. Our set time was nine-thirty, and it was only around six o'clock in the evening. The band and I decided to hang out backstage for a while and discuss

the show that night. I was very excited, as always, because I was on my way to living my dream. When our promoter called me over to discuss the ticket sales everything changed.

Good sensory details/explanation of situation

(6) I walked though the smoky club, passing the dimly lit mixing board and into the lobby. I rounded the corner and opened the weathered door to the coat room. That was Paul's office. I walked in, we exchanged business smiles, and I handed him the money. When I told him how many tickets we had sold he gave me a double-take. I asked what was wrong, and he said that he was not ready for that small an amount of tickets sold. At that point I started to get a little angry. When I reminded him of our phone conversation earlier in the week, he flat out denied that we even discussed ticket sales. After he was done calling me a liar he proceeded to tell me that we owed him money for the tickets that we could not sell. That is where I put my foot down. I could not believe that he was looking at my eyes and lying to my face. My band was giving him business and he was questioning me on something that he knew about. We exchanged a few four letter words and after a few minutes he backed down and said we had to go on around seven-thirty. That was two hours before we were supposed to go on. That meant that everyone coming to see us would miss our set and I would have to stand outside to tell them that. The fans would not appreciate losing twelve dollars and going out of their way to get to the club. The repercussion of that is they would be reluctant to purchase more tickets to see the band in the future.

Note different treatment of Paul—more sympathetic/even identification

(7) Part of the reason that Paul would want to take money from bands is that he was not a rich man. He was also growing older, around thirty-five. He spent everyday of his life booking shows for young bands that never draw a huge crowd. Paul gets paid on the number of people that come into the club. He was not a rich man to say the least. He could also just be tired of having to deal with teenage bands. Paul could have been depressed and disgruntled about his job and this was his way of venting the anger. Earlier in his life, Paul might have seen himself as a successful promoter, but now that he is not could be part of a problem within himself. I believe that the reason Paul is trying to scam bands is because he was trying to deal with not living his dream. It was very similar to what I soon realized after this incident.

Note greater description of feelings

(8) We reluctantly began playing our set. Somewhere in the middle I was so caught up in playing, that I forgot about the incident. Playing music is a form of therapy for me. I just drift away into my own world where everything is less harsh. My mind went blank and my emotions let loose. I never play with my eyes open because I feel my way though the music. After the set we loaded

our equipment into the cars. Then I had to wait outside of the club to tell anyone coming to see us that we had already played. That was one night that I will never forget.

Increased complexity of perspective; begins explicitly to locate it in larger cultural contexts, but could still use more detail; begins to infuse past story with present perspective; band members are now recognized as part of conflict situation

(9) The reason that I will never forget that evening is because that was the first time my heart was broken. I realized that I was alone in trying for my dream. My band mates did not care either way what direction the band went in. I did all of the scheduling, and promotion for Good Morning Richard. Up to that point in time all I did was anything to move my band closer to my goal. That night I learned that I could not trust anyone in the local music scene. I also realized that there were so many bands out there and the clubs did not care about any of them. All they wanted was their almighty dollar. I realized too that the musicians I had been listening to were all successful. They had made it. That gave me the feeling that anyone could, but now I could see all the musicians that weren't successful or weren't going to be because no one was going to support them. It took money as well as talent to succeed. To me it was about music, not money. From that point on I knew that my chances of becoming all that I dreamed of were slim because the clubs did not support the bands, and my band did not care about itself.

Note complexity of position/odd analogy

(10) To this very day it saddens me to think of never living my dream. I would do anything to have a chance. If by some miracle I do succeed, I would never work a day in my life. Music is never work, just an emotion that becomes as much a part of you as your pancreas. When one is hungry, they eat. A musician plays because he has to. I just could not live without it. The conflict I had was discovering that my dream was almost impossible to achieve. That realization was one of the toughest problems I had to learn to accept, but it is all part of having a dream. I play now for music's sake, never for fame. Music is the window into my heart. That is where someone can get to know my true self.

Note analysis of perspective before conflict

(11) One of the reasons that it was so hard to come to terms with not living my dream is because most of the people around me told me that I would never make it. My parents told me that musicians that I was looking up to at the time were "losers, bums, and drug addicts." Instead of making me turn away from music, it pushed me toward it. I wanted it that much more, just to prove that I could. I know that they were trying to do good, by wanting me to have a successful career, but they did not think that I could not be

happy doing anything else. My heart was in music and by their making a mockery of what I wanted to be, a deep trench was put in between us. . . .

Important points, but rather cliché in expression—needs more detail

(12) Conflicts exist whenever one is confronted by change. People, in general, do not like change because it scares them. Exploring the unknown is not supported by our society today. That is ingrained in our heads since birth. People are also inclined toward routine. Routine is good because it is not dangerous. One cannot get hurt by doing proven things. Even some popular sayings reinforce this, "Why fix what's not broke." In that respect, people fear change. When change occurs, whether it is external, or internal, one is conflicted. Every one of the student's papers that I read has some degree of change. It is also obvious that they fear that change. . . .

Some good points, but expressed in a rather clichéd fashion

(13) The bright side of being conflicted is the end result. Usually one comes out of a conflict being stronger. That will be an asset for future conflicts. One saying that is of the liberal persuasion is "There is no teacher like experience." Experience really is the best teacher because one can only learn from an experience. Of course a conflict that is unresolved can be detrimental, but usually it has a positive outcome. We change our minds about conflict because we grow.

As he had begun in earlier drafts, Matt writes explicitly about the conflicted nature of his dream. But in this final draft, Matt's description of the past is infused with his present understanding of it (see in particular paragraphs 7, 9, and 10). While Matt still clearly would love to hold onto his dream, his recognition of its naïveté and his understanding of why it cannot be fulfilled—at least on its terms before the conflict—is striking and quite moving. Although we would like to see Matt develop this integration of past and present perspectives more fully, his beginning to do so marks a new stage in his writing and thinking maturity. Matt's writing is starting to show his readers that experiences—including remembering past events in the present—all occur in contexts and that those contexts change over time.

Matt's process of writing these stages of his paper reveals two important developments. Not only was he able to put into words what had before only been feelings; his understanding of the entire conflict situation grew dramatically. A situation that looked fairly black and white at the beginning became complex. As Matt added an increasing number of details and began his analysis, he realized that he couldn't just divide up the good guys and the bad guys. Things weren't that simple. Matt's paper lets us begin to see the relationship of his and others' "personal" feelings and experiences to the larger culture. By his final draft, Matt's readers have a much greater understanding of the various perspectives involved. Matt himself has a much greater understanding of different positions, including his own.

Most important is the complexity of Matt's own position. He himself, as he acknowledges near the end, embodies conflicting perspectives. Even as he changes and becomes more realistic about the work it will take to develop a career in music, he still retains some of his early dreams. They have evolved; but they are still a part of him.

There are many places in which Matt could have improved on his paper. He repeatedly shies away from explicitly analyzing his relationship with dominant cultural representations. Why do you think he does this? Do you find yourself doing this in your paper? If so, why do you think you are? What do you think are the most successful aspects of Matt's paper? What parts do you think still need revision?

ॐ

Conclusion

Matt's paper gives us a glimpse at how history works. What seems on the surface to be unified is, in fact, fraught with contradiction, tension, and difference. Indeed, it is often the interaction of these different elements within the self—or within a culture—that motivates us to move in particular ways. Beliefs, assumptions, and practices do not usually change dramatically; more often, they evolve gradually over time. Anything that occurs in the present is subtly influenced by aspects of the past. Matt revealed some of this process to us.

Other texts—including our current culture—may not seem to reveal the past very obviously, and yet the influence and power of the past is there. We can often only begin to understand the present by studying the past. As we can understand Matt's current attitude about music only by understanding how it began and evolved, so too can we only understand our own perspectives, those of others, and indeed those of our whole culture, by going back, by looking for those traces that support, challenge, undermine, and redirect in diffuse ways the apparent unity of the present. As you begin to write your final draft, keep in mind your experiences as a reader, reading and interpreting Matt's paper and experiences. Keep in mind the places where Matt's paper struck you, positively and negatively. Write with your own readers in mind.

❧ 2 ❧

FASHION: SELVES AND SURFACES

Sherry Horton and Kathleen McCormick

The woman shall not wear that which pertaineth unto a man, neither shall a man put on a woman's garment; for all that do so are abomination unto the Lord thy God.
—DEUTERONOMY

Dress is the cultural metaphor for the body, it is the material with which we "write" or "draw" a representation of the body into our cultural context.
—ELIZABETH WILSON AND JULIET ASH, 1993

Fear of society, fear of oneself, fear of the power of clothing; fear is the reason fashion is so often dismissed as flippant and foolish.
—COLIN MCDOWELL, 1992

If menswear for women, earrings and skirts for men, navel and nipple rings for everyone, and tattoos on every part of the body, visible and invisible, are now part of the "mainstream," what buttons, envelopes, and borderlines are left to push?
—MARJORIE GARBER, 1995

❧

Introduction: Retaining Your Personal Voice with More Public Subjects

Chapter 1 introduced you to the experience of writing historical and cultural analyses of your own and others' personal conflicts; it also took you through the development of another student's analysis, as he worked through an assignment sequence. Starting with such a "private" text as an account of a personal conflict and then moving into the more "public realm"—as the later questions in the sequence required you to do—helps you maintain a strong sense of voice and investment in your writing.

Yet most college writing assignments ask you to begin working in a more public space: a disciplinary debate, a certain set of theories or ideas, a particular historical event. The rest of the book, therefore, asks you to analyze more obviously public subjects. But you are asked to link these public subjects with your personal experiences in ways that can make your writing engaging (and engaged) and can help you become a more critical reader, writer, and thinker.

Chapter 2 serves as a transition to the rest of the book. While you will likely not answer all of the questions in this chapter or even be assigned all of the readings, Chapter 2 continues the practice of defining a number of important concepts for you and of providing justifications for the writing assignments. These concepts will be relevant as you work with other chapters in the book. We also talk to you about reading strategies for written and visual texts, discussing ways for you to ask questions of texts that you may feel less familiar with or less comfortable with than the personal texts you worked on in Chapter 1. These will also be relevant to later chapters, and you may want to refer later to the discussions of them here. Apart from the definitions and justifications (which stop after this chapter) the organization here is basically the same as that of the following chapters.

This move to more public topics does not mean that you are to abandon your own voice or story—far from it. The skills you use in the rest of the book are an extension of those you used in Chapter 1. Starting with a personal text has obvious advantages, but the same discoveries, problems, and questions—as well as the same level of engagement—can and should occur with seemingly more objective topics. And just as they were in the first chapter, the assignments you are asked to work on in the rest of the book are *sequenced,* so you have a chance to work in gradual stages. We offer various suggestions for sequencing, but your instructor will determine what the best sequence is for your particular class.

☙

Reading the Signs around Us: Why Begin with Fashion?

We are surrounded by signs and symbols that we interpret all the time; and we continually produce signs and symbols for others to interpret. We indicate to people, often without saying a word, that we are approachable or unapproachable, that we like to ski, that we are well read. Within our own culture, we generally know the rules for sending signs or messages— a process called *encoding*—and for reading or interpreting messages—a process called *decoding*. Yet often we don't realize that we know these rules because, as we saw in Chapter 1, as part of our dominant ideology, they seem simply "normal" and "natural," just "the way things are." To begin to become critical readers, writers, and thinkers, we need to be able to articulate how and why we encode and decode signs in the ways we do, whether those signs are about race, beauty, social class, music, gender, or, in the case of this chapter, fashion.

What does it mean to say that something is a *sign?* A sign has a meaning that extends beyond what it literally is. So, for example, trees and bushes are not in themselves signs. When they are carefully trimmed and planted around the foundation of a building or on the grounds of a college campus, however, they begin to function as signs, suggesting affluence and perhaps pride. Ivy growing on the walls of school buildings suggests tradition and status, hence the term, *Ivy League.* Because ivy literally has no connection to status, when it suggests tradition, it is functioning as a sign in part of a symbol system rather than functioning literally. One can quite easily imagine a society in which ivy would have a different meaning attached to it.

Similarly, wearing black has certain meanings associated with it. These meanings change with the context, but since we are always in a context, the meaning at any given point is generally clear. What comes to your mind when you think of someone wearing black? Wearing black can mean that one is artsy and somewhat counterculture. In contrast, it can signify high fashion, sophistication, and status within the dominant culture, as in a *black tie reception.* Wearing black can also mean that one is in mourning (but because that custom is less common than it used to be, that may not be the first meaning you thought of).

We begin our study of signs with a look at fashion because it is relatively accessible, and many of you will probably find that you know more rules of encoding and decoding the fashion system than you might realize, especially when you focus on reading texts—whether printed or visual—with the help of a number of well-tested reading strategies.

∾

What Is Fashion?

How does fashion function as a sign system? The word *fashion* itself raises questions of definition. What do we mean by it? The *haute couture* fashion of Paris and New York? The glossy pages of *Vogue* or *GQ?* The "in" or trendy fashions that come and go on *Beverly Hills 90210* or MTV? Are school or sports uniforms a kind of fashion? How does the word *fashion* relate to the word *clothing?* Are they synonymous? What about the everyday clothes that most of us wear? Are these wardrobe staples fashion? How does any fashion item become mainstream, and why? Our definition of fashion throughout this chapter includes all of these types of clothing, but significant debate exists about what should be called *fashion*.

While people wear clothes for functional reasons, that is, to keep their bodies covered and protected, what they wear and how they wear it has meaning beyond its functionality. In other words, it has symbolic meaning as well as literal meaning. We often dress for others as much as for ourselves, to produce or project a certain identity.

Some insist that with fashion, "Anything goes!" We are free to throw on anything that's handy as we roll out of bed and race to class, to a job, or to an appointment. But most people also admit that at certain times they have agonized over getting dressed. "I have nothing to wear," we moan, staring at a closet bulging with everything from torn jeans to a prom dress or tuxedo. What are we worried about? That we won't "fit in" and be embarrassed that we don't? Or that we won't "stand out," and be embarrassed by that? Why does it matter so much what we choose to wear at any particular moment? How do we know how to dress? How do we learn and interpret the signs of fashion?

Turn now to Figure 2.1, "Anatomy of a Shredder," to get a sense of your knowledge of how to read or decode the signs of fashion. Finding words to describe a visual object—an ad or commercial, a painting or a photograph—is challenging. Practice doing some close observation with this contemporary photograph. A "shredder" is slang for a snowboarder. Of course, not all snowboarders dress like this, and no one individual necessarily displays all of these signs, but the point should be clear that the clothes of these "shredders" (the name, of course, is also a sign) do more than just provide functional covering for their bodies. They send out messages and suggest attitudes that people looking at them interpret. What are the meanings of these signs? The descriptions of the almost endless array of detailed signs do not directly explain their meaning, though they are clearly poking fun at the snowboarders. Why?

∾ Fastwrite 1

a. Take a minute and jot down some of the meanings of the fashion signs for you in Figure 2.1. Then explain why you think the snowboarders are being made fun of in the poster.

b. Create your own "Anatomy of a _____?" by listing five to seven signs of any current fashion style of your choice. Then quickly list the meaning of each of these signs to you and to people of your peer group. You may accompany your list with a magazine picture or a sketch of your own, but focus the fastwrite on enumerating some of the signs of the fashion style you have chosen and on having fun with it. Show yourself and your instructor that you already know how to decode what are actually fairly complex signs.

Anatomy of a Shredder

President of
Kurt Cobain Fan Club,
chapter 30

All clothing looks
like regular streetwear—
only difference is three
times the cost

Goggles have left
permanent marks
on forehead

Bleary eyes from
"second hand" smoke

Love beads bought from
ex-hippie garage sale

This is eighteen
years of growth

Graphic
makes the
board go
faster

Always hold
board as if
it's more
important
than your
girlfriend

Roomy
pockets
for hiding
six packs

Logos
stolen
from
Chevy van
circa '73

Gortex ™ pants so your butt
doesn't get wet when you're
sitting around looking cool

Boots designed to
look like sneakers

Wallet includes heavy chain,
lighter, no money, tickets to
Phish concert, and a map

Figure 2.1. Anatomy of a Shredder

⟋⟍

Locating Fashion in Larger Historical and Cultural Contexts

The "rules" and signs of fashion are complex and continually in flux, but they are not simply arbitrary; that is, they are not random and without cause. We can tell a lot about a culture, as well as a lot about individual people, by their clothes. And yet this move to cultural analysis after we individually decode a fashion style is not always easy.

While most people can readily attach a meaning to a contemporary article of clothing or style of dressing, they often see that meaning as not about the larger culture but more exclusively about the individual—he's a nerd; she's an art-type; they only listen to heavy metal. Because people have naturalized or accepted the fashion codes and range of choices as natural and normal, as the way things are, they tend not to ask *why* particular styles come to have certain meanings. Asking *why* is the beginning of cultural analysis.

The next examples in this chapter come from the past, up to two hundred years ago. That is because it is easier to see the connection of clothing (or any subject) to larger cultural values when we move to a period more distant in time from our own. The values of an older society and the clothes people wore are often significantly different from ours, and we will not have naturalized them; consequently, we are much more likely to ask why particular fashions of the past came to have certain meanings for the people who wore them.

Then, as you move to contemporary texts, you can become more analytical about them as you begin to see that our own values are situated in a particular time and place and are not universal. Further, you may discover some connections with the texts of the past that initially seemed so different.

Before you begin reading historical material about fashion, think about your own fashion history so that you can readily relate the concepts of change over time and of conflicting influences at one time period—from your work in Chapter 1—to the specific discussion of fashion in this chapter.

⟋⟍ Fastwrite 2

a. At the center of daily life is the decision of how to look and what to wear. (Am I dressed correctly? Will they like my outfit? How do I look? Do I look out of place?) How do these judgments shape our lives, our relationships with others, and our sense of self?

b. Fastwrite about fashion as it relates to your growing up. Beginning with your earliest memories of getting dressed up, sketch out some brief examples

Figure 2.2. Colonial American Fashion: 1700–1740

of how clothing has affected your life. What did you wear and why? Who gave this clothing to you? What clothing did you have for different occasions, activities, or events? When did you become conscious of choosing your own clothes or of feeling that you were not given a choice? When did your awareness of certain styles or trends and their significance first develop? When, if at all, did your sense of the "right" clothes for you change or evolve? What are the most important signs you want to send out today by the clothing you wear? What are their meanings for you?

Historical Questions

1. Compare and contrast the fashion signs of Figures 2.2 and 2.3. Describe as many of the continuities and changes in men's and women's fashion between the early eighteenth century and the middle nineteenth century as you can

Figure 2.3. Nineteenth-Century American Fashion: 1850

by what you see represented in these two pictures. To help you focus on individual signs, you might want to label particular details—such as the fabrics, the cut of the clothes, the stance of the men and the women, their hair and facial expression, and so on—as was done in Figure 2.1. Then, focusing on what you see to be the greatest point of change and the greatest point of continuity in men's and women's fashion, speculate about why you think certain changes occurred and why others did not. Suggest a possible link between these fashions and larger social values, beliefs, or practices in the United States at the time.

Definition

Historical Question: This question asks you to articulate and analyze *differences* in the clothing *of two periods from the past.* In doing so, you are practicing historical analysis: the comparison and contrast of beliefs, practices, and assumptions from different periods of time and the analysis of why those differences developed by exploring their larger social contexts. (See Figure 1.1 from the Introduction.)

Justification

Why study a more distant past that does not seem directly related to your experiences? This book often uses historical materials whose ideas are very different from those generally accepted today. It does so to accentuate *historical difference*. You are not being asked to accept the ideas from the past as valid today, but simply to try to understand why they seemed acceptable to people in a different period. The work you did in understanding and analyzing personal perspectives other than your own in Chapter 1 (think of Matt's work in trying to understand his promoter, Paul) will have prepared you in many ways for this kind of analysis.

2. Imagine yourself dressed in one of the outfits depicted in one of the pictures. Compare how you think you would feel being dressed in this outfit for an entire day, given your current lifestyle, with how a man or woman at the time might have felt.

Definition

Historical Question: This question asks you to articulate and analyze *differences in attitudes* toward clothing *between a past period in history and the present*. Like question 1, this question is an example of historical analysis because it asks you to compare two distinct historical periods. The difference with this question, however, is that it asks you to compare a period in the past with the present; question 1 asked you to compare two different periods from the past. (See Figure 1.1 from the Introduction.)

Justification

Such a comparison allows you to become more conscious of your own everyday assumptions and expectations—about lifestyle, freedom of movement, comfort, and so on—that you take for granted as normal or natural and that you might not think to discuss if they were not suddenly placed in an unfamiliar context.

Cultural Questions

1. Focusing on one couple in one of the two pictures, develop in more depth than you did above the values that might underlie the ways the man and woman are dressed. To help you access more of your knowledge about this time period, you might want to begin by fastwriting about the lives of the

people—individually and as a couple. Ask yourself some of the following questions. What do they do all day—together and separately? How do they live? What do others think of them? Why are they dressed this way? What do their other clothes look like? What are their interests? What opinions might they hold? Then reread what you wrote and explain the three or four most important details or signs of their clothing that suggested these larger values and beliefs to you.

Definition

Cultural Question: Although this question is about the past, it is an example of cultural analysis: the linking of a belief or practice—in this case, the way one dresses—to other beliefs, practices, and assumptions that are going on *at the same period of time.* (See Figure 1.2 from the Introduction.)

Justification

In American society, we tend to think much more in terms of the individual rather than the larger society. Therefore, it is more likely that you will be able to speculate about cultural values if you first attempt to visualize the people depicted as individuals. Also, the capacity to narrativize, that is, to tell a story, as we discussed in Chapter 1, is a powerful one. Writing a narrative may enable you to record details that you can later use for analytical purposes.

2. Find a picture of any contemporary couple—it can be a man and a woman, two men, or two women—and fastwrite about what you imagine their lifestyle and values might be. What particular signs of their clothing suggested certain meanings, that is, certain values and beliefs, to you? Why do you think the particular signs you focused on are linked in our contemporary society to the particular meanings you suggested? What aspects of our larger society's values help to code those signs in particular ways?

Definition

Cultural Question: Like the previous cultural question, this question is an example of cultural analysis because it asks you to link values and beliefs from *the same period of time.* The difference with this question, however, is that it focuses on the present; question 1 asked you to focus on a period in the past. Any question that asks you to focus on a single time period is defined throughout this book as cultural analysis. (See Figure 1.2 from the Introduction.)

Justification

It is always initially harder to see the values embedded in one's own cultural period than in a different period because one tends to naturalize the values of one's own time. However, juxtaposing this question with the previous question, which focused on an earlier time period, may enable some of your own values to become more apparent.

∾

Active Reading Strategies

In what follows are a variety of ideas for active reading. In reading more actively, you comprehend more while you are reading so that later, when you are writing, you are able to take up your own positions with a clearer sense of entering a conversation with what others have said on the subject. Try out all the different strategies when reading texts in this book and in your other classes as well. You will no doubt find some more helpful than others.

Questioning before You Start

Whenever you read a text, try to read it as "actively" as possible, that is, to think and reflect about what the author is saying, to draw connections between one part of the essay and another, and to make connections with your own experiences. You can develop an active stance toward a text even before you begin reading it. For example, think about what the phrase, *the great masculine renunciation,* might mean, especially in relation to Figures 2.2 and 2.3. Speculate. Look up the word *renunciation.* Define *the great masculine renunciation* in your own words. What questions come to mind as you think about this phrase that you want to answer by reading the text? What did men "renounce," and why was it a "great" renunciation?

Marking a Text and Writing a Summary

As you move from writing about conflicts you have personally experienced to reading and writing about other issues that affect your life, you need to talk about what reading means and about how you read texts that were written by others at more distant periods of time.

If you know before you start reading something that you will be writing about or taking a test on it, how does that affect the way you read? What strategies do you already use to record and remember a text's key ideas? Do you underline or highlight? Make marginal notes or marks? Write summaries on a separate page? Keep a reading log? However you make your notes, the goal is to record the author's points so that you will have them for easy reference as you prepare for class discussion or write an essay of your own.

We suggest that as you read you should wait until the end of a paragraph or section before underlining or highlighting and commenting. Often, ideas that seem important as you move line by line are clearer a paragraph or two later as the author continues to discuss them. Perhaps the author's extended examples of an abstract concept help you to understand it. Mark key ideas and their supporting evidence with a consistent method of notemaking that will catch your eye visually and help you quickly to recall the key points.

After you finish marking the text paragraph by paragraph, reread your marginal notes from the beginning. Do the key ideas that you noted in the margins synthesize into a coherent whole? If not, you may need to reread certain portions of the text. Then, use your marginal notes to write a summary of the whole reading selection. Your goal in summarizing is to condense several pages into a paragraph or two. Writing a summary can help you check to be sure you understand a text; it can also help you to remember it later.

Personal Response

Once you have a clear summary of the reading, you might write a personal response. Collect and record your own thoughts during or as soon after reading as possible, knowing that as the text's ideas fade with time, so will your own personal reactions to them. Talk back to the text you have just marked and summarized. Raise questions. Disagree. Offer confirming or counter examples from your own experiences.

Double-Entry Journal

One method of recording your own response is to experiment with what is called a *double-entry journal.* In a double-entry journal you write two kinds of notes in two columns or on two facing pages. On the left are the key ideas in the reading selection, with the page on which they occur, either directly quoted or paraphrased; on the right are your own thoughts about those ideas. Some students, preferring an easy-to-read method, write their double-entry journal on a word processor. A sample of a double entry journal on J. C. Flugel's "The Great Masculine Renunciation" occurs in Figure 2.4.

If you decide to use a double-entry journal when reading Flugel's essay, organize the left side to reflect the essay's four-part structure. Mark up the essay in the book and then, on the left side of your double-entry journal, paraphrase or quote passages that best express Flugel's key points from each section.

Experiment with ways to record these ideas. If you quote directly, be sure to put the page number in the margin next to the quotation. Even if

63 "Men gave up their right to all the brighter, gayer, more elaborate, and more varied forms of ornamentation, leaving these entirely to the use of women. . . . The Great Masculine Renunciation."

"Man abandoned his claim to be considered beautiful. . . . aimed at being only useful."

63 F. goes on to ask why the GMR happened. I'm going to outline this since after my first quick reading through I see that F's argument is well organized. He says, "Those who have duly considered the matter . . ."

A) political and social causes of the GMR, mainly the French Revolution with its focus on "Liberty, Equality, Fraternity."

[What were "special sumptuary laws"??? and "ancien regime"???]

B) Two ways the goals of the FR led to change in men's clothes:

(1) "doctrine of the brotherhood of man" meant that men should be brothers, and not show their differences in wealth and status.

Key words: "uniformity"—to get rid of class differences;

"simplification"–uniformity, all clothing would be simpler and therefore cost less.

(2) "the ideal of work had now become respectable." Previously, "Gentlemen" didn't do much of anything—made love and war!

63 So men had the *right* to wear ribbons and lace? Actually, we've already discussed in class the illustrations in this chapter showing how men's clothes changed then (@ 1800) and women's didn't. They were so ridiculous looking! Men looked like women! Stuff for Halloween! No guy would be caught dead in lace today, so what it means to look like a guy sure has changed.

—Why did men want to be *only* useful? F. says that men and women competed with each other for "splendour." Do we compete now? I don't think so—so much clothing is unisex. Actually, men and women both wore fancy decorations then, and now both sexes wear men-type stuff. So it's sort of the same but in a different way. Then, men and women in the same social class wore similar styles (we talked in class about nobles and peasants). Is that true now? I don't know, I don't think so. What does "renunciation" mean? And "decollete"?

64 The French Revolution was really important—also the American Revolution and the Industrial Revolution. All these revolutions meant that the leisure class (probably not a word that was used then) either didn't exist or went underground. And men went to work, built factories, cities, etc.

The middle class began. (The Civil War in 1860 is about where my last history course ended!) So these are political and economic factors that affected men a lot, but not women because almost all women kept their same domestic roles. They weren't involved in politics or work.

Figure 2.4. Double-Entry Journal on J. C. Flugel's "The Great Masculine Renunciation," 63–68.

65 "Such a change can only have been brought about by the operation of very powerful psychical inhibitions."
Key statements here:
—"modern man has a far sterner and more rigid conscience than has modern woman." (!!!???).
—"modern man's clothing. . . devotion to duty, renunciation, and self-control."
—"Fixed system of his clothing . . . strict adherence to the social code."
65 & 66 "Social nature of the Sex Differentiation Implied."
"greater uniformity of costume →greater sympathy between one individual and another, and between one class and another→removes certain socially disintegrating factors that are liable to be produced by differences in clothing."
Flugel answers my question: If men's clothes are dull, they also don't feel the envy and jealousy that women feel. So F. says class differences persist in women's clothes, but not in men's. Men don't show their wealth by clothes; women do.
66 F. asks 2 questions:
(1) why haven't women's clothes been affected like men's?
(2) how can men stand it? "What has happened to the psychological tendencies (Narcissistic, exhibitionistic, etc.) which formerly found expression in the decorative aspects of their dress?"
Answers: men only were affected because "of a more general difference between the sexes."
And why? Possibilities—"innate greater susceptibility to group influences in the male" OR "natural division of labour between the sexes"

65 What does F. mean by this? I have no idea what he's talking about. Men have more of a conscience than women? Give me a break! Men feel more duty and self control? Not likely! Well, maybe he means a stereotype like the businessman's suit and hat that, like in old movies, makes them all look alike. It makes me think that men are or have been much more conformist than women. True? I'll bring this up in class.

66 Now I get it. Women can compete with each other with clothes, and show their individuality. So men can't show individuality by clothes? True now, or not? I think the suit as a uniform for work is going out, although women do wear suits. We now have Casual Fridays, and my Dad doesn't wear a tie to work any more.

66 F. seems to say that men are more sociable, more involved in society, and thus pay more attention to fitting in with others. Women are more self-loving, pay more attention to themselves. And this is natural. Is it? I need to know more about Freud—maybe we'll discuss him in class. Is narcissism a psychological principle that is considered true for all human beings—more true for women than men? FIND OUT ABOUT THIS!

you paraphrase using your own words to translate Flugel's, whenever you use his particular terms, such as *uniformity* and *simplification,* use quotation marks to indicate that they are his words. On the right side of the journal record some of your immediate responses and questions.

Charts

Another visual notemaking method is a diagram, map, or flowchart. Your instructor may ask you to experiment with several different notemaking systems until you find one that suits you.

J . C .   F L U G E L

The Great Masculine Renunciation

Psychoanalyst J. C. Flugel (1884–1955) wrote *The Psychology of Clothes* in 1930, from which this essay is taken, after giving a series of talks on the subject for the British Broadcasting Corporation in 1928. Flugel is credited with formulating the phrase *the great masculine renunciation* to describe the remarkable change in men's clothing during the early 1800s.

At the end of the eighteenth century . . . there occurred one of the most remarkable events in the whole history of dress, one under the influence of which we are still living, one, moreover, which has attracted far less attention than it deserves: men gave up their right to all the brighter, gayer, more elaborate, and more varied forms of ornamentation, leaving these entirely to the use of women, and thereby making their own tailoring the most austere and ascetic of the arts. Sartorially, this event has surely the right to be considered as "The Great Masculine Renunciation." Man abandoned his claim to be considered beautiful. He henceforth aimed at being only useful. So far as clothes remained of importance to him, his utmost endeavours could lie only in the direction of being "correctly" attired, not of being elegantly or elaborately attired. Hitherto man had vied with woman in the splendour of his garments, woman's only prerogative lying in *décolleté* and other forms of erotic display of the actual body; henceforward, to the present day, woman was to enjoy the privilege of being the only possessor of beauty and magnificence, even in the purely sartorial sense.

What were the causes of this Great Renunciation? Those who have duly considered the matter seem to be in the main agreed that these causes were primarily of a political and social nature, and that, in their origin, they were intimately associated with the great social upheaval of the French Revolution. One of the purposes of decorative dress was . . . to emphasise distinctions of rank and wealth—distinctions which, in the fifteenth, sixteenth, and seventeenth centuries, the aristocracy had often endeavoured to preserve by means of special sumptuary laws. But distinctions of this kind were among the chief of those that the French Revolution, with its world-echoing slogan of "Liberty, Equality, Fraternity," aimed at abolishing. It is not surprising, therefore, that the magnificence and elaboration of costume, which so well expressed the ideals of the *ancien régime* should have been distasteful to the new social tendencies and aspirations that found expression in the Revolution.

There were, in particular, two ways in which these new aspirations tended to produce a simplification in the dress of the male sex. In the first place, the doctrine of the brotherhood of man was obviously incompatible with garments which, by their very nature and associations, emphasised the differences in wealth and station between one man and another. The new social order demanded something that expressed rather the common humanity of all men. This could only be done by means of a greater **uniformity** of dress, a uniformity achieved particularly by the abolition of those distinctions which had formerly divided the wealthy from the poor, the exalted from the humble; since these distinctions consisted largely in a greater elaboration and costliness of aristocratic costume as compared with that of the lower classes, the change in question implied at the same time a greater **simplification** of dress, by a general approximation to more plebeian standards that were possible to all. This tendency to greater simplification was powerfully reinforced by a second aspect of the general change of ideals which the Revolution implied—by the fact that the ideal of work had now become respectable. Formerly, all work connected with economic activities of any kind—the production or distribution of useful commodities—was considered degrading to the dignity of those classes who chiefly set the fashion. There were relatively few activities—the practice of arms, together with that of political or amorous intrigue, being perhaps the most important—that were considered worthy of a gentleman. The really significant moments of life were those that were passed on the field of battle or in the drawing-room, for both of which tradition had decreed a costly and elegant attire. With the new ideals of the Revolution (ideals which, in the main, became more and more consolidated as the nineteenth century progressed) a man's most important activities were passed, not in the drawing-room, but in the workshop, the counting-house, the office— places which had, by long tradition, been associated with a relatively simple costume. As commercial and industrial ideals conquered class after class, until they finally became accepted even by the aristocracies of all the more progressive countries, the plain and uniform costume associated with such ideals has, more and more, ousted the gorgeous and varied garments associated with the older order, until now it is only in such archaic features of social life as are represented by Court ceremonies, that anything resembling the former brilliance and variety is to be seen. . . .

If the causes that have produced the very remarkable change here in question may be conveniently considered as primarily social, it is of course true that such a change can only have been brought about by the operation of very powerful psychical inhibitions. It is, indeed, safe to say that, in sartorial matters, modern man has a far sterner and more rigid conscience than has modern woman, and that man's morality tends to find expression in his clothes in a greater degree than is the case with woman. Hence it is not surprising that . . . modern man's clothing abounds in features which symbolise his devotion to the principles of duty, of renunciation, and of self-control. The whole relatively 'fixed' . . . system of his clothing is, in fact, an outward and visible sign of the strictness of his adherence to the social code. . . .

Social Nature of the Sex Differentiation Implied.   The world has undoubtedly become aesthetically the poorer for this change, as the result of which brightness and contrast have been replaced by drabness and similarity; but there can be little doubt that the drastic reduction of the decorative element in male costume has really, to some extent, achieved its aim. Greater uniformity of costume has really been accompanied by greater sympathy between one individual and another, and between one class and another; not so much, it would appear, because the wearing of the same general style of clothes in itself produces a sense of community (this is strongly marked only in cases where a particular costume or uniform distinguishes a particular body of persons from the population as a whole— as with a military uniform), but because it removes certain socially disintegrating factors that are liable to be produced by differences in clothes. How severe these disrupting influences may be can be readily seen by comparing woman's and men's clothes at the present day. Take any ordinary social function. The men are dressed in a dull uniformity of black and white, 'the very embodiment of life's prose,' as one writer has it (though this same sombre costume is not without its admirers). But if there is a lack of romance, there is also absent the envy, the jealousy, the petty triumphs, defeats, superiorities, and spitefulnesses engendered by the— doubtless more poetical—diversity and gaiety of the women's costumes. One woman can seriously hurt another, even to the point of making a permanent enemy of her, by being better or more fashionably dressed upon some significant occasion. As long as individuality is permitted, women struggle with one another for wearing the 'latest' or most costly frocks. The snobbery of wealth may even take a purely quantitative form, and it may—and often does—become a point of honour to wear a different dress each day (or several different dresses each day, according to the varying occasions of morning, afternoon, and night). The more wealthy women have thus a great advantage over their poorer sisters, who can often ill afford so long a sequence of costumes. With men the superiority of this kind conferred by wealth is obviously much reduced; a man can, for instance, safely wear the same dress suit for months or years in succession. The richer man, who could afford to wear a different smoking jacket every night, would have little gain, since only the closest inspection would reveal such differences as there might be between one jacket and another.

If such be, indeed, the chief influences that have led to the abandonment of all serious attempt at the ornamental rôle by the male sex, two questions naturally present themselves to us. In the first place, why did not these influences affect women's costume in the same way as that of men? In the second place, how have men been able to bear the sacrifice that the new order has imposed upon them? What has happened to the psychological tendencies (Narcissistic, exhibitionistic, etc.) which formerly found expression in the decorative aspects of their dress? . . .

With regard to the first question, we may perhaps regard the fact that the Great Renunciation was confined to one sex as a particular consequence of a more general difference between the sexes. Taking the history of humanity as a whole, there can be little doubt that men have played a greater part in social life, and have been more easily influenced by social factors, than have women. Whether we seek evidence from the secret societies of primitive peoples or the corresponding associations—political, social, or economic—of the present day, we find almost everywhere that the male sex takes a greater interest and plays a more active part in group life than does the female. Whether this is due, to some extent, to an innate greater susceptibility to group influences in the male, or whether it is entirely a consequence of the natural division of labour between the sexes and the traditions that have arisen in consequence, is a point on which we have no exact knowledge[1] and which we have fortunately no need to discuss here. But if we grant, as we surely must, the general fact of the greater sociability of men, and their greater participation in group life, it is not surprising that if social and political influences have been the chief factors in bringing about the greater uniformity and lesser decorativeness of men's clothes, these factors should have produced a lesser effect on the costume

[1] The whole question is discussed elsewhere by the present writer, 'Sexual and Social Sentiments,' *British Journal of Medical Psychology*, 1927, vol. vii, p. 139.

of women; such lesser effect would be only one consequence among many others of the smaller rôle of social influences in the life of women. It is interesting to note, too, that the tendencies which have undoubtedly constituted formidable obstacles to the standardisation and simplification of women's costumes on the lines adopted by men (obstacles which might conceivably have prevented the social factors having these effects on women's costume, even if these factors had been equally strong in both sexes) are those which elsewhere have proved highly antagonistic to social influences, *i.e.* Narcissism and sexual competition. Women are, perhaps by nature and certainly in virtue of our social and sexual traditions, more Narcissistic than men,[2] and these traditions have at the same time imposed upon women—in many societies at any rate—a somewhat keener sexual rivalry than among men.[3] Here, as elsewhere, a high development of social feeling may demand some sacrifice of Narcissism and of sexual jealousy; the adoption of sober clothing by men has undoubtedly meant such a sacrifice, and it would seem that the more active part now being played in social life by women may demand, and indeed is demanding, some very similar sacrifice on their part also. For there can be little doubt that women are in certain respects now following in men's footsteps, and are themselves tending to adopt a more uniform and less decorative costume, at any rate for the working hours of life.[4]

Effects on Male Psychology.—The second of the two above-mentioned questions—the question as to how man has been able to tolerate the giving up of display—is one that is less easy to answer by simple reference to a general tendency. It is a question that has, of course, much in common with all problems concerned with the renunciation of a source of satisfaction—problems which have figured largely in the psycho-analytic studies of neuroses that have, of recent years, contributed so greatly to our understanding of all mental change and mental development. In general, it would

---

[2] Cf. Freud, *Collected Papers*, vol. iv. p. 44. The wearing of more distinctive and decorative clothes in its turn, of course, fosters this relatively greater Narcissism of women, so that a vicious circle is usually established.

[3] Cf. Flügel, *op. cit.* p. 155.

[4] The fact that those women who have entered the active walks of life are now, on the whole, less differentiated in dress from other women than were their predecessors of, say, forty years ago, is due partly to the fact that the ideal of work is now common to far more women than it was then (in this respect women have undoubtedly approximated to men); partly to the fact that, owing to economic circumstances and to the spread of this ideal, a sexually more 'normal' type of woman is adopting work as a 'career'; partly, again, to a general change of attitude towards sex and, in particular, to a lessening of the apparent incompatibility between the ideals of work and of sex (an incompatibility the former strength of which is well brought out in Reginald Berkeley's play, *The Lady with a Lamp*, where the heroine, Florence Nightingale, conceives that the due performance of the work to which she is called demands the sternest repression of her sex life and of all hopes and ideals associated therewith).

seem that, when a satisfaction is denied, the desires connected with the satisfaction are either inhibited or displaced (*i.e.* find some other outlet); often both inhibition and displacement play a part. Such would seem to be the case with the clothes renunciation here in question. Recent investigations by the present writer have corroborated the impression which may be gained from the daily press, that many members of the male sex are indeed profoundly dissatisfied with their own costume, and compare it very unfavourably with women's. It is probable, indeed, that further more intensive study would reveal deep-lying psychological difficulties and inefficiencies that are the indirect consequences of these dissatisfactions.

On the other hand, the energy that formerly expressed itself in clothes has probably, to some extent, been successfully employed in other directions. A greatly increased interest in the external world has been made possible by the fact that work in many new forms has, during the last 130 years, become respectable to members of the fashionable world. 'Work,' with all its attendant preoccupations, has thus, to some extent, ousted interest in 'showing off'. . . .

Another subtle psychological change may consist in the projection of the exhibitionistic desire on to a person of the opposite sex. A man will usually feel proud when he appears in public accompanied by a beautiful or well-dressed woman, and, although this pride is itself of complex structure, one important element certainly lies in the vicarious display which he is thus permitted (just as he may feel a vicarious shame if his companion is ill-dressed).[5]

Historical Questions

1. Flugel has strong opinions about the effects of the "great masculine renunciation." In this selection, he first explains the causes of the renunciation and then its social and psychological effects on both men and women. Compare and contrast the effects Flugel discusses with your observations of the social and psychological effects of a current fashion. Which aspects of Flugel's argument do you find most useful? Least useful? Try to explain this by discussing one relevant point of similarity and one relevant point of difference between Flugel's time and today.

2. Compare the reasons Flugel suggests to explain "sartorial differences between the sexes" with some of your views on why men and women of your age group today often wear sexually distinctive clothing. Choose one concept that Flugel mentions (such as sexual rivalry or inhibition) or another that

---

[5] In certain cases this tendency may take the extreme form of a husband demonstrating the beauties of his wife's naked body to his friends, as in the classical story of Candaules and Gyges, as told by Herodotus (i. 10), Sadger (82).

interests you and apply it to men and women in your peer group. Do you find Flugel's perspective still relevant? How? What social conditions today are similar to those in the 1920s that could explain the relevance of these concepts? What social conditions have changed that may make these concepts seem less relevant? Explain using two to three specific examples.

Justification

These two questions assume that you have closely read and understood Flugel's argument. But note that the questions themselves do not just ask you for a summary. They require you to apply Flugel's ideas to aspects of contemporary fashion and then to analyze the usefulness of these ideas with reference to similarities or differences in social conditions between the 1920s and today. You will only be able to do this if you have gone through those necessary stages of first understanding the fundamental premises of Flugel's arguments.

Cultural Questions

1. Flugel suggests that a variety of social factors worked together to enable the change in men's fashion to occur as rapidly as it did at the end of the eighteenth century. Although any cultural practice, such as fashion, is always *overdetermined*, when a variety of forces intersect, they help support change and make it seem natural. With specific reference to Flugel's text, discuss the ways in which different ideals at the end of the eighteenth century— related to democracy, work, and gender differentiation—combined to create a general acceptance of men's wearing pants and generally less ornate clothing.

Definition

Overdetermination: No one social factor *causes* people to take certain actions (this cause and effect relationship is called *determination*) because any situation is *overdetermined*; that is, there are many causes for a particular action, sometimes working together and sometimes working against each other. On a personal level, we are all surrounded by such a wealth of complex and contradictory ideological forces that we must continually negotiate among them. A change in men's fashion, therefore, was not fully "determined" by the social situation (if that were the case, every man in that time period would have begun to dress in exactly the same way); nor is it fully controlled by an individual's personal feelings or "subjectivity." Rather, it is overdetermined: A complex of social forces impinge on individuals.

To use an example, until about 1800, knee breeches were the common dress for men in the American colonies and were seen as normal clothing.

By 1800, the wearing of these short pants was no longer an apparently neutral act; rather, as the colonies began to forge a separate identity and a new way to govern, as reflected in the new Constitution, wearing short pants became a sign of allegiance to British aristocracy. Nonetheless, knee breeches remained popular among a minority, a sign of an earlier connection to a noble class.

A variety of factors all converged to bring about a change in men's fashion. These included beliefs about democracy as well as about masculinity; it became more prevalently thought that men should not wear fabrics or styles that could be associated with "femininity." Further, there was an increasing assumption that clothing should be appropriate for work (a very unaristocratic activity!). So no single factor caused this change in men's dress: It was overdetermined. But obviously, the greater the number of social factors sending out the same message, the greater the likelihood that individuals accept that message as natural and normal.

2. Develop an example of an individual man living at the end of the eighteenth century who decides to join in "the great masculine renunciation." What might consciously motivate him as he decides to change the kinds of clothes he wears? (We can call these conscious ideas about the self *personal* factors.) What larger social factors—which he may or may not be conscious of—might make him want to wear these new clothes? What personal and larger social factors might make him want to resist wearing them and stick instead to the *dominant* fashion?

3. What is your position on the social and psychological values embedded in men's suits in the United States today? How do you think men should dress when they are at work? Why do you think what you do? Try to relate your perspective to larger values within the culture. Now think about other possible perspectives on suits that could exist today besides yours. What arguments can be made today that might support the *residual* image of the dark, somber suit for men? What arguments can be made for other types of men's clothing? When is it acceptable for men today to wear *archaic* styles such as those depicted in Figure 2.2? What is *emergent* clothing for men today? What values are embedded in it?

Definition

Dominant, archaic, residual, emergent: Within any culture during any historical period, there is flux and tension. No culture is ever fully unified in its beliefs or practices, although at any given point, certain beliefs and practices are more accepted than others. The concept of cultural *dominance*, and the terms *archaic*, *residual*, and *emergent*, which are used throughout this book, are drawn from the work of the British cultural theorist and literary critic, Raymond Williams, whose views we summarize here. They are discussed in much more detail in many of his books, including *The Long Revolution* (1961) and *What I Came to Say* (1989). These terms, which are widely used in sociology and literary criticism, give us a framework for understanding the dynamic ways in which a culture operates as it continuously attempts to maintain stability and balance in the face of ever-changing views, feelings, and social pressures.

All societies consist of archaic, residual, and emergent experiences, beliefs, values, social structures—all of these together are called the *material practices* of a culture. Most practices are residual, derived from the past and, therefore, representing stability and continuity. They are upheld and identified by the dominant class or groups of that society—what we frequently refer to as *the dominant*. There are invariably some archaic practices as well, ones that most members of the society know are outmoded but that hang on in some ways of speaking or behaving as when we say "the sun rose this morning," a phrase derived from a now archaic view of the universe in which it was believed that the sun went round the earth and therefore "rose" each morning. Archaic practices are sometimes regarded with nostalgia, as in contemporary U.S. society when we sometimes think of the British monarchy, its supposed dignity, and (as in the case of the late Princess Diana) its glamour and fashion. Monarchy is not a natural part of a republic like the United States, which was created in the eighteenth century precisely to reject monarchy and replace it with liberal democracy; yet we sometimes revere and even feel nostalgic for the trappings of the archaic system we have rejected.

Williams explains that the dominant practices are the ones that are embodied in the majority of the society or within its ruling or most powerful class. They are often beliefs, values, ways of behavior, and experiences that we take for granted. We may regard them as normal or commonsensical or even universally true. Of course, what is dominant varies greatly from one society to another, and (most importantly) within one society across time.

One of the reasons this book stresses historical analysis is precisely so we can see and understand how what seems at one point in time to be natural or even apparently universally true can be challenged and replaced by alternatives. Even only one century ago, the dominant belief in Europe and the United States was that women were inferior to men, that they did not have men's reasoning powers, and that they, therefore, should have little or no say in how society was run. Until passage of the Nineteenth Amendment in 1920, U.S. women did not have the vote. It is not that there were no other views, but these alternative views were not dominant. They were marginal and often regarded as odd, revolutionary, or even seditious or heretical. Yet now, of course, these marginal views are dominant. The older, formerly dominant views have not ceased to exist, but they in turn have become marginal and even, to some (perhaps most) of us, archaic.

Williams clearly explains this process. He writes that in the inevitable changes that occur in the material practices of any society, there are always new fashions, explanations, or experiences emerging. They start usually on the margins of a culture. Some of these stay on the margins; they excite the interest of small groups of people but never become part of the dominant, just as some fashions long remain identifying marks of some groups of people but never become part of the mainstream. But some marginal practices do become part of the dominant. They "emerge." These emergent practices we might think of as the growing points of social change.

Which practices are genuinely emergent? We know only by looking back and studying what happened in history. The genuinely emergent, Williams argues, must be distinguished from what is simply a new element within the dominant. Thus, to take the example discussed above, changing the fabric of knee breeches in the early nineteenth-century United States would not have been enough to make them emergent. Emergent practices are those that are being developed, usually unconsciously, out of a new set of social interactions, as societies change. They often are very different from and actively challenge the dominant. They may themselves become dominant eventually, as trousers did, but that is not an inevitable process. They start at the margins of society, as in the case of longer, looser pants worn by farmers and slaves, and may eventually become less marginal. But they may never become central. Like the wearing of trousers, all dominant practices were once emergent; but not all emergent practices (like men's wearing skirts) become dominant.

In our example, political revolution against British regulation and interference in colonial affairs led to resistance to all things British, including breeches, lace, and wigs for men. American colonists gradually put away the dominant-residual fashions that represented their past connection and allegiance to British culture and donned clothing that better reflected their emergent political beliefs and goals. But resistance to British rule was still only one of a number of factors leading to this change in men's fashions. As we discussed above, actions are always overdetermined. A change in the conception of work for men and an increased desire for gender differentiation in dress were other factors that helped to create the desire for men to change their dominant fashion. British men also stopped wearing breeches, lace, and wigs: while this clothing did not have the negative *colonial* connotations in Britain that it had in the American colonies, it nonetheless symbolized effeminacy and a lack of commitment to progress and the work ethic.

Figure 2.5. Amelia Bloomer, 1851

∾ **Fastwrite 3**

Look closely at Figure 2.5, which shows Amelia Bloomer in the "new" short dress and Turkish pant or "bloomers." Writing quickly, explain the signs of the Bloomer outfit, as you did in your discussion of the shredders in Figure 2.1. Then discuss the meaning that you imagine might have been attached to this outfit in the 1850s. Finally, discuss why you think certain meanings became attached to bloomers. Remember, as we saw in our discussion of men's breeches, the meaning of an article of clothing, like any text, changes, depending on the historical context in which it occurs. How might bloomers have been connected to larger social issues in the 1850s?

ᔕᔕᔕᔕ

IDA HUSTED HARPER

Amazing Reactions to Women in Bloomers (1898)

Ida Husted Harper (1851–1931) was a journalist and women's suffragist. Soon after marrying in 1871, she began sending articles secretly and under a male pseudonym to the *Terre Haute Saturday Evening Mail*, a weekly newspaper in Indiana. Later she became editor-in-chief of the *Terre Haute Daily News*. After handling press relations during the women's suffrage fight in California in 1896, Susan B. Anthony, a leader in the movement for women's suffrage, asked Mrs. Harper to become her official biographer. For several years, Mrs. Harper lived in Anthony's home in Rochester, New York, writing the *Life and Work of Susan B. Anthony* (1898), from which the following is extracted.

Hon. Gerrit Smith, of Peterboro, N.Y., the wealthy and influential reformer and philanthropist, became an earnest advocate of this costume, and his daughter, Elizabeth Smith Miller, a beautiful and fashionable woman, was the first to put it on. In Washington she wore it, made of the most elegant materials, during all her father's term in Congress. She was soon followed by his cousin, Elizabeth Cady Stanton, and with this social sanction it was adopted in 1851 and '52 by a small number, including Lucy Stone, Amelia Bloomer, Dr. Harriet Austin, Celia Burleigh, Charlotte Wilbour, the Grimké sisters, probably less than one hundred in the whole country. In order to be entirely relieved from the care of personal adornment, they also cut off their hair. Miss Anthony was the very last to adopt the style. In May, 1852, she wrote Lucy Stone that Mrs. Stanton had offered to make her a present of the costume, but she would not wear it. In December she wrote again, dating her letter from Mrs. Stanton's nursery, "Well, at last I am in short skirt and trousers!" At this time she also sacrificed her abundant brown tresses.

The world was not ready for this innovation. There were no gymnasiums or bicycles to plead for the appropriateness of the costume and it was worn chiefly by women who preached doctrines for which the public was no better prepared than for dress reform. The outcry against it extended from one end of the country to the other; the press howled in derision, the pulpit hurled its anathemas and the rabble took up the refrain. On the streets of the larger cities the women were followed by mobs of men and boys, who jeered and yelled and did not hesitate to express their disapproval by throwing sticks and stones and giving three cheers and a tiger ending in the loudest of groans.[1] Sometimes these demonstrations became so violent that the women were obliged to seek refuge in a store and, after the mob had grown tired of waiting and dispersed, they would slip out of the back door and find their way home through the alleys. Their husbands and children refused to be seen with them in public, and they were wholly ostracized by other women. Mrs. Bloomer was at this time publishing a paper called the *Lily*, which was the organ for the reforms of the day. Its columns were freely used to advocate the short dress, the paper thus became the target of attack and, because the costume had no distinctive name, it was christened with that of the editor, much to her grief. Later a substitute for the trousers was adopted, consisting of high shoes with buttoned gaiters fitting in the tops and extending up over the leg, and an effort was made to change the name to the "American costume," but the people would not have it and "Bloomer" it will remain for all time. An extract from one of her unpublished letters will show how all the women felt on this subject. After protesting against connecting it with the question of woman's rights, she says:

> It is only one of our rights to dress comfortably. Many have put on the short dress who have never taken any part in the woman's rights movement and who have no idea they are going to be any less womanly by such a change. I feel no more like a man now than I did in long skirts, unless it be that enjoying more freedom and cutting off the fetters is to be like a man. I suppose in that

---

[1]At the top of their voices they shouted such doggerel as this:

"Heigh ho,
Thro' sleet and snow,
Mrs. Bloomer's all the go.
Twenty tailors take the stitches,
Plenty of women wear the breeches,
Heigh ho,
Carrion crow!"

And this:

"Gibbery, gibbery gab,
The women had a confab
And demanded the rights
To wear the tights.
Gibbery, gibbery gab."

respect we are more mannish, for we know that in dress, as in all things else, we have been and are slaves, while man in dress and all things else is free. I admit that we have "got on the pantaloons," but I deny that putting them on is going to make us any the less womanly or any the more masculine and immodest. On the contrary, I feel that if all of us were less slaves to fashion we would be nobler women, for both our bodies and minds are now rendered weak and useless from the unhealthy and barbarous style of dress adopted, and from the time and thought bestowed in making it attractive. A change is demanded and if I have been the means of calling the attention of the public to it and of leading only a few to disregard old customs and for once to think and act for themselves, I shall not trouble myself about the false imputations that may be cast upon me.

Amelia Bloomer

Mrs. Bloomer wore the costume eight years, but very few held out one-fourth of that time. With the exception of Gerrit Smith, all the prominent men, Garrison, Phillips, Channing, May, were bitterly opposed to the short dress and tried to dissuade the women from wearing it by every argument in their power. The costume, however, was adopted as a matter of principle, and for it they suffered a martyrdom which would have made burning at the stake seem comfortable. It requires far more heroism to bear jibes and jeers for one's personal appearance than for one's opinions. No pen can describe what these women endured for the two or three years in which they tried to establish this principle, through such sacrifices as only a woman can understand. So long as they were upheld by the belief that they were giving strength to the cause they loved, they bravely submitted to the persecution, but when they realized that they were injuring instead of helping it, endurance reached its limit. Mrs. Stanton was the first to capitulate, and as she had tried to induce the others to wear the costume so she endeavored to persuade them to abandon it. She wrote to Miss Anthony and Lucy Stone: "I know what you must suffer in consenting to bow again to the tyranny of fashion, but I know also what you suffer among fashionable people in wearing the short dress; and so, not for the sake of the cause, nor for any sake but your own, take it off! We put it on for greater freedom, but what is physical freedom compared with mental bondage?" In agony of spirit as to whether the cause was helped or hindered by wearing it, and ready to put aside all personal feeling in the matter, Miss Anthony appealed to Lucy Stone, who answered:

Now, Susan, it is all fudge for anybody to pretend that a cause which deserves to live is impeded by the length of your skirt. I know, from having tried through half the Union, that audiences listen and assent just as well to one who speaks truth in a short as in a long dress; but I am annoyed to death by people who recognize me by my clothes, and when I travel get a seat by me and bore me for a whole day with the stupidest stuff in the world. Then again, when I go to each new city a horde of boys pursue me and destroy all comfort. I have bought a nice new dress, which I have had a month, and it is not made because I can't decide whether to make it long or short. Not that I think any cause will suffer, but simply to save myself a great deal of annoyance and not feel when I am a guest in a family that they are mortified if other persons happen to come in. I was at Lucretia Mott's a few weeks ago, and her daughters took up a regular labor with me to make me abandon the dress. They said they would not go in the street with me, and when Grace Greenwood called and others like her, I think it would have been a real relief to them if I had not been there. James and Lucretia defended me bravely.

This was received by Miss Anthony while at the Albany convention, and she wrote:

Your letter caused a bursting of the floods, long pent up, and after a good cry I went straight to Mrs. Stanton and read it to her. She has had a most bitter experience in the short dress, and says she now feels a mental freedom among her friends that she has not known for two years past. If Lucy Stone, with all her power of eloquence, her loveliness of character, who wins all that hear the sound of her voice, can not bear the martyrdom of the dress, who can? Mrs. Stanton's parting words were, "Let the hem out of your dress to-day, before to-morrow night's meeting." I have not obeyed her but have been in the streets and printing offices all day long, had rude, vulgar men stare me out of countenance and heard them say as I opened the door, "There comes my Bloomer!" O, hated name! I have been compelled to attend to all the business here, as at Rochester. There every one knew me, knew my father and brother, and treated me accordingly, but here I am known only as one of the women who ape men—coarse brutal men! Oh, I can not, can not bear it any longer.

To this Lucy Stone replied:

I am sure you are all worn out or you would not feel so intensely about the dress. I never shed a tear over it in my life or came within a thousand ages of martyrdom on account of it; and to be compelled to travel in rain and snow, mud and dirt, in a long dress would cost me more in every respect than the short dress ever did. I don't think I can abandon it, but I will have two skirts. I have this feeling: Women are in bondage; their clothes are a great hindrance to their engaging in any business which will make them pecuniarily independent, and since the soul of womanhood never can be queenly and noble so long as it must beg bread for its body, is it not better, even at the expense of a vast deal of annoyance, that they whose lives deserve respect and are greater than their garments should give an example by which woman may more easily work out her own emancipation? . . . It is a part of the "mint, anise and cumin," and the weightier matters of justice and truth occupy my thoughts more.

She did abandon the costume, however, before the year was ended, as did most of the others. The establishment of gymnasiums and the encouragement of athletic sports among women eventually made a short dress an acknowledged necessity, and the advent of the bicycle so thoroughly swept away the old prejudice that the word "Bloomers" no longer strikes terror to the heart, nor does the wearing of a short skirt ostracise a woman and destroy her good works. Miss Anthony wore hers a little over a year. It was not very different from the bicycle dress of the present day, the skirt reaching almost to the shoe tops and made of satin or heavy merino, and yet for years afterwards she was described as attending meetings in the "regulation bombazine Bloomers," and it was impossible to convince people to the contrary until they had seen her with their own eyes. She herself said in regard to it: "I felt the need of some such garments because I was obliged to be out every day in all kinds of weather, and also because I saw women ruined in health by tight lacing and the weight of their clothing; and I hoped to help establish the principle of rational dress. I found it a physical comfort but a mental crucifixion. It was an intellectual slavery; one never could get rid of thinking of herself, and the important thing is to forget self. The attention of my audience was fixed upon my clothes instead of my words. I learned the lesson then that to be successful a person must attempt but one reform. By urging two, both are injured, as the average mind can grasp and assimilate but one idea at a time. I have felt ever since that experience that if I wished my hearers to consider the suffrage question I must not present the temperance, the religious, the dress, or any other besides, but must confine myself to suffrage." With the exception of that one year, Miss Anthony always has been particular to follow, in a modified and conservative form, the prevailing styles, and has fought strenuously the repeated efforts to graft any kind of dress reform on the suffrage movement.

Historical Questions

1. Compare and contrast the public reaction to the short skirt and trousers for women in the 1850s with a similar example of public outcry against a

more recent fashion. Discuss the reasons which the dominant explicitly gave for its opposition to each of these fashions. Then, speculate about what you think might be some unstated, underlying reasons for such violent reactions to a style of clothing.

Justification

This question asks you to compare a particular type of cultural dynamic—the dominant trying to suppress the emergent—in two different historical periods. The public outcry against bloomers discussed in the reading suggests that what a person wears can obviously be of great significance to a whole society. Thus the topic of fashion can be more serious than one might initially think. This question extends your use of the concepts of dominant, residual, and emergent as analytical tools to understand change and conflict within a society.

2. How do the arguments in favor of and against women's wearing bloomers that Harper reports connect to any aspects of the pre-1850s history of relations between the sexes that you know about? Given what you know of the history of male-female relations in the United States up to the 1850s, was it surprising that the dominant culture would not support women's wearing pants? Explain, giving two to three specific examples.

Justification

The question asks you to draw on your knowledge about gender relations prior to the mid-nineteenth century. Although you may not have explicitly studied this subject, if you were educated in the United States, you have studied U.S. history in school; have read U.S. literature; and have probably seen films or plays about the pre-1850s United States. Bring knowledge gained in other contexts to bear on your work here. This act of connecting different sources of information and using knowledge for new purposes is a vital part of learning to think critically.

Cultural Questions

1. Choose two very different perspectives from this reading and write in the first-person voice of those perspectives. You might choose Lucy Stone, Susan B. Anthony, Elizabeth Cady Stanton, their husbands or children, men or women in their audiences, even the street boys. Imagine, for example, what the street boys' parents said at home about the suffragists in trousers. Give full voice to the assumptions behind the positions you choose on the issue of women in pants.

Justification

This assignment requires a kind of role-playing that enables you to develop a more detailed understanding of different perspectives, particularly ones you do not feel sympathetic toward. In trying to actually think like a particular person, you begin to glimpse the complex systems of beliefs and practices in which that person may have been enmeshed. While you don't have to end up agreeing with the perspective, you can develop a much fuller understanding of how it could have developed and been sustained, given a particular set of cultural circumstances.

2. Develop a *symptomatic reading* of the violent reactions to the bloomer costume. To do this, first imagine what the opponents of the bloomer costume are *literally* saying about it; that is, what are their *explicitly articulated* objections? Then, focusing on two or three passages (for example, the doggerel, the extracts from any of the letters, or the cartoon in Figure 2.6 that follows the Harper essay, p. 83), speculate on what some of the underlying and unarticulated fears, tensions, and anxieties were in these explicit objections.

Definition

Symptomatic reading: Symptomatic comes from *symptom*, which is what a doctor observes in a patient's condition or behavior that suggests an illness lies "under the surface." A doctor cannot simply accept a symptom such as a patient's cough literally; that is, the doctor cannot simply say "my patient just happens to cough a lot" and leave it at that. Rather, the doctor must read the symptom as a sign of something else and try to analyze and hypothesize about what it could mean.

The doctor may try to detect a pattern between the cough and other aspects of the patient's behavior (does the patient smoke?), history (was the patient asthmatic as a child?), or current situation (does the patient live near a source of pollen?). The answer the doctor comes up with to explain the patient's cough may be superficial: There is pollen in the air. But the cough may be an indication of something deeper in the patient's history, social interactions, or heredity. Whatever the answers, they rarely lie on the surface. The recognition of the symptoms calls the doctor to investigate.

When readers do symptomatic readings of texts, they are similarly attentive, looking for something that disrupts the surface. In medicine, it might be a nagging cough or a rash. In the text, it might be a disruption in language or tone, or a stray remark, or an unexplained contradiction. Having recognized a symptom—say a contradiction in the text—you should not read it literally but rather as a sign, a symptom, of something else.

Then, like the doctor, you might look at the text's larger history (what was going on in historical periods before the text was written?) or at issues that were current at the time when the text was written. This approach helps you gain insight into what the symptom could mean.

Developing a symptomatic reading of Ida Harper's text. Let us review the process of symptomatic reading in relation to portions of Harper's text. A text's language and tone and its method of presenting its position can be as important as the actual position itself. Let's begin with one of the doggerel examples:

> Gibbery, gibbery gab,
> The women had a confab
> And demanded the rights
> To wear the tights.
> Gibbery, gibbery gab.

The symptom we are looking at here is the contradiction between the trivializing form and tone, as indicated by the doggerel, and the seriousness of the topic as indicated by the dramatic public outcry and demonstrations against bloomers. Why are the "mobs of men and boys" using a childish rhyme to deal with a serious topic?

Let's think of an analogy. When people make jokes at funerals, they are often expressing anxiety about themselves and their own mortality. It is fairly obvious what the speaker here is anxious about: the unthinkable thought that women are aggressively claiming more rights than they should.

The overall tone, the word choice, and the doggerel form all suggest that women's idea of wearing pants is both a ridiculous and a trivial issue. And yet, for a brief moment, one line suggests that women have power and strength. Although there is actually no such word as *gibbery,* it certainly suggests *gibberish,* which means meaningless or unintelligible language. *Gab* means idle talk, and even today *gabbing* is a term more frequently applied to women's talk than to men's. The sing-song quality of the doggerel makes it sound even more meaningless.

A *confabulation* is a discussion; the reduction of the term to *confab,* particularly in its rhyming with *gab,* also makes it seem silly, suggesting that the women might have thought it was important, but that the speakers know it was not.

What did the women do at their gibbery, gabbing confab? If we take this one line at a time, we can see the doggerel beginning to reveal perhaps more than it intends. We discover a contradiction in tone that may be a symptom of something else. Women are said to have *demanded the rights.* This, of course, is exactly what women were doing at the time—particularly demanding the right to vote, but also demanding to be thought of more generally as equal citizens under the law who should have property rights, the right to advanced education, and so on.

Demand is a word that doesn't quite fit with *gab* or *gibber*. It is a word with an edge that suggests strength and authority. Of course, the next line attempts to undermine this strength by saying that what women demanded rights for was *to wear the tights*. But the strength connoted by the word *demanded* can still echo for us as a possible tonal contradiction that might be important as we try to analyze why someone would have been motivated to write this doggerel in the first place. The anxiety underlying *demanded their rights* seems to seep through the text's attempts to trivialize women's actions because the tone and the power of the phrase stand out in contrast to the rest of the doggerel.

∾ Fastwrite 4

Turn to the letter by Amelia Bloomer that Harper quotes. On the surface, she appears to contradict herself: While she argues in large part that wearing bloomers will not make women more masculine, at a couple of points Bloomer suggests that it might:

> I feel no more like a man now than I did in long skirts, unless it be that enjoying more freedom and cutting off the fetters is to be like a man. I suppose in that respect we are more mannish, for we know that in dress, as in all things else, we have been and are slaves, while man in dress and all things else is free.

How would you characterize the tone of this paragraph? What does Bloomer's tone tell you about her status in the society at the time? About the likelihood that her desires will be met? If you were to read the paragraph literally, you might simply assume that Bloomer was rather incoherent in her writing because she contradicts herself. But try to read Bloomer's contradiction as a symptom of something else. Why do you think she spends so much time saying that wearing pantaloons won't make women more masculine, only to suggest in the middle of the paragraph that they just might? How could she say something that might give fuel to her opposition?

Can you be certain that your symptomatic reading is correct? The answer is no. You must take care that you do not jump to conclusions too quickly. Symptomatic reading requires that you do a very close reading of the particular text, and that you study it in relation to other texts and other ideas of its historical moment. Make sure, therefore, that you have read Harper's text carefully. You may want to look for patterns among a series of texts before you attempt a detailed symptomatic reading of any of them.

∾ **Further Research**

At times you may want to do more research before you fully develop a symptomatic reading so that you can look more carefully for patterns among texts. While suggestions for possible research are usually offered at the end of each chapter, here are two brief samples of further research to help you see how your symptomatic readings can be developed and extended as you learn more about a subject.

1. How does Figure 2.6 depict the women in bloomers? Compare this cartoon with the picture of Amelia Bloomer in Figure 2.5. What concerns or anxieties is the cartoon displaying? Compare it with the doggerel in Harper's article.

Figure 2.6. "Bloomer Costumes or Woman's Emancipation"

AMELIA BLOOMER
Female Attire: An Exchange with the *Seneca County Courier* (1851)

Amelia Bloomer (1818–1894) was a temperance reformer, women's rights editor, and suffragist. In 1849, as an officer in the Ladies' Temperance Society, she began printing "a little temperance paper" called the *Lily*, which soon evolved into a general women's rights paper. The two excerpts that follow are from the February 1851 issue of the *Lily*. The first is an editorial from the *Seneca County Courier* entitled "Female Attire"; the second is Amelia Bloomer's response.

"Female Attire," by the editor of the *Seneca County Courier*

The attention of the World's Fair, soon to be held in London, is to be called to the subject of improvement in the attire of females. That there is abundant room as well as necessity for improvement in the respect we firmly believe. We favor such reform for the reason that it would contribute greatly to the comfort, happiness and convenience of the sex; considerations to which we are always allve [sic].

With regard to means proposed to protect the persons of females from the chills of winter, and thus preserve their health and promote their comfort and convenience, it seems as though but one opinion should prevail. Who has not been pained to witness the inconvenience attending the act of entering a carriage or alighting? Ten to one but the dress is soiled, if not utterly ruined. This can scarcely be avoided, to say nothing of the indelicate exposure which is often unavoidable. Then how painful to the sensitive female must it be to strive to walk, her dress flapping in the breeze and assuming all the gyrations of a ship's sails in a storm. Many inconveniences—many a shock to the delicate female might be obviated—great addition to her comfort be wrought, by the substitution of a mode of dress having in view these considerations. A pair of Turkish pantaloons, wide, and nearly meeting the shoe, of such material and texture as the season demanded, and of a hue adapted to the taste of the wearer; and a garment neatly fitting the person, buttoned, or permanently closed on all sides, extending just below the knee, of a material and texture that would ward off the chilly atmosphere, colored and ornamented to suit the fancy of the wearer, and held by a girdle highly wrought and ornamented; a head-gear not subject to be crushed and destroyed by every slight contact with other objects, yet neat. What reasonable person could object to the substitution of such a costume for that now worn.

Amelia Bloomer's Reply

Really, we are surprised that the cautious editor of the *Seneca County Courier* has so far overcome his opposition to women's rights as to become himself an advocate of their wearing the pantaloons! This goes a step or two beyond what the most clamorous of the women claim on the subject of their rights. Had *we* broached this subject the cry would have been raised on all sides, "She wants to wear the pantaloons," and a pretty hornet's nest we should have got into. But now that our cautious editor of the *Courier* recommends it, we suppose there will be no harm in our doing so. And what is the dress, which we are to don at the bidding of our self-constituted lords and guardians? As near as we can get at it, it is simply a sack-coat and pantaloons, and a cap or hat similar to those worn by men. One thing we object to on the start, and that is having the coat entirely closed. Men like to display a handsome vest, and nicely plaited shirt-bosom, and why may we not have the same privilege? Nothing is said about our hair, whether we shall have it cut short—or about our boots, whether we shall wear them after the fashion of men.—The latter, we think, ought not to have been omitted. We go for high thick boots that are impervious to cold or wet, as an important preservation of health. Really, ladies, will it not be nice? We shall no longer have our dresses drabbled in the mud, or half the depth of them wet with snow. In getting in and out of carriages we need have no fears of the wheels, and we can even sit down in a puddle of tobacco-juice without endangering our Sunday suit. Yet the convenience of the thing is nothing when compared to the health and comfort. Small waists and whalebones can be dispensed with, and we shall be allowed breathing room; and our forms will be what nature made them. We are so thankful that men are beginning to undo some of the mischief they have done us. Fashion plates, songs, and stories have ever spoken their admiration of our small waists, our delicate features, and our small well-shaped feet, and we have been simple enough to gratify their taste at the sacrifice of health and comfort. Now if they will sing another tune women will no doubt be willing to dance after it, when they have once learned the steps they are to take.

We remember a year ago a great deal was said by the gentlemen of the press about Fanny Kemble's "*male attire.*" She was ridiculed, laughed at, and condemned for being so *masculine* as to put on pantaloons. And yet the dress worn by her which caused so great excitement, was precisely the same as that recommended above. This only shows that women should not dare to make a change in their costume till they have the consent of men—for they claim the right to prescribe for us in the fashion of our dress as well as in all things else.

2a. Why do you think the editor of the *Seneca County Courier* suggested that women wear the short dress and Turkish trousers? What evidence can you find in this brief letter to the *Lily* that might be symptomatic of the position many people at that time would have taken toward the idea of women in pants?

b. Analyze Bloomer's response to the *Courier* editorial, paying careful attention to her tone. What does it reveal about her attitude toward the controversy surrounding the short dress and trousers for women? If her perspective can be said to be emergent regarding women's fashions, define what you think the dominant position would have been for both men and women in the 1850s.

⮾⮾⮾⮾

ANNE HOLLANDER

Sex and Suits: The Power of Form (1994)

With this reading, we leap forward into the 1990s for another perspective on fashion. Anne Hollander (b. 1943) is an art historian and a Fellow of the New York Institute for the Humanities. Her books include *Seeing Through Clothes* (1978) and *Moving Pictures* (1989). In the following selection from her most recent book, *Sex and Suits* (1994), she argues for the sexual and aesthetic power of the suit for both men and women.

Modern long trousers came into existence as another example of startling and subversive male fashion. They chiefly derived from the French Revolutionary working-man's *sans-culotte* costume, although they were also worn by British common sailors and colonial slave-laborers, and had been occasionally used by gentlemen both for active sportswear and for leisure in those same colonies. But apart from their exciting plebeian connotations, they created an undemanding loose alternative to the close-fitting silk knee-breeches and skin-tight doeskin pantaloons of the late eighteenth century—clothes which had shown off the male legs and crotch without much room for compromise.

Trousers did not require a perfect body, and they had a nicely daring, casual look in themselves. They were instantly modified from their working-class simplicity and assimilated into the subtle tailoring scheme already developed for the elegant male coat of the new nineteenth century. The tube-like coverings for the legs answered harmoniously to the tube-like sleeves of the coat; and when the coat-skirts began consistently to veil the clearly delineated crotch of earlier days, the brilliantly colored necktie asserted itself, to add a needed phallic note to the basic ensemble.

The modern masculine image was thus virtually in place by 1820, and it has been only slightly modified since. The modern suit has provided so perfect a visualization of modern male pride that it has so far not needed replacement, and it has gradually provided the standard costume of civil leadership for the whole world. The masculine suit now suggests probity and restraint, prudence and detachment; but under these enlightened virtues also seethe its hunting, laboring, and revolutionary origins; and therefore the suit still remains sexually potent and more than a little menacing, its force by no means spent during all these many generations. Other ways for men to dress now share the scene with suits, so suits have shifted their posture; but they remain one true mirror of modern male self-esteem. . . .

The classical foundation for modern male tailoring has had another long-lasting effect. Just like ancient nude statues, men gradually came to look similar; and to desire to look similar. The greater uniformity among clothed men that characterizes the last two centuries, by comparison with the variety among women, was inaugurated at this same epoch. It was then another attribute of antique and natural virtue, representing the brother-hood of moral clarity and evenness of temper, and yet paradoxically offering a way to focus on the individual. Right now at the end of this century when world leaders come together, all wear similar suits that display the uniform desire for international harmony, even while each face appears all the more distinctive, clearly aware of separate responsibility. The individual tailoring for each suit also shows the flexible possibilities of a single scheme when faced with very different bodies, and the varieties of the same style desired by men of different cultures.

It had first become clear in the early part of the nineteenth century that when all men wear a white tie and a black tailcoat in the evening, the individual character of each man is made more important, not less; and a curious effect then occurs in mixed company. If each woman at the ball is carefully wearing something different, the different costumes are what you see first across the room, making a variable scene; but consequently the faces might as well be all the same, just as if the same doll were dressed in many different ways. When two women wear the same dress, however, the first thing you see is how different the actual women really look.

The Romantic movement was in fact already generating the notion of Woman as a creature who may appear in many guises but who always has the same nature. "Woman" became a sort of single primitive force, encoun-tered by individual men in the form of dramatically varied samples which were nonetheless believed to be only superficially different, sisters under the differently colored skin. This notion was partly responsible for the marked division, in clothes of the later Romantic period, between masculine solidarity about uniform style and dim color, and a feminine diversity largely based on vigorous polychromy. Mid-nineteenth-century paintings by Frith and indeed by Monet and Manet show groups of multicolored ladies blooming like varieties of flowering shrubbery among sturdy, dun-colored, tree-trunk-like gentlemen with distinctive faces. . . .

French and English Neo-classicism show how similar forms may be used to express different ideas. The way the same Neo-classic formal revi-sions in art quickly and simultaneously affected fashion in France and in England demonstrates that a quick rise of a certain form in fashion initially reflects the power of the form itself, not the political idea it comes to embody. We have suggested that a certain fashion may often precede a shift in politics and cultural attitude, to show an esthetic, almost physical desire for basic change rather than to reflect new ideas after they arise. The new form is adopted first out of a desire to change an extant style in a way that satisfies the psyche first, by satisfying the eye without taking on the burden of rational excuses and political adhesions. A social and political meaning necessarily gets attached to the fashion afterwards, to rationalize the unconscious need; and later the meaning can seem to have been what forced the change.

But if the formal simplicities of antiquity looked wonderful to both the French and the English at the same time, at a period in history when they were so widely different in cultural situation and social aim, the need to adopt antique forms must have arisen out of neither the one nor the other set of current social ideals. It must have come from an esthetic longing common to both, without reference to any immediate political applications, a need to change the look of things into something radically old and new at once. Unmodified antique looks must have had a satisfying emotional meaning that was deeper than any society's current social references. The thrilling union of well-thumbed Classical form with a new raw sexuality, a new creative originality and a new brute truthfulness would certainly satisfy; and it would be easy to ally it later with any current potency, whether of finance, commerce, war or politics.

The erotic character of the new masculine mode in the first decade of the nineteenth century was intensified by its demanding qualities. The more simply fitted clothes of Baroque times had been easier to wear for everybody. Perfectly fitting clothes and neckwear now required elegant posture and movement, which had to look effortless since they were invoking and allegedly imitating nature. In the days of stiff doublets and ruffs, prescribed deportment was itself stiff, and nobody wearing them pretended to behave naturally, that is, slackly and undesignedly. But in the Neo-classic climate, the wearer showed his potency by the ease with which he seemed unaware of the difficulty of his clothes and exhibited a transcendent nonchalance.

As always, the tension created by such a fusion of opposites—the effortless effort—had a strong erotic charge in itself. It was another example of the kind of sexual heroism evident in the graceful female management of trains, hoopskirts, corsets and extreme high heels, as it once had been in the tight, trussed-up, padded and very short male doublets of the early Renaissance. In fact the appeal of the modern suit in our period is still its combined look of comfort and crispness, with its neat collar and tie that perpetually defy the forces of hot weather, hard work and high anxiety, its unruffled tailored envelope suggesting an invincible physical aplomb, including sexual. No sweat-suits, cycling gear, or wrinkled khakis can hope to convey such a superior level of ease.

In its original Neo-classic or Dandy form, however, the modern masculine costume proved too extreme to do all its classicizing work at once,
and to evoke the innate heroism of every man. Not only the corpulent but
the seriously busy could not hold the perfectly natural Classical pose for
very long. The fashion had begun among the seriously idle, some of whom
had the leisure to align their physical behavior with the high artistic standard of the tailoring. Very soon it became obvious that modifications in
the tailoring were necessary, to preserve the same high standard while
demanding less contribution from the man himself. Idle or not, he should
not be required to muster all the original creative zeal of the Brummellian
pioneers. By 1815, trousers had largely replaced the sleek, demanding pantaloons, and men's arms and legs became similarly clad in smooth cylinders
of yielding fabric. The modern "suit" was now in existence, meaning the
unified abstraction of shape that is its defining characteristic; but it still
did not have to be made of the same fabric for trousers and coat, except
in evening dress. Waistcoats could also still be separate.

Trousers had been another informal fashion that looked rather bunchy
and sloppy the way the "frock" had done, until tailors refined and formalized
them to match the smooth new abstraction made out of the country coat.
The new, elegant trousers were often strapped under the instep for a more
perfect vertical fit. By 1830, the "frock coat," an elegant version of the old
modest country frock, had become correct for daytime wear in cities. Its
full skirt and closed front concealed the crotch and created a clothed shape
for business and professional men that was soberer than the original nude
mode, with its explicit genital focus. Daytime coats thereafter all veiled the
crotch; formal morning dress and evening wear kept to the older and nuder
idea, until the tuxedo was invented to keep even the nocturnal male in
harmony with his business self. . . .

Trousers for respectable women were publicly unacceptable except for
fancy dress and on the stage, and they were not generally worn even invisibly
as underwear until well on in the nineteenth century. At that period the
common adoption of underpants by women seems to represent the first
expression of the collective secret desire to wear pants, only acceptably
brought out on the surface with the bicycling costumes of the 1890's, and
only finally confirmed in the later twentieth century with the gradual
adoption of pants as normal public garments for women.

Anomalous persons like George Sand and Joan of Arc made their
temporary sensations in a virtual vacuum; a few movements like that of
Amelia Bloomer in the nineteenth century came and went. Pants were still
a forbidden borrowing from the male, so unseemly that they could only
be generally hidden until their time finally came. After those millennia of
dresses, dividing the legs of respectable women with a layer of fabric seemed
like sexual sacrilege. Consequently pants on women figured, naturally

enough, in soft-core pornography since the eighteenth century, and they were often worn for seductive purposes by fast ladies in elegant society ever since the sixteenth. Trousers had certainly been worn by female mine-workers, fisherfolk and agricultural laborers, and naturally by dancers and acrobats, and actresses or singers in "breeches" parts; but the low status of all these female occupations kept women's pants firmly associated with lowness in general, or else with the Mysterious East, which had its own dubious associations.

The twentieth-century modernization of women was altogether a laggard development, since it came a hundred years later than the great innovations, created for men by English tailors, that still form the basis of modern male dress. At that period, just as with plate armor only better, the male body received a complete new envelope that formed a flattering modern commentary upon its fundamental shape, a simple and articulate new version that replaced the naked frame, but this time without encasing it, upholstering it, stiffening it, or overdecorating it. The modern suit, although it still hid every inch of skin, now skimmed the surface and moved in counterpoint to the body's movement, making a mobile work of art out of the combination.

At that same time female fashion was also temporarily pared down, thinned out and simplified; but it continued throughout the next hundred years with the primitive, disguising long-dress-and-careful-head-dress formula. Fashion was still steadily rearranging the proportions of the female body and avoiding much reference to its actual composition, just as female costume had been doing ever since the first big trailing skirts of the fourteenth century. Nineteenth-century fashionable changes for women became even more distracting on the surface, as the changes in men's clothes continued to be a matter of subtly altering the basic tailored shape and its basic fabrics. The sartorial drama between the sexes became more acute than it had ever been. . . .

It's clear that modernizing clothes for women has meant copying men's clothes, directly or indirectly, one way or another. To even the balance, however, we can see that many men in the last third of this century have already taken up the formerly female game of finding pleasure in expressive multiple guises. In one man's closet, the new, colorful leisure versions of active gear make sharp contrasts with well-cut business suits and formal sportswear like tweed jackets, classic shirts lie next to extreme sweatshirts, and everything is meant for wear in the same urban milieu. We may now find the curious spectacle of a man privately at ease fifteen stories above the city street, sipping wine and reading Trollope in a warm room furnished with fragile antiques and Persian rugs, dressed in a costume suitable for roping cattle on the plains or sawing up lumber in the North woods. Once, only women and children offered such visual effects.

Apart from such curiosities, however, the new male freedom has produced a pleasing richness of variety similar to the modern female one, though not entirely the same and still not quite so broad. But handbags, necklaces and earrings have lost their taboo for men, just as all parts of male dress have long since lost their outrageousness for women; they are licensed dress-ups when they aren't practical or elegant. Both sexes play changing games today, because for the first time in centuries men are learning clothing habits from women, instead of the other way around.

Some of what men are taking up, it must be noted, is simply male trappings that have long since gone out of use *except* by women. Purses and earrings, long hair and brilliant scarves, fanciful hats and shoes may be safely regenerated as male habits, since they have been in storage below the surface as very old and vigorous masculine traditions in the West. It does seem unlikely, however, that ancient Western female effects—voluminous skirts, creative décolletage for chest, back, and arms, bonnets or veils for the head—are likely to be taken up very soon by ordinary Western men. Men have relearned from women mainly how to be mutable and multiple, decorative and colorful, and to rediscover their hair; but the most ancient female symbolic material still remains largely taboo.

The female move to male gear, on the other hand, which was always a partial affair in the past and a firm part of the feminine erotic tradition, has lately been fully completed, and society has thoroughly internalized it. Trousers and tailoring and short hair are now wholly female in themselves, and women wearing them no longer look masculine. Women can moreover no longer imitate men specifically to be taken seriously, because male clothes are already female, too. But it follows that current male clothes have less of a uniquely masculine meaning even when men wear them, and therefore they may safely take on new flavors formerly called feminine. It's clear that during the second half of this century, women finally took over the total male scheme of dress, modified it to suit themselves, and have handed it back to men charged with immense new possibilities.

Even conventional men who don't wear long hair or earrings do wear brilliant shirts, sweaters, socks, hats and scarves in arresting shapes and colors recently seen only on women. Many modish tailored trousers, jackets and waistcoats for men are abandoning their careful dependence on tradition and branching out into the expressive exaggerations devised for women's use of them. There has recently been a mode for trousers that begin to expose the underpants and appear to fall off the hips, in an unprecedented allusion to the female vocabulary of décolletage. Male street fashion from many sources has at last had an effect on middle-class males, as it once had only on women. The general idea of fantasy and pleasure seems to have re-entered male dress through female influence—that is, through a new acknowledgment and recognition of female reality that has permitted that influence to function.

The qualities of mutability in surface design that were associated with female habits of dress for two centuries no longer need to represent weakness and madness along with attractiveness, and men no longer have to fear them. There are new eyes for the gaudy old devices that once clothed male power before the modern era, in part because bright hues, vivid hair, glitter, and skin-tight fit are attributes of the great current heroes of sport and entertainment who command vast fees and global attention. The look of male sexual potency in the post-modern world is able to float free of those austere visions of masculinity, solidified in the nineteenth century, that discredited any richness of fantasy in dress by calling it feminine. . . .

In our present period of exchange, hair may be worn very short by women or very long by men without either looking transsexual, only extreme. Men not only wear long hair, they tie it back with the decorative clips and ribbon-decked elastics formerly used only by women—but it's noticeable that they usually don't wear Alice in Wonderland hairbands, which derive from hoods and veils and so far remain distinctly feminine. Headbands around the brow, by contrast, are unisex. Both sexes shave their heads, dye their hair purple or wear dreadlocks; anyone, in the androgynous infant spirit, may safely imitate the hairdressing associated with other-worldly fantasy, or seize on any headgear from other cultures. One new mode shown on strong and virtuous men in recent films is a classic tailored suit and tie, worn with a ponytail or the long curly hair once the property of girls. Even among the new male freedoms, the suit still goes down well—perhaps because it, too, has become the property of girls.

The intense power of deliberately androgynous looks has lately asserted itself publicly among adored popular performers, visually confirming the ancient idea that pleasure in sexuality may be richer if the two sexes are allowed to acknowledge their erotic affinities and are not kept stringently divided. The world has moreover finally learned that gay men and women are just as various in personal styles of dress as all other free citizens are; and so straight men and women may make new fashions out of old signals once narrowly perceived as homosexual, modes that are now attached to such former associations only by sympathy and irony, as the modern habit of fashion has taught us to use them.

Historical Questions

1. Not only do Hollander (1994) and Flugel (1930) have different interpretations of the suit, they also have significantly different assumptions about the relationship of fashion to the larger society. While Flugel argues that the suit arose out of particular political circumstances—related to ideals of

democracy, work, and gender differentiation—Hollander suggests that fashion is largely driven by aesthetic considerations and that "it may often precede a shift in politics and cultural attitudes." Reread each of their essays, taking notes on passages in which they discuss their assumptions about the relationship of fashion to the larger culture. Where are their arguments most similar? Where are they most different? Discuss what in their different sets of assumptions you find most helpful in developing historical and cultural analyses of fashion.

Justification

Analyzing assumptions underlying positions and avoiding right/wrong assessments. When you are trying to think critically, it is important that you not just react to different arguments, but that you assess the assumptions underlying those arguments. (Remember the discussion in Chapter 1 about avoiding simplistic right/wrong analyses of positions in a conflict.) Although Flugel and Hollander have significantly different positions and underlying assumptions, note that we do not ask you to simply "take sides," that is, to say that one of them is right and one of them is wrong, or that one of them is helpful and one of them is not. Rather, we ask you to find places where their arguments overlap as well as where they differ and then to develop a synthesis of the best of both of their positions.

While you can certainly lean more heavily toward one than the other if you wish, this type of analysis prevents you from dismissing a position that you might not immediately agree with. It encourages genuine dialogue among positions, and it also gives you the capacity to begin to theorize for yourself, to build on their arguments for a purpose of your own.

2. Compare Hollander's explanation of the nineteenth-century objection to women in pants with your analysis of Harper's explanations. Try to account for a significant point of agreement and a significant point of disagreement in the various analyses by exploring two or three assumptions that underlie them.

Justification

This question asks you not only to link Hollander's contemporary position with positions from the past, but it also gives you the opportunity to consider it in relation to an analysis you wrote earlier.

Cultural Questions

1. Focus on Hollander's writing style and specific use of language. For example, how many times do you notice her use of words and phrases like "a needed phallic note," and "sexually potent and more than a little menacing." How

does her choice of words relate to her key ideas? What does she mean when she talks about "modern male pride" and "mirror of modern male self-esteem" or "sexual sacrilege" and "sexual heroism?" Translate these phrases and others that you notice into your own words. Connect her specific words to her key ideas. Why does Hollander love the suit? Read a passage symptomatically to develop a connection between Hollander's writing and 1990s U.S. culture.

Justification

Language, like clothing, is a sign system. This question asks for a symptomatic reading of Hollander's language. Consider how her language is not simply functional—that is, neutrally conveying her thoughts—but rather itself part of a sign system (not unlike fashion). Recall the discussion of the snowboarders (see Figure 2.1); their clothes did not simply cover and protect their bodies. By wearing a certain type of pants, jackets, and boots, they send a particular set of messages. The same is true of language.

2. Develop a symptomatic reading of Hollander's analysis of the links between nineteenth-century fashion and Neoclassicism and Romanticism. What does she literally say about the ways in which those artistic and intellectual trends affected or reflected what men and women wore? What does her analysis suggest about her beliefs and assumptions about gender roles and fashion at the time she was writing? About some of the larger cultural tensions and issues at the time she was writing?

∞ Fastwrite 5

What do you know about the problems of eating disorders? Use specific examples wherever possible. How would you characterize the relationship between cultural representations of women and the self-image of individual women? Explain whether you think that men have equivalent cultural representations. Compare your sense of the dominant ideal male image with what you think is the dominant ideal female image today.

∾∾∾∾

JOHN DARNTON

Skeletal Models Create Furor over British Vogue (1996)

John Darnton (b. 1941) writes about political and cultural issues for the *New York Times*. A distinguished journalist, he won the Pulitzer Prize and George Polk award in 1982 for coverage of political turmoil in Poland. This article appeared in the *Times* on June 3, 1996.

Figure 2.7   Trish Goff. This photo appeared in British *Vogue* but was used only on the contents page and at a small size (1/8 page).

After stepping into a minefield of controversy over the connection between fashion and health, the Swiss watch manufacturer Omega reversed its decision to stop advertising in a British fashion magazine that used what it called "skeletal" models.

Giles Rees, the British marketing manager for the Omega Watch Corporation, a unit of the SMH Swiss Corporation, said on Thursday that his company would cease advertising in the British edition of *Vogue*, saying its emphasis on ultra-thin models, typified by two features in the June issue, could encourage young women to develop eating disorders.

But a day later he reversed his position, saying that the company's chairman, Nicholas Hayek, believed "it is not in anybody's interest to influence the editorial position of any given media."

Stephen Quinn, the magazine's publisher, said that the reversal "was a complete victory" for Condé Nast, the Advance Publications unit that owns the magazine. "It's good news in terms of editorial independence and the fact that advertising revenue will continue," Mr. Quinn said Friday, according to the Associated Press.

Mr. Rees's original letter to the magazine excoriated it for two editorial features in the June issue in which photos of two well-known models, Trish Goff and Annie Morton, show them as unusually thin. Mr. Rees said that he was "appalled" by the "extremely distasteful" pictures of the models—not just because they were so thin but because the layouts "made every effort to accentuate this attribute."

Miss Morton, in an eight-page spread on bandeau tops, tiny shorts and rubber skirts, shows a boyish figure and a rather sickly demeanor, described by a blurb as taking "body consciousness to a new extreme." Advice follows on achieving such a look: "All that's required is a well-toned physique and a cool attitude."

Caught off guard, the British *Vogue* first suggested that Omega was upset because a photo spread of watches, including one Omega, was intentionally printed out of focus, apparently for artistic reasons.

Then as the controversy gathered steam, the magazine's editor, Alexandra Shulman, released a statement saying that it used the same models as other magazines, that they "tend to be in their late teens and still, naturally, extremely thin," and that they "also tend to flesh out as time goes on."

The magazine added: "As the fashion bible, we are acutely concerned about the dangers of appearing to promote unnaturally slim models."

Those in the fashion trade and magazine business said that models— particularly British ones—have been getting slimmer. This trend has accelerated since 1992 and 1993 when Kate Moss, the British model, became the paradigm for the latest waif look popularized by fashion magazines and most prominently by Calvin Klein ads.

But this was the first time those industries recalled a major advertiser objecting publicly to the models' appearance because their appearance might encourage unhealthy behavior such as eating disorders. More often, editors and readers complain about the advertisements for reasons from sexual innuendo to encouragement of habits like smoking.

For a long time, casual observers have linked the trend of ultra-thin fashion models to a rise in eating disorders, theorizing that in setting new standards of slimness that are impossible for most people to meet, the models are encouraging obsessive dieting and extreme weight loss.

Anorexia nervosa, a sometimes fatal eating disorder characterized by self-induced starvation and excessive exercise, pre-dates fashion's focus on emaciated female bodies, but few psychologists doubt that the imperative to be thin, emphasized daily in ads, movies and on television, contributes heavily to eating disorders.

"The desire to fit the cultural ideal of thinness drives many women to diet severely," said Dr. Terence Wilson, a psychologist at Rutgers University. "In some vulnerable young women, this leads to bingeing and purging, or to self-starvation."

While not discounting the publicity about super-thin celebrities as a factor, researchers also tend to paint a more complicated picture of the disorders—involving low self-esteem, extreme perfectionism, a sense of loss of control and perhaps sexual confusion.

What is not in dispute is the widespread nature of the problem. Recent studies indicate that 1 in 10 college students suffers to a significant degree from anorexia, bulimia nervosa or binge eating. Although most by far are young women, there are signs that the problem is gaining among young men as well.

Some researchers believe that the disorder, once associated largely with middle- and upper-middle class teen-age girls, is now increasingly reported among preadolescent girls, adolescent boys and older women. The National Association for Anorexia Nervosa and Assorted Disorders, based in Highland Park, Ill., estimated that seven million females and a million males in the United States suffer from eating disorders.

But still, the most susceptible group appears to be young women at the beginning of puberty. That seems to cast the body image epitomized by models as the main villain.

"These girls, especially at adolescence, are watching women and they are watching the culture's fascination with models," said Marie Wilson, president of the Ms. Foundation for Women, which has been supporting research and programs involving girls and their body images for years.

Ms. Wilson said that a new study, done by the foundation with Seventeen magazine, of 500 young men and women between the ages of 13 and 21 turned up the intriguing finding that 5 percent of girls and 12 percent of boys said they judged others on appearance but that 30 percent of girls and 33 percent of boys believed others judged them by appearance.

"One-third of girls said that weight is something they worry about, compared to 17 percent of boys," she said.

Susie Orbach, a therapist who specializes in treating eating disorders and the author of "Fat is a Feminist Issue" and of "Hunger Strike," recalled that the first modern model who was shockingly thin was the British Twiggy, in the Swinging London of the 1960's. "The difference was she gave off the appearance of being happy"—he was a working-class girl breaking into the upper-class esthetic of being so rich you don't eat.

"Today it's more sinister. It's about the confusion of femininity, and who women are, and the conjunction of women insisting they can be taken seriously in the world, and the resistance to that which says, 'You can go as far as you like, baby, but you'll still feel insecure about your bodies.'"

In the June issue, Miss Goff was photographed lounging around and running across a beach in a spread on action wear. In one photograph on the Contents page, as she gazes at the camera with a towel around her neck and with a bare midriff, she looks especially gaunt.

The layout with Miss Morton is in keeping with a new fashion trend here, described by one newspaper as the "skimpy, thrown-together, post-Trainspotting junkie look." "Train Spotting" is a new British film about the lives of drug addicts in England's bleak north.

After the British press picked up the story Friday, various groups rushed to support Omega's stand. "We're pleased that this has happened and by the reaction to it," said Joanna Vincent, head of the Eating Disorders Association, a charity counseling organization here. "We've been saying for a long time that the use of these kind of models promotes anorexia and bulimia. I find if (sic) difficult to know what's in the minds of these fashion advertisers when they choose them."

Nothing but fashion goes through their minds, said the models' agents.

"This controversy is ridiculous," said Corinne Nicolas of Elite Model Management, the agent for the 19-year-old Trish Goff. "The girl looks no different. She eats well, and in her entire career she has looked the same."

"If you look right now at all the magazines, the trend is for thin girls. That's what's selling. There was a time when the girls were voluptuous. But today a girl who is busty and voluptuous won't sell. The advertisers are the ones who decide. They hire our talent."

David Bonnouvrier, Miss Morton's agent at DNA Model Management, said he was "amused" by the furor. "Anyone who knows Annie knows she's the most normal person you could meet. She drinks beer. We go to dinner and I can tell you, she's not a cheap date."

He said her measurements were: 34-24-34. Asked what her weight was, he said: "I'd have to get back to you on that."

Historical Questions

1. In his first sentence, Darnton refers to "a minefield of controversy over the connection between fashion and health." Flugel and Harper also discuss this connection. Compare and contrast the issues raised by one or two of these authors with those raised by Darnton as a way to assess dominant patterns or trends that have developed over time in relation to men's and women's health and fashion.

SUGGESTED PROCESS FOR WRITING COMPARATIVE HISTORICAL AND CULTURAL ESSAYS

1. Go back for a focused rereading of the authors of your choice.
2. Categorize the authors' basic arguments.
3. Relate the authors' arguments to the dominant values of the time in which they are writing.
4. Stay open-minded. Remind yourself that this question, like all of the questions in this book, can be answered in a number of ways. There is not one right answer.
5. Put it all together. When you write your essay, be sure to use the various details that you have discovered to support your larger historical and cultural claims. Keep in mind that your essay needs to explicitly articulate those larger claims. So, your final draft will need both details and larger "point sentences" that explain your overall historical and cultural analyses.

---

2. Discuss two or three varied examples from the popular culture between the 1960s and the present that focus on the connection between fashion, the body, and adolescent development. You could focus on particular individuals—perhaps models, actors, or actresses—who represent a certain style of fashion, or you could focus on particular fashion trends that have affected or reflected teenagers' appearances over the last forty years. Explain the signs of each fashion and what the meanings of those signs are supposed to be for those who wear the fashion and for those who view it. Then speculate briefly on a possible link between each fashion trend and some of the events that were going on in the larger society at the time the trend was popular.

Justification

This question asks for something which so far we have done in detail only with fashions from a more distant time period—it asks you to analyze the effects of the fashion on the wearer. J. C. Flugel introduced the notion that the clothes one wore could have a profound psychological effect on a person. Ida Husted Harper demonstrated the effects of wearing clothing that the dominant society did not approve of. Darnton and others he cites suggest that skeletal models encourage eating disorders. But in this question, you are asked to take up the role of theorist as you determine which fashions you will focus on, what you think their effects might be on viewers and wearers, and why a culture would seek to produce those effects in people.

Cultural Questions

1. Clarify the controversy behind this article by taking up the perspectives of one or two of the major parties involved, such as the British *Vogue* publisher and editor, the British marketing manager, or the chairman of the Omega Watch Corporation. Make a statement from them in your own words that explains their stance and why—at least on the surface—they think they have it.

   Darnton then deepens his discussion of the controversy by bringing other perspectives into his article. Briefly take up the perspective of one or two of the sources Darnton interviewed for the article: Dr. Terence Wilson, psychologist at Rutgers University; Marie Wilson, president of the Ms. Foundation for Women; Susie Orbach, a therapist and popular author; Joanna Vincent, head of the Eating Disorders Association; and the two models' agents, Corinne Nicolas and David Bonnouvrier. What do you imagine are the underlying assumptions of the sources you are discussing? How do they complicate the initial controversy? Which perspectives are you able to identify or sympathize with? Explore why.

Justification

   Avoiding right/wrong assessments—doing more complex cultural analysis. This question—like some you have already answered and many others that occur throughout the book—asks you to explore and analyze a number of the perspectives involved rather than jump to a conclusion that one is right and the rest are wrong.

   The contradictory nature of the self. Note that you are asked to discuss those perspectives you are sympathetic to only *after* you look carefully at a variety of the perspectives represented. Quite likely, you will find yourself sympathetic to more than one perspective, even to contradictory perspectives. As we saw in our discussion of dominant, residual, and emergent beliefs and practices, any particular historical period is made up of contradictory beliefs.

Individuals are also often conflicted. For example, in a magazine whose audience is supposedly working women, you may find fashion photographs in which the woman is carrying a briefcase but also wearing a thigh-high skirt and a low-cut blouse. Such a photograph obviously sends out contradictory messages, suggesting to the viewer that working women should look businesslike but also look sexually available to the men with whom they work.

Throughout this book we ask you to articulate and analyze the historical and cultural antecedents of conflicts such as these. We do this not so that you will be able to rid yourself of them—to do so fully is impossible—but so that you can begin to see that they are not just personal but are rooted deeply in cultural representations and practices. Once conscious of this, you then develop an increased capacity to negotiate them.

2. Study the signs of the photograph of Trish Goff in Figure 2.7. What meanings do you attach to them? Develop a symptomatic reading of skeletal models, comparing and contrasting this ideal of the female body and the types of fashions that are appropriate for it with the male ideal and male fashions presented by Hollander in "Sex and Suits." What kinds of clothes do skeletal models wear? What image of the self and what larger cultural values about women do they suggest? How do the kinds of clothes described by Hollander for contemporary stylish men compare with those worn by female skeletal models? What image of the self and what larger cultural values about men do they suggest?

Justification

This question asks that the skeletal models described by Darnton and the postmodern sexually potent men, described by Hollander, be read as symptoms of something else—of tensions, anxieties, pressures, contradictions, and so on within our culture.

∾ **Fastwrite 6**

Look closely at the ad in Figure 2.8. Writing quickly, list the signs of the look projected here. Then discuss the meaning that you imagine is attached to these signs. How is a person supposed to feel when looking at these models? How is a person supposed to feel when wearing the clothing depicted? How do you feel when you look at this advertisement? Briefly explore the ways these representations are attached to other attitudes, beliefs, and practices in the 1990s. Finally, compare them to the attitudes and practices suggested by the snowboarders in Figure. 2.1.

Figure 2.8. Nineties Advertising: Sex and Unisex

MARJORIE GARBER

Pushing Borderlines: Gender Crossover (1995)

Marjorie Garber is a Professor of English at Harvard University, where she also directs the Center for Literary and Cultural Studies. She is the author of two books on Shakespeare and two on fashion, *Vested Interests* (1992) and *Vice Versa* (1995), from which this selection is taken.

The mainstream success of such advertising campaigns as Calvin Klein jeans and underwear has confounded neat categorical distinctions between straight and gay consumers, and can contribute, in fact, to destabilizing not only the market but also the individual. Photographer Bruce Weber's homoerotic studies of men in Calvin's jeans and briefs "made people wonder about their own sexuality," Weber noted. A male college student who encountered one of the underwear ads confided to his father that he found it disturbing: "It makes a man attracted to another man." But straight and bisexual women also found Calvin's (and Weber's) muscle-y seminude men attractive. The print advertisements, whatever their overt or covert target audience, were being read *bisexually*.

Here, too, was a paradox. The more borders to patrol, the more border crossings. And if, as I believe, the act of crossover is itself, as the word implies, a "transgression," the exciting guilty pleasures of transgressing, of intruding and spying and misbehaving, added to the eroticism of the occasion. With a broad wink to those in the know, the Weber ads barely "passed" as straight—and simultaneously invited trespass *by* straights into an aesthetic (and an erotic) that was, in baring almost everything, clearly also coded gay. But to *call* these ads "bisexual" would, oddly, have robbed them of some of their erotic power, which seemed to inhere in the possibility of transgression. Giving permission to break a rule, as many parents learn, does not always give pleasure, and in fact may take the desired pleasure away. And if luxury items like nameplate boxer shorts and $50-an-ounce perfume are already in the category of "transgression" because of their cost and seductive superfluousness, one more transgression, advertising logic suggests, may make the pleasure even more exquisite, the object even more "necessary."

Take one apparent example of manifest superfluousness in design, the fly front on the boxer shorts Calvin Klein designed for women. When it first appeared on the market, "men's underwear" for women was startling and titillating to some. To others, the "masculine boxer shorts" and "wide-waistband briefs that looked like jockstraps for girls" were the realization of a desire they had forgotten they had ever had. . . . *Time* magazine wondered, in an article on "Calvin's New Gender Benders," why Klein retained the same design for women as for men, despite key differences in anatomy. "It's sexier with the fly," Klein answered. It was, too. Eighty thousand pairs of women's boxer shorts were sold in ninety days.

To underrate clothing and fashion as political statements would be to refuse to look at history—and to deny ourselves a lot of fun. Twentieth-century designers have played both cautiously and at times outrageously with gender crossover, as numerous "fashions of the nineties" articles reflect. On the brink of a new century, pundits try to predict sexual and social trends of the future through futuristic developments in clothing style. "Fashion has served a more complex function for lesbians and gays than it has for heterosexuals" over the last twenty-five years, according to the gay and lesbian publication *The Advocate*. "After all, has the straight community ever developed an idea such as color-coded handkerchiefs that cue others to the wearer's sexual proclivities?"

"In fashion, at least, the drama of sexual ambiguity has reached its dénouement, taking the skirts and flowing manes at the men's shows in stride," declared the "Runways" page in the Sunday *New York Times*, announcing that "androgyny, 1980's style, is over"—in case you hadn't noticed. In the 1970s, Mick Jagger and David Bowie could still scandalize an audience with costumes that hinted at the feminine. By the eighties, Boy George and Annie Lennox had become "fashion's role-reversal models," while designers offered what the *Times* chose to describe as "asexual equality" in clothing, with fabric draped loosely over male and female genitals. But with the much-touted "mainstreaming of gay culture"—a phrase one reads a great deal these days—fashion items like leather pants and ear studs have become de rigueur in the world of cool style, while very short hair for women, and long or very short hair for men, has again come to signify "liberation" and gender defiance without any sense that it is really threatening the order of things. As the *Times*'s Suzy Menkes noted, "It is the idea of breaking a sexual code that is upsetting." And the gym-tightened torsos of open-shirted males and small-boned "waif" females play with sexual codes but don't break them—at least when designers like Gaultier, Versace, Armani, Matsuda, and Paul Smith are in charge.

"What I love about fashion is that it's so tied into psychology and sociology," says Calvin Klein. Fashion photographer Bruce Weber once tried to convince Gianni Versace to design a kilt for male models, but Versace, the master of leather- and bondagewear, demurred: no "skirt" for men in his collection. Meanwhile, in the *Village Voice,* a dominatrix took on Madonna's *Sex* for its failure to distinguish between a dominant and a submissive shoe, the *New York Post* ran a three-part article on dominatrixes and their slaves, and a reporter quipped that "the United States is fast becoming a country in which mainstream readers can be expected to know the difference between a seven-inch and a nine-inch patent-leather heel." Body piercing "went mainstream" when supermodel Christy Turlington displayed a ring in her navel in a London fashion show, and the next day Naomi Campbell did the same. "In our culture, body piercing has origins in the gay scene and fetish scene," said Teena Maree, a Los Angeles piercer who caters to the London club world, "but the origins of body piercing are dotted all over the planet."

Tattoos have also crossed over. "Once the preserve of macho males (and gay men) wanting to tout their virility," they are now part of the teen scene, the preteen crowd (wash-off-able tattoos were very big for a while among the ten-year-old set), and the high-fashion world. Model Eve Salvini became famous for the tattoo on her bald head, and photographic exhibits of body tattoos have been shown in galleries from Los Angeles to New York. If menswear for women, earrings and skirts for men, navel and nipple rings for everyone, and tattoos on every part of the body, visible and invisible, are now part of the "mainstream," what buttons, envelopes, and borderlines are left to push?

Historical Questions

1. In the 1920s, Flugel argued that one of the major reasons for sexually distinctive dress was to create heterosexual stimulation and to guard against possible "ambi-sexual" or homosexual attraction. He argued that society's bias against homosexuality was so powerful that "it would be idle" to propose that men and women should wear less sexually distinctive clothing. He hoped, however, that at some time in "the future the fuller and more general recognition of the psychological grounds" for sexually distinct clothing would "eventually lead humanity to deal with the question in a more unprejudiced way than is at present possible." Garber contends that fashion today is characterized "by gender crossover." Do you think the "more unprejudiced" time Flugel spoke of has arrived? Focus on two to three specific examples of contemporary gender bender or unisex fashion to support your position, comparing what you think Flugel wanted with what you imagine are the psychological effects of wearing and viewing this type of fashion.

2. Until well into the eighteenth century, fashion was characterized by cross-gender emulation of the type you saw in Figure 2.2. The nineteenth century saw a dramatic separation of male and female fashion: While the dominant social forces worked together to create a change in men's fashion, we have seen that those forces worked against women's changing their fashion. Today, as Garber and Hollander argue, there is once again great overlap in the clothing of men and women. Why do you think that is? Analyze why, in our current historical period, we accept similarities in dress between men and women. Do you agree with Garber that crossover fashion is dominant today? Compare and contrast today's crossover fashion with what you know of the eighteenth century's crossover fashion. Are there significant similarities in the views of gender and fashion between the late twentieth century and the eighteenth century that enable men and women in both periods to emulate each other's fashions, or do you think other factors account for the similarity in dress? Give two to three specific examples as you argue your point.

Justification

Both of these questions require you to deepen your analysis of a contemporary type of fashion by placing it in a broader historical and analytical context. We often tend to imagine that developments within our own social formation are different from anything in the past. Here we ask you to explore what similarities might exist between our current cultural period and two other historical periods: the 1920s in which Flugel voiced the hope that less sexually distinctive clothing would eventually be favored and the eighteenth century in which men and women did actually share many similar styles.

Cultural Questions

1. Both Garber and Hollander suggest that many *parallel cultures* contribute to the fashion scene so that "crossing over" is occurring not only with gender but in relation to social class, race, ethnicity, and sexuality as gay culture, street fashion, and ethnic attire have all begun to have an increasingly powerful effect on mainstream American fashion. Discuss one specific example of a fashion that a parallel group has contributed to mainstream fashion. Pay particular attention to the subtle details of their codes, like color, fabric, shape or volume, and decoration. Then discuss a specific example of a fashion of one parallel culture that has not been adopted by the mainstream. Finally, speculate about why certain fashion items have been absorbed or *appropriated* into mainstream culture and why others have not.

Definitions

   Parallel culture: within any culture, there are a great number of groups that do not identify with the dominant culture. These groups, usually called *subcultures*, are referred to here as *parallel cultures*, a term that has recently gained more currency because it does not imply that these groups are somehow below (*sub*) the dominant group. At times an individual may identify both with the dominant culture and with a particular parallel culture, but a parallel culture is usually marked by some significant points of difference with the dominant culture.

   A parallel culture must have a sufficient number of members or a certain status within the dominant culture to constitute a group. It also must have sufficiently distinct practices from the dominant to be seen as different. A person may belong to one or more cultures at a given time. And what is deemed a parallel culture also changes over time.

   Appropriate: to appropriate is to take or make use of something for one's own purposes. In the sense we are using the term, the dominant takes something from a parallel culture and adapts it in ways that it becomes the property of the dominant; it is no longer, then, a distinctive attribute of the parallel culture. One can argue that an act of appropriation works positively to integrate the parallel culture into the mainstream and to gradually alter the mainstream.

   For example, until the last decade or two, soccer was not seen as a viable American sport. It was regarded somewhat suspiciously as "European" and insufficiently "masculine" to be taken seriously. Yet because it was not seen as a rough sport, it began to be introduced to children, and girls were allowed to play. This has led not only to a significant rise in general interest in the sport, but it has also been instrumental in changing the involvement of American girls in team sports. Thus, taking a sport from another country and using it for a purpose of our own has had positive effects on American youth and has also increased American interest in international sports.

The dominant's appropriating something from a parallel culture is more often seen as negative, however, because the meaning attached to the object appropriated is often changed by the dominant culture, and the parallel culture then feels that a symbol of its identity has been taken away. It is also possible, as we will see in the next reading, for a subculture to appropriate something from the dominant.

Justification

This question requires you to look at one of the ways in which ideology works—the appropriation of a parallel culture's fashion. It asks you to read the appropriation—or the lack of appropriation—symptomatically, that is, as a symptom of the larger culture's attitude toward the group. At times the dominant takes or appropriates aspects of the emergent and works to pull it into the dominant. Why would that be? At other times, however, the dominant rejects an aspect of the emergent by failing to acknowledge it or by labeling it as taboo. While the reasons that any fashion becomes dominant are overdetermined, you can get a glimpse of the relationship of the parallel group to the dominant by such an analysis.

2. Answer Garber's final question: "What buttons, envelopes, and borderlines are left to push?" Why do you think there is a desire in fashion to always push against the dominant? What do you think will be the next emergent trend in the world of body images, media, and fashion? Make your predictions with reference to a current trend you have observed, explaining the larger social beliefs, expectations, and assumptions that you think will support the new fashion.

Justification

In our discussion of dominant, residual, and emergent beliefs, we pointed out the distinction that Raymond Williams makes between that which is emergent and that which is merely a new embodiment of the dominant. This question asks you to assess what is seen as emergent in fashion today and to explore the values underlying it. Does the emergent today represent a genuine change in certain values or beliefs, or is it simply a remaking of older values? Based on your assessment of current trends, you should now be able to speculate on what you think the next fashion trend will be. Analyzing where that trend will come from, what it might mean to the group from which it comes, and how its meaning might change when it becomes a recognized "fashion" will help you to develop your skills in understanding the process of appropriation more fully.

❦❦❦

MICHIKO KAKUTANI

Common Threads (1997)

Michiko Kakutani, a distinguished journalist, received a Pulitzer prize in 1998. She writes book reviews and feature articles on cultural issues for the *New York Times*. This article appeared in the *Times* on February 16, 1997.

Central Park West. A cold, sunny day. In front of the Museum of Natural History, there's a motley crowd of folks milling about: a busload of tourists here to show their kids the dinosaurs, a group of homeboys on their way somewhere and some bored-looking private-school kids lounging on the steps waiting for someone or something. The odd thing is that everyone is dressed almost exactly alike—lots of puffy ski jackets, lots of polo shirts, lots of Gore-Tex and polar fleece. Designer logos (DKNY, Nautica, Ralph Lauren, North Face, Tommy Hilfiger) are de rigueur, as are bright Crayola colors. Industrial-strength sneakers and high-tech hiking boots are big; so are baseball caps and ski hats. The whole scene looks suspiciously like a tailgate party at an Ivy League football game.

What's going on here? Not so long ago, it was hard to imagine hip young kids—black or white—even deigning to look at the sort of clothes that soccer moms and their golfer husbands wear to the country club or ski slopes. For Panthers, hippies and punks alike, subversive dressing that sneered at bourgeois notions of class and taste was the rule: tattered jeans, worn leather coats, combat boots, military fatigues, tie-dyed T-shirts.

So what's behind this new preppy revolution? Well, a few years back, rappers and hip-hop kids got rid of their gold chains and urban commando gear and started dressing . . . well, suburban, wearing classic sportswear straight from the "Leave It to Beaver" era: rugby shirts, khakis, Windbreakers. Black and camouflage green gave way to primary colors and racing stripes, and the vogue for athletic gear expanded from designer sweat suits to two-tone varsity jackets, E.M.S. ski jackets, fishing vests and Polartec pants. The rap impresario Russell Simmons opened a classy SoHo boutique called Phat Farm, selling sportswear with a rural motif (T-shirts emblazoned with log cabins and cows), and a Georgia designer named Charles Walker Jr. began marketing a line of clothing described as "Afrocentric preppy" (its slogan: "We Don't Play Polo").

Part of this development is simply a testament to hip-hop's post-modernist esthetic. In much the same way that rap music appropriates disco and funk, as well as street noise and sound bites, hip-hop's sampling of preppy styles is a way of reinventing—or, as academics would say, recontextualizing—the past.

This appropriation comes with a kind of spin. Just as some rap songs play upon popular caricatures of blacks—exaggerating stereotypes of sexual prowess and lawlessness—so "badd" becomes good and "nigga" a word of empowerment. Hip-hop prep similarly winks at mainstream culture. The clothes, after all, aren't worn the way white-bread suburbanites wear them. They're worn more than a couple of sizes too big, pants pulled down prison-style on the hips, shirts hanging to the knees. They're mixed and matched in a wild cacophony of styles—ski clothes paired with basketball sneakers, golf togs paired with hiking boots. All in all, a sly cartoon of upscale dressing.

Hip-hop prep, however, isn't meant simply as an ironic comment on the good life; it also represents an earnest yearning after the American dream. In Russell Simmons's words: "Ghetto kids want to escape, so they wear things that represent success." More and more rap videos these days purvey sleek images of material success. Forget the Panthers' attacks on capitalism. Forget gangsta rap put-downs of bourgeois Huxtable blacks. Dr. Dre's latest video, "Been There, Done That," depicts a ballroom full of elegant couples doing the tango, while LL Cool J's new video, "Ain't Nobody," shows cheerfully attired rappers playing golf and snowmobiling.

Yet for the white kids known as wiggers, who spurn the moneyed life of their parents, being black means being hip and rebellious. Like Norman Mailer and Carl Van Vechten before them, these cultural tourists romanticize the very ghetto life that so many black kids want to escape. Instead of the terrible mortality rate for young black males, they see the glamour of violence. Instead of the frustration of people denied jobs and hope and respect, they see the verbal defiance of that frustration. Perhaps this is why the most violent of gangsta rap has found its largest audience among white suburban males. Such music not only commodifies the worst sorts of black stereotypes but at the same time enables white teen-agers to co-opt black rage as a metaphor for their own adolescent angst.

Rap started out as a kind of reportage, a means of testifying to the reality of life on the streets, but as promoters and producers began to realize its marketability, something began to change. Some performers were packaged as gangsters for the voyeuristic consumption of honkies; others were promoted as avatars of a new domesticated brand of rap, offering the beat and pulse of the original with none of its grittiness or threat.

Meanwhile, slick magazines like Vibe—started by Time Warner and Quincy Jones—tried to turn hip-hop into a life style, an attitude, a look that could be acquired through the right clothes. Hence, the white kids from Chapin and Dalton hanging out on Central Park West, outfitted in their Hilfiger jeans, their DKNY oversize parkas, their $150 Nikes, speaking fluent ebonics and doing their best to be young black teenagers, even as their role models, the homeboys from uptown, don the same clothes as a talisman of the better life they wish they had.

At an age when nearly all kids feel powerless, the class war becomes a kind of looking-glass world. Rich white kids, guilty about their privileged lives and fearful of being wimps, equate power—and authenticity—with the streetsmart, badman swagger of the homeboys, while poor black kids, facing dead-end jobs and unemployment lines, equate power with money and bourgeois comforts. Everyone looks in the mirror and covets what the other side has—or, at least, the clothes the other side is wearing.

Historical Question

Kakutani says there is a "new preppy revolution," and gives one reason for it as "hip-hop's post-modernist esthetic." This new style is a "sly cartoon of upscale dressing," according to the author, which has been appropriated "with a kind of spin." Kakutani suggests that this style can be read as both ironic and serious. Describe what you see as the two or three key signs of this fashion and then analyze each sign from both an ironic and a serious perspective. What do you think is the most accurate interpretation of the appropriation of preppy clothing by poor African American urban youth? Remember to historicize your analysis of the "preppy revolution" within the larger history of African American status and dress since the 1960s.

Justification

This question requires you to explore the effects of appropriation when a parallel culture appropriates something from the dominant. As we saw above, the effects of appropriation vary depending on the meaning attached to the fashion item and the power relations between the appropriating group and the group whose fashions are being appropriated.

Cultural Question

Similar to Garber's discussion of gender crossovers, Kakutani describes social class crossovers: Both authors focus on how ideas, behaviors, and practices from parallel cultures enter the dominant. Garber writes about the "mainstreaming of gay culture," and Kakutani focuses not only on urban African Americans' adopting preppy styles, but also on the adoption of African American music, style, and language by white suburbanites. What do you think are some of the larger consequences of the dominant's adopting fashions from gay cultures and African American cultures? For example, will the identity of the minority cultures be diluted? Will the beliefs and values of the dominant culture be expanded? Will there be greater tolerance? Will there be a reaction against the minority cultures and therefore less tolerance? Focus on two or three specific examples as you develop your position.

Justification

Before answering this question you may want to review the discussion of parallel cultures above and the discussion of dominant, residual, and emergent. This question asks you to take up a position of your own on the process of appropriation of minority cultures by the dominant. While you may change your mind in later chapters, or even when writing one of the assignment sequences for this chapter, it is important that you think carefully about the complexity of interactions that occur within any cultural period. We focus this question, therefore, on two fashion trends that are influential now and that you may be participating in. In this question, try to link those trends to larger cultural beliefs and attitudes and to explore their potential consequences.

∾ Assignment Sequence 1: Fashion and Identity

The clothing you wear functions as a complex sign system for others to interpret; your clothing helps to construct the identity and the sense of self that you represent to yourself and project to others. But clothing is more than just a personal statement. Our individual preferences, as sociologist Fred Davis notes, reflect "deeper historical and cultural forces, characterized by tensions over gender roles, social status, and the expression of sexuality." The concerns that we have about our own clothing choices, therefore, while personal, are also symptomatic of larger cultural concerns, tensions, and contradictions.

Essay Question

Discuss three moments in your life in which you wore different styles of clothing. What were the signs of these clothes? What or who were you trying to look like? What or who were you trying not to look like? How did you want to be "read"? How did others read you? What was your primary concern at each of these three moments? Describe what your concerns and styles said about you personally. Then analyze your different concerns and styles symptomatically by demonstrating how they connect to some of the tensions and concerns within our contemporary culture and within our larger history—not only about clothing, but also about social class, race, or gender.

Justification

This question is the umbrella or overarching question. All assignment sequences will have an umbrella question. Like many umbrella questions in this book, it is quite broad. Your answers, however, need to be detailed and focused. The question asks you to stand back and use the material you have written about for a purpose of your own rather than simply to rehash what you have already written. You will need to be selective when writing this essay; use material relevant to your particular areas of focus.

Review Questions

A list of suggested questions to review before beginning this essay follows. This list is meant only to suggest review options. You may focus on only a subset of the questions, decide that other questions should be added, or construct your own sequence of questions. We encourage you to choose what you believe is the most appropriate review strategy.

1. Fastwrite 2 (pages 54-55)
2. Figures 2.2 and 2.3, Historical Question 2 (pages 55-57)
3. Ida Husted Harper, Historical Question 1 (pages 78-79)
4. John Darnton, Cultural Question 2 (page 101)
5. Fastwrite 6 (page 101)
6. Marjorie Garber, Cultural Question 1 (page 106)
7. Michiko Kakutani, Cultural Question 1 (pages 110-111)

Justification

In reviewing the suggested questions or those you came up with, you will not necessarily be using what you wrote earlier in these questions verbatim, though you may adapt certain parts; rather, you will look at the insights you developed in answer to each of these questions and will draw on those insights to answer the umbrella question.

Questions for Further Reflection

After you go over your responses to the review questions and as you are beginning to draft your paper, consider the following questions to help you synthesize your developing ideas and address the primary question of this assignment sequence.

1. Study your closet by making a list of its contents. Categorize and analyze your list. What specific dominant-residual and emergent fashions influence you and why? What cultural markers do they represent?

2. What specific messages do you receive about how you should dress from the dominant culture and from one or more parallel cultures to which you belong? List these messages and the various sources of these messages. Which of their suggestions are consistent? Which are contradictory? If any of these messages come from printed sources such as advertisements, try to get samples of these. Refer to specific examples of these in your paper.

3. When you are reviewing your answers to earlier questions from Chapter 2, ask yourself not only why you relate to particular historical conflicts but also why you don't relate to some others. What might this tell you about your sense of yourself and the way you represent your identity in the clothes you wear? What might it also tell you about the dominant preoccupations of our culture today?

Justification

The questions in this section give you extra help in applying and revising—genuinely reseeing—the material you wrote earlier to help develop your answer to the umbrella question.

❧ Assignment Sequence 2: The Politics of Pants and Cross-Gender Dressing

Until well into the eighteenth century, fashion was characterized by cross-gender emulation of the type you saw in Figure 2.2. The nineteenth century saw a dramatic separation of male and female fashion: While the dominant social forces worked together to create a change in men's fashion, we have seen that those forces worked against women's changing their fashion. Today, there is significant overlap in the clothes of men and women, and yet we know that in any given moment, there are always points of tension and contradiction. Do you agree with Garber that "crossover" fashion is dominant today? Do you think it is emergent? Do you believe that we are still influenced by residual beliefs today?

gender roles → political

✓ Essay Question

Analyze why, in our current historical period, we accept many similarities in dress between men and women when, in the nineteenth century, attempts at emulation were met with disgust and disdain. How has the meaning of crossover fashion changed over time from the eighteenth century to the present? To answer this, discuss particular signs of such fashion in each period, then explain what they meant, and why they meant what they did. Finally, discuss the extent to which you believe attitudes have changed over time. In what circumstances are attitudes most different from those of the nineteenth century? In what circumstances are they most similar? Develop a number of specific examples in which you analyze the tensions and contradictions today surrounding male and female clothing. Relate those points of tension to the history of gendered fashion that you have studied in this chapter.

Justification

While the umbrella question in sequence 1 took you in the direction of a personal application of the material read, this question stays closer to the postreading questions. This question enables you to deepen and extend your postreading analyses, however, by asking you to use your knowledge of the history of men's and women's fashion to uncover some of the tensions and contradictions within contemporary notions of gendered dressing, contradictions that Hollander and Garber avoid because of their desire to demonstrate historical change. While there has been significant change, exploring continuities with the past as well as differences enables you to develop a fuller understanding of the tensions in our contemporary period among dominant, residual, and emergent attitudes toward gendered dressing.

Review Questions

A list of suggested questions to review before beginning this essay follows. This list is meant only to suggest review options. You may focus on only a subset of the questions, decide that other questions should be added, or construct your own sequence of questions. We encourage you to choose what you believe is the most appropriate review strategy.

1. Figures 2.2 and 2.3, Historical Question 1 (pages 55-56)
2. J. C. Flugel, Historical Question 2 (pages 68-69)
3. Ida Husted Harper, Cultural Question 2 (page 80)
4. Further Research Question 2 (page 85)
5. Anne Hollander, Historical Question 1 (pages 92-93)
6. Anne Hollander, Historical Question 2 (page 93)
7. Marjorie Garber, Historical Question 1 (page 105)

Questions for Further Reflection

After you go over your responses to the review questions and as you are beginning to draft your paper, consider the following questions to help you synthesize your developing ideas and address the primary question of this assignment sequence.

1. Study your closet by making a list of its contents. Categorize and analyze your list according to gender. Which specific items of clothing would you call "crossover" items? Why do you have clothing that in some sense relates to just one or to both genders?

2. What specific messages do you receive about how you, as a man or woman, should dress from the dominant culture and from one or more parallel cultures to which you belong? List these messages and the various sources of these messages. Which of their suggestions are consistent? Which are contradictory? If any of these messages come from printed sources such as advertisements, try to get samples of these. Refer to specific examples of these in your paper.

3. When you are reviewing your answers to earlier questions from Chapter 2, ask yourself not only why you relate to particular historical conflicts about clothing for men and women but also why you don't relate to some others. What might this tell you about your sense of yourself and the way you represent gender in the clothes you wear? What might it also tell you about the dominant preoccupations concerning gender in American culture today?

ॐ

For Further Research

Printed Texts

Boscagli, Maurizia. *Eye on the Flesh: Fashions of Masculinity in the Early Twentieth Century.* Boulder: Westview, 1996.

Brubach, Holly. "The Athletic Esthetic." *The New York Times Magazine* 23 June 1996: 48-51.

Craik, Jennifer. *The Face of Fashion: Cultural Studies in Fashion.* New York: Routledge, 1994.

Davis, Fred. *Fashion, Identity, and Culture.* Chicago: U Chicago P., 1992.

Garber, Marjorie. *Vested Interests: Cross-Dressing and Cultural Anxiety.* New York: Routledge, 1992.

Hollander, Anne. *Seeing Through Clothes.* Berkeley: U of California P., 1978.

———. *Sex and Suits: The Evolution of Modern Dress.* New York: Knopf, 1994.

Kidwell, Claudia Brush, and Valerie Steele. *Men and Women: Dressing the Part.* Washington: Smithsonian, 1989.

Lurie, Alison. *The Language of Clothes.* New York: Random, 1981.

McDowell, Colin. *Dressed to Kill: Sex, Power and Clothes.* London: Hutchinson, 1992.

Neimark, Jill, et al. "The Beefcaking of America: Turning Men into Objects of Desire." *Psychology Today.* Nov. 1994: 32-38.

Rand, Erica. *Barbie's Queer Accessories*. Durham: Duke UP, 1995.

Rubinstein, Ruth P. *Dress Codes: Meanings and Messages in American Culture.* Boulder: Westview, 1995.

Williams, Raymond. *The Long Revolution*. London: Chatto, 1961.

———. *Marxism and Literature*. London: Verso, 1977.

———. *What I Came to Say*. London: Hutchinson, 1989.

Wilson, Elizabeth. *Adorned in Dreams: Fashion and Modernity*. Berkeley: U of California, 1985.

Wilson, Elizabeth and Juliet Ash, eds. *Chic Thrills: A Fashion Reader*. Berkeley: U of California, 1993.

Wilson, Elizabeth and Lou Taylor. *Through the Looking Glass: A History of Dress from 1869 to the Present Day*. London: BBC, 1989.

Films/Videotapes

Clueless. Dir. Amy Heckerling. Perf. Alicia Silverstone. Paramount, 1995.

Dangerous Liaisons. Dir. Stephen Frears. Perf. Glenn Close, John Malkovich, Warner Bros., 1988.

The Eighteenth Century Woman. Prod. and dir. Suzanne Bauman and Jim Burroughs. ABC Video Enterprises and the Metropolitan Museum of Art, 1982.

The Famine Within. Dir. Katherine Gilday. PBS, 1990.

Unzipped. Dir. Douglas Keeve. Fashion documentary. Miramax Films, 1995.

PART II
Absorbing Stories, Creating Identities

❧ 3 ❧

FAMILY PORTRAITS: CHANGING ROLES

Donald Jones and Kerry Beckford

*[The word] family has an especially significant social history. . . .
In none of the pre-seventeenth century senses, can we find the distinctive modern sense of a small group confined to immediate
blood relations. . . . Yet it is clear that between the seventeenth and
nineteenth centuries the sense of the small kin-group, usually living in one house, came to be dominant so . . . in the twentieth century there has been an invention of terms . . . the distinction
between nuclear family and extended family.*
—RAYMOND WILLIAMS, 1977

*Until the middle of the [nineteenth] century, children were cus-
tomarily placed in the custody of their fathers (not their mothers)
when marital dissolutions occurred. Under common law, children
were viewed as the fathers' possessions, and it was assumed men
could make satisfactory arrangements for their children's care.*
—MICHAEL LAMB, 1982

*If the decade of the 1950's was the "heyday" of the nuclear family,
it was also a historical aberration. The social stability of the 1950's
was less the result of that decade's family forms or values than its
unique socioeconomic and political climate.*
—STEPHANIE COONTZ, 1995

*The very nature of white institutions works against the black
extended family as it attempts to fulfill its collective responsibilities
and functions within the context of Afro-American values. [Imag-
ine] what black college freshmen go through trying to explain the
income of their multiple extended family parents divided by the
number of cousins, siblings, nieces, nephews, and fictional kin to
college financial aid officers.*
—JOSEPH WHITE, 1984

119

‎

Introduction: "Spying" a Family

Before you begin reading the following introductory thoughts, try developing some images of your own family.

⌇ Fastwrite 1

a. *Family Images:* The modern British poet Christopher Isherwood compared himself to a camera as he began to collect ideas for his poetry. He wrote, "I am a camera with its shutter open, quite passive, recording, not thinking. . . . Some day all of this will have to be developed carefully, fixed [and] printed." Like Isherwood, can you open your mind's shutter, your creative camera, to capture several images of your family? Rather than creating a posed group portrait with everyone standing still, shoulder to shoulder, saying "cheese," try to get some "candid" shots that create some realistic images of your family life. Fastwrite one or two descriptive images that record a moment of your family members in action and that reveal their roles within your family.

b. *Analysis:* After you finish writing your descriptive images, briefly analyze their significance. In more fastwriting, explore three or four of the following questions:

1. Were your images generally positive or negative?
2. Were your images typical of or unusual for your family?
3. Who did you include (and exclude)? Why?
4. What is the expected role of each member of your family?
5. How do these roles match those expected by society in general? How do they differ?
6. What internal and external forces can pull this family together and push it apart?

c. *Defining the Family:* Now that you have described one or two significant images of your own family, how would you define the contemporary American family? What is a family?

In the film, *When Harry Met Sally,* Sally recounts a time when she was caring for a friend's child. The child would say "I spy a family" whenever she saw a man, woman, and a child. Can you "spy" a family? What is a *family?* The form and function of families have changed so greatly in the United States that many contemporary families would seem very strange to past generations, just as their family structures would seem unusual to many of us today.

The colonial family, for example, often consisted not only of parents and children, but also of other relatives, indentured servants, apprentices, and journeymen. Most of the members of this colonial family lived in the same dwelling, and they all ate their meals together regularly. This family was less defined by blood relationships and more by household membership. (The word *family* was a synonym for *household* in the English spoken during the sixteenth and seventeenth centuries.) Because the male head of this household and his assistants often worked as well as lived in the same dwelling, there was little distinction between a father's economic and domestic roles. He frequently treated his children like workers and his helpers like children. Apprentices, for example, had to promise not only to work for their master but also to obey his commands concerning their conduct. Apprentices could not leave the house without their master's permission. Would you want to live in a family under these conditions? What might be some of the advantages over your family life today? What might be some of the disadvantages?

Since colonial times, the size of U.S. families has steadily decreased. In 1790, most families had seven or more members living in one house. By 1890, less than half of all families were as large, and many had only three members. The definition of *family*, however, had changed as well; servants and apprentices were no longer considered family members. By 1970, three-quarters of all U.S. families had three members or fewer in the same household. Multiple factors account for this: Grandparents frequently no longer lived with their adult children; couples chose to have fewer children, and some couples chose not to have children at all; many divorces created single-parent families; and young adult children began leaving home and moving into their own households at an earlier age, often before marriage.

With these differences in numbers, there have also been much more complex changes in the roles of family members. For example, while we take for granted that most mothers naturally want to bond with their babies soon after birth, this was not always the case. In colonial times, when many babies did not survive birth or did not live beyond age two, mothers delayed forming emotional bonds with their babies because their survival was too uncertain. Only since the late nineteenth century, with its significant decrease in infant mortality, have mothers been expected to nurture their infants emotionally soon after birth. (It is now even suggested that mothers can begin to bond while the baby is still in the womb.)

The role of fathers also has changed greatly. When the United States was primarily an agrarian society, fathers worked side by side with their wives and children and were in their families' company most of the time. Since the industrialization and urbanization of the United States in the eighteenth century, however, the place of work has moved away from the home and the fields. Fathers became expected to be the primary providers for their families (until recently) and had to labor long hours away from their wives and children.

As these historical changes suggest, multiple and often conflicting perspectives now exist on what a family is and what the expected role of each member is. Every reading in this chapter provides a "snapshot" of one or more perspectives in what is a much larger "family album." This chapter is not intended to be a definitive history of family in the United States. It instead is designed to make you question your own assumptions and those of others about what a family is, has been, and will be. This chapter encourages you to ask and answer these questions about the family's form and function by requiring you to consider your beliefs in relation to readings that offer past and present perspectives.

For example, Frederick Douglass examines the effects nineteenth-century slavery had on the families of both master and slave. According to Joseph White, the residual effects of slavery have helped to create African-American families that are very different from other contemporary family units. Should religious and legal institutions recognize these and other alternative family structures, such as the gay family, especially when college financial aid or corporate health benefits are at stake? Before that question can be answered, two even more basic ones must be considered: Who should decide what a family is? For whom should they decide? Before you examine the perspectives of others on these issues, consider where you "spy" a family and why.

∞ Fastwrite 2

a. Brainstorm a list of as many television shows as you can recall that offer images of families. Include current shows as well as older shows that you have seen. Once you have compiled this list, ask yourself what these shows tell you about recent conceptions of the family. To answer this analytical question, you may want to group programs that are similar or different. What patterns of similarity and difference do you notice?

b. Once you have compiled a list and connected a number of shows, try being more deliberate in your analysis by answering one or two of the following questions in another fastwrite:

  1. How are the images of these TV families similar to and different from your images of your family (from fastwrite 1)?
  2. Has your conception of your family been influenced by these television programs? If so, how?
  3. What other sources have influenced your understanding of the family?

c. How do you think the size and membership of families have changed over the last hundred years or so? What may have been some of the causes of these changes?

❧ Fastwrite 3

What is your response to the photograph (Figure 3.1) of the multigenerational Munger family? Analyzing three or four specific details of the photograph, describe how this family conforms to or challenges American ideals of the family.

Figure 3.1. Climbing the Family Tree

PETER STEARNS

Reinventing the Family (1979)

During the nineteenth century, industrialization fundamentally changed the circumstances in which agrarian families, such as the family described in the introduction, had lived. The relocation of many jobs from farm to factory affected the definition of a father and every other member of the family. Peter Stearns (b. 1936) is Dean of Humanities and Social Sciences and Professor of History at Carnegie Mellon University. He has written many historical studies, including several books on gender and the history of the European labor market, including *European Society in Upheaval* (1967). In *Be a Man: Males in Modern Society* (1979), from which this reading is taken, Stearns examines the relationship between work issues and family formations.

Many a factory office started in the early nineteenth century as a husband-wife operation, with the woman doing the books in the traditional manner of the business class. But now the wife was gone; only small retail shops retained the traditional male-female cooperation in the workplace, and when women were reintroduced into offices after 1870, they came as subordinates. The offices offered none of the physical challenge of the mines or the machine shops. But they offered a kind of mental challenge: the male as aggressive business competitor (a new image which retained traditional hunting or warlike qualities, though in a sublimated fashion) and the male as master of rational knowledge, an old image in Western society which now became increasingly important. . . . Industrialization heightened the importance of gender; for men, it heightened the importance of defining the criteria of manhood and of fulfilling those criteria.

We know that women were greatly affected by industrialization and not just as passive victims. It caused them to initiate a host of changes in home and family of vital importance, some of them relevant in the long run to employment situations as well. (An openness to household technology has, for example, been associated with the early female monopoly of paid typewriting, against the resistance of tradition-minded male scribes.) But for a full century industrialization steadily converted non-agricultural production to a male sphere. Women and children worked in the textile factories, of course, and whenever cloth or metal goods could still be produced in the home, women were employed in large numbers. In largely household economies such as that in France, by 1900 some 30 percent of the manufacturing labor force was female. But until the rise of chemical industries the key growth industries were almost wholly male. Textile industrialization primarily involved putting labor in factories, not creating new labor, and its workforce steadily decreased as a percentage of the whole. Not only mining but also metalwork and metallurgy, construction, railroading, and shipping were predominantly male.

Furthermore, outside the workplace, gender distinctions also increased with the advent of industrialization. It became increasingly important to make sure that boys knew they were boys, and girls girls. Changes in children's costume eroded the unisex of preindustrial childhood; the skirt, for men, was now confined to infancy alone. The decline of the wig emphasized different gender hairstyles in adulthood. A growing female concern with slenderness accentuated different bodies. The male domination of most nineteenth-century trade unions was less novel, for earlier producer guilds were typically grouped by gender. But division or new leisure activities by sex was revealing. Working-class bars, race tracks, and sports were heavily masculinized, and there was little male-female contact in leisure apart from courtship. Middle-class patterns were more complex, but the rise of men's clubs shows the increase in gender distinction of leisure activities. . . .

The combined impact of early industrial technology and demography explains in part the increase in gender distinctions, for more was involved than a conveniently visible categorization. Many of the early machines did not significantly reduce the need for physical strength, and in few cases they even enhanced it. Women had always been able to spin by hand, and they could run the smaller new machines. But the largest spinning machines required, until the 1840s, the manual activation of heavy machine parts, and were almost uniformly reserved for men. Still more important, the early technology did not significantly apply to many production areas of growing importance. Rails helped haul coal, and in England girls did mine work alongside boys for a while; but there were no new machines at the pitface for hewing coal. The construction industry was unchanged by mechanization until electric and gasoline motors allowed power saws and, even more important, lifting equipment; the same applies to dockwork. In metallurgy, the growing size of blast furnaces and new skills such as puddling actually increased demands on physical strength.

Early industrialization occurred in a period when families in most social classes had a growing number of children surviving early infancy, compared to the situation before c. 1750. This resulted either from a decline in infant and child mortality, as in the middle class, or primarily from a higher birth rate (working class). The nineteenth century itself did not witness further gains in the reduction of infant mortality (though child mortality declined), but the century did preach, particularly for the middle classes, the need for increased care for children. With childrearing demands actually rising, both objectively and subjectively, a family specialization of labor became virtually a necessity, and of course it greatly heightened gender differentiation. Middle-class and working-class families alike developed a belief that married women should not work outside the home. The special responsibility of men for breadwinning made sense in the early nineteenth century. It had partial sanction in tradition, it followed from the demands for physical strength and dealing with strangers in the new industrial setting—both male roles by custom—and with the exacting functions of women in the home. Men had to be trained, with new emphasis, in their special responsibilities, and they were given to understand that some specially male rewards accompanied them; hence, perhaps, the importance of distinguishing male from female at a very early age. But by the late nineteenth century, the gender ethic of male superiority had taken on a life of its own. Men barred women from jobs the latter could perfectly well handle. Working-class wives continued to sacrifice their own comfort, even their basic diet, to make sure the male was sufficiently well fed and psychologically bolstered to go out to work in the outside world, a functional division that may have given some sense of purpose or satisfaction to both parties but one that had no basis in objective necessity. . . .

The increasing awareness of gender that accompanied industrialization made functional sense in a number of ways. Division of labor, not new in any event, seemed imposed by early industrial technology and the concomitant demands of a rising birth rate. Men had to be readied to go out to work, in contrast to women who, our images of factory girls notwithstanding, mainly confined their labors to a domestic setting as servants and wives. The new importance of dressing boys as boys owed much to work, for trousers were much safer than loose garments in the factory or mine. Attention to the schooling of men, their disproportionate advance in literacy, technical training and, in the middle classes, higher education, so pronounced in the first two-thirds of the nineteenth century, had its base in the increasingly distinctive economic roles of the two sexes.

There was also a psychic aspect to the new importance of gender, a significant hedge against the pressures of industrial life. Arduous, dangerous work might be endured as a demonstration of manliness, pitting one's strength against matter, one's brain against the complexities of machine design or bridge construction. Certainly there was scant time to think of alternatives when the work was done alongside one's fellow men, when complaint might seem unmanly. Women had their own stake in manliness.

Their own sustenance, and that of their children, depended on the male breadwinner. Their standing in the community owed much to the manliness of husband or father. Quickly and durably, manhood drew new strength from the forces of industrialization.

Men did not of course realize how fully they were identifying manhood and work. Most would have defined manhood in terms of family as least as much as in terms of economy. And family, in turn, with the addition of an early period of sexual freedom, was seen in terms of a masculine tradition little more adapted from tradition than the male association with strength and skill. Before the late nineteenth century, the image of patriarchalism lingered tenaciously. Yet, never automatic or easy, patriarchalism was harder than ever to attain, for several reasons.

Family expectations of men changed and helped confuse a patriarchal role. As courtship became freer of economic criteria, particularly in the working class, a man just might fall in love with his wife and modify patriarchal dominance over her for romantic reasons. A desire to see the family as a refuge and the woman as a haven, articulated most clearly in middle-class literature, suggested a family that a man might choose to rest in rather than to rule. More immediately, the same division of labor that made the man breadwinner outside the home gave the wife increasing control of the family. A man might seek and claim dominance, but he was simply not present for day-to-day decisions ranging from allocation of money to raising of children. Patriarchalism in this situation would be rather hollow, though man and wife might both, for their own reasons, pay lip service to it. . . .

It is not surprising, in this situation, that the definition of manhood tended to rigidify for a time. It was too vulnerable to challenge in practice to be very flexible in theory. The unmanly man was detested at least as vehemently in the nineteenth century as before. Homosexuality, increasingly shorn of religious proscription, became a mental illness; there was little relaxation against it in community custom. Hostility toward men who opted to become poets or artists increased, though a larger number of men could now choose these roles. In middle-class tirades against bohemianism, a host of male anxieties were expressed: envy of men who did not seem to accept a full, manly responsibility for proper breadwinning; concern that one's sons, in an age when paternal authority seemed to count for less, might slip away toward essentially feminine roles; a concern that manhood itself might be eroded if beauty or sensuality replaced tough realism. In its relaxation of community controls, the nineteenth century provided more outlets in fact for diverse male behavior than had been possible for the general run of men in preindustrial society. But this only increased the rigor with which most men, in working class and middle class alike, held to basic notions of what a real man should be.

For a time at least the option of being a gentle man, always a subordinate theme in Western culture, lost much of its viability. Romanticism gave some currency to the tearful, aesthetic man, but the consumers of this kind of romanticism turned out to be disproportionately women (supplemented by some of the dreaded bohemians). Moreover, the importance of Christianity to males declined, in two senses. Exposed to a competitive, acquisitive economic world and, often, to a secular education, many men lost an active religious sense. Male recruitment to the clergy declined. In many villages (France is a classic if extreme case), and even more in working-class communities, regular church attendance was left to women. And as the practice of religion fell more into women's hands—part of a new family division of labor, in one sense—so it could become more feminized and still less relevant to men's definitions of manliness. The image of God the father lost ground. Female saints won a new vogue in many Catholic countries, and the worship of Mary increased even more. Protestantism softened. Its churches became filled with songs and with flowers, the latter arranged by the women. The view of death itself softened, as women gained or were forced to take new responsibility for mortality. Much of this was all to the good. Death, beginning with infant death, became less a matter of God's stern will to be endured than something to be lamented, wept over, ultimately combatted. More than men, women proved ready to submit human frailty to medical treatment, and from 1850 onward hospitals and doctors gained a disproportionate number of patients from the female population and those in female charge. Ultimately, men themselves might be softened by a religion defined in more emotional terms or a new sympathy for illness and death. Through most of the nineteenth century, however, the image of manhood did not keep pace with these developments and may even have been rigidified by them, for gentleness—a sense of yielding to emotion and a sensitivity to the emotions of others—was defined more completely as a female specialty than ever before. . . . One of the ways to understand the legacy of the nineteenth century, the legacy of the first reactions to industrial society, is to realize that for a time men and women really did become more different than they had been in Western agricultural society (or were still, on the farms). Except in the family-run shops and crafts of the cities—and there were many of these—urban men and women spent an unprecedented amount of time apart from each other. Until the late nineteenth century, few business and professional offices had women working even in subordinate positions. Large branches of manufacturing involved no women at all, while in an industry like textiles men and women usually labored in different rooms. Sex separation in many schools reduced contact among the young. Recreation alone commonly provided the chance to unite men and women, but there was little time for it in early industrialization, and men often chose to take some of their leisure apart as well, developing their central definition of leisure in terms of maleness.

The simple fact was that, while both genders underwent some very common pressures—the cities, a commercial economy—their experiences differed substantially, and their perspectives diverged as well. Much more than women, men had to develop a new sense of time. This is a familiar theme in labor history, but its gender implications have not been assessed. In the factories and offices men were subjected to the clock, responsible for integrating small units of time into their daily lives. The worker had at most fifteen minutes' leeway from the first factory bell, or he would be locked out for half a day and fined as well as losing pay. Most women's work followed older rhythms, punctuated only by brief contacts with man's time: getting the man up and off, and later getting children away to school. Women's time was the day, not the hour or minute and, in pregnancy, women had more contact than men with even a more basic flow of time. The nineteenth century echoed traditional claims that women were closer to nature than men, a claim initially rooted in women's multitude of natural functions—from menstruation to childbirth—and men's greater exposure to their fellows outside the home, to a literally manmade world. Women's naturalness was not always held to be a vice, but inevitably the characterization had a rather patronizing air to it. Yet in the nineteenth century (not, it must be stressed, inevitably or forever), there was actually some truth to it. For better or worse, with varying degrees of success, men were plunged into a new level of social organization faster than women. Along with mother-in-law jokes, the early industrial revolution saw the basis for the long and only semi-humorous dispute between the sexes about punctuality. Men and women operated on different clocks.

They also operated according to different notions of work. Men gradually learned, many with great reluctance, that work was something to be done with considerable intensity. Middle-class businessmen set goals for themselves; factory workers had quotas set for them. In compensation, by the later nineteenth century, work was increasingly finite: do your job fast and you will have some nonwork time left over. Family work, in contrast, stretched endlessly through the day, but it could be accomplished with more self-determined breaks for rest or socializing. Men did not necessarily work harder than women, but they thought they did, for they could not see women putting in the intensity that they associated with work. Women did not necessarily work harder than men, but they thought they did, as they saw men's work terminate when theirs never seemed to. . . . The new need for the care of a loving woman was an important addition to the arsenal of nineteenth-century manhood. Men were quick to admit that only this support made the burdens of more traditional manhood. carried on in the strange world outside the home, endurable. As Horace Bushnell, the Congregational minister, put it: Americans need "a place of quiet, and some quiet minds, which the din of our public war never embroils . . . Let a little of the sweetness and purity . . . of life remain." "God made the woman to be a help for man." . . .

Part of the revised definition of gender came from churchmen and their wives, who saw no profit in attacking capitalism directly but who deplored many of its consequences and who invented the female principle as a possible modification. Essentially traditionalist in social outlook, they nevertheless saw no way to harness the new man of business to older values of economic restraint. So they commended to him the love of a good woman. And to women they gave a truly attractive moralizing role. But moralizing and sexuality don't mix, at least for traditionalist Christian ministers who had additional reasons for urging sexual restraint in the visible sexual "immorality" of young people in the lower classes.

The wives and daughters of businessmen might share a sense of discomfort in the urban, industrial world around them. (So might many sons, some of whom abandoned business; but it was probably harder for a middle-class male to criticize business behavior because of its association with manliness.) Hence women developed and advertised their nurturing spirit, increasingly taking over key charitable functions. They followed here a sensible division of middle-class labor, just as they were to represent their families on the boards of cultural institutions. But without confronting the male world head-on, charitable women promoted the idea that men are naturally harsh—had they not created conditions of appalling poverty?—and the corollary: that women are naturally soothing, beneficent. Women writers, more commonly the daughters or wives of ministers than in the business world themselves, painted vivid pictures of the industrial life that men made—because as men they could not help themselves—and the bounty that a charitable woman could bestow. There were also to be sure grasping, shallow women in the popular novels of women like Mrs. Gaskell, and men of subtle goodness (though usually rather one-dimensional men; the interesting characters of nineteenth-century novels are disproportionately female). Overall, the picture of stern, if just, men (God the Father) balanced precariously by feminine compassion won considerable currency.

Businessmen themselves largely accepted the new gender definition; certainly they constructed no alternative view. Many men vaguely perceived their wives' charitable efforts as appropriate if token modifications of their own capitalist strivings. . . . Men were the individualists in the world of competition and struggle. Women, kept at home, retained a sense of collective interest, expressing themselves through devotion to the family. When they moved onto a wider stage, as in the reform and charity movements in which they figured so prominently, they projected the values of an older society, in which individual self-interest required modification.

Since the men themselves long retained some feel for these same values, though little ability to act upon them, it was easy to see women as representing not only a different but a higher social principle. . . . Businessmen recognized that they were consumed by a market mentality which, while fully justified, was not appropriate as the moral basis of the family. Here was the domestic translation of their uneasiness about their competitive values. The wife and mother was necessary not just as subordinate, but as a counterweight to provide the family with a sweetness and tenderness that the man felt necessary but beyond his powers to provide. Certainly the women involved saw every reason to keep the taint of commerce at the doorstep. It was no mean role to be civilizing agent in the new commercial wilderness.

This gender division, formed because of the time constraints on men in the early industrial revolution and because of their hesitations over the ultimate validity of the competitive values they trumpeted in public, naturally perpetuated itself. The businessman's son would typically be taught to imitate his father and prepare for the roughness of the new economy, but he would also learn that there are other values in life beyond profit and expansion. He should be ready to grant women's importance as bearers of these values, just as he readily granted the importance of his gentle mother. What started in male indecision and anxiety in an immensely difficult period of transition to the new economy was erected as a durable, gender-based duality in the middle-class world.

Historical Questions

1. Discuss two ways in which the sons of the nineteenth-century industrial families learned to act masculine and the daughters learned to act feminine. How do you think these lessons in gender and the way they were taught to sons and daughters in the nineteenth century compare and contrast with those learned by children in families today?

2. Discuss two to three similarities and differences between the nineteenth-century family described by Stearns and the colonial family described in the introduction, focusing on the relationship between parents and children and the distinction between public and private. Explain which of these families you would prefer to be in, giving two to three reasons why you prefer one over the other.

Cultural Questions

1. In what ways did the roles that became dominant during the nineteenth century for men as husbands and fathers restrict some previous behaviors

as well as require some new ones? Why might these restrictions and require-ments have seemed logical and even desirable for many nineteenth-century men to assume? Why might some nineteenth-century men have objected to these restrictions and requirements?

2. In what ways did the roles that became dominant during the nineteenth century for women as wives and mothers restrict some past behaviors as well as require some new ones? Why do you think these restrictions and requirements might have seemed logical and even desirable for many nine-teenth-century women to assume? Why might some nineteenth-century women have objected to these restrictions and requirements?

∾ Fastwrite 4

The following poem was found in a keepsake book like those kept by many nineteenth-century girls and women. As in modern day high school yearbooks, friends would sign their names and write messages to the book's owner. On March 20, 1857, a male named Eliot March copied the following poem by Mary N. Paul for a female friend named Olive Jane.

> There is a pleasure in domestic life
> There is comfort in domestic cares,
> None know but they who share them: joys
> Which speak God's wisdom, love, and goodness, who
> Of old ordained the sweet relationships of home.
> Let me live, while live I may
> Surrounded by the joys, the cares and comforts
> Of a gladsome home, made such by blooming faces.
> And fond hearts, and God my Father's blessing.
> And I ask, no purer, sweeter cup of earth-born
> In this dark vale of tears; for O There is,
> There is sweet pleasure in domestic life!
> There is rich comfort in domestic cares;
> There is fond rapture in domestic bliss,
> None know but they who share them, and our God—
> Their author, unto whom be endless praise!

After reading the poem several times and considering the context in which it was copied, answer two or three of the following questions:

1. How do you react to the theme of this poem? Why? Discuss two or three phrases or lines in particular.
2. Why might Eliot March have chosen this particular poem to transcribe in Olive Jane's keepsake book?
3. How did Olive Jane probably react when she read this poem? Why?
4. Would you ever want to give or receive this poem? Why or why not?

↬↬↬↬

L O U I S A   M A Y   A L C O T T

Conquering Themselves So Beautifully (1868)

When the novel *Little Women* was published in 1868–69, Louisa May Alcott (1832–1888) received great popular and critical praise, which has continued until today. Yet this success was neither easy nor overnight. Raised in an intellectual but financially pressed family, Alcott struggled to create her position within her family and to establish herself professionally at a time when women writers were just beginning to be accepted in the United States. Traces of this personal and professional struggle are found in *Little Women* and its sequel *Little Men* (1871), as well as in many of Alcott's other writings.

"Christmas won't be Christmas without any presents," grumbled Jo, lying on the rug.

"It's so dreadful to be poor!" sighed Meg, looking down at her old dress.

"I don't think it's fair for some girls to have lots of pretty things, and other girls nothing at all," added little Amy, with an injured sniff.

"We've got father and mother, and each other, anyhow," said Beth, contentedly, from her corner.

The four young faces on which the firelight shone brightened at the cheerful words, but darkened again as Jo said sadly,—

"We haven't got father, and shall not have him for a long time." She didn't say "perhaps never," but each silently added it, thinking of father far away, where the fighting was.

Nobody spoke for a minute; then Meg said in an altered tone,—

"You know the reason mother proposed not having any presents this Christmas, was because it's going to be a hard winter for every one; and she thinks we ought not to spend money for pleasure, when our men are suffering so in the army. We can't do much, but we can make our little sacrifices, and ought to do it gladly. But I am afraid I don't;" and Meg shook her head, as she thought regretfully of all the pretty things she wanted.

"But I don't think the little we should spend would do any good. We've each got a dollar, and the army wouldn't be much helped by our giving that. I agree not to expect anything from mother or you, but I do want to buy Undine and Sintram for myself; I've wanted it *so* long," said Jo, who was a bookworm.

"I planned to spend mine in new music," said Beth, with a little sigh, which no one heard but the hearth-brush and kettle-holder.

"I shall get a nice box of Faber's drawing pencils; I really need them," said Amy, decidedly.

"Mother didn't say anything about our money, and she won't wish us to give up everything. Let's each buy what we want, and have a little fun; I'm sure we grub hard enough to earn it," cried Jo, examining the heels of her boots in a gentlemanly manner.

"I know *I* do,—teaching those dreadful children nearly all day, when I'm longing to enjoy myself at home," began Meg, in the complaining tone again.

"You don't have half such a hard time as I do," said Jo. "How would you like to be shut up for hours with a nervous, fussy old lady, who keeps you trotting, is never satisfied, and worries you till you're ready to fly out of the window or box her ears?"

"It's naughty to fret,—but I do think washing dishes and keeping things tidy is the worst work in the world. It makes me cross; and my hands get so stiff, I can't practise good a bit." And Beth looked at her rough hands with a sigh that any one could hear that time.

"I don't believe any of you suffer as I do," cried Amy; "for you don't have to go to school with impertinent girls, who plague you if you don't know your lessons, and laugh at your dresses, and label your father if he isn't rich, and insult you when your nose isn't nice."

"If you mean *libel* I'd say so, and not talk about *labels*, as if pa was a pickle-bottle," advised Jo, laughing.

"I know what I mean, and you needn't be 'statirical' about it. It's proper to use good words, and improve your *vocabilary*," returned Amy, with dignity.

"Don't peck at one another, children. Don't you wish we had the money papa lost when we were little, Jo? Dear me, how happy and good we'd be, if we had no worries," said Meg, who could remember better times.

"You said the other day you thought we were a deal happier than the King children, for they were fighting and fretting all the time, in spite of their money."

"So I did, Beth. Well, I guess we are; for though we do have to work, we make fun for ourselves, and are a pretty jolly set, as Jo would say."

"Jo does use such slang words," observed Amy, with a reproving look at the long figure stretched on the rug. Jo immediately sat up, put her hands in her apron pockets, and began to whistle.

"Don't, Jo; it's so boyish."

"That's why I do it."

"I detest rude, unlady-like girls."

"I hate affected, niminy piminy chits."

"Birds in their little nests agree," sang Beth, the peace-maker, with such a funny face that both sharp voices softened to a laugh, and the "pecking" ended for that time.

"Really, girls, you are both to be blamed," said Meg, beginning to lecture in her elder sisterly fashion. "You are old enough to leave off boyish tricks, and behave better, Josephine. It didn't matter so much when you were a little girl; but now you are so tall, and turn up your hair, you should remember that you are a young lady."

"I ain't! and if turning up my hair makes me one, I'll wear it in two tails till I'm twenty," cried Jo, pulling off her net, and shaking down a chestnut mane. "I hate to think I've got to grow up and be Miss March, and wear long gowns, and look as prim as a China-aster. It's bad enough to be a girl, any-way, when I like boy's games, and work, and manners. I can't get over my disappointment in not being a boy, and it's worse than ever now, for I'm dying to go and fight with papa, and I can only stay at home and knit like a poky old woman;" and Jo shook the blue army-sock till the needles rattled like castanets, and her ball bounded across the room.

"Poor Jo; it's too bad! But it can't be helped, so you must try to be contented with making your name boyish, and playing brother to us girls," said Beth, stroking the rough head at her knee with a hand that all the dishwashing and dusting in the world could not make ungentle in its touch.

"As for you, Amy," continued Meg, "you are altogether too particular and prim. Your airs are funny now, but you'll grow up an affected little goose if you don't take care. I like your nice manners, and refined ways of speaking, when you don't try to be elegant; but your absurd words are as bad as Jo's slang."

"If Joe is a tom-boy, and Amy a goose, what am I, please?" asked Beth, ready to share the lecture.

"You're a dear, and nothing else," answered Meg, warmly; and no one contradicted her, for the "Mouse" was the pet of the family.

As young readers like to know "how people look," we will take this moment to give them a little sketch of the four sisters, who sat knitting away in the twilight, while the December snow fell quietly without, and the fire crackled cheerfully within. It was a comfortable old room, though the carpet was faded and the furniture very plain, for a good picture or two hung on the walls, books filled the recesses, chrysanthemums and Christmas roses bloomed in the windows, and a pleasant atmosphere of home-peace pervaded it.

Margaret, the eldest of the four, was sixteen, and very pretty, being plump and fair, with large eyes, plenty of soft, brown hair, a sweet mouth, and white hands, of which she was rather vain. Fifteen-year-old Jo was very tall, thin, and brown, and reminded one of a colt; for she never seemed to know what to do with her long limbs, which were very much in her way. She had a decided mouth, a comical nose, and sharp, grey eyes, which appeared to see everything, and were by turns fierce, funny, or thoughtful. Her long, thick hair was her one beauty; but it was usually bundled into a net, to be out of her way. Round shoulders had Jo, big hands and feet, a fly-away look to her clothes, and the uncomfortable appearance of a girl who was rapidly shooting up into a woman, and didn't like it. Elizabeth,— or Beth, as everyone called her,—was a rosy, smooth-haired, bright-eyed girl of thirteen, with a shy manner, a timid voice, and a peaceful expression, which was seldom disturbed. Her father called her 'Little Tranquillity,' and the name suited her excellently; for she seemed to live in a happy world of her own, only venturing out to meet the few whom she trusted and loved. Amy, though the youngest, was a most important person, in her own opinion at least. A regular snow-maiden, with blue eyes, and yellow hair curling on her shoulders; pale and slender, and always carrying herself like a young lady mindful of her manners. What the characters of the four sisters were we will leave to be found out. . . .

"Glad to find you so merry, my girls," said a cheery voice at the door, and actors and audience turned to welcome a stout, motherly lady, with a "can-I-help-you" look about her which was truly delightful. She wasn't a particularly handsome person, but mothers are always lovely to their children, and the girls thought the gray cloak and unfashionable bonnet covered the most splendid woman in the world.

"Well, dearies, how have you got on to-day? There was so much to do, getting the boxes ready to go to-morrow, that I didn't come home to dinner. Has any one called, Beth? How is your cold, Meg? Jo, you look tired to death. Come and kiss me, baby."

While making these maternal inquiries Mrs. March got her wet things off, her hot slippers on, and sitting down in the easy-chair, drew Amy to her lap, preparing to enjoy the happiest hour of her busy day. The girls flew about, trying to make things comfortable, each in her own way. Meg arranged the tea-table; Jo brought wood and set chairs, dropping, overturning, and clattering everything she touched; Beth trotted to and fro between parlor and kitchen, quiet and busy; while Amy gave directions to every one, as she sat with her hands folded.

As they gathered about the table, Mrs. March said, with a particularly happy face, "I've got a treat for you after supper."

A quick, bright smile went round like a streak of sunshine. Beth clapped her hands, regardless of the hot biscuit she held, and Jo tossed up her napkin, crying, "A letter! a letter! Three cheers for father!"

"Yes, a nice long letter. He is well, and thinks he shall get through the cold season better than we feared. He sends all sorts of loving wishes for Christmas, and an especial message to you girls," said Mrs. March, patting her pocket as if she had got a treasure there. . . .

They all drew to the fire, mother in the big chair with Beth at her feet, Meg and Amy perched on either arm of the chair, and Jo leaning on the back, where no one would see any sign of emotion if the letter should happen to be touching.

Very few letters were written in those hard times that were not touching, especially those which fathers sent home. In this one little was said of the hardships endured, the dangers faced, or the homesickness conquered; it was a cheerful, hopeful letter, full of lively descriptions of camp life, marches, and military news; and only at the end did the writer's heart overflow with fatherly love and longing for the little girls at home.

"Give them all my dear love and a kiss. Tell them I think of them by day, pray for them by night, and find my best comfort in their affection at all times. A year seems very long to wait before I see them, but remind them that while we wait we may all work, so that these hard days need not be wasted. I know they will remember all I said to them, that they will be loving children to you, will do their duty faithfully, fight their bosom enemies bravely, and conquer themselves so beautifully, that when I come back to them I may be fonder and prouder than ever of my little women."

Everybody sniffed when they came to that part; Jo wasn't ashamed of the great tear that dropped off the end of her nose, and Amy never minded the rumpling of her curls as she hid her face on her mother's shoulder and sobbed out, "I *am* a selfish pig! but I'll truly try to be better, so he mayn't be disappointed in me by and by."

"We all will!" cried Meg. "I think too much of my looks, and hate to work, but won't any more, if I can help it."

"I'll try and be what he loves to call me, 'a little woman,' and not be rough and wild; but do my duty here instead of wanting to be somewhere else," said Jo, thinking that keeping her temper at home was a much harder task than facing a rebel or two down South.

Beth said nothing, but wiped away her tears with the blue army-sock, and began to knit with all her might, losing no time in doing the duty that lay nearest her, while she resolved in her quiet little soul to be all that father hoped to find her when the year brought round the happy coming home.

Mrs. March broke the silence that followed Jo's words, by saying in her cheery voice, "Do you remember how you used to play Pilgrim's Progress when you were little things? Nothing delighted you more than to have me tie my piece-bags on your backs for burdens, give you hats and sticks, and rolls of paper, and let you travel through the house from the cellar, which was the City of Destruction, up, up, to the house-top, where you had all the lovely things you could collect to make a Celestial City."

"What fun it was, especially going by the lions, fighting Apollyon, and passing through the Valley where the hobgoblins were," said Jo.

"I liked the place where the bundles fell off and tumbled down stairs," said Meg.

"My favorite part was when we came out on the flat roof where our flowers and arbors, and pretty things were, and all stood and sung for joy up there in the sunshine," said Beth, smiling, as if that pleasant moment had come back to her.

"I don't remember much about it, except that I was afraid of the cellar and the dark entry, and always liked the cake and milk we had up at the top. If I wasn't too old for such things, I'd rather like to play it over again," said Amy, who began to talk of renouncing childish things at the mature age of twelve.

"We never are too old for this, my dear, because it is a play we are playing all the time in one way or another. Our burdens are here, our road is before us, and the longing for goodness and happiness is the guide that leads us through many troubles and mistakes to the peace which is a true Celestial City. Now, my little pilgrims, suppose you begin again, not in play, but in earnest, and see how far on you can get before father comes home."

"Really, mother? where are our bundles?" asked Amy, who was a very literal young lady.

"Each of you told what your burden was just now, except Beth; I rather think she hasn't got any," said her mother.

"Yes, I have; mine is dishes and dusters, and envying girls with nice pianos, and being afraid of people."

Beth's bundle was such a funny one that everybody wanted to laugh; but nobody did, for it would have hurt her feelings very much.

"Let us do it," said Meg, thoughtfully. "It is only another name for trying to be good, and the story may help us; for though we do want to be good, it's hard work, and we forget, and don't do our best."

"We were in the Slough of Despond to-night, and mother came and pulled us out as Help did in the book. We ought to have our roll of directions, like Christian. What shall we do about that?" asked Jo, delighted with the fancy which lent a little romance to the very dull task of doing her duty.

"Look under your pillows, Christmas morning, and you will find your guide-book," replied Mrs. March.

They talked over the new plan while old Hannah cleared the table; then out came the four little workbaskets, and the needles flew as the girls made sheets for Aunt March. It was uninteresting sewing, but to-night no one grumbled. They adopted Jo's plan of dividing the long seams into four parts, and calling the quarters Europe, Asia, Africa and America, and in that way got on capitally, especially when they talked about the different countries as they stitched their way through them.

At nine they stopped work, and sung, as usual, before they went to bed. No one but Beth could get much music out of the old piano; but she had a way of softly touching the yellow keys, and making a pleasant accompaniment to the simple songs they sung. Meg had a voice like a flute, and she and her mother led the little choir. Amy chirped like a cricket, and Jo wandered through the airs at her own sweet will, always coming out at the wrong place with a crook or a quaver that spoilt the most pensive tune. They had always done this from the time they could lisp

"Crinkle, crinkle, 'ittle 'tar,"

and it had become a household custom, for the mother was a born singer. The first sound in the morning was her voice, as she went about the house singing like a lark; and the last sound at night was the same cheery sound, for the girls never grew too old for that familiar lullaby.

Jo was the first to wake in the gray dawn of Christmas morning. No stockings hung at the fireplace, and for a moment she felt as much disappointed as she did long ago, when her little sock fell down because it was so crammed with goodies. Then she remembered her mother's promise, and slipping her hand under her pillow, drew out a little crimson-covered book. She knew it very well, for it was that beautiful old story of the best life ever lived, and Jo felt that it was a true guide-book for any pilgrim going the long journey. She woke Meg with a "Merry Christmas," and bade her see what was under her pillow. A green-covered book appeared, with the same picture inside, and a few words written by their mother, which made their one present very precious in their eyes. Presently Beth and Amy woke, to rummage and find their little books also,—one dove-colored, the other blue; and all sat looking at and talking about them, while the East grew rosy with the coming day.

In spite of her small vanities, Margaret had a sweet and pious nature, which unconsciously influenced her sisters, especially Jo, who loved her very tenderly, and obeyed her because her advice was so gently given.

"Girls," said Meg, seriously, looking from the tumbled head beside her to the two little night-capped ones in the room beyond, "mother wants us to read and love and mind these books, and we must begin at once. We used to be faithful about it; but since father went away, and all this war trouble unsettled us, we have neglected many things. You can do as you please; but *I* shall keep my book on the table here, and read a little every morning as soon as I wake, for I know it will do me good, and help me through the day."

Then she opened her new book and began to read. Jo put her arm round her, and, leaning cheek to cheek, read also, with the quiet expression so seldom seen on her restless face.

"How good Meg is! Come, Amy, let's do as they do. I'll help you with the hard words, and they'll explain things if we don't understand," whispered Beth, very much impressed by the pretty books and her sisters' example.

"I'm glad mine is blue," said Amy; and then the rooms were very still while the pages were softly turned, and the winter sunshine crept in to touch the bright heads and serious faces with a Christmas greeting.

Historical Questions

1. From the descriptions of the four daughters in the March family, what can you infer about the expected appearances and activities of young nineteenth-century women? How might these expectations have enabled these females to function well within their families and beyond as they became adults? In what ways have these expectations changed or remained the same for young women today?

2. Why do you think Mr. March assumed his daughters would "conquer themselves so beautifully" and Mrs. March asked them to "begin [their game] again, not in play, but in earnest?" What nineteenth-century beliefs do you think made these requests seem reasonable and beneficial to Mr. and Mrs. March? How do you interpret Jo's immediate and subsequent reactions to her father's letter and her mother's proposed "game"? How would you react to similar messages from each of your parents?

3. How do you interpret the final scene of this excerpt in which Jo and her sisters piously and passively read the guide-books given to them by their mother? To what degree do you think the girls have acceded to their parents' wishes that they should conform to the dominant ideology for daughters in a middle-class nineteenth-century family? Why do you think Jo and her sisters decided to act as they have? When have you, likewise, decided to conform—to some degree—to the dominant ideology for daughters or sons in your family, and why did you decide to do so? How does your decision relate to Jo's and her sister's?

Cultural Questions

1. Consider the words and deeds of Meg, Jo, Beth, and Amy during their father's absence. Discussing each of the March sisters in turn, develop a symptomatic reading of the dominant nineteenth-century expectations for young women and daughters by exploring particular passages in which they conform to the dominant and other passages in which they chafe against it. What does the tension between conformity and resistance in these characters suggest about the relationship of nineteenth-century women to the dominant ideology?

2. In what ways is Mr. March able, during his absence, to fulfill the dominant nineteenth-century ideology of fatherhood, as Stearns described it? In what ways does Mr. March fail to fulfill this role? How do you think his extended absence from the house compares and contrasts

with the effects of a nineteenth-century father's typical daytime absence? What larger cultural anxieties about the roles of men do you feel the character of Mr. March might have helped nineteenth-century readers to cope with? Explain your imagined sense of a nineteenth-century reader's reaction in relation to two or three specific passages from the text.

3. In what ways do you think Mrs. March maintains the dominant nineteenth-century ideology of motherhood? In what ways does she transgress from this role? How does Mr. March's extended absence affect her traditional roles and responsibilities? What larger cultural anxieties about the roles of women do you feel the character of Mrs. March might have helped nineteenth-century readers to cope with? Explain your imagined sense of a nineteenth-century reader's reaction in relation to two or three specific passages from the text.

Figure 3.2. An Image of a U.S. Family

∾ **Fastwrite 5**

Consider this photograph (Figure 3.2) of a nineteenth-century African-American family. What do you imagine was their social status? Were they free or were they slaves? How does your image of this family conform to or challenge your idea of African-American families of the nineteenth century? In what ways do you think this image is similar to or different from the dominant American family of that time?

FREDERICK DOUGLASS

Families Enslaved (1845)

As an escaped slave, Frederick Douglass (1817–1895) joined the abolitionist movement and quickly became one of the leading figures of this antislavery movement. To oppose those who claimed that enslaved Africans in the United States were intellectually and morally inferior, Douglass wrote eloquent speeches and essays to prove his own rationality and the brutality of slavery. When Northern abolitionists like William Lloyd Garrison tried to control Douglass too much, he rebelled against them and founded his own antislavery newspaper. This reading is excerpted from Douglass's first autobiography, the 1845 *Narrative*, a text that he twice revised later in life to oppose continuing racial injustice.

I was born in Tuckahoe, near Hillsborough, and about twelve miles from Easton, in Talbot county, Maryland. I have no accurate knowledge of my age, never having seen any authentic record containing it. By far the larger part of the slaves know as little of their age as horses know of theirs, and it is the wish of most masters within my knowledge to keep their slaves thus ignorant. I do not remember to have ever met a slave who could tell of his birthday. They seldom come nearer to it than planting-time, harvest-time, cherry-time, spring-time, or fall-time. A want of information concerning my own was a source of unhappiness to me even during childhood. The white children could tell their ages. I could not tell why I ought to be deprived of the same privilege. I was not allowed to make any inquiries of my master concerning it. He deemed all such inquiries on the part of a slave improper and impertinent, and evidence of a restless spirit. The nearest estimate I can give makes me now between twenty-seven and twenty-eight years of age. I come to this, from hearing my master say, some time during 1835, I was about seventeen years old.

My mother was named Harriet Bailey. She was the daughter of Isaac and Betsey Bailey, both colored, and quite dark. My mother was of a darker complexion than either my grandmother or grandfather.

My father was a white man. He was admitted to be such by all I ever heard speak of my parentage. The opinion was also whispered that my master was my father; but of the correctness of this opinion, I know nothing; the means of knowing was withheld from me. My mother and I were separated when I was but an infant—before I knew her as my mother. It is a common custom, in the part of Maryland from which I ran away, to part children from their mothers at a very early age. Frequently, before the child has reached its twelfth month, its mother is taken from it, and hired out on some farm a considerable distance off, and the child is placed under the care of an old woman, too old for field labor. For what this separation is done, I do not know, unless it be to hinder the development of the child's affection toward its mother, and to blunt and destroy the natural affection of the mother for the child. This is the inevitable result.

I never saw my mother, to know her as such, more than four or five times in my life; and each of these times was very short in duration, and at night. She was hired by a Mr. Stewart, who lived about twelve miles from my home. She made her journeys to see me in the night, travelling the whole distance on foot, after the performance of her day's work. She was a field hand, and a whipping is the penalty of not being in the field at sunrise, unless a slave has special permission from his or her master to the contrary—a permission which they seldom get, and one that gives to him that gives it the proud name of being a kind master. I do not recollect of ever seeing my mother by the light of day. She was with me in the night. She would lie down with me, and get me to sleep, but long before I waked she was gone. Very little communication ever took place between us. Death soon ended what little we could have while she lived, and with it her hardships and suffering. She died when I was about seven years old, on one of my master's farms, near Lee's Mill. I was not allowed to be present during her illness, at her death, or burial. She was gone long before I knew any thing about it. Never having enjoyed, to any considerable extent, her soothing presence, her tender and watchful care, I received the tidings of her death with much the same emotions I should have probably felt at the death of a stranger.

Called thus suddenly away, she left me without the slightest intimation of who my father was. The whisper that my master was my father, may or may not be true; and, true or false, it is of but little consequence to my purpose whilst the fact remains, in all its glaring odiousness, that slave-holders have ordained, and by law established, that the children of slave women shall in all cases follow the condition of their mothers; and this is done too obviously to administer to their own lusts, and make a gratification of their wicked desires profitable as well as pleasurable; for by this cunning arrangement, the slaveholder, in cases not a few, sustains to his slaves the double relation of master and father.

I know of such cases; and it is worthy of remark that such slaves invariably suffer greater hardships, and have more to contend with, than others. They are, in the first place, a constant offence to their mistress. She is ever disposed to find fault with them; they can seldom do any thing to please her; she is never better pleased than when she sees them under the lash, especially when she suspects her husband of showing to his mulatto children favors which he withholds from his black slaves. The master is frequently compelled to sell this class of his slaves, out of deference to the feelings of his white wife; and, cruel as the deed may strike any one to be, for a man to sell his own children to human flesh-mongers, it is often the dictate of humanity for him to do so; for, unless he does this, he must not only whip them himself, but must stand by and see one white son tie up his brother, of but few shades darker complexion than himself, and ply the gory lash to his naked back; and if he lisp one word of disapproval, it is set down to his parental partiality, and only makes a bad matter worse, both for himself and the slave whom he would protect and defend.

Every year brings with it multitudes of this class of slaves. It was doubtless in consequence of a knowledge of this fact, that one great states-man of the south predicted the downfall of slavery by the inevitable laws of population. Whether this prophecy is ever fulfilled or not, it is never-theless plain that a very different-looking class of people are springing up at the south, and are now held in slavery, from those originally brought to this country from Africa; and if their increase will do no other good, it will do away the force of the argument, that God cursed Ham, and therefore American slavery is right. If the lineal descendants of Ham are alone to be scripturally enslaved, it is certain that slavery at the south must soon become unscriptural; for thousands are ushered into the world, annually, who, like myself, owe their existence to white fathers, and those fathers most fre-quently their own masters.

I have had two masters. My first master's name was Anthony. I do not remember his first name. He was generally called Captain Anthony—a title which, I presume, he acquired by sailing a craft on the Chesapeake

Bay. He was not considered a rich slaveholder. He owned two or three farms, and about thirty slaves. His farms and slaves were under the care of an overseer. The overseer's name was Plummer. Mr. Plummer was a miserable drunkard, a profane swearer, and a savage monster. He always went armed with a cowskin and a heavy cudgel. I have known him to cut and slash the women's heads so horribly, that even master would be enraged at his cruelty, and would threaten to whip him if he did not mind himself. Master, however, was not a humane slaveholder. It required extraordinary barbarity on the part of an overseer to affect him. He was a cruel man, hardened by a long life of slaveholding. He would at times seem to take great pleasure in whipping a slave. I have often been awakened at the dawn of day by the most heart-rending shrieks of an own aunt of mine, whom he used to tie up to a joist, and whip upon her naked back till she was literally covered with blood. No words, no tears, no prayers, from his gory victim, seemed to move his iron heart from its bloody purpose. The louder she screamed, the harder he whipped; and where the blood ran fastest, there he whipped longest. He would whip her to make her scream, and whip her to make her hush; and not until overcome by fatigue, would he cease to swing the blood-clotted cowskin. I remember the first time I ever witnessed this horrible exhibition. I was quite a child, but I well remember it. I never shall forget it whilst I remember any thing. It was the first of a long series of such outrages, of which I was doomed to be a witness and a participant. It struck me with awful force. It was the blood-stained gate, the entrance to the hell of slavery, through which I was about to pass. It was a most terrible spectacle. I wish I could commit to paper the feelings with which I beheld it. . . .

As to my own treatment while I lived on Colonel Lloyd's plantation, it was very similar to that of the other slave children. I was not old enough to work in the field, and there being little else than field work to do, I had a great deal of leisure time. The most I had to do was to drive up the cows at evening, keep the fowls out of the garden, keep the front yard clean, and run of errands. . . .

I was seldom whipped by my old master, and suffered little from any thing else than hunger and cold. I suffered much from hunger, but much more from cold. In hottest summer and coldest winter, I was kept almost naked—no shoes, no stockings, no jacket, no trousers, nothing on but a coarse tow linen shirt, reaching only to my knees. I had no bed. I must have perished with cold, but that, the coldest nights, I used to steal a bag which was used for carrying corn to the mill. I would crawl into this bag, and there sleep on the cold, damp, clay floor, with my head in and feet out. My feet have been so cracked with the frost, that the pen with which I am writing might be laid in the gashes.

We were not regularly allowanced. Our food was coarse corn meal boiled. This was called *mush*. It was put into a large wooden tray or trough, and set down upon the ground. The children were then called, like so many pigs, and like so many pigs they would come and devour the mush; some with oyster-shells, others with pieces of shingle, some with naked hands, and none with spoons. He that ate fastest got most; he that was strongest secured the best place; and few left the trough satisfied.

I was probably between seven and eight years old when I left Colonel Lloyd's plantation. I left it with joy. . . .

The ties that ordinarily bind children to their homes were all suspended in my case. I found no severe trial in my departure. My home was charmless; it was not home to me; on parting from it, I could not feel that I was leaving any thing which I could have enjoyed by staying. My mother was dead, my grandmother lived far off, so that I seldom saw her. I had two sisters and one brother, that lived in the same house with me; but the early separation of us from our mother had well nigh blotted the fact of our relationship from our memories. I looked for home elsewhere, and was confident of finding none which I should relish less than the one which I was leaving. If, however, I found in my new home hardship, hunger, whipping, and nakedness, I had the consolation that I should not have escaped any one of them by staying.

Historical Questions

1. During the nineteenth century, U.S. literature flourished as "sentimental novels" became very popular, especially with white, middle-class women much like Mrs. Marsh and her daughters, the main characters of *Little Women*. These novels appealed to their readers' emotions or sentiments by depicting "worthy" characters who usually learned to be more moral through undergoing various trials and tribulations. The lessons learned by these characters often reinforced the dominant ideology that Stearns describes. Consider Douglass's portrayal of his mother in relation to the conception of a "proper mother" that a nineteenth-century reader of sentimental novels might have. Focusing on two to three passages, describe how this nineteenth-century reader might have reacted to Douglass's description of his mother and his relationship with her. How do you respond to Douglass's portrayal of his mother and his maternal relationship? Compare and contrast three to four key assumptions that your response and that of your imagined nineteenth-century reader depend on.

2. Consider your imagined nineteenth-century reader's probable conception of a father's proper role. Focusing on two to three passages, describe how this reader might have reacted to Douglass's relationship with his apparent father. How do you respond to this relationship? Compare and contrast

three to four key assumptions that your response and that of your imagined nineteenth-century reader depend on.

3. Consider the image Douglass presents of himself as a child who was kept ignorant of his exact birthdate and his parentage as well as denied proper clothing, nutrition, and housing. What do you think might have been the reasons that slave owners subjected Douglass (and other enslaved African Americans) to this psychological and material deprivation? What do you think might have been some of the actual effects on Douglass? Can you think of any similar deprivations to which any particular modern day group is subjected? If so, who enforces these? What do you think might be some of the contemporary reasons for as well as some of the effects of such psychological and material deprivations?

Cultural Questions

1. In "Conquering Themselves So Beautifully," Mr. March was absent from his family because he was fighting in the Civil War. If Mr. March had died during the war, what do you think Jo and his other daughters' reactions would have been? How might they compare to Douglass's actual response to his mother's death? Why do you think Douglass includes his responses to the news of his mother's death within his examination of slavery? How might he have expected a white, middle-class, nineteenth-century reader to react to his responses?

2. Discuss three or four significant ways in which the families of both enslaved Africans and owners were affected by slavery. Why do you think Douglass includes a discussion of some of the effects on the owners' families as part of his biography? In discussing the punishments that were frequently given to the slave owner's biracial children, develop first a literal explanation for why the slave owner would deem such a punishment necessary. Then, looking at the larger institution of slavery as well as at the material details of the punishment, develop a symptomatic reading of some of the possible causes for the punishment. What values and beliefs in his readers might Douglass have been trying to appeal to?

3. Consider the dominant beliefs about nineteenth-century fatherhood and motherhood in relation to Douglass's presentation of his mother and his supposed father. At approximately the same time that Douglass wrote his *Narrative*, Alcott and other American women writers were beginning to question the dominant ideology of the family. What do you think Douglass's position is on the ideology of the family? In what ways is he trying to support or challenge the dominant concepts of the family? How might the different social positions that Douglass and Alcott occupy affect their relationships to the dominant ideology?

〜〜〜

MARY WILKINS FREEMAN

The Revolt of "Mother" (1891)

When a professor praised her short stories, Mary Wilkins Freeman (1852–1930) responded, "[I] wrote my little stories about the types [of people] I knew." Freeman displays her knowledge of these "types" in part by having her characters—such as Sarah Penn in this story—speak in a regional dialect. Freeman knew too well the life of Mrs. Penn, for she too struggled against poverty and an increasingly unsupportive husband. Though many critics now regard her as much more than the writer of "little stories," Freeman received little acclaim before her final years. She was a prolific writer who published thirteen novels, and many of her finest works are gathered in two short story collections entitled *A Humble Romance* (1887) and *A New England Nun* (1891), from which this selection comes.

"Father!"

"What is it?"

"What are them men diggin' over there in the field for?"

There was a sudden dropping and enlarging of the lower part of the old man's face, as if some heavy weight had settled therein; he shut his mouth tight, and went on harnessing the great bay mare. He hustled the collar on to her neck with a jerk.

"Father!"

The old man slapped the saddle upon the mare's back.

"Look here, father, I want to know what them men are diggin' over in the field for, an' I'm goin' to know."

"I wish you'd go into the house, mother, an' 'tend to your own affairs," the old man said then. He ran his words together, and his speech was almost as inarticulate as a growl.

But the woman understood; it was her most native tongue. "I ain't goin' into the house till you tell me what them men are doin' over there in the field," said she.

Then she stood waiting. She was a small woman, short and straight-waisted like a child in her brown cotton gown. Her forehead was mild and benevolent between the smooth curves of gray hair; there were meek downward lines about her nose and mouth; but her eyes, fixed upon the old man, looked as if the meekness had been the result of her own will, never of the will of another.

They were in the barn, standing before the wide open doors. The spring air, full of the smell of growing grass and unseen blossoms, came in their faces. The deep yard in front was littered with farm wagons and piles of wood; on the edges, close to the fence and the house, the grass was a vivid green, and there were some dandelions.

The old man glanced doggedly at his wife as he tightened the last buckles on the harness. She looked as immovable to him as one of the rocks in his pasture-land, bound to the earth with generations of blackberry vines. He slapped the reins over the horse, and started forth from the barn.

"*Father!*" said she.

The old man pulled up. "What is it?"

"I want to know what them men are diggin' over there in that field for."

"They're diggin' a cellar, I s'pose, if you've got to know."

"A cellar for what?"

"A barn."

"A barn? You ain't goin' to build a barn over there where we was goin' to have a house, father?"

The old man said not another word. He hurried the horse into the farm wagon, and clattered out of the yard, jouncing as sturdily on his seat as a boy.

The woman stood a moment looking after him, then she went out of the barn across a corner of the yard to the house. The house, standing at right angles with the great barn and a long reach of sheds and out-buildings, was infinitesimal compared with them. It was scarcely as commodious for people as the little boxes under the barn eaves were for doves.

A pretty girl's face, pink and delicate as a flower, was looking out of one of the house windows. She was watching three men who were digging over in the field which bounded the yard near the road line. She turned quietly when the woman entered.

"What are they digging for, mother?" said she. "Did he tell you?"

"They're diggin' for—a cellar for a new barn."

"Oh, mother, he ain't going to build another barn?"

"That's what he says."

A boy stood before the kitchen glass combing his hair. He combed slowly and painstakingly, arranging his brown hair in a smooth hillock over his forehead. He did not seem to pay any attention to the conversation.

"Sammy, did you know father was going to build a new barn?" asked the girl.

The boy combed assiduously.

"Sammy!"

He turned, and showed a face like his father's under his smooth crest of hair. "Yes, I s'pose I did," he said, reluctantly.

"How long have you known it?" asked his mother.

"'Bout three months, I guess."

"Why didn't you tell of it?"

"Didn't think 'twould do no good."

"I don't see what father wants another barn for," said the girl, in her sweet, slow voice. She turned again to the window, and stared out at the digging men in the field. Her tender, sweet face was full of a gentle distress. Her forehead was as bald and innocent as a baby's, with the light hair strained back from it in a row of curl-papers. She was quite large, but her soft curves did not look as if they covered muscles.

Her mother looked sternly at the boy. "Is he goin' to buy more cows?" said she.

The boy did not reply; he was tying his shoes.

"Sammy, I want you to tell me if he's goin' to buy more cows."

"I s'pose he is."

"How many?"

"Four, I guess."

The girl went to the sink, and began to wash the dishes that were piled up there. Her mother came promptly out of the pantry, and shoved her aside. "You wipe 'em," said she; "I'll wash. There's a good many this mornin'."

The mother plunged her hands vigorously into the water, the girl wiped the plates slowly and dreamily. "Mother," said she, "don't you think it's too bad father's going to build that new barn, much as we need a decent house to live in?"

Her mother scrubbed a dish fiercely. "You ain't found out yet we're women-folks, Nanny Penn," said she. "You ain't seen enough of men-folks yet to. One of these days you'll find it out, an' then you'll know that we know only what men-folks think we do, so far as any use of it goes, an' how we'd ought to reckon men-folks in with Providence, an' not complain of what they do any more than we do of the weather."

"I don't care; I don't believe George is anything like that, anyhow," said Nanny. Her delicate face flushed pink, her lips pouted softly, as if she were going to cry.

"You wait an' see. I guess George Eastman ain't no better than other men. You hadn't ought to judge father, though. He can't help it, 'cause he don't look at things jest the way we do. An' we've been pretty comfortable here, after all. The roof don't leak—ain't never but once—that's one thing. Father's kept it shingled right up."

"I do wish we had a parlor."

"I guess it won't hurt George Eastman any to come to see you in a nice clean kitchen. I guess a good many girls don't have as good a place as this. Nobody's ever heard me complain."

"I ain't complained either, mother."

"Well, I don't think you'd better, a good father an' a good home as you've got. S'pose your father made you go out an' work for your livin'? Lots of girls have to that ain't no stronger an' better able to than you be."

Sarah Penn washed the frying-pan with a conclusive air. She scrubbed the outside of it as faithfully as the inside. She was a masterly keeper of her box of a house. Her one living-room never seemed to have in it any of the dust which the friction of life with inanimate matter produces. She swept, and there seemed to be no dirt to go before the broom; she cleaned, and one could see no difference. She was like an artist so perfect that he has apparently no art. To-day she got out a mixing bowl and a board, and rolled some pies, and there was no more flour upon her than upon her daughter who was doing finer work. Nanny was to be married in the fall, and she was sewing on some white cambric and embroidery. She sewed industriously while her mother cooked, her soft milk-white hands and wrists showed whiter than her delicate work.

"We must have the stove moved out in the shed before long," said Mrs. Penn. "Talk about not havin' things, it's been a real blessin' to be able to put a stove up in that shed in hot weather. Father did one good thing when he fixed that stove-pipe out there."

Sarah Penn's face as she rolled her pies had that expression of meek vigor which might have characterized one of the New Testament saints. She was making mince-pies. Her husband, Adoniram Penn, liked them better than any other kind. She baked twice a week. Adoniram often liked a piece of pie between meals. She hurried this morning. It had been later than usual when she began, and she wanted to have a pie baked for dinner. However deep a resentment she might be forced to hold against her husband, she would never fail in sedulous attention to his wants.

Nobility of character manifests itself at loop-holes when it is not provided with large doors. Sarah Penn's showed itself to-day in flaky dishes of pastry. So she made the pies faithfully, while across the table she could see, when she glanced up from her work, the sight that rankled in her patient and steadfast soul—the digging of the cellar of the new barn in the place where Adoniram forty years ago had promised her their new house should stand.

The pies were done for dinner. Adoniram and Sammy were home a few minutes after twelve o'clock. The dinner was eaten with serious haste. There was never much conversation at the table in the Penn family. Adoniram asked a blessing, and they ate promptly, then rose up and went about their work.

Sammy went back to school, taking soft sly lopes out of the yard like a rabbit. He wanted a game of marbles before school, and feared his father would give him some chores to do. Adoniram hastened to the door and called after him, but he was out of sight.

"I don't see what you let him go for, mother," said he. "I wanted him to help me unload that wood."

Adoniram went to work out in the yard unloading wood from the wagon. Sarah put away the dinner dishes, while Nanny took down her curl-papers and changed her dress. She was going down to the store to buy some more embroidery and thread.

When Nanny was gone, Mrs. Penn went to the door. "Father!" she called.

"Well, what is it!"

"I want to see you jest a minute, father."

"I can't leave this wood nohow. I've got to git it unloaded an' go for a load of gravel afore two o'clock. Sammy had ought to helped me. You hadn't ought to let him go to school so early."

"I want to see you jest a minute."

"I tell ye I can't, nohow, mother."

"Father, you come here." Sarah Penn stood in the door like a queen; she held her head as if it bore a crown; there was the patience which makes authority royal in her voice. Adoniram went.

Mrs. Penn led the way into the kitchen, and pointed to a chair. "Sit down, father," said she; "I've got somethin' I want to say to you."

He sat down heavily; his face was quite stolid, but he looked at her with restive eyes. Well, what is it, mother?

"I want to know what you're buildin' that new barn for, father?"

"I ain't got nothin' to say about it."

"It can't be you think you need another barn?"

"I tell ye I ain't got nothin' to say about it, mother; an' I ain't goin' to say nothin'."

"Be you goin' to buy more cows?"

Adoniram did not reply; he shut his mouth tight.

"I know you be, as well as I want to. Now, father, look here"—Sarah Penn had not sat down; she stood before her husband in the humble fashion of a Scripture woman—"I'm goin' to talk real plain to you; I never have sence I married you, but I'm goin to now. I ain't never complained, an' I ain't goin' to complain now, but I'm goin' to talk plain. You see this room here, father; you look at it well. You see there ain't no carpet on the floor, an' you see the paper is all dirty, an' droppin' off the walls. We ain't had no new paper on it for ten year, an' then I put it on myself, an' it didn't cost but ninepence a roll. You see this room, father; it's all the one I've had to work in an' eat in an' sit in since we was married. There ain't another woman in the whole town whose husband ain't got half the means you have but what's got better. It's all the room Nanny's got to have her company in; an' there ain't one of her mates but what's got better, an' their fathers not so able as hers is. It's all the room she'll have to be married in. What would you have thought, father, if we had had our weddin' in a room no better than this? I was married in my mother's parlor, with a carpet on the floor, an' stuffed furniture, an' a mahogany card-table. An' this is all the room my daughter will have to be married in. Look here, father!"

Sarah Penn went across the room as though it were a tragic stage. She flung open a door and disclosed a tiny bedroom, only large enough for a bed and bureau, with a path between. "There, father," said she—"there's all the room I've had to sleep in forty year. All my children were born there—the two that died, an' the two that's livin'. I was sick with a fever there."

She stepped to another door and opened it. It led into the small, ill-lighted pantry. "Here," said she, "is all the buttery I've got—every place I've got for my dishes, to set away my victuals in, an' to keep my milk-pans in. Father, I've been takin' care of the milk of six cows in this place, an' now you're goin' to build a new barn, an' keep more cows, an' give me more to do in it."

She threw open another door. A narrow crooked flight of stairs wound upward from it. "There, father," said she, "I want you to look at the stairs that go up to them two unfinished chambers that are all the places our son an' daughter have had to sleep in all their lives. There ain't a prettier girl in town nor a more ladylike one than Nanny, an' that's the place she has to sleep in. It ain't so good as your horse's stall; it ain't so warm an' tight."

Sarah Penn went back and stood before her husband. "Now, father," said she, "I want to know if you think you're doin' right an' accordin' to what you profess. Here, when we was married, forty year ago, you promised me faithful that we should have a new house built in that lot over in the field before the year was out. You said you had money enough, an' you wouldn't ask me to live in no such place as this. It is forty year now, an' you've been makin' more money, an' I've been savin' of it for you ever since, an' you ain't built no house yet. You've built sheds an' cow-houses an' one new barn, an' now you're goin' to build another. Father, I want to know if you think it's right. You're lodgin' your dumb beasts better than you are your own flesh an' blood. I want to know if you think it's right."

"I ain't got nothin' to say."

"You can't say nothin' without ownin' it ain't right, father. An' there's another thing—I ain't complained; I've got along forty year, an' I s'pose I should forty more, if it wa'n't for that—if we don't have another house. Nanny she can't live with us after she's married. She'll have to go somewheres else to live away from us, an' it don't seem as if I could have it so, noways, father. She wa'n't ever strong. She's got considerable color, but there wa'n't ever any backbone to her. I've always took the heft of everything off her, an' she ain't fit to keep house an' do everything herself. She'll be all worn out inside of a year. Think of her doin' all the washin' an' ironin' an' bakin' with them soft white hands an' arms, an' sweepin'! I can't have it so, noways, father."

Mrs. Penn's face was burning; her mild eyes gleamed. She had pleaded her little cause like a Webster; she had ranged from severity to pathos; but her opponent employed that obstinate silence which makes eloquence futile with mocking echoes. Adoniram arose clumsily.

"Father, ain't you got nothin' to say?" said Mrs. Penn.

"I've got to go off after that load of gravel. I can't stan' here talkin' all day."

"Father, won't you think it over, an' have a house built there instead of a barn?"

"I ain't got nothin' to say."

Adoniram shuffled out.

Nanny came home with her embroidery, and sat down with her needlework. She had taken down her curl-papers, and there was a soft roll of fair hair like an auerole over her forehead; her face was as delicately fine and clear as porcelain. Suddenly she looked up, and the tender red flamed all over her face and neck. "Mother," said she.

"What say?"

"I've been thinking—I don't see how we're goin' to have any—wedding in this room. I'd be ashamed to have his folks come if we didn't have anybody else."

"Mebbe we can have some new paper before then; I can put it on. I guess you won't have no call to be ashamed of your belongin's.'

"We might have the wedding in the new barn," said Nanny, with gentle pettishness. "Why, mother, what makes you look so?"

Mrs. Penn had started, and was staring at her with a curious expression. She turned again to her work, and spread out a pattern carefully on the cloth. "Nothin'," said she.

Presently Adoniram clattered out of the yard in his two-wheeled dump cart, standing as proudly upright as a Roman charioteer. Mrs. Penn opened the door and stood there a minute looking out. . . .

The barn was all completed ready for use by the third week in July. Adoniram had planned to move his stock in on Wednesday; on Tuesday he received a letter which changed his plans. He came in with it early in the morning. "Sammy's been to the post-office," said he, "an' I've got a letter from Hiram." Hiram was Mrs. Penn's brother, who lived in Vermont.

"Well," said Mrs. Penn, "what does he say about the folks?"

"I guess they're all right. He says he thinks if I come up country right off there's a chance to buy jest the kind of a horse I want." He stared reflectively out of the window at the new barn.

Mrs. Penn was making pies. She went on clapping the rolling-pin into the crust, although she was very pale, and her heart beat loudly.

"I dun' know but what I'd better go," said Adoniram. "I hate to go off jest now, right in the midst of hayin', but the ten-acre lot's cut, an' I guess Rufus an' the others can git along without me three or four days. I can't get a horse round here to suit me, nohow, an' I've got to have another for all that wood-haulin' in the fall. I told Hiram to watch out, an' if he got wind of a good horse to let me know. I guess I'd better go."

"I'll get out your clean shirt an' collar," said Mrs. Penn calmly.

She laid out Adoniram's Sunday suit and his clean clothes on the bed in the little bedroom. She got his shaving-water and razor ready. At last she buttoned on his collar and fastened his black cravat.

Adoniram never wore his collar and cravat except on extra occasions. He held his head high, with a rasped dignity. When he was all ready, with his coat and hat brushed, and a lunch of pie and cheese in a paper bag, he hesitated on the threshold of the door. He looked at his wife, and his manner was defiantly apologetic. "*If* them cows come to-day, Sammy can drive 'em into the new barn," said he; "an' when they bring the hay up, they can pitch it in there."

"Well," replied Mrs. Penn.

Adoniram set his shaven face ahead and started. When he had cleared the door-step, he turned and looked back with a kind of nervous solemnity. "I shall be back by Saturday if nothin' happens," said he.

"Do be careful, father," returned his wife.

She stood in the door with Nanny at her elbow and watched him out of sight. He eyes had a strange, doubtful expression in them; her peaceful forehead was contracted. She went in, and about her baking again. Nanny sat sewing. Her wedding-day was drawing nearer, and she was getting pale and thin with her steady sewing. Her mother kept glancing at her.

"Have you got that pain in your side this mornin'?" she asked.

"A little."

Mrs. Penn's face, as she worked, changed, her perplexed forehead smoothed, her eyes were steady, her lips firmly set. She formed a maxim for herself, although incoherently with her unlettered thoughts. "Unsolicited opportunities are the guide-posts of the Lord to the new roads of life," she repeated in effect, and she made up her mind to her course of action.

"S'posin' I *had* wrote to Hiram," she muttered once, when she was in the pantry— "s'posin' I had wrote, an' asked him if he knew of any horse? But I didn't, an' father's goin' wa'n't none of my doin'. It looks like a providence." Her voice rang out quite loud at the last.

"What you talkin' about, mother?" called Nanny.

"Nothin'."

Mrs. Penn hurried her baking; at eleven o'clock it was all done. The load of hay from the west field came slowly down the cart track, and drew up at the new barn. Mrs. Penn ran out. "Stop!" she screamed—"stop!"

The men stopped and looked; Sammy upreared from the top of the load, and stared at his mother.

"Stop!" she cried out again. "Don't you put the hay in that barn; put it in the old one."

"Why, he said to put it in here," returned one of the hay-makers, wonderingly. He was a young man, a neighbor's son, whom Adoniram hired by the year to help on the farm.

"Don't you put the hay in the new barn; there's room enough in the old one, ain't there?" said Mrs. Penn.

"Room enough," returned the hired man, in his thick, rustic tones. "Didn't need the new barn, nohow, far as room's concerned. Well, I s'pose he changed his mind." He took hold of the horses' bridles.

Mrs. Penn went back to the house. Soon the kitchen windows were darkened, and a fragrance like warm honey came into the room.

Nanny laid down her work. "I thought father wanted them to put the hay into the new barn?" she said, wonderingly.

"It's all right," replied her mother.

Sammy slid down from the load of hay, and came in to see if dinner was ready.

"I ain't goin' to get a regular dinner to-day, as long as father's gone," said his mother. "I've let the fire go out. You can have some bread an' milk an' pie. I thought we could get along." She set out some bowls of milk, some bread and a pie on the kitchen table. "You'd better eat your dinner now," said she. "You might jest as well get through with it. I want you to help me afterward."

Nanny and Sammy stared at each other. There was something strange in their mother's manner. Mrs. Penn did not eat anything herself. She went into the pantry, and they heard her moving dishes while they ate. Presently she came out with a pile of plates. She got the clothes-basket out of the shed, and packed them in it. Nanny and Sammy watched. She brought out cups and saucers, and put them in with the plates.

"What you goin' to do, mother?" inquired Nanny, in a timid voice. A sense of something unusual made her tremble, as if it were a ghost. Sammy rolled his eyes over his pie.

"You'll see." . . .

At five o'clock in the afternoon the little house in which the Penns had lived for forty years had emptied itself into the new barn.

Every builder builds somewhat for unknown purposes, and is in a measure a prophet. The architect of Adoniram Penn's barn, while he designed it for the comfort of four-footed animals, had planned better than he knew for the comfort of humans. Sarah Penn saw at a glance its possibilities. These great box-stalls, with quilts hung before them, would make better bedrooms than the one she had occupied for forty years, and there was a tight carriage-room. The harness-room, with its chimney and shelves, would make a kitchen of her dreams. The great middle space would make a parlor, by-and-by, fit for a palace. Up-stairs there was as much room as down. With partitions and windows, what a house would there be! Sarah looked at the row of stanchions before the allotted space for cows, and reflected that she would have her front entry there.

At six o'clock the stove was up in the harness-room, the kettle was boiling, and the table set for tea. It looked almost as home-like as the abandoned house across the yard had ever done. The young hired man milked, and Sarah directed him calmly to bring the milk to the new barn. He came gaping, dropping little blots of foam from the brimming pails on the grass. Before the next morning he had spread the story of Adoniram Penn's wife moving into the new barn all over the little village. Men assembled in the store and talked it over, women with shawls over their heads scuttled into each other's houses before their work was done. Any deviation from the ordinary course of life in this quiet town was enough to stop all progress in it. Everybody paused to look at the staid, independent figure on the side track. There was a difference of opinion with regard to her. Some held her to be insane; some, of a lawless and rebellious spirit.

Friday the minister went to see her. It was in the forenoon, and she was at the barn door shelling pease for dinner. She looked up and returned his salutation with dignity, then she went on with her work. She did not invite him in. The saintly expression of her face remained fixed, but there was an angry flush over it.

The minister stood awkwardly before her, and talked. She handled the pease as if they were bullets. At last she looked up, and her eyes showed the spirit that her meek front had covered for a lifetime.

"There ain't no use talkin', Mr. Hersey," said she. "I've thought it all over an' over, an' I believe I'm doin' what's right. I've made it the subject of prayer, an' it's betwixt me an' the Lord an' Adoniram. There ain't no call for nobody else to worry about it."

"Well, of course, if you have brought it to the Lord in prayer, and feel satisfied that you are doing right, Mrs. Penn," said the minister, helplessly. His thin gray-bearded face was pathetic. He was a sickly man; his youthful confidence had cooled; he had to scourge himself up to some of his pastoral duties as relentlessly as a Catholic ascetic, and then he was prostrated by the smart.

"I think it's right jest as much as I think it was right for our forefathers to come over from the old country 'cause they didn't have what belonged to 'em," said Mrs. Penn. She arose. The barn threshold might have been Plymouth Rock from her bearing. "I don't doubt you mean well, Mr. Hersey," said she, "but there are things people hadn't ought to interfere with. I've been a member of the church for over forty year. I've got my own mind an' my own feet, an' I'm goin' to think my own thoughts an' go my own ways, an' nobody but the Lord is goin' to dictate to me unless I've a mind to have him. Won't you come in an' set down? How is Mis' Hersey?"

"She is well, I thank you," replied the minister. He added some more perplexed apologetic remarks; then he retreated.

Towards sunset on Saturday, when Adoniram was expected home, there was a knot of men in the road near the new barn. The hired man had milked, but he still hung around the premises. Sarah Penn had supper all ready. There were brownbread and baked beans and a custard pie; it was the supper Adoniram loved on a Saturday night. She had a clean calico, and she bore herself imperturbably. Nanny and Sammy kept close at her heels. Their eyes were large, and Nanny was full of nervous tremors. Still there was to them more pleasant excitement than anything else. An inborn confidence in their mother over their father asserted itself.

Sammy looked out of the harness-room window. "There he is," he announced, in an awed whisper. He and Nanny peeped around the casing. Mrs. Penn kept on about her work. The children watched Adoniram leave the new horse standing in the drive while he went to the house door. It was fastened. Then he went around to the shed. That door was seldom locked, even when the family was away. The thought how her father would be confronted by the cow flashed upon Nanny. There was a hysterical sob in her throat. Adoniram emerged from the shed and stood looking about in a dazed fashion. His lips moved; he was saying something, but they could not hear what it was. The hired man was peeping around a corner of the old barn, but nobody saw him.

Adoniram took the new horse by the bridle and led him across the yard to the new barn. Nanny and Sammy slunk close to their mother. The barn doors rolled back, and there stood Adoniram, with the long mild face of the great Canadian farm horse looking over his shoulder.

Nanny kept behind her mother, but Sammy stepped suddenly forward, and stood in front of her.

Adoniram stared at the group. "What on airth you all down here for?" said he. "What's the matter over to the house?"

"We've come here to live, father," said Sammy. His shrill voice quavered out bravely.

"What"—Adoniram sniffed—"what is it smells like cookin'?" said he. He stepped forward and looked in the open door of the harness-room.

Then he turned to his wife. His old bristling face was pale and frightened. "What on airth does this mean, mother?" he gasped.

"You come in here, father," said Sarah. She led the way into the harness-room and shut the door. "Now, father," said she, "you needn't be scared. I ain't crazy. There ain't nothin' to be upset over. But we've come here to live, an' we're goin' to live here. We've got jest as good a right here as new horses an' cows. The house wa'n't fit for us to live in any longer, an' I made up my mind I wa'n't goin' to stay there. I've done my duty by you forty year, an' I'm goin' to do it now; but I'm goin' to live here. You've got to put in some windows and partitions; an' you'll have to buy some furniture."

"Why, mother!" the old man gasped.

"You'd better take your coat off an' get washed—there's the wash-basin—an' then we'll have supper."

"Why, mother!"

Sammy went past the window, leading the new horse to the old barn. The old man saw him, and shook his head speechlessly. He tried to take off his coat, but his arms seemed to lack the power. His wife helped him. She poured some water into the tin basin, and put in a piece of soap. She got the comb and brush, and smoothed his thin gray hair after he had washed. Then she put the beans, hot bread, and tea on the table. Sammy came in, and the family drew up. Adoniram sat looking dazedly at his plate, and they waited.

"Ain't you goin' to ask a blessin', father?" said Sarah.

And the old man bent his head and mumbled.

All through the meal he stopped eating at intervals, and stared furtively at his wife; but he ate well. The home food tasted good to him, and his old frame was too sturdily healthy to be affected by his mind. But after supper he went out, and sat down on the step of the smaller door at the right of the barn, through which he had meant his Jerseys to pass in stately file, but which Sarah designed for her front house door, and he leaned his head on his hands.

After the supper dishes were cleared away and the milk-pans washed, Sarah went out to him. The twilight was deepening. There was a clear green glow in the sky. Before them stretched the smooth level of field; in the distance was a cluster of hay-stacks like the huts of a village; the air was very cool and calm and sweet. The landscape might have been an ideal one of peace.

Sarah bent over and touched her husband on one of his thin, sinewy shoulders. "Father!"

The old man's shoulders heaved: he was weeping.

"Why, don't do so, father," said Sarah.

"I'll—put up the—partitions, an'—everything you—want, mother."

Sarah put her apron up to her face; she was overcome by her own triumph.

Adoniram was like a fortress whose walls had no active resistance, and went down the instant the right besieging tools were used. "Why, mother," he said, hoarsely, "I hadn't no idee you was so set on't as all this comes to."

Historical Questions

1. Consider when and how each family member learns about Adoniram's plans to build a new barn. In what ways might each family member's knowledge about the barn be related to his or her position within this family structure? Compare and contrast your analysis of the Penn family with your own family: How does the position of members of your family determine what they can decide and know about your family's plans? What factors—beliefs, assumptions, and expectations—might explain the similarities or the differences between the structure of the Penn family and your own?

2. Consider Sammy's later defense of his mother and the move when he explains, "We have come here to live, father." What beliefs and values underlie his position? For example, is Sammy trying to defend his mother's right to make this move against his father's wishes? Is he simply assuming that he must defend his mother because she cannot do so for herself? Discuss these values with reference to two or three passages from the text. How would you respond in your own life to a female's "revolt" against male authority? What do you assume motivates Mrs. Penn to make this move? How does this assumption affect your feelings about this revolt? What motive do you think some of the characters attributed to Mrs. Penn and why do you think they would do so?

3. Sarah tells Nanny, "we [women] know only what men-folks think we do," yet when we look at Sarah more symptomatically, we see that she often knows much more than what Adoniram thinks she does. Thus, even when Sarah acts like a traditional wife, she also seems to be questioning that role. This is just one example of the contradictory beliefs that might exist within a given historical moment and of the contradictory roles that an individual might take up. Focusing on two to three specific passages, develop a symptomatic reading in which you explore some of the ways in which Sarah explicitly prepares Nanny to be a traditional nineteenth-century wife and yet implicitly warns her about the difficulties of being obedient. Why do you think she offers her daughter such apparently contradictory advice? Using one or two particular examples from your life, discuss ways your parents prepared you to fulfill your expected roles within the family and also (perhaps unconsciously) taught you to question them. Why, with

reference to the workings of the larger ideology, do you think these contradictory lessons can be taught simultaneously?

Cultural Questions

1. Consider the opening scenes of the story in relation to Stearns's description of the expected roles of fathers, mothers, sons, and daughters in many nineteenth-century U.S. families. In what ways does each family member fulfill his or her expected role as described by Stearns? In what ways do they fail to fulfill these roles? How might the roles these characters take up suggest places where Stearns's portrayal of nineteenth-century families needs to be questioned or complicated?

2. Note the varied reactions of Sarah's neighbors and her husband to her revolt. What do the responses of the hired man, the minister, and other townspeople reveal about the dominant ideology concerning nineteenth-century wives and mothers? What do Adoniram's initial and later reactions to the move suggest about his belief in and his ability to move beyond this ideology? Compare and contrast the range of Adoniram's responses within and outside dominant gender beliefs to Sarah's. What does this comparison suggest about the relation between an individual's status within the dominant and his or her ways of negotiating it?

3. In Mary Paul's poem (see fastwrite 4), religion functions as a conservative social influence; it is one part of the dominant ideology that helps to maintain some of its other aspects. In this reading, how is Christianity used both to defend and to question Sarah Penn's unexpected actions? What does this contradictory use of Christianity suggest about the relationships between the beliefs that together form the dominant ideology?

∾ Fastwrite 6

Alcott, Douglass, and Freeman each examine contemporary beliefs about the family, especially the role of parents in their children's lives. Before you continue reading further selections, reflect on your own beliefs by answering one or two of the following questions in several minutes of rapid writing. Use specific situations rather than vague generalizations.

1. When have your parents conformed to or departed from the traditional expectations for mothers and fathers?
2. In what ways have you already or do you think you might conform to or depart from traditional expectations for parents?
3. What social influences might most encourage you to conform to or depart from the traditional conceptions of fatherhood and motherhood?

ᐳᐳᐳᐳ

DAN QUAYLE

Restoring Basic Values (1992)

James Danforth Quayle III (b. 1947) served as the Republican Vice President of the United States from 1989–93 in the administration of George Bush. Following a series of speeches by Quayle in May and June 1992, the definition of *family* became a central issue of the 1992 U.S. presidential campaign. The speeches sparked such great controversy that "family values" became the theme of that year's Republican National Convention. In May 1992, Vice President Dan Quayle delivered this speech to the well-to-do members of the Commonwealth Club of California.

As you may know, I've just returned from a week-long trip to Japan. I was there to commemorate the 20th anniversary of the reversion of Okinawa to Japan by the United States, an act that has made a lasting impression on the Japanese.

While I was there, Japan announced its commitment to join with the United States in assisting Eastern and Central Europe with a 400 million dollar aid package. We also announced a manufacturing technology initiative that will allow American engineers to gain experience working in Japanese businesses.

Japan and the United States are allies and partners. Though we have our differences, especially in the area of trade, our two countries—with 40 percent of the world's GNP—are committed to a global partnership in behalf of peace and economic growth.

But in the midst of all of these discussions of international affairs, I was asked many times in Japan about the recent events in Los Angeles. From the perspective of many Japanese, the ethnic diversity of our culture is a weakness compared to their homogenous society. I begged to differ with my hosts. I explained that our diversity is our strength. And I explained that the immigrants who come to our shores have made, and continue to make, vast contributions to our culture and our economy.

It is wrong to imply that the Los Angeles riots were an inevitable outcome of our diversified society. But the question that I tried to answer in Japan is one that needs answering here: What happened? Why? And how do we prevent it in the future?

One response has been predictable: Instead of denouncing wrongdoing, some have shown tolerance for rioters; some have enjoyed saying "I told you so;" and some have simply made excuses for what happened. All of this has been accompanied by pleas for more money.

I'll readily accept that we need to understand what happened. But I reject the idea we should tolerate or excuse it.

When I have been asked during these last weeks who caused the riots and the killing in L.A., my answer has been direct and simple: Who is to blame for the riots? The rioters are to blame. Who is to blame for the killings? The killers are to blame. Yes, I can understand how people were shocked and outraged by the verdict in the Rodney King trial. But there is simply no excuse for the mayhem that followed. To apologize or in any way to excuse what happened is wrong. It is a betrayal of all those people equally outraged and equally disadvantaged who did not loot and did not riot—and who were in many cases victims of the rioters. No matter how much you may disagree with the verdict, the riots were wrong. And if we as a society don't condemn what is wrong, how can we teach our children what is right?

But after condemning the riots, we do need to try to understand the underlying situation.

In a nutshell: I believe the lawless social anarchy which we saw is directly related to the breakdown of family structure, personal responsibility and social order in too many areas of our society. For the poor the situation is compounded by a welfare ethos that impedes individual efforts to move ahead in society, and hampers their ability to take advantage of the opportunities America offers.

If we don't succeed in addressing these fundamental problems, and in restoring basic values, any attempt to fix what's broken will fail. But one reason I believe we won't fail is that we have come so far in the last 25 years.

There is no question that this country has had a terrible problem with race and racism. The evil of slavery has left a long legacy. But we have faced racism squarely, and we have made progress in the past quarter century. The landmark civil rights bills of the 1960's removed legal barriers to allow full participation by blacks in the economic, social and political life of the nation. By any measure the America of 1992 is more egalitarian, more integrated, and offers more opportunities to black Americans—and all other minority group members—than the America of 1964. There is more to be done. But I think that all of us can be proud of our progress.

And let's be specific about one aspect of this progress: This country now has a black middle class that barely existed a quarter century ago. Since 1967 the median income of black two parent families has risen by 60 percent in real terms. The number of black college graduates has skyrocketed. Black men and women have achieved real political power—black mayors head 48 of our largest cities, including Los Angeles. These are achievements.

But as we all know, there is another side to that bright landscape. During this period of progress, we have also developed a culture of poverty—some call it an underclass—that is far more violent and harder to escape than it was a generation ago.

The poor you always have with you, Scripture tells us. And in America we have always had poor people. But in this dynamic, prosperous nation, poverty has traditionally been a stage through which people pass on their way to joining the great middle class. And if one generation didn't get very far up the ladder—their ambitious, better-educated children would.

But the underclass seems to be a new phenomenon. It is a group whose members are dependent on welfare for very long stretches, and whose men are often drawn into lives of crime. There is far too little upward mobility, because the underclass is disconnected from the rules of American society. And these problems have, unfortunately, been particularly acute for Black Americans.

Let me share with you a few statistics on the difference between black poverty in particular in the 1960's and now.

—In 1967 68 percent of black families were headed by married couples. In 1991, only 48 percent of black families were headed by both a husband and wife.

—In 1965 the illegitimacy rate among black families was 28 percent. In 1989, 65 percent—two thirds—of all black children were born to never-married mothers.

—In 1951 9.2 percent of black youth between 16-19 were unemployed. In 1965, it was 23 percent. In 1980 it was 35 percent. By 1989, the number had declined slightly, but was still 32 percent.

—The leading cause of death of young black males today is homicide.

It would be overly simplistic to blame this social breakdown on the programs of the Great Society alone. It would be absolutely wrong to blame it on the growth and success most Americans enjoyed during the 1980's. Rather, we are in large measure reaping the whirlwind of decades of changes in social mores.

I was born in 1947, so I'm considered one of those "Baby Boomers" we keep reading about. But let's look at one unfortunate legacy of the "Boomer" generation. When we were young, it was fashionable to declare war against traditional values. Indulgence and self-gratification seemed to have no consequences. Many of our generation glamorized casual sex and drug use, evaded responsibility and trashed authority. Today the "Boomers" are middle-aged and middle class. The responsibility of having families has helped many recover traditional values. And, of course, the great majority of those in the middle class survived the turbulent legacy of the 60's and 70's. But many of the poor, with less to fall back on, did not.

The intergenerational poverty that troubles us so much today is predominantly a poverty of values. Our inner cites are filled with children having children; with people who have not been able to take advantage of educational opportunities; with people who are dependent on drugs or the narcotic of welfare. To be sure, many people in the ghettos struggle very hard against these tides—and sometimes win. But too many feel they have no hope and nothing to lose. This poverty is, again, fundamentally a poverty of values.

Unless we change the basic rules of society in our inner cities, we cannot expect anything else to change. We will simply get more of what we saw three weeks ago. New thinking, new ideas, new strategies are needed.

For the government, transforming underclass culture means that our policies and programs must create a different incentive system. Our policies must be premised on, and must reinforce, values such as: family, hard work, integrity and personal responsibility.

I think we can all agree that government's first obligation is to maintain order. We are a nation of laws, not looting. It has become clear that the riots were fueled by the vicious gangs that terrorize the inner cities. We are committed to breaking those gangs and restoring law and order. As James Q. Wilson has written, "Programs of economic restructuring will not work so long as gangs control the streets."

Some people say "law and order," are code words. Well, they are code words. Code words for safety, getting control of the streets, and freedom from fear. And let's not forget that, in 1990, 84 percent of the crimes committed by blacks were committed against blacks.

We are for law and order. If a single mother raising her children in the ghetto has to worry about drive-by shootings, drug deals, or whether her children will join gangs and die violently, her difficult task becomes impossible. We're for law and order because we can't expect children to learn in dangerous schools. We're for law and order because if property isn't protected, who will build businesses?

As one step on behalf of law and order—and on behalf of opportunity as well—the President has initiated the "Weed and Seed" program—to "weed out" criminals and "seed" neighborhoods with programs that address root causes of crime. And we have encouraged community-based policing, which gets the police on the street so they interact with citizens.

Safety is absolutely necessary. But it's not sufficient. Our urban strategy is to empower the poor by giving them control over their lives. To do that, our urban agenda includes:

—Fully funding the Home-ownership and Opportunity for People Everywhere program. HOPE—as we call it—will help public housing residents become home-owners. Subsidized housing all too often merely made rich investors richer. Home ownership will give the poor a stake in their neighborhoods, and a chance to build equity.

—Creating enterprise zones by slashing taxes in targeted areas, including a zero capital gains tax, to spur entrepreneurship, economic development, and job creation in inner cities.

—Instituting our education strategy, AMERICA 2000, to raise academic standards and to give the poor the same choices about how and where to educate their children as rich people.

—Promoting welfare reform to remove the penalties for marriage, create incentives for saving, and give communities greater control over how the programs are administered.

These programs are empowerment programs. They are based on the same principles as the Job Training Partnership Act, which aimed to help disadvantaged young people and dislocated workers to develop their skills to give them an opportunity to get ahead. Empowering the poor will strengthen families. And right now, the failure of our families is hurting America deeply. When families fail, society fails. The anarchy and lack of structure in our inner cities are testament to how quickly civilization falls apart when the family foundation cracks. Children need love and discipline. They need mothers and fathers. A welfare check is not a husband. The state is not a father. It is from parents that children learn how to behave in society; it is from parents above all that children come to understand values and themselves as men and women, mothers and fathers.

And for those concerned about children growing up in poverty, we should know this: marriage is probably the best anti-poverty program of all. Among families headed by married couples today, there is a poverty rate of 5.7 percent. But 33.4 percent of families headed by a single mother are in poverty today.

Nature abhors a vacuum. Where there are no mature, responsible men around to teach boys how to be good men, gangs serve in their place. In fact, gangs have become a surrogate family for much of a generation of inner-city boys. I recently visited with some former gang members in Albuquerque, New Mexico. In a private meeting, they told me why they had joined gangs. These teenage boys said that gangs gave them a sense of security. They made them feel wanted, and useful. They got support from their friends. And, they said, "It was like having a family." "Like family"—unfortunately, that says it all.

The system perpetuates itself as these young men father children whom they have no intention of caring for, by women whose welfare checks support them. Teenage girls, mired in the same hopelessness, lack sufficient motive to say no to this trap.

Answers to our problems won't be easy.

We can start by dismantling a welfare system that encourages dependency and subsidizes broken families. We can attach conditions—such as school attendance, or work—to welfare. We can limit the time a recipient gets benefits. We can stop penalizing marriage for welfare mothers. We can enforce child support payments.

Ultimately, however, marriage is a moral issue that requires cultural consensus, and the use of social sanctions. Bearing babies irresponsibly is, simply, wrong. Failing to support children one has fathered is wrong. We must be unequivocal about this.

It doesn't help matters when prime time TV has Murphy Brown—a character who supposedly epitomizes today's intelligent, highly paid, professional woman—mocking the importance of fathers, by bearing a child alone, and calling it just another "lifestyle choice."

I know it is not fashionable to talk about moral values, but we need to do it. Even though our cultural leaders in Hollywood, network TV, the national newspapers routinely jeer at them, I think that most of us in this room know that some things are good, and other things are wrong. Now it's time to make the discussion public.

It's time to talk again about family, hard work, integrity and personal responsibility. We cannot be embarrassed out of our belief that two parents, married to each other, are better in most cases for children than one. That honest work is better than hand-outs—or crime. That we are our brothers' keepers. That it's worth making an effort, even when the rewards aren't immediate.

So I think the time has come to renew our public commitment to our Judeo-Christian values—in our churches and synagogues, our civic organizations and our schools. We are, as our children recite each morning, "one nation under God." That's a useful framework for acknowledging a duty and an authority higher than our own pleasures and personal ambitions.

If we lived more thoroughly by these values, we would live in a better society. For the poor, renewing these values will give people the strength to help themselves by acquiring the tools to achieve self-sufficiency, a good education, job training, and property. Then they will move from permanent dependence to dignified independence.

Shelby Steele, in his great book, *The Content of Our Character,* writes "Personal responsibility is the brick and mortar of power. The responsible person knows that the quality of his life is something that he will have to make inside the limits of his fate. . . . The quality of his life will pretty much reflect his efforts."

I believe that the Bush Administration's empowerment agenda will help the poor gain that power, by creating opportunity, and letting people make the choices that free citizens must make.

Though our hearts have been pained by the events in Los Angeles, we should take this tragedy as an opportunity for self-examination and progress. So let the national debate roar on. I, for one, will join it. The president will lead it. The American people will participate in it. And as a result, we will become an even stronger nation.

Historical Questions

1. Choose one of the families presented in the nineteenth-century readings by Alcott, Douglass, or Freeman. Using two or three of Quayle's major points concerning the contemporary family, explain whether you think Quayle would approve or disapprove of this nineteenth-century family.

2. Using specific passages from each of the texts, compare and contrast Quayle's contemporary definition of the family with the nineteenth-century family described by Stearns. Stearns explains the development of the nineteenth-century family in relation to economic and social changes. Following Stearns's method, explore some of the economic and social factors that could explain or complicate Qualye's definition of the contemporary family.

Cultural Questions

1. How do your family images compare and contrast with Quayle's definition of the contemporary U.S. family? Review your fastwrite 1 from this chapter. Using some of your images from fastwrite 1 or other memories of your family life, explain your two or three strongest points of agreement and disagreement with Quayle's analysis of the problems of and solutions for the family.

2. Quayle discusses the need to "change the basic rules of society," yet he does not specifically identify those rules. What rules are Quayle referring to? Explain why you agree or disagree with him that these rules need to be changed? Who do you think should be responsible for determining these rules and for whom should they be determined?

3. Discuss some specific types of contemporary families that might not match Quayle's definition. What social institutions, policies, and beliefs would have to change to include those families? Explain whether you would support such changes.

4. Consider whom Quayle does and does not blame for the national problems he discusses in his speech. Why do you think Quayle makes such distinctions? Explain whether you agree with his assignment of blame.

❧ Fastwrite 7

Fastwrite for ten minutes on what you imagine to be the family roles and relationships of the four people in the photograph in Figure 3.3. Does this

Figure 3.3. Another Image of a U. S. Family

family represent a dominant, emergent, or residual family to you? Discuss the beliefs and assumptions about the family that influence the roles and relationships you envision.

∿∿∿∿

D A V I D   O S B O R N E

Beyond the Cult of Fatherhood (1985)

"The Cult of True Womanhood" is the label one scholar gives to the training many nineteenth-century women received in domesticity, passivity, and piety. In the following essay, David Osborne (b. 1951) alludes to this label as he examines the cultural lessons many men receive about fatherhood. Yet when the Osbornes' first child was born, he took on most of the child care responsibilities.

Since that untraditional beginning, the Osborne family has flour-ished, with three additional children and career success for both parents. Rose Osborne has pursued a successful medical career, and David Osborne has published the well-received book *Re-Inventing Government* (1992). The following essay originally appeared in *Ms.* magazine.

If I ever finish this article, it will be a miracle. Nicholas woke up this morning with an earache and a temperature, and I spent half the day at the doctor's office and pharmacy. Another ear infection.

Nicholas is my son. Twenty months old, a stout little bundle of energy and affection.

I will never forget the moment when I realized how completely Nick would change my life. My wife is a resident in obstetrics and gynecology, which means, among other things, that she works 100 hours a week, leaves the house every day by six and works all night several times a week, and often all weekend too. I'm not a househusband; I take Nick to day care five days a week. But I come about as close to house-husbandry as I care to. I am what you might call a "nontraditional" father.

Nick was three weeks old when I learned what that actually meant. Rose had just gone back to work, and Nick and I were learning about bottles. I don't remember if it was Rose's first night back or her second, but she wasn't home.

I stayed up too late; I had not yet learned that, with a baby in the house, you grab sleep whenever you can—even if it means going to bed at nine. Just as I drifted off, about 11:30, Nick woke up. I fed him and rocked him and put him back to sleep. About 2 A.M. he woke again, crying, and I rocked him for 45 minutes before he quieted down.

When he started screaming at four, I was in the kitchen by the time I woke up. As every parent knows, the sound of an infant—your infant—screaming sends lightning bolts up the spine. Bells ring in the head: nerves jangle. Racing against my son's hunger, I boiled water, poured it into the little plastic sack, slipped the sack into the plastic bottle, put on the top, and plunged the bottle into a bowl of cold water to cool it. I had not yet learned that in Connecticut, where I live, the water need not be sterilized. (Fathers are the last to know.)

It takes a long time to boil water and cool it back to body temperature, and I was dead on my feet even before the screams rearranged my vertebrae. By the time the water had cooled, I was half-crazed, my motions rapid and jerky. I mixed in the powdered formula and slipped the nipple back on. I ran toward Nick's room, shaking the bottle as hard as I could to make sure it was thoroughly mixed. As I reached his crib, the top flew off—and the contents sprayed all over the room.

At that point, I lost it. I swore at the top of my lungs, I stomped around the room, I slammed the changing table, and I swore some more. That was when I realized what I had gotten myself into—and how much I had to learn. . . .

My day starts about 6:30 or 7 A.M., when Nick stands up in his crib and calls out for me. I stumble into his room, pick him up, give him a kiss and a "Good morning, Pumpkin," and carry him back to bed. I lay him down on his mother's empty pillow, lie down beside him, and sometimes I drowse again before it's really time to get up. But most mornings Nick is ready to start his day, and he gradually drags me up toward consciousness. He smiles at me, climbs up on me, and rests his head against my cheek—even kisses me if I'm really lucky, or sits on my bladder and bounces, if I'm not. I tickle him, and he laughs and squirms and shrieks for more.

Sometimes he lies there for a few minutes, thinking his little boy thoughts, before sliding himself backward off the bed and going in search of something to do. Often he arrives back with a toy or two and asks to be picked "Up! Up!" Then he plays for a few minutes, making sure to keep an eye on my progress toward wakefulness. When he has waited long enough, he hands me my glasses, takes my hand, and pulls me out of bed.

While I shower, Nick plays in the bathroom, sitting on the floor with his toys. By the time I'm dressed, the kettle is whistling, and he's ready for breakfast. We always eat together, he has hot cereal, I have cold cereal, and often we share a bagel. I wish you could hear him say "cream cheese."

The rough times come on weekends. After 24 hours, I'm ready to be hung out on the line to dry. After 48 hours, I'm ready to pin medals on women who stay home every day with their kids. For single mothers, I'm ready to build monuments. . . .

Don't let anyone tell you otherwise: traditional mothers work harder than anyone else can even imagine. They are on duty 24 hours a day, 365 days a year. I remember wondering, as a youth, why my own mother always rushed around with such urgency when she was cooking or cleaning. To me, she was like a woman possessed. Now I do the same thing. When you have a young child (or two, or three), you have very little time to get the dishes done, or cook dinner, or vacuum, or do the laundry so when you get a moment, you proceed with all possible haste. If your children are asleep, they might wake up. If they're playing, they might get bored and demand your attention.

In any case, it is on weekends alone with Nick that I feel the full brunt of child-rearing. Consider a typical weekend: Nick wakes at 7:00, and we lie in bed and play for half an hour before getting up. But this morning he feels feverish, so I take his temperature. It is 101.6—not high for a young child, but a fever nonetheless. The first thing I do is call Maureen, who takes care of him during the week. Both of her kids have a bug, and I want to find out what the symptoms are, to see if Nick has the same thing. From what we can tell, he does. On that basis, I decide to give him Tylenol for the fever, rather than taking him in to the pediatrician to see if he's got an ear infection. Besides, he wants to lie down for a nap at 10:00, before I have decided, and doesn't wake until 1:00. By then the office is closed.

After lunch he feels much better—cool, happy, and bubbling. We play with his lock-blocks for a while, then watch a basketball game. He's very cuddly, because he's not feeling well. After the game it's off to the bank and grocery store. He falls asleep on the way home, at 5:45. It's an awkward time for a nap, but he only sleeps until 6:30. He wakes up crying, with a high fever, feeling miserable.

To get him to swallow more Tylenol, which he hates, I promise him ice cream. I give him half an ice-cream sandwich while I rush around the kitchen cooking dinner, and when he finishes it, he cries for the other half. I tell him he can have it after he eats his dinner. But when dinner is ready, he won't eat; he just sits there pointing at the freezer, where the ice cream is, and wailing. This is a major tantrum—hot tears, red face. I can't help but sympathize, though, because it's born of feeling absolutely wretched. How should I respond? I don't want to give in and teach him he can get his way by screaming. I try to comfort him by holding him in my lap, but he just sobs. Finally I take him into his room and rock him, holding him close. Gradually the sobs subside, and after 10 minutes I take him back into the kitchen, hold him on my lap, and feed him myself. He doesn't eat much, but enough to deserve his ice cream.

Though Nick gets over the incident in no time, I am traumatized. The fever is frightening—it has hit 102 by dinnertime, and it only drops to 101.4 by 8 P.M. Should I have taken him to the doctor? Will he spike a really high fever tonight? Am I being too relaxed? And what will Rose say? I cannot stop worrying; I feel heartsick as I read him his bedtime stories, though he cools down as he drifts to sleep in my arms. Would a mother feel so uncertain, I wonder? Do mothers feel adequate at moments like this? Or am I in a father's territory here?

Sunday morning Nick wakes at 6:30 and devours his breakfast, but pretty soon his temperature begins to rise. I call our pediatrician, who reassures me that it doesn't sound like an ear infection, and that I'm doing the right thing. Still, Nick isn't feeling well, and it makes him more demanding. He wants to be held; he wants me with him constantly; he insists that I do what he wants me to do and cries if I balk. It is a wearing day. He naps late, and when I wake him at seven, he is again miserable—temperature at 102.4, crying, refusing to let me change his diaper. But after more Tylenol and a good dinner he feels better.

I haven't heard from Rose all weekend, so I decide to call her at the hospital. She is furious that I haven't taken Nick to the doctor. A child who gets ear infections as often as he does has to be checked, she yells at me. He could blow out an eardrum! And why haven't I called her—she's his mother, for God's sake! I'm exhausted, I've been busting my hump all weekend, alone, doing the best I can, and now I'm being abused. I don't like it. My first impulse is to hang up on her, but instead I hand the phone to Nicholas, who has a long talk with her. He says "Mommy!" she says "Nicholas!" and he laughs and laughs.

Rose may be right, I know, but that doesn't help my anger. We part tersely, and I promise to take him to the pediatrician the next morning before I leave for California on an article assignment. After that's out of the way, Nick and I have a good evening. We read books, and several times he leads me into his room to get another handful. A short bath, more books, then off to bed. He wants to take two of his trucks to bed with him—a new wrinkle—but I finally convince him to say "night-night" to his trucks and turn out the lights. . . .

Two nights later I call Rose. When I ask how she is, she bursts into tears. Nicholas has fallen at Maureen's and cut his forehead on a metal toy. Rose was caught in an ice storm between the hospital and home, so Maureen had to take her own kids to a neighbor's and rush Nick to the pediatrician's office for stitches. They gave him a local anesthetic, but he screamed the whole time.

"I feel so awful," Rose sobs, over and over. "I should have been there. I just feel awful." Guilt floods in, but it is nothing to match Rose's guilt. This is one of the differences I have discovered between mothers and fathers.

Rose has felt guilty since the day she went back to work—the hardest single thing I've ever watched her do. Deep inside her psyche lies a powerful message that she belongs at home, that if she is not with her child she is terribly irresponsible.

I feel guilty only occasionally. When I dropped Nick off at day care the first day after returning from California, and he sobbed because he thought I was leaving him again, the guilt just about killed me. I turned into a classic mother: as soon as I got home, I called to see if he was still crying. (He was.) Two guilt-ridden hours later I called again, desperate to hear that everything was fine. (It was.)

Deep within my psyche, however, the most powerful message is that I belong at work, that if I am not out making my mark on the world I am worth nothing.

The contradiction between family and career is nothing new; it is perhaps the central unresolved conflict in the lives of American women today. What I did not expect was the force with which that conflict would erupt in my life.

Like an addict, I now find myself squeezing in every last minute of work that I can. I wait until the last possible instant before rushing out the door to pick Nick up in the afternoon. I dart out to my study while he naps on weekends, using a portable intercom to listen for his cries. At night I compulsively page through old newspapers that pile up because I can no longer read them over breakfast, afraid I've missed something important. As I hit deadline time, I pray that Nicholas doesn't get sick. I have even tried writing on a Saturday afternoon, with Nick playing in my studio. That experiment lasted half an hour, at which point he hit the reset button on the back of my computer and my prose was lost to the ages.

This frantic effort to keep up is clearly not good for me, but I cannot seem to abandon it. I constantly feel as if I live in a pressure cooker. I long for a free day, even a free hour. But my career has taken off just as my responsibilities as a father have hit their peak, and I cannot seem to scale down my commitment to either.

When Nick was four months old, I took him to a Christmas party, one Saturday when Rose was working. After an hour or so he got cranky, so I took him upstairs with a bottle. A little girl followed, and soon her brother and sister—equally bored by the goings-on downstairs—had joined us. It wasn't long before Dad came looking for them.

We introduced ourselves and talked for a bit. His wife, it turned out, was also a doctor. The curious part came when I asked what he did. First he told me all the things he had done in the past: carpentry, business, you name it. Then he said he'd done enough—he was about 40—and felt no need to prove himself any more. Finally he told me he stayed at home with the kids. And frankly, he pulled it off with far more dignity and less stammering than I would have, had our places been reversed.

I don't think I could do what he does. If I were to stay home full-time with Nick, I would quickly lose my self-esteem, and within months I would be deep into an identity crisis. Part of the reason I love my role as a father is that I am secure in my role as a writer. Without that, I would not feel good enough about myself to be the kind of father I am. . . .

We are in a Burger King, in Fall River, Massachusetts. We are not having a good day. We drove two hours to shop in the factory outlets here, and all but a handful are closed because it's Sunday.

Nick likes Burger King, but he's not having a great day either. He has recently learned about tantrums, and as we get ready to leave, he decides to throw one. He doesn't want to leave; he doesn't want to put on his coat;

he just doesn't want to be hauled around any more. So he stands up and wails.

Rose is mortified; she takes any misbehavior in public as an advertisement of her failings as a mother. It triggers all her guilt about working. This time, the timing couldn't be worse, because she is already on edge.

Our tantrum strategy is generally to let him yell, to ignore him, and thus to teach him that it does no good. But in a public restaurant, I don't have the stamina to ignore him, so I cross the room to pick him up.

Rose orders me away from him, in no uncertain terms. There are no negotiations, no consultations. We are going to do this her way or no way.

That lights my fuse, of course, and after simmering for 10 minutes, I bring it up. "Let it go," she tells me, almost in tears over Nicholas. "It's not important."

It's not important.

Ah, the double bind. You're in charge one day, playing mother and father all wrapped into one, depended upon to feed him and clothe him and change him and bathe him and rock him and meet his every need. And the next day you're a third wheel, because Mom is around. You are expected to put in the long hours, but to pretend in public that you don't, for fear of undercutting your wife's sense of self-worth as a mother. How could she be doing her job, her psyche seems to whisper, if she's letting someone else make half the decisions and give half the care? There are many double binds in modern relationships, and this is the one I like the least. . . .

This is the first time I've ever been part of a woman's world. I'm not really a part of it, of course; the chasm between the sexes is too wide to step across so lightly. But when it comes to children, I have instant rapport with most mothers. We talk about the same things, think about the same things, joke about the same things. With men, it is almost never that way, even when the men are fathers and the subject is kids. We can share enthusiasms, but the sense of being there, on the inside—the unspoken understanding that comes out of shared experience—that is missing.

In fact, most men don't have the slightest idea what my life with Nick is like. When I tell colleagues—even those with children—that I have no time to read, or to watch television, I get blank stares. (I never tell mothers that; they already know. Who has time to read?) One friend, also a writer, stopped in the middle of a recent conversation and said, "You have Nick at home while you're working, don't you? What do you do with him?" No such thought could pass a mother's lips.

None of this would have been possible had I not been forced into taking care of Nick on my own much of the time. In fact, my entire relationship with Nick would have been different had I not been forced off the sidelines. I am convinced that in our society, when Mom is home with the kids, it is almost impossible for Dad to be an equal partner in their upbringing, even if he wants to be.

I believe this because for three weeks, while Rose was home after Nick's birth, it felt impossible to me. Rose had carried Nick for nine months; Rose had been through labor; and Rose was nursing him. For nine months he had listened to her heartbeat, felt her pulse, been a part of her being. Now he hunted her scent and drank from her body, and the bond between them was awesome. I was like some voyeur, peeking through the window at an ancient and sacred rite.

Then Rose went back to work, and I had no choice but to get off the sidelines. I *had* to get Nick dressed in the morning. I *had* to feed him. I *had* to burp him and rock him and change him and get up with him in the night. He may have wanted his mother, but she wasn't there.

Gradually, it all began to come naturally. I learned to carry him on my (nonexistent) hip and do anything—or any combination of things—with one hand. I learned to whip up a bottle in no time, to change a diaper and treat diaper rash and calm his tears.

Even on vacation, it is remarkably easy to slip back into a traditional role—for both Rose and me. But the day Rose goes back to work, I am always yanked back to reality. I complain a lot, but in truth, this is my great good fortune.

Last night Nick asked to go to the beach—"Go? Beach? Go? Beach?" I walked him the two blocks down, one of his hands firmly in mine, the other proudly holding the leash for Sam, our dog. We played on the swings for a long time, then strolled along the beach while Sam went swimming. It was that very still hour before dark, when the world slows to a hush, and little boys and girls slowly wind down. It was almost dark when we returned. Nick asked his daddy to give him his bath, then his mommy to put him to bed.

This morning when I woke he was lying beside me, on his mother's empty pillow. I looked over and he gave me a big smile, his eyes shining with that special, undiluted joy one sees only in children. Then he propped himself up on his elbows, leaned over and kissed me. If there are any better moments in life, I've never found them.

Historical Questions

1. Review Stearns's analysis of the conditions that led to the greater division between fathers and mothers during the nineteenth century. Discuss three specific examples of the nineteenth-century expectations for fathers and mothers that David and Rose Osborne consciously try to challenge. Then, focusing on one or two specific moments when

David and Rose feel uncertain about their nontraditional roles, develop a symptomatic reading of how that uncertainty is linked to the presence of residual nineteenth-century expectations for parents in the late twentieth century.

2. David describes himself as a "nontraditional father" and in *Little Women*, Jo is identified as a "tomboy," and yet both of them still retain some conventional notions about father–child relations. With reference to two specific passages, discuss how David and Jo each demonstrate some belief in *both* traditional and nontraditional expectations for fathers and children. Then, with reference to the larger cultures that helped to produce them, speculate on one to two specific reasons why David and Jo might each maintain these contradictory beliefs. Finally, given the differences between their historical periods and their sex, explain whether it is easier or harder for David to be unconventional.

3. Consider David's description of his time at home with Nick. With specific textual references discuss how this description confirms, complicates, or contradicts the portrayal of domestic life in Mary Paul's nineteenth-century poem (see fastwrite 4). What can you infer about the social conditions and gender expectations of the nineteenth versus the twentieth century by comparing each writer's presentation of domestic life?

Cultural Questions

1. According to Stearns, industrialism and demographics affected nineteenth-century assumptions about manhood. Following the example of Stearns's analysis, discuss two to three contemporary economic and social conditions that you believe influenced David and Rose Osborne's decision to assume nontraditional parental roles.

2. With specific reference to his speech, develop two or three arguments that Quayle might use to support or disagree with the Osbornes' decision. For example, how might Quayle respond to the argument that economic and social conditions justify the Osbornes' decision? Then, reading more symptomatically, discuss one key underlying assumption of Quayle's and one of Osborne's that could account for their agreement or disagreement. What is your position on the Osborne family's organization? What arguments might you use to defend it? What arguments to criticize it? What is a key underlying assumption of yours that you might not have discussed explicitly but that helps you maintain your position? Whose position seems most dominant in America to you today—yours, Quayle's, Osborne's, or some combination? Why?

3. When are David and Rose most successful in assuming nontraditional roles for fathers and mothers? When are they least successful? What do their

successes and failures suggest about an individual's ability to defy traditional conceptions of motherhood and fatherhood?

4. During the nineteenth century, industrialism often separated the man's workplace from the home, so the relationship between child and father and between child and mother changed. Discuss two or three specific ways in which contemporary changes in the workplace have changed David's and Rose's relationships with Nick. Explain whether you agree with David that even the most nontraditional father can never replace a mother's bond with her child.

观观观

R I C H A R D   G O L D S T E I N

The Gay Family (1986)

Richard Goldstein (b. 1944) is a senior editor at the *Village Voice* and the author of *Reporting the Counterculture* (1989). He has written about a variety of social aspects of U.S. society such as the media, popular culture, and politics. The following is an excerpt from his article "The Gay Family" (1986) in which he offers the greatest challenge to the traditional family of any of the readings included in this chapter.

For Rosemary Dempsey and Maggie Wales, raising five children in the home they share has been a struggle whose rewards are barely hinted at by the plate that sits above their mantel: a gift from all their children, it reads, "Happy 10th Anniversary."

They can vividly recall the day in 1979 when their vacation in Florida was interrupted by a phone call from the friend they'd left the kids with: Maggie's cat had died, and not only that; five years after he relinquished custody, Rosemary's husband had suddenly appeared and taken his children. They drove all night, arrived at her husband's home the next afternoon, and found her son "hiding in a closet in his pajamas" and her daughter "crying hysterically." They brought the kids back, only to be confronted by two policemen who sheepishly arrested Dempsey. A first year law student (now a prominent attorney in custody law), she spent that day and night in jail.

It's the nightmare every gay parent lives with: the specter of the state stepping in. "You ask yourself," Rosemary says, "should we just stop and let them have the kids? Because it sure is painful for them. But then, the message you give is that they're not worth fighting for." So they went to trial, assembling a parade of neighbors to testify on their behalf and rallying feminist groups to their defense, with signs that read "Save Rosemary's Babies." The judge handed down a landmark ruling: though these children were being raised in "an unconventional household," there was not "a scintilla of evidence from which the court could infer that Dempsey's sexual orientation was adversely affecting them." She was not to be denied custody on the sole basis of her sexuality.

All's well that ends well, except this ordeal did not. Two weeks later, a new set of court papers arrived; this time, Maggie's husband was suing for custody of *his* kids on similar grounds. And this time, another judge ruled differently: Maggie could see her three children for a month every summer, on three weekends out of four, and on alternate holidays. But for the rest of the year, it was in the best interest of the children to live with their heterosexual dad.

Maggie and Rosemary are still very much a family, with scrapbooks full of pictures and the usual braggadocio: "Two kids from this household have won the mayor's award for academic excellence; one is president of his class and too popular for his own good." Their relationship, which began shortly after both women left their husbands, has the flinty, tempered quality of a boulder. "The kids have always known that we loved each other," Maggie says. "Their main concern was whether we were each gonna be there for them." They have been through a lot together, and it has sealed not just their union but their politics. "What often comes up in these trials is that it's wrong to expose kids to values that are different from the dominant society's," Rosemary insists. "When they saw that they couldn't get us on lesbian sexuality, the main thrust was our involvement in the feminist movement. They won't put you in jail for fighting to change society—but they might take your kids."

Despite the cultivated image of homosexuals as emotional nomads, most gay people, at some point in their lives, establish a stable, central relationship. And, despite all that Oscar Wilde[1] has said about marriage ("It's as demoralizing as cigarettes and far more expensive"), there is nothing new about gay people holding Ceremonies of Union, holy or otherwise. Historians have uncovered ample evidence of homosexual marriage rites, performed in private, sometimes by renegade clergy and occasionally with one party in drag. Half-camp, half-yearning, and all fantasy, these elaborate fetes were part of the high romanticism of gay life before Stonewall,[2] when,

---

[1]*Oscar Wilde:* Irish poet, dramatist, novelist, and social critic (1854–1900).

[2]*Stonewall:* the Stonewall or Christopher Street riots of June 1969 in Greenwich Village, New York City, a watershed event in gay activism. After police closed the Stonewall Inn, a dance bar frequented by flamboyant and unconventional homosexuals, the crowd attacked the police with cobblestones and bottles. Several nights of disorder and demonstrations followed.

as diarist Donald Vining recalls with some disdain, "we thought pairing up was what homosexuals *did*." ("Monogamy," he hastens to add, "was seldom part of the deal.")

What is new is the public nature of these ceremonies, and the active participation of family and clergy. Not since the year 342, when homosexual marriage was outlawed in Europe (it had flourished in the Roman Empire, largely among the aristocracy; Nero married two men, one of whom was accorded the status of an empress), has an established religion performed such ceremonies. But in 1984, the Unitarian/Universalist Association voted overwhelmingly to permit its ministers to marry congregants of the same sex. Reverend Robert Wheatly has married many homosexual couples, especially of the Catholic faith, at his Unitarian church in Boston. "To sanctify a relationship satisfies a very human need," he says. "It adds a dimension of integrity and longevity." Individual Quaker meetings will perform such ceremonies, and so will individual rabbis. "If a gay couple have, despite all the prejudices, managed to build an enduring relationship, it deserves to be recognized," says Yoel Kahn of San Francisco, who presided over Paul and Scott's union. And the Metropolitian Community Church, an openly gay denomination with over 200 congregations worldwide, will conduct "a ceremony of holy union" for lesbians and gay men who have lived together for at least a year.

Despite his antipathy to gay marriage, Vining put me in touch with two friends who, as he described it, "wear the ring." One of the pair, a professor at City College, describes a ceremony performed for him and his lover in 1969, by a Presbyterian minister who had been arrested in Selma, Alabama, several years earlier. "The civil rights movement was the coattail we were riding on," he recalls, "not the Stonewall riot." Their ceremony—along with a full communion service—was held in the chapel, before the entire congregation. As a guitarist played and sang "The Impossible Dream," the pair were pronounced "mate and spouse." "We gave our rings to the minister, who blessed them and put them on our hands. Then we went to his home for a reception with his wife and kids."

"Were you embarrassed?" I asked.

"Judging from the photos, we were scared to death. After the exchange of rings, it was clear we could kiss, and *that* was embarrassing. We *did* kiss, but gingerly, and when the service was over, we dashed into the back room and kissed good."

Times have changed. Last year, two male stockbrokers planning to marry registered a china pattern in their names at Bloomingdale's. They were reflecting the three A's of gay life in the '80s: aging, assimilation, and AIDS. As the Stonewall generation enters midlife, along with the rest of the baby boom, the entire culture is pushing couplehood. The gay response, in less tragic times, might be to combine the stability of a spouse with the serendipity of sexual adventures; but AIDS has ushered in monogamy, and the bond which suddenly carries with it obligations of denial and restraint makes gay male couplehood more like traditional marriage than it ever was. The energy that gay culture once poured into erotic enterprise—as well as the elaborate chains of "kinship" sex can forge—all must be redirected. If the predictions are correct, and 180,000 people, most of them gay men, perish from AIDS over the next five years, the survivors will be very different people, with values antithetical to those associated with the disease. The urge for couplehood is only the most visible component of that change: the real reconstitution going on in gay culture today involves the broader, trickier terrain of family.

The change is hardly limited to gay men. Among lesbians, "couplism," a heresy second only to "looksism" in some circles, is definitely making a comeback; but, as with gay male pairings, the return to a discarded tradition often has a radical edge. The lesbian couple of the '80s may well "choose children," often through artificial insemination. Heterosexual women have had to struggle for the right *not* to have children, but dykes are supposed to be sterile. They must defend their choice to bear children against social and legal pressures as binding as the system that tracks straight women toward motherhood.

No one knows how many of the 20,000 women inseminated each year are unmarried, but "turkey baster babies" have become a staple of what's being referred to as the "lesbian baby boom." The apotheosis of self-directed motherhood, A.I., confers on women an extraordinary degree of autonomy. As Joy Schulenberg writes in *Gay Parenting*, all that's required "is an ovulating woman, 1 cc. of viable sperm, a cheap piece of equipment, and some very basic knowledge of female anatomy." In the hands of lesbians, A.I. can become an instrument for appropriating the act of conception itself. "I inseminated LeAnn myself," one woman told Schulenberg, "and it was the most beautiful act of love I have ever done."

The contours of gay family, in this setting, have very little to do with the conventional heterosexual paradigm: there may be one or two mommies, sometimes a daddy or uncle, and sometimes, a profusion of parents who have no blood relation to the child. The collectivism of the '60s and '70s, when groups of women marshalled their meager assets and ample resources to care for each other, is being adapted to the tasks of parenting. In the lesbian enclave of Park Slope, a "mommies group" meets monthly, with nine women, two of whom have already borne children. They exchange information and energy, bolstering each other against reservations about raising a child in an unorthodox setting, and all the burdens that come of being out on the edge.

Not everyone is happy about the lesbian baby boom. "I'm horrified by it," says one woman whose lover is six months pregnant. "For me, part of being a lesbian is not being baby centered, and it seems to me that the lesbian world is becoming more baby centered every hour." At this rate, the Michigan Womyn's Music Festival, a sort of lesbian Woodstock, will soon have to drop its rule prohibiting males over the age of seven from mingling with women and girls.

All these changes are occurring at a time when the gay rights movement is having its most tangible success—at least in cities where homosexuals have translated their ample presence into political clout. Among urban professionals, at any rate, there is probably less onus attached to being openly gay than at any time in American history; Paul and Scott, for example, were able to get a "marriage discount" on their joint mortgage from the bank where Paul works because it has a non-discrimination hiring policy.

In the face of such relative equity, gay life is becoming increasingly demystified and, in the process, it is losing its compensatory—if colorful— edge. As distinctions become more subtle (among the young it sometimes seems that lesbians and gay men are Yuppies with brighter eyes), much of what used to seem inherent about homosexuality—its argot, costumes, inflection, and gait—is slipping away, leaving men who love men and women who love women but who are fundamentally different from heterosexuals in no other respect.

So much in gay tradition mocks the institutions of heterosexuality that what often goes unnoticed is the yearning to lead an ordinary life—to play a role in society without hiding one's sexuality. As the stereotypes drop away and new options open up, gay people are discovering a more authentically individual relationship to social conventions. "We're strong enough as a movement to support people's real life choices," says one lesbian mother-to-be.

The gay family is shorthand for a new institution, one that bears little resemblance to the patriarchal structure most of us were raised in. Homosexuals are, by definition, outside that structure, and given our status, when we try to appropriate the tradition of forming families, we end up creating something new.

Do gay families subvert the family? A more salient question might be, is the family subverting itself? By now, the statistics have been drummed into our fornicating brains: the average American marriage lasts 9.4 years; nearly 20 percent of all children are born to unwed mothers; four out of 10 children born in the '70s will spend some time in single-parent households. Depending on whether you like what you see, these figures epitomize either the crisis of family life or its evolution. In any case, the change has created a new class of single parents and their lovers—millions of people, most of them straight. The battle being waged on this cutting edge of gay liberation has implications for all unmarried people, since, when it comes to employee benefits, at least, gay couples are usually treated like heterosexuals "living in sin."

For most gay couples, the struggle has less to do with subverting the patriarchy than with getting a lover's children covered on your health plan. But symbolism is never far from the surface. As Nan Hunter, newly appointed director of the ACLU's[3] Lesbian and Gay Rights Project, observes: "The idea that other kinds of relationships would be accorded some of the economic breaks of marriage, or that other kinds of relationships can provide a loving atmosphere for the raising of children, is deeply frightening for society."

So far, activists have had their greatest success in the private sector. In 1982, the *Village Voice*'s union won health coverage for live-in "spouse equivalents" of its rank and file. Similar plans have been adopted by several small companies, and some progressive unions are considering raising the issue in collective bargaining. But when San Francisco's Board of Supervisors passed a bill in 1982 that would have extended benefits to the "domestic partners" of city workers and authorized a municipal registry for them, it was as if a line had been crossed. Gay rights, yes; gay power, reluctantly; but subsidizing relationships out of wedlock, never! Mayor Dianne Feinstein vetoed the bill.

But similar measures have passed in Berkeley and West Hollywood, a newly constituted city whose politics are dominated by homosexuals and retirees. For both groups, the benefits of domestic partnership legislation are more than financial: hospitals and convalescent homes must extend full visitation rights to live-in lovers. The AIDS crisis has heightened the urgency of these issues for gay male couples: suddenly, the power to make life-and-death decisions about a lover's medical treatment seems worth fighting for.

So does the right to grieve. In California, a railroad worker denied funeral leave to mourn his male lover, who had died of AIDS, sued and won time off. Retaining shared assets after a lover's death is another point of contention, especially when those possessions include a rent-controlled or stabilized apartment. A judge in New York recently ruled that a man who had lived with and cared for his male lover through a terminal struggle with AIDS was, in effect, a relative, and could continue to reside in their apartment, though his name is not on the lease. The case is currently being appealed.

---

[3]*ACLU*: the American Civil Liberties Union.

. . . In California, where court decisions affirming the validity of relationships outside marriage date back to 1921, gay adoptive parents meet relatively little resistance. In New York, the governor's executive order prohibiting discrimination in state services has been interpreted to apply to foster care and adoption. Gay people can and do adopt children here, but their road is seldom an easy one.

It's difficult, in any case, for a single male to adopt; the old wisdom is that men make poor care providers, so agencies are especially loath to place infants with "bachelors." But Rubén is an exception: a physician who has lived with his lover, an executive, for 19 years, he's the kind of adoptive parent any agency would relish—except for the fact that he's gay. But in New York, the subject of sexuality rarely comes up in adoption proceedings; officially, gay couples are treated like other unmarried couples: only one member can qualify as the legal parent. Even though the agency knew Rubén was a single male in his mid forties who lived with a male roommate, it had no immediate reservations about placing a three-week-old boy in his care—the procedure took all of four days.

Then the trouble began. When Rubén went to Family Court to have the adoption certified, the judge noticed the reference to a roommate and drew her own conclusions; she asked for a second home study. A probation officer visited Rubén and popped the question: Was he gay? His heart stopped. "I decided to be honest. I had heard that this was not supposed to be a deterrent to adoption, so I swallowed hard and said yes."

What followed was a two-year ordeal, during which the probation officer, the original agency, and the judge wavered over whether to certify the adoption. The court ordered two more home studies, called in a child psychologist, appointed an attorney to represent the child. "Through all those proceedings," Rubén remembers, "nobody said this shouldn't happen; but one thing or another kept standing in the way. And I began to sense that they were looking for a reason to say no."

Meanwhile, the child was bonding with his new family—calling Rubén "daddy" and the lover "father." Rubén's mother, who took to the child immediately, began to feel as if her grandson were only temporary. On more than one occasion, Rubén says, he was tempted to take "my kid and run away to Canada." But he stuck it out, in part because he understood that the longer a child lives in its adoptive home, the harder for a court to take it away. "It would have been devastating for him to be removed," Rubén says.

Finally, two weeks after the boy's second birthday, the adoption was finalized. "In retrospect, it seems they all wanted to see that every *i* was dotted, in case a problem came up afterward," he says. The final hearing in Family Court took all of five minutes, at the end of which, the judge looked up at Rubén's son and said, "Take good care of your father."

What about the children. Will they be insecure? Enraged? Gay? The latter question is often thrust at gay parents in the form of an accusation, but the evidence, scanty as it is, says otherwise. "At this stage, I tentatively suggest that children being raised by . . . homosexual parents do not differ appreciably from children raised in more conventional family settings," says Richard Greene, a professor of psychiatry and psychology at Stony Brook. All the children in his study were able to "comprehend and verbalize the atypical nature of their parents' lifestyles and to view that atypicality in the broader perspective of the cultural norm." Greene thinks that the formation of a sexual identity has more to do with interactions outside the home than with a parent's personal choice of a mate.

But that doesn't mean the children of gay people are *never* gay. The director of a camp for children of "alternative families" (mostly the daughters of lesbians), says: "My sense is that most of these kids will probably end up heterosexual—but not strictly so. They're more open-minded. A lot of them say they're bisexual, or that they don't know yet." There are anxieties peculiar to the situation: "Most kids go through a particularly homophobic period in junior high school. They're very judgmental. The girls are very into makeup and badly want to have boyfriends." The sons of gay men are even more likely than other adolescent boys to experience profound anxieties about their sexual identity. The best adjustment, a University of Alberta study suggests, is made by children whose parents are candid about sexuality and live in a stable relationship.

One gay father, interviewed in *Psychology Today*, remembers telling his sons when they were both 15. "I told them bluntly and then explained what it was all about," he said. "They wept—then they coped."

Gay families face a situation that is, in many ways, analogous to what interracial families confronted a generation ago. The children are typically more circumspect, especially about confiding in their peers. But the bonds they form are strong and their sense of social justice keen. "What he assimilates at this point is that anyone can love anyone—and it's not just a right but a fact," says one lesbian mother about her nine-year-old son. "He also knows that some people try to prevent it from happening, and that we're struggling for freedom just as they're struggling for freedom in South Africa."

All the gay parents interviewed for this article describe their children as self-directed and unafraid to speak out. It's a trait many gay parents cultivate from their own tribulations—a determination to make your own decisions and a drive to remake the world in your own terms. Even Rubén notices that, at three, his son has a "strong will. He's not a follower. So I'm hoping that, if he sees my situation is right for me, then he'll be able to deal with what the world thinks of it."

. . . If there's one thing gay parents have in common, it's a design for living. They are deliberate and determined, almost to a fault—it comes with the territory.

Julie Greenberg, 29, is a rabbinical student and a lesbian. In about a month, she intends to become pregnant with her first child. The semen, donated by a close friend, is waiting in the sperm bank for her. She calls it "alternate conception."

"I have 100 percent custody," she says. "I will do all the work and take the responsibility. But I would like the child to have a relationship with a father figure, and I intend to foster it." So the child will call the donor "daddy," and Julie will call him "Sam." A contract between them will enumerate his rights and responsibilities, which include some financial support.

Though some women insist on an anonymous donor—it avoids the prospect of a custody battle by the biological father—there's an evident risk to that approach: there's no way to evaluate an unknown donor's health. More often, the donor is known—a dear friend—and though he will never become "the man of the house," he will play a role in the child's life. Sam is heterosexual, but for many lesbians, the dear friend who is willing to be present but not dominant is a gay man who has tested negative for HTLV-III antibodies. (The odds of passing AIDS on to a woman and child via A.I. are not to be ignored.) The baby signifies not just a bond between its lesbian coparents, but between male and female homosexuals, one of the least acknowledged and most abiding relationships in gay life.

If the formation of families ever does become significant for homosexuals, A.I. will be one reason why. It requires neither medical intervention nor approval by the state, nor the capacity to function heterosexually. I know two gay men among my circle of friends who have entered into contractual relationships with women, intending to be the primary parent of the child that evolves. More commonly, lesbians enter into contractual relationships with men for a child who will be raised by the mother and her female lover. Julie intends to be "a single mother living in a feminist community. They'll contribute bits and pieces. And we'll be poor".

It remains to be seen how a congregation, even one willing to break with Jewish tradition, will react when it becomes apparent that its rabbi is pregnant and unmarried. But Julie is optimistic: "They don't necessarily have to deal with the fact that I'm a lesbian," she says, "but I'm hoping they'll be receptive to another form of Jewish family. We're saying there's no such thing as *the* family; there are various forms of family—single parents by choice, single parents not by choice, shared custody arrangements, collective networks. . . ."

Can a family be formulated by contract? In a sense, the point is moot: there's no more binding way for a mother and "father-figure" to declare their intentions; there aren't even words to describe such a relationship. Gay families are always coming up against the boundaries of language, which affirm their position on the edge of social change. And being on that edge carries a special burden: with no models or precedents, you don't know how to prepare for what the future may hold. So contracts and rituals take on an almost mystical significance. (Julie plans to appropriate an ancient fertility rite; she will stand among her friends and call forth a *neshuma*, or soul, into the world.)

Reba is six months pregnant now. When the baby arrives, by the terms of a 12-page contract, she will be the parent who makes all the decisions about its care. Ray will have custody of the child on weekends, alternate Wednesdays, and for three weeks every summer. "I'm still uncertain about what to call myself," he says. "I'm the daddy/uncle." Reba's lover Katy has taken to calling herself the "sometime-mommy," although she's tempted by the term "daddy" because, she says, "I want the privilege. I haven't had a biological desire to be a mother. I've always felt the family system as I know it is overwhelming, too nuclear. So the idea of sharing is all that makes this appealing to me."

Katy's parents have been drumming their fears into her head: What if Reba runs off and sticks her with a kid that isn't even "your own"? And Reba's parents resent the presence of another woman whose rights vis-à-vis their grandchild are uncodified. "I mean, they hung up the phone when they heard the baby was going to carry Katy's father's name," Reba recalls. "They asked me *not* to name it after *tanta Mascha*.[4] I realize my family's been bargaining with me about what to tell people. At best, they're gonna have to concoct a story about their daughter having an illegitimate child. At worst, they'll have to admit that their daugher is a lesbian mother."

Spend some time with the gay family and you may feel transported to the summer of love. But these "hippies" are a lot less innocent. They understand that progress is not inevitable, and they've learned to watch their backs. This counterculture is emerging at a time of mixed signals. Courts and agencies are distinctly more tolerant of unorthodox parenting arrangements, but the culture is lurching right-ward; judges can be replaced.

Given the uncertainties, gay families are easier to imagine than to maintain. Under stress, some will fall apart. Father-figures will breach their contracts. Children will suffer. Priests will proclaim, "They tampered with God's will." Friends will mutter, "I told you so."

And the world will change.

---

[4]*tanta Mascha*: Aunt Mascha.

∽ **Fastwrite 8**

Fastwrite for ten minutes on the kinds of nontraditional families you are willing to accept and the kinds you are unwilling to accept. Then, reread what you have written and discuss the beliefs, assumptions, and expectations about the family on which your answer is based.

Historical Questions

1. Goldstein argues that when homosexuals "try to appropriate the tradition of forming families, we end up creating something new." In what ways does Rosemary and Maggie's family fulfill or disrupt the traditional family life represented—at least in part—by the nineteenth-centuries stories "Conquering Themselves So Beautifully" and "The Revolt of Mother?" In what ways might their life have been different if Rosemary and Maggie tried to maintain their alternative lifestyle in the nineteenth century?

2. Consider Stearns's explanation that gender roles became more distinct during the nineteenth century. With references to Stearns's and Goldstein's texts, trace two or three connections between contemporary intolerance of homosexuality and nineteenth-century beliefs about masculinity and femininity. Do contemporary concepts of masculinity and femininity create more or less tolerance of homosexuality than existed in the nineteenth century? Discuss with reference to one or two specific examples.

3. Goldstein asserts that "Gay families face a situation that is . . . analogous to what interracial families confronted a generation ago." For example, just as people worried about the children of interracial parents in the past, so too some argue against homosexual parents today by asking, "But what will happen to the children?" Using the information provided by Goldstein, what arguments in favor of or against gay families could you make based on the effects on the children involved? Following Goldstein's discussion, what do you think the present level of acceptance for the children of interracial families, in comparison to the past, suggests about the future acceptance of the children of gay families?

Cultural Questions

1. When William Bennett nominated Dan Quayle to be the Republican candidate for vice president again in 1992, he was even more explicit than Quayle had been in his support of traditional families. Bennett, for example, stated that "Marriage and parenthood should be held up because between marriage between husband and wife and in fatherhood and motherhood come blessings that cannot be won any other way." Consider the family

values or "blessings" advocated by Quayle and Bennett. In what ways do the gay families described by Goldstein fulfill or fail to fulfill these values? In answering this question, be sure to consider the diversity of gay families represented by Rosemary Dempsey, Rubén, Julie Greenberg, and others in this reading.

2. Compare and contrast some of the characteristics of the two kinds of nontraditional families presented in this chapter: the nontraditional parenting of Dave and Rose Osborne and the various gay parents presented by Goldstein. What effect, if any, does you think that an increase in nontraditional, heterosexual parents like Rose and Dave Osborne could have on other nontraditional types of parenting? In developing your answer, set these specific examples within the larger context of the workings of the U.S. ideology of the family: what you think are really the dominant beliefs about families in America today and how the dominant might be changing to accommodate more emergent conceptions of the family. Feel free to bring in other examples from the media and your own experiences to develop your essay.

3. When Goldstein mentions the "stresses" that will "cause some [gay families] to fall apart," he is suggesting that altering certain social policies could enable gay families to function more easily. What institutional changes— in such areas as government policies, religious beliefs and practices, education, and so on—could make it easier for gay families to function well? Explain whether any of these changes are likely to occur. In answering this question, consider not only Goldstein's essay but also the general social attitude towards gay families as suggested by their depiction in television, on talk radio, and in film.

∽ Assignment Sequence 1: Complex Contexts Defining the Family

Each of the definitions of the family presented by the readings takes shape in a complex historical context. Douglass, for example, describes the impact of slavery on nineteenth-century southern families, and Goldstein analyzes the influence of governmental policies on modern gay families. Any attempt to define what the family is, has been, and will be must take into account these larger contexts.

Essay Question

Within the complex emotional, religious, economic, and legal context of the family today, how should the family be defined and what institutional influences can strengthen or weaken this preferred definition of the modern family?

∾ Fastwrite 9

Before answering this complex question, analyze its parts. Before reviewing the readings for detailed information, reread the question above and underline several phrases that represent key parts of the larger answer you will be developing. Then pick two or three of these phrases and fastwrite your immediate impressions: What do you think right now? Finally, pause to see connections among the phrases and a possible order that you might want to follow in developing your essay. How are your initial impressions related? To explain them to a reader, where would your explanation have to begin and end?

Review Questions

A list of suggested questions to review before beginning this essay follows. This list is meant only to suggest review options. You may focus on only a subset of the questions, decide that other questions should be added, or construct your own sequence of questions. We encourage you to choose what you believe is the most appropriate review strategy.

1. Frederick Douglass, Cultural Question 3 (page 147)
2. Mary Wilkins Freeman, Cultural Question 3 (page 161)
3. Dan Quayle III, Cutural Question 2 (page 168)
4. David Osborne, Cultural Question 1 (page 177)
5. David Osborne, Cultural Question 2 (page 177)
6. Richard Goldstein, Cultural Question 1 (page 188-89)
7. Richard Goldstein, Cultural Question 2 (page 189)

Questions for Further Reflection

1. With which of the many definitions of *family* presented in this chapter do you most agree and disagree? Why? On what specific assumptions are your agreement and disagreement based? In what ways have you changed or retained these assumptions during your reading and writing for this chapter (see your fastwrites 1 and 2)?

2. What is the relationship between a family's ability to function well and the emotional, religious, economic, and legal contexts in which it functions? Use two to three specific family structures to examine these contextual relationships.

3. Dominant ideologies often are defended as the "natural," the "obvious," and the "only way." Yet these beliefs usually benefit some and hurt others. What groups and institutions have benefited from the dominant ideologies of the family during the nineteenth and twentieth centuries? How have

they benefited? What other groups and institutions have been hurt by the dominant ideologies? How have they been hurt? How have some groups changed their status in relation to the dominant ideology over the last century, and what have been the effects on them of these changes?

∾ Assignment Sequence 2: Parental Roles

As demonstrated by the readings, the proper roles of parents have been the subject of great debate, and there is no clear development from one view to another across time. In Freeman's late-nineteenth-century story, for example, Sarah Penn rejects the dominant nineteenth-century conception of a mother; yet Quayle, in his contemporary speech, condemns nontraditional parents such as the television character Murphy Brown.

Essay Question

Within the diversity of past and present answers about motherhood and fatherhood, what do you think are the proper roles of each parent today?

∾ Fastwrite 10

To begin answering this complex question, it is important to analyze its parts. Before you begin reviewing the readings for detailed information, reread the question above and underline several phrases that you think represent key parts of the larger answer you will be developing. Then pick two or three of these phrases and fastwrite your immediate impressions: What do you think right now? Finally, pause to see connections among the phrases and a possible order that you might want to follow in developing your essay. How are your initial impressions related, and in order to explain them to a reader, where would your explanation have to begin and end?

Review Questions

A list of suggested questions to review before beginning this essay follows. This list is meant only to suggest review options. You may focus on only a subset of the questions, decide that other questions should be added, or construct your own sequence of questions. We encourage you to choose what you believe is the most appropriate review strategy.

1. Peter Stearns, Cultural Question 1 (page 131)
2. Peter Stearns, Cultural Question 2 (page 132)
3. Louisa May Alcott, Cultural Question 3 (page 141)
4. Mary Wilkins Freeman, Cultural Question 2 (page 161)

5. David Osborne, Cultural Question 3 (page 177)
6. Richard Goldstein, Historical Question 1 (page 188)

Questions for Further Reflection

1. Review your fastwrite 6. What assumptions about the proper roles of mothers and fathers did you present in this fastwrite? How have your beliefs about each parent's proper role changed or remained the same? Why?

2. Within the array of opinions presented by these readings, with whom do you find yourself most agreeing or disagreeing? Why? Whose position do you feel most ambivalent about? On what supporting beliefs, such as religious ones, do your various reactions depend?

3. How have the social and economic contexts of parenthood changed over time? What definitions of fatherhood and motherhood have been made possible or improbable by these changing contexts?

4. What are the responsibilities of a mother towards the family? What are the responsibilities of a father towards the family? Who do you think can and cannot fulfill these responsibilities? Why?

ॐ

For Further Research

Books and Articles

Carter, Betty and Joan Peters. "Remaking Marriage and Family." *MS.* Nov./Dec. 1996: 57–65.

Stephanie Coontz. "The American Family and the Nostalgia Trap." *Phi Delta Kappa* 76.7 (Mar. 1995): K1–K19.

———. *The Way We Never Were.* New York: Basic, 1992.

Edleman, Marian Wright. *The Measure of Our Success: A Letter to My Children and Yours.* Boston: Beacon, 1992.

Elkind, David. "The Future of Childhood." *Psychology Today* May/June 1992: 38–41.

Hareven, Tamara. "American Families in Transition: Historical Perspectives on Change." *Normal Family Processes.* Ed. Froma Walsh. New York: Guilford, 1982. 446–66.

Jack, Roger. "An Indian Story." *Dancing on the Rim of the World.* Ed. Andrea Lerner. Sun Tracks: U of Arizona, 1990. 101–11.

Kantrowitz, Barbara. "Gay Families Come Out." *Newsweek* 4 Nov. 1996: 51–57.

Laslett, Peter. *The World We Have Lost.* New York: Scribner's, 1965.

Quindlen, Anna. "Digging a Divide." *New York Times* 14 June 1992: E19.

Rich, Adrienne. "The Anger of a Child." *Of Woman Born.* New York: Norton, 1976.

Simmons, Thomas. "Motorcycle Talk." *The Unseen Shore.* New York: Beacon, 1991. 42-45.

Skolnick, Arlene. *Embattled Paradise: The American Family in an Age of Uncertainty.* New York: Basic, 1991.

Tan, Amy. "Two Kinds." *The Graywolf Annual Seven: Stories from the American Mosiac.* Ed. Scott Walker. St. Paul: Graywolf, 1990. 188–201.

Walker, Alice. "Father." *Living by the Word.* New York: Harcourt, 1981. 9–17.

White, Joseph. "Black Family Life." *The Psychology of Blacks.* Englewood Cliffs: Prentice-Hall, 1984. 60–70.

Whitehead, Barbara Dafoe. "Dan Quayle was Right."*Atlantic Monthly* Apr. 1993: 47–84.

———. "Ties That Don't Bind—Where Have All the Parents Gone?" *New Perspectives Quarterly* 7 (Winter 1990): 30–34.

Visual Texts

Films

Life with Father. Dir. Michael Curtiz. Perf. William Powell and Irene Dunne. Warner Bros., 1947.

Little Women. Dir. Gillian Armstrong. Perf. Winona Ryder, Claire Danes, and Susan Sarandon. Columbia, 1994.

Ordinary People. Dir. Robert Redford. Perf. Donald Sutherland and Mary Tyler Moore. Paramount, 1980.

Crooklyn. Dir. Spike Lee. Perf. Alfre Woodard and Delroy Lindo. Universal, 1994.

Television Documentary

An American Family, a twelve-part documentary. Prod. Alan and Susan Raymond. Perf. William and Pat Loud and children, Lance, Delilah, Grant, and Kevin. PBS. WNET, New York. 1 Jan. 1973, 29 Mar. 1973.

Television Shows

The Cosby Show (NBC)
Full House (ABC)
Leave it to Beaver
Married . . . with Children (FOX)
Roseanne (ABC)

BEAUTY AND THE BEAST: THE TALES WITHIN US

Leta Marks

Fairy tales were cultivated to assure that young people would be properly groomed for their social functions. The mark of beauty for a female is to be found in her submission, obedience, humility, industry, and patience; the mark of manliness is to be found in his self-control, politeness, reason, and perseverance.

—JACK ZIPES, 1994

The Oedipal love of Beauty for her father, when transferred to her future husband, is wonderfully healing. . . . [F]airy tales subtly offer suggestions on how to deal constructively with these inner experiences.

—BRUNO BETTELHEIM, 1976

Beauty has to learn to love the beast in him, in order to know the beast in herself . . . . The beast [is] authentic, fully realized sexuality.

—MARINA WARNER, 1994

Disney's version features a Beast who looks ugly and acts even uglier . . . . What is the message to little girls when Belle manages to transform this Beast? . . . That women are responsible for male anger and violence. What a heart-warming fable! Why, it's a regular training film for the battered women of tomorrow!

—KATHI MAIO, 1995

❧

Introduction: Why Study a Fairy Tale?

❧ Fastwrite 1

Reflect for a moment on the very different responses to *Beauty and the Beast* offered in the passages quoted above. What assumptions do these writers have about the effects that reading fairy tales—and *Beauty and the Beast* in particular—have on children? How do their positions strike you? Do you find them

Figure 4.1. Disney's Belle and the Beast. From *Beauty and the Beast.* Walt Disney. Adapted from the film by Teddy Slaterd. Illustrated by Ron Dias and Ric Gonzalez, 1991.

familiar? Surprising? Unusual? What assumptions do you have about the effects of fairy tales on children?

Why include *Beauty and the Beast* in a chapter of a college textbook dealing with the serious business of critical reading, writing, and thinking? Will analyzing a beloved story ruin it? In looking at the title of this chapter, perhaps some of these thoughts flashed through your mind.

The opening quotations suggest that analyzing fairy tales can be anything but child's play. Fairy tales are the subject of much critical debate. Readers offer startlingly different interpretations of how *Beauty and the Beast* in particular affects its audience. Psychologists, journalists, pop culture enthusiasts, literary critics, among others, not only argue about the meaning of *Beauty and the Beast,* they also suggest—though in very different ways—that fairy tales serve important purposes in helping children absorb the values and beliefs of a culture.

Beauty and the Beast has evolved over time in different versions from the early Roman myth of *Cupid and Psyche* to a "classic" children's story of various cultures, to contemporary theatrical and film versions, and even to a television series. In the process, the Beast has changed its animal form many times; the hurdles Beauty has had to overcome in developing a relationship with the Beast have been altered dramatically over time; new characters have been added, such as Gaston in the Disney version; and in one version included here, it is Beauty who is physically transformed, not the Beast.

Why has the story evolved in particular ways at different periods? What can the endurance of the story over time, as well as the particular changes it has undergone, tell us about the people who have read and reread, written and rewritten it? As archeologists dig for shards of colorful glass or pottery to try to glimpse aspects of the lived experiences, beliefs, and practices of past cultures, so too can we examine details such as these from various versions of *Beauty and the Beast*. These details have been left for us by people from different moments and different cultures, and they can help us glimpse and speculate about how they lived and loved, what they hoped for, and what they feared.

If fairy tales mean to initiate children into the values and beliefs of a culture, then different versions of a single story across the centuries may help give us insights into both the changing and enduring values of people over time. They may let us glimpse the historical tensions that existed below the surface of other cultures, and perhaps allow us to see some of the tensions within our own historical moment. Observing these tensions, however, requires a variety of critical reading skills. Fairy tales are often taken as "just stories" rather than as vehicles for imagining particular values, values that we often absorb unconsciously. But, as discussed in previous chapters, readers take better control over what they believe and why they believe it once they are able to analyze the assumptions that underlie even the most innocent and apparently neutral-looking texts.

Fairy tales initiate children into a culture's dominant belief structures in various ways: sometimes directly and literally in a manner that is obvious, at least to an adult reader, but sometimes in more subtle and indirect ways that might require a symptomatic reading to be uncovered. In this chapter, we include different versions of *Beauty and the Beast* as well as various critical readings of it so that you can increase the diversity of perspectives from which you initiate a symptomatic reading. You do not have to agree with all (or any) of the critical readings included here, but we do ask you to grapple with them and then to develop critical and symptomatic readings of your own.

Is *Beauty and the Beast* meant to teach young girls that when they grow up, they will see that their love for their father and their husband is complementary? Does it teach young boys that girls will love and nurture them even if they act "beastly"? Does it suggest to young girls that they have power in the world, power even to save their fathers? Does it teach boys that they need to have material wealth? That they need to show (or hide) their emotions? Does it teach young girls that they should be subservient to other people's wishes? To what extent does it suggest that the move into the sexual will be pleasurable for women? For men? What does it teach girls and boys about relationships with mothers and sisters? About relationships with each other?

Readers of *Beauty and the Beast* have suggested a variety of answers to these questions. As you trace the history of *Beauty and the Beast*, note the preoccupations that change over time and place and ask why, for example, Psyche is forbidden to look at Cupid; why Disney portrays Belle with a book in her hand; why the Beast's beastliness varies so dramatically, and why, in some versions, Beauty is tested to prove her character and her skills.

As you read each version of *Beauty and the Beast*, keep some of the following questions in mind as you try to determine what each story might tell you about the culture that produced it. Working with even one or two of these questions can help you to focus your reading so that you become more conscious of the values the story wants you to absorb, and more critical and thoughtful before you take them in. Further, reading with these questions in mind helps to prepare you for the historical and cultural questions that come after the readings.

1. What are the underlying assumptions in the story about gender roles and behavior, courtship and marriage customs? What are the desires, expectations, values, and beliefs of the characters?
2. Which gender or class of people has the most power and control over its individual lives and over the lives of others?
3. What is the nature of the Beast? How is he described?
4. What do we know about Beauty's character and behavior? What are her attributes?
5. What is the purpose of the story, and for what audience is it intended? What are its underlying themes? Is there a moral or lesson stated or implied? How might readers at the time have reacted to it? How does this compare with your reaction?

∾ Fastwrite 2

a. Write about your earliest memories of *Beauty and the Beast* and your reaction to the story. Was your first experience of the story in a film or written version? Who told you the story, read it to you, or took you to see it? Recall and describe details of images you remember and any characters or situations you identified with or particularly enjoyed or disliked. Why do you think these particular scenes or characters stand out in your mind? What, do you recall, was your overall feeling about the story as it unfolded?

b. If you are unfamiliar with *Beauty and the Beast*, read the Beaumont version of the story reprinted later in this chapter. (Although this version was written in 1745, it forms the basis of much of the Disney version and so gives you the closest sense of the popular contemporary rendition of the story.) Or watch the Disney film or read the Disney Golden Book version, which Disney would not give us permission to include in this book. Fastwrite about your impressions of whatever version of *Beauty and the Beast* you end up choosing; discuss the images, characters, and situations that strike you and that you particularly identified with, enjoyed, or disliked. Why did these particulars stand out for you? What is your overall feeling about the story as it unfolds?

LUCIUS APULEIUS

Cupid and Psyche (A.D. 150)

This first reading, an early forerunner of the *Beauty and the Beast* fairy tale, was told by Apuleius, a Roman writer born in Madaura, a colony of Rome, about C.E. 125. Apuleius studied rhetoric in Carthage and philosophy in Athens. His most famous work, written in C.E. 150, *The Golden Ass* (known also as *Metamorphosis*), contains a collection of stories combining moral lessons, humor, magic, and fantasy, one of which is *Cupid and Psyche*.

There was once a king who had three daughters, all lovely maidens, but the youngest, Psyche, excelled her sisters so greatly that beside them she seemed a very goddess consorting with mere mortals. The fame of her surpassing beauty spread over the earth, and everywhere men journeyed to gaze upon her with wonder and adoration and to do her homage as though she were in truth one of the immortals. They would even say that Venus herself could not equal this mortal. As they thronged in ever-growing

Figure 4.2. Eros and Psyche, engraving by William Blake, 1796.

numbers to worship her loveliness no one any more gave a thought to Venus herself. Her temples were neglected; her altars foul with cold ashes; her favorite towns deserted and falling in ruins. All the honors once hers were now given to a mere girl destined some day to die.

It may well be believed that the goddess would not put up with this treatment. As always when she was in trouble she turned for help to her son, that beautiful winged youth whom some call Cupid and others Love, against whose arrows there is no defense, neither in heaven nor on the earth. She told him her wrongs and as always he was ready to do her bidding. "Use your power," she said, "and make the hussy fall madly in love with the vilest and most despicable creature there is in the whole world." And so no doubt he would have done, if Venus had not first shown him Psyche, never thinking in her jealous rage what such beauty might do even to the God of Love himself. As he looked upon her it was as if he had shot one of his arrows into his own heart. He said nothing to his mother, indeed he had no power to utter a word, and Venus left him with the happy confidence that he would swiftly bring about Psyche's ruin.

What happened, however, was not what she had counted on. Psyche did not fall in love with a horrible wretch, she did not fall in love at all. Still more strange, no one fell in love with her. Men were content to look and wonder and worship—and then pass on to marry someone else. Both her sisters, inexpressibly inferior to her, were splendidly married, each to a king. Psyche, the all-beautiful, sat sad and solitary, only admired, never loved. It seemed that no man wanted her.

This was, of course, most disturbing to her parents. Her father finally traveled to an oracle of Apollo to ask his advice on how to get her a good husband. The god answered him, but his words were terrible. Cupid had told him the whole story and had begged for his help. Accordingly Apollo said that Psyche, dressed in deepest mourning, must be set on the summit of a rocky hill and left alone, and that there her destined husband, a fearful winged serpent, stronger than the gods themselves, would come to her and make her his wife.

The misery of all when Psyche's father brought back this lamentable news can be imagined. They dressed the maiden as though for her death and carried her to the hill with greater sorrowing than if it had been to her tomb. But Psyche herself kept her courage. "You should have wept for me before," she told them, "because of the beauty that has drawn down upon me the jealousy of Heaven. Now go, knowing that I am glad the end has come." They went in despairing grief, leaving the lovely helpless creature to meet her doom alone, and they shut themselves in their palace to mourn all their days for her.

On the high hilltop in the darkness Psyche sat, waiting for she knew not what terror. There, as she wept and trembled, a soft breath of air came through the stillness to her, the gentle breathing of Zephyr, sweetest and mildest of winds. She felt it lift her up. She was floating away from the rocky hill and down until she lay upon a grassy meadow soft as a bed and fragrant with flowers. It was so peaceful there, all her trouble left her and she slept. She woke beside a bright river; and on its bank was a mansion stately and beautiful as though built for a god, with pillars of gold and walls of silver and floors inlaid with precious stones. No sound was to be heard; the place seemed deserted and Psyche drew near, awestruck at the sight of such splendor. As she hesitated on the threshold, voices sounded in her ear. She could see no one, but the words they spoke came clearly to her. The house was for her, they told her. She must enter without fear and bathe and refresh herself. Then a banquet table would be spread for her. "We are your servants," the voices said, "ready to do whatever you desire."

The bath was the most delightful, the food the most delicious, she had ever enjoyed. While she dined, sweet music breathed around her: a great choir seemed to sing to a harp, but she could only hear, not see, them.

Throughout the day, except for the strange companionship of the voices, she was alone, but in some inexplicable way she felt sure that with the coming of the night her husband would be with her. And so it happened. When she felt him beside her and heard his voice softly murmuring in her ear, all her fears left her. She knew without seeing him that here was no monster or shape of terror, but the lover and husband she had longed and waited for.

This half-and-half companionship could not fully content her; still she was happy and the time passed swiftly. One night, however, her dear though unseen husband spoke gravely to her and warned her that danger in the shape of her two sisters was approaching. "They are coming to the hill where you disappeared, to weep for you," he said; "but you must not let them see you or you will bring great sorrow upon me and ruin to yourself." She promised him she would not, but all the next day she passed in weeping, thinking of her sisters and herself unable to comfort them. She was still in tears when her husband came and even his caresses could not check them. At last he yielded sorrowfully to her great desire. "Do what you will," he said, "but you are seeking your own destruction." Then he warned her solemnly not to be persuaded by anyone to try to see him, on pain of being separated from him forever. Psyche cried out that she would never do so. She would die a hundred times over rather than live without him "But give me this joy," she said: "to see my sisters." Sadly he promised her that it should be so.

The next morning the two came, brought down from the mountain by Zephyr. Happy and excited, Psyche was waiting for them. It was long before the three could speak to each other; their joy was too great to be expressed except by tears and embraces. But when at last they entered the palace and the elder sisters saw its surpassing treasures; when they sat at the rich banquet and heard the marvelous music, bitter envy took possession of them and a devouring curiosity as to who was the lord of all this magnificence and their sister's husband. But Psyche kept faith; she told them only that he was a young man, away now on a hunting expedition. Then filling their hands with gold and jewels, she had Zephyr bear them back to the hill. They went willingly enough, but their hearts were on fire with jealousy. All their own wealth and good fortune seemed to them as nothing compared with Psyche's, and their envious anger so worked in them that they came finally to plotting how to ruin her.

That very night Psyche's husband warned her once more. She would not listen when he begged her not to let them come again. She never could see him, she reminded him. Was she also to be forbidden to see all others, even her sisters so dear to her? He yielded as before, and very soon the two wicked women arrived, with their plot carefully worked out.

Already, because of Psyche's stumbling and contradictory answers when they asked her what her husband looked like, they had become convinced that she had never set eyes on him and did not really know what he was. They did not tell her this, but they reproached her for hiding her terrible state from them, her own sisters. They had learned, they said, and knew for a fact, that her husband was not a man, but the fearful serpent Apollo's oracle had declared he would be. He was kind now, no doubt, but he would certainly turn upon her some night and devour her.

Psyche, aghast, felt terror flooding her heart instead of love. She had wondered so often why he would never let her see him. There must be some dreadful reason. What did she really know about him? If he was not horrible to look at, then he was cruel to forbid her ever to behold him. In extreme misery, faltering and stammering, she gave her sisters to understand that she could not deny what they said, because she had been with him only in the dark. "There must be something very wrong," she sobbed, "for him so to shun the light of day." And she begged them to advise her.

They had their advice all prepared beforehand. That night she must hide a sharp knife and a lamp near her bed. When her husband was fast asleep she must leave the bed, light the lamp, and get the knife. She must steel herself to plunge it swiftly into the body of the frightful being the light would certainly show her. "We will be near," they said, "and carry you away with us when he is dead."

Then they left her torn by doubt and distracted what to do. She loved him; he was her dear husband. No; he was a horrible serpent and she loathed him. She would kill him—She would not. She must have certainty—She did not want certainty. So all day long her thoughts fought with each other. When evening came, however, she had given the struggle up. One thing she was determined to do: she would see him.

When at last he lay sleeping quietly, she summoned all her courage and lit the lamp. She tiptoed to the bed and holding the light high above her she gazed at what lay there. Oh, the relief and the rapture that filled her heart. No monster was revealed, but the sweetest and fairest of all creatures, at whose sight the very lamp seemed to shine brighter. In her first shame at her folly and lack of faith, Psyche fell on her knees and would have plunged the knife into her own breast if it had not fallen from her trembling hands. But those same unsteady hands that saved her betrayed her, too, for as she hung over him, ravished at the sight of him and unable to deny herself the bliss of filling her eyes with his beauty, some hot oil fell from the lamp upon his shoulder. He started awake: he saw the light and knew her faithlessness, and without a word he fled from her.

She rushed out after him into the night. She could not see him, but she heard his voice speaking to her. He told her who he was, and sadly bade her farewell. "Love cannot live where there is no trust," he said, and flew away. "The God of Love!" she thought. "He was my husband, and I, wretch that I am, could not keep faith with him. Is he gone from me forever? . . . At any rate," she told herself with rising courage, "I can spend the rest of my life searching for him. If he has no more love left for me, at least I can show him how much I love him." And she started on her journey. She had no idea where to go; she knew only that she would never give up looking for him.

He meanwhile had gone to his mother's chamber to have his wound cared for, but when Venus heard his story and learned that it was Psyche whom he had chosen, she left him angrily alone in his pain, and went forth to find the girl of whom he had made her still more jealous. Venus was determined to show Psyche what it meant to draw down the displeasure of a goddess.

Poor Psyche in her despairing wanderings was trying to win the gods over to her side. She offered ardent prayers to them perpetually, but not one of them would do anything to make Venus their enemy. At last she perceived that there was no hope for her, either in heaven or on earth, and she took a desperate resolve. She would go straight to Venus; she would offer herself humbly to her as her servant, and try to soften her anger. "And who knows," she thought, "if he himself is not there in his mother's house." So she set forth to find the goddess who was looking everywhere for her.

When she came into Venus' presence the goddess laughed aloud and asked her scornfully if she was seeking a husband since the one she had had would have nothing to do with her because he had almost died of the burning wound she had given him. "But really," she said, "you are so plain and ill-favored a girl that you will never be able to get you a lover except by the most diligent and painful service. I will therefore show my good will to you by training you in such ways." With that she took a great quantity of the smallest of the seeds, wheat and poppy and millet and so on, and mixed them all together in a heap. "By nightfall these must all be sorted," she said. "See to it for your own sake." And with that she departed.

Psyche, left alone, sat still and stared at the heap. Her mind was all in a maze because of the cruelty of the command; and, indeed, it was of no use to start a task so manifestly impossible. But at this direful moment she who had awakened no compassion in mortals or immortals was pitied by the tiniest creatures of the field, the little ants, the swift-runners. They cried to each other, "Come, have mercy on this poor maid and help her diligently." At once they came, waves of them, one after another, and they labored separating and dividing, until what had been a confused mass lay all ordered, every seed with its kind. This was what Venus found when she came back, and very angry she was to see it. "Your work is by no means over," she said. Then she gave Psyche a crust of bread and bade her sleep on the ground while she herself went off to her soft, fragrant couch. Surely if she could keep the girl at hard labor and half starve her, too, that hateful beauty of hers would soon be lost. Until then she must see that her son was securely guarded in his chamber where he was still suffering from his wound. Venus was pleased at the way matters were shaping.

The next morning she devised another task for Psyche, this time a dangerous one. "Down there near the riverbank," she said, "where the bushes grow thick, are sheep with fleeces of gold. Go fetch me some of their shining wool." When the worn girl reached the gently flowing stream, a great longing seized her to throw herself into it and end all her pain and despair. But as she was bending over the water she heard a little voice from near her feet, and looking down saw that it came from a green reed. She must not drown herself, it said. Things were not as bad as that. The sheep were indeed very fierce, but if Psyche would wait until they came out of the bushes toward evening to rest beside the river, she could go into the thicket and find plenty of the golden wool hanging on the sharp briars.

So spoke the kind and gentle reed, and Psyche, following the directions, was able to carry back to her cruel mistress a quantity of the shining fleece. Venus received it with an evil smile. "Someone helped you," she said sharply. "Never did you do this by yourself. However, I will give you an opportunity to prove that you really have the stout heart and the singular prudence you make such a show of. Do you see that black water which falls from the hill yonder? It is the source of the terrible river which is called hateful, the river Styx. You are to fill this flask from it." That was the worst task yet, as Psyche saw when she approached the waterfall. Only a winged creature could reach it, so steep and slimy were the rocks on all sides, and so fearful the onrush of the descending waters. But by this time it must be evident to all the readers of this story (as, perhaps, deep in her heart it had become evident to Psyche herself) that although each of her trials seemed impossibly hard, an excellent way out would always be provided for her. This time her savior was an eagle, who poised on his great wings beside her, seized the flask from her with his beak and brought it back to her full of the black water.

But Venus kept on. One cannot but accuse her of some stupidity. The only effect of all that had happened was to make her try again. She gave Psyche a box which she was to carry to the underworld and ask Proserpine to fill with some of her beauty. She was to tell her that Venus really needed it, she was so worn-out from nursing her sick son. Obediently as always Psyche went forth to look for the road to Hades. She found her guide in a tower she passed. It gave her careful directions how to get to Proserpine's palace; first through a great hole in the earth, then down to the river of death, where she must give the ferryman, Charon, a penny to take her across. From there the road led straight to the palace. Cerberus, the three-headed dog, guarded the doors, but if she gave him a cake he would be friendly and let her pass.

All happened, of course, as the tower had foretold. Proserpine was willing to do Venus a service, and Psyche, greatly encouraged, bore back the box, returning far more quickly than she had gone down.

Her next trial she brought upon herself through her curiosity and, still more, her vanity. She felt that she must see what that beauty-charm in the box was: and, perhaps, use a little of it herself. She knew quite as well as Venus did that her looks were not improved by what she had gone through, and always in her mind was the thought that she might suddenly meet Cupid. If only she could make herself more lovely for him! She was unable to resist the temptation; she opened the box. To her sharp disappointment she saw nothing there; it seemed empty. Immediately, however, a deadly languor took possession of her and she fell into a heavy sleep.

At this juncture the God of Love himself stepped forward. Cupid was healed of his wound by now and longing for Psyche. It is a difficult matter to keep Love imprisoned. Venus had locked the door, but there were the windows. All Cupid had to do was to fly out and start looking for his wife. She was lying almost beside the palace, and he found her at once. In a moment he had wiped the sleep from her eyes and put it back into the box. Then waking her with just a prick from one of his arrows, and scolding her a little for her curiosity, he bade her take Proserpine's box to his mother and he assured her that all thereafter would be well.

While the joyful Psyche hastened on her errand, the god flew up to Olympus. He wanted to make certain that Venus would give them no more trouble, so he went straight to Jupiter himself. The Father of Gods and Men consented at once to all that Cupid asked—"Even though," he said, "you have done me great harm in the past—seriously injured my good name and my dignity by making me change myself into a bull and a swan and so on . . . . However, I cannot refuse you."

Then he called a full assembly of the gods, and announced to all, including Venus, that Cupid and Psyche were formally married, and that he proposed to bestow immortality upon the bride. Mercury brought Psyche into the palace of the gods, and Jupiter himself gave her the ambrosia to taste which made her immortal. This, of course, completely changed the situation. Venus could not object to a goddess for her daughter-in-law; the alliance had become eminently suitable. No doubt she reflected also that Psyche, living up in heaven with a husband and children to care for, could not be much on the earth to turn men's heads and interfere with her own worship.

So all came to a most happy end. Love and the Soul (for that is what Psyche means) had sought and, after sore trials, found each other; and that union could never be broken.

∾   **Fastwrite 3**

Jot down your observations about the relationship of the two lovers, noting passages that describe or suggest their passion. You can use what you write here when you read later versions of *Beauty and the Beast* and compare them to this story.

Historical Questions

1. Although this story is regarded as the "source" of *Beauty and the Beast* as it has come down to us over the centuries, there are many differences between it and later versions. Quickly list a number of differences and similarities that you observe between "Cupid and Psyche" and the version you are most familiar with. Focusing on what you see as one important difference, explain why contemporary versions may have evolved away from that particular aspect of the original story. Then, concentrating on what you see as one important similarity, explain why you think that aspect of the story has endured throughout the centuries. Discuss the evolution of the story in relation to one aspect of our society's larger beliefs, values, and practices.

2. What is the significance of the taboo that forbids Psyche from looking at her lover? Why is Cupid, in contrast, able to see Psyche and admire her beauty? What do these different rules suggest about the dominant attitudes toward sexuality during the time when the story was created? Do these rules or aspects of them still exist today? Have they been replaced by different attitudes and standards? Give two or three examples from your personal contemporary experience, from magazines, television, or any other contemporary text.

3. All of the female characters—including a goddess—in the story are presented as Psyche's antagonists. With specific reference to the text, explore literally why each of them pits herself against Psyche. Then, read the text more symptomatically and explore the larger context of women's status in the world of the story to suggest other reasons why female characters might be represented as reacting to Psyche as they do. What assumptions about women's power and control are suggested by these antagonistic relationships? Do these assumptions or aspects of them still exist today, or have different beliefs and behaviors replaced them? Explain your position with one or two specific examples from your everyday life.

Cultural Questions

1. Myths and fairy tales may reveal psychological insights about a society's attitude toward family dynamics. Look back at the particular passages in

the story that explicitly discuss the relationships between Venus and Cupid and between Psyche and her family. What main assumptions does the story state directly about parent-child relationships, both when the child is at home and when children leave home to get married? Then, read more symptomatically to discover one or two other assumptions about parent-child relations that the story does not discuss explicitly but that it nonetheless takes for granted; these unstated assumptions are often at the core of a society's belief system.

2. Explore the tasks that Venus asks Psyche to perform by comparing them to those that a male hero such as Odysseus, Jason, or Theseus in a Greek or Roman myth might have had to perform. What challenges does a male hero typically have to face on a quest to win his beloved? Give two to three specific examples. In what way are they similar to the particular tasks Psyche has to perform? In what ways are they different? What does this comparison suggest about early conceptions of the male and the female?

3. By observing how a fairy tale represents the natural world in relation to the roles of women and men, we can gain insights into beliefs about the power relations within the social and cosmic order of the time in which it was written. Explore some of the details about social hierarchies, the natural world—especially the details dealing with the power of those who assist Psyche—and the gods. With specific references to the text, discuss what these details suggest about power relations, beliefs, and values in the world in which the story was told.

J A C O B   A N D   W I L H E L M   G R I M M

The Lady and the Lion (1812)

Jacob Grimm (1785–1863), a linguist, and Wilhelm Grimm (1786–1859), a librarian, traveled around Germany, their homeland, listening to older women tell folktales that had been passed down orally from generation to generation. In the process of writing them down, the brothers transformed these narratives into literary fairy tales, publishing them in 1812 for a middle-class audience. Over the years, they revised their earlier editions and attempted to make them more appealing by imitating the natural voices of the narrator and characters. While recognizing the important contribution the Grimm brothers made by preserving these old folk-

Figure 4.3. Lady leading Lion, from Grimm's "The Lady and the Lion." Illustrated by Arthur Rackham, 1812.

tales, some recent scholars are quick to point out that in the process of writing these tales down, the Grimm brothers, understandably, added to them many nineteenth-century preoccupations. Thus, the Grimm fairy tales contain a "layering" of historical beliefs, values, and concerns.

There was once a Man who had to take a long journey, and when he was saying good-bye to his daughters he asked what he should bring back to them.

The eldest wanted pearls, the second diamonds, but the third said, 'Dear father, I should like a singing, soaring lark.'

The father said, 'Very well, if I can manage it, you shall have it'; and he kissed all three and set off. He bought pearls and diamonds for the two eldest, but he had searched everywhere in vain for the singing, soaring lark, and this worried him, for his youngest daughter was his favourite child.

Once his way led through a wood, in the midst of which was a splendid castle; near it stood a tree, and right up at the top he saw a lark singing and soaring. 'Ah,' he said, 'I have come across you in the nick of time'; and he called to his Servant to dismount and catch the little creature. But as he approached the tree a Lion sprang out from underneath, and shook himself, and roared so that the leaves on the tree trembled.

'Who dares to steal my lark?' said he. 'I will eat up the thief!'

Then the Man said, 'I didn't know that the bird was yours. I will make up for my fault by paying a heavy ransom. Only spare my life.'

But the Lion said, 'Nothing can save you, unless you promise to give me whatever first meets you when you get home. If you consent, I will give you your life and the bird into the bargain.'

But the Man hesitated, and said, 'Suppose my youngest and favourite daughter were to come running to meet me when I go home!'

But the Servant was afraid, and said, 'Your daughter will not necessarily be the first to come to meet you; it might just as well be a cat or a dog.'

So the Man let himself be persuaded, took the lark, and promised to the Lion for his own whatever first met him on his return home. When he reached home, and entered his house, the first person who met him was none other than his youngest daughter; she came running up and kissed and caressed him, and when she saw that he had brought the singing, soaring lark, she was beside herself with joy. But her father could not rejoice; he began to cry, and said, 'My dear child, it has cost me dear, for I have had to promise you to a Lion who will tear you in pieces when he has you in his power.' And he told her all that had happened, and begged her not to go, come what might.

But she consoled him, saying, 'Dear father, what you have promised must be performed. I will go and will soon soften the Lion's heart, so that I shall come back safe and sound.' The next morning the way was shown to her, and she said good-bye and went confidently into the forest.

Now the Lion was an enchanted Prince, who was a Lion by day, and all his followers were Lions too; but by night they reassumed their human form. On her arrival she was kindly received, and conducted to the castle. When night fell, the Lion turned into a handsome man, and their wedding was celebrated with due magnificence. And they lived happily together, sitting up at night and sleeping by day. One day he came to her and said, 'To-morrow there is a festival at your father's house to celebrate your eldest sister's wedding; if you would like to go my Lions shall escort you.'

She answered that she was very eager to see her father again, so she went away accompanied by the Lions.

There was great rejoicing on her coming, for they all thought that she had been torn to pieces and had long been dead.

But she told them what a handsome husband she had and how well she fared; and she stayed with them as long as the wedding festivities lasted. Then she went back again into the wood.

When the second daughter married, and the youngest was again invited to the wedding, she said to the Lion, 'This time I will not go alone, you must come too.'

But the Lion said it would be too dangerous, for if a gleam of light touched him he would be changed into a Dove and would have to fly about for seven years.

'Ah,' said she, 'only go with me, and I will protect you and keep off every ray of light.'

So they went away together, and took their little child with them too. They had a hall built with such thick walls that no ray could penetrate, and thither the Lion was to retire when the wedding torches were kindled. But the door was made of fresh wood which split and caused a little crack which no one noticed.

Now the wedding was celebrated with great splendour. But when the procession came back from church with a large number of torches and lights, a ray of light no broader than a hair fell upon the Prince, and the minute this ray touched him he was changed; and when his wife came in and looked for him, she saw nothing but a White Dove sitting there. The Dove said to her, 'For seven years I must fly about the world; every seventh step I will let fall a drop of blood and a white feather which will show you the way, and if you will follow the track you can free me.'

Thereupon the Dove flew out of the door, and she followed it, and every seventh step it let fall a drop of blood and a little white feather to show her the way. So she wandered about the world, and never rested till the seven years were nearly passed. Then she rejoiced, thinking that she would soon be free of her troubles; but she was still far from release. One day as they were journeying on in the accustomed way, the feather and the drop of blood ceased falling, and when she looked up the Dove had vanished.

'Man cannot help me,' she thought. So she climbed up to the Sun and said to it, 'You shine upon all the valleys and mountain peaks, have you not seen a White Dove flying by?'

'No,' said the Sun, 'I have not seen one; but I will give you a little casket. Open it when you are in dire need.'

She thanked the Sun, and went on till night, when the Moon shone out. 'You shine all night,' she said, 'over field and forest, have you seen a White Dove flying by?'

'No,' answered the Moon, 'I have seen none; but here is an egg. Break it when you are in great need.'

She thanked the Moon, and went on till the Night Wind blew upon her. 'You blow among all the trees and leaves, have not you seen a White Dove?' she asked.

'No,' said the Night Wind, 'I have not seen one; but I will ask the other three Winds, who may, perhaps, have seen it.'

The East Wind and the West Wind came, but they had seen no Dove. Only the South Wind said, 'I have seen the White Dove. It has flown away to the Red Sea, where it has again become a Lion, since the seven years are over; and the Lion is ever fighting with a Dragon who is an enchanted Princess.'

Then the Night Wind said, 'I will advise you. Go to the Red Sea, you will find tall reeds growing on the right bank; count them, and cut down the eleventh, strike the Dragon with it and then the Lion will be able to master it, and both will regain human shape. Next, look round, and you will see the winged Griffin, who dwells by the Red Sea, leap upon its back with your beloved, and it will carry you across the sea. Here is a nut. Drop it when you come to mid-ocean; it will open immediately and a tall nut-tree will grow up out of the water, on which the Griffin will settle. Could it not rest, it would not be strong enough to carry you across, and if you forget to drop the nut, it will let you fall into the sea.'

Then she journeyed on, and found everything as the Night Wind had said. She counted the reeds by the sea and cut off the eleventh, struck the Dragon with it, and the Lion mastered it; immediately both regained human form. But when the Princess who had been a Dragon was free from enchantment, she took the Prince in her arms, seated herself on the Griffin's back, and carried him off. And the poor wanderer, again forsaken, sat down and cried. At last she took courage and said to herself: 'Wherever the winds blow, I will go, and as long as cocks crow, I will search till I find him.'

So she went on a long, long way, till she came to the castle where the Prince and Princess were living. There she heard that there was to be a festival to celebrate their wedding. Then she said to herself, 'Heaven help me,' and she opened the casket which the Sun had given her; inside it was a dress, as brilliant as the Sun itself. She took it out, put it on, and went into the castle, where every one, including the Bride, looked at her with amazement. The dress pleased the Bride so much that she asked if it was to be bought.

'Not with gold or goods,' she answered; 'but with flesh and blood.'

The Bride asked what she meant, and she answered, 'Let me speak with the Bridegroom in his chamber to-night.'

The Bride refused. However, she wanted the dress so much that at last she consented; but the Chamberlain was ordered to give the Prince a sleeping draught.

At night, when the Prince was asleep, she was taken to his room. She sat down and said: 'For seven years I have followed you. I have been to the Sun, and the Moon, and the Four Winds to look for you. I have helped you against the Dragon, and will you now quite forget me?'

But the Prince slept so soundly that he thought it was only the rustling of the wind among the pine-trees. When morning came she was taken away, and had to give up the dress; and as it had not helped her she was very sad, and went out into a meadow and cried. As she was sitting there, she remembered the egg which the Moon had given her; she broke it open, and out came a hen and twelve chickens, all of gold, who ran about chirping, and then crept back under their mother's wings. A prettier sight could not be seen. She got up and drove them about the meadow, till the Bride saw them from the window. The chickens pleased her so much that she asked if they were for sale. 'Not for gold and goods, but for flesh and blood. Let me speak with the Bridegroom in his chamber once more.'

The Bride said 'Yes,' intending to deceive her as before; but when the Prince went to his room he asked the Chamberlain what all the murmuring and rustling in the night meant. Then the Chamberlain told him how he had been ordered to give him a sleeping draught because a poor girl had been concealed in his room, and that night he was to do the same again. 'Pour out the drink, and put it near my bed,' said the Prince. At night she was brought in again, and when she began to relate her sad fortunes he recognised the voice of his dear wife, sprang up, and said, 'Now I am really free for the first time. All has been as a dream, for the foreign Princess cast a spell over me so that I was forced to forget you; but heaven in a happy hour has taken away my blindness.'

Then they both stole out of the castle, for they feared the Princess's father, because he was a sorcerer. They mounted the Griffin, who bore them over the Red Sea, and when they got to mid-ocean, she dropped the nut. On the spot a fine nuttree sprang up, on which the bird rested; then it took them home, where they found their child grown tall and beautiful, and they lived happily till the end.

∾ **Fastwrite 4**

How would you describe the ideal attributes of a woman today? What characteristics, attitudes, and ways of being should she possess? In what ways does the Lady in this story fit your description? How do you think others would classify your description? Residual? Dominant? Emergent? Explain briefly.

Historical Questions

1. In both "Cupid and Psyche" and "The Lady and the Lion," the male character is under the power of a strong female (Cupid by Venus, his mother, and the Lion prince by the "foreign princess"). And yet this male character also has the power to command some other characters to follow his bidding.

With close reference to two or more relevant passages from each of the fairy tales, compare and contrast the ways in which the male character is freed from the control of a female force and is able to exert his power over others. Then, reading symptomatically, explore what the predicaments of these men suggest about the psychological anxieties that men might have been experiencing in the two different historical periods. How do they seem similar? How do they seem different? How might these representations be relevant to male readers of the stories today?

2. In "The Lady and the Lion," the heroine marries the prince (Lion) and has a child; yet the prince has become the prospective bridegroom of another princess. With reference to the behavior of the husband, the foreign princess, and the role the Lady has to play in resolving the story, explore what this triangle might imply about marriages during the time of the story. Then juxtapose the triangle in this story with the triangle of Psyche, Venus, and Cupid in "Cupid and Psyche," comparing and contrasting what you feel are the most striking representations of males and females in the two stories. To what extent do any of these representations seem relevant to male-female interactions in today's world? If you find them relevant, briefly explain why with one or two contemporary examples.

3. In both stories, the heroine must undergo enormous tasks to win her beloved. Compare the tasks of the heroines in "The Lady and the Lion" and "Cupid and Psyche," the difficulties they encounter, and the help they receive. With reference to particular passages, explore which of the two, in your mind, is the greater heroine. Explain your criteria for heroism. Explore what the effects might be on readers today of the particular types of representation of heroism embodied in Psyche and the Lady.

Cultural Questions

1. In this version of the *Beauty and the Beast* story, we begin to see a development of the father's relationship with the heroine that is expanded in later versions and that became the focus of much critical discussion in the latter part of the twentieth century. When her father tells her that she must leave and go to the Lion, the Lady replies, "I will go and will soon soften the Lion's heart, so that I shall come back safe and sound." What assumptions is the daughter represented as having about herself, her father, and the male Lion? What assumptions does the father have about himself as a father and about his youngest daughter? Why do you think she is represented as being so confident about her capacity to tame the Lion? Why does she wants to come back home quickly?

2. In the beginning of the story, the elder sisters wanted the father to bring them diamonds and pearls while the youngest desired a singing, soaring lark. Additionally, the Princess who competes for the heroine's husband is dazzled by a dress "as brilliant as the sun itself." What

values underlie these contrasting desires? What social and economic class associations do they have? Which values does the story approve of, and what lessons it is trying to teach readers? What, if any, contradictions among these values can you observe? Now, step back and think about the historical periods in which the story was first told and then finally written down. What economic developments were occurring, and where do you think the tellers of the story fit in terms of their social and economic class?

3. Consider the following passage: "On her arrival she was kindly received, and conducted to the castle. When night fell, the Lion turned into a handsome man, and their wedding was celebrated with due magnificence. And they lived happily together, sitting up at night and sleeping by day. One day he came to her and said, 'To-morrow there is a festival at your father's house to celebrate your eldest sister's wedding; if you would like to go my Lions shall escort you.' " Develop a symptomatic reading of this and other passages to explore the values about work, behavior, and general lifestyle of the story. In your analysis, go beyond reading the story literally and explore what is not explicitly stated but is nonetheless assumed or implied by particular details, tone, and word choices. Who do you think the audience is for this story? Compare and contrast the lessons the story teaches directly through its plot line with those it might teach indirectly through its language and tone.

MADAME LE PRINCE DE BEAUMONT

Beauty and the Beast (1745)

In the seventeenth and eighteenth centuries, *Beauty and the Beast* became a popular subject for women writers who wrote many different renditions of the story. Beaumont's is the best known today. Madame le Prince de Beaumont (1711–1780), the wife of a French aristocrat, published a collection of fairy tales in 1745 intended to teach moral lessons to students. She adapted the fairy tales and used them when she served as a governess in England. This version of *Beauty and the Beast* may seem most familiar to readers today because Disney used Beaumont's story line as the basis for its book and film, and Jean Cocteau, the famous French writer, also incorporated many elements from Beaumont's plot into his film version of the story.

Figure 4.4. "Beauty and Beast," adapted from *Beauty and the Beast,* Madame de Beaumont. Illustrated by Diane Goode, 1978.

Once upon a time there lived a merchant who was extremely rich. He had six children, three sons and three daughters. And since he was a sensible man, he spared no expense upon their education, but gave them all kinds of tutors. His daughters were very beautiful, but the youngest was especially admired by everybody. When she was little she was known as *the beautiful child,* and this name remained with her, causing her sisters to be very jealous.

Beauty, as she came to be called, was not only prettier than her sisters, but she was also much nicer. The two older girls were very arrogant because of their wealth. They gave themselves ridiculous airs playing the great ladies, declining to receive the other merchants' daughters and associating only with aristocrats. Every day they went off to balls, to plays or for strolls, laughing at their little sister who spent most of her time reading good books.

Since the girls were known to be rich, they were sought in marriage by many a well-to-do merchant. The two eldest said they would never marry unless they could find a duke, or at least a count. But Beauty thanked those who wished to marry her, and said that she was too young at present and that she wished to keep her father company for several years yet.

All of a sudden the merchant lost his wealth. Nothing remained to him but a small country house, very far from the city. Weeping, he told his children they must move to this house where, by working the land, they might just manage to live.

The two elder girls replied that they would not leave the city, for they had several suitors who would be happy to marry them, even though they had lost their fortunes. But the good ladies were mistaken. Now that they were poor, their suitors slighted them. They were loved by no one because of their arrogance. People declared that they did not deserve pity; in fact, everyone thought it was a good thing that their pride was humbled. "Let them play the great ladies while tending their sheep!" they said. At the same time, however, everybody added, "As for Beauty, we grieve for her misfortune, she is so kind."

There were several worthy gentlemen who would have married Beauty, though she had not a penny. But she told them she could not abandon her poor father and that she intended to follow him to the country, to comfort him and help him to work.

When they had settled in their country house, the merchant and his three sons started to till the land. Beauty rose at four o'clock every morning, and hurried to clean the house and prepare the family meals. At first, she found it very hard, for she was not accustomed to such work; but at the end of two months she grew stronger, and the hard toil gave her perfect health. When she had leisure, she read, played the harpsicord, or sang while she spun.

Her two sisters, on the other hand, were bored to death. They never rose before ten o'clock in the morning, and they strolled about all day, lamenting the loss of their beautiful clothes and their former acquaintances. "Look at our little sister," they said to each other. "Her soul is so base and so stupid that she is quite content with this miserable situation."

The good merchant did not share the opinion of his two daughters. He knew that Beauty was more suited to shine in society than her sisters. He admired the girl's virtue, especially her patience. As for her sisters, not content with letting her do all the work of the house, they insulted her at every opportunity.

The family had been living in seclusion for a year when the merchant received a letter informing him of the arrival of a ship on which he had some merchandise. The news nearly turned the heads of the two older girls, for they thought they might finally escape their dull life in the country. When they saw their father ready to leave the house, they begged him to bring them back dresses, furs, hats and all sorts of trinkets. Beauty asked for nothing, thinking to herself that all the money the merchandise might yield would never be enough to buy her sisters gifts.

"You have asked for nothing," said her father.

"You are so kind to think of me," she replied, "you might bring me a rose, for there are none here."

The good merchant set off. But when he arrived at his destination, he discovered there was a law suit over his merchandise. After much trouble, he started for home, poorer than he had been before. Only thirty miles from his house, as he was thinking with pleasure of seeing his children again, the merchant came to a great forest. It was snowing horribly and he lost his way. The wind was so strong that he was thrown twice from his horse. When night fell he thought he would either die of hunger and cold or else be eaten by wolves, which he could hear howling all around him.

Suddenly, through a long avenue of trees, he saw a light in the distance. He hastened toward it on foot and discovered a great castle, all lit; but he was astonished to find the courtyards deserted. His horse saw a large open stable and went in. Finding hay and oats in readiness, the poor animal, who was nearly dying of hunger, ate eagerly. The merchant tied him in the stable, and walked toward the house. There was not a soul to be seen. He entered a large hall where he found a roaring fire and a table laden with meats, but the table was set only for one. The rain and snow had soaked him to the bone, so he drew near the fire to dry himself. "The master of this house or his servants will surely forgive the liberty I have taken," he thought, "and doubtless someone will be here soon."

He waited a considerable time; but eleven o'clock struck and still nobody came. No longer able to resist his hunger, he took some chicken and ate it in large mouthfuls, trembling. Then he drank several glasses of wine, and becoming bolder, left the hall and passed through many magnificently furnished apartments until he came to a chamber which had a very good bed. As midnight had struck, and he was very tired, he closed the door, and went to sleep.

It was ten o'clock the next morning before he awoke, and he was greatly surprised to find a new suit of clothes in place of his own, which was quite spoiled. "Surely," he said to himself, "this castle must belong to some good fairy, who has taken pity on my misfortune."

He looked out the window. The snow had vanished and arbors of roses met his view. He returned to the great hall where he had supped the night before, and found a small table with a cup of chocolate on it.

"I thank you, Madam Fairy," he said aloud, "for having the goodness to think of my breakfast."

Having drunk his chocolate, the merchant went to look for his horse.

As he passed under an arbor of roses, he recalled that Beauty had asked for one, and he plucked a branch on which there were several blooms. At that very moment, he heard a dreadful noise, and he saw coming toward him a beast so horrible that he nearly fainted from fright.

"You are most ungrateful!" the monster said to him in a terrible voice. "I have saved your life by receiving you into my castle, and, in return, you steal my roses which I love better than all things in this world! For this offense you must die!"

The merchant threw himself on his knees and wrung his hands. "My lord, forgive me, I did not think to offend you by picking a rose for one of my daughters."

"I am not called 'my lord,'" replied the monster, "but the Beast. I have no love for compliments, but prefer people to say what they think; therefore, do not try to move me with your flatteries. However, you have told me that you have daughters. I will forgive you on the condition that one of them comes of her own choice to die in your place. Don't argue with me! Be gone. And if your daughter should refuse to die in your place, swear that you will return in three months."

The good man had no intention of sacrificing one of his daughters to this vile monster; but he thought that at least he would have the pleasure of embracing them one more time. He swore to return, and the Beast told him he could go when he wished. "But," he added, "do not leave empty-handed. Return to the chamber where you slept and there you will find an empty chest. Fill it with whatever you wish and I will send it to your home."

The Beast withdrew, leaving the good man to reflect that if he must die, he would have the comfort of leaving something for his poor children.

The merchant returned to the chamber where he had slept. There he found a great quantity of gold coins and filled the chest the Beast had spoken of. He found his horse in the stable and set forth from the castle, as down-hearted now as he had been joyful when he entered.

The horse, of his own accord, took one of the forest roads, and in a few hours the good man arrived at his little house. His children gathered around him; but instead of welcoming their embraces, the merchant burst into tears. In his hand he held the branch of roses he had brought for Beauty, and he gave it to her saying, "Beauty, take these roses; it is dearly that I must pay for them."

Thereupon he recounted his fatal adventure. The two older girls made a great fuss and shouted insults at Beauty, because she did not cry at all.

"It would be quite useless to weep," Beauty said. "Why should I lament the death of my father? He shall not perish. Since the monster will accept one of his daughters, I will offer myself to his fury. I am very happy, for in doing so I shall save my father and prove my affection for him."

"No, sister," said her three brothers, "you will not die. We shall go and find this monster, and will perish under his blows if we cannot kill him."

"Have no such hopes, my children," said their father. "The power of this Beast is so great that there is no escaping him. I am touched by Beauty's goodness, but I will not expose her to certain death. I am old and have not long to live. I shall lose but a few years."

"I assure you, father," said Beauty, "that you will not go to the castle without me; you cannot prevent me from following you. I would rather be devoured by this monster than die of the grief which your death would cause me." It was useless. Beauty was determined to leave for the great castle.

The merchant was so grieved by the thought of losing his daughter that he quite forgot the chest he had filled with gold. No sooner had he closed his chamber door and prepared for bed than, to his great surprise, he found it by his bedside! He decided not to tell his children that he had become so rich, for his elder daughters would have wanted to return to the city, and he had resolved to die in the country. He did, however, confide his secret to Beauty, who told him that during his absence several gentlemen had called and that two of them had courted her sisters. She begged her father to let them marry, for she was of such a kind nature and she loved them.

When Beauty set off with her father, her two sisters rubbed their eyes with an onion so as to appear tearful. The merchant and her brothers wept freely while Beauty held back her tears, so as not to add to their sorrow.

The horse set out on the road to the castle, and by evening Beauty and her father beheld it, all lit up as before. Their horse went unguided to the open stable, and the good man and the girl entered the great hall. There they found the table magnificently set for two people. The merchant had not the heart to eat, but Beauty, forcing herself to appear calm, sat down and served him. "The Beast must be anxious to fatten me up," she thought to herself, "since he has provided us with this splendid reception."

When they had finished supper, they heard a terrible noise. Knowing that it was the Beast, the merchant bid a tearful farewell to his poor daughter. Beauty could not help but tremble at the hideous apparition, but she did her best to calm herself.

"Have you come of your own free will?" the Beast asked.

"Yes" she replied softly.

"You are indeed kind," said the Beast, "and I am much obliged. You, good man, will leave tomorrow morning. Never think of returning here again. Farewell, Beauty."

"Farewell, Beast," she answered, and immediately the monster withdrew.

Beauty and her father went to bed, thinking they would not sleep at all, but they had scarcely lain down when they fell sound asleep.

In her dreams there appeared to Beauty a lady who said to her, "Your virtuous heart pleases me, Beauty. In saving the life of your father, you have performed a good deed which shall not go unrewarded."

When Beauty awoke, she told her father of her dream. He was somewhat consoled by it, yet wept bitterly when it came time for him to leave.

When he had gone, Beauty sat down in the great hall and cried too. She was certain the Beast would eat her that very evening, but regaining her courage, she decided to grieve no more during the short time she had to live.

She made up her mind to explore the splendid castle and was greatly surprised when she came upon a door, above which was written, "Beauty's Room." She hastened to open the door, and was dazzled by the magnificence within. What surprised her most was a large library, a harpsicord and several books of music. "They are anxious that I should not be bored," she murmured. "If I had but one day to live, surely they would not have made such provisions for me."

This idea gave her fresh courage. Opening the bookcase, she removed a book and read these words, written in golden letters:

"Your wish is my command, you are mistress of all here."

"Alas!" she sighed, "I wish only to see my poor father."

Saying this, she glanced at a great mirror and saw her own home, where her father was just arriving. He looked down-cast as her brothers and sisters went to meet him. The joy the ladies felt at the loss of their sister was only too obvious. In an instant the vision faded. Beauty could not help but think that the Beast had been very kind, and that she had nothing more to fear from him.

At noon, she found the table set, and during her dinner she heard an excellent concert, though she saw no one. But in the evening, as she was about to sit down at the table, she heard the terrible noise the Beast made, and trembled in spite of herself.

"Beauty," said the monster, "may I watch you eat your supper?"

"You are master here," Beauty said, quaking.

"No," replied the Beast. "You alone are mistress here. You have but to tell me to leave. If my presence disturbs you, I shall go immediately. Tell me, do you not find me very ugly?"

"I do," said Beauty, "since I must be truthful; but I think you are also very kind."

"You are right that I am ugly," said the Beast; "and besides my ugliness, I have no wit. I know very well that I am but a fool."

"A fool," answered Beauty, "is not aware he lacks wit; a fool never realizes it."

"Sup well, Beauty," the Beast said. "And try to amuse yourself in your castle, for everything here is yours. I should be sorry to know you were unhappy."

"You are very generous," said Beauty. "I am well pleased with your kind heart; when I think of that, you no longer seem so ugly to me."

"Oh yes," answered the Beast, "my heart is good, but I am a monster."

"There are many men more monstrous than you," said Beauty, "and I prefer your form to those men who hide a false, corrupt and ungrateful heart."

"Had I wit enough," said the Beast, "I would make a fine compliment to thank you; but being so stupid, I can only say that I am most grateful."

Beauty ate well, her fear of the Beast nearly gone. But she nearly died of fright when he asked her:

"Beauty, will you be my wife?"

She waited for some time before replying, fearing her refusal would anger him. At last she said, "No, Beast!"

The poor monster sighed a sigh which hissed frightfully, the sound echoing through the castle walls. But Beauty was reassured when he said, "Farewell, then, Beauty," and took his leave from the hall, though turning from time to time to look at her. Alone, Beauty felt touched by this poor Beast. "What a pity he is so ugly," she thought, "for he is so good."

Beauty spent three quiet months living in the castle. Every evening, the Beast paid her a visit, entertaining her with much good sense, but never with what one might call wit. Every day, Beauty discovered some new kindness in the monster. Seeing him so often she became accustomed to his ugliness, and far from dreading the moment of his visit, she would glance frequently at the clock to see if it was nine o'clock, for the Beast never failed to appear at that hour.

Only one thing troubled Beauty. Each evening, before retiring, the Beast always asked her to be his wife, and seemed overcome by grief when she refused. One day she said to him:

"You distress me, Beast. I wish I could marry you, but I cannot allow you to hope that will ever be. I will always be your friend. Be content with that."

"I must," said the Beast. "I know I am very horrible, but I love you very much. I should be happy knowing you will stay here. Promise you will never leave me."

Beauty blushed at these words. She had seen in her mirror that her father was sick with grief at having lost her, and she wished to see him once again. "I would gladly promise never to leave you; but I have so great a desire to see my father that I should die of sorrow if you should refuse me."

"I would rather die myself than cause you grief," said the monster. "I will send you to your father. You will remain with him, and your Beast will die of sorrow."

"No," said Beauty, crying, "I am too fond of you to cause your death. I promise to return in eight days. You have shown me that my sisters are married and my brothers have joined the army. My father is lonely; let me stay with him for one week."

"You shall be there tomorrow morning," said the Beast. "But remember your promise. When you wish to return you have only to lay your ring on a table before you go to bed. Farewell, Beauty."

As usual, the Beast sighed as he said these words, and Beauty went to bed quite sad for having grieved him.

When she awoke the next morning, she found herself in her father's house. She rang the little bell at her bedside, and it was answered by a maid, who gave a great cry at seeing her. Hearing the noise, Beauty's father came running and nearly died with the joy of seeing his daughter again. Their embraces lasted for more than a quarter of an hour. When their joy had subsided, Beauty realized she had no clothes to wear; but the maid told her that she had just discovered a great chest filled with gold dresses, studded with diamonds. Beauty was grateful to the good Beast for his attention. She selected the plainest of the gowns and told the maid to pack up the others, so she might send them as presents to her sisters. She had hardly finished speaking when the chest disappeared. Her father told her that he thought the Beast must wish her to keep them all for herself, and in an instant, dresses and chest returned to where they had just been.

While Beauty was dressing, she learned that her sisters had been summoned and had arrived with their husbands. Both were very miserable. The eldest had married a most handsome gentleman, but he was so in love with his own good looks that he admired himself from morning 'til night. The second married a man of wit, but he used it only to insult everybody, his wife first and foremost. The sisters were sick with envy when they saw their sister dressed like a princess, more beautiful than the dawn. In spite of her caresses, they could not hide their envy, and it grew worse when she told them how happy she was. The jealous pair descended into the garden weeping bitterly.

"Why should this little creature be happier than we are? Are we not more agreeable than she?"

"Sister," said the elder, "I have a plan. Let us try to detain her longer than the eight days. Her stupid Beast will be so enraged at her for having broken her word, that he will very likely devour her."

"You are right, sister," said the other. "Therefore, we must show her as much kindness as possible if we wish the plan to succeed."

Having decided on this plot, they returned to the house and made a great fuss over Beauty. When the eight days had passed, the two sisters tore their hair and made such a dreadful scene at her departure that she promised to remain eight more days with them.

At the same time, Beauty reproached herself for the grief she was causing her poor Beast, whom she cared for with all her heart. She longed to see him again. On the tenth night of her stay in her father's house, she dreamed she was in the castle garden, where she saw the Beast lying on the grass, nearly dead, reproaching her for her ingratitude. Beauty woke with a start, and burst into tears.

"Am I not very wicked to cause so much grief to a Beast who has shown me so much kindness? Is it his fault that he is so ugly, and has so little wit? He is good, and that is worth more than the rest. Why did I not wish to marry him? I should be happier with him than my sisters are with their husbands. It is neither beauty nor wit in a husband that makes a woman happy; it is goodness of character, virtue, kindness; and the Beast has all of these qualities. It is true that I do not love him; but he has my esteem, friendship and respect. I must not make him miserable or I shall regret it all my life."

With these words, Beauty lay her ring on the table. No sooner had she returned to her bed than she was fast asleep. When she awoke the next morning she saw with joy that she was in the Beast's castle. She dressed in her very best to please him, and nearly died of impatience the entire day, waiting for nine o'clock that evening. When the hour struck the Beast did not appear. Fearing she had caused his death, Beauty ran throughout the castle in despair. She searched everywhere for him. At last, recalling her dream, she ran to the garden near the canal. There she found the poor Beast unconscious. Thinking him dead, and forgetting her horror, she threw herself on his body. Finding his heart still beating, she took some water from the canal and poured it on his face.

The beast opened his eyes.

"You forgot your promise," he whispered. "The grief I felt at your loss made me resolve to die of hunger; but I die content since I have the pleasure of seeing you again."

"No, my Beast, you shall not die," said Beauty. "Live and be my husband. From this moment, I give you my hand and swear to be yours alone. Alas, I thought I felt only friendship for you, but the grief I feel convinces me that I cannot live without you."

Beauty had scarcely pronounced these words when the castle suddenly sparkled with lights. Fireworks, music—everything proclaimed a great event; but all these splendors were lost on her. She turned toward her dear

Beast, still trembling for his danger. What a surprise she had! The Beast had vanished, and she saw at her feet a prince, who thanked her for having ended his enchantment. Though this prince commanded her full attention, she could not keep from asking what had become of the Beast.

"You see him at your feet," said the prince. "An evil fairy condemned me to retain that form until a beautiful girl should consent to marry me, and she forbade me to betray any sign of wit. In the whole world, only you were generous enough to be moved by the goodness of my character. In offering you my crown, I cannot discharge the obligation I owe you."

Beauty, happily surprised, gave her hand to the prince and helped him rise. Together they went to the castle, and Beauty was overjoyed to find that her father and all her family had been brought to the great hall by the beautiful lady in her dream.

"Beauty," said this lady, who was a fairy, "come and receive the reward of your noble choice. You preferred virtue to beauty and wit and you surely deserve to find all these qualities in one person. You shall become a great queen. I hope that the throne will not diminish your virtues. As for you, ladies," she said to Beauty's two sisters, "I know your hearts and the malice they contain. You shall become two statues, retaining all your feelings under the stone which envelops you. You shall stand before the gates of your sister's castle, for I can think of no greater punishment than for you to witness her happiness. You shall not return to your former state until you recognize your faults. But I fear that you shall remain statues forever."

With a tap of her wand, they were all transported to the prince's kingdom, where his subjects received him joyfully. The prince married Beauty and they lived together in happiness for a very long time.

❧   Fastwrite 5

How would you describe the ideal attributes of a man today? What characteristics, attitudes, and ways of being should he possess? In what ways does Beaumont's Beast embody these characteristics? How do you think others would classify your description? Residual? Dominant? Emergent? Explain briefly.

Historical Questions

1. With specific reference to two or three passages about Beauty's family and then about the Beast, explore the perspectives about social class, economic class, and general behavior that you think the story portrays. Which perspectives does it approve of? Reflect back to the situations and styles of life

described in a previous version. With two or three explicit references, explore how Beaumont's treatment of social class, economic class, and behavior compares with one of the other versions you have read. How do you react to this particular strand of the story's evolution?

2. Compare and contrast the psychological family dynamics operating in this version of the story with one of the other versions you have read. In what ways has Beauty's relationship with her father and her siblings evolved? Areas you might want to focus on in this version include: Beauty's unwillingness to leave home and marry; her devotion to her father; her relationship her sisters; her family's overall role in leading her to marry the Beast.

3. In Beaumont's adaptation, as in all of the versions included in this chapter thus far, the heroine displays attributes that move in two contradictory directions: courage, which suggests strength of will and independence, and, contradictorily, a capacity for self-sacrifice and submission to the will of others. In this version, for example, Beauty offers to go to the Beast to save her father's life, demonstrating courage and submission in the same action. Trace the evolution of these two sides of Beauty's character in two or three versions presented in the chapter so far. Do you think, for example, that she becomes more courageous with each version? More submissive and self-sacrificing? More contradictory? Develop your position with specific references to each of the texts. Then briefly explore, with one contemporary example, how the particular pattern of Beauty's evolution that you have charted out relates to roles women are expected to play today.

Cultural Questions

1. This is the first version of *Beauty and the Beast* in this chapter in which the female character does not become intimate with or marry the Beast almost immediately after meeting him. Much of the story, in fact, revolves around his repeated marriage requests and her refusal. One obvious reason for the difference in her reaction is that the Beast in this version does not turn into a man at night. So, in terms of the plot, her reaction to him is understandable. Yet, from a symptomatic standpoint, it is useful to explore why this change in the plot line of the story might have occurred in the first place. Focusing on two to three specific passages, explore what larger social concerns and anxieties about marriage and sexual passion might be being addressed by a plot line in which the Beast's princely form is not revealed until the end of the story.

2. "The grief I felt at your loss made me resolve to die of hunger; but I die content since I have the pleasure of seeing you again." With specific references to some of the many men in this story—the Beast, the father, the brothers, the suitors, and the sisters' husbands—explore the representations

of men's emotions and concerns in this version of *Beauty and the Beast*. What, literally, are the concerns of these different men? What range of attributes do they exhibit? Which of these attributes does the text encourage the reader to approve of? Which is it critical of? Then, focusing on what you think are two or three of the most important characteristics of men in this version, explore what some of the larger social issues, concerns, and practices may have been at the time the story was written that could have influenced the author to create these particular representations of men.

3. Read the story symptomatically to determine who its intended reader might be. As specifically as possible, give a profile of the reader's age, gender, and social class by demonstrating how three to four particular passages of the story address this person's (or this person's parents') concerns. As one way to answer this question, try assuming the voice and beliefs of Beaumont. Try writing an advice column for an eighteenth-century magazine addressing young women's or young men's concerns about love and marriage. Using the directions below as a starting-off point, try writing this first for young women and then for young men. Who does it seem to fit best? Why?

Instruct young women or young men in what characteristics to look for in a spouse. What should they expect from their spouse? Explain proper and improper behavior for the young person both during and after courtship. Explain what characteristics the opposite sex is looking for and will most admire in them and what they should expect from marriage.

BRUNO BETTELHEIM

Resolution and Restoration in Beauty and the Beast (1975)

The Uses of Enchantment: The Meaning and Importance of Fairy Tales, from which this selection is taken, was written in 1975 by Bruno Bettelheim (1903–1990), a well-known child psychiatrist. The book was widely read and applauded at that time. Prior to its publication, some people had voiced concerns about the impact of violence on children reading Grimm's fairy tales. Bettelheim challenged that concern by taking the position that reading these tales helps children to mature psychologically. In his book he explains that, as in "violent" play therapy, children subconsciously identify with the plights of the characters and assuage their own anxieties, aggression, and desires by witnessing the resolution of these emotions in others. Bettelheim's theory continues to create much debate and controversy among critics.

Figure 4.5. Beauty and Beast by Jean Cocteau, 1946.

No other well-known fairy tale makes it as obvious as "Beauty and the Beast" that a child's oedipal attachment to a parent is natural, desirable, and has the most positive consequences for all, if during the process of maturation it is transferred and transformed as it becomes detached from the parent and concentrated on the lover. Our oedipal attachments, far from being only the source of our greatest emotional difficulties (which they can be when they do not undergo proper development during our growing up), are the soil out of which permanent happiness grows if we experience the right evolution and resolution of these feelings.

This story suggests Beauty's oedipal attachment to her father not only by her asking him for a rose, but also by our being told in detail how her sisters went out enjoying themselves at parties and having lovers while Beauty always stayed home and told those who courted her that she was too young to marry and wanted "to stay with her father a few years longer." Since Beauty joins the Beast only out of love for her father, she wishes to have an asexual relation with it.

The Beast's palace in which all of Beauty's wishes are immediately fulfilled, . . . is a narcissistic fantasy typically engaged in by children. It is a rare child who has not at some time wished for an existence where nothing is demanded of him and all of his desires are met as soon as he expresses them. The fairy story tells that such a life, far from being satisfying, soon becomes empty and boring—so much so that Beauty comes to look forward to the evening visits of the Beast, which at first she dreaded.

If nothing happened to interrupt such a narcissistic dream life, there would be no story; narcissism, the fairy tale teaches, despite its seeming attractiveness, is not a life of satisfactions, but no life at all. Beauty comes to life when she learns that her father needs her. In some versions of the tale he has fallen seriously ill; in others he pines away for her, or in some other way is in great distress. This knowledge shatters Beauty's narcissistic non-existence; she begins to act and then she—and the story—come to life again.

Thrown into a conflict between her love for her father and the Beast's needs, Beauty deserts the beast to attend her father. But then she realizes how much she loves the Beast—a symbol of the loosening of ties to her father and transference of her love to the Beast. Only after Beauty decides to leave her father's house to be reunited with the Beast—that is, after she has resolved her oedipal ties to her father—does sex, which before was repugnant, become beautiful.

This foreshadows by centuries the Freudian view that sex must be experienced by the child as disgusting as long as his sexual longings are attached to his parent, because only through such a negative attitude toward sex can the incest taboo, and with it the stability of the human family, remain secure. But once detached from the parent and directed to a partner of more suitable age, in normal development, sexual longings no longer seem beastly—to the contrary, they are experienced as beautiful.

"Beauty and the Beast," in illustrating the positive aspects of a child's oedipal attachment while showing what must happen to it as he grows up, well deserves the praise Iona and Peter Opie bestow on it in their survey of *The Classic Fairy Tales*. They call it "the most symbolic of the fairy tales after Cinderella, and the most satisfying."

"Beauty and the Beast" begins with an immature view which posits man to have a dual existence as animal and as mind—symbolized by Beauty. In the process of maturation, these artificially isolated aspects of our humanity must become unified; that alone permits us to attain complete human fulfillment. In "Beauty and the Beast" there are no longer any sexual secrets which must remain unknown, the discovery of which necessitates a long and difficult voyage of self-discovery before the happy ending can be gained. On the contrary, in "Beauty and the Beast" there are no hidden secrets, and it is highly desirable that the Beast's true nature be revealed. Finding out what the Beast is really like or, to put it more correctly, what a kind and loving person he really is, leads right to the happy ending. The story's essence is not just the growth of Beauty's love for the Beast, or even her transferring her love for her father to the Beast, but her own growth in the process. From believing that she must choose between her love for her father and her love for the Beast, Beauty moves to the happy discovery that seeing these two loves in opposition is an immature view of things. By transferring her original oedipal love for her father to her future husband, Beauty gives her father the kind of affection most beneficial to him. This restores his failing health and provides him with a happy life in proximity to his beloved daughter. It also restores the Beast to his humanity, and then a life of marital bliss for him and Beauty becomes possible.

The marriage of Beauty to the former Beast is a symbolic expression of the healing of the pernicious break between the animal and the higher aspects of man—a separation which is described as a sickness, since, when separated from Beauty and what she symbolizes, first her father and then the Beast nearly die. It is also the end point of an evolution from a self-centered, immature (phallic-aggressive-destructive) sexuality to one that finds its fulfillment in a human relation of deep devotion: the Beast is about to die because of the separation from Beauty, who is both the beloved female and Psyche, our soul. This is an evolution from a primitive selfish-aggressive sexuality to one which finds its fulfillment as part of a loving relation freely engaged in. That is why the Beast accepts Beauty's substitution for her father only after she assures it that she voluntarily takes his place, and why it asks her repeatedly to marry it, but accepts without recrimination her rejection and makes no move toward her before she spontaneously declares her love for it.

Translating the poetic language of the fairy tale into the pedestrian language of psychoanalysis, the marriage of Beauty and the Beast is the humanization and socialization of the id by the superego. How apt, then, that in "Cupid and Psyche" the offspring of this union is Pleasure or Joy, an ego that provides us with the satisfactions we need for a good life. The fairy tale, unlike the myth, doesn't need to spell out the benefits of the union of the two protagonists. It uses a more impressive image: a world where the good live in happiness, and the evil ones—the sisters—are not beyond redemption . . . .

∾   **Fastwrite 6**

What is your predominant response to Bettelheim's position? How does reading *Beauty and the Beast* with Bettelheim's theory in mind affect the perspective on the story that you developed when you first began this chapter?

Historical Questions

1. According to Bettelheim, "Beauty deserts the Beast to attend her father. But then she realizes how much she loves the Beast—a symbol of the loosening of ties to her father and transference of her love to the Beast." Describe and analyze Bettelheim's assumptions about the anxiety of an adolescent—particularly a female—about breaking from the opposite-sexed parent and entering a sexual relationship. Then, with specific reference to different versions you have read, describe one or two instances in which the story line confirms Bettelheim's assumptions and one or two instances in which his assumptions could be challenged. Briefly sketch out a view of female sexuality presented in one of the versions that challenges Bettelheim's view. Do you prefer Bettelheim's version or the one you have articulated that challenges it? Why?

2. According to Bettelheim, the beastliness of the Beast is a manifestation of Beauty's negative attitude toward sex, which, he contends, is necessary to maintain the incest taboo until a child is ready to transfer her love to a person outside the family. For Bettelheim, the Beast is not literally a beast but is a symptom of Beauty's feelings about her sexuality. With reference to some of the different versions you have read, discuss two to three positive and two to three negative implications of reading the Beast as a manifestation of Beauty's fears rather than as either a literal beast or a manifestation of something else.

3. Bettelheim does not directly address the development of male sexuality, but theoretically the same points hold—a young man must separate from his mother to enter into a healthy sexual relationship with another woman. "Cupid and Psyche" presents a fairly developed depiction of Cupid's relationship with his mother, Venus. Following Bettelheim, develop a psychoanalytic reading of Cupid's sexual maturation over the course of the story that would parallel the reading Bettelheim develops of Beauty. Be sure to take into account such details as Cupid's devotion to his mother, his not allowing Psyche to look at him, his appearing to her only at night, and his conferring with Jupiter. Then think back to your first response to "Cupid and Psyche" and compare it to your reading of the story from Bettelheim's perspective. In what ways does Bettelheim's perspective change your initial response? In what ways does your initial response affect your use of Bettelheim?

Cultural Questions

1. Develop a symptomatic reading of Bettelheim's position. What are his explicit assumptions? What assumptions are unstated but nonetheless taken for granted about *Beauty and the Beast*? About male and female behavior and sexuality? In what ways do his views work to challenge dominant ideas about gender roles and sexuality today? In what ways do they work to confirm them? Develop your analysis of Bettelheim with two to three contemporary examples.

2. What assumptions does Bettelheim make about the universality of "narcissistic fantasies"? Are these universal or do you think they vary from individual to individual or over time? With specific reference to two different versions of the fairy tale you have read and to your own experience, analyze the "narcissistic fantasies" of various characters as well as some of your own childhood narcissistic fantasies. To what extent do these fantasies seem to depend on such cultural factors as gender, social and economic class, age, and moral values? To what extent do these fantasies transcend the social and enter the "universal" realm? What are some of the implications of arguing that such fantasies are socially produced or that they are universal?

JACK ZIPES

Beauty and the Beast: *A Lesson in Submission* (1994)

Jack Zipes (b. 1937) is a professor of German at the University of Florida and a writer and lecturer on fairy tales. His books, *Breaking the Magic Spell: Radical Theories of Folk and Fairy Tales* (1979) and *Fairy Tale as Myth/Myth as Fairy Tale* (1994), focus on the relationship of fairy tales to the social and political conditions of the culture that produced them. He argues that fairy tales not only reflect the values and beliefs of a culture, but also often perpetuate dominant values and beliefs through explicit or implicit assumptions and messages. The following is extracted from *Fairy Tale as Myth/Myth as Fairly Tale.*

Up through 1700, there was no literary fairy tale for children. On the contrary, children like their parents *heard* oral tales from their governesses, servants, and peers. The institutionalizing of the literary fairy tale, begun in the salons during the seventeenth century, was for adults and arose out of a need by aristocratic women to elaborate and conceive other alternatives in society than those prescribed for them by men. The fairy tale was used in refined discourse as a means through which women imagined their lives might be improved. As this discourse became regularized and accepted among women and slowly by men, it served as the basis for a literary mode that was received largely by members of the aristocracy and haute bourgeoisie. This reception was collective and social, and gradually the tales were changed to introduce morals to children that emphasized the enforcement of a patriarchal code of *civilité* to the detriment of women, even though women were originally the major writers of the tales. This code was also intended to be learned first and foremost by children of the upper classes, for the literary fairy tale's function excluded the majority of children who could not read and were dependent on oral transmission of tales.

Most scholars generally agree that the *literary* development of the children's fairy tale *Beauty and the Beast*, conceived by Madame Le Prince de Beaumont in 1756 as part of *Le Magasin des Enfants*, translated into English in 1761 as *The Young Misses Magazine Containing Dialogues between a Governess and Several Young Ladies of Quality, Her Scholars*, owes its origins to the Roman writer Apuleius, who published the tale of *Cupid and Psyche* in *The Golden Ass* in the middle of the second century A.D. . . . [1]

Madame Le Prince de Beaumont did an excellent job of condensing and altering the tale in 1756 to address a group of young misses, who were supposed to learn how to become ladies. In effect, the code of the tale was to delude them into believing that they would be realizing their goals in life by denying themselves.

This theme of self-denial, which had very little to do with the female autonomy aristocratic women had sought in the seventeenth century, is closely connected to the *changing* social function of the fairy tale and its inclusion of tales written explicitly for children. First of all, it should be noted once again that the origins of the fairy tale for children can . . . be associated . . . with the change in the institution of the fairy tale created by women. As we have seen, the fairy tale served the social function of representation in aristocratic circles in the latter half of the seventeenth century. During the first part of the eighteenth century, the fairy tale was

---

1. For the most complete history of this development, see Betsy Hearne, *Beauty and the Beast: Visions and Revisions of an Old Tale* (Chicago: University of Chicago Press, 1989). I have also commented on this development in my book *Fairy Tales and the Art of Subversion* (London: Heinemann, 1983), 32–44.

separated from its representative function and became more an artwork that depicted the possibilities for self-realization and was intended mainly for reading audiences of the aristocracy and bourgeoisie. At the same time, writers began to introduce didactic tales and fairy tales with strong messages for children in primers and collections intended for young audiences of the aristocracy and bourgeoisie.

With regard to the "origins" of the fairy tale for children, it is practically impossible to give an exact date, but it is more than likely that, given the shifts in the institution of the fairty tale itself, the fairy tale for children arose in the 1720s and 1730s through the distribution of chapbooks for a broad audience including children. Madame Le Prince de Beaumont's tale was highly unusual because it was one of the first fairy tales, if not the first, written expressly for children, and we must not forget that it was also first published within a book that has a governess tell different kinds of lessons and tales to a group of girls in her charge. Madame Le Prince de Beaumont herself was a governess in London during the time she wrote her book, and she based its structure on the way she organized the day that she spent with her wards. As Patricia Clancy has pointed out,

> she put into practice and perfected many of Fénelon's recommendations on teaching girls. But Fénelon never realised the connection between moral and intellectual education, and mme de Beaumont was thus more ambitious for their minds than he. The lessons were pleasantly interspersed with a good deal of teataking and the atmosphere was friendly, even intimate. Her method of teaching was based on free debate and gentle persuasion, which nevertheless did not always avoid some clash of wills. They usually began with one of her fairy tales from which she extrapolated a moral through elaboration and questions, then proceeded to a practical demonstration of physics, history, or geography, or else a commentary on a passage from the Old Testament.[2]

Clearly, there is a shift in the social function of the literary fairy tale as it began to be scripted for children: it was to instruct in an amusing way and was now received by children of the upper classes in the home where lessons were taught by private tutors or by governesses. Moreover, some of the fairy tales were evidently used in schools or in schooling the children of the upper classes. That boys were to be treated differently than girls is apparent from the structure and contents of Madame de Beaumont's book, or in other words, *Beauty and the Beast* originated as a sexspecific tale intended to inculcate a sense of good manners in little girls.

---

2. "A French Writer and Educator in England: Mme Le Prince de Beaumont," *Studies on Voltaire and the Eighteenth Century* 201 (1982): 201–2.

What is this good sense? The sense to sacrifice one's life for the mistakes of one's father, learn to love an ugly beastman if he is kind and has manners, keep one's pledge to a beast, no matter what the consequences may be. When confronted by her sisters, who accuse her for not being concerned about her father who is sentenced to death for picking a rose, Beauty responds: "Why should I lament my father's death when he is not going to perish? Since the monster is willing to accept one of his daughters, I intend to offer myself to placate his fury, and I feel very fortunate to be in a position to save my father and prove my affection for him." [3]

Beauty is selfless, and perhaps that is why she has no name. She is nameless. All girls are supposed to become "beauties," i.e., selfless and nameless. There is a false power attributed to Beauty as a virtue. By sacrificing oneself, it is demonstrated, the powers that be, here the fairies, will reward her with a perfect husband. The most important thing is to learn to obey and worship one's father (authority) and to fulfill one's promises even though they are made under duress. Ugliness is associated with bad manners like those of her sisters. The beast is not ugly because his manners are perfect. Beauty and the Beast are suited for one another because they live according to the code of civility. They subscribe to prescriptions that maintain the power of an elite class and patriarchal rule.

Madame Le Prince de Beaumont's classic fairy tale enables us to see key features of how the fairy tale was institutionalized for children. The framing conditions of this institutionalization are: (1) the social function of the fairy tale must be didactic and teach a lesson that corroborates the code of civility as it was being developed at that time; (2) it must be short so that children can remember and memorize it and so that both adults and children can repeat it orally; this was the way that many written tales worked their way back into the oral tradition; (3) it must pass the censorship of adults so that it can be easily circulated; (4) it must address social issues such as obligation, sex roles, class differences, power, and decorum so that it will appeal to adults, especially those who publish and publicize the tales; (5) it must be suitable to be used with children in a schooling situation; and (6) it must reinforce a notion of power within the children of the upper classes and suggest ways for them to maintain power.

Of course, there is a more positive reading of *Beauty and the Beast* and the role it played in the institutionalization of the fairy tale. In her day, Madame Le Prince de Beaumont was a progressive thinker who contributed a great deal to raising the esteem of girls and women in England and France. Patricia Clancy explains that "Mme le Prince de Beaumont

---

3. "Beauty and the Beast" in *Beauties, Beasts and Enchantment: Classic French Fairy Tales*, trs. Jack Zipes (New York: NAL, 1989), 237.

would by no means have been considered a radical in her own country, yet what she saw and experienced in England fired her with a reforming zeal for both the status and the education of women in society. With her as with most other feminist reformers, the two went hand in hand, and she never ceased to deplore the fact that men denied women education which would make them virtuous, then reviled them for their moral shortcomings."[4] Her primary goal in writing *Beauty and the Beast* was to celebrate the virtuous behavior of her heroine, who courageously chooses to sacrifice herself for the sake of her father. But Beauty's actions give rise to a certain ambivalence that undermines the intentions of Madame Le Prince de Beaumont: Beauty can be admired for her courage and simultaneously deprecated for submitting to the will of two men, her father and the beast. It would seem that she actually seeks to be dominated and to be praised for her submission as a virtuous and courageous act.

Beauty's ambivalent position can be attributed to Madame Le Prince de Beaumont's own ambivalence as reformer who did not want to alter the structure of the family or society and yet wanted to improve the status of women. Therefore, Madame Le Prince de Beaumont rationalized her own compromising role and the submission of women as female desire in her fairy tale. This rationalization of desire is what makes *Beauty and the Beast* so powerful and explains how her version assumed mythic proportions in the eighteenth century and continues to exercise such a compelling appeal up to the present. . . .

If we look . . . at Madame Le Prince de Beaumont's version of *Beauty and the Beast* in relation to the Oedipus complex and how girls were socialized to desire domination and boys to dominate, we must begin with the fact that Beauty is already in bonds or bonded by the time that we are introduced to her. She lives in a master/slave relationship with her father and accepts all his decisions without question, for he is the ultimate male authority. She has no other model or option because the mother is conveniently dead, wiped out, effaced. In fact, Beauty has already become a type of *Ersatz*-mother, and because of her *willingness* to be dominated and to serve, she is easily exploited by the father.

It is because of Beauty's desire to please the father that she does not hesitate to sacrifice herself to the Beast. In other words, it is not a great step for Beauty to move to the Beast's castle because she is merely exchanging one master for another. What is difficult is the adjustment to the new surroundings and the face of the new master. Once she learns that she can be comfortable in the new surroundings, she is willing to give up her father. In effect, she is placated and pacified because her "new" life, which is really

---

4. "A French writer and Educator in England: Mme Le Prince de Beaumont," 198.

not so new, will be richer and more comfortable. But her position will not be much different, for she is to be the nurturer, the one who sacrifices her body for the desire of the Beast. It is the Beast who *wants* her. She must learn that his desire is her desire just as she had learned that her father's desire was her desire. We are left then with Beauty as an exemplary figure who predicates all her desires on how she can please men, and all this seems reasonable, for they apparently cannot live without her.

Yet, this conclusion is all illusion, for her identity is determined by them. Her function in life is predetermined. Beauty must learn to tame her own desires to fit a male civilizing code in such a way that she appears to be the agent of her own desires. However, in complying with the Beast's desire, she is complying with her father and the socio-psychological pre-scriptives that promise rewards for masochistic behavior. The reward is a move up the social ladder: Beauty comes from the mercantile class and will be symbolically ennobled by marrying the Beast/prince. But her noble action, self-sacrifice for father and Beast, will only strengthen the bonds of domination that will constrain her for the rest of her life. Moreover, it should be stressed that the Beast is also portrayed in a stereotypical "oedi-pal" manner that rationalizes his will/desire to dominate. Why must he have a virginal daughter to compensate for the father's trespass? Why must he manipulate her to rescue him? Why does he have to be the provider, the keeper of her castle? Why can't he find a way to nurture himself from within? The fact is—if we can speak about facts—Beast's desires have also been scripted or pre-scripted, for he ostensibly knows no other way to win a woman than through power and emotional blackmail. The Beast must play upon preconditioned sentiments in Beauty to feel fulfilled and to become whole as the transformed prince born to rule.

In most of the standard illustrations of *Beauty and the Beast,* Beauty is depicted as compassionate, kind, and considerate. It is through her great compassion and her selfdenial that she assumes heroic proportions. The key image in most of the illustrated versions of Madame Le Prince de Beaumont's tale from the eighteenth century to the present reveal Beauty, full of pity leaning over some enormous furry creature or cuddling a freak-ish monster. What is interesting in all these illustrations is that they also bring out what boys are socialized to expect from young women: total abandonment, nurturing, mercy, obedience, responsibility. No matter what the male/beast is portrayed to resemble—and the imaginations of artists have drawn great pleasure in conceiving the most outlandish creatures imaginable—the female is supposed to curb her disgust and learn to love the Beast for his dignity and power. Or she is supposed to learn to love her chains and bonds. The illustrations in most books generally underline the thesis that the male is a beast despite his noble sentiments and can change with a submissive and tender wife. Males are not supposed to find the tenderness and compassion within themselves; they obtain such sustenance through emotional blackmail and manipulation.

The sentimental if not melodramatic scene of Beauty holding and seemingly rescuing the Beast at the end of the tale is a picture that has been impressed upon our imagination and scripted in thousands of books since Madame Le Prince de Beaumont printed her story in 1756. It was almost immediately frozen as a myth because it complied so "beautifully" with the prescriptions and desires of the male middle class that was solidifying its power in Europe and North America. Fairy tales do not become mythic unless they are in almost perfect accord with the underlying principles of how the male members of society seek to arrange object relations to satisfy their wants and needs. The fairy tales must seem natural and celebrate submission by the opposite sex or the dominated so that the dominated can feel the beauty of their actions.

This is not to say that the dominant pattern and constellation of the fairy tale, frozen as myth, has not been questioned or subverted. Betsy Hearne has pointed to the numerous endeavors by gifted writers and illustrators to suggest alternatives to the rationalization of female submission in the tale. For instance, Albert Smith wrote a mock verse rendition of *Beauty and the Beast* (1853),[5] in which the tone and style of the poem undermined the traditional message of the tale. Even more subversive was Guy Wetmore Carryl's poem, "How Beauty Contrived to Get Square with the Beast," (1902).[6] Here the gambling father, John Jeremy Platt, loses a large amount of money in a card game and obliges his daughter, the beautiful Guinevere, to marry F. Ferdinand Fife, coarse, excessively fat, and rich, to save her father from disgrace. However, the clever and feisty Guinevere drives Ferdinand bonkers and eventually to his death. Over seventy years later, Angela Carter picked up the notion of the decadent father in *The Tiger's Bride* (1979)[7] and elaborated it in a brilliant and unique manner that depicted the mutual fulfillment of desire by two sensual individuals. In commenting on this tale, Sylvia Bryant has argued that the transformation "centers on the girl, not the beast, thus presenting a challenge to the Oedipal myth,"[8] for Carter rewrote the traditional social/sexual patterns, turning them inside out and

5. *Beauty and the Beast*, illustr. Alfred Crowquill (London: Orr, 1853).

6. In *Grimm Tales Made Gay*, illustr. Albert Levering (Boston: Houghton, Mifflin, 1902), 65–70. There is a wonderful moral to this poem that reads:

> Predicaments often are found
> That beautiful duty is apt to get round:
> But greedy extortioners better beware
> For dutiful beauty is apt to get square!

7. See *The Bloody Chamber and Other Stories* (London: Gollancz, 1979).

8. "Re-Constructing Oedipus Through 'Beauty and the Beast,'" *Criticism* 31 (Fall, 1989): 448.

against themselves to offer the possibility for mutual understanding and respect for otherness. But Carter's work should not be viewed as an isolated or exceptional achievement.

Indeed, it is not by chance that the mythic Oedipus complex came under heavy attack and careful scrutiny during the 1970s when great changes occurred in the family and socialization processes of western countries. Given the questioning of traditional roles in the family, changes at the work place, and the reshaping of stereotypical social and gender expectations, the ideological status quo of the oedipal myth has been compelled to undergo reformation. Consequently, there were many other rescriptings of the frozen mythic constellation of *Beauty and the Beast* such as Janosch's "The Singing, Springing Liontattikin" (1972),[9] Olga Broumas's "Beauty and the Beast" (1977),[10] Robin McKinley's *Beauty* (1978),[11] Sara Henderson Hay's "Sequel" (1982),[12] Tanith Lee's "Beauty" (1983),[13] Peter Redgrove's "The Rose of Leo Mann" (1989),[14] and Gwen Strauss's "The Beast" (1990).[15] All of these versions are very different from one another, but they share a questioning attitude toward the manner in which the fairy tale has become mythicized to impart stereotyped roles of gender behavior in the service of patriarchal rule.

Of course, it is important to bear in mind that they represent the extreme side of the fairy tale as institution within which a heated debate about sexuality and role models has evolved in the last three hundred years. The voices of the traditional and dominant side of the debate since Madame de Beaumont's 1756 tale have continually reproduced the oedipal mythic features to reinforce the theme of female submission and male domination. One need only look at the key versions that have marked our imaginations and served the domestication of desire to verify this tendency. Significant here are Charles Lamb's poem *Beauty and the Beast: or a Rough Outside with a Gentle Heart* (1811),[16] Walter Crane's picture book *Beauty and the Beast* (1875),[17] Andrew Lang's story of "Beauty and the Beast" in *Blue Fairy Book* (1889),[18] and Sir Arthur Quiller-Couch and Edmund

9. In *Not Quite as Grimm* (London: Abelard-Schuman, 1974).

10. In *Beginning with O* (New Haven: Yale Univ. Press, 1977).

11. *A Retelling of the Story of Beauty and the Beast* (New York: Harper and Row, 1978).

12. In *Story Hour* (Fayeteville: Univ. of Arkansas Press, 1982).

13. In *Red as Blood, or Tales of the Sisters Grimmer.* (New York: DAW, 1983).

14. In *The One Who Set Out to Study Fear* (London: Bloomsbury, 1989).

15. In *Trail of Stones* (London: Julia MacRae Books, 1990).

16. See the interesting reprint, *Beauty and the Beast*, ed. Andrew Lang (London: Leadenhall Press, 1886).

17. (London: Routledge, 1875).

18. (London: Longmans, Green and Co., 1889).

Dulac's depiction of "Beauty and the Beast" in *The Sleeping Beauty and Other Tales from the Old French* (1910).[19] All of these renditions have been reproduced countless times up to the present along with thousands of duplications of Madame Le Prince de Beaumont's version as the classical tale, as a means to show how we should script our libidinal urges.

Historical Questions

1. For Zipes, unlike Bettelheim, the Beast is not simply a manifestation of Beauty's fears, but is an all too real male figure produced by particular cultural values about gender. Zipes argues that the Beast—in his role as provider, in his desire to win Beauty, in his inability to nurture himself—is a product of a long history within European and North American culture that prescribes and constrains men's roles as well as women's. Tracing the evolution of the story in some of the versions you have read, explore whether you feel the Beast's role has become more or less stereotypical over time. What evidence do you find in various of the versions to support Zipes's position that the Beast conforms to stereotypical masculine roles? What evidence do you find in any of the versions that would modify or go against Zipes's position, suggesting, perhaps, that the Beast is a more complex character.

2. Zipes suggests in this essay and discusses more explicitly in some of his other work that fairy tales not only work to confirm dominant assumptions of a culture, but that they were initially "rooted in a historically explicable desire to overcome oppression and change society" (*Breaking* 30). These underlying subversive messages, Zipes contends, are present—often contradictorily—in most fairy tales, even those that on the surface appear to support the dominant values of a culture. Discuss two to three passages from any version of *Beauty and the Beast* in which a desire to change certain values—or even an implied critique of some dominant belief or practice— seems most apparent. In each instance, compare the weight of the subversive messages to the weight of the messages that affirm the status quo to speculate about the extent to which readers or listeners at the time might have recognized and understood the implied social critique.

3. Zipes contends that Beaumont's *Beauty* is the product of contradictory impulses within French society at the time it was written: between emergent forces, in which women were seeking greater autonomy, and dominant-residual forces, which still encouraged submission and self-denial in women. He argues that the dominant-residual theme of self-denial wins out. How do your readings of Beaumont and one or two other versions of *Beauty and the Beast* compare with Zipes's? (You might want to review

19. (London: Hodder and Stoughton, 1910).

your answer to Beaumont H3, about the balance between the heroine's courage and submission in the versions you have read.) Develop a response to Zipes, arguing with him and agreeing with him wherever you see fit. Try to address Zipes on his own terms, that is, suggest relationships between the different representations of Beauty and what you think might have been the dominant and emergent forces of the societies in which the different versions were written.

Cultural Questions

1. Zipes contends that if a fairy tale is to achieve the status of "myth" within a culture, as *Beauty and the Beast* has, it must be in "almost perfect accord" with the beliefs, and the "wants and needs" of those who are the dominant group. It must make those beliefs and needs seem both natural and attractive to its readers, even to the point of "celebrat[ing] submission" of a dominated group so that "the dominated can feel the beauty of their actions." Go back to your first fastwrite or to any of your essays that address social class or gender. How did you respond to Beauty? To the idea of her marrying the Beast? To the representation of material wealth, taste, and social graces? Did you react as Zipes says the myth wants you to? If so, why do you think you did? If not, why do you think you did not?

2. Zipes's work on *Beauty and the Beast* is situated within the historical: It analyzes different versions of the story, explores the relationship of those versions to the dominant values of the time in which they were written, and studies the effects the stories might have on their readers. Bettelheim's analysis, in contrast, is situated in the transcendent and universal: He focuses on what he argues are universals of human development—aspects of our growth that transcend time and place and that are common to all readers. These two methodologies are both well-respected, but they clearly take us in very different directions. Choose one aspect of *Beauty and the Beast* about which both Zipes and Bettelheim write—such as Beauty's decision to marry the Beast, the meaning of the Beast, or Beauty's relationship with her father—and compare and contrast not only their different positions on the subject, but what you see as the *implications* of their positions for our understanding of ourselves and for our teaching of children today. Explain which position or which aspects of each of their positions you find to be most important.

3. Use Zipes's theory to develop an analysis of two contemporary texts or situations: these can be drawn from your personal experience, a television show you have watched, a play you have seen, a book you have read, and so on. One of the examples should be within the dominant and work, as Zipes suggests, to make the oppression of a particular group seem beautiful and natural. One should go against the dominant, representing oppression as something exploitative, perhaps ugly, and wrong. With specific reference

to Zipes's essay, analyze how his theory can help to explain the different representations you are analyzing.

∾ **Fastwrite 7**

To fully work with the following article, you need to see the Disney film that Warner is reviewing. While watching the film, pay particular attention to its depiction of passion and intimacy, its representation of Belle and the Beast, its attitude toward social class, and its depiction of the character of Gaston, whom Disney introduces for the first time. When you finish viewing the film, fastwrite for ten to fifteen minutes, first about your general response to the film and then about one of the areas of focus mentioned here.

MARINA WARNER

Go! Be a Beast (1994)

Marina Warner (b. 1946), a prize-winning writer of fiction, history, and criticism, has taught in London, Ulster, Rotterdam, and Los Angeles and has lectured in many countries on the subject of female myths and symbols. She appears regularly on British radio and television. Her books include *Monuments and Maidens; The Allegory of the Female Form* (winner of the Fawcett Prize, 1986) and *The Lost Father* (nominated for the Booker Prize in 1988). *From the Beast to the Blond* (1994), from which this selection is drawn, focuses on the tellers of fairy tales, particularly those tales with "family dramas at their heart."

The cuddliness of the teddy bear, the appeal of domesticated sexuality, also informs the present trend towards celebrating the male. In Tim Burton's film *Edward Scissorhands* (1990), the outcast hero does harm, entirely inadvertently: like Frankenstein's monster, he has been made by a mad scientist but left half finished, with cutlery for hands. As a metonymy of maleness and its fumbling connection to the world of others, the scissorhands capture eloquently the idea of the redeemed male beast in current circulation. By the 1990s, the perception of the social outcast, the exile from humankind in the form of a beast, had undergone such a sea-change that any return to full human shape might have degraded rather than redeemed the hero, limited his nobility rather than restored it.

In the same year, the Disney film animation, *Beauty and the Beast*, one of the biggest box-office draws of all time, ran the risk of dramatic collapse when the Beast changed into the prince. No child in my experience preferred the sparkling candy-coloured human who emerged from the enchanted monster; the Beast had won them. Linda Woolverton and the team who collaborated on the film had clearly steeped themselves in the tale's history, on and off screen; prolonged and intense production meetings, turning over every last detail of representation and narrative, can almost be heard over the insouciant soundtrack. This fairytale film is more vividly aware of contemporary sexual politics than any made before; it consciously picked out a strand in the tale's history and deliberately developed it for an audience of mothers who grew up with Betty Friedan and Gloria Steinem, who had daughters who listened to Madonna and Sinead O'Connor. Linda Woolverton's screenplay put forward a heroine of spirit who finds romance on her own terms. Beneath this prima facie storyline, the interpretation contained many subtexts, both knotty and challenging, about changing concepts of paternal authority and rights, about permitted expressions of male desire, and prevailing notions in the quarrel about nature/nurture. Above all, the film placed before the 1990s audience Hollywood's cunning domestication of feminism itself.

Knowing as the film is, it could not avoid the trap that modern retellings set: the Beast steals the show. While the Disney version ostensibly tells the story of the feisty, strong-willed heroine, and carries the audience along on the wave of her dash, her impatient ambitions, her bravery, her self-awareness, and her integrity, the principal burden of the film's message concerns maleness, its various faces and masks, and, in the spirit of romance, it offers hope of regeneration from within the unregenerate male. The graphic intensity given to the two protagonists betrays the weight of interest: Beauty is saucer-eyed, dainty, slender, and wears a variation on the pseudo-medieval dresses of both Cinderella and Snow White, which, as in *Cinderella*, turn into *ancien régime* crinolines–cum–New Look débutante gowns for the scene of awakening love when she dances with the Beast. Her passage from repugnance to attraction also follows a movement from village hall to castle gate, in the conventional upwardly mobile style of the twentieth- century fairy tale. The animators have introduced certain emancipated touches: she is dark-haired, a book worm and walks with a swing. The script even contains a fashionable bow in the direction of self-reflexiveness, for Belle likes reading fairy tales more than any other kind of book, and consequently recognizes, when she finds herself in the Beast's castle, the type of story she is caught in.

But next to the Beast, this Belle is a lacklustre creature. He held the animators' full attention: the pneumatic signature style of Disney animation suited the Beast's character as male desire incarnate. He embodies the Eros figure as phallic toy. The Beast swells, he towers, he inflates, he tumesces. Everything about him is big, and apt to grow bigger: his castle looms, its furnishings dwarfed by its Valhalla-like dimensions. His voice thunders, his anger roars to fill the cavernous spaces of his kingdom. We are shown him enraged, crowding the screen, edge to edge, like a face in a comic strip; when he holds Belle he looks as if he could snap her between his teeth like a chicken wing. His body too appears to be constantly burgeoning; poised on narrow hooves and skimpy legs, the Disney Beast sometimes lollops like a big cat, but more often stands erect, rising to an engorged torso, with an enormous, craggy, bull-like head compacted into massive shoulders, maned and shaggy all over, bristling with fangs and horns and claws that almost seem belittled by the creature's overall bulk.

The Beast's sexual equipment was always part of his charm—hidden or otherwise (it is of course scattered by synecdoche all over his body in the Disney cartoon). When Titania fell in love with Bottom the weaver, the associations of the ass were not lost on the audience.[1] But the comic— and its concomitant, the pathetic—have almost entirely slipped away from this contemporary representation of virility.

Whereas Bottom, even in his name, was a figure of fun, and the Golden Ass, his classical progenitor, a ruefully absurd icon of (male) humanity, the contemporary vision of the Beast tends to the tragic. The new Disney Beast's nearest ancestor is the Minotaur, the hybrid offspring of Pasiphae and the bull, and an ancient nightmare of perverted lust, and it is significant that Picasso adopted the Minotaur as his alter ego, as the embodiment of his priapism, in the vigour of youth as well as the impotence of old age. But the real animal which the Disney Beast most resembles is the American buffalo, and this tightens the Beast's connections to current perceptions of natural good—for the American buffalo, like the grizzly, represents the lost innocence of the plains before man came to plunder. So the celluloid Beast's beastliness thrusts in two contradictory directions; though he is condemned for his 'animal' rages, he also epitomizes the primordial virtues of the wild.

The Beast's longstanding identity with masculine appetite nevertheless works for him rather than against him, and interacts with prevailing ideas of healthy male sexuality. The enterprise of the earlier fairytale writers, to try to define their own desires by making up stories about beasts who either denied them or fulfilled them, has been rather lost to sight. The

---

1. This passage contains a discussion of *A Midsummer Night's Dream* by William Shakespeare (ed).

vindication of the Beast has become the chief objective; the true lovableness of the good Beast the main theme. The Disney cartoon has double-knotted the lesson in contemporary ecological and sexual politics, by introducing a second beast, another suitor for Belle's love, the human hunk Gaston. Gaston is a killer—of animals—and remains one; he is a lyncher, who preys on social outcasts (suspected lunatics and marginals), he wants to breed (he promises Belle six or seven children), and he is capable of deep treachery in pursuit of his own interests. The film wastes no sympathy on Gaston—though his conceit inspires some of its cleverest and funniest lyrics.

The penalty for Gaston's brutishness is death: he falls off a high crag from the Beast's castle. In the film, he takes the part of the real beast, the Calvinist unredeemed damned beast: socially deviant in his supremacist assumptions, unsound on ecology in both directions, abusing the natural (the forest) and culture (the library). What is above all significant about this caricature is that he is a man in a man's shape, Clark Kent as played by Christopher Reeve. The Disney version is pitiless towards Gaston; self-styled heart throbs who fancy themselves Supermen are now the renegades, and wild men in touch with nature and the beast within the exemplars.

He is moreover one of the rustics whom the sophisticated Belle despises in her opening song ('I want much more than they've got planned'), an anthem for the Me-generation; this Disney, like its predecessors, does not question the assumption that the Beast's princeliness must be material and financial. His credit card, with his social status, is no doubt bigger than Gaston's, too.

In *Edward Scissorhands*, the heroine also acts quickly, with gallantry and courage, to save this outcast from a mob; but he is fatally hampered by his hybrid form, halfway between the automaton and the creaturely; his weapon hands encumber him with man-made technology and cut him off from the desirable aspects of the human, which derive from what is perceived as natural, as animal. The further the cinematic outcast lies from the machine, the more likely his redemption; the Beast as cyborg, as in the *Terminator* movies, represents the apocalyptic culmination of human ingenuity and its diabolical perversion. Whereas, to a medieval spectator, the Devil was represented as close to the animal order in his hooved hairiness, and a bloodless and fleshless angel in gleaming armour approximated the divine artefact, the register of value has been turned topsy-turvy since the eighteenth century and the wild man has come into his own as an ideal. The evolution of the Beast in fairy tale and his portraits in film illustrate this profound shift in cultural values as well as sexual expectations.

The most significant plot change to the traditional story in the Disney film concerns the role of Beauty's father, and it continues the film's trend towards granting Beauty freedom of movement and responsibility for the rescue of the Beast and for his restoration to fundamental inner goodness. The traditional fairy tale often includes the tragic motif that, in return for his life, the father promises the Beast the first thing to greet him when he returns home; as in the story of Jephthah in the Bible (Jg. 11: 12), his daughter, his youngest and most dear, rushes to the gate to meet him, and the father has to sacrifice her. In the eighteenth-century French fairy story, which focussed on the evils of matrimonial customs, the father hands over Belle to the Beast in exactly the same kind of legal and financial transaction as an arranged marriage, and she learns to accept it. Bruno Bettelheim takes a governessy line on the matter: Beauty, learning to relinquish her Oedipal attachment to her father, should be grateful to her father for giving her away and making the discovery of sexuality possible.

Linda Woolverton's script sensibly sets such patriarchal analysis aside, and instead provides subplots to explain away the father's part in Beauty's predicament, as well as supplying Beauty herself with all the wilfulness and determination to make her mistress of her own fate. The Disney studio, sensitive to the rise of children's rights, has replaced the father with the daughter as the enterprising authority figure in the family. The struggle with patriarchal plans underlies, as we shall see, the plots of many other familiar tales.

In popular versions, 'Beauty and the Beast' offers a lesson in female yielding and its satisfactions. The Beast stirs desire, Beauty responds from some deep inner need which he awakens. (There are echoes here of 'Sleeping Beauty' too.) The Beast, formerly the stigmatizing envelope of the fallen male, has become a badge of the salvation he offers; Beauty used to grapple with the material and emotional difficulties of matrimony for young women; now she tends to personify female erotic pleasures in matching and mastering a man who is dark and hairy, rough and wild, and, in the psychotherapist Robert Bly's phrase, in touch with the Inner Warrior in himself.

In her encounter with the Beast, the female protagonist meets her match, in more ways than one. If she defeats him, or even kills him, if she outwits him, banishes or forsakes him, or accepts him and loves him, she arrives at some knowledge she did not possess; his existence and the challenge he offers is necessary before she can grasp it. The ancient tale of 'Cupid and Psyche' told of their love; apart from the child Pleasure whom Psyche bore, their other descendants—the tales in the Beauty and the Beast group—number among the most eloquent testaments to women's struggles, against arranged marriage, and towards a definition of the place of sexuality in love. The enchantments and disenchantments of the Beast have been a rich resource in stories women have made up, among themselves, to help, to teach, to warn.

Historical Questions

1. Warner writes that the Disney *Beauty and the Beast* has "replaced the father with the daughter as the enterprising authority figure in the family." With specific reference to Warner's argument and to the Disney film, explore whether you agree with Warner that the role of the father is diminished in this version and that Beauty takes on a more authoritative role. Compare Warner's analysis of the father-daughter interactions in the Disney version with your own sense of them and with comparable scenes from one or two other versions, exploring some of the ways in which the evolution of the father-daughter relationship could be connected to larger social assumptions about family roles, responsibilities, or adolescent sexuality.

2. Warner contends that sexual pleasure plays a much more significant role in the Disney version than in previous versions. She sees Belle as personifying "female erotic pleasures" in "matching and mastering" the Beast, and she argues that the Beast can be seen as "male desire incarnate." Return to any essays you have written about the representations of love and passion in various versions of *Beauty and the Beast* and then compare a version of your choice with the Disney film. How does your analysis compare with Warner's? Where do you agree? Disagree? What aspects of your position might be used to change or modify Warner's? What aspects of her position might you use to modify your position? What underlying assumptions do you share with Warner? What assumptions of yours differ from hers?

3. Warner contends that Belle dismisses Gaston because of his "rustic" background and because the Beast's "credit card, with his social status, is no doubt bigger than Gaston's." Compare and contrast the assumptions underlying Warner's analysis of social class in Disney's *Beauty and the Beast* to Zipes's analysis of it in older versions. To what extent does Disney's version, in comparison to any older version of your choice, work to maintain the power of an elite class? Discuss two or three specific examples from the Disney film in developing your argument.

Cultural Questions

1. In her analysis of the Disney film, Warner states that "this fairytale film is more vividly aware of contemporary sexual politics than any made before" because it seems directed to an audience of mothers who lived through the feminist movement. What assumptions does Warner make about the film's audience and about how successfully Disney deals with contemporary feminist sexual politics? With specific reference to Warner, Zipes, and the Disney film, compare and contrast the analysis that you think Zipes would

develop of Disney's Belle with the analysis Warner develops and with your own position on how submissive or independent you think Belle is.

2. Warner suggests that the juxtaposition of Gaston and the Beast attempts to resolve a number of our tensions in America about what masculinity is and how it should be expressed: "Self-styled heart throbs who fancy themselves Supermen are now the renegades, and wild men in touch with nature and the beast within the exemplars." What assumptions has Warner made about the male side of "sexual politics," and what assumptions does she make about contemporary viewers' attitudes about the subject of masculinity? How do you respond to the representations of masculinity in the film? Develop a response to Warner's argument in which you clearly articulate what you believe are the values and concerns underlying Disney's representations of Gaston and the Beast and the most likely response of viewers to them.

3. Bettelheim interprets Belle's wishing to leave the village and her subsequent enjoyment of the rich life of the castle as an example of a fulfillment of her "narcissistic fantasies." How would Warner respond to this interpretation? How might she interpret Belle's reasons for wanting to stay at the castle? Would she find the values underlying them consistent or conflicting with the values Belle exhibits at other points in the story? Develop your own reading—in dialogue with Warner and Bettelheim—of why Belle wants to stay in the castle. In developing your own position and evaluating theirs, analyze the *implications* of their positions and of your own for the kind of understanding readers can develop of Belle's motivations.

ANGELA   CARTER

From *The Tiger's Bride* (1979)

Angela Carter (1940–1992) is an award winning writer of fiction, drama, and criticism. Her novels include *The Magic Toy Shop* (1967, winner of the John Llewellyn Rhys Prize) and *Nights at the Circus* (1985, winner of the James Tait Black Memorial Prize). She is particularly well known for her feminist fairy tales, some of which are collected in *The Bloody Chamber* (1979, Cheltenham Festival of Literature Award), from which the following selection is taken.

My father lost me to the Beast at cards. The candles dropped hot, acrid gouts of wax on my bare shoulders. I watched with the furious cynicism peculiar to women whom circumstances force mutely to witness folly, while my father, fired in his desperation by more and yet more draughts of the firewater they call "grappa," rids himself of the last scraps of my inheritance. When we left Russia, we owned black earth, blue forest with bear and wild boar, serfs, cornfields, farmyards, my beloved horses, white nights of cool summer, the fireworks of the northern lights. What a burden all those possessions must have been to him, because he laughs as if with glee as he beggars himself; he is in such a passion to donate all to the Beast.

Everyone who comes to this city must play a hand with the *grand seigneur*; few come. They did not warn us at Milan, or if they did, we did not understand them— . . .

"La Bestia" said our landlady, gingerly fingering an envelope with his huge crest of a tiger rampant on it, something of fear, something of wonder in her face. And I could not ask her why they called the master of the place "La Bestia"—was it to do with that heraldic signature?—because her tongue was so thickened by the phlegmy, bronchitic speech of the region I scarcely managed to make out a thing she said except, when she saw me: "Che bella!"

Since I could toddle, always the pretty one, with my glossy, nut-brown curls, my rosy cheeks. And born on Christmas Day—her "Christmas rose," my English nurse called me. The peasants said: "The living image of her mother," crossing themselves out of respect for the dead. My mother did not blossom long, bartered for her dowry to such a feckless sprig of the Russian nobility that she soon died of his gaming, his whoring, his agonizing repentances. And the Beast gave me the rose from his own impeccable if outmoded buttonhole when he arrived, the valet brushing the snow off his black cloak. This white rose, unnatural, out of season, that now my nervous fingers ripped, petal by petal, apart as my father magnificently concluded the career he had made of catastrophe. . . .

My senses were increasingly troubled by the fuddling perfume of Milord, far too potent a reek of purplish civet at such close quarters in so small a room. He must bathe himself in scent, soak his shirts and underlinen in it; what can he smell of, that needs so much camouflage?

I never saw a man so big look so two-dimensional, in spite of the quaint elegance of the Beast, in the old-fashioned tailcoat that might, from its looks, have been bought in those distant years before he imposed seclusion on himself; he does not feel he need keep up with the times. There is a crude clumsiness about his outlines, that are on the ungainly, giant side; and he has an odd air of self-imposed restraint, as if fighting a battle with himself to remain upright when he would far rather drop down on all fours. He throws our human aspirations to the godlike sadly awry, poor fellow; only from a distance would you think the Beast not much different from any other man, although he wears a mask with a man's face painted most beautifully on it. Oh, yes, a beautiful face; but one with too much formal symmetry of feature to be entirely human: one profile of his mask is the mirror image of the other, too perfect, uncanny. He wears a wig, too, false hair tied at the nape with a bow, a wig of the kind you see in old-fashioned portraits. A chaste silk stock stuck with a pearl hides his throat. And gloves of blond kid that are yet so huge and clumsy they do not seem to cover hands.

He is a carnival figure made of papier-mâché and crepe hair; and yet he has the Devil's knack at cards.

His masked voice echoes as from a great distance as he stoops over his hand and he had such a growling impediment in his speech that only his valet, who understands him, can interpret for him, as if his master were the clumsy doll and he the ventriloquist.

The wick slumped in the eroded wax, the candles guttered. By the time my rose had lost all its petals, my father, too, was left with nothing.

"Except the girl."

Gambling is a sickness. My father said he loved me, yet he staked his daughter on a hand of cards. He fanned them out; in the mirror, I saw wild hope light up his eyes. His collar was unfastened, his rumpled hair stood up on end, he had the anguish of a man in the last stages of debauchery. The drafts came out of the old walls and bit me; I was colder than I'd ever been in Russia, when nights are coldest there. . . .

You must not think my father valued me at less than a king's ransom; but at *no more* than a king's ransom.

It was cold as hell in the parlor. And it seemed to me, child of the severe North, that it was not my flesh but, truly, my father's soul that was in peril.

My father, of course, believed in miracles; what gambler does not? In pursuit of just such a miracle as this, had we not traveled from the land of bears and shooting stars?

So we teetered on the brink.

The Beast bayed; laid down all three remaining aces.

The indifferent servants now glided smoothly forward as on wheels to douse the candles one by one. To look at them you would think that nothing of any moment had occurred. They yawned a little resentfully; it was almost morning, we had kept them out of bed. The Beast's man brought his cloak. My father sat amongst these preparations for departure, staring on at the betrayal of his cards upon the table.

The Beast's man informed me crisply that he, the valet, would call for me and my bags tomorrow, at ten, and conduct me forthwith to the Beast's palazzo. . . .

Where my father had been red as fire, now he was white as the snow that caked the windowpane. His eyes swam; soon he would cry.

"'Like the base Indian,'" he said; he loved rhetoric. "'One whose hand,/ Like the base Indian, threw a pearl away/Richer than all his tribe . . .' I have lost my pearl, my pearl beyond price."

At that, the Beast made a sudden, dreadful noise, halfway between a growl and a roar; the candles flared. The quick valet, the prim hypocrite, interpreted unblinking: "My master says: If you are so careless of your treasures, you should expect them to be taken from you."

He gave us the bow and smile his master could not offer us and they departed.

I watched the snow until, just before dawn, it stopped falling; a hard frost settled, next morning there was a light like iron.

The Beast's carriage, of an elegant if antique design, was black as a hearse and it was drawn by a dashing black gelding who blew smoke from his nostrils and stamped upon the packed snow with enough sprightly appearance of life to give me some hope that not all the world was locked in ice, as I was. . . .

The valet sat up on the box in a natty black-and-gold livery, clasping, of all things, a bunch of his master's damned white roses as if a gift of flowers would reconcile a woman to any humiliation. He sprang down with preternatural agility to place them ceremoniously in my reluctant hand. My tear-beslobbered father wants a rose to show that I forgive him. When I break off a stem, I prick my finger and so he gets his rose all smeared with blood. . . .

I drew the curtains to conceal the sight of my father's farewell; my spite was sharp as broken glass.

Lost to the Beast! And what, I wondered, might be the exact nature of his "beastliness"? My English nurse once told me about a tiger man she saw in London, when she was a little girl, to scare me into good behavior, for I was a wild wee thing and she could not tame me into submission with a frown or the bribe of a spoonful of jam. If you don't stop plaguing the nursemaids, my beauty, the tiger man will come and take you away. They'd brought him from Sumatra, in the Indies, she said; his hinder parts were all hairy and only from the head downward did he resemble a man.

And yet the Beast goes always masked; it cannot be his face that looks like mine. . . .

But if this young lady was not a good little girl and did not eat her boiled beet root, then the tiger man would put on his big black traveling cloak lined with fur, just like your daddy's, and hire the Erlking's galloper of wind and ride through the night straight to the nursery and—

Yes, my beauty! GOBBLE YOU UP!

How I'd squeal in delighted terror, half believing her, half knowing that she teased me. And there were things I knew that I must not tell her. In our lost farmyard, where the giggling nursemaids initiated me into the mysteries of what the bull did to the cows, I heard about the wagoner's daughter. Hush, hush, don't let on to your nursie we said so; the wagoner's lass, harelipped, squint-eyed, ugly as sin, who would have taken her? Yet, to her shame, her belly swelled amid the cruel mockery of the ostlers and her son was born of a bear, they whispered. Born with a full pelt and teeth; that proved it. But when he grew up, he was a good shepherd, although he never married, lived in a hut outside the village and could make the wind blow any way he wanted to, besides being able to tell which eggs would become cocks, which hens. . . .

Old wives' tales, nursery fears! I knew well enough the reason for the trepidation I cozily titillated with superstitious marvels of my childhood on the day my childhood ended. For now my own skin was my sole capital in the world and today I'd make my first investment.

We had left the city far behind us and were now traversing a wide, flat dish of snow where the mutilated stumps of the willows flourished their ciliate heads athwart frozen ditches; mist diminished the horizon, brought down the sky until it seemed no more than a few inches above us. As far as eye could see, not one thing living. How starveling, how bereft the dead season of this spurious Eden in which all the fruit was blighted by cold! And my frail roses, already faded. I opened the carriage door and tossed the defunct bouquet into the rucked, frost-stiff mud of the road. Suddenly a sharp, freezing wind arose and pelted my face with a dry rice of powdered snow. The mist lifted sufficiently to reveal before me an acreage of half-derelict facades of sheer red brick, the vast man-trap, the megalomaniac citadel of his palazzo.

It was a world in itself but a dead one, a burned-out planet. I saw the Beast bought solitude, not luxury, with his money.

The little black horse trotted smartly through the figured bronze doors that stood open to the weather like those of a barn and the valet handed me out of the carriage onto the scarred tiles of the great hall itself, into the odorous warmth of a stable, sweet with hay, acrid with horse dung. An equine chorus of neighings and soft drummings of hooves broke out beneath the tall roof, where the beams were scabbed with last summer's swallows' nests; a dozen gracile muzzles lifted from their mangers and turned towards us, ears erect. The Beast had given his horses the use of the dining room. The walls were painted, aptly enough, with a fresco of horses, dogs and men in a wood where fruit and blossom grew on the bough together.

The valet tweaked politely at my sleeve. Milord is waiting.

Gaping doors and broken windows let the wind in everywhere. We mounted one staircase after another, our feet clopping on the marble.

Through archways and open doors I glimpsed suites of vaulted chambers opening one out of another like systems of Chinese boxes into the infinite complexity of the innards of the place. He and I and the wind were the only things stirring; and all the furniture was under dust sheets, the chandeliers bundled up in cloth, pictures taken from their hooks and propped with their faces to the walls as if their master could not bear to look at them. The palace was dismantled, as if its owner were about to move house or had never properly moved in; the Beast had chosen to live in an uninhabited place. . . .

Milord has his aerie high above the house, a small, stifling, darkened room; he keeps his shutters locked at noon. I was out of breath by the time we reached it, and returned to him the silence with which he greeted me. I will not smile. He cannot smile. . . .

The valet coughed. To him fell the delicate task of transmitting to me his master's wishes. . . .

"My master has but one desire."

The thick, rich, wild scent with which Milord had soaked himself the previous evening hangs all about us, ascends in cursive blue from the smoke hole of a precious Chinese pot.

"He wishes only—"

Now, in the face of my impassivity, the valet twittered, his ironic composure gone, for the desire of a master, however trivial, may yet sound unbearably insolent in the mouth of a servant and his role of go-between clearly caused him a good deal of embarrassment. He gulped; he swallowed, at last contrived to unleash an unpunctuated flood.

"My master's sole desire is to see the pretty young lady unclothed nude without her dress and that only for the one time after which she will be returned to her father undamaged with bankers' orders for the sum which he lost to my master at cards and also a number of fine presents such as furs, jewels and horses—"

I remained standing. During the interview, my eyes were level with those inside the mask, that now evaded mine as if, to his credit, he was ashamed of his own request even as his mouthpiece made it for him. Agitato, molto agitato, the valet wrung his white-gloved hands.

"Desnuda—"

I could scarcely believe my ears. I let out a raucous guffaw; no young lady laughs like that! my old nurse used to remonstrate. But I did. And do. At the clamor of my heartless mirth, the valet danced backward with perturbation, palpitating his fingers as if attempting to wrench them off, expostulating, wordlessly pleading. I felt that I owed it to him to make my reply in as exquisite a Tuscan as I could master.

"You may put me in a windowless room, sir, and I promise you I will pull my skirt up to my waist, ready for you. But there must be a sheet over my face, to hide it; though the sheet must be laid over me so lightly that it will not choke me. So I shall be covered completely from the waist upward, and no lights. There you can visit me once, sir, and only the once. After that I must be driven directly to the city and deposited in the public square, in front of the church. If you wish to give me money, then I should be pleased to receive it. But I must stress that you should give me only the same amount of money that you would give to any other woman in such circumstances. However, if you choose not to give me a present, then that is your right."

How pleased I was to see I struck the Beast to the heart! For, after a baker's dozen hearbeats, one single tear swelled, glittering, at the corner of the masked eye. A tear! A tear, I hoped, of shame. The tear trembled for a moment on an edge of painted bone, then tumbled down the painted cheek to fall, with an abrupt tinkle, on the tiled floor.

The valet, ticking and clucking to himself, hastily ushered me out of the room. A mauve cloud of his master's perfume billowed out into the chill corridor with us and dissipated itself on the spinning winds.

A cell had been prepared for me, a veritable cell, windowless, airless, lightless, in the viscera of the palace. The valet lit a lamp for me; a narrow bed, a dark cupboard with fruit and flowers carved on it, bulked out of the gloom.

"I shall twist a noose out of my bed linen and hang myself with it," I said.

"Oh, no," said the valet, fixing upon me wide and suddenly melancholy eyes. "Oh, no, you will not. You are a woman of honor." . . .

Time passed but I do not know how much; then the valet woke me with rolls and honey. I gestured the tray away but he set it down firmly beside the lamp and took from it a little shagreen box, which he offered to me.

I turned away my head.

"Oh, my lady!" Such hurt cracked his high-pitched voice! He dexterously unfastened the gold clasp; on a bed of crimson velvet lay a single diamond earring, perfect as a tear.

I snapped the box shut and tossed it into a corner. . . .

"Very well," said the valet, put out. And indicated it was time for me to visit my host again. He did not let me wash or comb my hair. There was so little natural light in the interior of the palace that I could not tell whether it was day or night.

You would not think the Beast had budged an inch since I last saw him; he sat in his huge chair, with his hands in his sleeves, and the heavy air never moved. I might have slept an hour, a night, or a month, but his sculptured calm, the stifling air, remained just as had been. The incense rose from the pot, still traced the same signature on the air. The same fire burned.

Take off my clothes for you, like a ballet girl? Is that all you want of me?

"The sight of a young lady's skin that no man has seen before—" stammered the valet.

I wished I'd rolled in the hay with every lad on my father's farm, to disqualify myself from this humiliating bargain. That he should want so little was the reason why I could not give it; I did not need to speak for the Beast to understand me.

A tear came from his other eye. And then he moved; he buried his cardboard carnival head with its ribboned weight of false hair in, I would say, his arms; he withdrew his, I might say, hands from his sleeves and I saw his furred pads, his excoriating claws.

The dropped tear caught upon his fur and shone. And in my room for hours I hear those paws pad back and forth outside my door.

When the valet arrived again with his silver salver, I had a pair of diamond earrings of the finest water in the world; I threw the other into the corner where the first one lay. The valet twittered with aggrieved regret, but did not offer to lead me to the Beast again. Instead, he smiled ingratiatingly and confided: "My master, he say: Invite the young lady to go riding." . . .

"I'll run away, I'll ride to the city."

"Oh, no," he said. "Are you not a woman of honor?" . . .

The doors of the hall let the bright day in; I saw that it was morning. Our horses, saddled and bridled, beasts in bondage, were waiting for us, striking sparks from the tiles with their impatient hooves while their stablemates lolled at ease among the straw, conversing with one another in the mute speech of horses. A pigeon or two, feathers puffed to keep out the cold, strutted about, pecking at ears of corn. The little black gelding who had brought me here greeted me with a ringing neigh that resonated inside the misty roof as in a sounding box and I knew he was meant for me to ride.

I always adored horses, noblest of creatures, such wounded sensitivity in their wise eyes, such rational restraint of energy at their high-strung hindquarters. I lirruped and hurumphed to my shining black companion and he acknowledged my greeting with a kiss on the forehead from his soft lips. There was a little shaggy pony nuzzling away at the *trompe l'oeil* foliage beneath the hooves of the painted horses on the wall, into whose saddle the valet sprang with a flourish as of the circus. Then the Beast, wrapped in a black fur-lined cloak, came to heave himself aloft a grave gray mare. No natural horseman he; he clung to her mane like a shipwrecked sailor to a spar.

Cold, that morning, yet dazzling with the sharp winter sunlight that wounds the retina. There was a scurrying wind about that seemed to go with us, as if the masked, immense one who did not speak carried it inside his cloak and let it out at his pleasure, for it stirred the horses' manes but did not lift the lowland mists. . . .

A profound sense of strangeness slowly began to possess me. I knew my two companions were not, in any way, as other men, the simian retainer and the master for whom he spoke, the one with clawed forepaws who was in a plot with the witches who let the winds out of their knotted handkerchiefs up towards the Finnish border. I knew they lived according to a different logic than I had done until my father abandoned me to the wild beasts by his human carelessness. This knowledge gave me a certain fearfulness still; but, I would say, not much. . . . I was a young girl, a virgin, and therefore men denied me rationality just as they denied it to all those who were not exactly like themselves, in all their unreason. . . .

We came to the bank of the river, that was so wide we could not see across it, so still with winter that it scarcely seemed to flow. The horses lowered their heads to drink. The valet cleared his throat, about to speak; we were in a place of perfect privacy, beyond a brake of winter-bare rushes, a hedge of reeds.

"If you will not let him see you without your clothes—"

I involuntarily shook my head.

"—you must, then, prepare yourself for the sight of my master, naked."

The river broke on the pebbles with a diminishing sigh. My composure deserted me; all at once I was on the brink of panic. I did not think that I could bear the sight of him, whatever he was. The mare raised her dripping muzzle and looked at me keenly, as if urging me. The river broke again at my feet. I was far from home.

"You," said the valet, "must."

When I saw how scared he was I might refuse, I nodded.

The reed bowed down in a sudden snarl of wind that brought with it a gust of the heavy odor of his disguise. The valet held out his master's cloak to screen him from me as he removed the mask. The horses stirred.

The tiger will never lie down with the lamb; he acknowledges no pact that is not reciprocal. The lamb must learn to run with the tigers.

A great, feline, tawny shape whose pelt was barred with a savage geometry of bars the color of burned wood. His domed, heavy head, so terrible he must hide it. How subtle the muscles, how profound the tread. The annihilating vehemence of his eyes, like twin suns.

I felt my breast ripped apart as if I suffered a marvelous wound.

The valet moved forward as if to cover up his master now the girl had acknowledged him, but I said: "No." The tiger sat still as a heraldic beast, in the pact he had made with his own ferocity to do me no harm. He was far larger than I could have imagined, from the poor, shabby things I'd seen once, in the Czar's menagerie at Petersburg, the golden fruit of their eyes dimming, withering in the far North of captivity. Nothing about him reminded me of humanity.

I therefore, shivering, now unfastened my jacket, to show him I would do him no harm. Yet I was clumsy and blushed a little, for no man had seen me naked and I was a proud girl. Pride it was, not shame, that thwarted my fingers so; and a certain trepidation lest this frail little article of human upholstery before him might not be, in itself, grand enough to satisfy his expectations of us, since those, for all I knew, might have grown infinite during the endless time he had been waiting. The wind clattered in the rushes, purled and eddied in the river.

I showed his grave silence my white skin, my red nipples, and the horses turned their heads to watch me also, as if they, too, were courteously curious as to the fleshly nature of women. Then the Beast lowered his massive head. Enough! said the valet with a gesture. The wind died down, all was still again.

Then they went off together, the valet on his pony, the tiger running before him like a hound, and I walked along the riverbank for a while. I felt I was at liberty for the first time in my life. Then the winter sun began to tarnish, a few flakes of snow drifted from the darkening sky, and when I returned to the horses, I found the Beast mounted again on his gray mare, cloaked and masked and once more, to all appearances, a man, while the valet had a fine catch of waterfowl dangling from his hand and the corpse of a young roebuck slung behind his saddle. I climbed up on the black gelding in silence and so we returned to the palace as the snow fell more and more heavily, obscuring the tracks that we had left behind us.

The valet did not return me to my cell but, instead, to an elegant if old-fashioned boudoir with sofas of faded pink brocade, a jinn's treasury of Oriental carpets, tintinnabulation of cut-glass chandeliers. Candles in antlered holders struck rainbows from the prismatic hearts of my diamond earrings, that lay on my new dressing table at which my attentive maid stood ready with her powder puff and mirror. Intending to fix the ornaments in my ears, I took the looking glass from her hand, but it was in the midst of one of its magic fits again and I did not see my own face in it but that of my father; at first I thought he smiled at me. Then I saw he was smiling with pure gratification.

He sat, I saw, in the parlor of our lodgings, at the very table where he had lost me, but now he was busily engaged in counting out a tremendous pile of banknotes. My father's circumstances had changed already; well-shaven, neatly barbered, smart new clothes. A frosted glass of sparkling wine sat convenient to his hand beside an ice bucket. The Beast had clearly paid cash on the nail for his glimpse of my bosom, and paid up promptly, as if it had not been a sight I might have died of showing. Then I saw my father's trunks were packed, ready for departure. Could he so easily leave me here?

There was a note on the table with the money, in a fine hand. I could read it quite clearly. "The young lady will arrive immediately." Some harlot with whom he'd briskly negotiated a liaison on the strength of his spoils? Not at all. For at that moment, the valet knocked at my door to announce that I might leave the palace at any time hereafter, and he bore over his arm a handsome sable cloak, my very own little gratuity, The Beast's morning gift, in which he proposed to pack me up and send me off.

When I looked at the mirror again, my father had disappeared and all I saw was a pale, hollow-eyed girl whom I scarcely recognized. The valet asked politely when he should prepare the carriage, as if he did not doubt that I would leave with my booty at the first opportunity. . . .

"Leave me alone," I said to the valet.

He did not need to lock the door now. I fixed the earrings in my cars. They were very heavy. Then I took off my riding habit, left it where it lay on the floor. But when I got down to my shift, my arms dropped to my sides. I was unaccustomed to nakedness. I was so unused to my own skin that to take off all my clothes involved a kind of flaying. I thought the Beast had wanted a little thing compared with what I was prepared to give him; but it is not natural for humankind to go naked, not since first we hid our loins with fig leaves. He had demanded the abominable. I felt as much atrocious pain as if I was stripping off my own underpelt. . . .

I huddled in the furs I must return to him, to keep me from the lacerating winds that raced along the corridors. I knew the way to his den without the valet to guide me.

No response to my tentative rap on his door.

Then the wind blew the valet whirling along the passage. He must have decided that if one should go naked, then all should go naked; without his livery, he revealed himself, as I had suspected, a delicate creature, covered with silken moth-gray fur, brown fingers supple as leather, chocolate muzzle, the gentlest creature in the world. He gibbered a little to see my fine furs and jewels as if I were dressed up for the opera and, with a great deal of tender ceremony, removed the sables from my shoulders. The sables thereupon resolved themselves into a pack of black, squeaking rats that rattled immediately down the stairs on their hard little feet and were lost to sight.

The valet bowed me inside the Beast's room.

The purple dressing gown, the mask, the wig, were laid out on his chair; a glove was planted on each arm. The empty house of his appearance was ready for him but he had abandoned it . . . .

A candle stuck by its own grease to the mantelpiece lit two narrow flames in the pupils of the tiger's eyes.

He was pacing backward and forward, backward and forward, the tip of his heavy tail twitching as he paced out the length and breadth of his imprisonment between the gnawed and bloody bones.

He will gobble you up.

Nursery fears made flesh and sinew; earliest and most archaic of fears, fear of devourment. . . .

He went still as stone. He was far more frightened of me than I was of him.

I squatted on the wet straw and stretched out my hand. I was now within the field of force of his golden eyes. He growled at the back of his throat, lowered his head, sank onto his forepaws, snarled, showed me his red gullet, his yellow teeth. I never moved. He snuffed the air, as if to smell my fear; he could not.

Slowly, slowly he began to drag his heavy, gleaming weight across the floor towards me.

A tremendous throbbing, as of the engine that makes the earth turn, filled the little room; he had begun to purr.

The sweet thunder of this purr shook the old walls, made the shutters batter the windows until they burst apart and let in the white light of the snowy moon. Tiles came crashing down from the roof; I heard them fall into the courtyard far below. The reverberations of his purring rocked the foundations of the house, the walls began to dance. I thought: It will all fall, everything will disintegrate.

He dragged himself closer and closer to me, until I felt the harsh velvet of his head against my hand, then a tongue, abrasive as sandpaper. "He will lick the skin off me!"

And each stroke of his tongue ripped off skin after successive skin, all the skins of a life in the world, and left behind a nascent patina of shining hairs. My earrings turned back to water and trickled down my shoulders; I shrugged the drops off my beautiful fur.

✑ Fastwrite 8

This story is consciously written with an awareness of the *Beauty and the Beast* tradition, and it breaks with it in somewhat more radical ways than the other versions you have read. Fastwrite about your predominant response to the story. Then, quickly discuss any three details of the story that particularly strike you. Why do they strike you?

Historical Questions

1. "My father lost me to the Beast at cards." Compare the representation of the father in "The Tiger's Bride" with two to three other versions of the story. Begin by analyzing the plots of the stories: How does the father lose his daughter to the Beast in other versions? What similarities and differences do you find with the way the father loses the heroine in Carter's version?

Then, focus on the language and details used to describe the father. In what ways are these similar? In what ways different? Explore the effects of Carter's language on readers familiar with other versions of the story. How do you respond to her representation of the father? Why did you react in the ways you did? Why do you think Carter portrayed him as she did? In what ways might Carter's representation of the father affect your reading of other versions of the story?

2. In many of the versions included in this chapter, the Beast makes various requests of the heroine. Yet none seem as explicitly sexual as what she is asked in "The Tiger's Bride," even though in some versions, she becomes intimate with the Beast early on in the story. Develop a symptomatic reading of La Bestia's request in "The Tiger's Bride" in which you explore it as a symptom of: (a) issues that were unarticulated but still present in one or two earlier versions; and (b) tensions or issues in sexual relationships today. For example, why does La Bestia ask to look at the heroine? Why does she find this request so shocking? Why does he show himself to her? What contemporary issues in male-female relations today might such actions be symptomatic of?

3. In the other versions we have read, the Beast is transformed into a human form. In this version, the heroine is transformed into a beast. How do you interpret this transformation, and what does it imply about the strength or submission of Carter's Beauty. Compare and contrast the interplay of the themes of female self-denial and autonomy in Carter's version with those in two other versions. Be sure to explain how (or whether) definitions of autonomy and self-denial have changed over time and what definition of these terms you are using.

4. Objects can have different meanings attached to them when they are placed in different contexts. This version of *Beauty and the Beast* has its share of treasure chests, expensive objects, lavish living quarters, and gifts from the Beast, and yet, because the Beast does not transform into a prince, these objects do not get to be used by the couple. They do not form part of Beauty's reward for loving the Beast. The only person who gains use of some of them is the heroine's father. Compare the values regarding social class imbedded in this version with two or three other versions. Then analyze the effects on you of Carter's representations of social class and wealth, exploring why the story has the effects on you that it does.

Cultural Questions

1. Zipes quotes Sylvia Bryant who argues that Carter's "The Tiger's Bride" constitutes a "challenge to the Oedipal myth," which guided Bettelheim's interpretation that the Beast is a symbol of the young girl's fear of sexuality.

Focusing on three or four specific passages from "The Tiger's Bride" and on relevant passages from Bettelheim, explore whether you think that the story does challenge the Oedipal myth. If so, explore the effects of that challenge on the reader. If not, explore how the story might confirm the myth, even while it appears to some to rewrite it.

2. Only twelve years passed between the writing of "The Tiger's Bride" and the production of Disney's *Beauty and the Beast,* and yet, in many ways, it is more different from the Disney version than stories written over two hundred years ago. Focusing on three or four aspects of the two stories, develop a cultural analysis that explores why they might be so different. Who is the audience for each of the stories? What lessons do they teach? What is their relationship to dominant, residual, and emergent notions of gender, sexuality, and marriage?

∾ Assignment Sequence 1: The Evolution of Gender Roles

Definitions of family and marriage and beliefs about gender roles and sexuality continue to be significant issues generating contemporary debate. *Beauty and the Beast,* in all its different variations, has appealed to writers and readers throughout history because it addresses these issues in ways that generally lead—at least on the surface—to a resolution of conflict, though the specific nature of the conflict and the particular resolutions have changed significantly over time. Studying the history of this fairy tale enables us to glimpse some of the historical *antecedents* of our contemporary debates about gender, the family, and sexuality, as we discover why certain social conditions in the past could have helped to produce particular positions. Such a study also enables us to glimpse some of the *implications* of the different positions we might take up as we explore what their consequences were for men and women in the past as they are played out in different versions of *Beauty and the Beast.*

Essay Question

Describe what you feel are the most significant contemporary debates about gender roles—definitions of masculinity and femininity. What views are dominant? What views are emergent? Where do you stand? Use your knowledge of the various versions of *Beauty and the Beast* to analyze the historical antecedents and implications of these debates. Then take up a position that you can defend by arguing that your position has better consequences than those of other positions. How you define "better" will be determined by your long held values and beliefs, but also should be influenced by the ideas you have developed while reading and writing about the texts in this chapter.

Review Questions

A list of suggested questions to review before beginning this essay follows. This list is meant only to suggest review options. You may focus on only a subset of the questions, decide that other questions should be added, or construct your own sequence of questions. We encourage you to choose what you believe is the most appropriate review strategy.

1. Jacob and Wilhelm Grimm, Historical Question 1 (page 212)
2. Madame le Prince de Beaumont, Historical Question 3 (page 225)
3. Madame le Prince de Beaumont, Cultural Question 2 (page 225)
4. Bruno Bettelheim, Historical Question 1 (page 230)
5. Jack Zipes, Historical Question 1 (page 239)
6. Jack Zipes, Historical Question 3 (page 239)
7. Marina Warner, Cultural Question 2 (page 247)

You may want to focus this essay on family and marriage or on sexual passions rather than on definitions of masculinity and femininity. If so, try the following review questions:

Family and Marriage

1. Lucius Apuleius, Cultural Question 1 (page 206)
2. Jacob and Wilhelm Grimm, Historical Question 2 (page 213)
3. Jacob and Wilhelm Grimm, Cultural Question 1 (page 213)
4. Madame le Prince de Beaumont, Historical Question 2 (page 225)
5. Bruno Bettelheim, Historical Question 2 (page 230)
6. Marina Warner, Historical Question 1 (page 246)
7. Angela Carter, Historical Question 1 (page 258)

Sexual Passion

1. Lucius Apuleius, Historical Question 2 (page 206)
2. Madame le Prince de Beaumont, Cultural Question 1 (page 225)
3. Bruno Bettelheim, Cultural Question 1 (page 231)
4. Marina Warner, Historical Question 2 (page 246)
5. Angela Carter, Historical Question 2 (page 259)
6. Angela Carter, Historical Question 3 (page 259)

Questions for Further Reflection

1. This section asks you to use material you have read and written on *Beauty and the Beast* to develop an argument about some aspect of contemporary

gender relations. While the general focus is gender relations, it is up to you to determine the exact focus that you want to take up. Spend some time brainstorming about gender issues that matter most to you. Do some quick fastwrites.

2. Look at the essays you have written on the various versions of *Beauty and the Beast*, focusing on areas in which you felt you developed some genuine insight, that is, you saw something by the end that you did not see at the beginning. Use these points to start developing connections between contemporary issues that matter to you and issues raised by *Beauty and the Beast*.

3. Use the knowledge you have gained from studying *Beauty and the Beast* to articulate a perspective of your own. Your knowledge is not only content knowledge, but also knowledge of a method of analysis that locates particular concerns, assumptions, conflicts, and beliefs within larger historical contexts. Apply the methods of analysis—analyzing the interplay of dominant, residual, and emergent forces, and reading symptomatically—as you develop your own argument. In this process, you will be transforming information that you have to create new knowledge that is meaningful to you; you will not simply be rehashing what you wrote before.

❧   Assignment Sequence 2: Representations of Social and Economic Class Distinctions: Responses and Implications

While fairy tales are rooted historically in a desire to change society, most tend to reinforce dominant beliefs more than they challenge them. Most of the versions of *Beauty and the Beast* encourage readers to accept social and economic class distinctions as normal and natural and to place a high value on material wealth.

Essay Question

Explore the extent to which you, as a reader of the various versions of *Beauty and the Beast*, are attracted to those elements of the story that reinforce or that work against dominant social class distinctions. Are you interested only in aspects that reinforce the dominant or only in emergent aspects? Or are you attracted, somewhat contradictorily, to some of both? What particular elements in what particular stories attract you? Particular behaviors? Lifestyles? Taste? Representations of material wealth? Explore your various responses to the different stories to look for patterns. Then, develop a symptomatic reading of your responses, exploring the antecedents of them in your own experiences—personal, familial, educational—and the implications of maintaining your pattern of responses for your interactions with people from social classes different from the one to which you belong.

Review Questions

A list of suggested questions to review before beginning this essay follows. This list is meant only to suggest review options. You may focus on only a subset of the questions, decide that other questions should be added, or construct your own sequence of questions. We encourage you to choose what you believe is the most appropriate review strategy.

1. Lucius Apuleius, Cultural Question 3 (page 207)
2. Jacob and Wilhelm Grimm, Cultural Question 2 (page 213)
3. Jacob and Wilhelm Grimm, Cutural Question 3 (page 214)
4. Madame le Prince de Beaumont, Historical Question 1 (page 224)
5. Jack Zipes, Cultural Question 1 (page 240)
6. Marina Warner, Historical Question 3 (page 246)
7. Angela Carter, Historical Question 4 (page 259)

Questions for Further Reflection

1. Look for patterns across a number of your different readings. These patterns may not be immediately obvious when you reread some of your essays. Take notes and mark up the essays you have written just the way you would mark up a text in a book to begin to sort and categorize your responses. You may need to freewrite to help you determine what it was that most interested you in a particular story and what its relationship—and yours— is to the dominant.

2. When you begin to explore the antecedents of your responses to particular elements of the story, allow yourself to move freely among as many of the factors that influence you as possible—family, friends, television and other aspects of the media, school, advertising, and so on. Keep in mind that no one is completely consistent; thus, your own social class and upbringing may not always be reflected in the aspects of the story to which you gravitate. Often, however, it is in those contradictions that the most complex symptomatic analysis can develop, so do not shy away from them.

3. Once you have analyzed as fully as you can why you have the responses that you do, explore their implications. Begin by looking at their implications within each of the versions of *Beauty and the Beast* that you are writing about. For example, which characters in which versions did you particularly like? Which did you disdain? When did you find yourself wishing that a particular event would or would not occur? When you see the implications

of particular class assumptions within the narrow constraints of a story, you begin to glimpse the possible implications they have for you in your own world. Think about interactions you have had with people whom you consider to be in a different social class from yourself. How do you regard them? How do you act toward them? What do you think about them? What patterns might you be able to detect between your responses to the different characters in *Beauty and the Beast* and your responses to people you know in different social classes? What are the possible implications of these patterns for your encounters with new people in the future?

∾

For Further Research

Other Versions of the Beauty and the Beast Tale

Arnott, Kathleen. *The Snake Chief: African Myths and Legends*. Ed. Joan Kiddell-Monroe. New York: Oxford UP, 1990.

Calvino, Italo. "Belinda and the Monster." *Italian Folktales Selected and Retold by Italo Calvino*. Trans. George Martin. New York: Harcourt, 1980.

Heath-Stubbs, John. "Beauty and the Beast." *Collected Poems, 1943–1987*. Manchester: Manchester Carcanet, 1988.

Johnson, A. E., trans. "Ricky of the Tuft." *Perrault's Complete Fairy Tales*. Illus. W. Heath Robinson. New York: Dodd, 1977.

Lynch, P. J., ill., and George Webbe Dasent. *East O' the Sun and West O' the Moon*. Cambridge, MA: Candlewick, 1995.

Mayer, Fanny Hagin. "The Monkey's Son in Law." *Ancient Tales in Modern Japan: An Anthology of Japanese Folktales*. Bloomington: Indiana UP, 1985.

Slaterd, Teddy. *Beauty and the Beast*. Adapted from the Walt Disney film. Illus, Ron Dias and Ric Gonzalez. Golden Book. Racine, WI: Western, 1991.

Critical Texts

Cocteau, Jean and Marie Leprince de Beaumont. *Beauty and the Beast: Diary of a Film*. New York: Dover, 1972.

Deacot, Jean. "Preface." *Beauty and the Beast: Scenario and Dialogues by Jean Cocteau*. Dir. Jean Cocteau. Prod. Andre Paulve. Ed and ann. by Robert M. Hammond. New York: New York UP, 1970.

Hearne, Betsy. *Beauty and the Beast: Visions and Revisions of an Old Tale*. Chicago: U of Chicago P, 1991.

Zipes, Jack. *Breaking the Magic Spell*. New York: Routledge, 1993.

———. *Don't Bet on the Prince: Contemporary Feminist Fairy Tales in North American and England*. New York: Routledge, 1989.

————. *Fairy Tales and the Art of Subversion: The Classical Genre for Children and the Process of Civilization.* New York: Routledge, 1988.

Visual Texts

Beauty and the Beast. Dir. Jean Cocteau. Home Vision, 1993.
Beauty and the Beast. Dir. Gary Trousdale, Kirk Wise. Buena Vista [Disney], 1991.
Edward Scissorhands. Dir. Tim Burton. Perf. Johnny Depp. Twentieth Century Fox, 1990.

Audio

Beauty and the Beast: Broadway Musical Soundtrack. Walt Disney Pub, 1994.

∿ 5 ∿

QUESTIONING U.S. HIGH SCHOOLS: WHAT TO TEACH AND HOW TO LEARN

Sherry Horton and Donald Jones

Schooles.
It being one chiefe project of that old deluder Sathan, to keepe men from knowledge of the Scriptures . . . [it is] ordered by this Courte and Authority thereof, that euery Towneshipp within this Juriss-diction, after the Lord hath increased them to the number of fifty householders, shall then forthwith appoint one within theire Towne to teach all such children as shall resorte to him, to read and write.
—CODE OF LAWS ESTABLISHED BY THE [CONNECTICUT] GENERAL COURT, 1650

The good Education of youth has been esteemed by wise men of all ages, as the surest foundation of the happiness both of private families and of commonwealths. . . . They [should] learn those things that are likely to be the most useful and most ornamental. [With] regard being had to the several professions for which they are intended.
—BENJAMIN FRANKLIN, 1749

[Education is the] great equalizer of the condition of men—the balance wheel of the social machinery.
—HORACE MANN, 1848

In teaching women we have two choices: to lend our weight to the forces that indoctrinate women to passivity [and] self-depreciation . . . or to consider what we have to work against, as well as with, in ourselves, in our students, in the content of the curriculum in the structure of the institution [and] in the society at large.
—ADRIENNE RICH, 1979

The great majority of American children attend schools that are largely segregated—that is, where almost all of their fellow students are of the same racial background as they are.
—JAMES COLEMAN, 1966

∽

Introduction: Why are High Schools the Way They Are?

∽ **Fastwrite 1**

Describe in detail a specific scene, either one from your actual memory or a composite picture based on several recollections, that represents a significant aspect of your high school education. Imagine your pen is a video camcorder and collect impressions of the setting, the characters, the actions and inactivity, and the sounds and the silences. What are your dominant thoughts and feelings toward your high school learning? What scene best represents these feelings? Where were you? What was (and was not) happening?

What memories came to mind when you wrote fastwrite 1? Some students talk about an exceptional teacher who inspired them. Others recount that endless last class of the day. Still others describe an average class with the activity interrupted by too many announcements, or an unusual event that taught them something about friendship, failure, or grief. As you and your classmates examine your high school experiences, whether they were recent or thirty years ago and whether you were content or critical, you begin to uncover some important issues about one area of U.S. cultural history, its schools.

Education is always a major source of debate in the U.S., both locally and nationally. Whether to open at 8:37 or 8:52 A.M., whether to desegregate schools by busing children outside their neighborhoods, whether to give school vouchers—educational issues affect everyone. And everyone has an opinion to express. Naysayers in the media spit out failures: Fourth graders don't read well enough, eighth graders perform poorly in math, and high school students can't compete with international students on standard measures like the SAT. The remedy? National standards, some say, including Bill Clinton, who made them a priority in his second term in office. The issue of national standards is partly a debate over whether there should be local or state or national control of public schools. Which type of control do you advocate? What do you think are the implications of standardized curriculum and performance testing?

Another debate is about equality of educational opportunity, which raises the spectre of bias—unequal learning opportunities based on socioeconomic status, gender, race, or ethnicity. Urban schools, with large minority populations, are said to be the worst in the country; wealthy, predominantly white suburban schools, the best. Girls are said to suffer in silence in coed classrooms. Opinions about rural

America are divided, no doubt because there is significant diversity in the quality of education students receive there. Some believe that one remedy to unequal educational opportunity is choice. What does that mean? Charter schools? Busing to integrate children, black and white, rich and poor, who then go home to different neighborhoods and perhaps very different expectations? What are the implications of these and other possibilities?

Why are high schools the way they are? Answers to particular problems and practices existing today can't be found by looking just at the current scene. Since the educational stage was set over one hundred years ago, we need to understand the past to understand the present. When and how did high schools begin? Who has determined their goals, methods, and structures, and why?

Until the end of the nineteenth century, secondary schools existed for the privileged few and were run privately as elite preparatory schools for university training in the religious, medical, and legal professions. By the turn of the century, when requests for admission to secondary schools skyrocketed, the National Education Association realized it needed to address the impact of rapid social changes in schooling, to admit more students, and to alter curriculum. Yet in a report from 1893, the merit of "new" subjects like English and French was debated, while the value of traditional courses like Greek and Latin remained unquestioned. What subjects to teach, how to teach, and whom to give access to the best schools—issues hotly debated today—also concerned Americans over one hundred years ago. The answers to these questions have differed radically depending on their cultural and historical contexts, or "the needs of the society to be served," as a 1918 report asserts. What are our most pressing needs as a society today? To help you consider possible answers to this question, explore two or three of the questions in the next fastwrite assignment.

◌ Fastwrite 2

Whether your high school experience was positive or negative, average or atypical, answer two or three of these questions. (If you wrote on fastwrite 1, you may want to focus your answers here on the experience you described there.) Figures 5.1 and 5.2 may help you to remember particular high school experiences, roles, or attitudes.

1. What were the predominant attitudes and roles of the teachers in your high school?
2. What were the predominant attitudes and roles of the students in your high school?
3. What was your predominant attitude and role in your high school?

Figure 5.1. Following traditional patterns of education.

4. What kinds of situations promoted or prevented positive learning experiences?
5. What better contribution could you or others have made to learning in your high school?

THEODORE R. SIZER

What High School Is (1984)

Theodore Sizer (b. 1932) is one of America's leading educational reformers. As the author of *Horace's Compromise: The Dilemma of the American High School* (1984) and *Horace's School: Redesigning the American High School* (1992), he has examined the goals and methods of American high schools. As chair of the Coalition of Essential Schools, Sizer has helped individual schools engage in similar self-examination and enact necessary reforms. In this first

Figure 5.2. Creating knowledge through student-centered activities.

reading, excerpted from *Horace's Compromise*, Sizer describes the daily experience of a fictional student to analyze what America's modern high schools are accomplishing and what they are not.

Mark, sixteen and a genial eleventh-grader, rides a bus to Franklin High School, arriving at 7:25. It is an Assembly Day, so the schedule is adapted to allow for a meeting of the entire school. He hangs out with his friends, first outside school and then inside, by his locker. He carries a pile of textbooks and notebooks; in all, it weighs eight and a half pounds.

From 7:30 to 8:19, with nineteen other students, he is in Room 304 for English class. The Shakespeare play being read this year by the eleventh grade is *Romeo and Juliet*. The teacher, Ms. Viola, has various students in turn take parts and read out loud. Periodically, she interrupts the (usually halting) recitations to ask whether the thread of the conversation in the play is clear. Mark is entertained by the stumbling readings of some of his classmates. He hopes he will not be asked to be Romeo, particularly if his current steady, Sally, is Juliet. There is a good deal of giggling in class, and much attention paid to who may be called on next. Ms. Viola reminds the class of a test on this part of the play to be given next week.

The bell rings at 8:19. Mark goes to the boys' room, where he sees a classmate who he thinks is a wimp but who constantly tries to be a buddy. Mark avoids the leech by rushing off. On the way, he notices two boys engaged in some sort of transaction, probably over marijuana. He pays them no attention. 8:24. Typing class. The rows of desks that embrace big office machines are almost filled before the bell. Mark is uncomfortable here: typing class is girl country. The teacher constantly threatens what to Mark is a humiliatingly female future: "Your employer won't like these erasures." The minutes during the period are spent copying a letter from a handbook onto business stationery. Mark struggles to keep from looking at his work; the teacher wants him to watch only the material from which he is copying. Mark is frustrated, uncomfortable, and scared that he will not complete his letter by the class's end, which would be embarrassing.

Nine tenths of the students present at school that day are assembled in the auditorium by the 9:18 bell. The dilatory tenth still stumble in, running down aisles. Annoyed class deans try to get the mob settled. The curtains part; the program is a concert by a student rock group. Their electronic gear flashes under the lights, and the five boys and one girl in the group work hard at being casual. Their movements on stage are studiously at three-quarter time, and they chat with one another as though the tumultuous screaming of their schoolmates were totally inaudible. The girl balances on a stool; the boys crank up the music. It is very soft rock, the sanitized lyrics surely cleared with the assistant principal. The girl sings, holding the mike close to her mouth, but can scarcely be heard. Her light voice is tentative, and the lyrics indecipherable. The guitars, amplified, are tuneful, however, and the drums are played with energy.

The students around Mark—all juniors, since they are seated by class—alternately slouch in their upholstered, hinged seats, talking to one another, or sit forward, leaning on the chair backs in front of them, watching the band. A boy near Mark shouts noisily at the microphone-fondling singer, "Bite it . . . ohhh," and the area around Mark explodes in vulgar male laughter, but quickly subsides. A teacher walks down the aisle. Songs continue, to great applause. Assembly is over at 9:46, two minutes early.

9:53 and biology class. Mark was at a different high school last year and did not take this course there as a tenth-grader. He is in it now, and all but one of his classmates are a year younger than he. He sits on the side, not taking part in the chatter that goes on after the bell. At 9:57, the public address system goes on, with the announcements of the day. After a few words from the principal ("Here's today's cheers and jeers . . ." with a cheer for the winning basketball team and a jeer for the spectators who made a ruckus at the gymnasium), the task is taken over by officers of ASB (Associated Student Bodies). There is an appeal for "bat bunnies." Carnations are for sale by the Girls' League. Miss Indian American is coming. Students are auctioning off their services (background catcalls are heard) to earn money for the prom. Nominees are needed for the ballot for school bachelor and school bachelorette. The announcements end with a "thought for the day. When you throw a little mud, you lose a little ground."

At 10:04 the biology class finally turns to science. The teacher, Mr. Robbins, has placed one of several labeled laboratory specimens—some are pinned in frames, others swim in formaldehyde—on each of the class-room's eight laboratory tables. The three or so students whose chairs circle each of these benches are to study the specimen and make notes about it or drawings of it. After a few minutes each group of three will move to another table. The teacher points out that these specimens are of organisms already studied in previous classes. He says that the period-long test set for the following day will involve observing some of these specimens— then to be without labels—and writing an identifying paragraph on each. Mr. Robbins points out that some of the printed labels ascribe the speci-mens names different from those given in the textbook. He explains that biologists often give several names to the same organism.

The class now falls to peering, writing, and quiet talking. Mr. Robbins comes over to Mark, and in whispered words asks him to carry a requisition form for science department materials to the business office. Mark, because of his "older" status, is usually chosen by Robbins for this kind of errand. Robbins gives Mark the form and a green hall pass to show to any teacher who might challenge him, on his way to the office, for being out of a classroom. The errand takes Mark four minutes. Meanwhile Mark's group is hard at work but gets to only three of the specimens before the bell rings at 10:42. As the students surge out, Robbins shouts a reminder about a "double" laboratory period on Thursday.

Between classes one of the seniors asks Mark whether he plans to be a candidate for schoolwide office next year. Mark says no. He starts to explain. The 10:47 bell rings, meaning that he is late for French class.

There are fifteen students in Monsieur Bates's language class. He hands out tests taken the day before: "C'est bien fait, Etienne . . . c'est mieux, Marie . . . Tch, tch, Robert . . ." Mark notes his C+ and peeks at the A– in front of Susanna, next to him. The class has been assigned seats by M. Bates; Mark resents sitting next to prissy, brainy Susanna. Bates starts by asking a student to read a question and give the correct answer. "James, question un." James haltingly reads the question and gives an answer that Bates, now speaking English, says is incomplete. In due course: "Mark, question cinq." Mark does his bit, and the sequence goes on, the eight quiz questions and answers filling about twenty minutes of time.

"Turn to page forty-nine. Maintenant, lisez apres moi . . ." and Bates reads a sentence and has the class echo it. Mark is embarrassed by this and mumbles with a barely audible sound. Others, like Susanna, keep the decibel count up, so Mark can hide. This I-say-you-repeat drill is interrupted once by the public address system, with an announcement about a meeting for the cheerleaders. Bates finishes the class, almost precisely at the bell, with a homework assignment. The students are to review these sentences for a brief quiz the following day. Mark takes note of the assignment, because he knows that tomorrow will be a day of busy-work in French class. Much though he dislikes oral drills, they are better than the workbook stuff that Bates hands out. Write, write, write, for Bates to throw away, Mark thinks.

11:36. Down to the cafeteria, talking noisily, hanging out, munching. Getting to Room 104 by 12:17: U.S. history. The teacher is sitting cross-legged on his desk when Mark comes in, heatedly arguing with three students over the fracas that had followed the previous night's basketball game. The teacher, Mr. Suslovic, while agreeing that the spectators from their school certainly were provoked, argues that they should neither have been so obviously obscene in yelling at the opposing cheerleaders nor have allowed Coke cans to be rolled out on the floor. The three students keep saying that "it isn't fair." Apparently they and some others had been assigned "Saturday mornings" (detentions) by the principal for the ruckus.

At 12:34, the argument appears to subside. The uninvolved students, including Mark, are in their seats, chatting amiably. Mr. Suslovic climbs off his desk and starts talking: "We've almost finished this unit, chapters nine and ten . . ." The students stop chattering among themselves and turn toward Suslovic. Several slouch down in their chairs. Some open notebooks. Most have the five-pound textbook on their desks.

Suslovic lectures on the cattle drives, from north Texas to railroads west of St. Louis. He breaks up this narrative with questions ("Why were the railroad lines laid largely east to west?"), directed at nobody in particular and eventually answered by Suslovic himself. Some students take notes. Mark doesn't. A student walks in the open door, hands Mr. Suslovic a list, and starts whispering with him. Suslovic turns from the class and hears out this messenger. He then asks, "Does anyone know where Maggie Sharp is?" Some one answers, "Sick at home"; someone else says, "I thought I saw her at lunch." Genial consternation. Finally Suslovic tells the messenger, "Sorry, we can't help you," and returns to the class: "Now, where were we?" He goes on for some minutes. The bell rings. Suslovic forgets to give the homework assignment.

1:11 and Algebra II. There is a commotion in the hallway: someone's locker is rumored to have been opened by the assistant principal and a narcotics agent. In the five-minute passing time, Mark hears the story three times and three ways. A locker had been broken into by another student. It was Mr. Gregory and a narc. It was the cops, and they did it without Gregory's knowing. Mrs. Ames, the mathematics teacher, has not heard anything about it. Several of the nineteen students try to tell her and start arguing among themselves. "O.K., that's enough." She hands out the day's problem, one sheet to each student. Mark sees with dismay that it is a single, complicated "word" problem about some train that, while traveling at 84 mph, due west, passes a car that was going due east at 55 mph. Mark struggles: Is it $d = rt$ or $t = rd$? The class becomes quiet, writing, while Mrs. Ames writes some additional, short problems on the blackboard. "Time's up." A sigh; most students still writing. A muffled "Shit." Mrs. Ames frowns. "Come on, now." She collects papers, but it takes four minutes for her to corral them all.

"Copy down the problems from the board." A minute passes. "William, try number one." William suggests an approach. Mrs. Ames corrects and cajoles, and William finally gets it right. Mark watches two kids to his right passing notes; he tries to read them, but the handwriting is illegible from his distance. He hopes he is not called on, and he isn't. Only three students are asked to puzzle out an answer. The bell rings at 2:00. Mrs. Ames shouts a homework assignment over the resulting hubbub.

Mark leaves his books in his locker. He remembers that he has homework, but figures that he can do it during English class the next day. He knows that there will be an in-class presentation of one of the *Romeo and Juliet* scenes and that he will not be in it. The teacher will not notice his homework writing, or won't do anything about it if she does.

Mark passes various friends heading toward the gym, members of the basketball teams. Like most students, Mark isn't an active school athlete. However, he is associated with the yearbook staff. Although he is not taking "Yearbook" for credit as an English course, he is contributing photographs. Mark takes twenty minutes checking into the yearbook staff's headquarters (the classroom of its faculty adviser) and getting some assignments of pictures from his boss, the senior who is the photography editor. Mark knows that if he pleases his boss and the faculty adviser, he'll take that editor's post for the next year. He'll get English credit for his work then.

After gossiping a bit with the yearbook staff, Mark will leave school by 2:35 and go home. His grocery market bagger's job is from 4:45 to 8:00, the rush hour for the store. He'll have a snack at 4:30, and his mother will save him some supper to eat at 8:30. She will ask whether he has any homework, and he'll tell her no. Tomorrow, and virtually every other tomorrow, will be the same for Mark, save for the lack of the assembly: each period then will be five minutes longer. . . .

The basic organizing structures in schools are familiar. Above all, students are grouped by age (that is, freshman, sophomore, junior, senior), and all are expected to take precisely the same time—around 720 school days over four years, to be precise—to meet the requirements for a diploma.

When one is out of his grade level, he can feel odd, as Mark did in his biology class. The goals are the same for all, and the means to achieve them are also similar.

Young males and females are treated remarkably alike; the schools' goals are the same for each gender. In execution, there are differences, as those pressing sex discrimination suits have made educators intensely aware. The students in metalworking classes are mostly male; those in home economics, mostly female. But it is revealing how much less sex discrimination there is in high schools than in other American institutions. For many young women, the most liberated hours of their week are in school.

School is to be like a job: you start in the morning and end in the afternoon, five days a week. You don't get much of a lunch hour, so you go home early, unless you are an athlete or are involved in some special school or extracurricular activity. School is conceived of as the children's workplace, and it takes young people off parents' hands and out of the labor market during prime-time work hours. Not surprisingly, many students see going to school as little more than a dogged necessity. They perceive the day-to-day routine, a Minnesota study reports, as one of "boredom and lethargy." One of the students summarizes: School is "boring, restless, tiresome, puts ya to sleep, tedious, monotonous, pain in the neck."

The school schedule is a series of units of time: the clock is king. The base time block is about fifty minutes in length. Some schools, on what they call modular scheduling, split that fifty-minute block into two or even three pieces. Most schools have double periods for laboratory work, especially in the sciences, or four-hour units for the small numbers of students involved in intensive vocational or other work-study programs. The flow of all school activity arises from or is blocked by these time units. "How much time do I have with my kids" is the teacher's key question.

Because there are many claims for those fifty-minute blocks, there is little time set aside for rest between them, usually no more than three to ten minutes, depending on how big the school is and, consequently, how far students and teachers have to walk from class to class. As a result, there is a frenetic quality to the school day, a sense of sustained restlessness. For the adolescents, there are frequent changes of room and fellow students, each change giving tempting opportunities for distraction, which are stoutly resisted by teachers. Some schools play soft music during these "passing times," to quiet the multitude, one principal told me.

Many teachers have a chance for a coffee break. Few students do. In some city schools where security is a problem, students must be in class for seven consecutive periods, interrupted by a heavily monitored twenty-minute lunch period for small groups, starting as early as 10:30

A.M. and running to after 1:00 P.M. A high premium is placed on punctuality and on "being where you're supposed to be." Obviously, a low premium is placed on reflection and repose. The student rushes from class to class to collect knowledge. Savoring it, it is implied, is not to be done much in school, nor is such meditation really much admired. The picture that these familiar patterns yield is that of an academic supermarket. The purpose of going to school is to pick things up, in an organized and predictable way, the faster the better.

What is supposed to be picked up is remarkably consistent among all sorts of high schools. Most schools specifically mandate three out of every five courses a student selects. Nearly all of these mandates fall into five areas—English, social studies, mathematics, science, and physical education. On the average, English is required to be taken each year, social studies and physical education three out of the four high school years, and mathematics and science one or two years. Trends indicate that in the mid-eighties there is likely to be an increase in the time allocated to these last two subjects. Most students take classes in these four major academic areas beyond the minimum requirements, sometimes in such special areas as journalism and "yearbook," offshoots of English departments.

Press most adults about what high school is for, and you hear these subjects listed. *High school? That's where you learn English and math and that sort of thing.* Ask students, and you get the same answer. High school is to "teach" these "subjects."

What is often absent is any definition of these subjects or any rationale for them. They are just there, labels. Under those labels lie a multitude of things. A great deal of material is supposed to be "covered"; most of these courses are surveys, great sweeps of the stuff of their parent disciplines.

While there is often a sequence *within* subjects—algebra before trigonometry, "first-year" French before "second-year" French—there is rarely a coherent relationship or sequence *across* subjects. Even the most logically related matters—reading ability as a precondition for the reading of history books, and certain mathematical concepts or skills before the study of some of physics—are only loosely coordinated, if at all. There is little demand for a synthesis of it all; English, mathematics, and the rest are discrete items, to be picked up individually. The incentive for picking them up is largely through tests and, with success at these, in credits earned.

Coverage within subjects is the key priority. If some imaginative teacher makes a proposal to force the marriage of, say, mathematics and physics or to require some culminating challenges to students to use several subjects in the solution of a complex problem, and if this proposal will take "time" away from other things, opposition is usually phrased in terms of what may be thus forgone. If we do that, we'll have to give up colonial history.

We won't be able to get to programming. We'll not be able to read *Death of a Salesman*. There isn't time. The protesters usually win out.

The subjects come at a student like Mark in random order, a kaleidoscope of worlds: algebraic formulae to poetry to French verbs to Ping-Pong to the War of the Spanish Succession, all before lunch. Pupils are to pick up these things. Tests measure whether the picking up has been successful.

The lack of connection between stated goals . . . and the goals inherent in school practice is obvious and, curiously, tolerated. Most striking is the gap between statements about "self-realization and mental and physical growth" or "moral and ethical values" —common rhetoric in school documents—and practice. Most physical education programs have neither the time nor the focus really to ensure fitness. Mental health is rarely defined. Neither are ethical values, save at the negative extremes, such as opposition to assault or dishonesty. Nothing in the regimen of a day like Mark's signals direct or implicit teaching in this area. The "schoolboy code" (not ratting on a fellow student) protects the marijuana pusher, and a leechlike associate is shrugged off without concern. The issue of the locker search was pushed aside, as not appropriate for class time.

Most students, like Mark, go to class in groups of twenty to twenty-seven students. The expected attendance in some schools, particularly those in low-income areas, is usually higher, often thirty-five students per class, but high absentee rates push the actual numbers down. About twenty-five per class is an average figure for expected attendance, and the actual numbers are somewhat lower. There are remarkably few students who go to class in groups much larger or smaller than twenty-five.

A student such as Mark sees five or six teachers per day; their differing styles and expectations are part of his kaleidoscope. High school staffs are highly specialized: guidance counselors rarely teach mathematics, mathematics teachers rarely teach English, principals rarely do any classroom instruction. Mark, then, is known a little bit by a number of people, each of whom sees him in one specialized situation. No one may know him as a "whole person"—unless he becomes a special problem or has special needs.

Save in extracurricular or coaching situations, such as in athletics, drama, or shop classes, there is little opportunity for sustained conversation between student and teacher. The mode is a one-sentence or two-sentence exchange: *Mark, when was Grover Cleveland president? Let's see, was 1890 . . . or something . . . wasn't he the one . . . he was elected twice, wasn't he? . . . Yes . . . Gloria, can you get the dates right?* Dialogue is strikingly absent, and as a result the opportunity of teachers to challenge students' ideas in a systematic and logical way is limited. Given the rushed, full quality of the school day, it can seldom happen. One must infer that careful probing of students' thinking is not a high priority. How one gains . . .

"the ability to make decisions, to solve problems, to reason independently, and to accept responsibility for self-evaluation and continuing self-improvement" without being challenged is difficult to imagine. One certainly doesn't learn these things merely from lectures and text-books.

Most schools are nice places. Mark and his friends enjoy being in theirs. The adults who work in schools generally like adolescents. The academic pressures are limited, and the accommodations to students are substantial. For example, if many members of an English class have jobs after school, the English teacher's expectations for them are adjusted, downward. In a word, school is sensitively accommodating, as long as students are punctual, where they are supposed to be, and minimally dutiful about picking things up from the clutch of courses in which they enroll.

This characterization is not pretty, but it is accurate, and it serves to describe the vast majority of American secondary schools. "Taking subjects" in a systematized, conveyer-belt way is what one does in high school. That this process is, in substantial respects, not related to the rhetorical purposes of education is tolerated by most people, perhaps because they do not really either believe in those ill-defined goals or, in their heart of hearts, believe that schools can or should even try to achieve them. The students are happy taking subjects. The parents are happy, because that's what they did in high school. The rituals, the most important of which is graduation, remain intact. The adolescents are supervised, safely and constructively most of the time, during the morning and afternoon hours, and they are off the labor market. That is what high school is all about.

Historical Questions

1. In the second quotation at the beginning of this chapter, Benjamin Franklin praises "good Education . . . as the surest foundation of [private and public] happiness," suggesting that education should be a highly personal process, benefiting both the individual and the state. Yet more than two centuries later, Sizer criticizes the modern high school for being an impersonal "conveyor belt" designed for "taking subjects." Compare your images of eighteenth- and nineteenth-century education, such as the little red schoolhouse and the stick for corporal punishment, with your memories of high school. Do you agree or disagree with Sizer that high schools have become more impersonal? Why? What organizational structures in high schools today make them more or less personal than schools of an earlier time?

2. Define a positive learning experience. In which of Mark's five classes do you think the students are most engaged in positive learning? In which class is their experience most negative? Reread the quotations at the beginning of this chapter and speculate both about how definitions of a positive learning experience have changed over time, and about how Sizer's role as

a contemporary school reformer might have influenced his portrayal of a typical American high school.

Cultural Questions

1. Sizer claims that his characterization of Mark's high school is "accurate" and that "it serves to describe the vast majority of American secondary schools." Do you think Sizer's fictional description is accurate? Discuss two or three similarities and two or three differences between Sizer's description of American high schools and your own experiences (or those of people you know).

2. The title "What High School Is" creates an implied question that Sizer does not answer immediately. After presenting some of the goals that high schools claim to fulfill, Sizer suggests what he feels are the actual purposes of high schools. Focusing on two or three of his major points and bringing in examples of your own, explore whether you agree with Sizer's suggestions. What might be some of the cultural and economic reasons for the contradictions between the stated and actual goals of high schools today?

3. Although this reading primarily follows Mark, it also suggests several other perspectives, such as the viewpoints of the administrators, the teachers, the more motivated students, and the parents. Focusing on two or three of these groups, explore how they might evaluate the quality of this high school. On what evidence and what assumptions about high school learning would they base their evaluation? Develop a short dialogue between two of these different representatives on an aspect of high school that you think is important.

DR. CHARLES ELIOT et al.

In the Beginning . . . The 1893 Report of the Committee of Ten (1893)

In 1890, only 6.7 percent of fourteen- to seventeen-year-olds attended high school. But as enrollment grew, the National Educational Association (NEA) appointed "The Committee of Ten" to determine the purpose and subjects of secondary schools. As the president of Harvard University, Charles Eliot (1834–1926) chaired the committee consisting of the national commissioner of education, the headmasters of two prestigious private schools, one public school principal, a professor from Oberlin, and the presidents of five leading universities, such as Vassar and Michigan. Their ideas sparked debates about high schools that persist today.

To the National Council of Education.

Every gentleman named on the Committee of Ten accepted his appointment; and the Committee met, with every member present, at Columbia College, New York City, from the 9th to the 11th of November, 1892, inclusive. . . .

Questions for the Conferences

The Committee of Ten, after a preliminary discussion on November 9th, decided on November 10th to organize Conferences on the following subjects: 1. Latin; 2. Greek; 3. English; 4. Other Modern Languages; 5. Mathematics; 6. Physics, Astronomy, and Chemistry; 7. Natural History (Biology, including Botany, Zoology, and Physiology); 8. History, Civil Government, and Political Economy; 9. Geography (Physical Geography, Geology, and Meteorology). They also decided that each Conference should consist of ten members. They then proceeded to select the members of each of these Conferences, having regard in the selection to the scholarship and experience of the gentlemen named, to the fair division of the members between colleges on the one hand and schools on the other, and to the proper geographical distribution of the total membership. After selecting ninety members for the nine Conferences, the Committee decided on an additional number of names to be used as substitutes for persons originally chosen who should decline to serve, from two to four substitutes being selected for each Conference. . . .

The Committee next adopted the following list of questions as a guide for the discussions of all the Conferences, and directed that the Conferences be called together on the 28th of December:

1. In the school course of study extending approximately from the age of six years to eighteen years—a course including the periods of both elementary and secondary instruction—at what age should the study which is the subject of the Conference be first introduced?
2. After it is introduced, how many hours a week for how many years should be devoted to it?
3. How many hours a week for how many years should be devoted to it during the last four years of the complete course; that is, during the ordinary high school period?

4. What topics, or parts, of the subject may reasonably be covered during the whole course?
5. What topics, or parts, of the subject may best be reserved for the last four years?
6. In what form and to what extent should the subject enter into college requirements for admission? Such questions as the sufficiency of translation at sight as a test of knowledge of a language, or the superiority of a laboratory examination in a scientific subject to a written examination on a text-book, are intended to be suggested under this head by the phrase "in what form."
7. Should the subject be treated differently for pupils who are going to college, for those who are going to a scientific school, and for those who, presumably, are going to neither?
8. At what stage should this differentiation begin, if any be recommended?
9. Can any description be given of the best method of teaching this subject throughout the school course?
10. Can any description be given of the best mode of testing attainments in this subject at college admission examinations?
11. For those cases in which colleges and universities permit a division of the admission examination into a preliminary and a final examination, separated by at least a year, can the best limit between the preliminary and final examinations be approximately defined?

The Committee further voted that it was expedient that the Conferences on Latin and Greek meet at the same place. Finally, all further questions of detail with regard to the calling and the instruction of the Conferences were referred to the Chairman with full power. . . .

Unanimity of the Conferences

All the Conferences sat for three days; their discussions were frank, earnest, and thorough; but in every Conference an extraordinary unity of opinion was arrived at. The nine reports are characterized by an amount of agreement which quite surpasses the most sanguine anticipations. Only two Conferences present minority reports, namely, the Conference on Physics, Astronomy, and Chemistry, and the Conference on Geography; and in the first case, the dissenting opinions touch only two points in the report of the majority, one of which is unimportant. In the great majority of matters brought before each Conference, the decision of the Conference was unanimous. When one considers the different localities, institutions, professional experiences, and personalities represented in each of the Conferences, the unanimity developed is very striking, and should carry great weight. . . .

Number and Variety of Changes Urged

The Council and the public will doubtless be impressed, at first sight, with the great number and variety of important changes urged by the Conferences; but on a careful reading of the appended reports it will appear that the spirit of the Conferences was distinctly conservative and moderate, although many of their recommendations are of a radical nature. The Conferences which found their tasks the most difficult were the Conferences on Physics, Astronomy, and Chemistry; Natural History; History, Civil Government, and Political Economy; and Geography; and these four Conferences make the longest and most elaborate reports, for the reason that these subjects are today more imperfectly dealt with in primary and secondary schools than are the subjects of the first five Conferences. The experts who met to confer together concerning the teaching of the last four subjects in the list of Conferences all felt the need of setting forth in an ample way what ought to be taught, in what order, and by what method. They ardently desired to have their respective subjects made equal to Latin, Greek, and Mathematics in weight and influence in the schools; but they knew that educational tradition was adverse to this desire, and that many teachers and directors of education felt no confidence in these subjects as disciplinary material. Hence the length and elaboration of these reports. In less degree, the Conferences on English and Other Modern Languages felt the same difficulties, these subjects being relatively new as substantial elements in school programs.

The Committee of Ten requested the Conferences to make their reports and recommendations as specific as possible. This request was generally complied with; but, very naturally, the reports and recommendations are more specific concerning the selection of topics in each subject, the best methods of instruction, and the desirable appliances or apparatus, than concerning the allotment of time to each subject. The allotment of time is a very important matter of administrative detail; but it presents great difficulties, requires a comprehensive survey of the comparative claims of many subjects, and in different parts of the country is necessarily affected by the various local conditions and historical developments. Nevertheless, there will be found in the Conference reports recommendations of a fundamental and far-reaching character concerning the allotment of program time to each subject. . . .

Earlier Introduction of Subjects

Anyone who reads these nine reports consecutively will be struck with the fact that all these bodies of experts desire to have the elements of their several subjects taught earlier than they now are; and that the Conferences on all the subjects except the languages desire to have given in the elementary schools what may be called perspective views, or broad surveys, of their respective subjects—expecting that in later years of the school course parts of these same subjects will be taken up with more amplitude and detail. The Conferences on Latin, Greek, and the Modern Languages agree in desiring to have the study of foreign languages begin at a much earlier age than now—the Latin Conference suggesting by a reference to European usage that Latin be begun from three to five years earlier than it commonly is now. The Conference on Mathematics, wish to have given in elementary schools not only a general survey of arithmetic, but also the elements of algebra, and concrete geometry in connection with drawing. The Conference on Physics, Chemistry, and Astronomy urge that these studies should constitute an important part of the elementary school course from the very beginning. The Conference on Natural History wish the elements of botany and zoology to be taught in the primary schools. The Conference on History wish the systematic study of history to begin as early as the tenth year of age, and the first two years of study to be devoted to mythology and to biography for the illustration of general history as well as of American history. Finally, the Conference on Geography recommended that the earlier course treat broadly of the earth, its environment and inhabitants, extending freely into fields which in later years of study are recognized as belonging to separate sciences.

In thus claiming entrance for their subjects into the earlier years of school attendance, the Conferences on the newer subjects are only seeking an advantage which the oldest subjects have long possessed. The elements of language, number, and geography have long been imparted to young children. As things now are, the high school teacher finds in the pupils fresh from the grammar schools no foundation of elementary mathematical conceptions outside of arithmetic; no acquaintance with algebraic language; and no accurate knowledge of geometrical forms. As to botany, zoology, chemistry, and physics, the minds of pupils entering the high school are ordinarily blank on these subjects. When college professors endeavor to teach chemistry, physics, botany, zoology, meteorology, or geology to persons of eighteen or twenty years of age, they discover that in most instances new habits of observing, reflecting, and recording have to be painfully acquired by the students—habits which they should have acquired in early childhood. The college teacher of history finds in like manner that his subject has never taken any serious hold on the minds of pupils fresh from the secondary schools. He finds that they have devoted astonishingly little time to the subject; and that they have acquired no habit of historical investigation, or of the comparative examination of different historical narratives concerning the same period of events. It is inevitable, therefore, that specialists in any of the subjects which are pursued in the high schools or colleges should earnestly desire that the minds of young children be stored with some of the elementary facts and principles of their subject; and that all the mental habits, which the adult student will surely need, begin to be formed in the child's mind before the age of fourteen. It follows, as a matter of course, that all the Conferences except the Conference on Greek, make strong suggestions concerning the programs of primary and grammar schools—generally with some reference to the subsequent programs of secondary schools. They desire important changes in the elementary grades; and the changes recommended are all in the direction of increasing simultaneously the interest and the substantial training quality of primary and grammar school studies.

Correlation of Subjects

If anyone feels dismayed at the number and variety of the subjects to be opened to children of tender age, let him observe that while these nine Conferences desire each their own subject to be brought into the courses of elementary schools, they all agree that these different subjects should be correlated and associated one with another by the program and by the actual teaching. If the nine Conferences had sat all together as a single body, instead of sitting as detached and even isolated bodies, they could not have more forcibly expressed their conviction that every subject recommended for introduction into elementary and secondary schools should help every other; and that the teacher of each single subject should feel responsible for the advancement of the pupils in all subjects, and should distinctly contribute to this advancement.

On one very important question of general policy which affects profoundly the preparation of all school programs, the Committee of Ten and all the Conferences are absolutely unanimous. Among the questions suggested for discussion in each Conference were the following:

1. Should the subject be treated differently for pupils who are going to college, for those who are going to a scientific school, and for those who, presumably, are going to neither?
2. At what age should this differentiation begin, if any be recommended?

A Simplification of Programs

The first question is answered unanimously in the negative by the Conferences, and the second therefore needs no answer. The Committee of Ten unanimously agree with the Conferences. Ninty-eight teachers, intimately concerned either with the actual work of American secondary schools, or with the results of that work as they appear in students who come to college, unanimously declare that every subject which is taught at all in a secondary school should be taught in the same way and to the same extent to every pupil so long as he pursues it, no matter what the probable destination of the pupil may be, or at what point his education is to cease. Thus, for all pupils who study Latin, or history, or algebra, for example, the allotment of time and the method of instruction in a given school should be the same year by year. Not that all the pupils should pursue every subject for the same number of years; but so long as they do pursue it, they should all be treated alike. It has been a very general custom in American high schools and academies to make up separate courses of study for pupils of supposed different destinations, the proportions of the several studies in the different courses being various. The principle laid down by the Conferences will, if logically carried out, make a great simplification in secondary school programs. It will lead to each subject's being treated by the school in the same way by the year for all pupils, and this, whether the individual pupil be required to choose between courses which run through several years, or be allowed some choice among subjects year by year.

Teachers More Highly Trained

Persons who read all the appended reports will observe the frequent occurrence of the statement that, in order to introduce the changes recommended, teachers more highly trained will be needed in both the elementary and the secondary schools. There are frequent expressions to the effect that a higher grade of scholarship is needed in teachers of the lower classes, or that the general adoption of some method urged by a Conference must depend upon the better preparation of teachers in the high schools, model schools, normal schools, or colleges in which they are trained. The experienced principal or superintendent in reading the reports will be apt to say to himself, "This recommendation is sound, but cannot be carried out without teachers who have received a training superior to that of the teachers now at my command." It must be remembered, in connection with these admissions, or expressions of anxiety, that the Conferences were urged by the Committee of Ten to advise the Committee concerning the best possible—almost the ideal—treatment of each subject taught in a secondary school course, without, however, losing sight of the actual condition of American schools, or pushing their recommendations beyond what might reasonably be considered attainable in a moderate number of years. The Committee believe that the Conferences have carried out wisely the desire of the Committee, in that they have recommended improvements, which, though great and seldom to be made at once and simultaneously, are by no means unattainable. The existing agencies for giving instruction to teachers already in service are numerous; and the normal schools and the colleges are capable of making prompt and successful efforts to supply the better trained and equipped teachers for whom the reports of the Conferences call. . . .

Requirements for Admission to College

One of the subjects which the Committee of Ten were directed to consider was requirements for admission to college; and particularly they were expected to report on uniform requirements for admission to colleges, as well as on a uniform secondary school program. Almost all the Conferences have something to say about the best mode of testing the attainments of candidates at college admission examinations; and some of them, notably the Conferences on History and Geography, make very explicit declarations concerning the nature of college examinations. The improvements desired in the mode of testing the attainments of pupils who have pursued in the secondary schools the various subjects which enter into the course will be found clearly described under each subject in the several Conference reports; but there is a general principle concerning the relation of the secondary schools to colleges which the Committee of Ten, inspired and guided by the Conferences, feel it their duty to set forth with all possible distinctness.

The secondary schools of the United States, taken as a whole, do not exist for the purpose of preparing boys and girls for colleges. Only an insignificant percentage of the graduates of these schools go to colleges or scientific schools. Their main function is to prepare for the duties of life that small proportion of all the children in the country—a proportion small in number, but very important to the welfare of the nation—who show themselves able to profit by an education prolonged to the eighteenth year, and whose parents are able to support them while they remain so long at school. There are, to be sure, a few private or endowed secondary schools in the country, which make it their principal object to prepare students for the colleges and universities; but the number of these schools is relatively small. A secondary school program intended for national use must therefore be made for those children whose education is not to be pursued beyond the secondary school. The preparation of a few pupils for college or scientific school should in the ordinary secondary school be the incidental, and not the principal object. At the same time, it is obviously desirable that the colleges and scientific schools should be accessible to all boys or girls who have completed creditably the secondary school course. Their parents often do not decide for them, four years before the college age, that they shall go to college, and they themselves may not, perhaps, feel the desire to continue their education until near the end of their school course. In order that any successful graduate of a good secondary school should be free to present himself at the gates of the college or scientific school of his choice, it is necessary that the colleges and scientific schools of the country should accept for admission to appropriate courses of their instruction the attainments of any youth who has passed creditably through a good secondary school course, no matter to what group of subjects he may have mainly devoted himself in the secondary school. As secondary school courses are now too often arranged, this is not a reasonable request to prefer to the colleges and scientific schools; because the pupil may now go through a secondary school course of a very feeble and scrappy nature— studying a little of many subjects and not much of any one, getting, perhaps, a little information in a variety of fields, but nothing which can be called a thorough training. Now the recommendations of the nine Conferences, if well carried out, might fairly be held to make all the main subjects taught in the secondary schools of equal rank for the purposes of admission to college or scientific school. They would all be taught consecutively and thoroughly, and would all be carried on in the same spirit; they would all be used for training the powers of observation, memory, expression, and reasoning; and they would all be good to that end, although differing among themselves in quality and substance.

Historical Questions

1. Sizer's "What High School Is" raises a key question that you may have addressed in fastwrite 1: Why should adolescents attend high school? With specific reference to the text, explore two or three purposes of high school education that the authors of this report suggest. Do any or all of these purposes still meet the needs of our country and its individuals today? How do they compare with Sizer's sense of the purpose of high school? Develop your position by referring to two or three specific similarities or differences between today's culture and the nineteenth-century United States.

2. Consider the nine subjects listed in the 1893 report as well as the relationship between them (note the established and the "relatively new" subjects). Compare the proposed course of study to your own high school curriculum. If you find similarities, discuss why you think some of the report's proposed courses might still be taught today. What needs did they serve in 1893? What needs do they serve today? If you found differences, analyze why particular changes might have been made. What academic or social needs might your high school curriculum have addressed that the 1893 one did not?

Cultural Questions

1. Develop a symptomatic reading of the construction of the Committee of Ten. Who were the people being asked to determine the future of American

education? Speculate about why these persons were asked. Can you think of others who might have been asked but who were not? From the composition of the committee, speculate about whose interests were being served and whose interests were being neglected.

2. Read the report symptomatically to determine which problems of education it is actually trying to resolve, focusing on implied problems as well as those explicitly discussed. Based on the language and tone with which various problems are presented and discussed, and on your analysis of the construction of the committee, which two or three problems could the committee's recommendations solve or help to solve? Which two or three will they be less likely to solve? Why?

3. Develop a symptomatic reading of the persuasiveness of this report. Focusing on two or three specific passages, explore how the authors' choice of language works to make their recommendations seem logical and desirable. What possible objections to their recommendations could the authors be trying to avoid? Explore the effects you think the language of the report might have had on two or three different possible readers of it: college professors; parents not planning to send their children to college; parents who wanted their children to attend college; students who are unsure about going to college; students who want to go on to college; students who definitely do not want to go to college; or whatever other group of readers you would like to represent.

∾ Fastwrite 3

Just twenty-six years after the first report on American education, another committee was formed to reconsider the aims and the means of secondary schooling. "Secondary education," this second report begins, "should be determined by the needs of the society to be served." Before reading the next report, review the first three quotations that begin this chapter on seventeenth-, eighteenth-, and nineteenth-century education, each of which claims to be serving society's needs. Then fastwrite to answer two of the following questions:

1. What social needs are each of these definitions of education trying to address?
2. In what ways are the high schools described in "What High School Is" and in your fastwrite 1 still trying to meet these past social needs? In what ways are they not trying to do so?
3. To what extent are social needs and individual "student needs" the same?
4. What social needs will secondary schools have to try to meet in the twenty-first century?

COMMISSION ON THE REORGANIZATION OF SECONDARY EDUCATION

"The Magnificent Seven" Cardinal Principles of Secondary Education: 1918

By 1910, enrollment in secondary schools had more than doubled, from one in fifteen fourteen- to seventeen-year-olds to better than one in seven. This explosion of students caused the National Education Association to appoint a new committee to rethink the earlier mission of high schools. Committee membership included five high school principals and one superintendent of schools, a professor of education, the dean of faculties at Berkeley, and the Massachusetts Deputy Commissioner of Education. While the committee's initial purpose was to encourage colleges to relax some of their entrance requirements, during the course of their work together, they focused on the broader mission of secondary education.

I. The Need for Reorganization

Secondary education should be determined by the needs of the society to be served, the character of the individuals to be educated, and the knowledge of educational theory and practice available. These factors are by no means static. Society is always in process of development; the character of the secondary school population undergoes modification; and the sciences on which educational theory and practice depend constantly furnish new information. Secondary education, however, like any other established agency of society, is conservative and tends to resist modification. Failure to make adjustments when the need arises leads to the necessity for extensive reorganization at irregular intervals. The evidence is strong that such a comprehensive reorganization of secondary education is imperative at the present time.

1. Changes In Society

Within the past few decades changes have taken place in American life profoundly affecting the activities of the individual. As a citizen, he must to a greater extent and in a more direct way cope with problems of community life, State and National Governments, and international relationships. As a worker, he must adjust himself to a more complex economic order. As a relatively independent personality, he has more leisure. The problems arising from these three dominant phases of life are closely interrelated and call for a degree of intelligence and efficiency on the part of every citizen that can not be secured through elementary education alone, or even through secondary education unless the scope of that education is broadened.

The responsibility of the secondary school is still further increased because many social agencies other than the school afford less stimulus for education than heretofore. In many vocations there have come such significant changes in the substitution of the factory system for the domestic system of industry; the use of machinery in place of manual labor; the high specialization of processes with a corresponding subdivision of labor; and the breakdown of the apprentice system. In connection with home and family life have frequently come lessened responsibility on the part of the children; the withdrawal of the father and sometimes the mother from home occupations to the factory or store; and increased urbanization, resulting in less unified family life. Similarly, many important changes have taken place in community life, in the church, in the State, and in other institutions. These changes in American life call for extensive modifications in secondary education.

2. Changes In The Secondary School Population

In the past 25 years there have been marked changes in the secondary school population of the United States. The number of pupils has increased, according to Federal returns, from one for every 210 of the total population in 1889–90, to one for every 121 in 1899–1900, to one for every 89 in 1909–10, and to one for every 73 of the estimated total population in 1914–15. The character of the secondary school population has been modified by the entrance of large numbers of pupils of widely varying capacities, aptitudes, social heredity, and destinies in life. Further, the broadening of the scope of secondary education has brought to the school many pupils who do not complete the full course but leave at various stages of advancement. The needs of these pupils cannot be neglected, nor can we expect in the near future that all pupils will be able to complete the secondary school as full-time students.

At present only about one third of the pupils who enter the first year of the elementary school reach the four-year high school, and only about one in nine is graduated. Of those who enter the seventh school year, only one half to two thirds reach the first year of the four-year high school. Of those who enter the four-year high school about one third leave before the beginning of the second year, about one half are gone before the beginning of the third year, and fewer than one third are graduated. These facts can no longer be safely ignored.

3. Changes In Educational Theory

The sciences on which educational theory depends have within recent years made significant contributions. In particular, educational psychology emphasizes the following factors:

Individual differences in capacities and aptitudes among secondary school pupils. Already recognized to some extent, this factor merits fuller attention.

The reexamination and reinterpretation of subject values and the teaching methods with reference to "general discipline." While the final verdict of modern psychology has not as yet been rendered, it is clear that former conceptions of general values must be thoroughly revised.

Importance of applying knowledge. Subject values and teaching methods must be tested in terms of the laws of learning and the application of knowledge to the activities of life, rather than primarily in terms of the demands of any subject as a logically organized science.

Continuity in the development of children. It has long been held that psychological changes at certain stages are so pronounced as to overshadow the continuity of development. On this basis secondary education has been sharply separated from elementary education. Modern psychology, however, goes to show that the development of the individual is in most respects a continuous process and that, therefore, any sudden or abrupt break between the elementary and the secondary school or between any two successive stages of education is undesirable.

The foregoing changes in society, in the character of the secondary school population, and in educational theory, together with many other considerations, call for extensive modifications of secondary education. Such modifications have already begun in part. The present need is for the formulation of a comprehensive program of reorganization, and its adoption, with suitable adjustments, in all the secondary schools of the Nation. Hence it is appropriate for a representative body like the National Education Association to outline such a program. This is the task entrusted by that association to the Commission on the Reorganization of Secondary Education.

II. The Goal of Education in a Democracy

Education in the United States should be guided by a clear conception of the meaning of democracy. It is the ideal of democracy that the individual and society may find fulfillment each in the other. Democracy sanctions neither the exploitation of the individual by society, nor the disregard of the interests of society by the individual. More explicitly—

The purpose of democracy is so to organize society that each member may develop his personality primarily through activities designed for the well-being of his fellow members and of society as a whole.

This ideal demands that human activities be placed upon a high level of efficiency; that to this efficiency be added an appreciation of the significance of these activities and loyalty to the best ideals involved; and that the individual choose that vocation and those forms of social service in which his personality may develop and become most effective. For the achievement of these ends democracy must place chief reliance upon education.

Consequently, education in a democracy, both within and without the school, should develop in each individual the knowledge, interests, ideals, habits, and powers whereby he will find his place and use that place to shape both himself and society toward ever nobler ends.

III. The Main Objectives of Education

In order to determine the main objectives that should guide education in a democracy it is necessary to analyze the activities of the individual. Normally he is a member of a family, of a vocational group, and of various civic groups, and by virtue of these relationships he is called upon to engage in activities that enrich the family life, to render important vocational services to his fellows, and to promote the common welfare. It follows, therefore, that worthy home membership, vocation, and citizenship demand attention as three of the leading objectives.

Aside from the immediate discharge of these specific duties, every individual should have a margin of time for the cultivation of personal and social interests. This leisure, if worthily used, will recreate his powers and enlarge and enrich life, thereby making him better able to meet his responsibilities. The unworthy use of leisure impairs health, disrupts home life, lessens vocational efficiency, and destroys civic mindedness. The tendency in industrial life, aided by legislation, is to decrease the working hours of large groups of people. While shortened hours tend to lessen the harmful reactions that arise from prolonged strain, they increase, if possible, the importance of preparation for leisure. In view of these considerations, education for the worthy use of leisure is of increasing importance as an objective.

To discharge the duties of life and to benefit from leisure, one must have good health. The health of the individual is essential also to the vitality of the race and to the defense of the Nation. Health education is, therefore, fundamental.

There are various processes, such as reading, writing, arithmetical computations, and oral and written expression, that are needed as tools in the affairs of life. Consequently, command of these fundamental processes, while not an end in itself, is nevertheless an indispensable objective.

And, finally, the realization of the objectives already named is dependent upon ethical character, that is, upon conduct founded upon right principles, clearly perceived and loyally adhered to. Good citizenship, vocational excellence, and the worthy use of leisure go hand in hand with ethical character; they are at once the fruits of sterling character and the channels through which such character is developed and made manifest. On the one hand, character is meaningless apart from the will to discharge the duties of life, and, on the other hand, there is no guarantee that these duties will be rightly discharged unless principles are substituted for impulses, however well intentioned such impulses may be. Consequently ethical character is at once involved in all the other objectives and at the same time requires specific consideration in any program of national education.

This commission, therefore, regards the following as the main objectives of education: 1. Health. 2. Command of fundamental processes. 3. Worthy home membership. 4. Vocation. 5. Citizenship. 6. Worthy use of leisure. 7. Ethical character.

The naming of the above objectives is not intended to imply that the process of education can be divided into separated fields. This can not be, since the pupil is indivisible. Nor is the analysis all inclusive. Nevertheless, we believe that distinguishing and naming these objectives will aid in directing efforts; and we hold that they should constitute the principal aims in education.

IV. The Role of Secondary Education in Achieving These Objectives

The objectives outlined above apply to education as a whole--elementary, secondary, and higher. It is the purpose of this section to consider specifically the role of secondary education in achieving each of these objectives.

For reasons stated in Section X, this Commission favors such reorganization that secondary education may be defined as applying to all pupils of approximately 12 to 18 years of age.

1. Health

Health needs can not be neglected during the period of secondary education without serious danger to the individual and the race. The secondary school should therefore provide health instruction, inculcate health habits, organize an effective program of physical activities, regard health needs in planning work and play, and cooperate with home and community in safeguarding and promoting health interests. . . .

2. Command of Fundamental Processes

Much of the energy of the elementary school is properly devoted to teaching certain fundamental processes, such as reading, writing, arithmetical computations, and the elements of oral and written expression. The facility that a child of 12 or 14 may acquire in the use of these tools is not sufficient for the needs of modern life. This is particularly true of the mother tongue. Proficiency in many of these processes may be increased more effectively by their application to new material than by the formal reviews commonly employed in grades seven and eight. Throughout the secondary school, instruction and practice must go hand in hand, but as indicated in the report of the Committee on English,[1] only so much theory should be taught at any one time as will show results in practice.

3. Worthy Home Membership

Worthy home membership as an objective calls for the development of those qualities that make the individual a worthy member of a family, both contributing to and deriving benefit from that membership.

This objective applies to both boys and girls. The social studies should deal with the home as a fundamental social institution and clarify its relation to the wider interests outside. Literature should interpret and idealize the human elements that go to make the home. Music and art should result in more beautiful homes and in greater joy therein. The coeducational school with a faculty of men and women should, in its organization and its activities, exemplify wholesome relations between boys and girls and men and women.

Home membership as an objective should not be thought of solely with reference to future duties. These are the better guaranteed if the school helps the pupils to take the right attitude toward present home responsibilities and interprets to them the contribution of the home to their development.

In the education of every high school girl, the household arts should have a prominent place because of their importance to the girl herself and to others whose welfare will be directly in her keeping. The attention now devoted to this phase of education is inadequate, and especially so for girls preparing for occupations not related to the household arts and for girls planning for higher institutions. The majority of girls who enter wage-earning occupations directly from the high school remain in them for only a few years, after which home making becomes their lifelong occupation. For them the high school period offers the only assured opportunity to prepare for that lifelong occupation, and it is during this period that they are most likely to form their ideals of life's duties and responsibilities. For girls planning to enter higher institutions—

our traditional ideals of preparation for higher institutions are particularly incongruous with the actual needs and future responsibilities of girls. It would

1. Bureau of Education, Bulletin, 1917, No. 2, "Reorganization of English in Secondary Schools."

seem that such high school work as is carefully designed to develop capacity for, and interest in, the proper management and conduct of a home should be regarded as of importance at least equal to that of any other work. We do not understand how society can properly continue to sanction for girls high school curriculums that disregard this fundamental need, even though such curriculums are planned in response to the demands made by some of the colleges for women.[2]

In the education of boys, some opportunity should be found to give them a basis for the intelligent appreciation of the value of the well-appointed home and of the labor and skill required to maintain such a home, to the end that they may cooperate more effectively. For instance, they should understand the essentials of food values, of sanitation, and of household budgets.

4. Vocation

Vocational education should equip the individual to secure a livelihood for himself and those dependent on him, to serve society well through his vocation, to maintain the right relationships toward his fellow workers and society, and, as far as possible, to find in that vocation his own best development.

This ideal demands that the pupil explore his own capacities and aptitudes, and make a survey of the world's work, to the end that he may select his vocation wisely. Hence, an effective program of vocational guidance in the secondary school is essential.[3] . . .

5. Civic Education

Civic education should develop in the individual those qualities whereby he will act well his part as a member of neighborhood, town or city, State, and Nation, and give him a basis for understanding international problems.

For such citizenship the following are essential: A many sided interest in the welfare of the communities to which one belongs; loyalty to ideals of civic righteousness; practical knowledge of social agencies and institutions; good judgment as to means and methods that will promote one social end without defeating others; and as putting all these into effect, habits of cordial cooperation in social undertakings. . . .

The comprehension of the ideals of American democracy and loyalty to them should be a prominent aim of civic education. The pupil should

2. Report of the Committee on the Articulation of High School and College, 1911.

3. For a comprehensive program of vocational guidance see a report of this Commission issued as Bureau of Education Bulletin, 1918, No. 19, "Vocational Guidance in Secondary Schools."

feel that he will be responsible, in cooperation with others, for keeping the Nation true to the best inherited conceptions of democracy, and he should also realize that democracy itself is an ideal to be wrought out by his own and succeeding generations.

Civic education should consider other nations also. As a people we should try to understand their aspirations and ideals that we may deal more sympathetically and intelligently with the immigrant coming to our shores, and have a basis for a wiser and more sympathetic approach to international problems. Our pupils should learn that each nation, at least potentially, has something of worth to contribute to civilization and that humanity would be incomplete without that contribution. . . .

6. Worthy Use Of Leisure

Education should equip the individual to secure from his leisure the re-creation of body, mind, and spirit, and the enrichment and enlargement of his personality.

This objective calls for the ability to utilize the common means of enjoyment, such as music, art, literature, drama, and social intercourse, together with the fostering in each individual of one or more special avocational interests. . . .

7. Ethical Character

In a democratic society ethical character becomes paramount among the objectives of the secondary school. Among the means for developing ethical character may be mentioned the wise selection of content and methods of instruction in all subjects of study, the social contacts of pupils with one another and with their teachers, the opportunities afforded by the organization and administration of the school for the development on the part of pupils of the sense of personal responsibility and initiative, and, above all, the spirit of service and the principles of true democracy which should permeate the entire school—principal, teachers, and pupils.

Specific consideration is given to the moral values to be obtained from the organization of the school and the subjects of study in the report of this Commission entitled, Moral Values in Secondary Education.[4] That report considers also the conditions under which it may be advisable to supplement the other activities of the school by offering a distinct course in moral instruction.

4. Bureau of Education Bulletin, 1917, No. 51.

Historical Questions

1. Explain how the "three dominant phases of life," as citizen, worker, and "relatively independent individual" cited at the beginning of this report justify the particular reorganization of secondary schools proposed in this report. Explore how these changes could have been used to justify one or two other types of reorganization proposals. With reference to one or two concerns of yours today, develop an example of an alternative reorganization proposal that you might develop today. Why do you think the committee in 1918 decided on the particular proposals it did?

2. Consider the recommendations of this report and the language used to present them (words, for example, such as *efficiency, worthy home membership*, and *fundamental processes*). In what ways does the tone of this report, as well as its specific recommendations, compare to the first report? How do the values and assumptions underlying these recommendations—concerning, for example, the purposes of secondary education, who should be educated, and the definitions of good citizenship—differ in these two reports?

3. In what ways might the recommendations of the "Cardinal Principles" help to resolve the problems Sizer identified in Mark's modern high school? Explain your answer with two or three specific examples.

Cultural Questions

1. Consider the social factors—political, economic, demographic, and so on—that may have led to the changes in high school organization proposed in this report. With reference to two or three specific passages in the report, discuss which of these social factors you think most explicitly influenced this committee. Then, reading more symptomatically, discuss one or two passages in which one of these factors is only implicitly referred to, but which you see as nonetheless being an important consideration for the committee. Finally, explore a larger cultural reason why certain factors could be discussed more overtly than others.

2. Unlike the 1893 report, this proposal mentions the secondary education of "girls." What cultural or political events, beliefs, and assumptions of the authors probably influenced the recommendations concerning "the education of every high school girl"? In a symptomatic reading of these recommendations, explain the expectations for U.S. women at that time.

෴

JOHN DEWEY

Between Traditional and Progressive Education
(1938)

John Dewey (1859–1952) is often associated with the progressive education of the 1920s and 1930s and is usually blamed for the "permissive" failure of this student-centered reform movement. Yet this leading American philosopher was one of the first and finest critics of educational theories that focused too much on either the student or the teacher. In works like *Democracy and Education* (1916), Dewey instead tried to consider the complex interactions between the student, the teacher, and the subject matter being taught. The following reading is from *Experience and Education* (1938), in which Dewey looks back on the successes and the failures of American education's traditions and reforms.

Mankind likes to think in terms of extreme opposites. It is given to formulating its beliefs in terms of *Either-Ors*, between which it recognizes no intermediate possibilities. When forced to recognize that the extremes cannot be acted upon, it is still inclined to hold that they are all right in theory but that when it comes to practical matters circumstances compel us to compromise. Educational philosophy is no exception. The history of educational theory is marked by opposition between the idea that education is development from within and that it is formation from without; that it is based upon natural endowments and that education is a process of overcoming natural inclination and substituting in its place habits acquired under external pressure.

At present, the opposition, so far as practical affairs of the school are concerned, tends to take the form of contrast between traditional and progressive education. If the underlying ideas of the former are formulated broadly, without the qualifications required for accurate statement, they are found to be about as follows: The subject-matter of education consists of bodies of information and of skills that have been worked out in the past; therefore, the chief business of the school is to transmit them to the new generation. In the past, there have also been developed standards and rules of conduct; moral training consists in forming habits of action in conformity with these rules and standards. Finally, the general pattern of school organization (by which I mean the relations of pupils to one another and to the teachers) constitutes the school a kind of institution sharply marked off from other social institutions. Call up in imagination the ordinary schoolroom, its time-schedules, schemes of classification, of examination and promotion, of rules of order, and I think you will grasp what is meant by "pattern of organization." If then you contrast this scene with what goes on in the family, for example, you will appreciate what is meant by the school being a kind of institution sharply marked off from any other form of social organization.

The three characteristics just mentioned fix the aims and methods of instruction and discipline. The main purpose or objective is to prepare the young for future responsibilities and for success in life, by means of acquisition of the organized bodies of information and prepared forms of skill which comprehend the material of instruction. Since the subject-matter as well as standards of proper conduct are handed down from the past, the attitude of pupils must, upon the whole, be one of docility, receptivity, and obedience. Books, especially textbooks, are the chief representatives of the lore and wisdom of the past, while teachers are the organs through which pupils are brought into effective connection with the material. Teachers are the agents through which knowledge and skills are communicated and rules of conduct enforced.

I have not made this brief summary for the purpose of criticizing the underlying philosophy. The rise of what is called new education and progressive schools is of itself a product of discontent with traditional education. In effect it is a criticism of the latter. When the implied criticism is made explicit it reads somewhat as follows: The traditional scheme is, in essence, one of imposition from above and from outside. It imposes adult standards, subject-matter, and methods upon those who are only growing slowly toward maturity. The gap is so great that the required subject-matter, the methods of learning and of behaving are foreign to the existing capacities of the young. They are beyond the reach of the experience the young learners already possess. Consequently, they must be imposed; even though good teachers will use devices of art to cover up the imposition so as to relieve it of obviously brutal features.

But the gulf between the mature or adult products and the experience and abilities of the young is so wide that the very situation forbids much active participation by pupils in the development of what is taught. Theirs is to do—and learn, as it was the part of the six hundred to do and die. Learning here means acquisition of what already is incorporated in books and in the heads of the elders. Moreover, that which is taught is thought of as essentially static. It is taught as a finished product, with little regard either to the ways in which it was originally built up or to changes that will surely occur in the future. It is to a large extent the cultural product of societies that assumed the future would be much like the past, and yet it is used as educational food in a society where change is the rule, not the exception.

If one attempts to formulate the philosophy of education implicit in the practices of the new education, we may, I think, discover certain common principles amid the variety of progressive schools now existing. To imposition from above is opposed expression and cultivation of individuality; to external discipline is opposed free activity; to learning from texts and teachers, learning through experience; to acquisition of isolated skills and techniques by drill, is opposed acquisition of them as means of attaining ends which make direct vital appeal; to preparation for a more or less remote future is opposed making the most of the opportunities of present life; to static aims and materials is opposed acquaintance with a changing world. . . . There is always the danger in a new movement that in rejecting the aims and methods of that which it would supplant, it may develop its principles negatively rather than positively and constructively. Then it takes its clew in practice from that which is rejected instead of from the constructive development of its own philosophy.

I take it that the fundamental unity of the newer philosophy is found in the idea that there is an intimate and necessary relation between the processes of actual experience and education. If this be true, then a positive and constructive development of its own basic idea depends upon having a correct idea of experience. Take, for example, the question of organized subject-matter—which will be discussed in some detail later. The problem for progressive education is: What is the place and meaning of subject-matter and of organization *within* experience? How does subject-matter function? Is there anything inherent in experience which tends towards progressive organization of its contents? What results follow when the materials of experience are not progressively organized? A philosophy which proceeds on the basis of rejection, of sheer opposition, will neglect these questions. It will tend to suppose that because the old education was based on ready-made organization, therefore it suffices to reject the principle of organization *in toto,* instead of striving to discover what it means and how it is to be attained on the basis of experience. We might go through all the points of difference between the new and the old education and reach similar conclusions. When external control is rejected, the problem becomes that of finding the factors of control that are inherent within experience. When external authority is rejected, it does not follow that all authority should be rejected, but rather that there is need to search for a more effective source of authority. Because the older education imposed the knowledge, methods, and the rules of conduct of the mature person upon the young, it does not follow, except upon the basis of the extreme

Either-Or philosophy, that the knowledge and skill of the mature person has no directive value for the experience of the immature. On the contrary, basing education upon personal experience may mean more multiplied and more intimate contacts between the mature and the immature than ever existed in the traditional school, and consequently more, rather than less, guidance by others. The problem, then, is: how these contacts can be established without violating the principle of learning through personal experience. The solution of this problem requires a well thought-out philosophy of the social factors that operate in the constitution of individual experience.

What is indicated in the foregoing remarks is that the general principles of the new education do not of themselves solve any of the problems of the actual or practical conduct and management of progressive schools. Rather, they set new problems which have to be worked out on the basis of a new philosophy of experience. The problems are not even recognized, to say nothing of being solved, when it is assumed that it suffices to reject the ideas and practices of the old education and then go to the opposite extreme. . . . Now we have the problem of discovering the connection which actually exists *within* experience between the achievements of the past and the issues of the present. We have the problem of ascertaining how acquaintance with the past may be translated into a potent instrumentality for dealing effectively with the future. We may reject knowledge of the past as the *end* of education and thereby only emphasize its importance as a *means*. When we do that we have a problem that is new in the story of education: How shall the young become acquainted with the past in such a way that the acquaintance is a potent agent in appreciation of the living present? . . . It is a great mistake to suppose, even tacitly, that the traditional schoolroom was not a place in which pupils had experiences. Yet this is tacitly assumed when progressive education as a plan of learning by experience is placed in sharp opposition to the old. The proper line of attack is that the experiences which were had, by pupils and teachers alike, were largely of a wrong kind. How many students, for example, were rendered callous to ideas, and how many lost the impetus to learn because of the way in which learning was experienced by them? How many acquired special skills by means of automatic drill so that their power of judgment and capacity to act intelligently in new situations was limited? How many came to associate the learning process with ennui and boredom? How many found what they did learn so foreign to the situations of life outside the school as to give them no power of control over the latter? How many came to associate books with dull drudgery, so that they were "conditioned" to all but flashy reading matter?

If I ask these questions, it is not for the sake of wholesale condemnation of the old education. It is for quite another purpose. It is to emphasize the fact, first, that young people in traditional schools do have experiences; and, secondly, that the trouble is not the absence of experiences, but their defective and wrong character—wrong and defective from the standpoint of connection with further experience. The positive side of this point is even more important in connection with progressive education. It is not enough to insist upon the necessity of experience, nor even of activity in experience. Everything depends upon the *quality* of the experience which is had. The quality of any experience has two aspects. There is an immediate aspect of agreeableness or disagreeableness, and there is its influence upon later experiences. The first is obvious and easy to judge. The *effect* of an experience is not borne on its face. It sets a problem to the educator. It is his business to arrange for the kind of experiences which, while they do not repel the student, but rather engage his activities are, nevertheless, more than immediately enjoyable since they promote having desirable future experiences. Just as no man lives or dies to himself, so no experience lives and dies to itself. Wholly independent of desire or intent, every experience lives on in further experiences. Hence the central problem of an education based upon experience is to select the kind of present experiences that live fruitfully and creatively in subsequent experiences.

Later, I shall discuss in more detail the principle of the continuity of experience or what may be called the experiential continuum. Here I wish simply to emphasize the importance of this principle for the philosophy of educative experience. A philosophy of education, like any theory, has to be stated in words, in symbols. But so far as it is more than verbal it is a plan for conducting education. Like any plan, it must be framed with reference to what is to be done and how it is to be done. The more definitely and sincerely it is held that education is a development within, by, and for experience, the more important it is that there shall be clear conceptions of what experience is. Unless experience is so conceived that the result is a plan for deciding upon subject-matter, upon methods of instruction and discipline, and upon material equipment and social organization of the school, it is wholly in the air. It is reduced to a form of words which may be emotionally stirring but for which any other set of words might equally well be substituted unless they indicate operations to be initiated and executed. Just because traditional education was a matter of routine in which the plans and programs were handed down from the past, it does not follow that progressive education is a matter of planless improvisation.

It is, accordingly, a much more difficult task to work out the kinds of materials, of methods, and of social relationships that are appropriate to the new education than is the case with traditional education. I think many of the difficulties experienced in the conduct of progressive schools and many of the criticisms leveled against them arise from this source. The difficulties are aggravated and the criticisms are increased when it is supposed that the new education is somehow easier than the old. This belief is, I imagine, more or less current. Perhaps it illustrates again the *Either-Or* philosophy, springing from the idea that about all which is required is *not* to do what is done in traditional schools.

I admit gladly that the new education is *simpler* in principle than the old. It is in harmony with principles of growth, while there is very much which is artificial in the old selection and arrangement of subjects and methods, and artificiality always leads to unnecessary complexity. But the easy and the simple are not identical. . . .

Here, again, the problem for the progressive educator is more difficult than for the teacher in the traditional school. The latter had indeed to look ahead. But unless his personality and enthusiasm took him beyond the limits that hedged in the traditional school, he could content himself with thinking of the next examination period or the promotion to the next class. He could envisage the future in terms of factors that lay within the requirements of the school system as that conventionally existed. There is incumbent upon the teacher who links education and actual experience together a more serious and a harder business. He must be aware of the potentialities for leading students into new fields which belong to experiences already had, and must use this knowledge as his criterion for selection and arrangement of the conditions that influence their present experience.

Because the studies of the traditional school consisted of subject-matter that was selected and arranged on the basis of the judgment of adults as to what would be useful for the young sometime in the future, the material to be learned was settled upon outside the present life-experience of the learner. In consequence, it had to do with the past; it was such as had proved useful to men in past ages. By reaction to an opposite extreme, as unfortunate as it was probably natural under the circumstances, the sound idea that education should derive its materials from present experience and should enable the learner to cope with the problems of the present and future has often been converted into the idea that progressive schools can to a very large extent ignore the past. If the present could be cut off from the past, this conclusion would be sound. But the achievements of the past provide the only means at command for understanding the present. Just as the individual has to draw in memory upon his own past to understand the conditions in which he individually finds himself, so the issues and problems of present *social* life are in such intimate and direct connection with the past that students cannot be prepared to understand either these problems or the best way of dealing with them without delving into their roots in the past. In other words, the sound principle that the objectives of learning are in the future and its immediate materials are in present experience can be carried into effect only in the degree that present experience is stretched, as it were, backward. It can expand into the future only as it is also enlarged to take in the past. . . .

I have been forced to speak in general and often abstract language. But what has been said is organically connected with the requirement that experiences in order to be educative must lead out into an expanding world of subject-matter, a subject-matter of facts or information and of ideas. This condition is satisfied only as the educator views teaching and learning as a continuous process of reconstruction of experience.

Historical Questions

1. Describe a specific example from your high school classroom experiences in which an instructor used traditional educational methods. Describe an example in which an instructor taught from a more progressive perspective. What made each of these learning situations effective or ineffective for you? Describe whether your evaluation of traditional and progressive educational methods agrees or disagrees with Dewey's judgments and explain why you hold the position you do.

2. Progressive education developed in the United States during the 1920s and 1930s, so the second report on the "Cardinal Principles" from 1918 marks the beginning of this student-centered reform movement. Use Dewey's discussion of traditional and progressive education to analyze three differences between the reports of 1893 and 1918.

3. According to Dewey, "the new education" that places significant attention on students' experiences is much harder for a teacher to practice than the traditional method. Considering the students of contemporary high schools, explore whether Dewey's new education is harder or easier for an instructor to practice. In explaining your position and why you hold it, make clear linkages between particular points from Dewey's text and at least two specific examples of contemporary high school students and teachers.

4. With specific references to each of the texts, compare the goals for education that Dewey proposes with the goals of traditional high schools described by Sizer. How might Dewey's "new" methods change the relationship between a student like Mark, his teachers, and the subjects taught?

Cultural Questions

1. Although Dewey criticizes progressive education, he prefers it to traditional education. With specific references to his text, analyze how Dewey's version of progressive education tries to correct some of its potential problems. Do you think it would be successful? Why or why not?

2. Dewey begins by criticizing the tendency to think in the simple terms of *Either-Ors*, yet he also treats traditional and progressive education as "extreme opposites." Develop a symptomatic reading in which you focus on two or three passages to explore the extent to which Dewey's own either-or thinking affects his analysis of traditional and progressive education.

3. How might proponents of traditional or progressive education in 1938 have responded to Dewey? What, for example, might they have said in defense of their positions? Construct a debate between Dewey and a traditional or progressive teacher in 1938. What key points might they have made, and what assumptions would underlie them?

ℭ **Fastwrite 4**

The previous three readings—the 1893 report, the 1918 report, and Dewey's "Between Traditional and Progressive Education"—have discussed the goals and methods of secondary education. The next three readings examine the ability of several schools to implement these and other educational recommendations successfully. Before you continue with the following readings, fastwrite your responses to one or more of these questions:

1. Choose one of the sets of recommendations you have read about. What factors would its successful implementation depend on?

2. What kinds of communities, i.e., which boards of education in which areas of the country, would be best or least be able to implement the recommendations you have focused on in the first question?

3. How equal or unequal have your educational opportunities been compared to students you have met from other schools?

4. What do you think are the causes of equal or unequal educational opportunities?

JONATHAN KOZOL

From *Savage Inequalities* (1991)

Jonathan Kozol (b. 1936) is a well-known educator and writer. A Rhodes Scholar and recipient of Guggenheim and Rockefeller fellowships, Kozol won the National Book Award in 1968 for *Death at an Early Age: The Destruction of the Hearts and Minds of Children in the Boston Public Schools. Savage Inequalities* (1991) was the result of his spending two years visiting schools and talking with children in thirty city neighborhoods all over the United States. Everywhere Kozol went, he found an incredible degree of racial segregation.

From the street, the school looks like a medieval castle; its turreted tower rises high above the devastated lots below. A plaque in the principal's office tells a visitor that this is the oldest high school in the Bronx.

The first things that one senses in the building are the sweetness, the real innocence, of many of the children, the patience and determination of the teachers, and the shameful disrepair of the surroundings. The principal is unsparing in her honesty. "The first floor," she tells me as we head off to the stairwell, "isn't bad—unless you go into the gym or auditorium." It's the top two floors, she says, the fourth and fifth floors, that reveal the full extent of Morris High's neglect by New York City's Board of Education.

Despite her warning, I am somewhat stunned to see a huge hole in the ceiling of the stairwell on the school's fourth floor. The plaster is gone, exposing rusted metal bars embedded in the outside wall. It will cost as much as $50 million to restore the school to an acceptable condition, she reports.

Jack Forman, the head of the English department, is a scholarly and handsome gray-haired man whose academic specialty is British literature. Sitting in his office in a pinstripe shirt and red suspenders, his feet up on the table, he is interrupted by a stream of kids. A tiny ninth grade student seems to hesitate outside the office door. Forman invites her to come in and, after she has given him a message ("Carmen had to leave—for an emergency") and gone to her next class, his face breaks out into a smile. "She's a lovely little kid. These students live in a tough neighborhood, but they are children and I speak to them as children."

Forman says that freshman English students get a solid diet of good reading: *A Tale of Two Cities, Manchild in the Promised Land,* Steinbeck's *The Pearl,* some African fiction, a number of Greek tragedies. "We're implementing an AP course ["advanced placement"—for pre-college students] for the first time. We don't know how many children will succeed in it, but we intend to try. Our mission is to stretch their minds, to give them every chance to grow beyond their present expectations.

"I have strong feelings about getting past the basics. Too many schools are stripping down curriculum to meet the pressure for success on tests that measure only minimal skills. That's why I teach a theater course. Students who don't respond to ordinary classes may surprise us, and surprise themselves, when they are asked to step out on a stage.

"I have a student, Carlos, who had dropped out once and then returned. He had no confidence in his ability. Then he began to act. He memorized the part of Pyramus. Then he played Sebastian in *The Tempest*. He had a photographic memory. Amazing! He will graduate, I hope, this June.

"Now, if we didn't have that theater program, you have got to ask if Carlos would have stayed in school."

In a sun-drenched corner room on the top floor, a female teacher and some 25 black and Hispanic children are reading a poem by Paul Laurence Dunbar. Holes in the walls and ceiling leave exposed the structural brick. The sun appears to blind the teacher. There are no shades. Sheets of torn construction paper have been taped to windowpanes, but the glare is quite relentless. The children look forlorn and sleepy.

> I know why the caged bird sings. . . .
> It is not a carol of joy. . . .

"This is your homework," says the teacher. "Let's get on with it."

But the children cannot seem to wake up to the words. A 15-year-old boy, wearing a floppy purple hat, white jersey and striped baggy pants, is asked to read the lines.

> I know what the caged bird feels . . .
> When the wind stirs soft through the
>   springing grass,
> And the river flows like a stream of glass. . . .

A 15-year-old girl with curly long red hair and many freckles reads the lines. Her T-shirt hangs down almost to her knees.

> I know why the caged bird beats his wing
> Till its blood is red on the cruel bars.

A boy named Victor, sitting at my side, whispers the words: "I know why the caged bird beats his wing. . . . His blood is red. He wants to spread his wings."

The teacher asks the children what the poet means or what the imagery conveys. There is no response at first. Then Victor lifts his hand. "The poem is about ancient days of slavery," he says. "The bird destroys himself because he can't escape the cage."

"Why does he sing?" the teacher asks.

"He sings out of the longing to be free."

At the end of class the teacher tells me, "Forty, maybe 45 percent out of this group will graduate."

The counseling office is the worst room I have seen. There is a large blue barrel by the window.

"When it rains," one of the counselors says, "that barrel will be full." I ask her how the kids react. "They would like to see the rain stop in the office," she replies.

The counselor seems to like the kids and points to three young women sitting at a table in the middle of the room. One of them, an elegant tall girl with long dark hair, is studying her homework. She's wearing jeans, a long black coat, a black turtleneck, a black hat with a bright red band. "I love the style of these kids," the counselor says.

A very shy light-skinned girl waits by the desk. A transfer from another school, she's with her father. They fill out certain transfer forms and ask the counselor some questions. The father's earnestness, his faith in the importance of these details, and the child's almost painful shyness stay in my mind later.

At eleven o'clock, about 200 children in a top-floor room are watching Forman's theater class performing *The Creation* by James Weldon Johnson. Next, a gospel choir sings—"I once was lost and now am found"—and then a tall black student gives a powerful delivery of a much-recited speech of Martin Luther King while another student does an agonizing, slow-paced slave ballet. The students seem mesmerized. The speaker's voice is strong and filled with longing.

"One day, the sons of former slaves and the sons of former slave-owners will be able to sit down together at the table of brotherhood."

But the register of enrollment given to me by the principal reflects the demographics of continued racial segregation: Of the students in this school, 38 percent are black, 62 percent Hispanic. There are no white children in the building.

The session ends with a terrific fast jazz concert by a band composed of students dressed in black ties, crimson jackets and white shirts. A student with a small trimmed beard and mustache stands to do a solo on the saxophone. The pianist is the same young man who read the words of Martin Luther King. His solo, on a battered Baldwin, brings the students to their feet.

Victor Acosta and eight other boys and girls meet with me in the freshman counselors' office. They talk about "the table of brotherhood"— the words of Dr. King that we have heard recited by the theater class upstairs.

"We are not yet seated at that table," Victor says.

"The table is set but no one's in the chairs," says a black student who, I later learn, is named Carissa.

Alexander, a 16-year-old student who was brought here by his parents from Jamaica just a year ago, says this: "You can understand things better when you go among the wealthy. You look around you at their school, although it's impolite to do that, and you take a deep breath at the sight of all those beautiful surroundings. Then you come back home and see that these are things you do not have. You think of the difference. Not at first. It takes a while to settle in."

I ask him why these differences exist.

"Let me answer that," says Israel, a small, wiry Puerto Rican boy. "If you threw us all into some different place, some ugly land, and put white children in this building in our place, this school would start to shine. No question. The parents would say: This building sucks. It's ugly. Fix it up. They'd fix it fast—no question.

"People on the outside," he goes on, "may think that we don't know what it is like for other students, but we *visit* other schools and we have eyes and we have brains. You cannot hide the differences. You see it and compare. . . .

"Most of the students in this school won't go to college. Many of them will join the military. If there's a war, we have to fight. Why should I go to war and fight for opportunities I can't enjoy—for things rich people value, for their freedom, but I do not *have* that freedom and I can't go to their schools?"

"You tell your friends, 'I go to Morris High,'" Carissa says. "They make a face. How does that make you feel?" She points to the floor beside the water barrel. "I found wild mushrooms growing in that corner."

"Big fat ugly things with hairs," says Victor.

Alexander then begins an explanation of the way that inequality becomes ensconced. "See," he says, "the parents of rich children have the money to get into better schools. Then, after a while, they begin to say, Well, I have this. Why not keep it for my children? In other words, it locks them into the idea of always having something more. After that, these things—the extra things they have—are seen like an *inheritance*. They feel it's theirs and they don't understand why we should question it.

"See, that's where the trouble starts. They get used to what they have. They think it's theirs by rights because they had it from the start. So it leaves those children with a legacy of greed. I don't think most people understand this."

One of the counselors, who sits nearby, looks at me and then at Alexander. Later he says, "It's quite remarkable how much these children see. You wouldn't know it from their academic work. Most of them write poorly. There is a tremendous gulf between their skills and capabilities. This gulf, this dissonance, is frightening. I mean, it says so much about the squandering of human worth. . . ."

I ask the students if they can explain the reasons for the physical condition of the school.

"Hey, it's like a welfare hospital! You're getting it for free," says Alexander. "You have no power to complain."

"Is money really everything?" I ask.

"It's a nice fraction of everything," he says.

Janice, who is soft-spoken and black, speaks about the overcrowding of the school. "I make it my business," she says, "to know my fellow students. But it isn't easy when the classes are so large. I had 45 children in my fifth grade class. The teacher sometimes didn't know you. She would ask you, 'What's your name?'"

"You *want* the teacher to know your name," says Rosie, who is Puerto Rican. "The teacher asks me, 'Are you really in this class?' 'Yes, I've been here all semester.' But she doesn't know my name."

All the students hope to go to college. After college they have ambitious plans. One of them hopes to be a doctor. Two want to be lawyers. Alexander wants to be an architect. Carissa hopes to be a businesswoman. What is the likelihood that they will live up to these dreams? Five years ago, I'm told, there were approximately 500 freshman students in the school. Of these, only 180 survived four grades and made it through twelfth grade to graduation; only 82 were skilled enough to take the SATs. The projection I have heard for this year's ninth grade class is that 150 or so may graduate four years from now. Which of the kids before me will survive?

Rosie speaks of sixth grade classmates who had babies and left school. Victor speaks of boys who left school during eighth grade. Only one of the children in this group has ever been a student in a racially desegregated school.

"How long will it be," I ask, "before white children and black and Hispanic children in New York will go to the same schools?"

"How long has the United States existed?" Alexander asks.

Janice says, "Two hundred years."

"Give it another two hundred years," says Alexander.

"Thank you," says Carissa.

At the end of school, Jack Forman takes me down to see the ground-floor auditorium. The room resembles an Elizabethan theater. Above the proscenium arch there is a mural, circa 1910, that must have been impressive long ago. The ceiling is crossed by wooden ribs; there are stained-glass windows in the back. But it is all in ruins. Two thirds of the stained-glass panes are missing and replaced by Plexiglas. Next to each of eight tall windows is a huge black number scrawled across the wall by a contractor who began but never finished the repairs. Chunks of wall and sections of the arches and supporting pillars have been blasted out by rot. Lights are falling from the ceiling. Chunks of plaster also hang from underneath the balcony above my head. The floor is filled with lumber, broken and upended desks, potato-chip bags, Styrofoam coffee cups and other trash. There is a bank of organ pipes, gold-colored within a frame of dark-stained wood, but there is no organ. Spilled on the floor beside my feet are several boxes that contain a "Regents Action Plan" for New York City's schools. Scattered across the floor amid the trash: "English Instructional Worksheets: 1984."

"Think what we could do with this," says Forman. "This kind of room was meant for theater and to hold commencements. Parents could enter directly from outside. The mural above the proscenium arch could be restored.

"This could be the soul of the school," he says. "Hopefully, three years from now, when Victor is a senior, we will have this auditorium restored. That's my dream: to see him stand and graduate beneath this arch, his parents out there under the stained glass."

From my notes: "Morris High could be a wonderful place, a centerpiece of education, theater, music, every kind of richness for poor children. The teachers I've met are good and energized. They seem to love the children, and the kids deserve it. The building mocks their goodness."

Like Chicago, New York City has a number of selective high schools that have special programs and impressive up-to-date facilities. Schools like Morris High, in contrast, says the *New York Times*, tend to be "most overcrowded" and have "the highest dropout rates" and "lowest scores." In addition, we read, they receive "less money" per pupil.

The selective schools, according to the *Times*, "compete for the brightest students, but some students who might qualify lose out for lack of information and counseling." Other families, says the paper, "win admission through political influence."

The *Times* writes that these better-funded schools should not be "the preserve of an unfairly chosen elite." Yet, if the experience of other cities holds in New York City, this is what these special schools are meant to be. They are *intended* to be enclaves of superior education, private schools essentially, within the public system.

New York City's selective admissions program, says the principal of nonselective Jackson High, "has had the effect of making Jackson a racially segregated high school. . . . Simultaneously, the most 'difficult' and 'challenging' black students [have been] *encouraged* to select Jackson. . . ." The plan, she says, has had the effect of "placing a disproportionate number" of nonachieving children in one school. Moreover, she observes, students who do not meet "acceptable standards" in their chosen schools are sent back to schools like Jackson, making it effectively a dumping ground for children who are unsuccessful elsewhere.

"The gerrymandered zoning and the high school selection processes," according to a resident of the Jackson district, "create a citywide skimming policy that we compare to orange juice—our black youngsters are being treated like the sediment." The city, she says, is "not shaking the juice right." But she may be wrong. In the minds of those who have their eyes on an effective triage process—selective betterment of the most fortunate— this may be exactly the right way to shake the juice.

Unfairness on this scale is hard to contemplate in any setting. In the case of New York City and particularly Riverdale, however, it takes on a special poignance. Riverdale, after all, is not a redneck neighborhood. It has been home for many years to some of the most progressive people in the nation. Dozens of college students from this neighborhood went south during the civil rights campaigns to fight for the desegregation of the schools and restaurants and stores. The parents of those students often made large contributions to support the work of SNCC and CORE. One generation passes, and the cruelties they fought in Mississippi have come north to New York City. Suddenly, no doubt unwittingly, they find themselves opposed to simple things they would have died for 20 years before. Perhaps it isn't fair to say they are "opposed." A better word, more accurate, might be "oblivious." They do not want poor children to be harmed. They simply want the best for their own children. To the children of the South Bronx, it is all the same.

The system of selective schools in New York City has its passionate defenders. There are those who argue that these schools *deserve* the preferential treatment they receive in fiscal areas and faculty assignment because of the remarkable success that they have had with those whom they enroll. One such argument is made by the sociologist and writer Nathan Glazer.

Noting that excellent math and science teachers are in short supply in New York City, Glazer asks, "If they are scarce, is their effectiveness maximized by scattering them" to serve all children "or by their concentration" so that they can serve the high-achieving? "I think there is a good argument to be made that their effectiveness is maximized by concentration. They, like their students, have peers to talk to and work with and to motivate them." While recognizing the potential for inequity, Glazer nonetheless goes on, "I would argue that nowhere do we get so much for so little . . . than where we bring together the gifted and competent. They teach each other. They create an institution which provides them with an advantageous . . . label."

The points that Glazer makes here seem persuasive, though I think he contemplates too comfortably the virtually inevitable fact that "concentration" of the better teachers in the schools that serve the "high-achieving" necessarily requires a dilution of such teachers in the schools that serve the poorest children. While disagreeing with him on the fairness of this policy, I am not in disagreement on the question of the value of selective schools and am not proposing that such schools should simply not exist. Certain of these schools—New York's Bronx High School of Science, for instance, Boston's Latin School, and others—have distinguished histories and have made important contributions to American society.

If there were a multitude of schools *almost* as good as these in every city, so that applicants for high school could select from dozens of good options—so that even parents who did not have the sophistication or connections to assist their children in obtaining entrance to selective schools would not see their kids attending truly *bad* schools, since there would be none—then it would do little harm if certain of these schools were even better than the rest. In such a situation, kids who couldn't be admitted to a famous school such as Bronx Science might be jealous of the ones who did get in, but would not, for this reason, be condemned to third-rate education and would not be written off by the society.

But that is not the situation that exists. In the present situation, which is less a field of education options than a battlefield on which a class and racial war is being acted out, the better schools function, effectively, as siphons which draw off not only the most high-achieving and the best-connected students but their parents too; and this, in turn, leads to a rather cruel, if easily predictable, scenario: Once these students win admission to the places where, in Glazer's words, the "competent" and "gifted" "teach each other" and win "advantageous" labels, there is no incentive for their parents to be vocal on the issues that concern the students who have been excluded. Having obtained what they desired, they secede, to a degree, from the political arena. The political effectiveness of those who have been left behind is thus depleted. Soon enough, the failure of their children and the chaos, overcrowding and low funding of the schools that they attend confirm the wisdom of those families who have fled to the selective schools. This is, of course, exactly what a private school makes possible; but public schools in a democracy should not be allowed to fill this role.

Historical Questions

1. Review the first three quotations at the start of this chapter from the seventeenth, eighteenth, and nineteenth centuries. How would the authors of each quotation would react to the conditions of Morris High School? On what one or two key beliefs about education do you think each of these reactions would depend?

2. What links can you discover between Kozol's experience of observing and talking with teachers and students at Morris High and the first two reports on secondary education from 1893 and 1918? Compare two or three of their underlying beliefs about education: what its content should be, what its function should be, its value for students, the role of teachers, their expectations of students, and so on.

3. Reread the quotation at the beginning of the chapter from the 1966 Coleman report focusing on racial segregation. Kozol's experiences in U.S. schools suggest that very little has changed over the last thirty years. If Kozol is right, what particular aspects of U.S. beliefs, values, and behaviors could account for the persistence of segregation and inequality in our schools? Focus on two or three areas and refer to specific materials you read earlier in the chapter for evidence of these beliefs, values, and behaviors.

Cultural Questions

1. Using various sources, from official reports to student responses, Kozol suggests several reasons for the economic inequalities of New York City public schools. According to the students interviewed, what factors best explain these inequalities? What factors do you think best explain the inequalities? Analyze the assumptions underlying the reasons for two of your points of agreement and two of your points of disagreement with the students in this reading selection.

2. Compare Morris High to your high school and to Sizer's composite high school. What similarities and differences in teaching methods and educational goals do you see among the institutions? Compare the specific values or beliefs that underlie these methods and goals. Which do you feel are most important? Why?

3. Look again at Kozol's discussion of his and Glazer's argument about elite, selective schools, and examine your assumptions about selective schools. Imagine that you are a member of a board of education, a superintendent or principal, teacher or parent, or a student who has the opportunity to vote on a proposal to include a selective high school in your local public system. What assumptions about tracking and high-achieving students would govern your decision? How would your assumptions about students relate to the conditions Kozol describes at schools like Morris High?

MYRA SADKER AND DAVID SADKER

Missing in Interaction (1994)

Myra Sadker (1943-1995) and David Sadker (b. 1942), professors of education at The American University in Washington, D.C., collaborated on more than a dozen federal equity grants, developed training programs to combat sexism and sexual harassment, and wrote six books and more than seventy-five articles before Myra Sadker's death from cancer in 1995. Much of their work focuses on sexism in education, as does their last book, *Failing at Fairness: How America's Schools Cheat Girls* (1994), from which "Missing in Interaction" is taken.

No Entrance

For almost two centuries American education, following European traditions, barred girls from school. Education was the path to professions and careers open only to men. During Colonial times, viewed as mentally and morally inferior, women were relegated to learning only domestic skills, though they hungered for more.

While formal histories say little, letters and diaries hint of women's desire for learning and the lack of opportunity to fulfill that desire. In the early 1700s a Virginia girl wrote to her brother who had been sent to England to study: "I find you have got the start of me learning very much, for you write better already than I expect to do as long as I live."[1] The parents of another Virginia girl, Mary Ball, searched to find a tutor for their able daughter. After four years they finally found a minister who agreed to live in their home and teach young Mary, the woman who would later give birth to George Washington.

But these were the lucky girls. Most received no education or just a few years in a dame school where they might learn to read the Bible. An analysis of documents reveals that only 30 percent of women during this time could even sign their names.[2] . . .

But by the late 1700s, new ideas were brewing. When the boys left for home, girls were smuggled into school to receive an hour's worth of instruction. Some public schools actually opened their doors to girls, but with severe restrictions. In 1767 a school in Providence, Rhode Island, advertised that it would teach both reading and writing to female children. The small print noted the hours of instruction: from six to seven-thirty in the morning and from four to six-thirty in the afternoon. Each female student was charged a hefty sum for this inconveniently timed education. By tucking girls' education around the boys' regular hours, the teachers acquired needed additional income. Other elementary schools provided winter instruction for boys and allowed the girls to attend in the summer, an off-season education at a discount rate. Thus, slowly, as the concept of democracy

1. Woody, Thomas. *A History of Women's Education in the United States*, vols. I and II. New York: Octagon Books, 1966, p. 273.

2. Greene, Maxine. *Landscapes of Learning*. New York: Teachers College Press, 1978, pp. 225–43.

Tannenbaum Deutsch, David. "The Polite Lady: Portraits of American Schoolgirls and Their Accomplishments, 1725–1830," *Antiques* 135 (March 1980), pp. 742–53.

was taking root, so was the notion that girls as well as boys should receive an education.[3]

Revolutionary Ideas

The new democracy enlarged the European view of women, for while a woman's place was still in the home, in America her role took on new dimensions. In those revolutionary times she was to nurture her children's intellectual development. America's mothers were the nation's first teachers, and it didn't take long for people to realize that before a woman could enlighten children, she had to be enlightened herself.

The current debate over "school choice" would pale in comparison to the entrepreneurial array of schools that flourished in America's early years. And some schools began to open their doors to girls, at least those whose parents were able and willing to pay. Noted educator Benjamin Rush created the Young Ladies Academy in Philadelphia to transform girls into strong and intellectually able mothers. Religious orders spread their educational philosophies in girls' schools built by Quakers, Moravians, and Catholics.

By the first half of the nineteenth century, some communities in Massachusetts began to experiment with the radical concept of high school education for girls. A high school for boys had already been established in Boston, and in the late 1820s the public demanded one for girls, too. But city leaders underestimated the interest, and there were far more applicants than spaces available. Three out of four girls were turned away. Facing growing public unrest, Boston's mayor had to explain why 75 percent of the girls applying could not attend high school, and he came up with a brilliant but painful solution: Disappointing everyone equally, he played no favorites and closed the high school. Girls who thirsted for more education would have to wait until after the election; with the mayor's defeat, their high school was finally reopened.[4]

While large cities struggled to establish separate high schools, smaller communities could not afford to build one high school for boys and another for girls. With true American ingenuity, towns and rural communities built one high school and then pretended that they had built two. Entering by separate doors, boys and girls went directly to their assigned single-sex area. Sometimes they went to different floors, or boys went to one side of the building and girls to the other. Frequently the girls were taught by women and the boys by men, so they continued to learn in their own

---

3. Axtell, James. *The School Upon a Hill: Education and Society in Colonial New England*, New Haven, CT: Yale University Press, 1974.

4. Higginson, J. *Common Sense About Women*. Quoted in Woody, *A History of Women's Education*, vol. 2, pp. 200–1.

Krug, Edward A. *The Shaping of the American High School*. New York: Harper & Row, 1964.

Cremin, Lawrence A. *The Transformation of the School: Progressivism in American Education, 1876–1957*. New York: Knopf, 1961.

sex-segregated worlds. But they were in the same school building at the same time—a revolutionary development!

These "mixed" schools, as they were called, stirred emotional debate. Critics worried that boys and girls learning together in one place would have dire consequences. Such a combustible mix, they warned, required close supervision. These worries only increased as, over several decades, "mixed" schools became "mixed" classrooms. Opponents to this burgeoning coeducation charged that boys and girls were headed for different destinies, and they should be educated separately for their distinct life paths. Offering girls and boys identical lessons would do little to encourage womanly interest and skill in domestic activities.

Advocates of coeducation argued that the presence of girls would refine boys' rough behavior and that these mixed schools and classrooms would develop better-educated females who, when they became mothers, could teach their own children more effectively. But the winning argument was economic: One school for boys and another for girls meant higher taxes. So coeducation came to America as the outcome of financial necessity.

Citizens discussed the sexual consequences and economic costs of coeducation, but no one evaluated the effectiveness of this new approach or the possibility that different books or teaching strategies might be needed now that girls had arrived. Coeducation happened because it was cheaper, but was it educationally better?[5] . . .

Missing in Interaction

"Candid Camera" would have a field day in elementary school. There would be no need to create embarrassing situations. Just set the camera to take a photograph every sixty seconds. Since classroom action moves so swiftly, snapshots slow down the pace and reveal subliminal gender lessons.

Snapshot #1	Tim answers a question.
Snapshot #2	The teacher reprimands Alex.
Snapshot #3	Judy and Alice sit with hands raised while Brad answers a question.
Snapshot #4	Sally answers a question.
Snapshot #5	The teacher praises Marcus for skill in spelling.
Snapshot #6	The teacher helps Sam with a spelling mistake.
Snapshot #7	The teacher compliments Alice on her neat paper.
Snapshot #8	Students are in lines for a spelling bee. Boys are on one side of the room and girls are on the other.

5. A comprehensive discussion of coeducation is provided in Keller, Arnold Jack, *A Historical Analysis of the Arguments for and Against Coeducational Public High Schools in the United States*. Unpublished doctoral dissertation, Columbia University, New York, 1971.

As the snapshots continue, the underlying gender messages become clear. The classroom consists of two worlds: one of boys in action, the other of girls' inaction. Male students control classroom conversation. They ask and answer more questions. They receive more praise for the intellectual quality of their ideas. They get criticized. They get help when they are confused. They are the heart and center of interaction. Watch how boys dominate the discussion in this upper elementary class about presidents.

The fifth-grade class is almost out of control. "Just a minute," the teacher admonishes. "There are too many of us here to all shout out at once. I want you to raise your hands, and then I'll call on you. If you shout out, I'll pick somebody else."

Order is restored. Then Stephen, enthusiastic to make his point, calls out.

STEPHEN: I think Lincoln was the best president. He held the country together during the war.

TEACHER: A lot of historians would agree with you.

MIKE (seeing that nothing happened to Stephen, calls out): I don't. Lincoln was okay, but my Dad liked Reagan. He always said Reagan was a great president.

DAVID (calling out): Reagan? Are you kidding?

TEACHER: Who do you think our best president was, Dave?

DAVID: FDR. He saved us from the depression.

MAX (calling out): I don't think it's right to pick one best president. There were a lot of good ones.

TEACHER: That's interesting.

KIMBERLY (calling out): I don't think the presidents today are as good as the ones we used to have.

TEACHER: Okay, Kimberly. But you forgot the rule. You're supposed to raise your hand.

The classroom is the only place in society where so many different, young, and restless individuals are crowded into close quarters for an extended period of time day after day. Teachers sense the undertow of raw energy and restlessness that threatens to engulf the classroom. To preserve order, most teachers use established classroom conventions such as raising your hand if you want to talk.

Intellectually, teachers know they should apply this rule consistently, but when the discussion becomes fast-paced and furious, the rule is often swept aside. When this happens and shouting out begins, it is an open invitation for male dominance. Our research shows that boys call out eight times more often than girls. Sometimes what they say has little or nothing to do with the teacher's questions. Whether male comments are insightful or irrelevant, teachers respond to them. However, when girls call out, there is a fascinating occurrence: Suddenly the teacher remembers the rule about raising your hand before you talk. And then the girl, who is usually not as assertive as the male students, is deftly and swiftly put back in her place.

Not being allowed to call out like her male classmates during the brief conversation about presidents will not psychologically scar Kimberly; however, the system of silencing operates covertly and repeatedly. It occurs several times a day during each school week for twelve years, and even longer if Kimberly goes to college, and, most insidious of all, it happens subliminally. This micro-inequity eventually has a powerful cumulative impact.

On the surface, girls appear to be doing well. They get better grades and receive fewer punishments than boys. Quieter and more conforming, they are the elementary school's ideal students. "If it ain't broke, don't fix it" is the school's operating principle as girls' good behavior frees the teacher to work with the more difficult-to-manage boys. The result is that girls receive less time, less help, and fewer challenges. Reinforced for passivity, their independence and self-esteem suffer. As victims of benign neglect, girls are penalized for doing what they should and lose ground as they go through school. . . .

Self-Censored

In our studies of classroom interaction, we document the silence of girls from grade school through graduate school; and in the AAUW survey, students report that girls are quieter, more hidden. Almost half of the boys, 48 percent, but only 39 percent of the girls said they speak up in class. The gender gap was wider on the question of arguing with teachers. Almost twice as many boys as girls, 28 percent versus 15 percent, said they always argued with teachers when they thought they were right.

Between 1986 and 1990, Lyn Mikel Brown and Carol Gilligan interviewed nearly one hundred girls between the ages of seven and eighteen at the single-sex Laurel School in Cleveland, Ohio.[6] Over the years they listened as these girls learned to censor themselves. Younger children spoke in clear, strong, authentic voices. As they moved up in grade, their voices

6. Weitzman, Lenore, and Diane Rizzo. *Biased Textbooks: A Research Perspective.* Washington, DC: The Research Center on Sex Roles in Education, 1974.

became modulated, softened, sometimes obliterated. Lively, outspoken, and able to express a range of feelings at seven and eight, they became more reticent as they grew older; they monitored themselves and one another with adult prescriptions for "good girl" behavior: "Be nice," "Talk quietly," "Be calm," "Cooperate."[7] As Jesse explained, "You should be nice to your friends and communicate with them and not . . . do what you want." While Jesse harbored strong feelings and felt the need "to get my anger out of me," she was "terrified" that speaking her feelings would "cause a ruckus,"[8] disrupt the peace and quiet, anger others, or make them turn away and withdraw their love and attention. So she concealed her feelings.

As the Laurel School girls grew older, they began to mask and deny their feelings with the phrase "I don't know." When Judy was interviewed at nine, she used "I don't know" four times. Her interview at ten years of age, one of comparable length, was riddled with the phrase. When the interviewer asked Judy if there was a way to talk over problems before they exploded, Judy stumbled and was disconnected from the feelings she had concealed within her: "I don't know. It's just like if—I don't know, it's like—I don't know. I can't even begin to explain it because I don't even know if I know what it is. So I can't really explain it. Because I don't know. I don't even know, like in my brain or in my heart, what I am really feeling. I mean, I don't know if it's pain or upsetness or sad—I don't know."[9]

Girls who have spent years submerging their honest feelings, afraid to speak them aloud, eventually become confused; they begin to wonder whether their feelings are real. Neeti, a quiet, pretty girl of Indian descent who was popular and had good grades, was shocked to discover that by fifteen she couldn't write an answer to the essay question "Who am I?" This was her explanation for not being able to respond: "The voice that stands up for what I believe in has been buried deep inside me."[10]

The girls in Linda Kramer's study of a southern rural middle school had been singled out as gifted. As a result they went to extraordinary lengths to blend in, even denying and consciously hiding their special gifts.

7. Weitzman, Lenore, et al. "Sex Role Socialization in Picture Books for Preschool Children," *American Journal of Sociology* 77:6 (1972), pp. 1125–50.

8. Feminists on Children's Literature. "A Feminist Look at Children's Books," *School Library Journal* 17:5 (January 1971), pp. 19–24.
    Graebner, Diane Bennett. "A Decade of Sexism in Readers," *Reading Teacher* 16:1 (October 1972), pp. 52–58.

9. McCracken, Glenn, and Charles Walcutt, eds. Lippincott Basic Reading Series, Book H, 1970.
    O'Donnell, M., and Van Roekel, eds. *Around the Corner,* Harper & Row, 1966.
    Robinson, Helen et al., eds. *Ventures,* Book 4, Scott Foresman, 1965
    Handforth, Thomas. *Mei Li.* New York: Doubleday, 1938.

These girls felt that to survive they had to censor what they did and said, literally silencing themselves:

OBSERVER: I hear you are an excellent singer.

ELLEN: No. Not really. Not excellent.

OBSERVER: Miss Hunt told me you sing well.

ELLEN: When I was in fifth or sixth grade, I had a lot of nerve. See, I didn't care what people thought of me then, because . . . I don't know. But when I was in fifth grade I sang "Tomorrow" in front of the whole school. And if I had any way of changing it, I would. . . .

OBSERVER: Because of that song?

ELLEN: I guess being up there by myself, people think it's weird. The boys think so. . . . I think I'd rather have friends and things than really be that good.[11]

One way to get noticed was to be called on in class. For a gifted girl, being asked a question was a no-win proposition: If she got it wrong, she looked dumb. But if she got it right, then people would dislike her for being too smart. One of the gifted girls was so nervous about this that she prayed every night that the teacher would not call on her. . . .

When children internalize success and externalize failure (the male approach), they are able to tackle new and challenging tasks with a mastery orientation, one that perseveres in the face of difficulty and leads to future achievement. Children who attribute success to effort and failure to lack of ability (the female approach) exhibit "learned helplessness." When con-

10. During the 1970s publishers developed and disseminated the following guidelines for the preparation of nonsexist materials:

Avoiding Stereotypes. College Division, Houghton Mifflin Co., Boston, MA.

Guidelines for Creating Positive Sexual and Racial Images in Educational Materials. Macmillan Publishing Co., New York, NY.

Guidelines for the Development of Elementary and Secondary Instructional Materials. Holt, Rinehart and Winston, New York, NY.

Guidelines for Eliminating Stereotypes from Instructional Materials, Grades K-12. School Department, Harper & Row, New York, NY.

Guidelines for Equal Treatment of the Sexes in McGraw-Hill Book Company Publications. McGraw-Hill, New York, NY.

Guidelines for Improving the Image of Women in Textbooks. Scott, Foresman & Co., Glenview, IL.

Statement on Bias-Free Materials. School Division, Association of American Publishers, New York, NY.

Suggestions for Developing Materials That Are Free of Racial, Sexual, Cultural and Social Bias. Science Research Associates, Chicago, IL.

11. Gritzner, Charles. *Exploring Our World, Past and Present.* Lexington, MA: D.C. Heath, 1991.

fronted with difficult academic material, they do not persist. "I think I can't," they say—and give up.[12]

Recent research clarifies the connection between self-esteem and academic achievement, especially in math and science. Girls and boys who enjoy science and math consider themselves more important, like themselves more, and feel better about their schoolwork and family relationships. They are also more likely to hold professional career goals. Thirty-one percent of girls in elementary school say they are good in math. By middle school, only 18 percent think they are mathematically capable.[13] When girls lose confidence in their ability to learn math and science, they avoid these subjects. When they believe they can't succeed, they become less willing to attempt new science and math tasks. As they have fewer and fewer experiences with math and science, they become less capable. As their competence withers, so does their self-esteem, and the vicious, connected cycle continues: attenuation of self-confidence that leads to loss of mental ability and results in the diminishment of self-confidence. The order of this downward spiral is crucial. The plunge in confidence comes first and is followed by the drop in achievement. It is during middle school that the fabled gender gap in math emerges and gets greater in science. The brightest girls suffer the most. In Lewis Terman's famous studies of gifted men and women, boys' IQs fell 3 points during adolescence. Girls dropped an eye-opening 13 points.[14]

12. Dweck, Carol, and Diane Gilliard. "Expectancy Statements as Determinants of Reactions to Failure: Sex Differences in Persistence and Expectancy Change," *Journal of Personality and Social Psychology* 32:6, pp. 1077–84.

Dweck, Carol, William Davidson, Sharon Nelson, and Bradley Enna. "Sex Differences in Learned Helplessness: II. The Contingencies of Evaluative Feedback in the Classroom, III. An Experimental Analysis," *Developmental Psychology* 14:3 (1978), pp. 268–76.

Ryckman, David, and Percy Peckham. "Gender Differences in Attributions for Success and Failure Situations Across Subject Areas," *Journal of Educational Research* 81 (November-December 1987), pp. 120–25.

Elliott, Elaine, and Carol Dweck. "Goals: An Approach to Motivation and Achievement," *Journal of Personality and Social Psychology* 54:1 (1988), pp. 5–12.

Levine, Gavrielle. "Grade Level Differences Between Females and Males in Mathematics Computation and Motivation Factors." Paper presented at the American Educational Research Association, Chicago, Illinois, 1991.

13. Researched by the Analysis Group, Greenberg-Lake. *Shortchanging Girls, Shortchanging America*. Commissioned by the American Association of University Women.

14. Sadker, Myra, David Sadker, and Susan Klein. "The Issue of Gender in Elementary and Secondary Education." In Grant, Gerald (ed.), *Review of Research in Education*, vol. 17. Washington, DC: American Educational Research Association, 1991.

Mullis, Ina, et al. *Trends in Academic Progress*. Washington, DC: U.S. Department of Education, 1991. Prepared by Educational Testing Service under contract with the National Center for Education Statistics.

Terman, L., and M. Oden. "The Promise of Youth." In Terman, L. (ed.), *Genetic Studies of Genius*, vol. 3. Stanford, CA: Stanford University Press, 1935.

By the end of middle school smart girls report they are more worried and afraid, and less encouraged and appreciated, than they were in elementary school.[15] Many see these changes as a form of adult betrayal:

> Until I was in junior high, my dad was my best friend. We read together and played chess together. He was proud of my intelligence, and he showed it. Then when I entered junior high, he began to show ambivalence toward my achievements. He still said "Great" when I got good grades, but he began asking me about boyfriends and praising me for looking pretty. Somehow this made me feel bad, but I never could express it. I was just frustrated with him and felt betrayed. He just wanted me to be like the other girls.[16]. . .

Poised on the edge of adolescence, girls struggle to keep their balance, retain their authenticity and vitality, and move on to emerge as secure and capable adults. But now so many pitfalls surround them: physical vulnerability, the closing of options, the emphasis on thin, pretty, and popular, the ascendancy of social success over academic achievement, the silencing of their honest feelings, the message that math and science are male domains, the short-circuiting of ability that renders them helpless, the subtle insinuations that boys are really the smart ones (they just don't try). Girls who succumb to these messages are at emotional and academic risk, in danger of losing not only their confidence and their achievement but the very essence of themselves.

Historical Questions

1. Although the exclusion of females from public education seems indefensible to most of us today, it seemed reasonable to earlier generations. With reference to some of the texts you have read in this chapter, discuss two or three of the cultural beliefs, values, and economic circumstances that made such exclusionary practices seem reasonable. Then explore two or three of the cultural and economic changes that made the education of females acceptable and seem necessary. In answering this, again return to some of the texts you have read in this chapter to cite specific examples. But remember that values are often not discussed explicitly, so you may have to read these texts symptomatically to discern why positions on educating females have changed over time.

2. Review the recommendations of the 1918 "Cardinal Principles" report for "the education of every high school girl." In what ways are the lessons

15. Kline, Bruce, and Elizabeth Short. "Changes in Emotional Resilience: Gifted Adolescent Females," *Roeper Review* 13:3 (1991), pp. 118–21.

16. Quoted in Barbara A. Kerr, *Smart Girls, Gifted Women*. Dayton: Ohio Psychology P (1985), p. 106.

learned by female students today, as described by the Sadkers, similar to and different from those proposed in the 1918 report?

3. Compare the Sadkers' description of girls' responses to educational settings and challenges with Dewey's description of the proper attitude and rules of conduct in traditional classrooms. What similarities or differences do you see? Account for these similarities or differences by analyzing two or three of the underlying assumptions of Dewey and the Sadkers about gender identity or roles or behaviors.

Cultural Questions

1. Discuss two or three ways in which the educational unfairness analyzed by the Sadkers is similar to the inequality examined by Kozol. Discuss two to three ways in which it is different. Then explore which type of unfairness you think will be easier to resolve by exploring some of the material and ideological factors underlying each.

2. According to the Sadkers, the refrain "Be nice . . . be a good girl" dominates the messages female students get from their families, teachers, and communities. From your own experiences, or, from observations of your sisters and female friends, what examples can you provide to confirm the authors' assertion of gender inequities in the classroom? What examples can you provide to question their position? What complex and perhaps contradictory assumptions about gender underlie your different examples?

3. At the end of "Missing in Interaction," the authors list many "pitfalls" that adolescent females face in high school. What social institutions other than schools help to create these potential problems? What do you think would have to be done to lessen or eliminate these pitfalls? Discuss one perspective that you have read about or experienced yourself which could support this process, one that would resist it, and one that would be ambivalent. What reasons might each perspective give for its position in relation to adolescent females?

CRCRCRCR

MIKE ROSE

Pasadena: Revised Images of Excellence (1996)

Mike Rose's (b. 1944) own educational career represents many of the strengths and weaknesses of U.S. education today. In the award-winning Lives on the Boundary: A Moving Account of the Struggles and Achievements of America's Educational Underclass (1989), Rose describes several dedicated teachers who enabled him to attain the literacy that other, more privileged students often acquire more easily. In his own career, Rose has become a gifted teacher and scholar who studies the problems and the possibilities of less advantaged students and schools. This reading is an excerpt from Rose's recent book Possible Lives: The Promise of Public Education in America (1996), in which he examines diverse examples of educational excellence.

Continue north from Monterey Park about six winding miles to the foothills of the San Gabriel mountains, and you'll enter Pasadena, located along the northeast rim of the LA Basin. It is linked to downtown Los Angeles by the first freeway built in California, the Arroyo Seco Parkway, a six-mile route built by the WPA and opened in 1940. Though Pasadena is now a middle-class community, it has a history of privilege. Founded in 1874 on the site of an old *rancho* by settlers from Indiana ("The California Colony of Indiana"), Pasadena would quickly develop from what John Muir called "an aristocratic little colony" of orange and lemon orchards, exotic gardens, and learned societies into a booming resort for people of means looking to ease the chill of Boston or Chicago. It hosted the Rose Parade (the first in 1890) and, from 1916, when football replaced chariot racing in the festivities, the Rose Bowl. The city was one of the wealthiest in California until its tourism was devastated by the Great Depression. It was saved—as were a number of other Southern California cities—by World War II, for a local polytechnic institute had developed into Cal Tech, a hub for the region's aerospace and electronics industries. To this day, a large number of residents have undergraduate and graduate degrees and hold managerial and professional positions. Until recently, the power base of the city was exclusively White. Though Mexican and Chinese immigrants were present from the first days of the settlement—employed primarily as field hands—and African Americans migrated in to fill jobs as hotel domestics and chauffeurs (developing eventually a small but active middle class), all non-Whites were strictly segregated in housing, schools, and medical facilities. Such patterns of segregation—restrictive covenants, separate schools—could be found in most Southern California suburbs.

In the last two decades, the demographic mix of Pasadena's citizenry has changed considerably. As the population increased (from 113,000 in 1970 to 132,000 in 1990), the White majority became a minority. The number of African Americans decreased slightly, as well. The Asian population expanded, and the Latino population has increased significantly (from 21,772 in 1980 to 35,912 in 1990), reflecting trends evident throughout Southern California. But the ethnic shifts in the Southland have been marked not only in Latino and Asian numbers. There is a growing Armenian population in Pasadena, migrating in from their point of entry in East Hollywood and Glendale. The 250,000 Armenians in Los Angeles County form the largest concentration outside their homeland.

Pasadena High School graduated its first class in 1890, moved and rebuilt two times to accommodate the city's boom cycles, and opened the doors of its newest campus in 1960. The large, well-equipped facility (it has two swimming pools) served a White middle- and upper-middle-class constituency until 1970, when the courts judged Pasadena to be in violation of school desegregation laws, and busing was mandated. The demographic changes, combined with busing and massive White flight to private schools, have yielded a current ethnic composition of 38 percent Hispanic, 32 percent African American, 25 percent Caucasian (many of whom are Armenian), and about 5 percent Asian. But these percentages do not tell the full story of Pasadena High School. Within the demographer's broad categories, there are forty-two nationalities represented on campus and thirty-eight languages spoken. And since the early 1970s, there has been a shift in class: PHS has the largest number of low-income students in the Pasadena school district, many of whom live in foster homes and/or public housing projects. A lot of these young people see little meaning in school, are regularly truant, are getting in trouble with the law, show all the signs of dropping out.

These problems have absorbed Principal Judy Codding. How, she wondered, could she develop services and programs that would "give our students hope that school can do something for them." One thing she did was establish two academies—one in Graphic Arts and one in Visual Arts and Design—small programs within the school that each enroll 100 to 150 students and attempt an integration of vocational and academic coursework. Such career-academic programs, which have been gaining national attention, can be little more than deceptive tracks away from college and toward low-level employment. But if they are carried out with integrity, they can provide an engaging curriculum, a feeling of specialness, and an expansion of opportunity. Ruby, a junior in the Graphic Arts Academy, saw it like this: the program will enable her to do two things she really wants to do—she wants to go to college, but she has to get a job to support herself. When she graduates, she figures, she'll be able to do both. To ensure that students like Ruby will be able to achieve such goals, Principal Codding has secured mentors and internships from the local printing industry, arranged for students to take courses during their senior year at nearby Pasadena City College, and established agreements so that course-work will be given credit at California State University at Los Angeles.

When I visited it, the Graphic Arts Academy was in its second exper-imental year. Students entered as sophomores and took some courses in the regular curriculum—a foreign language or physical education or an art elective—but the majority of their courses were taken with academy faculty, teachers chosen because of their skill in the classroom and their interest in creating an interdisciplinary curriculum. There were five: Ellen Abraham and Kirk Odegard taught humanities, Elaine Mirkin taught biol-ogy and mathematics, Mary Tsotsis handled chemistry, and Mark Hall was head of the Graphic Arts Lab. They met every week, and conferred on the fly, to develop ways to integrate their curricula: How can you teach human-ities or chemistry with an orientation toward graphic arts? What kind of projects can bring the disciplines together in fruitful ways? So, for example, early in their first term, sophomores wrote a haiku or limerick or quatrain in humanities, made their own paper in the Graphic Arts Lab—and tested its weight and thickness and determined its gloss and texture—and made the ink they used to letter their verse in chemistry, testing its reflective density, opacity, and absorbency. At the heart of the academy was one critical question: How is graphic arts a science, an art, and a language?

I was standing by the Heidelberg computerized printing press in the Graphic Arts Lab with Alena Bayramyan, a sophomore who, with her parents, had emigrated from Armenia. "This program is so special," she said. "The teachers don't want you to get a low grade. They really care about you. It's like we're a family." Alena was petite and full of feeling, and she had taken it on herself to walk me around the lab. It was a big room, white brick walls, lots of windows covered with blinds to regulate the light, a gray linoleum floor. Student-made signs with bright safety warnings were everywhere: DON'T RUN, KEEP HANDS AND LOOSE CLOTHING AWAY FROM ALL MACHINES, DO NOT THROW OBJECTS, and, by the door to the teacher's small office, DON'T MESS WITH MR. HALL! Alena had started us off at the entrance, where students were sitting at computers composing and formating text for their projects. Between the terminals were backpacks, bookbags, jackets and sweaters piled in small heaps, folders full of paper, a couple of dictionaries. Next came four "light tables," tables with opaque glass tops illuminated from below. Students were bent over the soft glow, laying out their negatives, using T-squares and triangles to get the images just right. Then came a long sink with curled negatives hanging from a string overhead, and then the darkroom—its red warning light on. "I'm just learning all of this," Alena said. "I can't wait to get really proficient at it."

Once past the darkroom, we paused at the electrostatic plate maker, a kind of high-intensity photocopying machine that created a plastic "plate" from the texts the students had made. "You have to be careful," Alena explained, "if you make it too hot, it'll burn." From there we passed the paper cutter, where two Armenian boys looked up long enough to tease Alena. "Don't you know," one said to me, "she's an illegal alien!" Alena rolled her eyes and sighed as if to say "How pathetic" and shot something back in Armenian—and we continued on to the Heidelberg printer.

On this day, the academy students were making business cards. Some had a personal slant, the student's name and phone number inscribed under or around a cartoon with a simple exhortation to call, to use the number, to dial and see what happens. Others were for a family business, an auto shop or wrecking yard or shoe repair. Dimple and Lynita, best friends, were over at the computers formating their cards, giving each other a little friendly grief, moving, occasionally, to the hiphop tape playing low on a portable recorder, Lynita now and then executing a gliding dance step. Three or four boys were in close over the light tables, their cheeks and foreheads illuminated a gentle gold, touching up scratches on their negatives with a fine brush—no talking here—or concentrating on a precise cut with an Exacto knife, squinting, biting a lip. The Graphic Arts Academy, according to its position paper, stressed "the central importance of learning how to learn, how to reason, and how to investigate complex issues that require collaboration, personal responsibility, and a tolerance for uncertainty." Two girls traded off at the darkroom. Over by the plate maker, Truc Pham was showing Jack Zabounian how to fuse an electrostatic plate without overheating it. And here at the printing press, the instructor, Mark Hall, stood back as Anthony Willis, a gifted cartoonist, was explaining to a sophomore named Davida how to run the machine. Alena, my guide, stepped to the back of the whirring printer, where sheets of business cards were flapping into a tray. "Hey, Davida," Alena asked, slipping a sheet quickly from the pile, "why did this corner come out so light?" "Oh," Davida answered, "that's cause the printer is still loading with ink—right, Anthony?" Anthony nodded and showed her how to adjust a knob on the side of the machine. Mr. Hall watched, arms folded across his lab coat. "Hey, Alena, see," Davida said, grabbing a new sheet. "Look at this—it's darker." Alena's eyes brightened. "Oh, OK, I got it!" "Tell me what just became clear to you, Alena," Mr. Hall said. A few feet away, a Lebanese-Armenian boy named Pierre (there are Lebanese, Egyptian, Iranian, kish, and Soviet Armenians in Los Angeles) was standing over the electrostatic plate maker, hesitating. "Hey, Mr. Hall," he called out, "I forgot—do I put this transparency face up or face down?" Mr. Hall looked up from the Heidelberg press. "Where's the light coming from, Pierre?" "Oh, yeah," Pierre said quickly, "yeah, yeah, OK, face down." The bell for lunch rang, and Alena and Davida and Anthony and Pierre and Jack Zabounian and Truc Pham kept working. Across the room, Dimple and Lynita walked over to the printer to get hard copies of their texts, and Lynita started picking, slowly, through the piles of clothing for her jacket, keeping an eye on the printer. Mr. Hall leaned over and tapped my shoulder. "I just love it," he said softly, "when the bell rings and nobody moves."

Mark Hall, thirty-one, six-one, a big man with glasses, both irreverent and sentimental, worked in the printing industry until three years ago, when he decided to become a teacher. "I just found that what I enjoyed most about the work I was doing was training new people. You know, we would hustle, push hard to get out advertising inserts—that's what we printed—and it hit me one day: So what if someone didn't get their Kmart ad? Who would care? They'd just miss that week's lining for their cat box. I wanted to work with someone or something that would matter to people, would make a difference in their lives, so I began to think about teaching. What I guess I like most about this program is that it gives kids a reason to come to school—and once they're here and with it, you have a better shot at everything else."

A few hundred feet south of the Graphic Arts Lab, the chemistry teacher Mary Tsotsis was preparing a class of academy sophomores to conduct experiments on polar and nonpolar materials. For a long time, Mary had been interested in developing ways to integrate the teaching of science and art, and the Graphic Arts Academy provided her the opportunity. She would select a procedure or problem in graphic arts and then focus on the chemistry involved, both concepts and techniques.

She began this day by reviewing for the class the defining characteristics of polarity and nonpolarity (the absence or presence of free electrons), and then asked why they, as future graphic artists, need to know "whether polar materials and nonpolar materials can mix." Billy, a sharp kid who could be a teacher's bad day, answered, "Because we'll be using lots of different materials when we make plates." He slid down in his chair, continuing, "We'll hafta know what'll mix, or we'll mess up." Mary nodded. She was formal, serious, dressed meticulously. "Yes," she said in slightly accented English—she was of Greek heritage—"you would mess up."

She asked the students to go to the small laboratory in the back of the room and begin the experiments. Along a wood counter was a row of neatly labeled polar materials (salt, water-based ink, hydrochloric acid, water, and water-based pigment) and a row of nonpolar materials: carbon tetrachloride, ink solvent, oil, and oil-based pigment—in this case, crayon shavings. Some of these would be found in a print shop; others were commonplace, thrown in to complicate the experiment. There was a tray of beakers behind the materials and, alongside the tray, a cabinet and a sink and draining rack filled with clean test tubes. In front of all this were several Formica-covered tables on which Mary's students began laying out large sheets of white paper. The sheets were lined with dark grids. Along the top and down the left side, the students had written the names of the polar materials—NaCl, water-based ink, HCl—and nonpolar materials, CCl_4, ink solvent, and so on. (Some boys wrote these names in the stylized tagger script you'd usually see in graffiti.) As the students began systematically mixing one material with another (a polar with a polar, a nonpolar with a polar), they were to place a drop of each mix in the appropriate square on the grid, thereby illustrating at a glance if a solution had resulted—a nice blot on white—or a bad mix—little clumps of salt or crayon or unblended streaks and stains. A graphic representation of data. Mary would put these sheets on the wall, and later—as the class created further displays of basic concepts and experimental results—they would be stored in a set of bulging portfolios of student work.

Around the room, the students were washing test tubes, holding them up to the windows for the glint of sunlight, checking for a bad rinse; mixing salt and water to prepare one of their polar materials; shaving more crayons, thin slivers of magenta and violet and black, to replenish their store of nonpolar oil-based pigment; cautiously filling droppers with hydrochloric acid or carbon tetrachloride or ink solvent; stirring solutions with glass rods—*tink, tink, tink*—squinting to see the results. There was chatter and school-yard news and crude flirtation and rebuff, lots of questions of Mrs. Tsotsis and of one another, and an occasional line from a song, sung under breath during the washing and stirring. And Mary Tsotsis walked from student to student, asking what they were doing and why and what they were finding out.

I had been with the academy students in other classes and walked around the school yard at lunchtime. Some of them would probably do well in a traditional academic program. Others would have a hard time of it, would get discouraged, and possibly not see the point of it all. And still others—four or five boys—would most likely end up in a continuation school . . . or worse. In the yard they challenged each other, pushing the verbal limits, and in some of their classes they jockeyed continually for the funny line, a desperate impulsivity, not laughing at one another's jokes, but elbowing for the delinquent limelight. A few boys bore so much anger, such a charged resistance to any authority, that the air seemed to pop when a teacher walked by their desks, trying in vain to cool them out.

But here in chemistry and in Mark Hall's Graphic Arts Lab, the work seemed to focus these students' energies and, at times, virtually demanded collaboration rather than street-culture combativeness. So while you certainly heard young people insulting each other, or, on the other hand, saw them congregating in small groups by gender or ethnicity or neighborhood affiliation, you also saw interaction around joint problems or projects, shared needs. Many of the tasks in Mary's or Mark's classes were hard to do alone, and because of the mix of backgrounds and interests and skill, some students would simply be more adept at the technology, some better artists, some in possession of a sharper eye, some quicker to grasp concepts behind procedures. Working together made sense. "You know," Mark had said to me, "sometimes I think the really big benefit of this program is social. It would be hard to prove—how would I get stats on such a thing—but I see some remarkable things happening with my students." By bringing together young people who would traditionally be in separate academic tracks and by integrating applied vocational and college-oriented curricula, the Graphic Arts Academy was creating an institutional and instructional space that encouraged the formation of a microsociety that valued both hand and brain.

But over the brief history of the academy's existence, the creation of that space had proven to be a challenge of the first order. To begin with, nowhere in their professional education are teachers taught how to work together, jointly solve problems, develop mutual curricula; teaching is defined as a highly individualized pursuit. The isolation is reinforced by the rigid borders our colleges and universities establish between disciplines; for all the current talk in higher education about "interdisciplinarity," chemists rarely interact with physicists, let alone social scientists or humanists. This conceptual insularity is, of course, passed on to those who will eventually move into the schools. Add to the problem society's class-laden distinction between manual work and mental work, demonstrated in school by the fierce gulf between vocational education and college preparation. (John Dewey called this distinction "the most deep-seated antithesis . . . in educational history.") And to all this, add one further complication: the linkages that Principal Judy Codding established with industry, with Pasadena City College, with Cal State LA—connections that will assist academy students as they move beyond high school, but that affect here and now the curriculum Mark and Mary and the others must develop for them. "We make a lot of mistakes," Mark told me. "It's not like we have the time to sit back and think all this through, troubleshoot it. We have to create it and teach it at the same time. You just hope it goes right."

And some things did go right. On a shelf by Mark Hall's office in the Graphic Arts Lab was a neat row of hand-bound books with multicolored cloth covers. The students had been reading Sandra Cisneros's *The House on Mango Street* in their humanities class, and they were asked to write a series of vignettes—following Cisneros's episodic style—about their name, their house, their neighbors, the language(s) they spoke, their first job, and so on. They were to write their own *Mango Street*. Since this structure allowed for a lot of variation, it occurred to the biology teacher that students could incorporate brief chapters on science that would thematically play off the autobiographical vignettes. So if you paged through, for example, Dimple's and Lynita's books, you'd find a chapter called "Tears" (about the death of a grandmother) followed by a brief chapter on the lacrimal glands, and a summary of genetics following a chapter on the family. Dimple's chapter on her name was accompanied by a definition of *dimple*. Lynita's chapter called "Me" was paired with an illustration of the human brain. The whole project took about three weeks, and at the end, the students had to plan, measure, illustrate, cut, lay out, and bind the book in the Graphic Arts Lab. When the teachers first came up with the idea, they were unsure about it. Could the students pull it off? Could it be sufficiently interdisciplinary? But once they introduced the project, it began to take shape, the students further developing it. Mark remembered the last few days, watching the students going from biologist to humanities teacher to graphic artist for help, working with them after school to get the binding right, driving Dimple and Lynita to the bus stop as the sky was turning deep blue.

Historical Questions

1. Describe the ways in which Mark Hall, Mary Tsotsis, and other instructors at the Graphic Arts Academy create new organizations of teacher-student-subject interactions and compare them to the interactions Dewey advocated. With specific reference to both texts, explain what Dewey's reactions might be to these reorganized interactions. Why do you think he would have these reactions?

2. A curriculum, like the one at the Graphic Arts Academy, seems unusual to many people. What are two or three advantages and two or three disadvantages of curricular innovations like those described at the Graphic Arts Academy? Then, with reference to at least two previous readings of your choice, explore why certain authors you have read would see such a curriculum as a positive innovation while others would see it as an unproductive change. If you were given the opportunity within your main area of study, would you have chosen to participate in a similar high school curriculum? Explain why or why not by linking your assumptions to Rose's and to the other authors you discussed.

3. In the "Cardinal Principles" report, the authors assert that "secondary education should be determined by the needs of the society to be served." What social needs is the Graphic Arts Academy curriculum trying to meet? Compare what you feel are the primary social needs addressed by the Graphic Arts Academy with those addressed in the "Cardinal Principles" report. What do you see as their major difference and major similarity? How does developing this comparison inform your sense of a current educational debate?

Cultural Questions

1. Analyze the tensions that Rose admits exist among the students in the Graphic Arts Academy. What creates them? What makes them similar to or different from tensions between students that you remember in your high school?

2. In an earlier book entitled *Lives on the Boundary* (1989), Rose describes how he developed from a disadvantaged student to an exceptional student and then to a gifted teacher. As Rose explains his current efforts to make educational programs more inclusive, he notes, "We are in the middle of an extraordinary social experiment: the attempt to provide education for all members of a vast pluralistic democracy." What social and economic factors make this experiment more or less likely to succeed at Pasadena High School? At Morris High School as described by Kozol?

3. In *Lives,* Rose asserts that "We'll need a revised store of images of educational excellence, ones . . . that celebrate the plural messy human reality of it." To what extent do you think that the teachers at the Academy are promoting educational excellence? Return to your first fastwrite and to your readings of Sizer, Kozol, and the Sadkers. What images of educational excellence do you now have? Describe two or three in detail.

❧ Assignment Sequence 1: On the Goals and Methods of High School Learning

As the reports of 1893 and 1918 demonstrate, educational goals change over time. Educators also propose different methods of teaching or "pedagogies," such as the three analyzed by Dewey. For Sizer, however, the central problem lies in the *relationship* between goals and methods, not in the goals or methods in isolation. The gap between what high schools claim as their stated goals and the actual methods of instruction employed is central to Sizer's critique of contemporary high schools. He, for example, contrasts the idealized goal of responsible citizenship, which assumes a capacity for active decision making and analysis, with the actual passivity encouraged in Mark by the methods of classroom instruction.

Essay Question

Considering Sizer's criticism, what do you think are the most important goals and the best methods of high school education? How should these ends and means be coordinated?

∾ Fastwrite 5

Before you begin reviewing the readings, trust in the strength of the knowledge you gained from work in this chapter. If someone asked you your opinion to this question in a friendly conversation, what would you say right now? As you fastwrite, let yourself ramble a bit, as we often do in informal conversation. Then stop and reread your quick response and consider the connections between your response and the readings. In this chapter, which writers agree or disagree with your opinion? On what specific assumptions does this agreement or disagreement depend?

Review Questions

A list of suggested questions to review before beginning this essay follows. This list is meant only to suggest review options. You may focus on only a subset of the questions, decide that other questions should be added, or construct your own sequence of questions. We encourage you to choose what you believe is the most appropriate review strategy.

1. Theodore R. Sizer, Cultural Question 2 (page 274)
2. The 1893 Report of the Committee of Ten, Historical Question 1 (page 297)
3. John Dewey, Historical Question 1 (page 304)
4. John Dewey, Historical Question 4 (page 304)
5. Jonathan Kozol, Cultural Question 2 (page 314)
6. Mike Rose, Historical Question 1 (page 332)
7. Mike Rose, Historical Question 2 (page 332)

Questions for Further Reflection

1. Considering your own high school experiences (see fastwrite 1) and those described by Sizer, Kozol, and Rose, do you agree that there are inconsistencies between the stated goals and actual methods of many contemporary high schools? Explain your reasons for agreeing or disagreeing and give specific examples to illustrate your points.

2. What historical and cultural developments explain the consistency or inconsistency between the contemporary ends and means of secondary education?

3. Considering the multiple answers to the questions of educational ends and means, what do you think are the most important goals and the most appropriate methods that should be maintained or established?

ᐅ Assignment Sequence 2: On the Relationship between School and Society

As an educational theorist, Dewey initially believed that better schooling would lead to the social reforms he desired, such as the furthering of democracy. Yet when he tried to implement his educational theories, Dewey found his task was much more difficult than he had considered because schools, as social institutions, are slow to change because of the "opposition of those who . . . realize [educational reform] would threaten their ability to use others for their own ends." Thus, the possibility of educational reform leading to social reform is complicated by the fact that schools share many of the same problems from which society in general suffers.

Essay Question

Based on your reading and writing in this chapter, to what degree do you think high schools can help resolve social problems?

ᐅ Fastwrite 6

Use the same fastwrite assignment as outlined in fastwrite 5 (p. 334).

Review Questions

A list of suggested questions to review before beginning this essay follows. This list is meant only to suggest review options. You may focus on only a subset of the questions, decide that other questions should be added, or construct your own sequence of questions. We encourage you to choose what you believe is the most appropriate review strategy.

1. The 1893 Report of the Committee of Ten, Cultural Question 2 (page 288)
2. The "Cardinal Principles" Report of 1918, Historical Question 1 (page 297)
3. Jonathan Kozol, Cutural Question 1 (page 314)

4. Myra and David Sadker, Cultural Question 2 (page 324)
5. Mike Rose, Historical Question 3 (page 333)

Questions for Further Reflection

1. Considering the reports of 1893 and 1918, fastwrite 3, and the reading by Rose, to what degree are schools able to change in order to address social needs?

2. Evaluate the quality of education offered by the high schools described by Kozol, the Sadkers, Rose, and you in fastwrite 1.

3. Considering the readings by Kozol and the Sadkers especially, what cultural beliefs do high schools challenge and reinforce? How equal or unequal do you think educational opportunity is in U.S. high schools?

ભ

For Further Research

Written Texts

American Association of University Women. *How Schools Shortchange Girls— The AAUW Report: A Study of Major Findings on Girls and Education.* New York: Marlowe, 1992.

Freire, Paulo. "The 'Banking' Concept of Education." *The Pedagogy of the Oppressed.* New York: Continuum, 1981.

Freire, Paulo, and Ira Shor. "Do First-World Students Need Liberating?" *A Pedagogy for Liberation: Dialogues on Transforming Education.* New York: Bergin, 1987.

Giroux, Henry A. *Border Crossings: Cultural Workers and the Politics of Education.* New York: Routledge, 1993.

Hirsch, E. D., Jr. *Cultural Literacy: What Every American Needs to Know.* New York: Vintage, 1987.

Illich, Ivan. *DeSchooling Society.* New York: Harper, 1970.

Kozol, Jonathan. *Death at an Early Age: The Destruction of the Hearts and Minds of Negro Children in Boston's Public Schools.* Boston: Houghton, 1967.

Lightfoot, Sara Lawrence. *The Good High School.* New York: Basic, 1983.

A Nation at Risk: The Full Account of the National Commission on Excellence in Education. Cambridge, MA: USA Research, 1984.

Ravitch, Diane. *The Troubled Crusade: American Education, 1945–1980.* New York: Basic, 1983.

Rodriguez, Richard. "The Achievement of Desire." *Hunger of Memory.* New York: Godine, 1982: 46-57.

Rose, Mike. *Lives on the Boundary: An Account of the Struggles and Achievements of America's Educational Underclass.* New York: Macmillan, 1989.

Sizer, Theodore R. *Horace's Compromise: The Dilemma of the American High School.* Boston: Houghton, 1984.

———. *Horace's School: Redesigning the American High School.* Boston: Houghton, 1992.

Tyack, David, and Larry Cuban, *Tinkering Toward Utopia: A Century of Public School Reform.* Harvard UP, 1995.

Films

Dangerous Minds. Dir. John N. Smith. Perf. Michelle Pfeiffer. Via Rosa, 1995.

Dead Poet's Society. Dir. Peter Weir. Perf. Robin Williams. Touchstone, 1989.

Fast Times at Ridgemont High. Dir. Amy Heckerling. Perf. Sean Penn. Universal, 1982.

Mr. Holland's Opus. Dir. Stephen Herek. Perf. Richard Dreyfus. Hollywood Pictures, 1995.

The Principal. Dir. Christopher Cain. Perf. James Belushi. TriStar, 1987.

Stand and Deliver. Dir. Ramon Menendez. Perf. Edward James Olmos. Warner Bros., 1987.

Up the Down Staircase. Dir. Robert Mulligan. Perf. Sandy Dennis, Alan J. Pakula. Warner Bros., 1967.

Documentaries

"Failing in Fairness 1." *Dateline.* Narr. Jane Pauley. Produced, Elizabeth Kavetas. Ed. Lynn Hertzog. NBC, 7 Apr. 1992.

"Failing in Fairness 2." *Dateline.* Narr. Jane Pauley. Prod. Elizabeth Kavetas. Ed. Lynn Hertzog. NBC, 8 Feb. 1994. To order, call 1-800-420-2626.

High School I (1968) and *High School II.* (1994) Dir., ed., and prod. Frederick Wiseman. 1994.

Television Shows

Beverley Hills 90210. Fox, 1989–91.

Boy Meets World. ABC.

Breaker High. WB.

Dawson's Creek. WB.

Fame. NBC, 7 Jan. 1982 to 4 Aug. 1983.

My So-Called Life. Prod. Bedford Falls. 1994.

Party of Five. Fox.

Room 222. ABC, 17 Sept. 1969 to 11 Jan. 1974.

Saved by the Bell. USA.

Sweet Valley High. UPN.

USA High. USA. (Focuses on an international school.)

Welcome Back, Kotter. Created Gabriel Kaplan and Alan Sacks. ABC, 9 Sept. 1975 to 10 Aug. 1979.

ॐ 6 ॐ

ELVIS PRESLEY: ANY WAY YOU WANT ME (THAT'S HOW I WILL BE)

ALAN G. SCHMIDT

No one has ever been more famous for being famous.
—NEW YORK TIMES EDITORIAL,
AUGUST 16, 1997

The three most identifiable names in the whole world are Jesus,
Coca-Cola, and Elvis.
—RON ROSENBAUM, 1995

Elvis helped liberate the country from the strictures of its puritan-
ical heritage while blurring the nation's black-white cultural
boundaries, making black music popular with white teenagers.
—DOUGLAS BRINKLEY, 1993

Anyone who idolizes Elvis and considers him a church are [sic]
sickies; they have the brains of gnats.
—JIMMY DENSON, 1994

Some people just have trouble believing that a piece of white
trash from the depths of the segregated South could have been
musically color blind. If Elvis hadn't been a Southerner . . .
maybe those who despise or ridicule him would be willing to
give him a break. But if he hadn't been a Southerner, he
wouldn't have been Elvis and probably wouldn't have sung
the blues with such natural feeling.
—FRANCIS DAVIS, 1995

The bad death did not diminish his life. With Elvis, it is
always better to hear the songs, watch the film clips and
movies that fill the airwaves at tribute times. From the first
performance, it was all there—the self-assurance, awareness,
and charm of a natural.
—JULIE BAUMGOLD, 1994

338

ᐰ

Introduction: Man Or Myth?

ᐰ **Fastwrite 1**

Fastwrite about your current perspective on Elvis Presley, using some of the following questions to guide your fastwrite. How much do you know about Elvis? Where did you learn it? On the radio? Television? Videos, tapes, or CDs? In any of the many new books coming out about Elvis? From visiting Graceland? Did you read about, watch, or listen to any of the events surrounding the twentieth anniversary of Elvis's death on August 16, 1997? What do you think of Elvis? Do you think your position is similar to that of your peers? What, in your opinion, is Elvis's contribution to culture? Is it a positive contribution? Be as specific as possible in representing your own perspective and your sources.

The 1950s. Memphis. Blues. Truck Driver. Mama's Boy. Country Music. Sun Records. King of Rock 'n' Roll. Sex. Hound Dog. Gospel Music. Blue Suede Shoes. Colonel Parker. Graceland. Ed Sullivan. Gold Suit. Television. Pink Cadillacs. Movies. Jailhouse Rock. Millionaire. The Army. Can't Help Falling In Love. Priscilla. Viva Las Vegas. The Comeback Special. Suspicious Minds. Lisa Marie. Richard Nixon. Aloha from Hawaii. Peanut Butter and Banana Sandwiches. Hunka Hunka Burnin' Love. Karate. Jumpsuits. Drugs. Fat. Dead. Legend. Myth. God.

When you think of Elvis Presley, how many of the terms above come to mind? There are some facts we all know about Elvis that are deeply embedded in our cultural language. Sometimes the facts contradict each other; for example, how is it that a man called by some a "mama's boy" could come to embody uninhibited sexual release? How could a boy with no formal musical education embrace country music, blues, and gospel and create something new from them? How could a poor boy become so wealthy so quickly? How did Elvis Presley then go on to become a cultural icon, a star, a legend, larger than life, even during his lifetime? The questions go on and on, and the more facts we discover about Elvis, the more conflicts we can find in his story. In fact, the story we think is *his* becomes a story about many of our own ideas and aspirations, about our whole culture. It becomes not just a personal story but what we call a *myth*.

Certainly, the statistics regarding Elvis's career are staggering. Elvis has had more number one records than anyone else in music. He has had more weeks at number one than any other entertainer. He has had more gold and platinum records. Elvis Presley is the only artist ever to have the same record at number one on the pop, country, and rhythm and blues charts

("Hound Dog/Don't Be Cruel"). The *annual* revenue on his music—twenty years after his death—is over one-quarter of $1 billion. Seven hundred thousand visitors annually to go Graceland, his Memphis home. During the first two weeks of August 1997, media coverage of the twentieth anniversary of Elvis's death was as intense as the coverage of any contemporary event; no doubt many of you witnessed some this coverage and heard a litany of facts about Elvis during that time.

The facts of Elvis Presley's life and career will only take us so far, however, because in the brief time since he first arrived on the scene, he has become a legend—the rags-to-riches version of the American Dream realized. And with the apparent realization of that dream, Elvis the man became a cultural icon, subject to the myth making of all of the United States. With this mythic status, his personal control over his own identity became less certain as various forces—with different values and goals— sought to create, market, and sell the icon to a "consuming" public with a vast variety of wants and needs. Indeed, in the years since his death, Elvis's life and career continue to take on new meanings, many of which might have seemed impossible to imagine back in those days when teenage girls swooned in adoration of him and their boyfriends tried to copy his mannerisms and clothing.

To understand this phenomenon, think of the ways in which our culture represents fame. Stories, often bordering on the impossible, emerge about the powers, beauty, goodness, riches, or wisdom of a person, stories that can come to represent less of that actual person and more of our culture's values, hopes, and ambitions. Think, perhaps, of sports heroes, movie stars, and some religious figures—"larger than life," as we sometimes say, or—going back in our history and to other cultures—miracle workers, saints, and gods. Think of what we refer to as the American Dream, stories and accounts of the United States that are embodiments of people's hopes and ambitions rather than exact descriptions of the land or of particular situations or achievements. The function of such objects of veneration has tradi- tionally been to embody a culture's most deeply felt hopes and fears, ambitions and desires. An actual person, especially after he or she dies, may have little actual connection with the stories that are told, retold, added to, collected, and passed on. His or her significance for us is what becomes important. That person has become a *myth*. Consider the figure of Elvis Presley primarily in such a context.

All "texts" relating to Elvis Presley (or to any other artist, musician, film star, dancer, composer, and so on) are secondary texts—that is, they are texts "about" Elvis. The primary texts for this chapter are Elvis's own works: his records, his films, and videos of his performances. Because of copyright costs, these important texts cannot be presented here; but even if they were, reading the words of a song is certainly not the same as listening to it or seeing the artist perform it. As you study Elvis, therefore, become familiar with some of his music. To assist you, we make suggestions throughout the chapter of songs or videos that you might want to listen to or watch. We indicate these with the icon of a musical note for a song or an eye for a video. Full references for these appear at the end of the chapter. We also give you specific pieces of information about Elvis's life throughout the chapter, at points where they are relevant to the text you are reading, rather than putting them all in the introduction. You might also want to do some research of your own. The Internet is a valuable source of information on Elvis; you might want to spend some time during the course browsing Web sites. Finally, a list of recommended works by and about Elvis appears at the end of the chapter.

By examining the complexity of such a seemingly entertainment-oriented topic as "Elvis Presley," you may come to see the complexity that lies behind the making of a cultural legend. You may also see the ways in which you might be involved in such legend-making. The phenomenon of "Elvis Presley" is still evolving and, in the course of your own lifetime, may develop further.

N E W   Y O R K   T I M E S

Elvis Forever (1997)

On August 16, 1997, the twentieth anniversary of Elvis Presley's death, when celebrations were being held at Graceland and in many other places throughout the country, and when television and radio were filled with tributes to Elvis, the *New York Times* ran the following editorial.

Elvis Presley was 42 years old when he died of cardiac arrhythmia at Graceland, his Memphis mansion, 20 years ago today. At the time, having been eclipsed by the Beatles, Elvis seemed very much older than his years—caught, in fact, in an irresolute, premature middle age. But now, looking across the years to Aug. 16, 1977, it becomes clear just how young Elvis was when he died.

Twenty years isn't only the distance between now and then: it's also the distance between the fullness of Elvis's mid-50's notoriety and his last breath. Not nearly enough time, and yet—thanks to the special relativity of fame—too much time, or so Elvis often made it seem.

Fame did not transform Elvis Presley. Elvis Presley transformed fame. His celebrity was purely personal. Once, it had something to do with his music, of course. But no one has ever been more famous for being famous. Elvis is often regarded as a victim of pure renown, but he understood celebrity. For all its absurdities, the late Elvis—the jump-suited, chrome-goggled, bespangled version so widely imitated—was at least an Elvis struggling with personal alchemy—the transformation of image, if not identity.

Virtually no one impersonates the young G.I. or the Sun Records recording artist. Elvis impersonators conjure up the man who was headed where only Liberace had gone before: toward a vision of the self as spectacle. The public Elvis who died in August 1977 was the incomplete creation of a private man who lacked the sustenance to outlive himself. When he was still a young man, he leaped ahead, musically speaking, to a place his fans would find comfortable when they grew middle aged. He died so that Neil Diamond might live.

What Elvis lacked, chiefly, was irony. What he possessed instead was sincerity, which is easily misread as self-parody. The nation has not had to memorialize Elvis Presley, except in postage stamps, because he did such a good job of it himself at Graceland. He created there a far more credible, because ultimately more honest, memorial than anyone else could ever have done.

But to look back past the Graceland years—to the young Elvis recording "Heartbreak Hotel," his first hit single—is to realize that Elvis embodied a virility that is not quite the same thing as masculinity. He was helplessly male without a manhood to grow into, and he was hopelessly American without knowing which America to inhabit, as his December 1970 meeting with President Richard Nixon—who knew something very different about personal alchemy—made clear. "The Drug Culture, the Hippie Elements, the S.D.S., Black Panthers, etc. do *not* consider me as their enemy or as they call it the Establishment," Elvis wrote to Nixon. Then he added, somewhat obliquely, "I call it America and I love it."

ॐ   **Fastwrite 2**

Fastwrite about your reaction to some of the details of this review; you might focus on its attitude toward Elvis and fame, his maleness, or his relationship to the United States. What is the tone of the review? What does it suggest about how Elvis is viewed in the United States today?

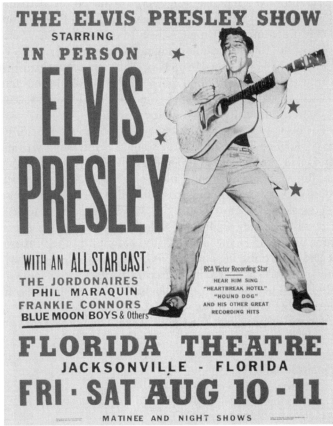

Figure 6.1.   Elvis Presley Show Poster, 1956.
Elvis was under a judge's orders not to bump and grind in his usual manner for these shows, and warrants for his arrest were prepared if he disobeyed. He performed moving only his little finger, and the crowds went wild anyway.

JACK   GOULD

TV: New Phenomenon (1956)

Elvis Presley began his recording career in 1954, with the release of "That's All Right, Mama" and "Blue Moon of Kentucky" on Sam Phillips's Sun Records label in Memphis. He quickly became a local, and then a regional star, and he attracted the attention of Colonel Tom Parker, who became his manager and signed him to a recording contract with RCA Records. His first RCA release, "Heartbreak Hotel," became his first million-selling record, early in 1956. He had performed on network television four times before the appearance on the *Milton Berle Show* reviewed in this article, and each appearance had increased his popularity with teenagers and the reaction against him by many adults.

For his appearance on the *Milton Berle Show* on June 5, 1956, Elvis performed his version of the song "Hound Dog," written by Jerry Leiber and Mike Stoller, and originally recorded by Willie Mae "Big Mama" Thornton, a blues singer. Wearing an unusually tailored jacket and forsaking his guitar, Elvis performed the song at its usual pace, then repeated the last verse several times at half speed while dancing wildly across the stage. No one had ever seen anyone perform like this on television before, and the controversy that had been bubbling about Elvis boiled over. The next day, the following review appeared in the *New York Times*. Critic Jack Gould (1914–1993) was the radio and television critic for the *Times* from 1944 to 1972 (which means that when he wrote this review, he was forty-two years-old, the age Elvis was when he died).

♪ "Don't Be Cruel"
♪ "Heartbreak Hotel"
♪ "Hound Dog"
♪ "That's All Right, Mama"
◉ Elvis '56

Elvis Presley is currently the entertainment world's most astonishing figure. The young man with the sideburns and mobile hips is the rage of the squealing teen-agers and his records are a top item in the never-never land of juke box operators and disk jockeys. By any reasonable standards of success he is big business.

Mr. Presley made another television appearance last night on the Milton Berle show over Channel 4; indeed the entire program revolved around the boy. Attired in the familiar oversize jacket and open shirt which are almost the uniform of the contemporary youth who fancies himself as terribly sharp, he might possibly be classified as an entertainer. Or, perhaps quite as easily, as an assignment for a sociologist.

Mr. Presley has no discernible singing ability. His specialty is rhythm songs which he renders in an undistinguished whine: his phrasing, if it can be called that, consists of the stereotyped variations that go with a beginner's aria in a bathtub. For the ear he is an unutterable bore, not nearly so talented as Frankie Sinatra back in the latter's rather hysterical days at the Paramount Theatre. Nor does he convey the emotional fury of a Johnnie Ray.

From watching Mr. Presley it is wholly evident that his skill lies in another direction. He is a rock-and-roll variation on one of the most standard acts in show business: the virtuoso of the hootchy-kootchy. His one specialty is an accented movement of the body that heretofore has been primarily identified with the repertoire of the blonde bombshells of the burlesque runway. The gyration never had anything to do with the world of popular music and still doesn't.

Certainly, Mr. Presley cannot be blamed for accepting the adulation and economic rewards that are his. But that's hardly any reason why he should be billed as a vocalist. The reason for his success is not that complicated.

∾

Postscript

The reaction to Elvis's performance was so strong that several weeks later when Elvis appeared on the *Steve Allen Show,* he sang "Hound Dog" standing still, dressed in a tuxedo, and singing to a basset hound. Elvis always considered this appearance the most embarrassing moment of his career. The day after the Allen show, Elvis finally recorded the song at the RCA studio in New York. Elvis insisted on doing over thirty takes of the song until he got the one he wanted, the one we know today. The single of "Hound Dog," backed with "Don't Be Cruel," went to the number one position on the pop, country, and rhythm and blues charts. Both songs often appear in "top 100 of all time" lists.

Historical Questions

1. Develop a symptomatic reading of Gould's review of Elvis, analyzing the language and tone of his review as well as the particular examples and details he includes. What is he literally saying about Elvis? Then, focusing on one or two specific examples, explore what Gould is also saying indirectly about Elvis, about himself, and about what he imagines are the dominant values at the time regarding music and entertainers. You might explore, for example, why he compares Elvis to a burlesque dancer or to Frank Sinatra, or why he describes Elvis's clothes as he does. What is your reaction to this review reading it today? Why do you have the reaction you do?

2. Compare and contrast aspects of the language and tone of Gould's *New York Times* review with the one written in the *Times* in 1997, forty-one years later.

Cultural Question

In the library, review the *New York Times* for June 6, 1956. Describe some of the other stories covered that day. How many names do you recognize? What seemed particularly important at that time? Try to find an article that attempts to predict the outcome of a world or national event. Were the predictions accurate? What does the location in the newspaper and the length of the review of Elvis's performance suggest to you about the paper's general view of Elvis? What "feel" do you have for this particular historical moment—what tensions, issues, contradictions are you sensing—based on your reading of the paper for one day?

∾   Fastwrite 3

What do you think is the role and the effectiveness of the daily news in shaping the dominant views of a culture? Develop your fastwrite with reference to a specific example.

STANLEY BOOTH

Situation Report: Elvis in Memphis, 1967 (1968)

The following article by Stanley Booth (b.1942) was originally published in *Esquire* magazine in February 1968. Booth was born in Georgia and graduated from Memphis State University in 1963. He is the author of numerous articles and books on rock 'n' roll, including *The True Adventures of the Rolling Stones* (1985) and *Rythm Oil: A Journey through the Music of the American South* (1991).

♪ "(Let Me Be Your) Teddy Bear"
♪ "Love Me Tender"
♪ "Milkcow Blues Boogie"
♪ "Mystery Train"

The time is the early '50s, and the scene is dull. Dwight Eisenhower is president, Perry Como is the leading pop singer. The world has changed (it changed in 1945), but the change is not yet evident. Allen Ginsberg is a market researcher for a San Francisco securities company. William Burroughs is in New Orleans, cooking down codeine cough syrup. Malcolm X, paroled from Massachusetts's Charlestown Prison, is working in a Detroit furniture store. Stokely Carmichael is skinny, insolent, and eleven years old.

It is, let us say, 1953. Fred Zinnemann rehashes the past with *From Here to Eternity*, and Laslo Benedek gives us, in *The Wild One*, a taste of the future. This is a movie with good guys and bad guys, and the good guys are the ones who roar on motorcycles into a town which is small, quiet, typically American, and proceed to take it apart. Their leader, Marlon Brando, will be called an anti-hero. But there is no need for the prefix. He is a new, really contemporary hero: the outcast.

Soon James Dean repeats the theme with even greater success. But Dean's career was absurdly short. 'You know he was dead before he knew who he was,' someone said. The outcasts of America were left without a leader.

Then, one Saturday night early in 1956 on a television variety program, a white singer drawls at the camera: 'Ladies and gentlemen, I'd like to do a song now, that tells a little story, that really makes a lot of sense—Awopbopaloobop—alopbamboom! Tutti-frutti! All rootie! Tutti-frutti! All rootie!'

Though nearly all significant popular music was produced by Negroes, a white rhythm-and-blues singer was not an entirely new phenomenon. Bill Haley and the Comets had succeeded with such songs as 'Shake, Rattle and Roll,' and 'Rock Around the Clock.' But the pudgy Haley, in his red plaid dinner jacket, did not project much personal appeal. This other fellow was something else.

He was not quite a hillbilly, not yet a drugstore cowboy. He was a Southern—in that word's connotation of rebellion and slow, sweet charm—version of the character Brando created in *The Wild One*. Southern high-school girls, the 'nice' ones, called these boys 'hoods.' You saw them lounging on the hot concrete of a gas station on a Saturday afternoon, or coming out of a poolroom at three o'clock of a Monday afternoon, stopping for a second on the sidewalk as if they were looking for someone who was looking for a fight. You even see their sullen faces, with a toughness lanky enough to just miss being delicate, looking back at you out of old photographs of the Confederate Army. They were not named Tab or Rock, nor even Jim, Bill, Bob. They all had names like Leroy, Floyd, Elvis. All outcasts, with their contemporary costumes of duck-ass haircuts, greasy Levis, motorcycle boots, T-shirts for day and black leather jackets for evening wear. Even their unfashionably long sideburns (Elvis's were *furry*) expressed contempt for the American dream they were too poor to be part of.

No one writing about Presley should forget the daring it took to be one of these boys, and to sing. A hood might become a mechanic or a house painter or a bus-driver or even a cop, but nobody would expect him to be a singer. If he tried it at all, he would have to have some of his own crowd playing with him; he'd have to sing some old songs his own people had sung before him; and he would have to sing them in his own way, regardless of what people might say about him.

'Mama, do you think I'm vulgar on the stage?'

'Son, you're not vulgar, but you're puttin' too much into your singin'. Keep that up and you won't live to be thirty.'

'I can't help it, Mama. I just have to jump around when I sing. But it ain't vulgar. It's just the way I feel. I don't feel sexy when I'm singin'. If that was true, I'd be in some kinda institution as some kinda sex maniac.'

These days, when asked about the development of his career, Elvis either ignores the question or refers it to 'my manager.' Generally speaking his manager is the person standing closest to him at the time. This is often Alan Fortas, officially the ranch foreman, a young man only slightly less stocky than a bull, with a history of hostility to reporters. When the Beatles visited Elvis in Hollywood, Fortas, not troubling to remember their names, addressed each of them as, 'Hey, Beatle!' They always answered, too: nobody wants to displease Alan.

A more voluble source of information is Dewey Phillips. During Elvis's early career Phillips was probably as close to him as anyone except his mother, Gladys. Now retired, Phillips was then one of the most popular and influential disc jockeys in the nation. He still speaks the same hillbilly jive he used as a broadcaster.

'Nobody was picking up on the ole boy back then. He was a real bashful kid, but he liked to hang around music. They'd chased him away from the switchboard at WMPS, and he'd come hang around Q. That's WHBQ, where I was doing my show, Red Hot and Blue, every night. Weekends, he'd come down to Sun Records—he'd cut that record, "My Happiness," for his mother, paid four dollars for it himself—and Sam Phillips, President of Sun, finally gave him a session. Tried to record a ballad, but he couldn't cut it. Sam got Bill Black, the piano player, and Scotty Moore, the guitarist, to see if they could work anything out with him.

'After a couple of tries, Elvis, Bill and Scotty fixed up a couple of old songs, "That's All Right, Mama," and "Blue Moon of Kentucky" so they sounded a little different. When Elvis began to cut loose with "That's All Right," Sam came down and recorded these son-of-a-guns. One night I played the record thirty times. Fifteen times each side. When the phone calls and telegrams started to come in, I got hold of Elvis's daddy, Vernon. He said Elvis was at a movie, down at Suzore's number two theater. Get him over here, I said. And before long Elvis came running in. Sit down, I'm going to interview you, I said. He said, "Mr. Phillips, I don't know nothing about being interviewed." Just don't say nothing dirty, I told him. 'He sat down, and I said I'd let him know when we were ready to start. I had a couple of records cued up, and while they played we talked. I asked him where he went to school, and he said "Humes." I wanted to get that out, because a lot of people listening had thought he was colored. Finally I said, All right, Elvis, thank you very much. "Aren't you gone interview me?" he asked. I already have, I said. The mike's been open the whole time. He broke out in a cold sweat.'

According to Phillips, Elvis at this time considered himself a country singer. 'Sam used to get him, Roy Orbison, Jerry Lee Lewis and Johnny Cash down at Sun and play Big Bill Broonzy and Arthur Crudup records for them, trying to get them on the blues thing, because he felt like that was going to be hot. One of Elvis's first public appearances was at a hillbilly jamboree at the downtown auditorium. Webb Pierce was there, and Carl Smith, Minnie Pearl, a whole houseful of hillbillies. Elvis was nervous, said he wanted me with him. But Sam and I were out at my house, drinking beer, or we had something going, and I missed the afternoon show. Elvis came looking for me, mad as hell. I asked him what he'd sung and he said, '"Old Shep" and "That's How My Heartaches Begin."''

What happened? 'Nothing.'

'So that night I went along with him and told him to open with "Good Rockin' Tonight" and not to sing any hillbilly songs. I introduced him and stayed onstage while he sang. He went into "Good Rockin'," started to shake, and the place just blew apart. He was nobody, didn't even have his name on the posters, but the people wouldn't let him leave. When we finally went off we walked past Webb Pierce, who had been waiting in the wings to go on. I smiled at him and he said, "You son of a bitch."'

The sales of Elvis's records enabled him to get more bookings, and Dewey Phillips bought him an old Lincoln sedan for $450 so he could play out-of-town jobs. Appearing in Nashville at a convention of the Country and Western Disc Jockeys' Association, he was seen— 'discovered,' by talent scouts for RCA Victor. In a moviehouse matinée in Texarkana, he was discovered by Thomas Andrew Parker, a latter-day Barnum out of W. C. Fields by William Burroughs. Parker, an illegal immigrant from Holland, had created a fictional canny background for himself: he had worked in his uncle's 'Great Parker Pony Circus,' dipped candied apples, shaved ice for snow cones, operated merry-go-rounds, even put in a stretch as dog-catcher in Tampa, Florida.

Astute techniques in these businesses had enabled Parker to rise in the world to a position of some prestige. The title 'Colonel' had been conferred upon him by, as he put it, 'a few governors.' He was managing the careers of such big-name country entertainers as Hank Snow and Eddy Arnold. But in all his years as a promoter, he had never found so promotable a commodity as Presley. He had seen Elvis at, for his purposes, just the right time. The demand for Elvis's records prompted RCA to offer $35,000 for Presley, lock, stock, and tapes. Sam Phillips accepted.

'Elvis knew he was going big time,' Dewey Phillips remembers, 'and he needed a manager. That was late spring of '55. He was the hottest thing in show business, and still just a scared kid. He had got his mother and daddy a nice house, they had three Cadillacs, and no phone. He asked me to be his manager. I told him I didn't know anything about managing. Then Colonel Parker came to town. He knew what he was doing. He didn't talk to Elvis. He went out to the house and told Gladys what he could do for the boy. That Parker is a shrewd moo-foo, man.'

Elvis's first appearances on network television, on the Tommy and Jimmy Dorsey Show in January and February 1956, changed him from a regional phenomenon into a national sensation. This might not have happened, the American public might simply have shuddered and turned away, had there not been a new group among them: teenagers, the enemy within. When the older generation, repelled by Presley's lean, mean, sexy image, attacked him from pulpits and editorial columns, banned him from radio stations, the teenagers liked him more than ever, and went out and bought his records. Entrepreneurs could not afford to ignore Presley. As one radio producer asked: How can you argue with the country's number-one recording star? Reluctantly, almost unwillingly, show business accepted Elvis. Ed Sullivan, who only a couple of months before had condemned Presley as 'unfit for a family audience,' now was obliged to pay him $50,000 for three brief appearances. However, Elvis was photographed only from the waist up, and his material was diluted by the addition of a ballad, 'Love Me Tender,' which oozed syrup.

Such attempts to make Elvis appear respectable were very offensive to the good old boys back in Memphis. Steve Allen, involved in a ratings battle with Sullivan, booked Presley, but assured the audience that they would see only 'clean family entertainment.' Elvis appeared and sang, standing still, wearing white tie and tails, with top hat and cane, but without a guitar. Just after the show went off the air, Dewey Phillips's telephone rang.

'Hello, you bastard,' Dewey said.

'How'd you know it was me?' asked Elvis.

'You better call home and get straight, boy. What you doing in that monkey suit? Where's your guitar?'

So when Elvis made his next hometown appearance (it was on July 4, 1956) he reassured his people. The occasion was a charity benefit and Colonel Parker had turned down paying engagements so that Elvis could be part of the show. His was the closing spot, and he was preceded by more than a hundred performers, including the orchestra of Bob Morris and Aaron Bluestein, the Admiral's Band of Navy Memphis, a barbershop quartet called the Confederates, Charlotte Morgan's dancing Dixie Dolls, and innumerable singers, by no means the least of which was one Helen Putnam, founder of Fat Girls Anonymous, who dedicated 'A Good Man Is Hard to Find' to Elvis.

After nearly three hours, with the audience so bored that it was on the point of having a religious experience, Dewey Phillips, who was master of ceremonies, said 'All right. Here he is,' and there he was, his hair hanging over his forehead, a wad of gum in his jaw. He wore a black suit, black shoes, black shirt, red tie, and red socks, clothes with so much drape and flash that they created a new sartorial category, somewhere on the other side of corny. He sang all the old songs in the old way, from 'That's All Right' to 'Blue Suede Shoes' to 'Heartbreak Hotel.' He sang until he was dripping with sweat, and when at last he spoke, his words were a promise to his friends, a gift of defiance to his enemies: 'I just want to tell y'awl not to worry—them people in New York and Hollywood are not gone change me none.'

Then his voice became a growl, an act of rebellion: 'You ain't nothin' but a houn' dog,' he sang, and proceeded to have sexual intercourse with the microphone.

If the police had not been there, forming a blue wall around the stage, the audience might have eaten Elvis's body in a eucharistic frenzy. They were his and he was theirs, their leader: it was an incandescent moment.

And the same time it was a climactic one. For as he stood there singing defiance at his natural enemies—those with power, prestige, money—the Humes High School hood, the motorcycle jockey, was gone, and in his place there was a star, with power, prestige, money. A few months from now at about three o'clock one morning, he would be standing with one of his hired companions outside the Strand Theatre on Main Street in Memphis when a couple of his high-street classmates would drive past, not going much of anywhere, just dragging Main. They would slow their car as they came alongside the Strand; they would see it was Elvis; and then, without a word, they would drive on. 'A few years ago,' Elvis said, 'they would have spoken to me.'

Elvis had tried to go on being himself. When Paramount offered him a movie contract with a clause forbidding him to ride motorcycles, he said 'I'd rather not make movies.' They let him keep his motorcycles. All that was really necessary was that he stop doing his thing and start doing theirs. His thing was 'Mystery Train,' 'Milkcow Blues Boogie.' Theirs was 'Love Me Tender,' 'Loving You,' 'Jailhouse Rock,' 'King Creole.'

Then he was drafted. The Army cut his hair, took away his fancy clothes, and Elvis let them. His country had served him well and he was willing to serve his country. He is nothing if not fair-minded.

While he was stationed in Fort Hood, Texas, Elvis moved his parents to a rented house in the nearby town of Killeen. His mother, who had been doing poorly for more than a year, worsened, and on August 8, 1958, Elvis put her on a train to Methodist Hospital in Memphis and requested the customary special leave.

It was refused. When Gladys's doctors, at Elvis's request, advised his command of the seriousness of his mother's illness they were told, in effect, 'If it were anybody else, there'd be no problem. It's standard procedure. But if we let Presley go everybody will yell special privilege.'

Days passed while Gladys Presley sank lower and lower. In spite of constant urging from Elvis and the doctors, the leave still was not granted. Finally, on the morning of August 12, Elvis decided that he had had enough. 'If I don't get a pass by two o'clock this afternoon,' he said, 'I'll be home tonight.'

The doctors reasoned with him, urged him to remember that he set an example for millions of other boys. But Elvis had made up his mind. A Humes High boy can be pushed only so far. They could only advise the command of Elvis's plans.

So naturally, the pass came through. The Army is not that dumb. Elvis had the same rights as any other American boy.

Back in Memphis Elvis fought his way through the crowds of newsmen outside the hospital. He was in his mother's room for only a few minutes; then he came out, walked down the hall to an empty waiting room, sank into a chair and cried.

His mother had been the one, perhaps the only one, who had told him throughout his life that even though he came from poor country people, he was just as good as anyone. His success had not surprised her, nor had it changed her. Shortly after Gladys Presley was buried, her husband and son were standing on the magnificent front steps at Graceland. 'Look, Daddy,' Elvis sobbed, pointing to the chickens his mother had kept on the lawn of the hundred-thousand-dollar mansion. 'Mama won't never feed them chickens no more.'

He never really got over his mother's death. He treasured for many years, in his office at Graceland, a lighted, fully decorated, artificial Christmas tree, a souvenir of the last Christmas the family spent together. He had the tree cared for all the time he was in Germany, where the Army had put him safely away.

Elvis liked Germany and both he and his father found wives there. When his tour of duty was ended, he came out with sergeant's stripes.

The whole thing was fictionally celebrated in *G.I. Blues*, a happy movie with a multi-million-dollar gross. One Elvis Presley film followed another: *Flaming Star, Wild in the Country, Blue Hawaii, Girls! Girls! Girls!, Kid Galahad, Follow That Dream, It Happened at the World's Fair, Fun in Acapulco, Viva Las Vegas, Kissin' Cousins, Roustabout, Girl Happy, Tickle Me, Harem Scarem, Frankie and Johnny, Paradise—Hawaiian Style, Spinout, Easy Come, Easy Go, Double Trouble, Speedway, Clambake.* They all have two things in common: none lost money, none is contingent at any point upon reality.

But this is not quite true; there is one reality which they reflect. In *Fun in Acapulco*, Elvis walks into a bar which is full of Mexicans, all of whom have good teeth. A mariachi band is playing. Elvis comes in on the chorus, and carries away the verse. Everyone applauds. The men smile and the girls turn on to him. They all think he is a hell of a fellow. One expects that at any moment he may produce a model plane and lead them out on to the lawn.

Elvis has fulfilled the American dream: he is young, rich, famous, adored. Hardly a day passes in Memphis without a politician wanting to name something after him. So far nothing has been found worthy of the honor. Presley has become a young man of whom his city and his country can be truly proud.

∾

Postscript

Dewey Phillips later told Booth that Elvis had asked him about this article, apparently hurt by its appraisal of him. Several months after the article was published, Elvis appeared before a live audience for the first time in eight years, taping what would come to be known as his "comeback special," which aired on NBC in December 1968. As a result of that special and the recordings that followed, Elvis's popularity rose to even greater heights.

∾ **Fastwrite 4**

Fastwrite about a major accomplishment of your life so far. What did you have to do to achieve it? How did this achievement—even in a small way—change your view of yourself? What new internal issues did it make you face? How did the achievement change others' attitudes toward you? How did others' changed attitudes toward you affect your sense of yourself? Would you wish to have done anything differently? Based on this achievement, what is your next goal in life?

Historical Questions

1. Booth ends his article by saying: "Elvis has fulfilled the American dream: he is young, rich, famous, adored." The American Dream is linked to certain definitions of the individual and of success, though these have changed over time. What do you think the American Dream meant for Elvis in 1956? What did it mean for Booth in 1968? What does it mean to you today? After you develop these three perspectives, compare two to three points of continuity and two to three points of difference among the perspectives. What might these similarities and differences say about our country's values and beliefs?

2. Think about Booth's assertion that it took "daring" for Elvis, as an outcast, to become a singer: "A hood might become a mechanic or a house painter or a bus-driver or even a cop, but nobody would expect him to be a singer." What roles do you think entertainers played in U.S. society in the 1950s? How do you think social class influenced a person's success at that time? In what ways have people's roles in music changed over the last few decades? To what extent is social class a factor in a person's successful singing career today? Explore the extent to which some of these changes over time could have resulted from Elvis's influence both as an individual and as a cultural icon.

Cultural Questions

As we saw in Chapter 1, "personal" identities are produced in interactions with others. While all people contain contradictory elements inside themselves—as their evolving values, goals, and desires may not always concur—these contradictions are heightened to enormous proportions both internally, within the self, and externally, in relation to others, when a person becomes a cultural icon. As people become "stars," their personal control over their identity becomes less certain, as various forces—with perhaps quite different values and goals—seek to create, market, and "sell" them to a "consuming" public with a vast variety of wants and needs. The following two questions ask you to explore some of the sources and effects of such contradictory positioning.

1. "Them people in New York and Hollywood are not gone change me none," Elvis told the hometown crowd in Memphis, even while people on both coasts and elsewhere were working frantically to transform him into a star. Choose two or three of the different groups who were projecting particular and contradictory identities on Elvis, for example, the boys he went to school with, television show hosts, his family, movie producers, music "managers," reviewers, audiences in different parts of the country. Explore first the particular identity each group was trying to project on Elvis, and second the values underlying those different identities. What do these constructions of

Elvis tell us about U.S. notions of individuality and success and about how the relationship between dominant and emergent forces might play out? Why did so many different groups wanted to construct "Elvis"?

2. Booth writes that "Elvis had tried to go on being himself." But what was that self? Booth goes on to note the irony that even as Elvis sang in Memphis on July 4, 1956 in "defiance at his natural enemies—those with power, prestige, money," he, in fact, had become a person with just those attributes. Write about what you imagine to be Elvis's deepest internal conflict about his identity between 1956, when he first became famous, and 1968, when this article was written. Describe the conflict in detail and then analyze two or three of the key values and beliefs that underlie it. In what ways is the conflict unique to a "star"? In what ways is it experienced by other more "ordinary" people? Finally, read the conflict symptomatically. What does it tell you about U.S. culture? About our beliefs and expectations? About the ways in which our culture enables and constrains us?

∾ **Fastwrite 5**

Examine the photograph shown in Figure 6.2 (p. 356), taken during Elvis's 1968 TV special. Discuss what it tells us about U.S. society both culturally and historically. Consider all aspects of the photo: the kinds of people who are there (and not there), what everyone is doing, the meanings of the principal and secondary characters in the photo, and the changes in society the photo represents. Based on what you know about the year 1968 in the United States, what values do you think this photo represents?

  ♪ "Burning Love"
  ♪ "Suspicious Minds"
  👁 The '68 Comeback

∾ **Fastwrite 6**

Before reading the next selection, describe the most memorable performance you have ever witnessed, whether it was a musical performance, an athletic performance, a portrayal of a character in a movie or a play, or a special feat such as skydiving or stunt flying. Use the most passionate language you can to describe the event, and fill your description with as much detail as possible. Do not limit your description to the performer alone; include the audience, the location, the conditions surrounding your presence at the event, and as much information as you can recall. Be sure to discuss the effect of the performance on you. Try writing your description in the present tense, as if the event is just happening.

Figure 6.2. Elvis Presley, 1968, during his "comeback" special on NBC-TV. Reviewing Elvis's performance, Jon Landau (who later became Bruce Springsteen's manager and producer) wrote, "There is something magical about watching a man who has lost himself, find his way home."

꩜

G R E I L   M A R C U S

Fanfare (1975)

The 1970s saw the flowering of *rock journalism,* articles about rock 'n' roll by writers who had grown up with the music, gone to college, and began their professional careers writing for one of the many new magazines devoted to the music that emerged in the late 1960s. These writers attempted to examine and explain rock 'n' roll in the broader context of American culture, contributing to magazines such as *Rolling Stone, Cream,* and *Crawdaddy.* Greil Marcus (b.1945) was one of these writers. His book, *Mystery Train: Images of America in Rock 'n' Roll Music,* was first published in 1975 (4th revised edition, 1997). The centerpiece of the book is the essay entitled "Presliad," which was devoted to Elvis. "Fanfare" is the opening section of the essay. Marcus is also the author of *Lipstick Traces: A Secret History of the Twentieth Century* (1989), *Dead Elvis: A Chronicle of a Cultural Obsession* (1991), *The Dustbin of History* (1995), and *Invisible Republic: Bob Dylan's Basement Tapes* (1997).

♪ "An American Trilogy" from *Elvis: Aloha from Hawaii*
♪ "You Gave Me a Mountain" from *Elvis: Aloha from Hawaii*
👁 *Elvis: Aloha from Hawaii*
👁 *Elvis: One Night with You*

Elvis Presley is a supreme figure in American life, one whose presence, no matter how banal or predictable, brooks no real comparisons. He is honored equally by long-haired rock critics, middle-aged women, the City of Memphis (they finally found something to name after him: a highway), and even a president. . . .

Presley's career almost has the scope to take America in. The cultural range of his music has expanded to the point where it includes not only the hits of the day, but also patriotic recitals, pure country gospel, and really dirty blues; reviews of his concerts, by usually credible writers, sometimes resemble Biblical accounts of heavenly miracles. Elvis has emerged as a great *artist,* a great *rocker,* a great *purveyor of shlock,* a great *heart throb,* a great *bore*, a great *symbol of potency*, a great *ham*, a great *nice person*, and, yes, a great American.

In 1954 Elvis made his first records with Sam Phillips, on the little Sun label in Memphis, Tennessee; then a pact was signed with Col. Tom Parker, shrewd country hustler. Elvis took off for RCA Victor, New York, and Hollywood. America has not been the same since. Elvis disappeared into an oblivion of respectability and security in the sixties, lost in inter-changeable movies and dull music; he staged a remarkable comeback as that decade ended, and now performs as the transcendental Sun King that Ralph Waldo Emerson only dreamed about—and as a giant contradiction. His audience expands every year, but Elvis transcends his talent to the point of dispensing with it altogether. Performing a kind of enormous victory rather than winning it, Elvis strides the boards with such glamour, such magnetism, that he allows his audience to transcend their desire for his talent. Action is irrelevant when one can simply delight in the presence of a man who has made history, and who has triumphed over it.

Mark now, the supreme Elvis gesture. He takes the stage with a retinue of bodyguards, servants, singers, a band, an orchestra; he applies himself vaguely to the hits of his past, prostrates himself before songs of awesome ickiness; he acknowledges the applause and the gasps that greet his every movement (applause that comes thundering with such force you might think the audience merely suffers the music as an excuse for its ovations); he closes with an act of show-biz love that still warms the heart; but above all, he throws away the entire performance.

How could he take it seriously? How could anyone create when all one has to do is appear? "He *looks* like Elvis Presley!" cried a friend, when the Big E stormed forth in an explosion of flashbulbs and cheers. "What a burden to live up to!" It is as if there is nothing Elvis could do to overshadow a performance of his myth. And so he performs from a distance, laughing at his myth, throwing it away only to see it roar back and trap him once again.

He will sing, as if suffering to his very soul, a song called "This Time, You [God, that is] Gave Me a Mountain," which sums up his divorce and his separation from his little girl. Having confessed his sins, he will stand aside, head bowed, as the Special Elvis Presley Gospel Group sings "Sweet, Sweet Feeling (In this Place)." Apparently cleansed of his sins, he will rock straight into the rhythm and blues of "Lawdy, Miss Clawdy" and celebrate his new-found freedom with a lazy grin. But this little melodrama of casual triumph will itself be a throwaway. As with the well-planned sets, the first-class musicians, the brilliant costumes, there will be little life behind the orchestration; the whole performance will be flaccid, the timing careless, all emotions finally shallow, the distance from his myth necessitating an even greater distance from the musical power on which that myth is based.

Elvis gives us a massive road-show musical of opulent American mastery; his version of the winner-take-all fantasies that have kept the world lined up outside the theaters that show American movies ever since the movies began. And of course we respond: a self-made man is rather boring, but a self-made king is something else. Dressed in blue, red, white, ultimately gold, with a Superman cape and covered with jewels no one can be sure are fake, Elvis might epitomize the worst of our culture—he is bragging, selfish, narcissistic, condescending, materialistic to the point of insanity. But there is no need to take that seriously, no need to take anything seriously. "Aw, shucks," says the country boy; it is all a joke to him; his distance is in his humor, and he can exit from this America unmarked, unimpressed, and uninteresting.

"From the moment he comes out of the wings," writes Nik Cohn, "all the pop that has followed him is made to seem as nothing, to be blown away like chaff." That is exactly what that first moment feels like, but from that point on, Elvis will go with the rest of it, singing as if there are no dangers or delights in the world grand enough to challenge him. There is great satisfaction in his performance, and great emptiness.

It is an ending. It is a sure sign that a culture has reached a dead end when it is no longer intrigued by its myths (when they lose their power to excite, amuse, and renew all who are a part of those myths—when those myths just bore the hell out of everyone); but Elvis has dissolved into a presentation of his myth, and so has his music. The emotion of the best music is open, liberating in its commitment and intangibility; Elvis's presentation is fixed. The glorious oppression of that presentation parallels the all-but-complete assimilation of a revolutionary musical style into the mainstream of American culture, where no one is challenged and no one is threatened.

History without myth is surely a wasteland; but myths are compelling only when they are at odds with history. When they replace the need to make history, they too are a dead end, and merely smug. Elvis's performance of his myth is so satisfying to his audience that he is left with no musical identity whatsoever, and thus he has no way to define himself, or his audience—except to expand himself, and his audience. Elvis is a man whose task it is to dramatize the fact of his existence; he does not have to create something new (or try, and fail), and thus test the worth of his existence, or the worth of his audience.

Complete assimilation really means complete acceptance. The immigrant who is completely assimilated into America has lost the faculty of adding whatever is special about himself to his country; for any artist, complete assimilation means the adoption of an aesthetic where no lines are drawn and no choices are made. That quality of selection, which is what is at stake when an artist comes across with his or her version of anything, is missing. When an artist gives an all-encompassing Yes to his audience (and Elvis's Yes implicitly includes everyone, not just those who say Yes to *him*), there is nothing more he can tell his audience, nothing he can really do for them, except maybe throw them a kiss.

Only the man who says No is free, Melville once wrote. We don't expect such a stance in popular culture, and those who do might best be advised to take their trade somewhere else. But the refusal that lurks on the margins of the affirmation of American popular culture—the margins where Sly Stone and Randy Newman have done their best work—is what gives the Yes of our culture its vitality and its kick. Elvis's Yes is the grandest of all, his presentation of mastery the grandest fantasy of freedom, but it is finally a counterfeit of freedom: it takes place in a world that for all its openness (Everybody Welcome!) is aesthetically closed, where nothing is left to be mastered, where there is only more to accept. For all its irresistible excitement and enthusiasm, this freedom is complacent, and so the music that it produces is empty of real emotion—there is nothing this freedom could be for, nothing to be won or lost.

At best, when the fans gather around—old men and women who might see their own struggles and failures ennobled in the splendor of one who came from the bottom; middle-aged couples attending to the most glamorous nightclub act there is; those in their twenties and thirties who have grown with Elvis ever since he and they created each other years ago (and who might have a feeling he and they will make their trip through history together, reading their history in each other)—at best, Elvis will confirm all who are there *as* an audience. Such an event, repeated over and over all across the land, implies an America that is as nearly complete as any can be. But what is it worth?

When Elvis sings "American Trilogy" (a combination of "Dixie," "The Battle Hymn of the Republic," and "All My Trials," a slave song), he signifies that his persona, and the culture he has made out of blues, Las Vegas, gospel music, Hollywood, schmaltz, Mississippi, and rock 'n' roll, can contain any America you might want to conjure up. It is rather Lincolnesque; Elvis recognizes that the Civil War has never ended, and so he will perform the Union.

Well, for a moment, staring at that man on the stage, you can almost believe it. For if Elvis were to bring it off—and it is easy to think that only he could—one would leave the hall with a new feeling for the country; whatever that feeling might be, one's sense of place would be broadened, and enriched.

But it is an illusion. A man or woman equal to the song's pretension would have to present each part of the song as if it were the whole story, setting one against each other, proving that one American really could make the South live, the Union hold, and slavery real. But on the surface and beneath it, Elvis transcends any real America by evading it. There is no John Brown in his "Battle Hymn," no romance in his "Dixie," no blood in his slave song. He sings with such a complete absence of musical personality that none of the old songs matter at all, because he has not committed himself to them; it could be anyone singing, or no one. It is in this sense, finally, that an audience is confirmed, that an America comes into being; lacking any real fear or joy, it is a throwaway America where nothing is at stake. The divisions America shares are simply smoothed away.

But there is no chance anyone who wants to join will be excluded. Elvis's fantasy of freedom, the audience's fantasy, takes on such reality that there is nothing left in the real world that can inspire the fantasy, or threaten it. What *is* left is for the fantasy to replace the world; and that, night after night, is what Elvis and his audience make happen. The version of the American dream that is Elvis's performance is blown up again and again, to contain more history, more people, more music, more hopes; the air gets thin but the bubble does not burst, nor will it ever. This is America when it has outstripped itself, in all of its extravagance, and its emptiness is Elvis's ultimate throwaway.

There is a way in which virtually his whole career has been a throwaway, straight from that time when he knew he had it made and that the future was his. You can hear that distance, that refusal to really commit himself, in his best music and his worst; if the throwaway is the source of most of what is pointless about Elvis, it is also at the heart of much of what is exciting and charismatic. It may be that he never took *any* of it seriously, just did his job and did it well, trying to enjoy himself and stay sane—save for those first Tennessee records, and that night, late in 1968, when his comeback was uncertain and he put a searing, desperate kind of life into a few songs that cannot be found in any of his other music.

It was a staggering moment. A Christmas TV special had been decided on; a final dispute between Colonel Parker (he wanted twenty Christmas songs and a tuxedo) and producer Steve Binder (he wanted a tough, fast, sexy show) had been settled; with Elvis's help, Binder won. So there Elvis was, standing in an auditorium, facing television cameras and a live audience for the first time in nearly a decade, finally stepping out from behind the wall of retainers and sycophants he had paid to hide him. And everyone was watching.

In the months preceding Elvis had begun to turn away from the seamless boredom of the movies and the hackneyed music of the soundtrack albums, staking out a style on a few half-successful singles, presenting the new persona of a man whose natural toughness was tempered by experience. The records—"Big Boss Man," "Guitar Man," "U.S. Male"—had been careful, respectable efforts, but now he was putting everything on the line, risking his comforts and his ease for the chance to start over. He had been a bad joke for a long time; if this show died, little more would be heard from Elvis Presley. Did he still have an audience? Did he still have anything to offer them? He had raised the stakes himself, but he probably had no idea.

Sitting on the stage in black leather, surrounded by friends and a rough little combo, the crowd buzzing, he sang and talked and joked, and all the resentments he had hidden over the years began to pour out. He had always said yes, but this time, he was saying no—not without humor, but almost with a wry bit of guilt, as if he had betrayed his talent and himself. "Been a long time, baby." He told the audience about a time back in 1955, when cops in Florida had forced him to sing without moving; the story was hilarious, but there was something in his voice that made very clear how much it had hurt. He jibed at the Beatles, denying that the heroes who had replaced him had produced anything he could not match, and then he proved it. After all this time he wanted more than safety; he and the men around him were nervous, full of adventure.

"I'd like to do my favorite Christmas song," Elvis drawls—squeals of familiarity from the crowd, the girls in the front rows doing their job, imitating themselves or their images of the past, fading into an undertone of giggles as the music begins. Elvis sings "Blue Christmas," a classically styled rhythm and blues, very even, all its tension implied: a good choice. He sings it low and throaty, snapping the strings on his guitar until one of his pals cries, "Play it dirty! Play it dirty!"—on a Christmas song! All right! But this is recreation, the past in the present, an attempt to see if Elvis can go as far as he once did. Within those limits it works, it is beautiful. The song ends with appropriate, and calculated, screams.

"Ah think Ah'll put a strap around this and stand up," Presley says. AHAHAHAHAHAHAHAHAAHAHA! God, what's that? Nervous laughter from a friend. Slow and steady, still looking around for the strap no one has bothered to hook onto the guitar, Elvis rocks into "One Night." In Smiley Lewis's original, it was about an orgy, called "One Night of Sin" (with the great lines, "The things I did and I saw/ Would make the earth stand still"); Elvis cleaned it up into a love story in 1958. But he has forgotten—or remembered. He is singing Lewis's version, as he must have always wanted to. He has slipped his role, and laughing, grinning, something is happening.

> . . . *The things I did and I saw, could make* . . .
> these dreams—*Where's the strap*?

Where's the strap, indeed. He falls in and out of the two songs, and suddenly the band rams hard at the music and Elvis lunges and eats it alive. No one has ever heard him sing like this; not even his best records suggest the depth of passion in this music. One line from Howlin' Wolf tells the tale: "When you see me runnin', you know my life is at stake." That's what it sounds like.

Shouting, crying, growling, lusting, Elvis takes his stand and the crowd takes theirs with him, no longer reaching for the past they had been brought to the studio to reenact, but responding to something completely new. The crowd is cheering for what they had only hoped for: Elvis has gone beyond all their expectations, and his, and they don't believe it. The guitar cuts in high and slams down and Elvis is roaring. Every line is a thunderbolt. *AW, YEAH!*, screams a pal—he has waited years for this moment.

UNNNNNNH! WHEW! When . . . I ain't nevah did no wrong!

And Elvis floats like the master he is back into "One night, with you," even allowing himself a little "Hot dog!", singing softly to himself.

It was the finest music of his life. If ever there was music that bleeds, this was it. Nothing came easy that night, and he gave everything he had—more than anyone knew was there.

Something of that passion spilled over into the first comeback album, *From Elvis in Memphis*; into "Suspicious Minds," the single that put him back on top of the charts; into his first live shows in Las Vegas; and then his nerves steadied, and Elvis brought it all back home again. You can still hear the intensity, the echo of those moments of doubt, in the first notes of most songs Elvis sings on stage—just before he realizes again that the crowd cares only that he is before them, and that anyway, the music would be his if he wanted it, that his talent is so vast it would be demeaning to apply it. So he will revel in his glory, acting the part of the King it has always been said he is; and if that is a throwaway, it is at least thrown at those who want it. A real glow passes back and forth between Elvis and his audience, as he shares a bit of what it means to transcend the world of weakness, failure, worry, age and fear, shows what it means for a boy who sprung from the poor to be godly, and shares that too.

I suppose it is the finality this performance carries with it that draws me back to Elvis's first records, made when there was nothing to take for granted, let alone throw away. Those sides, like "One Night," catch a world of risk, will, passion, and natural nobility; something worth searching out within the America of mastery and easy splendor that may well be Elvis's last word. The first thing Elvis had to learn to transcend, after all, was the failure and obscurity he was born to; he had to find some way to set himself apart, to escape the limits that could well have given his story a very different ending. The ambition and genius that took him out and brought him back is there in that first music—that, and much more.

Historical Questions

1. Marcus argues that Elvis achieved the American Dream of "winner take all," and yet he also argues that Elvis's performances, and indeed much of his career, had become empty, a "throwaway": "When an artist gives an all-encompassing Yes to his audience . . . there is nothing more he can tell his audience." Explore first what Marcus means by his assessment of Elvis's career. What were some of the major forces to which Elvis said Yes? Then, building on some of the analyses of Elvis you developed in the cultural questions on Booth, explore why Elvis Presley was motivated to say Yes to various demands placed on him.

2. Compare and contrast two or three of the major demands placed on Elvis in the 1950s and 1960s with some of the demands placed on individuals striving for success in the 1990s. Then focus on a specific person—someone in the music or entertainment field, a politician, or someone you know personally. To what extent does that person say Yes? Compare the effects of that Yes with Elvis's.

3. Develop a symptomatic reading of Marcus's implicit critique of the American Dream. Explore the language and details of his argument to analyze not only what he says literally about Elvis and about U.S. movie and music audiences in the 1950s and 1960s, but also what he implies about the nature of the American Dream itself and its effects on those who achieve it. To what extent do you think Marcus's analysis is true for the 1990s? Develop a response to his position, giving one or two specific contemporary examples.

Cultural Questions

1. Marcus uses the word *myth* frequently in his discussions of Elvis. How does Marcus describe the "myth of Elvis"? To help to develop a sense of how a myth gets created and perpetuated, write a paragraph describing Elvis from the perspective of two or three of the many groups of people who helped to create that myth—female or male teenagers attending movies, seeing concerts, or buying albums; middle-age male or female audiences; audiences from different regions of the country; religious groups; producers; promoters; the people who worked for Elvis, such as bodyguards or costume designers. Then explore the patterns that develop from these different perspectives.

2. For Marcus, Elvis's 1968 Christmas TV special was one of the most important moments in his career. Develop a symptomatic reading of the language and tone of Marcus's description of Elvis's performance. Why, literally, is he saying the performance was so outstanding? What else might he also be suggesting? What values about success, individualism, and the American Dream underlie Marcus's analysis? Where does Marcus position himself in

relation to dominant American values and beliefs? Where does he position Elvis?

3. Why do you think Marcus mentions such literary figures as Ralph Waldo Emerson and Herman Melville in this section of the essay? With reference to two or three specific passages, explore which characteristics of U.S. culture Marcus might be linking with Elvis by invoking these names. What might be Marcus's point in doing this in 1975? What effect might it have had on critical discussion of Elvis Presley?

∾ **Fastwrite 7**

Before reading the following obituary of Elvis, explore what you would want to be remembered for in your obituary. List these characteristics. Are there aspects of your life that you would prefer were forgotten? If so, list these. Then, in about three short paragraphs, write your obituary. You may want to compare yours with others' in your class to discover any patterns or trends. If you find such trends, read them symptomatically as indications of larger cultural values today. After you read Elvis's obituary, compare what you included in yours with what was included in his.

CLARK   PORTEOUS

A Lonely Life Ends on Elvis Presley Boulevard (1977)

This is the newspaper article about Elvis's death, written by Clark Porteous (1911–1997), from his hometown newspaper, the *Memphis Press-Scimitar*, August 17, 1977.

The King is dead.

Elvis Presley—the jiggling, jiving, rock 'n' roll king—lived just 42 years, seven months and eight days.

It was an exciting but frustrating life which ended in Baptist Hospital, where Elvis was pronounced dead at 3:30 P.M. yesterday of a heart attack.

Elvis made millions of dollars and literally was worshiped by millions of fans. But he was lonesome much of the time, paid a high price for privacy and could not do many things he would have liked to do because he always drew a crowd of admirers.

Elvis, with a pleasant singing voice and a new style, strumming a guitar and gyrating his pelvis—which brought him the name in early days of "Elvis the Pelvis"—made millions, was able to buy anything he wanted, yet happiness seemed to elude him.

Elvis gave away countless thousands, giving funds to numerous Memphis institutions just before Christmas every year. He would give his friends—and occasionally even strangers—expensive automobiles.

Yet as the years passed, many of his friends seemed to have faded away, not generally because they wanted to, but some said Elvis had changed.

Elvis Aron Presley was written about on his 40th birthday, and friends were quoted as saying he was "fat and forty" and refused to see anybody until his weight got down to his regular trim 180 pounds. He was staying in his mansion, Graceland, on Elvis Presley Boulevard, a part of Bellevue renamed by city fathers to honor Elvis.

He became more and more of a recluse in his last few years. Red West and other close friends, who used to be called the "Memphis Mafia," were no longer with him.

Elvis, already a living legend and somewhat of a folk hero to many, was found unconscious at Graceland at 2:30 P.M. yesterday.

Maurice Elliott, Baptist Hospital vice president, said Joe Esposito, Presley's road manager and long-time friend, called an ambulance and tried to revive Elvis with mouth-to-mouth resuscitation and heart massage until the ambulance arrived. Efforts to revive Presley continued in the ambulance and in the emergency room at Baptist Hospital.

Finally, according to Elliott, Dr. George C. Nichopoulos, Elvis's personal physician, discontinued efforts and pronounced the singer dead at 3:30. Nichopoulos indicated a heart attack and this was shown to be correct by an autopsy.

Elvis's friends, who followed the ambulance to the hospital, were overcome with grief and kept expressing hope that the king was not dead. Many nurses and others in the hospital had tears in their eyes when word spread that Elvis was really dead.

And at Graceland, fans gathered—many weeping—at a requiem in front of the gate which is decorated with musical notes.

The Presley epic started in a small frame house where he was born in Tupelo, Miss. Now an Elvis shrine, the house was built by his father and grandfather. He was the surviving member of twin boys whom his mother, Gladys Presley, named Elvis Aron and Jessie Garon. His twin died in infancy.

Elvis was grief-stricken when his mother died Aug. 14, 1958, while Elvis was serving in the Army in Texas. Mrs. Presley, who also died of a heart attack, was the same age as Elvis when he died—42. The 19th anniversary of her death was two days before Elvis died.

Elvis bade his mother farewell on a little wooded knoll in Forest Hill Cemetery, where he later placed an impressive white marble and rose-red granite memorial.

"Goodby, darling, goodby—I loved you so much," a sobbing Elvis said before leaving the burial site. "I lived my whole life just for you."

Elvis once recalled that in his boyhood his mother was very possessive of him, probably due to the loss of the twin. The Presleys had no other children.

"My mama never let me out of her sight," Elvis said. "I couldn't go down to the creek with the other kids. Sometimes, when I was little, I used to run off. Mama would whip me and I thought she didn't love me."

Elvis knew extreme poverty as well as extreme wealth.

His father, Vernon, who has shared in his son's success, did odd jobs and farmed in Tupelo, but the family was poor. When Elvis was 14, the family moved to Memphis. They lived in a one-room apartment on Alabama in North Memphis at first, later moved into Lauderdale Courts, one of the two first public housing projects built in Memphis in the mid-'30s.

Elvis went to Humes High, where he made such friends as Red West and George Klein. Elvis failed to make the Humes football team, but long after he became a big success, he liked to play touch football with his friends.

He remained partial to Humes and bought concert tickets for Humes alumni. On one occasion, *The Press-Scimitar* ran a story about a senior student at Humes who was living with her grandmother because her father, an Army career man, was stationed elsewhere.

The girl was told she had to pay tuition and she didn't have the money and was afraid she would not be able to graduate. That night a big black car drove up to the little North Memphis house and Elvis personally delivered far more than enough money for the girl to continue at Humes and also buy some nice clothes. Yes, Elvis remembered the tough times he had.

As a boy, Elvis never studied music, but he had an inexpensive radio which he would listen to for hours at a time. He remembered liking the Grand Ole Opry and records by cowboy singers such as Roy Acuff and Hank Snow. But a special favorite was sweet-singing Gene Austin.

"I sang some with my folks in the Assembly of God Church choir," Elvis said. "It was a small church so you couldn't sing too loud.

"Getting a guitar was Mama's idea. I beat on it a year or two and never did learn much about it. I still know only a few major chords. I don't read music, but I know what I like."

Elvis was graduated from Humes in 1953. He had been too small to make the football team, but he was interested in sports and learned to be an expert at karate. After graduation from Humes, Elvis worked on the assembly line of a precision tool company, then at a furniture factory making plastic tables and then as a truck driver for Crown Electric Co. He also ushered at Loew's State, a theater which was later to show many of his movies.

In the summer of 1953, Elvis took the step which led to fame and fortune. He had "just an urgin" and went to Sam Phillips's Sun Record Co. He paid to have a recording made for his mother. Elvis said "it sounded like somebody beating on a bucket lid." But Elvis was told he had an unusual voice and someone might call him.

Months passed and Elvis kept driving a truck for $35 a week. At night he attended a trade school, studying to be an electrician.

Then in the spring of 1955, lightning struck and Phillips called Elvis and asked him if he could come to the studio and record a ballad called "Without You." But Elvis just couldn't sing it the way Phillips wanted him to. After a coffee break, Elvis started singing a song with a rock 'n' roll beat. Phillips and the others liked it. The king was on his way to fame and fortune. He recorded "That's All Right, Mama" and "I Don't Care if the Sun Don't Shine," backed up by "Blue Moon of Kentucky."

Elvis's recordings first were played on radio station WHBQ. Elvis hid in a theater because he was afraid people would laugh at him. "Some did and some are still laughing, I guess," Elvis said later. But the record sold 7,000 copies in Memphis that first week.

A few months later, Col. Thomas A. Parker, a country slicker from Madison, Tenn., who likes to talk like a rube, agreed to manage Presley and Parker has had much to do with the phenomenal financial success of Presley. Parker craftily handled Presley appearances, kept him out of the limelight at times, helped build the Elvis mystique.

Parker, whose motto has been "Don't try to explain it, just sell it," did quite a job of selling Elvis. Col. Parker booked Elvis on tours with such established stars as Hank Snow and Andy Griffith. By the fall of 1955, Manhattan was beginning to hear about the swivel-hipped rock-and-roll singer. Col. Parker induced RCA to buy Elvis's contract from Phillips for $35,000, a price which turned out to be a great deal for RCA. Elvis got a $5,000 bonus for signing, more money than he had ever seen, but just a taste of what was coming.

In cities such as Jacksonville and Norfolk, Elvis swiveled out onto the stage wearing pink silk shirts, tight black pegged pants and cat boots over pink and black socks. He would stand for a moment like a figure in a wax museum. Then he would spraddle his long legs into a pivoting stance, take a few swipes at his guitar which rested against his then-flat belly and he would start swinging his hips in a sexual swirl. In fact, he was so sexy that when he appeared on TV on the Ed Sullivan show, the camera focused above his hips. The TV people believed it was too hot for the audience.

Parker began to sell Elvis with pink bunnies, Teddy bears, pennants, posters, cutouts and stacks of records. Parker often wore gaudy hats and sports shirts with "Elvis" embroidered on all sides.

Parker got 20th Century–Fox to put Elvis in films and the story is that when Parker talked to Buddy Adler, the production boss, about Elvis, Adler said, "Would $25,000 be all right?" Parker said that would be "just fine for me. Now how about the boy." He got the ante upped for Elvis, got $50,000 for a single TV appearance, which was a lot at that time. Parker said he considered it "his patriotic duty to keep Elvis in the 90 percent tax bracket," and he did. Parker got Elvis booked into Las Vegas and refused to accept a check, demanding cash in advance. And he got it.

He got Elvis signed for the Seattle World's Fair for $250,000. There were a series of inexpensive movies, with Elvis pleasing his growing horde of fans and finally learning to act just a bit. There were regular appearances at Las Vegas, concerts now and then, and the money rolled in.

Elvis lived in a nice house on Audubon, near the park, off Park Avenue. Then he bought the 18-room Graceland mansion on South Bellevue in Whitehaven. Graceland has been his home since. Elvis had other homes, but he said he would always live in Memphis, and he seemed to enjoy the privacy of Graceland with its music-note gate, stone fence and security guards to keep the public out. His uncle, Travis Smith, used to take cameras up to the mansion to take pictures for Elvis fans, when he felt like it.

There were almost always Elvis fans at the gate, fans from all over, fans who wanted blades of grass, leaves from Graceland as a souvenir.

The fans would wait for hours, hoping to get a glimpse of the king. Sometimes they would be rewarded. Sometimes Elvis would ride one of his many motorcycles, a tractor or other smaller vehicles around on his estate. Sometimes he would even go out the gate. On rare occasions—much less in recent years—he would stop and chat with his fans or sign autographs.

But when Elvis really wanted to go out, he would charter a skating rink, bowling alley, theater or other entertainment place and take his friends. He just couldn't make a public appearance alone fearful of being mobbed.

In later years, at concerts, Elvis would throw scarves out to the crowd, and these became prized souvenirs of those lucky enough to catch one.

Elvis's song hits rolled out regularly, with RCA Victor bringing out the first big one, "Heartbreak Hotel." It was followed by many more such as "Love Me Tender," "Blue Suede Shoes," "I Got a Woman," "I Want You, I Need You," "Jailhouse Rock," "Hard-headed Woman" and many others. And the one his fans never let him forget, "Hound Dog."

Elvis had a handsome face, which prompted Danny Thomas at a Memphis show for St. Jude Children's Hospital to call him "Doll Face." The show was at old Russwood Park, before it burned, and Elvis appeared and gyrated, but he could not sing because of a Parker contract clause. But as usual, Elvis brought down the house and was a hit in competition with such movie stars as Jane Russell and Susan Hayward.

At the peak of his career, in 1958, Elvis was called into the Army. The draft was still in effect and it became Elvis's turn. Despite all the money he was making and the enormous taxes he was paying Uncle Sam, he made no effort to avoid going into service at a buck private's meager pay.

At the old Kennedy Hospital on Getwell, now part of Memphis State University, Elvis took and easily passed his physical. He was a fine specimen of a young man at the time. He was extremely courteous and he remained polite to his elders and to women the rest of his life. He "sirred" reporters and others. Hedda Hopper, the Hollywood gossip columnist, said she once told Elvis, "Call me Hedda, Elvis. Everybody else does." She said he replied "Yes, ma'am, Mrs. Hopper."

Once on a movie set, Jackie Gleason visited Elvis on the set and scolded him for calling him "sir" and "mister." Elvis told Gleason that his mama had told him that anybody a year older than him was "mister" and "Mr. Gleason, you're one year older than I am, I think, sir."

Elvis asked no special favors in the Army and apparently got few. He was a good soldier. He got his eight weeks of basic training at Fort Hood, Tex. He was sent to Germany and came home only for his mother's funeral. He served in a tank outfit in Germany and was promoted to sergeant.

While in Germany, Elvis met a girl, Priscilla Beaulieu, daughter of an Air Force officer. Apparently there was a spark for Elvis from the very first for the teen-ager. Elvis, who had dated Anita Wood, Ann-Margaret and many others, brought Priscilla home to Graceland.

She finished growing up at Graceland and attended Immaculate Conception High School, being taken to and from school in one of the Presley fleet of cars. Elvis had been car crazy since he began to earn big money and always had a number of fine cars, including a $34,000 Rolls Royce, which in 1968 he gave to SHARE, Inc., a Hollywood women's charity group to sell to the highest bidder.

Graceland, like other Elvis homes, had pinball machines, pool tables, jukeboxes and other gadgets to keep the king from being bored. Elvis always was a night owl, liking to stay up most of the night and sleep away daylight hours.

There were often rumors that Elvis was married to Priscilla, but they were wrong. In early 1967, when found at a 160-acre ranch he was interested in buying, near Days, Miss., Elvis made a slip. A reporter asked Elvis if she could go inside the house at the ranch and Elvis smiled and said, "No, people are asleep in there. My father and mother-in-law." The reporter jumped on that at once and asked Elvis if he were married, and Elvis finally said he meant to say his stepmother. His father Vernon had remarried.

Priscilla was only 14 and Elvis 25 when he met her in Germany. They were married in 1967, in Las Vegas, and a year later had a daughter, Lisa, now 9 years old. Lisa is the presumptive heir to most of Elvis's millions. Though he and Priscilla were divorced in 1973, blaming his career for their long separations, there were some who believed the couple might get back together, had Elvis lived. Friends say they talked on the telephone almost every night and that Elvis missed both Lisa and Priscilla. They live in California.

Elvis had made such movies as *Love Me Tender, Loving You, Jailhouse Rock* and *King Creole* before going in the Army. After he got out, he made more movies. He showed talent as a half Navajo Indian rodeo cowboy in *Stay Away, Joe,* and other movies. But then Col. Parker, apparently fearing overexposure, took him out of movies. The Presley movies were big money makers and at one time it was reported Elvis would star in the movie version of Rudolf Valentino.

After taking Elvis out of movies, Col. Parker began to let him star in high-price TV appearances. Elvis became even richer, and in addition to Rolls Royces had at one time five Cadillacs—white, pink, blue, canary yellow and gold.

In the late 1960s, Elvis went into semiretirement after selling 400 million records and making 31 movies. Then he came back in 1972 and found his fans still faithful—though many of the fans who had swooned at his appearances had children of their own. Even younger fans still got goose bumps over the king of rock 'n' roll, though he was approaching 40.

Presley the car fan would buy as many as a half-dozen cars at a time and would give friends fine ones for Christmas presents. In September 1973, he went into Schilling Lincoln Mercury, 987 Union, and bought five Continental Mark IV's from Raymond Surber, a car salesman. It was a $60,000 sale.

But with all his cars and other gadgets with which to have fun, all his girl friends, his fame and fortune, some who knew Elvis best did not believe he ever really found happiness.

Recently, Presley bought a 707 jet and named it Lisa Marie for his daughter.

Elvis always appeared before sell-out houses at his infrequent Memphis concerts, just as in other cities. He had a concert scheduled at the Mid-South Coliseum Aug. 27 and it sold out so quickly that a second was added for Aug. 28, and it also sold out. So Elvis fans who had planned to see and hear him at the Coliseum will have to settle for the final appearance of the King, in a silent trip to Forest Hill Cemetery, where lies his beloved mother, who—like her famous son—died at age 42 on a hot August day.

Historical Questions

1. Explore what this obituary emphasizes and what it leaves out of the account of Elvis's life. Why do you think it has the focus it does? Explore how it might contribute to the myth of Elvis discussed by Marcus.

2. You have now read three different chronologies of Elvis's career: Booth's, Marcus's, and the one contained in this obituary. What key similarities and differences do you find in each account? In answering this question, explore how the time when each piece was written and the intended audience might have affected the particular information presented and withheld. What "factual information" about Elvis given in any of the three accounts do you think is most important in telling his story? What other information, which perhaps extends beyond the "facts," is necessary to understanding the creation of "the King of Rock 'n' Roll"? Briefly explain what your criteria are for deciding this.

Cultural Questions

1. Some have criticized the story of Elvis told in his obituary as not fully accurate. That Elvis first went to Sam Phillips to record for his mother's birthday, for example, has puzzled some because his mother's birthday was in April and Elvis made his first recording with Phillips in late summer. Also, some records indicate that Gladys Presley was forty-six when she died, not forty-two—Elvis's age at death—as the article states. Why might there be such discrepancies about such a famous and well-documented person?

2. Information about Elvis is written in a variety of different registers in this obituary—both in terms of the tone and the content. For example, on the one hand, it presents a significant amount of statistical information, including records sold, money made and given away, successful movies, and so on. On the other hand, it makes such simple statements as "Elvis lived in a nice house. . . ." Explore the obituary for further examples of these different registers. Then analyze why they are there and what their rhetorical effect might have been on the many who would have read it.

∾ Fastwrite 8

In a later section of "Presliad," Marcus refers to the photograph in Figure 6.3 as a representation of all that Elvis left out of his story. Historically and cul-

Figure 6.3. Gladys Presley, Elvis Presley, Vernon Presley, Tupelo, Mississippi, c. 1938. Elvis was born in a two-room house built by his father. His twin brother, Jesse Garon, was stillborn.

turally, what does that mean? How might knowing what an artist does *not* tell us alter our perception of what he or she has accomplished?

♪ "An American Trilogy" (from *Elvis: Aloha from Hawaii*)
♪ "Baby, Let's Play House"
♪ "Blue Moon of Kentucky"
♪ "Crying in the Chapel"
♪ "Peace in the Valley" (from *Elvis '56*)
👁 *Elvis: Aloha from Hawaii*
👁 *Elvis '56*

෴ **Fastwrite 9**

Before reading the next selection, in ten to fifteen minutes fastwrite as much as you can about what you feel are some of the key aspects of the American South: its history, culture, and contributions to American life, and its relationship to the rest of the United States.

LINDA RAY PRATT

Elvis, or the Ironies of a Southern Identity (1977)

Linda Ray Pratt (b. 1943) is a professor of English and graduate chair at the University of Nebraska at Lincoln and a past president of the American Association of University Professors. She has written on postmodernism as well as on Elvis Presley. The following article first appeared in a collection of essays edited by J. L. Tharpe, *Elvis: Images and Fancies* (1977).

Elvis was the most popular entertainer in the world, but nowhere as popular as in his native South. In the last years of his career, his audience in other parts of the country was generally centered in the original "fifties" fans whose youth and music were defined by Elvis, and in the lower or working class people who saw in Elvis some glamorized image of their own values. In the South, however, the pattern of Elvis's popularity tended to cut across age barriers and class lines which were themselves a less recognizable thing in a region in which almost no one is more than a generation or two away from poverty, and where "class" in small communities might have more to do with family and past status than with money. Among Southern youth, Elvis was not a relic from a musical past; he was still one of the vital forces behind a Southern rock, which though different now from his, still echoes the rhythms which his music had fused out of the region. His numerous concerts in the South could not exhaust the potential audience. At his death, leading politicians and ministers from the South joined the people on the street in eulogizing him. Local radio and television stations ran their own specials in addition to the syndicated or national programs. Halftime ceremonies at the Liberty Bowl were in tribute to him. When someone commented on national TV that the Presleys were "white trash," it was a regional slur, not just a personal one. The white

South expressed love, grief, and praise for Elvis from all age groups at virtually every level of the social, intellectual, and economic structures. The phenomenon of such widespread sectional regard and emotional intensity went beyond the South's usual pride in the success of "one of our own." The emotion became more puzzling if one listened to some of the reasons offered to explain it: Elvis loved his mother; Elvis's heart was broken; Elvis loved Jesus; Elvis was the American Dream. Such reasons for loving and mourning Elvis seemed strange because, on the surface at least, they were so tangential to Elvis himself or to the musical or cultural impact he unquestionably did have. How, in the face of his vitality and defiance of convention, could one love Elvis because he loved Jesus? And how, in a man expressing nothing if not undisguised sexuality, could one love Elvis because he was so good to his mother? But people, especially those beyond the age group of his original teen fans, often did say such things. Merle Haggard's "From Graceland to the Promised Land," with its emphasis on Elvis's mother's death and his faith in Jesus, is, after all, the perfect Southern folk song about Elvis. The South's involvement with Elvis is sincere, but most of the expressed reasons for it do not reach very far, and some of them seem patently false. They are the myths sent up to justify the emotion and to obscure its source. The emotions spring from associations with a reality the South collectively prefers to conceal and yet constantly experiences. The paradox of Elvis was that he was able simultaneously to reveal the reality of the modern South while concealing it in a myth of the American Dream. He was at once both "King" and outsider. . . .

The Elvis of the sentimental myth would never have changed musical or cultural history, but the authentic Elvis who did so was transformed into a legend obscuring what the man, the music, or the image really meant. Although some elements of the myth were commonly associated with Elvis throughout the country, in the South—particularly the white South—the myth was insisted upon and pushed to its extremes. . . .

Those who have argued that people projected onto Elvis anything they liked because his image was essentially vacuous are mistaken; if anything, the image is too rich in suggestion to be acknowledged fully or directly. . . .

C. Vann Woodward has said that the South's experience is atypical of the American experience, that where the rest of America has known innocence, success, affluence, and an abstract and disconnected sense of place, the South has known guilt, poverty, failure, and a concrete sense of roots and place ("The Search for Southern Identity" in *The Burden of Southern History*). These myths collide in Elvis. His American success story was always acted out within its Southern limitations. No matter how successful Elvis became in terms of fame and money, he remained fundamentally disreputable in the minds of many Americans. Elvis had rooms full of gold records earned by million-copy sales, but his best rock and roll records were not formally honored by the people who control, if not the public taste, the rewarding of the public taste. Perhaps this is always the fate of innovators; awards are created long after the form is created. . . .

Elvis's sheer commercial value commanded respect, but no amount of success could dispel the aura of strangeness about him. He remained an outsider in the American culture that adopted his music, his long hair, his unconventional clothes, and his freedom of sexual movement.

Although he was the world's most popular entertainer, to like Elvis a lot was suspect, a lapse of taste. It put one in beehives and leisure suits, in company with "necrophiliacs" and other weird sorts. The inability of Elvis to transcend his lack of reputability despite a history-making success story confirms the Southern sense that the world outside thinks Southerners are freaks, illiterates, Snopeses, sexual perverts, lynchers. I cannot call this sense a Southern "paranoia" because ten years outside the South has all too often confirmed the frequency with which non-Southerners express such views. Not even the presidency would free LBJ and Jimmy Carter from such ridicule. At the very moment in which Southerners proclaim most vehemently the specialness of Elvis, the greatness of his success, they understand it to mean that no Southern success story can ever be sufficient to satisfy a suspicious America. . . .

Compounding his case was the fact that Elvis didn't always appear fully white. Not sounding white was his first problem, and white radio stations were initially reluctant to play his records. Not to be clearly white was dangerous because it undermined the black-white rigidities of a seg-regated society, and to blur those definitions was to reveal the falseness at the core of segregation. Racial ambiguity is both the internal moral con-demnation and the social destruction of a racist society which can only pretend to justify itself by abiding by its own taboos. Yet all Southerners know, despite the sternest Jim Crow laws, that more than two hundred years of racial mixing has left many a Southerner racially ambiguous. White Southerners admit only the reality of blacks who have some white blood, but, of course, the knife cuts both ways. Joe Christmas and Charles Bon. Désirée's Baby. In most pictures, Elvis might resemble a blue-eyed Adonis, but in some of those early black and white photographs, his eyes sultry, nostrils flared, lips sullen, he looked just that—black and white. And he dressed like blacks. His early wardrobe came from Lansky Brothers in Memphis. Maybe truck drivers wore greasy hair and long sideburns, but only the blacks were wearing zoot suits and pegged pants with pink darts in them. Country singers might sequin cactus and saddles on satin shirts, Marty Robbins would put a pink carnation on a white sport coat, and Johnny Cash would be the man in black. Only Elvis would wear a pink sport coat with a black velvet collar. "The Memphis Flash," he was some-times called.

The music was the obvious racial ambiguity. Elvis's use of black styles and black music angered many Southern blacks who resented the success he won with music that black artists had originated but could not sell beyond the "race record" market of a segregated commercial world. In interviews today, these black blues musicians usually say that Elvis stole everything from them, an understandable complaint but one that never-theless ignores his fusion of black music with white country to create a genuinely new sound. He was the Hillbilly Cat singing "Blue Moon of Kentucky" and "That's All Right (Mama)." Elvis's role in fusing the native music of poor Southern whites and poor Southern blacks into rock and roll is the best known aspect of his career and his greatest accomplishment.

Students of rock always stress this early music, but the sentimental myth gives it less attention, though the records always sold better in the South than in any other region. The music in the myth is more often the love ballads and the Protestant hymns. Yet the music that was in reality most important to Southerners was the music most closely tied to Southern origins. . . . Rock and roll, taking inside it rhythm and blues and country, was the rhythm of Southern life, Southern problems, and Southern hopes. It is not coincidence that rock and roll emerged almost simultaneously with the civil rights movement, that both challenged the existing authority, and that both were forces for "integration."

The most stunning quality about Elvis and the music was the sexuality, yet the sentimental myth veers away from this disturbing complexity into the harmlessly romantic. Elvis might be "nice looking" or "cute" or perhaps "sexy," but not sexual. The sexuality he projected was complicated because it combined characteristics and appeals traditionally associated with both males and females. On one hand, he projected masculine aggression and an image of abandoned pleasure, illicit thrills, back alley liaisons and, on the other hand, a quality of tenderness, vulnerability, and romantic emo-tion. Andy Warhol captured something of this diversified sexuality in his portrait of Elvis, caught in a threatening stance with a gun in his hand but with the face softened in tone and line. The image made Elvis the perfect lover by combining the most appealing of male and female characteristics and satisfying both the physical desire for sensual excitement and the emo-tional need for loving tenderness. . . . In the South where sex roles are bound up with the remnants of a chivalric "way of life," open sexuality was allowable only in the "mysterious" lives of blacks, and permissible sexual traits in whites were rigidly categorized by sex. But the image of Elvis goes behind these stereotypes to some ideal of sexuality that combines the most attractive elements in each of them. . . .

Beyond the money, the power, the fame, there was always at some level this aspect of Elvis, the American Dream in its Southern variation. Like other great Southern artists, Elvis revealed those characteristics of our culture which we know better than outsiders to be part of the truth. In Elvis was also the South that is bizarre, or violent, or darkly mysterious, the South called the grotesque in Faulkner or O'Connor. Perhaps this is why a book like *Elvis: What Happened?* could not damage the appeal. The hidden terrors, pain, and excesses of the private life which the book reveals, despite its mean-spirited distortions, only make the image more compelling in its familiarity. Even his drug problem had a familiar Southern accent— prescription medicines, cough syrups, diet pills.

Elvis's South is not the old cotton South of poor but genteel aristocrats . . . . Elvis's South was the one that most Southerners really experience, the South where not even the interstate can conceal the poverty, where industrial affluence threatens the land and air which have been so much a part of our lives, where racial violence touches deep inside the home, where even our successes cannot overcome the long reputation of our failures. Even Graceland is not really beautiful. Squeezed in on all sides by the sprawl of gas stations, banks, shopping plazas, and funeral homes, Elvis's beloved home is an image of the South that has been "new" now for over fifty years.

Elvis evoked the South of modern reality with a fidelity he could not himself escape. The South rewarded him with its most cherished myths, but Elvis's tragedy was that he got caught in the contradictions. We only wanted to be able to claim that he was a good boy who loved Jesus. He apparently needed to become that, to live out the mythic expectations. He hungered for approval. The problem was that most of what Elvis really was could never be so transmogrified. He *was* the king of rock and roll, but he was uncomfortable with what the title implied. Linda Thompson has said that in his later years he hated hard rock. The further he moved from the conventions of the romantic myth, the more he proclaimed them. The more drugs he used, the more he supported law and order. When the counter culture he helped to usher in became widespread, he thought of helping the FBI as an undercover agent. How could he not be schizophrenic at the end, balancing the rock myth he created, the sentimental myth he adopted, and the emotional needs that made him like anyone else? He was destroyed by having to be what he was and wanting to be what he thought he ought to be. . . .

After Elvis died, it was necessary to deify him. It isn't, after all, very becoming to grieve for a rock idol who died, as *The New York Times* once put it, "puffy and drug-wasted." But saying what and why one grieved was difficult. The South has had a lot of practice mythologizing painful and ambiguous experiences into glamorous and noble abstractions. So it was from Graceland to the Promised Land. Rex Humbard told us that Elvis found peace in Jesus, and Billy Graham assured us that Elvis was in Heaven. Billy was even looking forward to visiting him there. A disc jockey playing "How Great Thou Art" reflects at the end of the record, "And he certainly was." In Tupelo the Elvis Presley Memorial Foundation is building a $125,000 Chapel of Inspiration in his memory. Memphis will put a 50-ton bronze statue on a river bluff. Priscilla wants their daughter to remember, most of all, his humbleness. He loved his Jesus, his daughter, his lost wife. He loved his daddy. He loved the South. He was a great humanitarian. "God saw that he needed some rest and called him home to be with Him," the tombstone reads. Maybe all of this is even true. The apotheosis of Elvis demands such perfection because his death confirmed the tragic frailty, the violence, the intellectual poverty, the extravagance of emotion, the loneliness, the suffering, the sense of loss. Almost everything about his death, including the enterprising cousin who sold the casket pictures to *National Enquirer,* dismays, but nothing can detract from Elvis himself. Even this way, he is as familiar as next door, last year, the town before. . . .

Southerners do not love the old Confederacy because it was a noble ideal, but because the suffering of the past occasioned by it has formed our hearts and souls, both good and evil. But we celebrate the past with cheap flags, cliché slogans, decorative license plates, decaled ash trays, and a glorious myth of a Southern "way of life" no one today ever lived. And Southerners do not love Elvis because he loved Jesus or anyone else. The Elvis trinkets, his picture on waste cans or paperweights or T-shirts or glowing in the dark from a special frame, all pay the same kind of homage as the trinkets in worship of the past. People outside the Elvis phenomenon may think such commercialization demeans the idol and the idolater. But for those who have habitually disguised the reality of their culture from even themselves, it is hard to show candidly what and why one loves. In impeccable taste. By the most sentimental people in history.

Historical Questions

1. Pratt discusses Elvis's "racial ambiguity"—his crossing of racial boundaries not only in his music, but also in his voice, his style of dress, and even in some of his early black and white photographs. While she sees this articulation of "racial mixing" as something that could only have happened in the 1950s in the South—where it had been an ongoing, if unacknowledged, practice for over two-hundred years—she also points out that Elvis's display was anathema to the racist values of the whole country at the time. How could Elvis have gained such popularity and almost instant stardom if he was going against such an entrenched belief system? Be sure to specifically discuss some of the complex ways in which the dominant and the emergent interact. Pratt asserts that rock 'n' roll eventually became a force for integration and was important to the success of the civil rights movement. To what extent do you think popular music today unites people of different races? Give two specific examples.

2. Consider the conflicts Pratt presents regarding Elvis's sexuality. Once again, we see that Elvis blurred distinctions that were generally rigidly adhered to within dominant U.S. values. Analyzing the interaction of dominant and emergent values, compare two to three ways in which the Elvis myth of sexuality crossed traditional male-female lines and how it was interpreted and even imitated by his fans. Then, compare Elvis's acts of sexual "blurring" in the 1950s with a famous person's today. How do you think the dominant within America today represents acts of sexual blurring to themselves? How do you represent these acts and react to them?

3. Pratt observes that in the last years of Elvis's career, except in the South, his fans divided along social class lines. Why do you think Southerners might have found it easier to consistently cross class lines in embracing Elvis than people living in other regions of the country? To help you answer this, explore the following: When people did cross class or regional lines to become Elvis fans, what images of Elvis and themselves do you think they were likely to have? Be as specific as you can about the attributes of the person and the specific social class and regional markers of Elvis to which they would be responding. Under what conditions might someone have been disturbed by the class differences or the regional differences that Elvis represented? What do your examples suggest about the relationship between social class and Southern identity during the span of Elvis's career? To what extent has that relationship changed in the twenty years since his death?

4. Consider Pratt's notion that "to like Elvis a lot was suspect, a lapse of taste." Why would she say that? Do you think that notion has changed in any way since this essay was written? If so, how? If not, why not? Compare Pratt's perspective with Francis Davis's at the opening of the chapter or the *New York Times* editorial from 1997. In what ways are Elvis's origins and accomplishments still in dispute? In what ways has he gained greater acceptance since Pratt wrote her article?

∾ Fastwrite 10

Compare and contrast the ambivalence felt about Elvis with another star of your own choosing. Where do you see the greatest points of commonality? Where do you see the greatest points of difference?

Cultural Questions

1. Pratt offers a somewhat different angle on Elvis from the writers included so far. She analyzes Elvis not only as an American, but as part of an American parallel culture, the South. She contends that Elvis's "American success story was always acted out within its Southern limitations." Consider two

to three significant details you have learned about Elvis's background and career from any of the previous essays. Then, compare how your reading of these details might change when you think about Elvis as Southern as opposed to thinking about him as simply American. Use specific points from Pratt's essay as well as your own knowledge of the U.S. South. What regional and national assumptions about the South are revealed in your reading? Which reading—Elvis as Southerner or Elvis as American—do you prefer? Why?

2. Pratt analyzes some of the tension between the sentimental myths of Elvis and the Elvis who changed music history. Focusing on two or three of these myths, analyze some of the larger belief systems that encouraged myth making, particularly in the South. You might want to draw on Gould's early review and on criticisms of Elvis discussed by either Booth or Marcus. What were some of the effects of the myth making on Elvis himself? Finally, move your discussion from the particulars of Elvis's career to speculate about why you think a society engages in such myth-making about its "stars."

RON ROSENBAUM

Among the Believers (1995)

Ron Rosenbaum (b. 1946) writes about U.S. popular culture. He has written for *Esquire, Commonweal, Harper's Bazaar,* and *Vanity Fair.* Among his books are *Manhattan Passions* (1988) and *Explaining Hitler* (1998). This essay was originally published in the *New York Times Magazine* on Sunday, September 24, 1995.

♪"Can't Help Falling in Love" (compare the versions on the *Comeback* and *Aloha* videos with the original single from 1961)
♪ "Hurt"
♪ "My Way" (from *Elvis: Aloha from Hawaii*)
👁*Elvis: Aloha from Hawaii*
👁*Elvis: The '68 Comeback Special*
👁*Why Elvis?*

It's death week here in Memphis, the week leading up to the mass veneration of Elvis Presley's grave, and the signature sound in the ambient soundtrack is a song called "Hurt." The city is swelling with pilgrims from all over the world. Tens of thousands of mourners, fans, impersonators, icon-sellers, former Elvis entourage members and hangers-on are flooding into this oven-baked Egyptian-named Mississippi River metropolis, the place that midwifed the birth of the blues on Beale Street and bore witness to the death of Elvis on his Graceland toilet. For days, a Canterbury-like fusion of carnival and spiritual impulses has been building toward the convergence on the grave in a climactic ceremony referred to simply as "Candlelight." It's the central ritual in Elvis Culture, a phenomenon that has lately transcended the familiar contours of a dead celebrity cult and has begun to assume the dimensions of a redemptive faith.

It began, the veneration ritual, with small gatherings at the gates of Graceland in the first few years after Elvis's death on Aug. 16, 1977. A few hundred fans lighting candles on Death Night has mushroomed to tens of

Figure 6.4. Graceland, Memphis, Tennessee, annual candlelight vigil commemorating the anniversary of Elvis's death. Each year in August, thousands of fans from all over the world remember Elvis by visiting his home. Some consider these admirers the disciples of a new religion evolving from Elvis's life and works.

thousands now. Despite the oppressive August heat in Memphis, the death ceremony eventually dwarfed the January birthday remembrance on the Elvis liturgical calendar and began expanding from a single night to a full weeklong pilgrimage and pageant. The corporate headquarters of Elvis Presley Enterprises at Graceland (representing the Estate, which is owned by Elvis's daughter, Lisa Marie) prefers calling it Elvis Week to Death Week and schedules a busy round of upbeat celebratory concerts, dances and the like. But for the deadly serious mourners who make the pilgrimage here from all continents (and from all age brackets), the central focus is on loss, on hurt, on the moment of grieving communion at the grave.

On the evening of the 15th of August, when the last light fades from the sky, the gates of Graceland will part and a solemn throng of worshipers bearing burning tapers will begin slowly flooding through the entrance to the estate, climbing the hill toward the grave site, dripping parafin wax and tears in their wake, as they wind their way up to the Meditation Garden, circle around to the flat bronze grave marker and pause there to commune with the spirit of the departed King.

I'd been hearing about the Death Night ceremony, about the way it's grown into a must-see sui generis American folk ritual, a fusion of our longing for spirituality and our lust for celebrity. Witnessing it will be, for me, the climax of two weeks' total immersion in Elvis Country (as the Mississippi-Tennessee realm of Elvis shrines is called) and in the larger domain of Elvis Culture. An odyssey that took me and the photographer James Hamilton south from Graceland to the birthplace shrine in Tupelo, Miss.; then to the cemetery in nearby Priceville, where we searched for the unmarked grave of Elvis's stillborn twin; next, west to Oxford, Miss., for a week-long encounter with academic theories of Elvis at the University of Mississippi's first International Conference on Elvis Presley, and finally, north on Highway 61 through the Delta and back to Memphis for Death Week.

One thing I've learned is that—dramatic as it is—Death Week is but the tip of the iceberg of Elvis Culture, a phenomenon whose dimensions can only be incompletely hinted at by citing numbers. According to Paul Williams, the vice president for Presley Affairs (among other things) at RCA, Elvis recently passed the *half-billion* mark in record sales, and the release next month of a new boxed set of his 70's recordings (which contains some stunning and heartbreaking reflections of the pain of his final years) will only add to this number, one that perhaps no artist in any medium has ever attained. The number of visitors making the pilgrimage to Grace-land every year has climbed to three-quarters of a million—making it, Graceland officials like to boast, the single most visited home in America, save for the White House. A White House, it hardly needs mentioning, now occupied by a sometime Elvis impersonator.

And speaking of impersonators—the lay priests of the Elvis religion—this peculiar phenomenon has become a remarkably pervasive fixture of the iconography of American culture. There are tens of thousands of amateur and professional impersonators belting out sweaty versions of "Viva Las Vegas" in gem-encrusted white jump suits all over America. A figure rivaled only, perhaps, by the number of reported appearances the real Elvis seems to be making—the "sightings," as they're called in Elvisian literature.

But more to the point than the quantity of Elvis manifestations is the quality, the intensity, of the posthumous devotion he inspires—the number of people who have "Elvis shrines" and "Elvis rooms" in their homes, who trade in icons like vials of Elvis sweat, buy and sell his hair and warts. It has become a truism that the three most identifiable names in the whole world are Jesus, Coca-Cola and Elvis. What's more remarkable is that, to some, Elvis has come to seem less like the soft drink—just another commodity—and more like a savior. Greil Marcus, the cultural critic who has long been the most prescient observer of the Presley phenomenon, has written (in "Dead Elvis") that "the identification of Elvis with Jesus has been a secret theme of the Elvis story at least since 1956." While Elvis himself disclaimed the comparison ("There is only one King," he piously averred), what he seems to offer to those who revere him is some kind of healing. Not necessarily physical healing (although there are reports of that) but healing for emotional travail. And not just for stereotypical Elvisians.

The sea change in the perception—and the demographics—of Elvis's spirituality can perhaps be traced to the release of Paul Simon's hugely successful "Graceland" album of 1986. That haunting title song—about a pilgrimage by an urban sophisticate in pain, a guy who's "blown apart" by the loss of love, going to Graceland with "the child of my first marriage," seeking some kind of secular spiritual succor for his pain at the place where the pain-racked body of Elvis Presley finally came to rest—suggested that the grace of Graceland was something accessible to all.

Similarly, Elvis culture has transcended the camp ridicule, the kitschy condescension, the hostile tell-all bios (whose portraits of a burned-out wreck of a hunk of burning love, crucifying himself with pills and self-pity, only fueled the compelling power of his suffering savior image). The pilgrimage to Graceland has become a way for all kinds of Americans to come to terms with all kinds of pain and loss.

I witnessed a particularly dramatic instance of the way this worked on the penultimate night of Death Week, when I attended an Elvis memorial dinner at the grand old Peabody Hotel. It was a charity benefit run by Marian Cocke, Elvis's one-time private nurse, one of the few people in the world to see at close hand just how badly hurt Elvis was at the end. (She was there at the hospital when he was pronounced dead.) You can tell instantly why Elvis would have called on Nurse Cocke when he was in pain: she radiates a kind of healing warmth that extends to all in her orbit. She told me something about the last few times Elvis had summoned her for help in the final days. Tormented by an inability to sleep that no amount of drugs could assuage, he'd asked her up to his bedroom suite. "He just wanted me to sit with him and hold his hand until he could fall asleep," she told me. And so she'd sit for hour after hour. It wasn't physical pain, Nurse Cocke told me, it was a deeper hurt, one that had been with him all his life, one that no amount of pink Cadillacs, gold records or little yellow pills could alleviate.

Nurse Cocke's memorial banquet featured a beautiful candlelight ceremony, but it was a moment during the entertainment afterward that crystallized for me my sense of the pain-filled transaction going on between Elvis and the Elvisians. Two highly professional Elvis impersonators sang, and what struck me most forcefully about their performances was the one song they both did that just stopped the show. It's a song not very well known to the casual Elvis observer like myself—I'd been hooked the first time I heard "Heartbreak Hotel" as a kid, but like many I'd lost interest by the time the Beatles arrived—a song Elvis recorded just a year before his death. But it has become one of those secret shared passions that marks a true Elvis initiate. A song that Elvis did in his most melodramatic quasi- operatical all-out soul-baring hold-nothing-back style. A song called, simply, "Hurt." . . . It's a hurt that seems to transcend the petty betrayals of the woman he's singing to. It's a bigger hurt: his own naked, personal pain.

So powerful, so popular was the song among the Elvisians at Nurse Cocke's banquet that it evoked an extraordinary outburst: The first impersonator did "Hurt" to cries and screams and whistles and then the second impersonator got up and—toward the end of his set—announced that he, too, had planned to do a version of "Hurt," but that since the previous impersonator had done it, he'd close with a different number.

Not a chance: A cry began to build from the audience. A few yelled: *No! No! Do Hurt!* But most simply cried out, *Hurt!* A chant began to build: *Hurt! Hurt! Hurt!* And it continued until he relented and sang it.

Hurt! Hurt! Hurt! It was a demand, a song request, yes, but in a sense it was more than that: it was a self-diagnosis. It was Elvis fans expressing what they, commoners, shared most deeply with the King: hurt. The pain of their lives, of life itself, a pain that was acute and unappeasable, whether experienced in Graceland or a trailer park; the kind of pain that pills and religions seek to minister to, the kind of pain that is the true source of the growing reach of the Elvis faith. . . .

Confinement, of course, can take many forms. But suddenly, last summer, the possibility arose that 18 years after his jailbreak from life, Elvis would face a form of confinement he could never have imagined: enshrinement in academia. The announcement that the University of Mississippi's highly regarded Center for the Study of Southern Culture was co-sponsoring what it intended as an annual conference of "Elvis scholars," a conference that would, moreover, feature Elvis impersonators, gospel preachers and "Memphis mafia" types touched off a brief firestorm of national controversy. While semiotic papers on Madonna have been a fixture of university "cultural studies" programs for some time, many found that the notion of Elvis scholarship transgressed the boundary between academic self-parody and outright scandal.

For the most part, the arguments that raged about the Elvis conference's right to exist were about the wrong questions. It all began as an attack by Faulkner people on Elvis people. Oxford, Miss., is the home of Faulkner's Rowan Oak homestead and of an annual genteel scholars' conference on his legacy at Ole Miss. Faulkner partisans denounced the university's decision to hold an Elvis conference as an act of lowbrow lese majeste to a high culture icon. Elvis conference organizers like Bill Ferris of the Southern Culture Center fired back—accusing the Faulkner people of the same "class-based snobbery," the prudish genteel contumely, that Elvis had endured when he burst upon the scene.

The fallacy on both sides was to insist that studying the Elvis Presley phenomenon meant equating "Hound Dog" with "Light in August." While some Elvis scholars at the conference were perfectly prepared to do just that, it's not the necessary consequence. A better way of looking at it is this: Few serious scholars would look askance at a conference of classical scholars on the subject of the Eleusinian Mystery Cults and their influence upon the reception of Christianity in the Hellenic world. And yet what were the Eleusinian mysteries but the equivalent of ecstatic rock-and-roll rites whose wild Dionysian chants, while not perhaps as elegant as Sophocles' choral laments, may have had more influence on Western culture. Just as Elvis's lyrics, while less sophisticated than Faulkner's prose, may—for better or worse—have had a more profound influence on our culture.

In fact, I found the Elvis conference itself a fascinating cultural barometer, in part because of the striking new image of Elvis that emerged from it: an Elvis who is no longer the victim of pathology. The scholars' Elvis has more in common with the one the fans cry out to: the Healing Elvis. This is Elvis as racial integrator, as gender-liberating sexual healer. The Multicultural Elvis is an even grander figure than the one the fans conceive of—an Elvis who heals not just personal pain in individual souls but painful rifts in the nation's soul, rifts not only between black and white but between sex and spirituality in America.

I began to detect the emerging contours of the Multicultural Elvis, the King as Martin Luther King, in my conversations with an Ole Miss English professor, Vernon Chadwick, about the conflicting theories of Elvis's sexuality—or what might be called the Leg Wiggle Controversy. Chadwick was the guiding spirit of the Ole Miss Elvis conference. As perhaps academia's foremost Elvis scholar, Chadwick is an interesting combination of good-natured, native-Mississippi good ol' boy and up-to-the-second Yale-lit-bred academic. He can deploy jargon du jour like *bricoleur* to describe Elvis as an assembler of clothing "signifiers," yet still get down with sublimely nonacademic Elvis devotees like the father-son impersonator team, Paul and Elvis Aaron Presley MacLeod, who have turned their home in Holly Springs, Miss., into a shrine called Graceland Too, open to the public 24 hours a day (my personal favorite stop in Elvis country).

Chadwick's academic exploration of Elvis grew out of his study of Melville. He told me about a paper he'd published on Melville's Polynesian romances ("Omoo," "Typee," etc.) as the forerunners of Elvis's cinematic Hawaiian trilogy ("Blue Hawaii," "Girls! Girls! Girls!" and "Paradise, Hawaiian Style") in their shared preoccupation with transgressive interracial, multicultural, social and sexual intercourse. Chadwick sees Elvis, in his Hawaiian oeuvre, as "the deconstructor of civilized prejudices and prohibitions," re-enacting "the anthropological function of the 'taboo man' first delineated by Melville in 'Typee.' " The taboo man being, like Elvis, a healing figure with "a special license . . . to cross boundaries—geographical, cultural, sexual, spiritual—otherwise inaccessible to the ordinary tribally regulated man."

But while Chadwick pays obeisance to Elvis as a sexual figure, his stance on the Leg Wiggle Question suggests that he and other Leg Wiggle Revisionists are not completely comfortable with Elvis's sexuality qua sexuality. . . .

"I'd defend myself this way," Chadwick said in response to my view that spiritualizing Elvis's sexuality was doing an Ed Sullivan job on him. "In Southern spirituality, spiritual exaltation is close to bodily release, and that bodily release implies as well a healthy spiritual and sexual concept."

Again the emphasis on wholesomeness, on health, on Elvis as a kind of singing Bill Moyers-Joseph Campbell figure. God forbid Elvis should be allowed to be purely sexy or—horrors—frankly and joyfully "dirty." . . .

I wondered at the importance Chadwick and other Elvis scholars at the conference attached to the wholesomeness of Elvis's sexuality—the tendency to see him as a saintly figure. (Or more: Chadwick even went so far as to tell a conference audience that Elvis's "Don't Be Cruel" was analagous to the Sermon on the Mount! Even academics can't resist the Elvis-Jesus analogy.) In part, I think it has something to do with the importance Elvis has for Southern liberal scholars seeking a redemptive vision of their native region, eager to find a source of health in a culture widely stereotyped as "redneck"—particularly on the even more contentious and significant question of race.

The whiteness of Elvis culture: It's not the first thing you notice on Death Night, but it's something you can't help seeing. While some black musicians like James Brown and B. B. King have paid tribute to the way Elvis opened up mainstream opportunities for them, judging by the crowds during Death Week the black public is comparatively indifferent.

Certainly, you notice other things on Death Night: the wheelchairs, for instance, the clutch of crippled Elvis pilgrims, many from overseas. Their passage here had been paid for by fan clubs who give Graceland-trip scholarships to the handicapped in search of healing for the soul, if not the body. And, yes, you notice the impersonators, many in father-son pairs. Then you notice the tears, the way the flickering candle flames are reflected in the tracks of the tears running down the faces of the pilgrims patiently standing in that serpentine line up the driveway to the Meditation Garden and the grave—the Elvis fan's stairway to heaven.

And you notice certain people you've seen before. The blond middle -aged woman you'd seen at the Ole Miss Elvis Conference, not an academic but a dedicated lay person. She'd become an Elvis fan, she had told me down there, not because of his music but because of his pain.

She'd identified with Elvis, she said, because she saw him—as she saw herself —as the victim of a dysfunctional alcoholic family. "If you study the family history," she told me, "you'd see: it was passed down." But unlike Elvis, she'd rescued herself, she said, with a 12-step program. And now by getting into Elvis's pain, she was somehow mourning her own and forgiving herself. I found her on Death Night lingering at the Meditation Garden after she'd knelt by the grave, her cheeks still streaked with tears, lingering there, crying, she said, because she was feeling his pain. It's an example of how exposés of Elvis's sins and vices, like his gargantuan prescription-drug abuse problem, often have the effect—particularly in a 12-step recovery and redemption-oriented culture—not of repelling but of drawing fans closer to him as fellow victim and sufferer.

You also notice the silent communion at the grave marker. The way so many stopped and seemed to engage in some kind of intense commu-nication with the man buried there. They don't think he's alive. I found very few who bought into the Elvis-faked-his-death-and-can-be-seen-buying-Big-Gulps-at-Kalamazoo-7-Eleven's theory. But they do think he's some kind of Living Presence. While it's true that many were just fervent fans paying their respects to a man whose music moved them, many more spoke of him as a kind of higher being, "up there in heaven," who hears their prayers, who understands them the way no one on earth could.

What kind of being are they talking about or talking to? I had an illuminating conversation on that question with Charles Reagan Wilson, professor of history at Ole Miss and author of a forthcoming book, "Judg-ment and Grace in Dixie: Southern Faiths From Faulkner to Elvis." Wilson says that for Elvis's religiously inclined followers, he occupies a kind of intermediary realm that "blurs the boundaries between the supernatural and the sacred, something like the way U.F.O.'s do for believers." That Elvis is a figure more than human, less than divine, with elements of St. Francis of Assisi and E.T.

Certainly, you can be impressed with the sincerity of the devotees and admire the improvisational rituals people devise to find ways of healing themselves. But you still can't help wondering at how few black faces there are. In the nearly four hours we spent drifting up and down the serpentine trail of tears—it was long after midnight when we left—we saw only one black family.

This is not to say that Elvis culture is racist, or that Elvis was racist. But it does make one skeptical about some of the more extreme claims made for the Multicultural Elvis of the Ole Miss conference, particularly the claim that Elvis had been the medium, the medicine man, through which black sexuality cured the pathologies of the white race.

Such was the expansive visionary claim made by one of the most eloquent speakers at the conference, Jon Michael Spencer, professor of music and American studies at the University of Richmond. Spencer, who is black, began his talk with a witty deconstruction of the Elvis scenes in "Forrest Gump." If you'll recall, the young Elvis is a boarder in the Gump home at the time Forrest is forced to wear complicated leg braces. Braces that force Forrest to walk in an elaborately syncopated knock-kneed fashion, a fashion that the young, pre-stardom Elvis takes careful note of.

Professor Spencer sees the Gump version of Leg Wiggle theory as an appropriation, an erasure of the culture that was the true origin of Elvis's gyrations: "Those syncopated leg and body movements are not attributable to Forrest Gump but to the rhythms that underlie African-American music. . . ." He will not even permit the Chadwick-Guralnick attribution of the Leg Wiggle to white gospel. No, Spencer insists: "What Elvis loved in white gospel was the rhythms of *black* gospel."

Spencer insists that it was a specifically black sexuality that Elvis displayed, that Elvis became the channel for, that Elvis broadcast to white America. That what Elvis accomplished was "the sexual seduction of whites into blackness." And that it was emphatically a therapeutic seduction—the Sexual Healing of White America. It's a healing Spencer describes in Jungian terms: "Elvis's injection of black rhythms into mainstream American culture accomplished the reconciliation of the unnatural binary oppositions between body and soul, flesh and spirit, spirit and nature."

But if white America was so profoundly and thoroughly healed by exposure to Elvis's black sexuality, would we really be as socially segregated a society as we still seem to be? On the way from the Elvis conference back to Memphis for Death Week, we'd driven up Highway 61, the blues highway (and the apocalyptic killing ground of the civil rights era in the famous Dylan song), in order to make a special pilgramage to the place I thought of as the real Heartbreak Hotel, the place where Bessie Smith died. It's now called the Riverside Hotel, but when the great blues lady was brought there after a car wreck on Highway 61 it was "a colored hospital," a place she bled to death in.

It was a sobering experience to see firsthand the appalling, unabated black poverty of the Delta. And it left me wondering about the optimistic vision of Spencer and the other academics at the Ole Miss conference. If Elvis so profoundly healed and integrated America, that Heartbreak Hotel where Bessie Smith died should have been as grand and as splendid a shrine as Graceland.

More curious and notable perhaps than the whiteness of the faces of Elvis culture is the whiteness—for want of a better word—of the music at its heart. Very early on, Elvis discovered that the power of big, bland ballads—weepy, syrupy crooner vehicles of the sort Pat Boone sang, songs like "Love Me Tender" and "Can't Help Falling in Love"—was far greater than the power of breakthrough rockers like "Mystery Train" and "Good Rockin' Tonight." That the power of the Leg Wiggle was exceeded by that of the tear jerk. And after 1958, with some exceptions (the brief "Suspicious Minds/ Burning Love" period), it was sentimental, soap-operatic ballads like "Are You Lonesome Tonight?" and "Unchained Melody," that became the heart of his work and the soul of the Elvis cult.

It was these songs, weepy, blatantly sentimental, sobbers like "You Gave Me a Mountain" and "Solitaire," that you heard pumped out over the speakers in the Memphis strip malls and souvenir shops during Death Week. It's these big broad Vegas soul ballads as suety with emotion as Elvis's peanut-butter-and-bacon diet, that the hard-core worshipers want to hear.

Vegas soul: It's a much-despised, even oxymoronic notion to some. But it's a powerful presence in mainstream American lives. While I never saw Elvis in Vegas, I once spent two weeks trying to figure out Wayne Newton's appeal there, watching two shows a night at the Aladdin Casino showroom and learning what Wayne had learned from Elvis. (Wayne has said he considers himself Elvis's true successor in Las Vegas.) What I learned from studying Wayne was the spell those big, shamelessly sentimental Vegas ballads cast over real people. Hard-bitten couples who'd been through a marriage or two, through rocky times—cheating, money trouble—and survived to celebrate, and after a few drinks and a few songs like "Lady," "My Way" and "The Impossible Dream," they reached an emotional communion that would inscribe these songs in their souls forever. Vegas soul is not the kind of breakthrough soul that rock critics rave about, but these people don't live rock critics' lives, and, for them, it works; it heals.

It is this Elvis, the Vegas Healer, not the Young Elvis, who is at the heart of the posthumous cult. America put the Young Elvis on its postage stamps; as the novelist Kay Sloan put it at the Ole Miss conference, it was the Young Elvis who empowered her generation of women to become "romantic revolutionaries," but it is the Late Elvis—the old, fat, sweaty Vegas Elvis—that America has taken to its heart. . . .

The question remains, though, what is it about the pain of the Man Behind the Curtain that Americans continue to be drawn to? One answer suggested itself to me in a conversation at the Sun Studio Cafe. This is the low-key, funky eating place next door to the now legendary hole-in-the-wall recording studio where many say rock-and-roll itself was invented by Sam Phillips, the place where Elvis was discovered or invented when Sam coaxed a sound out of him that hadn't been heard before. Sun is still a working studio (U2 made a pilgrimage to record there some years ago), as well as a shrine, and it has a kind of vitality that the mausoleumlike Graceland lacks.

A couple of pilgrims at the Sun Cafe were discussing the difference. "This is a place of life," one woman was saying, "while Graceland—I was just over there and it's so *sad.*"

"Sad because of what became of him?" I asked her.

"No," she said, "sad because of what became of *us.*"

But that's precisely why America has come to love and embrace the Late, Fat, Pain-Racked, Self-Destructive Elvis. It's a way of coming to terms with our own sense of loss, with what's become of us as a nation—the transition America has made from the young, vital, innocent pioneer nation we once were (the young, vital Elvis we put on our stamps) to the bloated colossus we feel we've become: the Fat Elvis of nations. For America, finding a way to love the fat, sweaty figure Elvis turned into, the heartbroken, pain- and pill-filled impersonator of greatness, may be our way of finding, in our *own* decline, some forgiveness, some humor, even some healing.

∽ Fastwrite 11

Most of you are probably familiar with Elvis impersonators, but there are other famous Americans—Abraham Lincoln, Mark Twain, Will Rogers, Emily Dickinson, Harry Truman, and Franklin D. Roosevelt, to name a few—who have been portrayed by actors on stage and in films. If you have ever witnessed one of these portrayals, discuss your feelings about it and what it meant to you. Whether you have witnessed such a performance or not, write a brief essay examining the kinds of characters who tend to be impersonated and what you think an audience expects and receives by witnessing such an event. Finally, discuss briefly why you think an actor would agree to such a role.

ELVIS CALENDAR

Here's a list of selected events for Elvis Week. See The Commercial Appeal's Web site for more information at http://www.gomemphis.com

MUSIC

Concerts and shows celebrating Elvis.

Through Aug. 17: Daily Activities at Graceland. Elvis music live every day. Noon-4 p.m. Graceland Plaza. Call 332-3322 or (800) 238-2000.

Through Aug. 17: Elvis: Legacy In Light. Laser graphics, lighting effects and more than 200 photographs choreographed to Elvis music. 1:30 and 3 p.m. Admission: $5.50. Memphis Pink Palace Museum (Sharpe Planetarium), 3050 Central. Call 320-6362.

Through Aug. 17: Daniel's Tribute — "Elvis If You Could See Me Now." A musical portrait of the life of Elvis Presley, starring Daniel Young. 7-9:15 p.m. (nightly) Tickets: $15/$20 at the door. Humes Jr. High School, 659 Manassas (off Jackson Ave). Call 526-2849.

Today: All The King's Music. El Vez and the Memphis Mariachis with Maggie Lewis & the Thunderbolts. Advance tickets $8, $15 at the gate. Gates open 6 p.m.; show 7 p.m. Overton Park Shell. Call 274-6046 or Ticketmaster, 525-1515.

Through Saturday: Elvis Tribute at the New Daisy. 7 p.m. (nightly) Elvis impersonators and other rock and roll performers; plus "The Ultimate Tribute" with Mike Albert and the Big 'E' Band at 8 p.m. Thursday, 7 p.m. Friday. New Daisy Theatre, 330 Beale. Call 525-8981 or (601) 342-4899.

Monday: All The King's Music. Billy Lee Riley with Gutbucket and North Mississippi All-Stars. Advance tickets $8, $15 at the gate. Gates open at 6 p.m.; show 7 p.m. Overton Park Shell. Call 274-6046 or Ticketmaster, 525-1515.

Monday-Saturday: Ron Starr and the Mystery Train. Performing rock/dance and R&B classics from the golden era of rock. 9 p.m. Ramada Inn-Airport, 1471 E. Brooks. Call 332-3500.

Wednesday: Good Rockin' Tonight VIII. Three concerts in one, each with special guests; separate shows by Carl Perkins, Ronnie McDowell and Terry Mike Jeffrey; also featured, D.J. Fontana and the Jordanaires. 7 p.m. Tickets: $35-$65. Mud Island Amphitheatre, downtown Memphis. Call (818) 991-3892.

TALK

Discussions and reminiscences about the King.

Today: George Klein's Memphis Mafia Reunion. Sixth annual reunion of friends and associates of Elvis who reminisce and answer questions. 7 p.m. Alfred's, 197 Beale. No reservations. Call 525-3711.

Tuesday: Elvis Presley Memorial Dinner Charity Event. Auction 3-6 p.m.; dinner 7 p.m. "A Tribute — We Remember You" guests include Sam and Knox Phillips, D.J. Fontana, Dick Grob, George Klein. Proceeds benefit Elvis Presley Endowed Scholarship Fund, Make-A-Wish Foundation, Elvis Presley

Trauma Center. The Peabody, 149 Union. Call 324-9612.

Wednesday: Conversations on Elvis at Humes. Friends, colleagues and family of Elvis share stories and answer questions at Elvis's alma mater. 2-4 p.m. Admission: $8. Tours available for $10. For details, call 344-8687 or (800) 948-8680.

Wednesday: Elvis's Hometown Fans Fan Club. Champagne brunch with authors and friends/family of Elvis, plus entertainment, 11 a.m.-1 p.m., cost $10. Also, a "Garden Party/Orion Sings Elvis" at 3 p.m., cost $12.50. Pick-up at Graceland Crossing shopping center starting at 2:15 p.m. Call 323-0739.

T.C.B.

Stuff to buy.

Through Friday: Elvis Jamboree '97. Elvis Collectors Show & Sale. Elvis fans gather from around the world to buy, sell and trade the rarest and most collectible of Elvis Presley nostalgia; includes original records, movie posters, RCA-Vegas concert memorabilia. 1-6 p.m. today through Friday. Free admission Wilson World-Graceland, 3677 Elvis Presley. Call 332-1000.

Monday: Booksigning. Neal and Janice Gregory sign copies of When Elvis Died. 7-9 p.m. Bookstar, 3410 Poplar. Call 323-9332.

Monday-Friday: Elvis Fan Club Festival. Tables with memorabilia, raffles, continuous videos, refreshments. 11 a.m.-6 p.m. Admission: $1 per day at the door, or $5 pass for all five days. Benefits Porter-Leath Children's Home and Tupelo Children's Mansion. Super 8 Inn, 3280 Elvis Presley. Call Fred Whobrey, (217) 875-3598.

Tuesday: Booksigning. Frank Coffey discusses and signs copies of his new book, The Complete Idiot's Guide to Elvis; Scotty Moore, Elvis's first guitarist and manager, and co-author James Dickerson read from, discuss and signs copies of their new book That's Alright, Elvis. 7:30-8:30 p.m. Bookstar, 3410 Poplar. Call 323-9332.

TOURS

Follow that dream along the Elvis trail.

Through Saturday: Overton Park Shell Tours. Tour where Elvis performed one of his earliest gigs. 9 a.m.-7 p.m. Bring your guitar and play on stage. Overton Park Shell, 1928 Poplar. Call 274-6046.Free, but $1 donation suggested.

Today: Elvis Presley Birthplace. Live music, welcome by Tupelo, Miss., officials, and more. 1-5:30 p.m. Tours of two-room house where Elvis was born, the memorial chapel, and the "Times & Things Remembered" Museum available daily. Call (601) 841-1245.

Today: Elvis's Hometown Fans Fan Club. Bus trip to Elvis's birthplace in Tupelo, Miss., cost $35, boarding 8 a.m. Graceland Crossing shopping center. Call 332-0739.

Through Aug. 17: Humes High School Tours. Guided tours of the school Elvis attended (now a junior high school). 10 a.m.-2 p.m. Admission: $2. Students conduct tours that include the Elvis A. Presley Auditorium, where Elvis once per-

formed. Call 579-3226.

Tuesday-Saturday: Kang Rhee Karate School Tours. Meet and talk with Kang Rhee, Elvis karate action photos. 11 a.m.-1 p.m. Kang Rhee, 706 Germantown Parkway (Trinity Commons shopping center). Call 757-5000. Free.

EVERYTHING ELSE

Other entertainments too singular, weird or wonderful to classify.

Through Aug. 17: "Patty Carroll's Ultimate Elvis Impersonator Extravaganza." Exhibition consists of fine photography, computer prints, plates, clocks and impersonator scarves. Closing reception Aug. 17 features a lecture by artist Patty Carroll and a booksigning of I Elvis by author Bill Henderson. Memphis College of Art, Overton Park. Call 726-4085.

Through Aug. 29: First Tennessee Heritage Collection Gallery. "William Eggleston's Graceland," a portfolio of 11 dye-transfer color photographs created in 1983 at the Graceland mansion. Open 8:30 a.m.-4 p.m. Monday-Friday, though Aug. 29. First Tennessee Bank, 165 Madison. Call 523-4382. Free.

Through Thursday: Elvis Movie Nights at Graceland. Elvis movies at the Bijou Theatre at Graceland Plaza. 7 p.m. Call 332-3322 or (800) 238-2000. Free.

Through Tuesday: Elvis River Boat Cruise & Dance Party. The Andy Childs Band performs all-Elvis music. 7 p.m. boarding; 8-11 p.m. cruise/dance. Admission: $20. Reservations recommended. Memphis Queen Line, Riverside Drive, downtown Memphis. Call 332-3322 or (800) 238-2000.

Through Saturday: Images of Elvis Inc.'s 11th annual impersonator Contest. Preliminaries today-Monday, Wednesday-Friday. Finals Friday and Saturday. Hours: 7 p.m. for all shows. Four Points Hotel By Sheraton, 2240 Democrat (at Airways). For more information/prices, call 342-4899 or 332-1130.

Through Aug. 17: Elvis: The Karate Years. Locked in a bank vault since it was produced more than 23 years ago, this never-before seen 30-minute documentary film features Elvis, in full karate attire, demonstrating and practicing his martial arts skills with friends and associates. 9 a.m.-4 p.m. (hourly). Tickets: $10 at the door, $5 age 11-younger. Hernando's Hide-A-Way, 3210 Old Hernando (at Brooks), one block south of Elvis Presley Blvd. Call 398-7496.

Through Aug. 17: Elvis International Forum 10th Anniversary Celebration. Activities include a raffle to benefit the Carl Perkins Center for the Prevention of Child Abuse, fan club gift packages for club charity efforts. 10 a.m.-4 p.m. Wilson World Hotel (Graceland). Call (818) 991-3892.

Monday: RCA Presentation Of Elvis's International Gold & Platinum Record Awards. 10:30 a.m. Presentation ceremony in the racquetball building on the Graceland mansion grounds. Live closed-circuit videoscreening of the ceremony. Free.

Tuesday: Dedication of Elvis

Statue on Beale. Statue of Elvis Presley is unveiled in a special ceremony. 10:30 a.m. 126 Beale across from Elvis Presley's Memphis club. Call 332-3322 or (800) 238-2000.

THE VIGIL, THE CONCERT, THE MANSION

The main events.

Friday: Annual Candlelight Vigil. Fans gather to pay tribute to Elvis. 9 p.m. Gates remain open until dawn. Free secured parking at Graceland Visitor Center complex. Free admission.

Saturday: Elvis in Concert '97 via video technology. 7 p.m. Tickets: $50, $70 and $80 plus Ticketmaster service charge. Mid-South Coliseum (Fairgrounds). Call 274-3982 or Ticketmaster, 525-1515.

Graceland, 3764 Elvis Presley Blvd.: Graveside free daily 6-7:30; then becomes part of mansion tour. Ticket office hours: 8:30 a.m.-5 p.m. Tours and attractions open until visits completed. Mansion tour includes several rooms, grounds, Elvis's trophy building, original business office and racquetball building. Admission: mansion tour $10, $9 seniors 62-older, $5 for age 7-12; free to age 6-younger. Separate tickets for Elvis Presley Automobile Museum, Lisa Marie jet and JetStar planes and Sincerely Elvis exhibition. Platinum Ticket package includes mansion tour, all attractions: $18.50, $16.65 for seniors 62-older, $11 for children 7-12; children 6-younger free. Discount rates available to 15+ groups and school field trips. Wheelchair accessible except for two basement rooms at mansion and on-board plane tours. Call 332-3322.

Figure 6.5. This is a list from the *Memphis Commercial Appeal*, Sunday, August, 10, 1997, of some of the events scheduled to be held in Memphis on the week of the twentieth anniversary of Elvis's death. Note the listing of an Internet address for more information.

Historical Questions

What a "star" signifies can change dramatically over time as audiences and cultural contexts change, which, in turn, place the star and his or her work in different ideological contexts. The following questions ask you to explore the beliefs and values that underlie some of the changing interpretations of Elvis.

1. Rosenbaum observes that while Elvis's roots are in black music, Elvis culture today is primarily white. Compare Rosenbaum's perception of Elvis's contemporary role as a force in racial harmony with Pratt's. What particular changes in the eighteen years between their two essays—both in terms of the reception of Elvis's music and in terms of race relations in America—might account for their different perspectives? Explain which perspective you agree with more and the criteria you use in making this assessment.

2. With specific reference to earlier articles in this chapter as well as to Rosenbaum's, develop an account of three to four different representations of Elvis's sexuality. Then, analyze why you think these representations developed and why they changed by linking them to the Elvis myth and to the ways in which the myth was related, at any given point, to dominant-residual and emergent forces within the culture at that time.

3. "The pilgrimage to Graceland has become a way for all kinds of Americans to come to terms with all kinds of pain and loss." Think about the implications of this statement. How far back in history do the antecedents of such behavior reach? Why has Elvis become a focal point for such quasi-religious fervor, the appeal of which is on the rise, as the twentieth anniversary celebrations indicated? Develop an analysis that attempts to explain this reaction to Elvis in which you use material from any earlier essays in the chapter dealing with the Elvis myth and the American Dream.

Cultural Questions

1. Focusing on three or four key passages, develop a symptomatic reading of Rosenbaum's essay. Explore not only some of the major statements Rosenbaum literally makes about Elvis and Elvis fans, but focus also on his language and tone. How do you feel about the people he talks about? Why do you think he chooses to represent them as he does? How, for example, might Pratt account for Rosenbaum's language and tone? How do you account for it?

2. Rosenbaum reports that the University of Mississippi's sponsoring an Elvis conference incensed a number of academics. How can you account for the various negative reactions to the conference described by Rosenbaum? What

assumptions about academic study, popular culture, and social class underlie these reactions? To what extent do you agree or disagree with these
negative reactions? Explain your position with a specific example and
explore the assumptions that underlie it.

3. The attraction to Elvis continues today. Thousands of people from vastly
different social class backgrounds—from academics, to fellow musicians
such as Paul Simon, to father-son impersonators—and people from other
countries travel to Graceland. To what extent have Elvis fans today transcended many of the social class barriers Pratt discussed in 1977? If you
believe that many of the barriers have been broken down, explain how you
think this has happened. If you think they have not, explain why you think
people from working class backgrounds throughout the country and the
world are more likely to be attracted to the Elvis myth.

∾   Assignment Sequence 1: Elvis's Relationship to and Effect on Dominant and Emergent Aspects of our Culture: Sexuality and Race

Dominant and emergent elements are always interacting within a cultural
period, and their interactions in one period affect the culture in years
to come in complex and often contradictory ways. Elvis Presley's career
epitomized the ways in which the dominant and the emergent confront
each other.

Essay Question

How was Elvis's work shaped by the larger culture, and how did he help shape
the larger culture? Focusing on one or two key moments in Elvis's career, explore
the relationship of his use of sexuality and race with reference to the following
questions: In what ways was Elvis within the dominant? In what ways did he
work to change or modify it? In what ways did the emergent qualities of his
work enter the dominant? In what ways did the dominant mute the emergent?
Then, turn to a contemporary singer that you listen to a lot and know a fair bit
about. Do you consider him or her more dominant or more emergent? Explain.
What relation might this singer's positioning today have to Elvis's interactions
with the dominant in terms of either sexuality or race?

Review Questions

A list of suggested questions to review before beginning this essay follows.
This list is meant only to suggest review options. You may focus on only a
subset of the questions, decide that other questions should be added, or construct your own sequence of questions. We encourage you to choose what you
believe is the most appropriate review strategy.

1. Jack Gould, Historical Question 1 (page 345)
2. Greil Marcus, Cultural Question 3 (page 365)
3. Fastwrite 5 (page 355)
4. Linda Ray Pratt, Historical Question 1 (page 379)
5. Linda Ray Pratt, Historical Question 2 (page 380)
6. Ron Rosenbaum, Historical Question 1 (page 393)
7. Ron Rosenbaum, Historical Question 2 (page 393)

You may want to focus this essay on social class or regionalism rather than sexuality and race. If so, try the following review questions.

Social Class

1. Stanley Booth, Historical Question 2 (page 354)
2. Linda Ray Pratt, Historical Question 3 (page 381)
3. Ron Rosenbaum, Cultural Question 2 (page 393)

Regionalism

1. Fastwrite 9 (page 374)
2. Linda Ray Pratt, Historical Question 3 (page 380)
3. Linda Ray Pratt, Cultural Question 2 (page 381)
4. Ron Rosenbaum, Cultural Question 1 (page 393)

Questions for Further Reflection

1. This essay not only asks you to put together pieces of some of the work you have done thus far, but it also asks you to stand back and try to get a larger picture, both of how societies change and of how they work to maintain dominant values. The composite picture you will develop will not be neat and clear because that is not how ideology works. You will not be able to say simply "the emergent won" or "the dominant triumphed." Interactions—especially over time—are much more subtle and gradual. Further, changes which appear to take hold at one moment may lose their appeal—as the dominant fights back or appropriates them for its own uses—and may not have as great a consequence in the long run. At other times, what looks like a subtle change may have significant long term implications. And, of course, sometimes, something that looks like a major change actually is one.

   Thus, once you decide on the particular career moment(s) of Elvis on which you want to focus and the areas you want to explore, try to develop a map or sketch of the tensions within each of those moments. Spend some time on this. Only then begin to look for patterns. Try to stay open-minded and remember that there is no single correct answer to this question. The patterns you discover will depend upon the pieces you choose to focus on.

2. Choose a singer whom you know a lot about. Before you being thinking about his or her relationship to Elvis, sketch out what you see are key attributes of the persona he or she represents. Fastwrite for 10–15 minutes about what this singer stands for and why you like his or her music. Then reread your work to see what emerges. Again, stay open. There may be connections that you will discover that will only surface by allowing yourself space to write and think.

∞ Assignment Sequence 2: The Evolution of Myths Surrounding Elvis

In his book, *Dead Elvis: A Chronicle of a Cultural Obsession* (1991), Greil Marcus writes that "in the diffusion of Elvis as a myth, the concentration of Elvis Presley as a person who once did interesting things has become irrelevant; . . . up against the perversity and complexity of Elvis's myth, its infinite circularity, capable of turning any merely human attribute into a phantasm, Elvis Presley's physical presence in a song is redundant after all."

Essay Question

Write an essay that in some way responds to Marcus. Discuss two to three key points in the evolution of the myths surrounding Elvis. How and why did they evolve over time, and how might they be linked to the myth of the American Dream? Why do you think Elvis Presley has had such myth making built around him? What is your take, as a student today, on Elvis? Then compare one aspect of the myths surrounding Elvis with a musician you listen to, a personal acquaintance, someone you have read about, or who is thought to have achieved the American Dream. Or compare one aspect of the myths surrounding Elvis with an achievement of your own, something that has caused others to "build myths" about you. Where do the myths most overlap? Where do they most diverge? What do you think the kinds of myths Americans make around successful people suggest about our culture?

Review Questions

A list of suggested questions to review before beginning this essay follows. This list is meant only to suggest review options. You may focus on only a subset of the questions, decide that other questions should be added, or construct your own sequence of questions. We encourage you to choose what you believe is the most appropriate review strategy.

1. Fastwrite 2 (page 342)
2. Stanley Booth, Historical Question 1 (page 354)
3. Stanley Booth, Cultural Question 1 (page 354)
4. Greil Marcus, Historical Question 3 (page 364)
5. Greil Marcus, Cultural Question 1 (page 364)
6. Clark Porteous, Historical Question 2 (page 372)
7. Ron Rosenbaum, Historical Question 3 (page 393)

Questions for Further Reflection

1. As you put this question together, explore places where more than one source talks about the same aspect of the myth. Do they agree? Why or why not? What underlying assumptions do they have? How do these fit with your assumptions?

2. Remember than you cannot address everything. A good essay has to be focused. Be willing to pick and choose what you will write about and then write about it in detail.

3. Develop the example of your own before you put the rest of the essay together. You may discover points in your own example that will help you to organize what you want to say about Elvis and about our society in general. While you may want to write about a famous person, do not shy away from writing about yourself if you have had an experience in which an achievement of yours did change the way people thought of you. In developing the comparison, you are not suggesting that you are on the road to becoming as famous as Elvis, but rather that you are looking for examples of myth making on a more personal level, which may make some of this material resonate to you in ways that it would not have if you had stayed with an example more distanced from yourself.

For Further Research

Written Texts

Chadwick, Vernon, Ed. *In Search of Elvis: Music, Race, Art, Religion.* Boulder: Westview P, 1997.

Coffey, Frank. *The Complete Idiot's Guide to Elvis.* New York: Alpha, 1997.

DeCurtis, Anthony, and James Henke. *The Rolling Stone Illustrated History of Rock 'n' Roll.* 3rd. ed. New York: Random, 1992.

Dundy, Elaine. *Elvis and Gladys*. New York: St. Martin's P, 1991.

Escott, Colin, and Martin Hawkins. *Good Rockin' Tonight: Sun Records and the Birth of Rock 'n' Roll*. New York: St. Martin's P, 1991.

Gordon, Robert. *The King on the Road: Elvis on Tour, 1954 to 1977*. New York: St. Martin's P, 1996.

Guralnick, Peter. *Last Train to Memphis: The Rise of Elvis Presley*. Boston: Little, Brown, 1994.

———. *Lost Highway: Journeys and Arrivals of American Musicians*. Boston: Godine, 1979.

Halberstam, David. *The Fifties*. New York: Villard, 1993.

Marsh, Dave. *Elvis*. New York: Times Books, 1982.

Pierce, Patricia Jobe. *The Ultimate Elvis: Elvis Presley Day by Day*. New York: Simon and Schuster, 1994.

Quain, Kevin, ed. *The Elvis Reader*. New York: St. Martin's P, 1992.

Rodman, Gilbert. B. *Elvis after Elvis: The Posthumous Career of a Living Legend*. London: Routledge, 1996.

Stanley, David E. *The Elvis Encyclopedia*. Santa Monica: General Publishing, 1994.

Videos

Elvis: Aloha from Hawaii. NTSC, 1973.

Elvis: The Great Performances. Vols. 1 and 2. Buena Vista Home Video, 1990.

Elvis: One Night with You. Lightyear Entertainment, 1992.

Elvis: The '68 Comeback Special. Lightyear Entertainment, 1991.

Elvis '56: In the Beginning. Lightyear Entertainment/BMG, 1995.

Why Elvis? WhiteStar/KULTUR, 1994.

The History of Rock 'n' Roll. 10 volumes. Time Life Video, 1995.

Recordings

"Elvis: Command Performances"—The Essential 60's Masters. Vol II. RCA, 1995.

"Elvis: From Nashville to Memphis"—The Essential 60's Masters." Vol. I. RCA, 1993.

"Elvis: The King of Rock 'n' Roll"—The Complete 50's Masters. RCA, 1992.

"Elvis: Walk a Mile in My Shoes"—The Essential 70's Masters. RCA, 1995.

"Elvis Presley: Amazing Grace—His Greatest Sacred Performances." RCA, 1994.

"Elvis Presley: If Every Day Was Like Christmas." RCA, 1994.

"Elvis Presley: The Million Dollar Quartet." RCA, 1990.

"Elvis Presley: The Top Ten Hits." RCA, 1987.
　　"Heartbreak Hotel"
　　"Hound Dog"
　　"Love Me Tender"
　　"Teddy Bear"
　　"Suspicious Minds"

"Burning Love"
"Crying in the Chapel"
"Can't Help Falling in Love"
"The Sun Sessions CD–Elvis Presley." RCA, 1987.
   "That's All Right, Mama"
   "Mystery Train"
   "Milkcow Blues Boogie"
   "Blue Moon of Kentucky"
   "Baby, Let's Play House"

PART III
Contesting People, Contested Spaces

∽ 7 ∽

THE AMERICAN CITY: DREAMS
AND NIGHTMARES

Sally Terrell and Cynthia Reik

*Those who labor in the earth are the chosen people of God. I view
cities as pestilential to the morals, the health, and the liberties of
man.*

—THOMAS JEFFERSON, 1800

*I have been fairly familiar with the streets of New York and Boston
for the last fifty years, and there is no fact . . . with which I have
been more impressed than the physical improvement which has
taken place in both men and women during that period. . . .
Whether this would hold good in the slums and low parts of the
town may be doubted, but there of course one looks for the refuse
and cast-off material of society.*

—F. J. KINGSBURY, 1895

*To me, a thirteen-year-old Black girl, stalled by the South
and Southern Black life style, the city was a state of beauty
and a state of freedom. [It] became for me the ideal of what
I wanted to be as a grownup. Friendly but never gushing,
cool but not frigid or distant, distinguished without the aweful
stiffness.*

—MAYA ANGELOU, 1969

*In the 'burbs, an entire generation has come of age thinking of
cities as badlands filled with crack, guns, and AIDS.*

—DANIEL LAZARE, 1992

*We have been knocking cities for at least 400 or 500 years as the
essence of decadence on the planet and yet so far, they've ended
up being a) the essence of decadence on the planet and b) the
essence of regeneration.*

—TOM PETERS, 1993

403

c✎

Introduction: City Visions

When was the last time you were in a U.S. city? Perhaps you've grown up in one, or perhaps you've never been in one at all. When you think about U.S. cities today, what comes to mind? A spectacular skyline at night? The hustle and bustle of people? A place to experience the best in entertainment, food, and culture? Or is your vision of the city darker? Do you develop images of poverty, crime, and violence? Does the city make you feel afraid? Excited? Some other combination of emotions? Where does your view of the city come from? Real-life experiences? Prime-time TV dramas? The evening news? How has the U.S. city changed over time? What tensions have existed within the city at different points? How do living spaces reflect the larger ideology—the beliefs, assumptions, hopes, and fears—of a society? You don't have to write about your ideas on these subjects yet; for now, just think about them.

The U.S. city as we know it has developed over the past one hundred years. Figures 7.1 and 7.2 show what the United States looked like before urbanization. Figure 7.1 shows the territories held by the United States in 1825. Note the vast "wilderness" in the west. Figure 7.2 is an 1859 railroad map of New England and the mid-Atlantic states, giving a sense of where

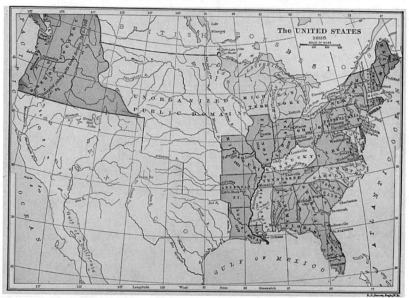

Figure 7.1. Map of U.S. in 1825 showing the development of the states east of the Mississippi and the unorganized territories to the west.

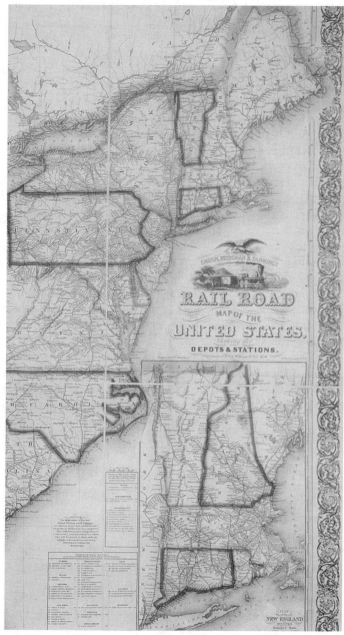

Figure 7.2. Map of the U.S. at approximately 1850, showing the railroad and canal routes in the Northeast.

most of the population lived. Even the relatively settled area of the country was quite sparsely populated.

In 1790, when the first federal census was taken, only one out of twenty of the nearly four million Americans lived in towns of 2,500 or more. Of the large cities, only Philadelphia (42,444) and New York (33,131) had over 25,000 people living in cities. The United States was primarily a nation of farmers, and its economy at that time depended on agriculture. It wasn't until the turn of the nineteenth century that urbanization happened on a larger scale. Although "cities" had existed for nearly seven thousand years, at no time before the nineteenth century did more than a small fraction of the population live in them.

Below is a description by De Witt Clinton, mayor of New York in 1825, of the construction of the Erie Canal. Consider that, at the time, elaborate predictions about the future development of great cities were common in bolstering community support for economic development programs.

> On the 4th of July, 1817, the work was commenced. The Champlain and the greater part of the Erie canal are now in a navigable state, and in less than a year the whole, comprising an extent of about four hundred and twenty-five miles, will be finished. Every year's experience will enhance the results in the public estimation, and benefits will be unfolded which we can now hardly venture to anticipate. As a bond of union between the Atlantic and Western states, it may prevent the dismemberment of the American empire. As an organ of communication between the Hudson, the Mississippi, the St. Lawrence, the great lakes of the north and west, and their tributary rivers, it will create the greatest inland trade ever witnessed. The most fertile and extensive regions of America will avail themselves of its facilities for a market. All their surplus productions, whether of the soil, the forest, the mines, or the water, their fabrics of art and their supplies of foreign commodities will concentrate in the city of New York, for transportation abroad or consumption at home. Agriculture, manufactures, commerce, trade, navigation, and the arts, will receive a correspondent encouragement. That city will, in course of time become the granary of the worked, the emporium of commerce, the seat of manufactures, the focus of great moneyed operations, and the concentrating point of vast, disposable, and accumulating capitals, which will stimulate, enliven, extend, and reward the exertions of human labour and ingenuity, in all their processes and exhibitions. And, before the revolutions of a century, the whole island of Manhattan, covered with habitations and replenished with a dense population, will constitute one vast city. (*A View of the Grand Canal*, 1825)

∽   **Fastwrite 1**

What can you infer about the state of the U.S. city in 1825 from Clinton's description? For example, what was seen as the primary function of cities at this time? Why would building a canal be so important? What factors would most contribute to changes in American living spaces? Based on what you know about cities today, to what extent were Clinton's predictions accurate?

Living in a city during this time was dramatically different from living in one today. Try to imagine how you would react to living in such a space. America's first cities had no housing or building regulations, no fire department, no public water supply, no garbage removal system. Roving herds of swine and goats routinely deposited waste, and there were rotting carcasses in the street. Public health was a large concern; many people used to farm life engaged in practices that were not sanitary when living in closer quarters, such as slaughtering animals in their basements. Viruses were often deadly because there was no cure for them yet.

With city living came the need for people to solve problems together to survive. The earliest forms of urban planning arose from this need for a collective response to city-dwellers' problems. Not only was American society inexperienced in dealing with the problems of masses of people sharing a small amount of living space, it also held the dominant view that life was still very much rooted in farming. As you will read, some of the early writers attach great significance to the differences between the city and country lifestyle. As Carl Bridenbaugh, a historian of the colonial American city, observes, "In these problems of town living, which affected the entire community, lay one of the vast differences between town and country society, and out of the collective efforts to solve these urban problems arose a sense of community responsibility and power that was further to differentiate the two ways of life."

The perceived differences between city and country went beyond the question of lifestyle preference and developed into a nationwide debate about the future direction of the United States. This debate in turn raised issues of the relationship between living spaces and moral character and social class. It also led to conflicting notions of the "American way of life" that challenged the residual ideology of wealth and privilege.

∾   **Fastwrite 2**

Take a few minutes and write about the living space you call home. By *living space,* we mean the place where you sleep, dwell, frequently eat, entertain, and think. If you live on or near a college campus, you can write about your dorm room or apartment or about your living space in your hometown. Describe it in as much detail as you can. How do you feel about your living space? Did you choose this living space? Why? If you didn't choose it, why do you think the person who chose it did? What would you change? What kind of living spaces do you prefer? Individual units separate from other people? The bigger the better? A space where lots of other people live nearby? City energy? Rural tranquillity? Now get up and look out the window. How is your current living space designed? What kinds of structures and land surround it? Why do you think this space was designed the way it was? In what ways does your living space reflect your lifestyle and your needs (physical, social, economic) at this point in your life?

You may not think of your living space preference as being important to anyone but yourself, but to some in early America the rapid growth of cities as living spaces appeared to threaten "fundamental" American values. For example, the distrust of the concentration of power in any one place—a major concern of the founding fathers—created an instinctive suspicion of cities as a possible threat to democratic principles. Still others saw cities as sinful places where saloons, prostitution, and disease corrupted the citizenry. Yet the inevitable effects of the Industrial Revolution enabled cities to flourish, and U.S. cities became havens of opportunity and brought the promise of a new life to thousands of immigrants. At the beginning of the twentieth century, it appeared that U.S. culture would, as Alexander Hamilton had predicted, be a manufacturing power carried on the backs of its cities.

So what happened? Why did so many U.S. cities fall apart socially, physically, and economically? Although there is significant disagreement in a variety of areas, most scholars agree that the following factors helped to cause American cities to decline. After World War II, the suburban housing market skyrocketed, and many of those who could afford to move out of the city did. Federal dollars were channeled to support new communities outside of city limits. Racial segregation played a large part in what happened to cities: because of redlining (racist real estate policies that prevented African-Americans from buying homes in suburban neighborhoods), only middle-class whites were able to live what became the American Dream: a single-family house with a white picket fence. The urban poor, who were and still are mostly comprised of minorities—were left behind. Eventually, as jobs—particularly entry-level positions in retail and manufacturing—moved to malls in the suburbs or to factories overseas, cities and their neighborhoods began to deteriorate. While some cities found ways to remain culturally and economically healthy, many others lost businesses and the middle-class people who worked in them to the suburbs.

The problems of the city are linked to some of the most sensitive and hotly debated issues in our country today: racial inequality, the class system in the United States, and contentions about personal versus collective responsibility as members of a democratic society. Yet even with their problems, U.S. cities share many assets: first-class museums, libraries, performance halls, ethnic restaurants, neighborhood festivals, social and religious diversity, and the abundance of public places. The authors in this chapter and your responses to them can help you to explore not only your views of U.S. cities and other living spaces but also your attitudes towards social problems and their solutions.

∾ **Fastwrite 3**

Return to some of the thoughts you had at the beginning of this introduction as well as to other ideas that developed while you were reading it. What are your predominant feelings about cities? (You may discuss a particular city or a city in a country other than the United States if you wish.) Do you like to be in the city? Why or why not? What are three or four of the most important things you have experienced, seen, read, or heard about cities? Who or what was the source of the information? (Was it personal experience? A story on the news? A movie or TV show? A novel or short story you read? A friend's or family member's story?) What image comes to mind when you think about a city near you or cities in general? To what extent did your choice of college or university have to do with the proximity to (or distance from) a city?

"What's Good about . . . ?" (1995)

These selections were originally part of background research for an issue of the *Utne Reader* devoted to the state of U.S. cities. The editors at the magazine were so impressed by the "deep loyalty the writers felt for their cities and the satisfaction they took in them," they decided to publish them in an article in 1995. Most of the writers report that they "fastwrote" their "What's Good about . . . ?" pieces not expecting to get them into print.

KALAMU YA SALAAM

What's Good about New Orleans? (1995)

Kalamu ya Salaam (b. 1947) is a widely published New Orleans' writer. He is a poet, dramatist, fiction writer, and music critic. Among his publications are seven books of poetry, two books of essays, and two children's books. He is also a senior partner of Bright Moments, the New Orleans-based public relations firm.

Salaam was the editor of *The Black Collegian Magazine* for thirteen years and an actor in the Free Southern Theater. Currently, he is working on an anthology of New Orleans poetry and editing an anthology of African-American literature.

What makes cities great is dreams and diversity: the clamor, clash, and confluence of conflicting cultures. All great cities are portals into which flow alien cultures and out of which fly local cultures.

People have always gravitated to or remained in great cities: partially for the money, for the glamour, for the cultural diversity, but at a subconscious level for the opportunity to become more than they are; for the opportunity to mix and mate outside of their immediate blood and cultural lines.

But what keeps me in New Orleans and what I like most about it is that it is so overwhelmingly black (which is also a reason many "whites" are leaving the city as quickly as they can). Not only is the population 65 percent black but also the historic culture and the day-to-day vibe is "black." For example, more than a few businesspeople from other places have commented about our "elastic" sense of time. What I'm saying is that even "white" people are "late" for business meetings in New Orleans (which are preferably two-hour luncheon tête-à-têtes). But blackness is more than simply the antithesis of "white." The significance of African-American culture permeates the identity of New Orleans. For example, on St. Patrick's Day, Irish-Americans march in a traditional secondline jazz-parade formation with umbrellas and no one here finds it the least bit strange. Where else would "white" Americans celebrate their "Eurocentric" roots by using an "Afrocentric" cultural expression?

ELLEN RYAN

What's Good about St. Paul? (1995)

Ellen Ryan (b. 1955) has worked as a community organizer since 1976 in various locations in New England, Appalachia, and the rural Midwest. She lives in St. Paul, Minnesota, and works as an organizer in small towns in the southeast part of the state. She is codirector of Regeneration Partnership, a small nonprofit organization.

The morning after the riots in South Central Los Angeles, I stepped out on the porch in my predominantly African-American neighborhood in St. Paul. The sunny day was strangely tense and quiet, with an absence of the usual street traffic. I noted my neighbor, an older African-American woman, leaning on her front gate. She waved and motioned to me to cross the street to talk to her. She told me her nephews were coming to help with yard work and asked to borrow my rake. I went to the garage for the rake and brought it to her. As she took it, she said, "I know you always put in a big garden in your own yard, but this year I want you to plant something in the community garden, a few tomatoes, maybe." She pointed to the vacant lot down the street that some people in the neighborhood had used for gardening the previous summer. "It's times like this all people have to stick together." I told her I'd save some plants for the garden and left for work.

That night I returned to get my rake. Her front yard was filled with garden tools. At the gate I met two more of my neighbors, a young African-American man and an elderly white woman, who like me had returned to pick up borrowed items. We started laughing when we saw each other, realizing simultaneously that our neighbor had spent the day borrowing tools all over the neighborhood, giving us reason to come out and greet each other and make gardening plans together that first angry, scary night after the tragedy in L.A.

CHELLIS GLENDINNING

What's Good about San Francisco? (1995)

Chellis Glendinning (b. 1947) is a psychologist and the author of *My Name is Chellis and I'm in Recovery from Western Civilization* (1994) and the Pulitzer Prize-nominated *When Technology Wounds* (1990). Glendinning no longer lives in the city, but in a traditional Indo-Hispano village in northern New Mexico.

What I like most about city living is café society. In fact, café society is one of the three major accomplishments of Western civilization (The other two are homeopathic medicine and figure-skating competition.)

I used to live in San Francisco's North Beach neighborhood *because* of café society. Think of the fine history of this accomplishment: Paris in the '20s and '30s, surrealism, the smell of coffee roasting, Italian pastries, Greenwich Village and North Beach in the '50s. Think of the soul, the literature, the philosophy and politics it engenders.

In North Beach I still recommend: Malvina's, Café Trieste, the Cigar Store.

RICHARD DAHL

What's Good about Boston? (1995)

Dick Dahl grew up on a farm in Minnesota and has lived in small towns and suburbs, but he prefers city life. For the last ten years he's lived in Boston, where he is a freelance journalist. He specializes in legal and medical issues and is a regular contributor to the *Boston Globe Magazine*. He also writes regularly on gun-violence prevention for a Web site that is operated by the Boston University School of Public Health.

The single most overwhelming reason I prefer city life is that I find human beings to be so infinitely fascinating. I like city living because I like the parade.

When it comes to Boston itself, the first special characteristic that comes to mind is the fact that it is a great city to traverse by foot. Not only does that set it apart from nearly every suburb in the United States, but it also differentiates it from most American cities. Boston predates the car by a couple of centuries. Thus, the thoroughfares are both narrow and winding, having been created long ago not by urban planners or traffic engineers, but by beings with a greater sensitivity to the lay of the land: Native Americans, wild animals, early settlers, and cows.

Harvard Square is one of my favorite urban places: the street musicians, the bookstores everywhere you turn, the chess players, the human potpourri. Harvard Square is one of those areas you go to when you feel like just hanging out somewhere. You take the Red Line subway and emerge directly into its center. You browse the musicians and then stop and listen to someone who catches your fancy. Then you check out a bookstore or two, pick up a copy of your hometown paper at the Out-Of-Town newsstand, grab a coffee and a spinach pie, and find a spot to sit back and watch the show of humanity.

∾   **Fastwrite 4**

Write your own "What's Good about . . . ?" for a city you live in, have lived in, or have visited.

Historical Questions   *2 Pages*

1. Although each of these writers is talking about the contemporary city, some of them also refer to much older values and hint at what their city might have been like at an earlier time. Focus on one or two selections and explore what has changed over time and what has remained the same within the particular city, both in terms of certain values and beliefs and in terms of the actual physical conditions of the city. What are one or two of the most important factors that could have led to change over time in these cities? What are one or two of the most important factors that could have enabled continuity to occur over time? ②

2. Look over fastwrite 4, your own "What's Good about . . . ?" Expand the fastwrite by developing an increased sense of the history of the city you wrote about for your readers. When was the city founded? What were its original industries? What groups of people settled there? Then, compare the city's beginnings and its development with its contemporary condition. What is its current population? What groups of people live there now? What is its physical condition? What is its business climate? Finally, explore the feelings you articulated about the city in your fastwrite by setting them in the expanded context of what has changed over time about this city and what has remained the same.

3. Which of the "What's Good about . . . ?" selections suggests the most compelling points of tension or conflict within city life today? Focusing on the discussion of that particular city and on one or two major points of conflict within it today, analyze why those conflicts might exist. What tensions does the piece suggest could have existed in that city's past? Compare and contrast one or two of its past and present tensions, exploring why you think those in the past existed and whether the reasons underlying them are similar or different from those in the present.

Cultural Questions

1. As they celebrate their cities, many of the writers suggest that certain relationships, events, and experiences can happen in a city that they don't think can happen anywhere else. Using two or three of the pieces, compare and contrast the differences that these writers suggest exist between living in the city and living in other kinds of spaces (suburbs, rural areas) with your own feelings and experiences about how life in the city is different from suburban or rural living.

2. In what ways is city living similar to suburban or rural living? Develop one or two arguments that counter the positions developed in the "What's Good About . . . ?" selections that suggest that living in the city is a fundamentally different experience from living elsewhere.

3. Most of the pieces either directly or indirectly describe problems with the contemporary U.S. city. Make a list of what you think are the two or three most significant problems discussed in the readings, and for each quickly jot down as many related issues that might create or compound the problem. Then, focusing on one specific problem in one city, discuss how you would go about starting to work on it if you lived there.

∽ **Fastwrite 5**

Before reading the next selection, fastwrite on the following question. Have you or anyone you know ever been involved with volunteer efforts or any form of community service? Fastwrite about the experience. If you have no experience with such activities, fastwrite about why you think you haven't gotten involved.

JANE ADDAMS

The Settlement House Concept and Individual Commitment (1910)

Jane Addams (1860–1935) was the founder of Hull-House in 1889, a settlement house that provided services for the poor in Chicago. Addams devoted her life to caring for the underprivileged and to fighting for the rights of workers, women, and children. Her work was an important part of the progressive movement, a reform movement between 1905 and 1920. Progressives held the view that the irresponsible actions of the rich were corrupting both public and private life. For her work, she was a co-winner of the Nobel Peace Prize for 1931. The following is a selection from her memoir, *Twenty Years at Hull-House*, first written in 1910 and reissued in 1960.

January 1884 found Miss Starr and myself in Chicago, searching for a neighborhood in which we might put our plans into execution. In our eagerness to win friends for the new undertaking, we utilized every opportunity to set forth the meaning of the Settlement as it had been embodied in Toynbee Hall, although in those days we made no appeal for money, meaning to start with our own slender resources. From the very first the plan received courteous attention, and the discussion, while often skeptical, was always friendly.

Halsted Street has grown so familiar during twenty years of residence that it is difficult to recall its gradual changes—the withdrawal of the more prosperous Irish and Germans, and the slow substitution of Russian Jews, Italians, and Greeks. A description of the street such as I gave in those early addresses still stands in my mind as sympathetic and correct.

Halsted Street is thirty-two miles long, and one of the great thoroughfares of Chicago; Polk Street crosses it midway between the stockyards to the south and the shipbuilding yards on the north branch of the Chicago River. For the six miles between these two industries the street is lined with shops of butchers and grocers, with dingy and gorgeous saloons, and pretentious establishments for the sale of ready-made clothing. Polk Street, running west from Halsted Street, grows rapidly more prosperous; running a mile east to State Street, it grows steadily worse, and crosses a network of vice on the corners of Clark Street and Fifth Avenue. Hull-House once stood in the suburbs, but the city has steadily grown up around it and its site now has corners on three or four foreign colonies. Between Halsted Street and the river live about ten thousand Italians—Neapolitans, Sicilians, and Calabrians, with an occasional Lombard or Venetion. To the south on Twelfth Street are many Germans, and side streets are given over almost entirely to Polish and Russian Jews. Still farther south, these Jewish colonies merge into a huge Bohemian colony, so vast that Chicago ranks as the third Bohemian city in the world. To the northwest are many Canadian-French, clannish in spite of their long residence in America, and to the north are Irish and first-generation Americans. On the streets directly west and farther north are well-to-do English-speaking families, many of whom own their houses and have lived in the neighborhood for years; one man is still living in his old farmhouse.

The policy of the public authorities of never taking an initiative, and always waiting to be urged to do their duty, is obviously fatal in a neighborhood where there is little initiative among the citizens. The idea underlying our self-government breaks down in such a ward. The streets are inexpressibly dirty, the number of schools inadequate, sanitary legislation unenforced, the street lighting bad, the paving miserable and altogether lacking in the alleys and smaller streets, and the stables foul beyond description. Hundreds of houses are unconnected with the street sewer. The older and richer inhabitants seem anxious to move away as rapidly as they can afford it. They make room for newly arrived immigrants who are densely ignorant of civic duties. This substitution of the older inhabitants is accomplished industrially also, in the south and east quarters of the ward. The Jews and Italians for the finishing for the great clothing manufacturers, formerly done by Americans, Irish, and Germans, who refused to submit to the extremely low prices to which the sweating system has reduced their successors. As the design of the sweating system is the elimination of rent from the manufacture of clothing, the "outside work" is begun after the clothing leaves the cutter. An unscrupulous contractor regards no basement as too dark, no stable loft too foul, no rear shanty too provisional, no tenement room too small for his workroom, as these conditions imply low rental. Hence these shops abound in the worst of the foreign districts where the sweater easily finds his cheap basement and his home finishers.

The houses of the ward, for the most part wooden, were originally built for the one family and are now occupied by several. They are after the type of the inconvenient frame cottages found in the poorer suburbs twenty years ago. Many of them were built where they now stand; others were brought thither on rollers, because their previous sites had been taken for factories. The fewer brick tenement buildings which are three or four stories high are comparatively new, and there are few large tenements. The little wooden houses have a temporary aspect, and for this reason, perhaps, the tenement-house legislation in Chicago is totally inadequate. Rear tenements flourish; many houses have no water supply save the faucet in the back yard, there are no fire escapes, the garbage and ashes are placed in wooden boxes which are fastened to the street pavements. One of the most discouraging features about the present system of tenement houses is that many are owned by sordid and ignorant immigrants. The theory that wealth brings responsibility, that possession entails at length education and refinement, in these cases fails utterly. The children of an Italian immigrant owner may "shine" shoes in the streets, and his wife may pick rags from the street gutter, laboriously sorting them in a dingy court. Wealth may do something for her self-complacency and feeling of consequence; it certainly does nothing for her comfort or her children's improvement nor for the cleanliness of anyone concerned. Another thing that prevents better houses in Chicago is the tentative attitude of the real estate men. Many unsavory conditions are allowed to continue which would be regarded with horror if they were considered permanent. Meanwhile, the wretched conditions persist until at least two generations of children have been born and reared in them.

In every neighborhood where poorer people live, because rents are supposed to be cheaper there, is an element which, although uncertain in the individual, in the aggregate can be counted upon. It is composed of people of former education and opportunity who have cherished ambitions and prospects, but who are caricatures of what they meant to be— "hollow ghosts which blame the living men." There are times in many lives when there is a cessation of energy and loss of power. Men and women of education and refinement come to live in a cheaper neighborhood because they lack the ability to make money, because of ill health, because of an unfortunate marriage, or for other reasons which do not imply criminality or stupidity. Among them are those who, in spite of untoward circumstances, keep up some sort of an intellectual life; those who are "great for books," as their neighbors say. To such the Settlement may be a genuine refuge. . . .

It is easy for even the most conscientious citizen of Chicago to forget the foul smells of the stockyards and the garbage dumps, when he is living so far from them that he is only occasionally made conscious of their existence but the residents of a Settlement are perforce constantly surrounded by them. During our first three years on Halsted Street, we had established a small incinerator at Hull-House and we had many times reported the untoward conditions of the ward to the city hall. We had also arranged many talks for the immigrants, pointing out that although a woman may sweep her own doorway in her native village and allow the refuse to innocently decay in the open air and sunshine, in a crowded city quarter, if the garbage is not properly collected and destroyed, a tenement-house mother may see her children sicken and die, and that the immigrants must therefore, not only keep their own houses clean, but must also help the authorities to keep the city clean.

We have in America a fast-growing number of cultivated young people who have no recognized outlet for their active faculties. They hear constantly of the great social maladjustment, but no way is provided for them to change it, and their uselessness hangs about them heavily. Huxley declares that the sense of uselessness is the severest shock which the human system can sustain, and that if persistently sustained, it results in atrophy of function. These young people have had advantages of college, of European travel, and of economic study, but they are sustaining this shock of inaction. They have pet phrases, and they tell you that the things that make us all alike are stronger than the things that make us different. They say that all men are united by needs and sympathies far more permanent and radical than anything that temporarily divides them and sets them in opposition to each other. If they affect art, they say that the decay in artistic expression is due to the decay in ethics, that art when shut away from the human interests and from the great mass of humanity is self-destructive. They tell their elders with all the bitterness of youth that if they expect success from them in business or politics or in whatever lines their ambition for them has run, they must let them consult all of humanity; that they must let them find out what the people want and how they want it. It is only the stronger young people, however, who formulate this. Many of them dissipate their energies in so-called enjoyment. Others not content with that, go on studying and go back to college for their second degrees; not that they are especially fond of study, but because they want something definite to do, and their powers have been trained in the direction of mental accumulation. Many are buried beneath this mental accumulation with lowered vitality and discontent. Walter Besant says they have had the vision that Peter had when he saw the great sheet let down from heaven, wherein was neither clean nor unclean. He calls it the sense of humanity. It is not philanthropy nor benevolence, but a thing fuller and wider than either of these. . . .

The Settlement, then, is an experimental effort to aid in the solution of the social and industrial problems which are engendered by the modern conditions of life in a great city. It insists that these problems are not confined to any one portion of a city. It is an attempt to relieve, at the same time, the overaccumulation at one end of society and the destitution at the other; but it assumes that this overaccumulation and destitution is most sorely felt in the things that pertain to social and educational advantages. From its very nature it can stand for no political or social propaganda. It must, in a sense, give the warm welcome of an inn to all such propaganda, if perchance one of them be found an angel. The one thing to be dreaded in the Settlement is that it lose its flexibility, its power of quick adaptation, its readiness to change its methods as its environment may demand. It must be open to conviction and must have a deep and abiding sense of tolerance. It must be hospitable and ready for experiment. It should demand from its residents a scientific patience in the accumulation of facts and the steady holding of their sympathies as one of the best instruments for that accumulation. It must be grounded in a philosophy whose foundation is on the solidarity of the human race, a philosophy which will not waver when the race happens to be represented by a drunken woman or an idiot boy. Its residents must be emptied of all conceit of opinion and all self-assertion, and ready to arouse and interpret the public opinion of their neighborhood. They must be content to live quietly side by side with their neighbors, until they grow into a sense of relationship and mutual interests. Their neighbors are held apart by differences of race and language which the residents can more easily overcome. They are bound to see the needs of their neighborhood as a whole, to furnish data for legislation, and to use their influence to secure it. In short, residents are pledged to devote themselves to the duties of good citizenship and to the arousing of the social energies which too largely lie dormant in every neighborhood given over to industrialism. They are bound to regard the entire life of their city as organic, to make an effort to unify it, and to protest against its over-differentiation.

It is always easy to make all philosophy point to one particular moral and all history adorn one particular tale; but I may be forgiven the reminder that the best speculative philosophy sets forth the solidarity of the human race; that the highest moralists have taught that without the advance and improvement of the whole, no man can hope for any lasting improvement in his own moral or material individual condition; and that the subjective necessity for Social Settlements is therefore identical with that necessity, which urges us on toward social and individual salvation.

Historical Questions

1. U.S. citizens in the nineteenth century did not believe that poverty was a problem that could be solved; their efforts in settlement houses were intended to alleviate, not eliminate, poverty. Focusing on two or three specific passages from "The Settlement House Concept," compare and contrast Addams's beliefs about poverty with what you think are the dominant beliefs about poverty today. Which beliefs are the same? Which are different? Then, as a start for a symptomatic reading, compare and contrast one assumption about the relationship of poverty to economic class, the function of government, or the structure of society that underlies Addams's perspective with one of your own today.

2. Some contemporary sociologists criticize nineteenth-century philanthropic efforts as self-serving, saying that those who professed to want to help people were actually seeking to reinforce the power of the wealthy over the poor. Reread Addams's description of her mission in founding Hull-House. Besides helping the poor, what were her goals? Discuss two or three ways in which the goals of philanthropy or volunteerism might be the same today. Discuss two or three ways in which they might be different. Explain whether you think the sociologists' criticisms of philanthropy and volunteerism are accurate for either the nineteenth or twentieth century.

3. Think of an example of a contemporary counterpart of Hull-House. In what ways is the contemporary counterpart an effective solution to some of the city's problems? In what ways is Addams's solution outdated? Explain your reasons for holding the views you do. For example, what factors contributing to the problem of poverty today do you think are the same as those at the turn of the century? What factors do you think are different?

4. How do you think Addams would have responded to the quotation from Thomas Jefferson at the beginning of this chapter? Write a response to Jefferson, adopting Addams's perspective. What aspects of the U.S. city—and the United States in general—might have changed over the one-hundred dred years separating the two writers?

Cultural Questions

1. Do a symptomatic reading of "The Settlement House Concept" to uncover some of the diverse and often conflicting perspectives about ways of living in the city that existed at the time within Chicago. Take up the position of one or two different groups of people Addams describes: an Italian immigrant family, a Polish or Russian Jew, or a "richer inhabitant." Trace as much as you can about what Addams says about them—implicitly as well as explicitly. What were their beliefs, goals, and aspirations? How did they interact with each other? How do you think they would have reacted to Addams's portrayal of them and her goals for Hull-House?

2. Hull-House was modeled after Toynbee Hall, a university settlement in England whose purpose was twofold: to educate young men during their residence at the house, thus functioning as a civic and educational institution, and to serve the poor in the surrounding community, thus having a communal function. The goals of Hull-House, therefore, were instruction in citizenship, not only service to the poor. Write a journal entry from the point of view of a young student living at Hull-House. What are you learning? How would you describe this form of education as compared with other kinds of education?

3. Take up the position of one of the immigrant groups you discussed in cultural question 1. How do you react to the journal entry written by the student in cultural question 2?

F . K .   K I N G S B U R Y

In Defense of the City: Observing Urban Progress (1895)

A professor of social science and president of the American Social Science Association, F. K. Kingsbury (1823–1910) delivered this speech in 1895 at a national convention of social scientists. In it, he was responding to the abundance of criticisms of cities, mainly by the clergy, who saw cities as places of moral decadence. The speech was published later in 1895 in the *Journal of Social Sciences* under the title, "The Tendency of Men to Live in Cities."

We must remember, too, that cities as places of human habitation have vastly improved within half a century. About fifty years ago neither New York nor Boston had public water, and very few of our cities had either water or gas, and horse railroads had not been thought of. When we stop to think what this really means in sanitary matters, it seems to me that the increase of cities is no longer a matter of surprise.

A few years since the great improvement of the lift or elevator added probably 10 per cent, actually, and much more than that theoretically, to the possibilities of population on a given amount of ground; and now within a very recent period three new factors have been suddenly developed which promise to exert a powerful influence on the problems of city and country life. These are the trolley, the bicycle, and the telephone. It is impossible at present to foresee just what their influence is to be on the question of the distribution of population; but this much is certain, that it adds from five to fifteen miles to the radius of every large town, bringing all this additional area into new relations to business centres. Places five or ten miles apart and all the intervening distances are rendered accessible and communicable for all the purposes of life as if they were in the next street. Already the bicycle has done more toward directing attention and effort to the improvement of ordinary highways than all that has been done before since the days of Indian paths. It is affecting the legislation of the country on the subject of roads. When we think of what this minimizing of distance means, we cannot help seeing that its influence must be immense, but just what no man can foretell. It is by such apparently unimportant, trifling, and inconspicuous forces that civilization is swayed and moulded in its evolutions and no man can foresee them or say whither they lead. . . .

I have been fairly familiar with the streets of New York and Boston for the last fifty years, and there is no fact in that connection with which I have been more impressed than the physical improvement which has taken place in both men and women during that period. The men are more robust and more erect, the women have greatly improved both in feature and carriage; and in the care and condition of the teeth in both sexes a surprising change has taken place. In Boston streets and streetcars it seems to me that you see a hundred good-looking women where you formerly saw one. Whether this would hold good in the slums and low parts of the town may be doubted, but there of course one looks for the refuse and cast-off material of society. . . .

It is to be noted that the attrition and constant opportunity for comparison which city life makes possible, and even compulsory, tend to make all the people who are subjected to its influence alike. They do and see and hear and smell and eat the same things. They wear similar clothes, they read the same books, and their minds are occupied with the same objects of thought. In the end they even come to look alike, as married people are sometimes said to do, so that they are at once recognized when they are seen in some other place; while people who live isolated lives think their own thoughts, pursue different objects, and are compelled to depend upon their own judgments and wills for the conduct of their daily lives. The consequence is that they develop and increase peculiarities of character and conduct to the verge of eccentricity, if not beyond it, and present all that variety and freshness of type, which we call originality, or individuality. They are much more dramatic, picturesque, and interesting in literature, perhaps not always in real life. I mention this in passing without any attempt to estimate fully the value of either development. Doubtless something is lost and something gained in either case, and probably much could be said in favor of each. Many persons have a great desire to get, as they say, "back to nature"; while others prefer mankind in the improved state, even with some sameness.

The ideal life, time out of mind, for all who could afford it, has been the city for action, the country for repose, tranquillity, recuperation, rest. . . . The country is a good place to rest in, especially if one can control his surroundings. The quiet, the calm, the peace, the pleasant color, the idyllic sights and sounds, all tend to allay nervous irritation, to tranquillize the soul, to repress the intellectual, and to invigorate the animal functions in a very remarkable degree. But this is not rustic life; it is only the country life of the city resident. But the tranquil appearance of a country town, the apparent simplicity and serenity of rural life, the sweet idyllic harmony of rural surroundings, are, as every one must know who has much experience, very deceptive. I remember in one of Dickens' stories a man who lives the life of a travelling showman, one Dr. Marigold, says, in substance, that temper is bad enough anywhere, but temper in a cart is beyond all endurance. The small jealousies and rivalries, the ambitions, bickerings and strifes of a small rural community, are greatly intensified by the circumscribed area in which they find their vent, and compared with the same human frailities in a larger sphere have all the drawbacks of temper in a cart. . . .

It would seem then, (1) that for economic reasons a large part of the work of the world must be done in cities, and the people who do that work must live in cities.

(2) That almost everything that is best in life can be better had in the city than elsewhere, and that, with those who can command the means, physical comforts and favorable sanitary conditions are better obtained there.

(3) That a certain amount of change from city to country is desirable, and is also very universally attainable to those who desire it, and is constantly growing more so.

(4) That the city is growing a better place to live in year by year; that in regard to the degenerate portion of mankind, the very poor, the very wicked, or the very indifferent, it is a question whether they are better off in the country; but, whether they are or not, their gregarious instincts will lead them to the city, and they must be dealt with there as part of the problem.

(5) That efforts to relieve the congested conditions of the city poor by deportation of children to the country are good and praiseworthy, but only touch the surface of things, and that city degeneration must mainly be fought on its own ground.

Historical Questions

1. As part of his defense of cities, Kingsbury celebrates the invention of the elevator, the trolley, the bicycle, and the telephone. One hundred years later, what two or three inventions would you name as having important consequences for our society's ideas about living space? How have these inventions affected your lifestyle and your sense of community? How have they affected cities and their function? Focusing on three or four specific passages of "In Defense of the City," compare and contrast your discussion of the effects of your century's new inventions with Kingsbury's discussion of his.

2. Update Kingsbury's comparison of the relative well-being of the city dweller and the country dweller. Who fares better now and why? Be sure to be articulate about the perspective from which you are writing: Are you from a city, the suburbs, or a more rural environment? Have you lived in different types of locations? Explore how your perspective affects your views of the city and the country. Kingsbury, for example, acknowledges that much of his discussion about the country is from the point of view of a city resident. Focusing on two or three passages from "In Defense of the City," compare and contrast the criteria you are using to evaluate city life versus country life with those Kingsbury used.

3. One obvious similarity between the "What's Good About . . . ?" pieces and Kingsbury's speech is that they celebrate the city's positive aspects. But because they were written at two very different periods in the history of the U.S. city, audience reactions to them may differ significantly. Compare and contrast one or two effects that you imagine Kingsbury's speech and the "What's Good About . . . ?" pieces might have on their respective readers. Briefly explain why you think audiences might have reacted as you are suggesting. What issues are on their minds? How do the texts address those issues?

Cultural Questions

1. Kingsbury was an academic, attached to a university, and he was listened to by other people like himself. How does his position as an academic affect what he says? What kind of criteria does he set up to evaluate the health of the city? As president of the organization, he must be using accepted language of the group at that time. What does the speech suggest to you about the science of sociology then?

2. Kingsbury writes about New York and Boston in 1895, roughly the same time Jane Addams was setting up Hull-House in Chicago in 1889. He talks of the tremendous improvements in sanitation, transportation, building and development, good health—and even good looks—of people in the city. Addams's work, in contrast, focuses on the continued problems in most of these areas. Yet there are some continuities in their underlying values and beliefs. Focusing on two to three particular passages from each of their essays, develop a symptomatic reading of the some of the tensions that existed at the turn of the century about the functions of cities and about who is responsible for maintaining them. What assumptions regarding such areas as human worth, economic class, and technology underlie their positions?

URBANISM COMMITTEE

The National Government Takes a Stand on America's Cities (1937–38)

In the 1930s, with the United States deep in the Depression, President Franklin Delano Roosevelt created numerous programs and federal agencies to address the country's economic and social problems. Among Roosevelt's most influential New Deal agencies were the Federal Housing Administration and the U.S. Housing Authority, both intended to channel funds into slum clearance and the construction of public housing for the poor as well as the construction of single-family housing outside of cities. In 1934, the same year as the creation of the FHA, Roosevelt issued an executive order to establish the National Resources Board (which consisted of the secretaries of the interior, war, agriculture, and commerce, as well as scholars in political science and economics) to study key national issues, including the condition of U.S. cities. The Urbanism Committee was a branch of this board, and in 1937 and 1938 it submitted a report entitled, "Our Cities: Their Role in the National Economy," from which the following selection is taken.

Both physically and socially the cities of the United States bear the imprint of private ownership of land and the absence of a sound long-term land policy. Our traditional procedure of settling communities by alloting homesteads to those that wanted them, and our time-sanctioned method of allowing their subdivision into uniform small lots which were sold to private owners to use, by and large, as their means, their tastes, and their needs dictated, have produced the characteristic features of the typical American city with its stereotyped, monotonous gridiron block pattern.

So phenomenal has the growth of our cities been that even the most optimistic first settlers seldom could envisage the future uses of the land that was to be had virtually for the asking, or the best uses to which it might be put. The city itself, although it generally retained through governmental provision a portion of the available area for public use, was induced, as the settlement grew, to squander its priceless heritage of land which should have been set aside for schools, parks, open spaces, streets and public buildings. The community generally was unable to foresee its own future public needs. Its citizens shortsightedly, or with the idea of private speculative gain, allowed the community to dispose of a substantial part of its holdings in order to "pay as it went" when its credit was poor or to avoid taxation of its inhabitants when their limited capital was profitably employable in pioneer, speculative ventures.

Nor were American cities, at least during the formative stages of their history, particularly concerned about the uses to which private owners put their land holdings or the structures they built upon them. Only a few had any sort of plan, and those that did allowed the growth of the city to run away with whatever plan there was. At any rate successive subdivisions and additions were mechanically joined to the existing settled area or some at some distance therefrom, without thought of the product. For the greater part of their history cities cared little how much of his land area the owner would occupy by buildings, the type of structures he would erect, the materials of which he would build them, or the uses to which he would put them. Building lines and street widths varied widely and arbitrarily. Order, safety, and beauty were of little consequence. Even where the original buildings were acceptable for the purpose for which they had been built, the expansion of the city soon produced the incentive to convert them to other and generally more intensive uses.

As the city grew and as new technological factors were introduced, it became increasingly difficult and costly to readapt the fundamental urban street and building pattern to changed needs. As a consequence, there has emerged a public attitude of placid resignation which too generally accepts what is as inevitable and irremediable. Even when disasters such as fires or earthquakes reduced the major part of the city to ruins, as in Chicago and San Francisco respectively, the rebuilding on the same site has usually been guided by little more than intensified speculative fervor.

While during the colonial period there was evidence of building restrictions and some indication of an interest in community design, the subsequent irresistible expansion and the undaunted spirit of private enterprise swept most of these away. Laws designed to curb the greed and heedlessness of the individual owner and speculator in the interests of order, health, safety, and public welfare were allowed to lapse and were resuscitated only when it was too late to repair most of the damage that had been done through generations of neglect.

As cities have grown big, they have also, in general, grown more sordid and uninhabitable. Building regulations and their enforcement came into use only after the evils of the tenements in the large cities had become glaringly manifest and had been exposed through arduous campaigns of urban social reform. It was not actually until the "muckrakers" through journalism, the social survey, and social research had awakened the public conscience in regard to some of the most disreputable phases of urban living, that legislation designed to mitigate the disastrous consequences of civic apathy and neglect was enacted and some effort made to enforce it. The tremendous growth of cities during the last half of the nineteenth century, the wreckage left behind by periodic depressions, and the appalling congestion in the urban slums helped to call attention to the social and individual cost of land gambling and to the absence of social control of housing and of the physical development of the community.

Today over 1,500 municipalities have building codes and the number of municipal zoning ordinances in force, which have increased phenomenally since 1916, has grown to over 1,300. Legislation authorizing city planning commissions now exists in 42 States, and county planning, which is essential to effective metropolitan planning, is authorized in 26 States.

The nonexistence or nonenforcement of rational land policies, combined with an overemphasis on individualistic enterprise and speculation, in the face of unparalleled growth and expansion, are the underlying factors in some of the most acute problems of urban life. Such problems include congestion of traffic, the herding of the low-income groups into dark, poorly ventilated dwellings, the contagion of blight near the heart of the city, the uneconomical, unsafe, and disorderly distribution of structures, a deficiency of public open spaces combined with a surplus of unused private space, undue concentration of land values, inequitable apportionment of local tax burdens, and inadequate public services. In varying degrees these are to be found in practically every city.

New methods of transportation have made unprecedented urban decentralization possible. The scale of the interior planning of our cities, however, has not been changed to conform with the new mobility. Great inconvenience and waste have resulted from our outmoded street system. These conditions have been among the factors which have produced blighted areas and slums, premature land subdivisions, and jerry-built potential slums. Disintegration of the general property tax resulting in differential rates of taxation and increasing exemptions of property both by type and use; the inefficiency of assessments generally, but improvement of some assessing techniques; confusion and inefficiency of collection practices; widespread use of special assessments; and the spread of rigid tax limits—these are probably the most outstanding recent trends in taxation which, for good or ill, directly affect urban land policies.

Even such instrumentalities as city planning and zoning and the control of subdivisions designed to lead to a more rational policy have often been infected by the speculative psychology of a perpetual land boom. Thus cities are induced to overzone land for uses to which it can never be put, and to extend utilities and services into areas long before they will be so densely inhabited as to warrant such expenditures. The losses, both financial and social, affect the private owner and developer as well as the public treasury, and must be underwritten ultimately by the general public in the form of tax arrears, the decline in public revenues, increasing cost of wasteful public services, and the support of a dependent and handicapped, if not socially dangerous, debtor population.

The growth and welfare of many individual cities shortly will be affected by Nation-wide population trends, by changes in methods of production, transportation and distribution, and even by national policies with reference to interstate commerce, tariffs, and international relations. Urban land policies, therefore, are not merely questions of local public opinion and legislation, but they are intimately related to State and National constitutions and laws and to other factors even more difficult to control. Cities will probably, unless present trends are reversed by large-scale rehabilitation of the blighted areas, continue to increase in density of population at the periphery and to decrease at the center. Land values most likely will follow the same course. . . .

In other countries throughout modern history, and in this country only recently or sporadically, the comprehensive planning of communities has been undertaken. Planned communities here and there have been developed by industry, governmental agencies, real-estate organizations, and philanthropic enterprises. . . .

A survey of 144 planned communities undertaken by this committee indicates the unmistakable success of planning. The industries involved recognize the value of the city plan as do the real-estate people. Such communities are comparatively free from overcrowding of buildings and of people. The residents of the better planned communities enjoy greater efficiency, greater safety, a more healthful environment, and, in great measure, live a more satisfying life. A high degree of social cohesion and community spirit is evident and a greater degree of self-sufficiency is found. Large departures from the plan are the exception. Unforeseen change is a much greater threat to a city plan than physical deterioration. The borders of the planned community are its weakest points; they should be protected from unsuitable development by such physical buffers as "green belts" and land acquisition on a generous scale. Except where all the homes are rented by an industrial company, they tend to become occupied by persons working elsewhere.

That there is a direct relationship between the definiteness and continuity of governmental policy and the success of a city plan can hardly be doubted. Under conditions of long-time unified control, intelligent planning may confidently be expected to be effective as a tool in the hands of those working for community welfare to prevent many of the ills and conflicts of purposes and interests otherwise likely to occur in the development and continued readaptation to changing conditions. These are essential elements in every form of social control of the urban structure, whether it be desired to obtain a more adequate urban existence through building regulation, zoning, planning, taxation, a rational land policy, or a combination of these devices. Until the Nation as a whole recognizes that land is a public utility instead of a speculative commodity, not much prospect exists either of obtaining adequate housing for the population or for reconstructing cities to make them fit for human living.

Historical Questions

1. A capitalist society generally relys on private enterprise, rather than strong government intervention, for development and growth. A democratic society values equal opportunities for all of its citizens. This report points to some of the tensions that exist within a capitalist democracy when privatization does not seem to have as its primary aim the good and general well-being of all citizens. With specific references to Kinsbury's essay, explore why you think that in 1895 he so extolled the virtues of private enterprise while dismissing the lack of equality this was causing and why the government, in 1937, adopted almost the opposite perspective. How do the arguments by each writer reflect changing perspectives in terms of who or what is responsible for addressing problems in U.S. cities?

2. Analyze some of the predictions of the 1937 committee in relation to a U.S. city of your choice. Explore two to three instances in which governmental intervention has succeeded in increasing the quality of life in this city and two to three instances in which it failed. In what ways might these successes and failures point to the tension between private enterprise and government regulation in ensuring fairness in living standards?

3. Addams might have written quite a different urbanism report at the turn of the century. With specific reference from her memoir and the report, explore how she would have responded to the idea of government policy determining land use, and how the Urbanism Committee might have responded to settlement houses as a way to solve some of the city's problems.

Cultural Questions

1. Develop a symptomatic reading of the Urbanism Committee report to explore the tension between private entrepreneurship and the common good by adopting the position of two or three different people the report refers to—for example, a builder, a slum dweller, a citizen filled with "civic apathy," a person living in a "planned community." What does the report say about these groups, implicitly as well as explicitly? Write one or two paragraphs from the perspective of each of the people you choose. What underlying values, expectations, and assumptions about their own and others' rights within living spaces might they each have? How might they have reacted to this report? What attitudes might they have toward each other?

2. What concerns would you like to see addressed if your family had to appear before the local zoning commission dealing with either your home or a place of business? Remember that zoning issues center on what residents can (and cannot do) with their property. Zoning also deals with commercial land use—what businesses are given land or space, how large their signs can be, and so on. If your family has had experience with local zoning, what was the experience like?

3. As part of a civilized society, rules—both written and unwritten—are established to ensure that people fulfill a responsibility to a larger community while having some freedom to make choices about their living spaces. For example, in most condominium communities, bylaws prohibit the use of barbecue grills on outside decks because of the fire hazard, not only to one individual unit, but to residents of the entire building. Look over your student handbook's rules for dorm life, the rules of your apartment lease, or the guidelines of the community in which you rent or own a home. Which rules are geared toward your personal safety? Which involve the

safety and interests of the larger community? If there are any rules you disagree with, discuss why you do. How does your overall response to the rules of your living space reflect your attitudes about community responsibility?

∾ **Fastwrite 6**

The population of the United States over the two hundred years of its existence has shifted from predominantly rural to mainly urban, and in the 1990s census for the first time it is chiefly suburban. How closely does your family's history mirror the national trends, or does it have quite a different pattern? How much did job opportunity affect the various moves your family made during the time you have lived in the United States?

MAYA ANGELOU

Gi' Me a Penny (1976)

Maya Angelou was born Marguerite Johnson on April 4, 1928, in St. Louis, Missouri, and grew up in racially segregated rural Arkansas. Despite her difficult and impoverished background, she has become an internationally renowned writer of the African-American experience. She was the first black woman to have an original screenplay produced in Georgia (1971). The author of over ten best-selling works, she is best known for her autobiographical volumes, particularly *I Know Why the Caged Bird Sings* (1970) and for her several books of poetry. She is a Pulitzer Prize winner and has had several National Book Award nominations; she was nominated for an Emmy Award for her acting in *Roots*. At the 1992 Presidential Inauguration, she read her ceremonial poem, "On the Pulse of Morning." She is currently a professor of American Studies at Wake Forest University in North Carolina. The following piece is a selection from the second volume in her autobiography, *Singin' and Swingin' and Gettin' Merry like Christmas* (1976).

Music was my refuge. I could crawl into the spaces between the notes and curl my back to loneliness.

In my rented room (cooking privileges down the hall), I would play
a record, then put my arms around the shoulders of the song. As we
danced, glued together, I would nuzzle into its neck, kissing the skin, and
rubbing its cheek with my own.

The Melrose Record Shop on Fillmore was a center for music, musicians, music lovers and record collectors. Blasts from its loudspeaker
poured out into the street with all the insistence of a false mourner at a
graveside. Along one wall of its dark interior, stalls were arranged like open
telephone booths. Customers stood playing their selections on turntables
and listening through earphones. I had two hours between jobs. Occasionally I went to the library or, if the hours coincided, to a free dance class
at the YWCA. But most often I directed myself to the melodious Melrose
Record Store, where I could wallow, rutting in music.

Louise Cox, a short blonde who was part owner of the store, flitted
between customers like a fickle butterfly in a rose garden. She was white,
wore perfume and smiled openly with the Negro customers, so I knew she
was sophisticated. Other people's sophistication tended to make me nervous and I stayed shy of Louise. My music tastes seesawed between the
blues of John Lee Hooker and the bubbling silver sounds of Charlie Parker.
For a year I had been collecting their records.

On one visit to the store, Louise came over to the booth where I was
listening to a record.

"Hi, I'm Louise. What's your name?"

I thought of "Puddin' in tame. Ask me again, I'll tell you the same."
That was a cruel childhood rhyme meant to insult.

The last white woman who had asked me anything other than "May
I help you?" had been my high school teacher. I looked at the little woman,
at her cashmere sweater and pearls, at her slick hair and pink lips, and
decided she couldn't hurt me, so I'd give her the name I had given to all
white people.

"Marguerite Annie Johnson." I had been named for two grandmothers.

"Marguerite? That's a pretty name."

I was surprised. She pronounced it like my grandmother. Not Mar-
garite, but Marg-you-reet.

"A new Charlie Parker came in last week. I saved it for you."

That showed her good business sense.

"I know you like John Lee Hooker, but I've got somebody I want you
to hear." She stopped the turntable and removed my record and put on
another in its place.

> "Lord I wonder, do she ever think of me,
> Lord I wonder, do she ever think of me,
> I wonder, I wonder, will my baby come back to me?"

The singer's voice groaned a longing I seemed to have known my life long. But I couldn't say that to Louise. She watched my face and I forced it still.

"Well, I ain't got no special reason here,
No, I ain't got no special reason here,
I'm gonna leave 'cause I don't feel welcome here."

The music fitted me like tailor-made clothes.

She said, "That's Arthur Crudup. Isn't he great?"; excitement lighted her face.

"It's nice. Thank you for letting me hear it."

It wasn't wise to reveal one's real feelings to strangers. And nothing on earth was stranger to me than a friendly white woman.

"Shall I wrap it for you? Along with the Bird?"

My salary from the little real estate office and the dress shop downtown barely paid rent and my son's baby-sitter.

"I'll pick them both up next week. Thank you for thinking of me." Courtesy cost nothing as long as one had dignity. My grandmother, Annie Henderson, had taught me that.

She turned and walked back to the counter, taking the record with her. I counseled myself not to feel badly. I hadn't rejected an offer of friendship, I had simply fielded a commercial come-on.

I walked to the counter.

"Thank you, Louise. See you next week." When I laid the record on the counter, she pushed a wrapped package toward me.

"Take these, Marg-you-reet. I've started an account for you." She turned to another customer. I couldn't refuse because I didn't know how to do so gracefully.

Outside on the evening street, I examined the woman's intention. What did I have that she wanted? Why did she allow me to walk away with her property? She didn't know me. Even my name might have been constructed on the spot. She couldn't have been seeking friendship; after all she was white, and as far as I knew, white women were never lonely, except in books. White men adored them, Black men desired them and Black women worked for them. There was no ready explanation for her gesture of trust.

At home I squeezed enough from the emergency money I kept in a drawer to repay her. Back at the store, she accepted the money and said, "Thanks, Marg-you-reet. But you didn't have to make a special trip. I trust you."

"Why?" That ought to get her. "You don't know me."

"Because I like you."

"But you don't know me. How can you like someone you don't know?"

"Because my heart tells me and I trust my heart."

For weeks I pondered over Louise Cox. What could I possibly have that she could possibly want?

Maybe she offered friendship because she pitied me. The idea was a string winding at first frayed and loose, then tightening, binding into my consciousness. My spirit started at the intrusion. A white woman? Feeling sorry for me? She wouldn't dare. I would go to the store and show her. I would roll her distasteful pity into a ball and throw it in her face. I would smash her nose deep into the unasked-for sympathy until her eyes dribbled tears and she learned that I was a queen, not to be approached by peasants like her, even on bended knees, and wailing.

Louise was bent over the counter talking to a small Black boy. She didn't interrupt her conversation to acknowledge my entrance.

"Exactly how many boxes have you folded, J.C.?" Her intonation was sober.

"Eighteen." The boy's answer matched her seriousness. His head barely reached the counter top. She took a small box from a shelf behind her.

"Then here's eighteen cents." She pushed the coins around counting them, then poured them into his cupped palms.

"O.K." He turned on unsure young legs and collided with me. He mumbled "Thank you."

Louise rounded the counter, following the little voice. She ran past me and caught the door a second after he slammed it.

"J.C." She stood, arms akimbo on the sidewalk, and raised her voice. "J.C., I'll see you next Saturday." She came back into the store and looked at me.

"Hi, Marg-you-reet. Boy, am I glad to see you. Excuse that scene. I had to pay off one of my workers."

I waited for her to continue. Waited for her to tell me how precious he was and how poor and wasn't it all a shame. She went behind the counter and began slipping records into paper jackets.

"When I first opened the shop, all the neighborhood kids came in. They either demanded that I 'gi' them a penny'"—I hated whites' imitation of the Black accent— "or play records for them. I explained that the only way I'd give them anything was if they worked for it and that I'd play records for their parents, but not for them until they were tall enough to reach the turntables."

"So I let them fold empty record boxes for a penny apiece." She went on, "I'm glad to see you because I want to offer you a job."

I had done many things to make a living, but I drew the line at cleaning white folks' houses. I had tried that and lasted only one day. The waxed tables, cut flowers, closets of other people's clothes totally disoriented me.

I hated the figured carpets, tiled kitchens and refrigerators filled with someone else's dinner leftovers.

"Really?" The ice in my voice turned my accent to upperclass Vivien
Leigh (before *Gone With the Wind*).

"My sister has been helping me in the shop, but she's going back to
school. I thought you'd be perfect to take her place."

My resolve began to knuckle under me like weak knees.

"I don't know if you know it, but I have a large clientele and try to
keep in stock a supply, however small, of every record by Negro artists.
And if I don't have something, there's a comprehensive catalog and I can
order it. What do you think?"

Her face was open and her smile simple. I pried into her eyes for hidden
meaning and found nothing. Even so, I had to show my own strength.

"I don't like to hear white folks imitate Negroes. Did the children
really ask you to 'gi' them a penny'? Oh, come now."

She said, "You are right—they didn't ask. They demanded that I 'gi'
them a penny." The smile left her face. "You say it."

"Give me a penny." My teeth pressed my bottom lip, stressing the *v*.

She reached for the box and handed me a coin. "Don't forget that
you've been to school and let neither of us forget that we're both grown-up.
I'd be pleased if you'd take the job." She told me the salary, the hours and
what my duties would be.

"Thank you very much for the offer. I'll think about it." I left the shop,
head up, back straight. I tried to exude indifference, like octopus ink, to
camouflage my excitement.

I had to talk to Ivonne Broadnax, the Realist. She was my closest friend.
Ivonne had escaped the hindrance of romantic blindness, which was my
lifelong affliction. She had the clear, clean eyes of a born survivor. I went
to her Ellis Street house, where she, at twenty-five, was bringing up an
eight-year-old daughter and a fifteen-year-old sister.

"Vonne, you know that woman that runs the record store?"

"That short white woman with the crooked smile?" Her voice was
small and keen and the sound had to force itself past white, even teeth.

"Yes."

"Why?"

"She offered me a job."

"Doing what?" I knew I could count on her cynicism.

"Salesgirl."

"Why?"

"That's what I've been trying to figure out. Why? And why me?"

Ivonne sat very still, thinking. She possessed a great beauty which she
carried nonchalantly. Her cupid's-bow lips pursed, and when she raised
her head her face was flushed pink and cream from the racing blood.

"Is she funny that way?"

We both knew that was the only logical explanation.

"No. I'm sure that she's not."

Ivonne bent her head again. She raised it and looked at me.

"Did you ask her?"

"No."

"I mean did you ask her for the job?"

"No. She offered it." I added just a little indignation to my answer.

Ivonne said, "You know white people are strange. I don't even know if they know why they do things." Ivonne had grown up in a small Mississippi town, and I, in a smaller town in Arkansas. Whites were as constant in our history as the seasons and as unfamiliar as affluence.

"Maybe she's trying to prove something." She waited. "What kind of pay she offering?"

"Enough so I can quit both jobs and bring the baby home."

"Well, take it."

"I'll have to order records and take inventories and all that." The odor of an improvement in my life had barely touched my nostrils and it made me jittery.

"Come on, Maya" (she called me by the family name). "If you could run a hook shop, you can run a record shop. . . .Tell her you'll take the job and then watch her like a hawk. You know white women. They pull off their drawers, lay down first, then scream rape. If you're not careful, she'll get weak and faint on you, then before you know it you'll be washing windows, and scrubbing the floor." We cackled like two old crones, remembering a secret past. The laughter was sour and not really directed at white women. It was a traditional ruse that was used to shield the Black vulnerability; we laughed to keep from crying.

I took the job, but kept Louise under constant surveillance. None of her actions went unheeded, no conversation unrecorded. The question was not if she would divulge her racism but when and how the revelation would occur. For a few months I was a character in a living thriller plot. I listened to her intonations and trailed her glances.

After two months, vigilance had exhausted me and I had found no thread of prejudice. I began to relax and enjoy the wealth of a world of music. Early mornings were given over to Bartok and Schoenberg. Midmorning I treated myself to the vocals of Billy Eckstine, Billie Holiday, Nat Cole, Louis Jordan and Bull Moose Jackson. A piroshki from the Russian delicatessen next door was lunch and then the giants of bebop flipped through the air. Charlie Parker and Max Roach, Dizzy Gillespie, Sarah Vaughan and Al Haig and Howard McGhee. Blues belonged to late afternoons and the singers' lyrics of lost love spoke to my solitude.

I ordered stock and played records on request, emptied ashtrays and dusted the windows' cardboard displays. Louise and her partner, David Rosenbaum, showed their pleasure by giving me a raise, and although I was grateful to them for the job and my first introduction to an amiable black-white relationship, I could exhibit my feelings only by being punctual in coming to the shop and being efficient at work and coolly, grayly respectful.

At home, however, life shimmered with beautiful colors. I picked up my son from the baby-sitter's every evening. He was five years old and so beautiful his smile could break the back of a brute.

For two years we had spun like water spiders in a relentless eddy. I had to be free to work for our support, but the baby-sitters were so expensive I had to have two jobs to pay their fees and my own rent. I boarded him out six days and five nights a week.

On the eve of my day off, I would go to the baby-sitter's house. First he'd grab the hem of my dress, then wrap his arms around my legs and hold on screaming as I paid the weekly bill. I would pry his arms loose, then pick him up and walk down the street. For blocks, as I walked, he would scream. When we were far enough away, he'd relax his strangle hold on my neck and I could put him down. We'd spend the evening in my room. He followed my every turn and didn't trust me to go to the bathroom and return. After dinner, cooked in the communal kitchen, I would read to him and allow him to try to read to me.

The next day was always spent at the park, the zoo, the San Francisco Museum of Art, a cartoon movie house or any cheap or free place of entertainment. Then, on our second evening he would fight sleep like an old person fighting death. By morning, not quite awake, he would jerk and make hurtful noises like a wounded animal. I would still my heart and wake him. When he was dressed, we headed back to the sitter's house. He would begin to cry a few blocks from our destination. My own tears stayed in check until his screams stabbed from behind the closed doors and stuck like spearheads in my heart.

The regularity of misery did nothing to lessen it. I examined alternatives. If I were married, "my husband" (the words sounded as unreal as "my bank account") would set me up in a fine house, which my good taste would develop into a home. My son and I could spend whole days together and then I could have two more children who would be named Deirdre and Craig, and I would grow roses and beautiful zinnias. I would wear too-large gardening gloves so that when I removed them my hands would look dainty and my manicure fresh. We would all play chess and Chinese checkers and twenty questions and whist. We would be a large, loving, hilarious family like the people in *Cheaper by the Dozen*.

Or I could go on welfare.

There wasn't a shadow of a husband-caliber man on my horizon. Indeed, no men at all seemed attracted to me. Possibly my façade of cool control turned them away or just possibly my need, which I thought well disguised, was so obvious that it frightened them. No, husbands were rarer than common garden variety unicorns.

And welfare was absolutely forbidden. My pride had been starched by a family who assumed unlimited authority in its own affairs. A grandmother, who raised me, my brother and her own two sons, owned a general merchandise store. She had begun her business in the early 1900's in Stamps, Arkansas, by selling meat pies to saw men in a lumber mill, then racing across town in time to feed workers in a cotton-gin mill four miles away.

My brother, Bailey, who was a year older than I and seven inches shorter, had drummed in my youthful years: "You are as intelligent as I am" —we both agreed that he was a genius—"and beautiful. And you can do anything."

My beautiful mother, who ran businesses and men with autocratic power, taught me to row my own boat, paddle my own canoe, hoist my own sail. She warned, in fact, "If you want something done, do it yourself."

I hadn't asked them for help (I couldn't risk their refusal) and they loved me. There was no motive on earth which would bring me, bowed, to beg for aid from an institution which scorned me and a government which ignored me. It had seemed that I would be locked in the two jobs and the weekly baby-sitter terror until my life was done. Now with a good salary, my son and I could move back into my mother's house.

A smile struck her face like lightning when I told her I had retrieved my son and we were ready to come home. There was a glaze over her eyes. It was unnerving. My mother was anything, everything, but sentimental. I admired how quickly she pulled her old self back in charge. Typically she asked only direct questions.

"How long will you all stay this time?"

"Until I can get a house for us."

"That sounds good. Your room is pretty much as you left it and Clyde can have the little room in back."

I decided that a little bragging was in order. "I've been working at the record shop on Fillmore and the people down there gave me a raise. I'll pay rent to you and help with the food."

"How much are they paying you?"

When I told her, she quickly worked out a percentage "O.K. You pay me that amount and buy a portion of food every week."

I handed her some cash. She counted it carefully. "All right, this is a month's rent. I'll remember."

She handed the money back to me. "Take this downtown and buy yourself some clothes."

I hesitated.

"This is a gift, not a loan. You should know I don't do business slipshod."

To Vivian Baxter business was business, and I was her daughter; one thing did not influence the other.

"You know that I'm no baby-sitter, but Poppa Ford is still with me looking after the house. He can keep an eye on Clyde. Of course you ought to give him a little something every week. Not as much as you pay the baby-sitters, but something. Remember, you may not always get what you pay for, but you will definitely pay for what you get."

"Yes, Mother." I was home.

∽   **Fastwrite 7**

Develop a quick sketch of what you think Angelou's living arrangements, financial opportunities, and opportunities for mobility would have been like had she been born in the middle of the nineteenth century as Addams was. What do you think Addams's situation might have been like had she been born in the late 1920s? As you sketch out the possible "other" lives these women might have had, you begin to explore the ways in which historical change may be experienced differently by people in parallel cultures within the same society.

Historical Questions

1. Angelou's writing both echoes and challenges the views of the city developed by Addams sixty years earlier. As women from different historical periods and different ethnic and economic backgrounds, they had very different relationships to the city. With specific references to their texts, explore the extent to which their different relationships to the city could be attributed to their living in different historical periods, to their social class, or to their racial differences. Which of the three factors do you think is most significant in understanding their different relationships to the city? Explain why. (Fastwrite 7 may provide a good starting point for answering this question.)

2. Throughout "Gi' Me a Penny," Angelou expresses significant distrust of white women. Develop a symptomatic reading of this distrust by linking it to the material circumstances of her living as part of a particular social class and ethnic group in the city. Focus on three or four passages in which Angelou explains her feelings about white women. What explicit reasons does she give for them? What other larger reasons may underlie them? To develop this symptomatic reading, relate Angelou's feelings to some of the points about the relationships between social class and ethnicity and one's living experiences in the city made by Kingsbury, the Urbanism Committee, or Addams.

3. Have you ever looked for and gotten a job? If so, why? If not, why not? Where did you look for employment? Be specific about the geographical location—city? Suburban mall? Countryside? How did you conduct your job search? Why do you think you were hired? In what ways was your job search similar to Angelou's? In what ways was it different? For example, to what extent did your racial or ethnic affiliation directly or indirectly affect your sense of your job prospects? To what extent do you feel that your and your potential employer's attitudes about racial or ethnic integration were affected by the geographical location of the place of work? In developing your comparison with Angelou about the relationship over time between where one lives, one's job prospects, and one's racial and ethnic affiliation, be sure to focus on three or four specific passages from her text.

Cultural Questions

1. The Urbanism Committee report was written in 1937 when Angelou was nine years old. If its proposals had been enacted by the city government of San Francisco, what effects might it have had on the chapter of Angelou's life presented here? In what ways do the proposals of the committee address some of the concerns Angelou might have had as a financially poor, single African-American mother living in the city in the late 1940s? What issues are not addressed?

2. Develop a symptomatic reading of two to three different characters' perspectives—other than Angelou's—in which you analyze how their particular social status and living conditions within the city might have affected certain of their attitudes. After reviewing Angelou's discussion of each individual, briefly fastwrite statements from the point of view of two or three of them about their attitudes toward trust, responsibility, work, or the city in general. What points of tension and points of continuity do you discover among the different perspectives? Focusing on one specific point, explore how particular material conditions of city living in San Francisco in the 1940s could have worked to support each of their particular perspectives. Use specific details from Angelou's text (as well as from other texts from this chapter if you wish) to support your analysis.

3. Write a brief story about an experience of your own that, like Angelou's, suggests your sense of connectedness with a particular geographical area. Then specifically analyze some of the ways in which the behavior, attitudes, and feelings you exhibit in the story are related to where it took place.

∾ Fastwrite 8

Before you read the following essay, quickly list what you believe are U.S. cities' main problems today and briefly explain how you think they should be solved.

ᏄᏇᏌᏇᏄᏇ

ADAM WALINSKY

Cities under Assault (1993)

Adam Walinsky (b. 1937) was a top aide and speech writer for Robert Kennedy. A lawyer, Walinsky made an unsuccessful bid for the office of state attorney general in New York in the early 1970s. He became interested in addressing the problem of crime in 1978 while working for Governor Hugh Carey. In 1982, he became the chief proponent of the Police Corps, a service program in which competitively selected high school seniors would receive federal financing for a college education; in return, they would serve four years as local police officers after graduation. The program has yet to receive congressional approval. The following selection was taken from a feature article entitled "The Crisis of Public Order," which appeared in the *Atlantic Monthly* in 1993.

For more than twenty years the children of the ghetto have witnessed violent death as an almost routine occurrence. They have seen it on their streets, in their schools, in their families, and on TV. They have lived with constant fear. Many have come to believe that they will not live to see twenty-five. These are often children whose older brothers, friends, and uncles have taught them that only the strong and the ruthless survive. Prison does not frighten them—it is a rite of passage that a majority of their peers may have experienced. Too many have learned to kill without remorse, for a drug territory or for an insult, because of a look or a bump on the sidewalk, or just to do it: why not?

These young people have been raised in the glare of ceaseless media violence and incitement to every depravity of act and spirit. Movies may feature scores of killings in two hours' time, vying to show methods ever more horrific; many are quickly imitated on the street. Television commercials teach that a young man requires a new pair of $120 sneakers each week. Major corporations make and sell records exhorting their listeners to brutalize Koreans, rob store owners, rape women, kill the police. Ashamed and guilt-ridden, elite opinion often encourages even hoodlums to carry a sense of entitlement and grievance against society and its institutions.

These lessons are being taught to millions of children as I write and you read. They have already been taught to the age groups that will reach physical maturity during the rest of this century.

The worst lesson we have taught these benighted children I have saved for last, because it is a lesson we have also taught ourselves: We will do almost anything not to have to act to defend ourselves, our country, or our character as people of decency and strength. We have fled from our cities, virtually abandoning great institutions such as the public schools. We have permitted the spread within our country of wastelands ruled not by the Constitution and lawful authority but by the anarchic force of merciless killers. We have muted our dialogue and hidden our thoughts. We have abandoned millions of our fellow citizens—people of decency and honor trying desperately to raise their children in love and hope—to every danger and degraded assault. We have become isolated from one another, dispirited about any possibility of collective or political action to meet this menace. We shrink in fear of teenage thugs on every street. More important, we shrink even from contemplating the forceful collective action we know is required. We abandon our self-respect and our responsibility to ourselves and our posterity.

How to change all this, how to recover heart and spirit, how to save the lives and souls of millions of children, and how to save ourselves from this scourge of violent anarchy—in short, how to deal with things as they are, how to respond to the implacable and undeniable numbers: this will be the real measure and test of our political system. But more than that, it will be the measure of our own days and work, the test of our own lives and heritage.

In the past decade 200,000 of our citizens have been killed and millions wounded. If we assume, with the FBI, that 47 percent of them were killed by friends and family members, that leaves 106,000 dead at the hands of strangers. Ten years of war in Vietnam killed 58,000 Americans. Over an equal period we have had almost the exact equivalent of two Vietnam Wars right here at home.

Whether fighting the war or fighting against the war, participants and opponents alike engaged Vietnam with fury and passion and a desperate energy. Were we to find such energy, such passion, now, how might we use it? Where would we start?

I suggest simplicity. If your territory and your citizens are under constant deadly assault, the first thing you do is *protect them.*

To do this we need forces. We need a very large number of additional police officers: at least half a million in the next five years, and perhaps more thereafter. We do not need more private police, who protect only the circumscribed property of better-off citizens who can afford to pay;

we need public police, whose mission is the protection of all citizens, and who are available for work in the ghettos and housing projects where most of the dying is taking place.

If we as a society expect black citizens to construct reasonable lives, we cannot continue to abandon so many of them and their children to criminal depredation. If we expect children to respect law and the rights of others, it would seem elementary that we must respect the law and their rights enough to keep them from getting murdered.

We need a larger police force not to imprison more of our fellow citizens but to liberate them. The police need not function as the intake valve of a criminal-justice system devoted to the production of more prison inmates, of whom we already have more than is healthy; their true role is to suppress violence and criminal activity, to protect public space that now serves as the playground and possession of the violent. The role of the police is to guard schools and homes, neighborhoods and commerce, and to protect life; they should represent the basic codes and agreements by which we live with one another. Today's vastly undermanned police forces, whose officers race from call to call, taking endless reports of crimes they were not around to prevent, do not control the streets. They do not exercise and cannot embody the authority for which we look to government. Rather, it is the most violent young men of the street who set the tone and filter the light in which the children of the city are growing. *That* is what we need at least half a million new officers just to begin to change.

Some will ask how we are to afford the $30 billion or so a year that this would cost. The question has a ready answer. We have a gross domestic product of more than $6 trillion, and a federal budget of more than $1.6 trillion. President Clinton has requested $261.4 billion for defense against foreign enemies who killed fewer than a hundred Americans in all of last year. It would be silly to suggest that the federal government should not or cannot spend an eighth as much—two percent of even a shrunken federal budget—to defend the nation against domestic enemies who killed more than 10,000 people who were strangers to them in 1994, and who will surely kill more in every year that lies ahead.

This is not a complete program, because this is not the time for a complete program. *We have to stop the killing.* Beyond doubt we must reform welfare, minimize illegitimacy, change the schools, strengthen employment opportunities, end racism. In the midst of this war, while the killing continues, all that is just talk. And dishonest talk besides: there can be no truth to our public discussions while whites are filled with fear of black violence, and blacks live every day with the fear and bitter knowledge that they and their children have been abandoned to the rule of criminals. If some foreign enemy had invaded New England, slaughtering its people and plundering its wealth, would we be debating agricultural subsidies and the future of Medicaid while complaining that the deficit prevented us from enlarging the Army or buying more ammunition? Would the budget really force us to abandon New Hampshire? Why is this case different?

Some people will say that I propose an army of occupation. But all too many black citizens already live in territories occupied by hostile bands of brigands. How can these citizens be freed except by forces devoted to their liberation?

It is true that the police, especially in the ghettos of older cities, have often been corrupt, brutal, and ineffective, although they are almost always better than most of their critics. The remedy for bad policing is for good people to join the police force and make it better: that is why the one truly promising feature of the 1994 crime bill is the creation of a prototype Police Corps, a police ROTC that will offer four-year college scholarships to the best and most committed of our young people in return for four years of police service following their graduation. Now and for many years into the future the opportunity to give the greatest service to one's fellow citizens will be as a member of a police force—the one truly indispensable agency of a free and civil government.

Others will say—not openly, because this kind of thing is never said openly—that it's hopeless, and that the best we can hope for is that the killers will kill one another and leave the rest of us alone. Indeed, a visitor from another planet might well conclude that only such a belief could explain our society's otherwise inexplicable passivity. History should save us from such vile and horrible thoughts. Despite all vicissitudes, within two generations of Emancipation black families had achieved levels of stability and nurture comparable or superior to those of many immigrant groups. The long history of black people in America has not been one of violent or cruel conduct beyond the national norm. Rather, it is a story of great heroism and dignity, of a steady upward course from slavery to just the other day.

The collapse of the black lower class is a creation not of history but of this generation. It has been a deliberate if misguided act of government to create a welfare system that began the destruction of black family life. It was the dominant culture that desanctified morality, celebrated license, and glorified fecklessness; as the columnist Joe Klein has observed, it is in moral conduct above all that the rich catch cold and the poor get pneumonia. It was stupidity and cowardice, along with a purposeful impulse toward justice, that led the entire governmental apparatus, the system of law enforcement and social control, to cede the black ghettos to self-rule and virtual anarchy in the 1960s and 1970s, and to abandon them entirely since. It is the evident policy of the entertainment industry to seek profit by exploiting the most degraded aspects of human and social character. None of this is necessary. All of it can be changed.

I have spoken of the need to change conditions among blacks, because they are experiencing the greatest suffering and the gravest danger today. But let none of us pretend that the bell tolls only for blacks; there is no salvation for one race alone, no hope for separate survival. At stake for all of us is the future of American cities, the promise of the American nation, and the survival of our Constitution and of American democracy itself.

Historical Questions

1. Walinsky blames the "collapse of the black lower class" on the welfare system and sees the problems he identifies as having begun in the 1960s: "The collapse of the black lower class is a creation not of history but of this generation." Compare Walinsky's description of the city's problems with some of those identified by Kingsbury, Addams, or the Urbanism Committee. In what ways are the problems Walinsky focuses on different from those of the past, as he suggests? In what ways are there connections between the present problems and those mentioned or implied in the earlier texts? Discuss one to two explicit examples of each of these.

2. In what ways might people's understanding of ghetto problems—and their sense of responsibility in changing them—differ depending on whether they see the problem as "a creation of history" or "a creation of this generation"? Fastwrite from the perspective of three different contemporary Americans of different races, social status, and age who live in different types of locations (include yourself as one of these). How might each of these people react to Walinsky's position that the welfare state is to blame for the collapse of the black lower class? What might their reactions be to the argument that the problems began much earlier?

3. Walinsky argues that the worst lesson we have taught children of the inner city (and our citizenry in general) is that it is all right to "do almost anything not to have to act to defend ourselves, our country, or our character as people of decency and strength." He seems to go beyond the specific problems of cities to raise a larger issue about the American character and American values. What do you think he means by this statement? Imagine the Urbanism Committee members (writing in 1937–39) or Angelou (writing about the 1940s) reading this statement. In what specific ways might their perspectives about the character of the American people in relation to city problems be similar to Walinsky's? In what ways might they be different? What could account for the differences and similarities you suggest?

Cultural Questions

1. Compare Walinsky's solutions to the city's problems with the ideas you came up with in fastwrite 8 about solving city problems. In what ways are

your solutions similar to Walinsky's? In what ways are they different? What does the comparison of your solutions with Walinsky's suggest about the values both of you have about equality, the personal responsibility of citizens for each other, and the value of public-government intervention versus private-philanthropic solutions. Focusing on one of the points that you and Walinsky differ on, compare the effects that each of your solutions might have on people living in the ghetto or on people living outside of it.

2. Different readers have different perspectives on such topics as crime, safety, and the role of the police in protecting the community, which causes them to respond differently to Walinsky's article. The article was written for the *Atlantic Monthly*, a newsmagazine primarily targeted toward so-called Eastern urban intelligentsia. Focusing on particular passages of your choice, explain what responses the article's primary reading audience might have had to it. Then, explore what responses nontypical readers of the magazine who are city residents might have had to the article. (In constructing the response of two to three city residents, consider differences in age, economic status, race, and gender.) Finally, how might this article affect someone who has never visited an American city before?

3. Write a letter to the editor of the *Atlantic Monthly* in response to Walinsky's article, either from your own point of view, from the point of view of someone you discussed in the previous question, or from the point of view of one of the writers of a "What's Good about . . . ?" piece.

∾ Fastwrite 9

Before reading the next essay, quickly fastwrite in response to the following questions. Have you ever been to New York City? If so, describe your trip: What were your expectations? What did you see and do? What impressions of the city were you left with? If you haven't been to New York City, would you like to go? Explain why or why not. What expectations of the city do you have? What would be "must sees" for you? From what sources have you developed your sense of New York City? If you currently live or have lived in New York City, explain what the city means to you.

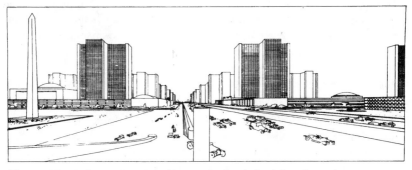

Figure 7.3. A Contemporary City, Le Corbusier's vision from the 1920s.

◆ JONATHAN FRANZEN
♦ *Why We Need Cities* (1996)

Jonathan Franzen (b. 1959) is a novelist whose first work, *The Twenty-Seventh City* (1988), gives a startling fictional account of St. Louis under siege by a police chief who uses terrorist tactics to convert those who oppose her plan to revitalize the city. Franzen is a frequent contributor to *The New Yorker*, *Harper's*, the *New York Times Book Review*, and the *Village Voice* where he reviews books and films. The following is extracted from a book review of Witold Rybcznski's *City Life* (1996) published in *The New Yorker* in 1996.

Two things that happened this year got me wondering why New York City and American cities in general still bother to exist. The first was a plane ride back East from St. Louis. I sat next to a smart, pleasant woman from Springfield, Missouri, who was taking her eleven-year-old son to see relatives in Boston. The son had already scored points with me by removing a book, rather than a Game Boy, from his backpack, and, when his mother told me that they were stopping in New York for two nights and that it was her son's first visit there, I asked what sights they planned to see. "We want to go to the Fashion Café," she said, "and we want to try to get on the 'Today' show. There's that window you can stand in front of? My son wants to do that." I said I hadn't heard about the window, and it certainly did sound interesting, but what about the Statue of Liberty and the Empire State Building? The woman gave me a funny look. "We'd love to see Letterman, too," she said. "Do you think there's any chance of getting tickets?" I told her she could always hope.

The second thing that happened, after this reminder that for the rest of the country New York is now largely a city of the mind—at best, a site for the voodoo transformation of image into flesh—was a walk I took down Silicon Alley, in lower Manhattan. Silicon Alley is that district where the romance between downtown hipsters and the digital revolution has emerged from upper-floor bedrooms and set up house behind plate glass; I could see girls with fashion-model looks who wouldn't be caught dead at the Fashion Café clustering around monitors while gurus with shaved heads helped them to configure. The Cyber Café, at 273 Lafayette Street, is a strange phenomenon. According to Web dogma, it ought not to exist. "Click, click through cyberspace," William J. Mitchell writes in his recent manifesto "City of Bits." "This is the new architectural promenade . . . a city unrooted to any definite spot on the surface of the earth, shaped by connectivity and bandwidth constraints rather than by accessibility and land values, largely asynchronous in its operation, and inhabited by disembodied and fragmented subjects who exist as collections of aliases and agents." Yet the Cyber Café—to say nothing of the thousands of clubs and galleries and bookstores and non-cyber cafés doing business within a mile of it—resembles nothing so much as an old-fashioned see-and-be-seen promenade.

Two New Yorks, then: one a virtual province of Planet Hollywood, the other a definite spot on the surface of the earth populated by young people who, even as they disembody and fragment themselves, cannot resist the urge to Be There. Between the New York of Springfield's imaginings and the New York of Lafayette Street is a disjunction that I feel well equipped to appreciate. I grew up in Missouri, and in the last fifteen years I've moved to New York six times. At no point was a job or a ready-made community waiting for me. As a self-employed writer, I can live anywhere I want, and it would make sense for me to choose an inexpensive place. Yet whenever I'm in one of those inexpensive places I feel compelled to reinflict New York on myself—this despite my fear of neighbors with televisions and pianos, my aversion to Gothamite provinciality, and my immunity to the city's "cultural vitality." When I'm here, I spend a lot of time at home; as a rule, I hit the museums and theatres only in a last-minute panic, before moving somewhere else. And, fond though I am of Central Park and the subways, I have no overpowering love for the Apple as a whole. The city has little of the soul-stirring desolation of Philadelphia, say, and none of the deep familiarity of Chicago, where I was born. What draws me back, again and again, is simply safety. Nowhere else am I safe from the question: Why *here*?

Manhattan, in particular, offers the reassurance of high rents, which means that this is a city people want to live in, not escape from. It's no accident that Parisians adore New York. Its orthogonal street grid notwithstanding, they feel right at home here, since one of the things that make Europe Europe is that its urban centers are still attractors, rather than repellers, of public life. Conversely, for an American Midwesterner like me, hungry for a feeling of cultural placement, New York is the next best thing to Europe.

Most North American metropolises are wildly centrifugal, however, and the contrast between our lifeless inner grids and Europe's thriving centers has prompted the architect and essayist Witold Rybczynski to ask, "Why aren't our cities like that?" His latest book, "City Life," is an examination of "urban expectations" in the New World. Although he devotes much of the book to explaining the different *look* of our cities, Rybczynski understands that "like that" means something deeper: an urban vitality, an at-homeness with the idea of living in cities. Washington, D.C., has Parisian-style diagonal boulevards, height uniformity, and monumental architecture, and yet no one would mistake the feel of a residential D.C. street at ten in the evening for the Fourteenth Arrondissement. Nor is there any mistaking *our country's current mood of hostility toward cities.* Upstate New York has taken revenge on Gotham in the person of George Pataki; planned cuts in Medicare, welfare, and other federal programs target city centers like ICBMs; and the groups that the Western and suburban Republicans now ascendant in Congress have identified as flies in the ointment—poor people, gay people, liberal élites, rap musicians, N.E.A.-sponsored performance artists, government bureaucrats—all happen to be concentrated in big cities.

"City Life" traces the provenance of this hostility. . . European towns were traditionally enclosed by walls of stone and walls of class; membership in the bourgeoisie (literally, "town dwellers") brought various jealously guarded privileges. American towns were open from the start. Surrounded by wilderness, Rybczynski says, "town builders reacted not by emphasizing the contrast between the natural and the man-made, but by incorporating natural elements in the town as much as possible, whether as green squares, tree-lined streets, or ample gardens." That the Colonial town became specifically "a celebration of the house," however, resulted from the accident of North America's being settled by the English and the Dutch, whose wealthier citizens, unlike their counterparts in other European countries, had a marked preference for individual home ownership. In America, even people of modest means could afford private ownership, and land was so plentiful that each house could have a private yard. . . .

In Rybczynski's telling of it, the first century and a half of post-Colonial American history was essentially a detour in the inevitable fulfillment of these proto-suburban ideals. Quaker practicality and a profusion of immigrants insured that Philadelphia, for example, which William Penn had laid out as a "green country town," quickly saw its spacious grid parcelled up by speculators and bricked up with row houses. It was Penn's grid, not his green vision, that became the norm for big American cities. In the absence of a belief in cities as unique repositories of culture, moreover, there was little to prevent American cities from becoming purely commercial enterprises. However much the country's urban gentry came to hunger for European refinements, attempts at making cities more "like Paris" — Daniel Burnham's plan for a more horizontal Chicago of parks and boulevards is perhaps the most famous—soon foundered on the economics of skyscrapers or sank beneath waves of immigration. As Rybczynski puts it, "the city profitable replaced the city beautiful."

Yet the city profitable worked. The first decades of this century were the heyday of urban life in America. I generally resist wishing I'd lived in an earlier era (I always imagine myself dying of some disease whose cure was just around the corner), but I make an exception for those years when the country's heart was in its cities—the years of Lou Gehrig and Harold Ross, Automats and skyscrapers, trolley cars, fedoras, and crowded train stations. I make this exception precisely because the era seems so anomalous, so extraneous to the continuum connecting Williamsburg Colonials and Tocqueville's urbane woodsmen to the far-flung tract-housing dwellers of today. It seems like a time when the country could have turned in a less wasteful, more public-spirited, more *European* direction.

The irony is that these decades were a time, perhaps the only time, when European cities were looking westward for inspiration. If there's a villain in "City Life," it's Le Corbusier, who, with what Rybczynski calls "a Warholian gift for self-promotion," toured the world publicizing his vision of the Radiant City of the future. "City Life" offers a nice contrast between the heroic descriptive work of the nineteenth-century Tocqueville and the malignant fatuity of the twentieth-century Le Corbusier, whose vision was prescriptive: superskyscrapers surrounded by grass and superhighways; a Cartesian separation of work from play, of housing from commerce. When Le Corbusier proposed razing six hundred acres of central Paris, he was ignored by everyone but his fellow French intellectuals. In America, however, his ideas influenced a generation of city planners and eventually inspired hundreds of "urban renewal" projects. In Manhattan, we still live with the radiance of N.Y.U.'s high-rises and East Harlem's projects.

Radiant City planning, whose wrong-headedness is old news now, by no means killed the American inner city single-handed. Kenneth T. Jackson concluded his study of American suburbanization, "Crabgrass Frontier," with an excellent analysis of the "residential deconcentration" of America. Jackson pinned the unique degree of American suburbanization on two fundamental causes: racial prejudice and inexpensive housing. Suburbs provide uneasy whites with a safe haven, and a variety of factors—high per-capita wealth, cheap land and transportation, government subsidies and tax breaks—have made flight affordable to the great middle class.

The most salient contemporary American urban expectations, therefore, are that core cities will be poor and non-white, and that the suburbs will be soothingly homogeneous. Rybczynski is strangely oblivious of these particular expectations. In "City Life's" final chapter, "The Best of Both Worlds," he celebrates the Philadelphia community of Chestnut Hill, which became a middle-class haven in the first decades of this century, when a local millionaire named George Woodward and his father-in-law built several hundred beautiful rental houses of Wissahickon schist. With medium population density, a parklike ambiance, and carefully planned architecture, the Woodward development showed the influence of the Hampstead Garden Suburb, a model development begun outside London in 1906. In "The Death and Life of Great American Cities," Jane Jacobs observed that garden cities, since they have neither the street life of real cities nor the privacy of real suburbs, succeed only if their residents are homogeneous and relatively affluent. Rybczynski, who now owns a house in Chestnut Hill, contradicts Jacobs by asserting that the community "has become more socially and economically heterogeneous." He extolls it as "a small town and a city both," as "an only slightly urbanized Arcadia" whose central shopping street, Germantown Avenue, is "precisely the sort of old-fashioned pedestrian district people find so attractive." He speaks of the "long" waiting list for Woodward-house rentals.

For a check on the reality of American cities, it's worth taking a closer look at the neighborhood Rybczynski calls home. The last time I moved to New York, it was from Philadelphia. My wife and I had heard about the waiting list for Woodward houses, and we were surprised when, at the interview required of all applicants, we were told that several houses were immediately available. Only later did we realize that every one of the dozens of families in Woodward houses on our block, in the substantially black city of Philadelphia, was white. At the closest good supermarket and the closest mall, both of which are in mixed neighborhoods, you will rarely see a shopper from Chestnut Hill. When I shopped at those places, I was struck by the exemplary warmth and courtesy with which I was treated. Knowing that a black male shopper at a predominantly white mall or supermarket would probably have had a quite different experience, I couldn't help wondering whether the courtesy wasn't meant to be *literally* exemplary. As in: We would like to be treated the way we are treating you.

The First Cities of European countries have tended to be capitals in every way—commercially, culturally, governmentally, and demographically. Early America, however, was so far-flung and so distrustful of concentrated authority that it was not until 1900 or so, when Wall Street and the big media had established themselves as the country's shadow government, that the four functions fully converged in New York. One measure of New York's enduring primacy is that it continues to act as a lightning rod for national resentment. When Americans rail against "Washington," they mean the abstraction of federal government, not the District of Columbia. New York is resented as an actual place—for its rudeness, its arrogance, its crowds and dirt, its moral turpitude, and so forth. Global resentment is the highest compliment a city can receive, and by nurturing the notion of the Apple as the national Forbidden Fruit such resentment guarantees not only that ambitious souls of the "If I can make it there, I'd make it anywhere" variety will gravitate toward New York but that the heartland's most culturally rebellious young people will follow. There's no better way of rejecting where you came from, no plainer declaration of an intention to reinvent yourself, than moving to New York; I speak from personal experience. . . .

During the nineteen-seventies and eighties, Rybczynski says, a new shopping center opened in the United States every seven hours. In "City Life" he asserts that as malls increasingly come to have hotels attached to them and museums and skating rinks and public libraries housed within them they are entitled to be considered "the new downtown." He marvels at the "variety" to be found in a shopping-center food court ("Tex-Mex, Chinese, Italian, Middle Eastern") and compares the scene to a sidewalk café. What ultimately attracts people to malls, he believes, is that they supply "a reasonable (in most eyes) level of public order; the right not to be subjected to outlandish conduct, not to be assaulted and intimidated by boorish adolescents, noisy drunks, and aggressive panhandlers." He adds, "It does not seem too much to ask." To "academic colleagues" who might object to the "hyperconsumerism" and "artificial reality" of malls, Rybczynski replies that "commercial forces have always formed the center of the American city" and that "it is unclear to me why sitting on a bench in the mall should be considered any more artificial than a bench in the park."

For my part, I'm willing to admit to an almost physical craving for the comforts of the suburban mall. Natural opiates flood my neural receptors when I step from the parking lot into the air lock. Inside, the lighting is subdued, and every voice sounds far away. Never mind that Waldenbooks rarely stocks Denis Johnson and Sam Goody has no Myra Melford; I have cash in my wallet, my skin is white, and I feel utterly, utterly welcome. Is this a community? Is the reality artificial, or am I part of a genuine promenade? I don't know. When I'm not being actively repelled by the purple and teal that are this year's favored suburban leisure-wear colors, I'm too busy enjoying the rush of purchase to pay much attention.

My craving for city life feels entirely different. It's often tinged with anxiety; I'm never entirely relaxed except at home; there's a world of difference between inside and outside. How is it possible that life in New York, whose buildings are like upwellings of pure molten capital, can be so much *less* beholden to the world of consumerism than life in the suburbs, which ostensibly offer more freedom and privacy? The answer is, narrowly, that cities represent an older, less advanced stage in the development of buying and selling, in which producers work cheek by jowl with consumers, and the whole economic mechanism is open to inspection and so is less susceptible to the seamless enchantment of modern sales pitches; and, more generally, that there's something in the very nature of cities which enforces adult responsibility. I don't mean to suggest that we city dwellers are any less mad for products than suburb dwellers are, or that the cleansing and police actions of various Business Improvement Districts are not, even now, transforming large swaths of Manhattan into out-door malls—only that it's far easier on the streets of New York to have experiences that have nothing to do with the spending of money than it is in the typical galleria.

Rybczynski is correct, nevertheless, in stressing that "civic" and "commercial" have always been near-synonyms in America. Although European cities, too, historically functioned as trading and manufacturing centers, they had more ancient functions as well: as fortifications, as the sites of cathedrals and universities, as the residences of princes, and, most important, as the embodiment of regional or national identities. Barcelona *is* Catalonia, and every new building erected there serves to make Catalonia's identity that much more glorious and concrete. It's impossible to imagine an American city being cherished in the same way, if only because we have no regional identities as coherent and enduring—as *tribal*—as the Catalonian. This country was populated largely by immigrants in search of freedom or economic opportunity, or both, and I suspect it's no accident that the heyday of American cities directly followed the decades of peak immigration. These immigrants were similar only in their rejection of the Old World and so could never develop urban fealties that extended beyond a given ethnic neighborhood. It was only a matter of time before they adopted the New World ideal of house-as-kingdom, with its implications that what you earn and what you buy matters far more than where you do it.

The real mystery, therefore, is not that we have so few cities "like Paris" but that we have any at all. However many Americans prefer the suburbs, there are still millions who expressly choose cities. "Yuppie" is not a kind appellation, but the people who put the "u" in the word remain impressive in their sheer numbers. Even the most woebegone urban centers—Syracuse in the Rust Belt, Colorado Springs in the midst of neo-Californian sprawl—manage a few blocks of mixed-use vitality. And many larger cities—New York, Boston, San Francisco, Chicago, Los Angeles, Seattle—have a clearly sustained critical mass. For better or worse, the most reliable measure of a city's vitality is whether rich people are willing to live in the center of it. Once upon a time, the middle class was the bellwether of urban vitality; in Mayor Giuliani's speeches, it still is. But, as Labor Secretary Robert Reich has observed, the term "middle class" today has a definition more sociological than economic. And the best definition might be "suburban."

However reliable the presence of the rich may be as an indicator, it's merely the final effect in a chain of causes which begins with a city's ability to attract young people. How long would the upper crust persevere on Park Avenue without the horde of young singles who fill Yorkville? How long would downtown remain a capital of culture without a constant infusion of young artists, students, and musicians? We hear a lot about the dependence of poor people on cities, but young people, especially creative young people, need them just as much. The suburbs may be an ideal place to spend a childhood, but people in the years between leaving the nest and building a nest of their own need a place to congregate. So cities will continue to see, at a minimum, heavy nighttime and weekend use—unless, of course, Netbrokered marriages become common; and the only thing more dismal to imagine than virtual courtship is daily life in the marriage of two people who would court that way. . . .

Jane Jacobs identified as a hallmark of city life the existence of privacy in heavy crowds—a privacy whose maintenance depends not on the pseudo-parental expedients of isolated houses and controlled shopping environments but on modes of civilized behavior best learned in public spaces like the sidewalk. That the country's widely decried "breakdown of civility" began at home rather than in so-called urban jungles can be confirmed at any movie theatre, where audiences accustomed to watching videos in the bedroom have forgotten how to shut up. In "Death and Life," Jacobs also quoted Paul Tillich, who believed that the city, by its very nature, "provides what otherwise could be given only by traveling; namely, the strange." Familiarity, whether of chain stores or of cookie-cutter subdivisions, erodes the autonomous intelligence and, in a weird way, undermines privacy. In the suburbs, I'm the stranger; I feel exposed. Only in a crowded, diverse place like New York, surrounded by strangeness, do I come home to myself.

I'm not so innocently enamored of cities, of course, as not to realize that the plate-glass windows of Silicon Alley serve purposes of display similar to those of the CRT screens behind them: that the hidden link between Fashion Café and Cyber Café is a culture of Being Seen. It's possible to worry, too, that young people who come to Manhattan seeking what I seek—literal centrality, the privacy of crowds, the satisfaction of being a fly in the ointment—will eventually be repelled by the miasma of Disney-fication that is hanging over SoHo and Fifty-seventh Street and creeping into the East Village and Times Square. For now, though, I work and sleep in a building that houses two dressmakers, a realtor, an antique dealer, a caterer, and a fish seller. When I lie on the floor and relax by listening to my breathing, I can hear the slower respirations of the city itself, a sound like the rumble of a surf: subway trains crowded with people who are teaching themselves how to be here.

Historical Questions

1. In 1895, Kingsbury wrote, "Facilities for travel make it as easy to get from city to country as from country to city; but the tide, except for temporary purposes, all sets one way." Franzen and Kingsbury both enthusiastically defend the choice of people to live in cities. Compare and contrast some of the reasons Franzen develops for why people today are drawn to the city (New York in particular) with reasons developed by Kingsbury over one hundred years before. What aspects of city life celebrated by Kingsbury and Franzen appear to have remained constant over the last one hundred years? What aspects of city life appear to have changed over the last one hundred years? Are you struck more by the differences or the similarities? Explain your position with three or four specific references to each of the two texts.

2. Wiltold Rybcyzinski—whose book, *City Life*, Franzen is reviewing—asks a question commonly asked about U.S. cities: Why aren't they more like European cities? Rybcyzinski and Franzen suggest that the reasons are largely threefold: the use of space in U.S. cities, from colonial times to the present; the more exclusive focus on commerce in U.S. cities; and the absence of ancient histories and functions in U.S. cities. Focusing on one of these three factors, explore some of the ways in which it could have led some American cities to become, in Franzen's words, "lifeless inner grids" in comparison to Europe's "thriving centers." Develop your essay with close reference to Franzen's comparison between American and European cities (which occurs in a number of places throughout his essay) and with reference to an older text—Addams or the Urbanism Committee report.

3. Franzen speaks of our government's "current mood of hostility toward cities," and he cites, as evidence, cuts in federal programs such as medicare and welfare, and attitudes of prejudice against the poor, gays, rap musicians,

and others who go against the norm who "happen to be concentrated in big cities." With reference to Addams, Kingsbury, the Urbanism report, or Angelou, develop a position on whether you think the government is more hostile today to cities and urban dwellers than it was in the past. (Remember that you do not have to simply disagree or simply agree with Franzen; you may argue for a more complex and nuanced position.)

Cultural Questions

1. Franzen's view of New York City clearly differs from those of the visitors from Missouri and the patrons of the Cyber Cafe. What assumptions about why one would visit or live in New York City underlie these perspectives, and how do they differ from Franzen's own? Compare and contrast these different assumptions with your own views and underlying assumptions about New York City. (Use some of your work from fastwrite 9 if you wrote on it.) Remember to take into account the sources from which you developed your perspective.

2. Although Franzen loves New York, he admits to being lured to suburban malls. Trace what you feel are three or four of Franzen's key comparisons of city living with suburban living to explore the values that underlie his preference for the city. What, for example, are some of the underpinnings for Franzen of a good quality of life? What does he imagine are some of the most productive ways for individuals to interact with their living spaces? Why do cities, according to Franzen, provide a better and more productive quality of life? Then return to fastwrites 2, 3, or 4, which ask you to explore some of your attitudes toward living spaces. Compare some of the key values underlying your position with Franzen's. Remember to explain why you hold the views that you do.

3. Imagine that you have been asked to serve on an urban renewal committee with Franzen and Walinsky to make plans for solving city problems. With close reference to both of their texts, sketch out a dialogue that might take place at one committee meeting. On what points would their agendas agree? Where would they differ? What assumptions about the city and those who live there lie beneath each of their perspectives?

ℕ **Fastwrite 10**

Before you read the following selection, fastwrite about whether you have ever experienced discrimination because of your skin color, the way you dress, your weight, your age, or some other reason. If you have, describe the experience in detail. Go on to discuss the ways in which the experience influenced your feelings about the place where it happened—the city or town, a particular

restaurant, a place of work, or school. If you have not ever experienced discrimination, why do you think you haven't? Discuss your lack of experience
with discrimination in relation to where you live.

⋘C O R N E L   W E S T

Waiting (1995)

Cornel West (b. 1953) is a professor of Afro-American Studies
and the Philosophy of Religion at Harvard University and is one
of the most prominent African-American educators in the United
States today. His philosophy of "prophetic pragmatism" —which
is concerned with addressing issues of racial oppression, violence,
sexism, and homophobia through the life of the mind—is reflected
in his many books on the issues of race and multicultural relations
in the United States. This selection is taken from *Race Matters*
(1995), his recent best-selling book about the state of race relations
in American society.

This past September my wife, Elleni, and I made our biweekly trek
to New York City from Princeton. I was in good spirits. My morning
lecture on the first half of Plato's *Republic* in my European Cultural Studies
course had gone well. And my afternoon lecture on W. E. B. Du Bois's
The Souls of Black Folk in my Afro-American Cultural Studies course had
left me exhausted yet exhilarated. Plato's powerful symbolism of Socrates'
descent to the great port of Piraeus—the multicultural center of Greek
trade and commerce and the stronghold of Athenian democracy—still
rang in my ears. And Du Bois's prescient pronouncement— "The problem
of the twentieth century is the problem of the color line"—haunted me.
In a mysterious way, this classic twosome posed the most fundamental
challenges to my basic aim in life: to speak the truth to power with love
so that the quality of everyday life for ordinary people is enhanced and
white supremacy is stripped of its authority and legitimacy. Plato's profound—yet unpersuasive—critique of Athenian democracy as inevitably
corrupted by the ignorance and passions of the masses posed one challenge,
and Du Bois's deep analysis of the intransigence of white supremacy in
the American democratic experiment posed another.

As we approached Manhattan, my temperature rose, as it always does when I'm in a hurry near the Lincoln Tunnel. How rare it is that I miss the grinding gridlock—no matter the day or hour. But this time I drove right through and attributed my good luck to Elleni. As we entered the city, we pondered whether we would have enough time to stop at Sweetwater's (our favorite place to relax) after our appointments. I dropped my wife off for an appointment on 60th Street between Lexington and Park avenues. I left my car—a rather elegant one—in a safe parking lot and stood on the corner of 60th Street and Park Avenue to catch a taxi. I felt quite relaxed since I had an hour until my next engagement. At 5:00 P.M. I had to meet a photographer who would take the picture for the cover of this book on the roof of an apartment building in East Harlem on 115th Street and 1st Avenue. I waited and waited and waited. After the ninth taxi refused me, my blood began to boil. The tenth taxi refused me and stopped for a kind, well-dressed, smiling female fellow citizen of European descent. As she stepped in the cab, she said, "This is really ridiculous, is it not?"

Ugly racial memories of the past flashed through my mind. Years ago, while driving from New York to teach at Williams College, I was stopped on fake charges of trafficking cocaine. When I told the police officer I was a professor of religion, he replied, "Yeh, and I'm the Flying Nun. Let's go, nigger!" I was stopped three times in my first ten days in Princeton for driving too slowly on a residential street with a speed limit of twenty-five miles per hour. (And my son, Clifton, already has similar memories at the tender age of fifteen.) Needless to say, these incidents are dwarfed by those like Rodney King's beating or the abuse of black targets of the FBI's COINTELPRO efforts in the 1960s and 1970s. Yet the memories cut like a merciless knife at my soul as I waited on that godforsaken corner. Finally I decided to take the subway. I walked three long avenues, arrived late, and had to catch my moral breath as I approached the white male photographer and white female cover designer. I chose not to dwell on this everyday experience of black New Yorkers. And we had a good time talking, posing, and taking pictures.

When I picked up Elleni, I told her of my hour spent on the corner, my tardy arrival, and the expertise and enthusiasm of the photographer and designer. We talked about our fantasy of moving to Addis Ababa, Ethiopia—her home and the site of the most pleasant event of my life. I toyed with the idea of attending the last day of the revival led by the Rev. Jeremiah Wright of Chicago at Rev. Wyatt T. Walker's Canaan Baptist Church of Christ in Harlem. But we settled for Sweetwater's. And the ugly memories faded in the face of soulful music, soulful food, and soulful folk.

As we rode back to Princeton, above the soothing black music of Van Harper's Quiet Storm on WBLS, 107.5 on the radio dial, we talked about what *race* matters have meant to the American past and of how much race *matters* in the American present. And I vowed to be more vigilant and virtuous in my efforts to meet the formidable challenges posed by Plato and Du Bois. For me, it is an urgent question of power and morality; for others, it is an everyday matter of life and death.

Historical Questions

1. Using at least three specific passages from West (writing in the 1990s) and Angelou (writing about the 1940s in the 1970s), discuss two or three ways in which race relations in the city have changed in the last fifty years and two or three ways in which they have remained the same. Discuss some of the factors that account for the changes and for the similarities over time. Feel free to refer to other texts you have read in this chapter.

2. In the first paragraph of his essay, West describes the ways Plato and W. E. B. Du Bois present challenges to how democracy works in society. Other essays in this chapter have also explored ways in which U.S. democratic ideals (such as that all men are created equal and have the right to life, liberty, and the pursuit of happiness) have not been realized, particularly in our cities. Using West's analysis of Plato and Du Bois and the experience he recounts and other texts of your own choosing (for example, Addams or Kingsbury on classism or Angelou or Walinsky on racism), explore one or two ways in which you think the tensions between U.S. democratic ideals and classism and racism have changed over time. Have these changes brought us closer to or further from our democratic ideals? How do these changes specifically relate to some of the problems in U.S. cities today?

3. Using Kingsbury or Angelou, and West, discuss some of the ways in which people mingle in the city, both positively and negatively, and how these ways of mingling have changed and how they have remained constant over time. Make a list of what you feel are three or four of the key relationships among people in the city as they appear in each text, including a brief description of the nature of the relationship. Once you have completed the list, discuss the contexts in which each of these relationships takes place. What are some of the factors of city life at different periods in history that have encouraged certain types of interactions and discouraged others?

Cultural Questions

1. West refers to his experience as an "everyday experience of black New Yorkers," though he also recognizes that for many it is "an everyday matter of life and death." West, thus, shares Walinsky's recognition of the violence

that is a part of the daily life of the urban poor, particularly the African-American urban poor. Compare and contrast West's and Walinsky's responses to this violence and the ways in which they attempt to address it. Analyze the implications of the very different types of solutions they pose for urban violence. Explain your position in their debate and why you hold the position you do.

2. Do a symptomatic reading of West's piece to uncover a sense of some of the diverse and often conflicting perspectives about ways of interacting in New York today. Take up the position of two or three different groups of people West describes—the taxi drivers who won't pick him up, the photographers, his wife, the woman who steps into the cab, the people at Sweetwater's, the Princeton police. What does West say about them, implicitly as well as explicitly? What are their beliefs about encountering and living with diversity in the city? How might they interact with each other? How would they react to West's response to them? Reviewing the perspectives you have sketched out, what suggestions do you have for developing more democratic interactions among these different perspectives?

3. When talking of New York City, Franzen speaks of the "privacy of crowds" and of "coming home" to himself in the city. The experience West recounts suggests that it is more difficult for an African-American male to experience such privacy and sense of selfhood in New York, or in any place in the United States, given "the intransigence of white supremacy." And yet, there are distinct pleasures that West takes in being in New York City. Compare and contrast two or three key points about city living that West and Franzen make. Are they more in agreement or disagreement? In what ways do their positions about New York City transcend their racial difference? In what ways are their positions linked to it? Based on your comparison and analysis, discuss the aspects of city life that you most value and explore some of the ways in which these may be connected to your racial background.

4. Race relations are a central issue not only in this text, but in several of the "What's Good about. . . ?" pieces. Focusing on specific passages from "Waiting" and from two or three of the "What's Good about. . . ?" pieces, discuss two important differences and two consistencies among them. What are the major assumptions underlying the issues of racial tension in each of the examples you have discussed? In what ways do these assumptions create, worsen, or reduce racial tensions? Are the experiences described in these texts similar to those one might experience in the suburbs or in rural areas? Based on your answer, what might you conclude about the influence of place on race relations in the United States today?

●●●~   **Assignment Sequence 1: On the Functions of the City and the People Responsible for Them**

From the quotations that open this chapter to West's meditation on the "everyday experiences of black New Yorkers," we see that the functions performed by the U.S. city have changed over time. The writers also develop different positions on who is responsible for the city's condition and the welfare of those who live there. For Addams, the question of responsibility involves joining together the poor and privileged classes in the spirit of volunteerism and civic education as the poor benefit from the services these volunteers provide. For Angelou, the central issues of self-reliance and racial prejudice supersede any considerations of help from a service such as Addams's Hull-House. And the residents of the cities in the "What's Good About . . . ?" pieces find individual reasons for living in the city, many revealed in the poignant and symbolic moments they describe. For each writer in this chapter, the function of the city is both public and personal, and the answers to who should be responsible for the well-being of the city range from grassroots action groups to the most complicated forms of government intervention.

Essay Question ●●●○○●●∙∙

Given the wide range of perspectives on the function of and responsibility for cities and the many ways in which the role of cities has changed over time, what do you see as the central function of the U.S. city today? Who should be responsible for making sure the city survives? Should it survive? As a living space, what purposes does it serve that other living spaces can't or don't?

1st part of Question → Kingsbury

Review Questions

A list of suggested questions to review before beginning this essay follows. This list is meant only to suggest review options. You may focus on only a subset of the questions, decide that other questions should be added, or construct your own sequence of questions. We encourage you to choose what you believe is the most appropriate review strategy.

1. Jane Addams, Historical Question 2 (page 419)
2. Jane Addams, Cultural Question 2 (page 420)
3. F. J. Kingsbury, Cultural Question 2 (page 426)
4. Urbanism Committee Report, Cultural Question 1 (page 431)
5. Jonathan Franzen, Historical Question 3 (page 456)
6. Cornel West, Historical Question 3 (page 460)

Questions for Further Reflection

1. Considering your own experience of cities and those described by Kingsbury, Franzen, and West, do you agree that there are certain fundamental aspects of the human condition that draw people to cities and thereby ensure that cities will always have a function in U.S. life? What reasons and specific examples lie behind your position?

2. What factors have influenced society's attitudes about the value of U.S. cities over time? What historical developments explain the different tensions in the city? How have people's reasons for being in cities changed over time?

3. Considering the multiple answers to the question of "who is responsible" for cities, who or what plays the most important role in caring for U.S. cities today?

∞ Assignment Sequence 2: On the Causes of City Problems and Solutions for Them

The problems of the U.S. city have evolved over time in their degree of severity and in the types of social tensions they reflect. Essays in this chapter explore ways in which U.S. democratic ideals have fallen short in our cities. The Urbanism Committee report, for example, explores some of the tensions between democratic ideals and capitalism; Addams explores tensions between democracy and classism; and Angelou, Walinsky, and West explore tensions between democracy and racism. Writers have identified many problems and have argued about their causes in proposing ideas for the continued improvement of city life. What do you see as the most pressing problems in the U.S. city right now? What are the major causes of these problems? To what degree do you think these problems can be solved? How should we go about solving them?

Essay Question

Write a proposal in which you argue for specific solutions for one or two of the most urgent problems in cities today. Be sure to explain the historical antecedents of the problem and how it has changed or evolved over time, and the different ways in which the problem might be viewed by different people both within the same historical period and over time. Finally, situate your proposal by careful reference to proposals of other contemporary writers.

Review Questions

A list of suggested questions to review before beginning this essay follows. This list is meant only to suggest review options. You may focus on only a subset of the questions, decide that other questions should be added, or construct your own sequence of questions. We encourage you to choose what you believe is the most appropriate review strategy.

1. Fastwrite 8 (page 444)
2. "What's Good About . . . ?", Cultural Question 3 (page 414)
3. Urbanism Committee, Historical Question 1 (page 430)
4. Maya Angelou, Historical Question 2 (page 440)
5. Adam Walinsky, Historical Question 1 (page 446)
6. Adam Walinsky, Historical Question 2 (page 446)
7. Cornel West, Historical Question 2 (page 460)

Questions for Further Reflection

1. Make a list of the various problems and solutions articulated by the different writers; include your work in fastwrite 8. What patterns do you see among them? Where do you find the most interesting intersections? How has your position developed from fastwrite 8? Choose a problem that you feel you now know a lot about and that you are interested in.

2. As you begin to develop your suggestions for solving the problem you are focusing on, think about whether it is possible to achieve an "ideal" city. What is an ideal city? What would it look like? What kind of housing would there be? What kinds of public spaces? What kinds of work? What kinds of interactions among people? What kinds of values? What aspects of life in the city would attract people to it?

3. What aspects of a city make a city most undesirable? How would your proposal attempt to address these?

∾

For Further Research

Written Texts

Girouard, Mark. *Cities and People: A Social and Architectural History.* New Haven: Yale UP, 1985.

Hayden, Dolores. *Redesigning the American Dream: The Future of Housing, Work, and Family Life.* New York: Norton, 1984.

Jacobs, Jane. *The Death and Life of Great American Cities.* New York: Random, 1961.

Kazin, Alfred. *A Walker in the City.* New York: Harcourt, 1951.

Langdon, Philip. *A Better Place to Live: Reshaping the American Suburb.* Amherst: U of Massachusetts P, 1994.

McKenzie, Evan. *Privatopia: Homeowner Associations and the Rise of Residential Private Government.* New Haven: Yale UP, 1994.

Mumford, Lewis. *The City in History: Its Origins, Its Transformations, and Its Prospects.* New York: Harcourt, 1961.

Rusk, David. *Cities without Suburbs.* Baltimore: Johns Hopkins UP, 1993.

Rybczynski, Witold. *City Life.* New York: Scribner, 1997.

Scully, Vincent. *American Architecture and Urbanism.* New York: Praeger, 1969.

Smith, Patricia. *Close to Death.* Cambridge: Zoland, 1993.

Terkel, Studs. *Division Street.* New York: Pantheon, 1967.

Trefil, James. *A Scientist in the City.* New York: Doubleday, 1994.

United States Federal Housing Administration. *Redlining and Disinvestment as a Discriminatory Practice in Residential Mortgage Loans.* Washington: GPO, 1977.

———. *The Structure and Growth of Residential Neighborhoods in American Cities.* Washington: GPO, 1939.

Wilson, Elizabeth. *The Sphinx in the City: Urban Life, the Control of Disorder, and Women.* Berkeley: U of California P, 1992.

Wilson, William Julius. *The Truly Disadvantaged: The Inner City, the Underclass and Public Policy.* Chicago: U of Chicago P, 1987.

Films

Atlantic City. Dir. Louis Malle. Perf. Burt Lancaster, Susan Sarandon. Paramount, 1981.

Chinatown. Dir. Roman Polanski. Perf. Jack Nicholson, Faye Dunaway, John Huston. Paramount, 1974.

Do the Right Thing. Dir. Spike Lee. Perf. Spike Lee, Danny Aiello, Ruby Dee, Ozzie Davis. Universal Studios Home Video, Facets Multimedia, Inc., 1989.

Manhattan. Dir. Woody Allen. Perf. Woody Allen, Diane Keeton, Meryl Streep. MGM, 1979.

Metropolis. Dir. Fritz Lang. Perf. Brigette Helm, Alfred Abel, Gustov Froehlich. Sinister Cinema, Nostalgia Family Video, Moore Video, 1926.

∾ 8 ∾

GALILEO TO GATES: HUMAN
REACTIONS TO TECHNOLOGY

Edward Klonoski

*Too often these days when I am trying to concentrate on tracking
down the moons of Jupiter, I see my parents. . . . They scrape a living, and underlying their poverty there is a sort of order. . . . How
could they take it, were I to tell them that they are on a lump of
stone ceaselessly spinning in empty space, circling around a second
rate star? What then, would be the use of their patience, their
acceptance of misery?*
—BERTOLT BRECHT, 1966

*Which scenario seems more conducive to democracy, which to
totalitarian rule: a world in which a few people control communications technology that can be used to manipulate the beliefs of
millions, or a world in which every citizen can broadcast to every
other citizen?*
—HOWARD RHEINGOLD, 1993

*The most exciting breakthroughs of the 21st century will not occur
because of technology but because of an expanding concept of what
it means to be human.*
—JOHN NAISBITT AND PATRICIA ABURDENE, 1990

*Networks are based on choice. When they get uncomfortable, it's
easy to opt out of them. Communities teach tolerance, co-existence,
and mutual respect. . . . I fear that calling a network a community
leads people to complacency and delusion, to accepting an inadequate substitute because they've never experienced the real thing
and they don't know what they're missing.*
—ERIC UTNE, 1995

466

ॐ
Introduction: Living With Our Tools

During the great technological revolutions in human history, lives are changed by new tools. For example, when we moved from hunting and gathering to farming and exchanged swords for plowshares, we also exchanged migrating for living in a fixed place. And when we shifted again from farming to manufacturing, we moved near the new factories, creating cities, nuclear families, and increasing immigration. New tools often prompt huge changes in how we live, and they are accompanied by intense debates about what is going on, whether the changes are good, and whether they should be allowed to occur.

In this century, tools such as cars, phones, television, and birth control have prompted such debates. As students of culture, we have at least a statistical idea of how these arguments turned out. We know that cars, phones, and TV "won" (the jury may still be out on birth control). But what exactly does winning mean? What were the original sides in the argument? As a way to experience what it is like to be in the middle of these debates, this chapter explores two such moments that share certain themes—one from 300 years ago and one that is going on right now. We examine the conflicts engendered by Galileo's telescope in 1633 and our own contemporary conflicting responses to cyberspace.

What implications did the telescope have for people of the seventeenth century? In what ways did it challenge dominant cultural assumptions, beliefs, and expectations? Watching how Renaissance culture grappled with the effects of a new technological tool gives us insights and points of comparison for understanding not only our new electronic tools but also the complex and often contradictory responses we have to them. Reactions to the telescope in the 1600s had much less to do with the planets and the stars than with the meanings and belief systems that had been developed around them. The telescope threatened to undermine people's sense of their place within the universe. Similarly, our reactions to technology today are not only about the technology but also about its potential to change our sense of ourselves in relation to the world.

In 1609, Galileo (1564–1642) heard about the invention of a telescope in Holland the previous year and began to build his own. Within a year he had improved its optics so that objects appeared thirty times closer than they did to the naked eye. When Galileo turned his new telescope on the heavens, he saw things that the science of his day could not explain— the craters on the moon, the phases of Venus, the moons of Jupiter. He set out to find explanations for the phenomena he saw in the theories of Copernicus.

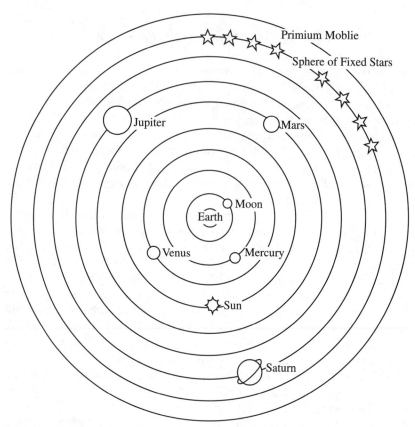

Figure 8.1. The Aristotelian Universe. All of the planets and stars revolve around the earth.

The astronomy of 1609 was based on three sources: Aristotle, Ptolemy, and the Bible. In the fourth century B.C.E.[*] Aristotle (384–322 B.C.E.) looked at the world and concluded that the earth was motionless, and that a series of perfect spheres rotated around it. These spheres were thought to hold the moon, the planets, and the stars and to be moved by the Primum Movens Immobile (the first Unmoved Mover). See Figure 8.1.

What astronomers saw in the night sky, however, did not perfectly support this theory. Planets sometimes seemed to reverse their direction

---

[*] B.C.E. refers to *before the common era* and C.E refers to the *common era*. These are the preferred terms for historical scholars because they do not mark time with the specifically Christian terms B.C. (*before Christ*) and A.D. (*anno domini, after the birth*).

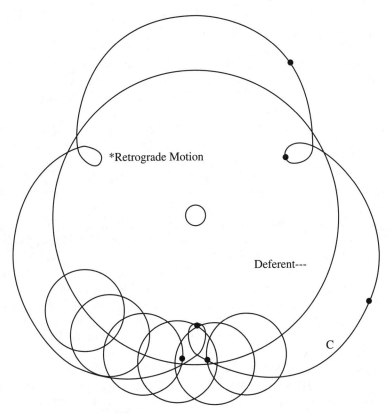

*Retrograde Motion

Deferent---

C

Figure 8.2. The Ptolemeic Universe. In Ptolemy's system, the deferent revolves in a perfect circle around the earth, while the epicycle in turn is revolving around the deferent. Line C represents the path a planet would follow around the earth.

or to change their brightness. The Greek astronomer Ptolemy (c. 150 B.C.E.) argued that celestial motion was a complex interaction of eccentric, or not perfectly circular orbits, and epicycles in which the center of one planet's orbit was thought to be rotating on the circumference of a larger circle. Using elaborate designs to describe the motions of the planets, Ptolemy was able to "save the appearance" that the earth was the center of the universe. The intricacies of Ptolemy's system suggest the ends to which a culture may go at times to resist change and maintain the status quo. See Figure 8.2.

The Bible supported the view of a stationary earth in such passages as Joshua's commanding the sun (not the earth) to stand still. This theory of a universe that moved in perfect circles around a stationary earth satisfied most, although not all, astronomers until Copernicus (1473–1543) began, by the early sixteenth century C.E., building an alternative "heliocentric" theory that proposed that the earth revolved around the sun.

When Galileo began producing evidence that challenged the Ptolemaic universe and, by extension, the accuracy of the Bible, the leading Renaissance authority—the pope—balked. Having observed that Jupiter's moons rotated around the planet itself and that Venus was not rotating around the earth, Galileo argued that it no longer made sense to assert that all celestial objects rotated around a stationary earth. What made more sense was a solar system that rotated around the sun. But the church was not ready to abandon two thousand years of astronomy, and Galileo was forced to recant.

Most people today know this much about Galileo's story. We also know that his explanation of what he saw was correct; it all looks so clear from our vantage point of three hundreds years later. But, had you lived in Galileo's time, how would you have viewed the news he brought back from his newfangled telescope? Remember, this was before pictures from the space shuttle; it was even before Newton began explaining gravity. Galileo was suggesting that what was known and accepted as commonsensical, natural, and normal was wrong, but he wasn't actually providing *proof* that his Copernican alternative was true.

Had you lived in the 1600s, would you have thought the telescope to be the devil's instrument as some did? Or would you have abandoned two thousand years of established "truth" to enter this new unproven Copernican universe? Or might you have been, like Galileo, terribly conflicted? As you will see, Galileo was aware that he did not have genuine proof that Copernicus's heliocentric theory was correct. Further, he was a devout Catholic who would not reject the authority of his church. So he was caught in the contradictory position of "knowing" that the earth was not stationary without having incontrovertible proof, and of wanting to try to prove the truth of his ideas without having these attempts be regarded as an attack against the Bible.

∾ Fastwrite 1

Look back at the quotation uttered by Little Monk from Brecht's play, *Galileo*, that opened this chapter and think about what you know about Galileo and what has been presented here so far. Imagine that you are living in Galileo's time. Taking up any role you'd like—devout Catholic, fellow astronomer, papal authority, even Galileo himself—write for ten minutes on what you feel about Galileo's discoveries and why you think you feel that way.

Today, we are creating a global communication network. *Should* we move wholeheartedly into a world linked by computers? How you and others answer this question depends on what you see its implications to be. Renaissance Europe questioned whether to accept the facts that tools like the telescope were discovering because to do so meant possibly disavowing assumptions about the world that had been accepted since the time of the ancient Greeks. While the consequences for us might not sound quite so dramatic, the material implications are profound. Will this network be good for the common person? Who should "own" it? While it will certainly increase our access to information, won't it simultaneously reduce our privacy? And if intelligent machines can replace people by performing their work, how will we earn our livings?

The capacity to network has happened very rapidly. Computers began as large, expensive devices that required a dedicated staff of servants called *operators*. These mainframe computers dominated the industry from the 1950s until the personal computer caught on in the early 1980s. By the late 1980s, users began to network these same personal computers, which were gaining power with each upgrade. Initially, these networks allowed a few machines to share printers and servers, but with startling rapidity, such local networks began linking to each other and the global network of networks that we call the *Internet* was born.

There are approximately 25 million nodes on the Internet representing about 110 million users. This phenomenon is growing at a rate of over one hundred percent a year and has a presence in nearly 150 countries. The creation of the World Wide Web server in the 1989, followed by the graphic browser Mosaic in 1993, brought pictures, colors, and sounds to the Internet. Today, we can send e-mail around the world in minutes, publish information on our own Web pages, use desktop computers to video conference, search databases around the planet for information, shop, or just explore. If this growth rate continues, the Internet will become ubiquitous.

Among the questions we must face as we enter the twenty-first century are whether this global network is a positive force, and, if so, how to mold and shape it. Just as Pope Urban was faced with the implications of the new universe Galileo discovered, so too are we faced with the implications of the new universe we have created. Neither he nor we know in advance if the changes that come from accepting these new universes will improve our lives. We can only try to understand our current situation using what we know about previous revolutions. By looking at the dominant, residual, and emergent perspectives that influenced Galileo's time, we may be able to build a clearer sense of the perspectives that shape ours.

∾ Fastwrite 2

Fastwrite for fifteen minutes on what experience you have using computers. What is your overall impression of how they affect your life? Quickly list as many instances as possible in your daily life in which you encounter or use a computer. For which of your examples did you in the past not use a computer? Focusing on one of these, compare and contrast the difference in your experiences using versus not using a computer. Then think about something you do regularly without a computer. How might using a computer change that task?

∾ Fastwrite 3

In 1632 Pope Urban VII summoned the sixty-eight year old Galileo Galilei (1564–1642) to Rome to defend his latest book, *Dialogue*, against the claim that it violated an injunction against teaching Copernican theories that had been placed on Galileo in 1616 by Cardinal Bellarmine. Before you begin reading the following selection, fastwrite on what you think the conflict between Galileo and the church was really about. If relevant, draw on what you already know about this and other conflicts between science and authority.

JEROME J. LANGFORD

The Trial of Galileo (1966)

Father Jerome Langford (b. 1937) has taught philosophy and theology at St. Thomas College, in St. Paul, Minnesota. In his own words, Langford chose to write his book *Galileo, Science and the Church* (1966), from which "The Trial of Galileo" is extracted, because "three centuries of myths, prejudiced accounts, and apologetics have distorted the facts and issues of the conflict and made the condemnation of Galileo a subject of enduring prominence."

On April 12, 1633, Galileo was brought to the Holy Office and the hearings began. A Dominican friar, Father Vincent Maculano da Firenzuola, as Commissary-General of the Holy Office, was in charge of prosecuting the case. The task must have been doubly hard on him, since he himself had admitted to Father Castelli in 1632, that he found the Copernican system quite acceptable and that the problem certainly could not be solved on the authority of Sacred Scripture.[1] But like Riccardi he had a job to do, and unlike Riccardi he was not going to bungle it.

The questioning began with Firenzuola asking Galileo whether or not he knew why he had been called before the Holy Office. He replied that he wasn't sure but it was probably because of his latest book. He was shown a copy of the *Dialogue* and admitted that he was the author. The Commissary-General then reviewed the events of 1616. He asked Galileo to recount the events surrounding the prohibition of Copernicus's *De revolutionibus*. The Florentine scientist answered that it had been decided that the Copernican opinion, if taken as an established fact, contradicted Holy Scripture and thus was permitted only as a hypothesis. This decision, he continued, was made known to him by Robert Cardinal Bellarmine. What, Firenzuola asked, had Cardinal Bellarmine told him? Galileo answered that the Cardinal informed him that the Copernican opinion, taken absolutely, must not be defended or held. Galileo then brought forth the certificate which the Cardinal had given him years before when he had asked for something in writing with which to protect his reputation. Firenzuola looked at the certificate and then asked if any other command had been given to him in 1616. Galileo said that he did not remember any other command. Did anyone command him not to "hold, defend, or teach in any way" the said opinion? As far as he could recall, Galileo answered, the only command which he had been given came from Cardinal Bellarmine and it was that he must not hold or defend the opinion. He did not remember the words "not to teach" or "in any way" but they might have been said. If they were, he had forgotten them. He had felt that there was no need to remember anything other than what was in Bellarmine's certificate, which he had saved all these years. Had he, the questioner went on, when seeking an *Imprimatur* for the *Dialogue*, revealed to the authorities that he had been given a command in 1616? Just what command the Commissary was referring to is not clear. Galileo was aware of only one instruction and that was from Cardinal Bellarmine. His answer was, at best, an evasion:

> I did not say anything about that command to the Master of the Palace when I asked for the *Imprimatur*. I did not think it necessary to say anything, because I had no doubts about it; for I have neither maintained nor defended in that book the opinion that the earth moves and that the sun is stationary, but have even demonstrated the opposite of the Copernican opinion and shown that the arguments of Copernicus are weak and inconclusive.[2]

That concluded the first hearing.

[1] Castelli to Galileo, October 2, 1632, *Opere*, XIV, 401–402.

[2] *Opere*, XIX, 341.

Five days later, on April 17, three theological Consultors of the Holy Office, who had been appointed to examine the text of the *Dialogue*, submitted their reports. They agreed that Galileo had taught the Copernican system. His book made it appear that a number of physical phenomena, among them the tides and the sunspots, which had already been explained in other ways, could be caused only by a stable sun and a moving earth. He had also, in their opinion, defended the Copernican doctrine. Not only had he ridiculed Aristotle and Ptolemy, he had also proposed new arguments with the intention of establishing the truth of the forbidden opinion. And he had held the Copernican doctrine. This, concluded the Consultors, was obvious in his work despite his testimony to the contrary. It was enough by way of evidence to point out that he mocked all who did not hold the Copernican theory. Surely Galileo did not consider himself numbered among the "mental pygmies" in which class he placed anyone who did not subscribe to the view of Copernicus.

The reports were filled with long quotations from the *Dialogue* confirming their conclusions. Historians have admitted freely that they were a just appraisal of Galileo's position.

Even so, there was not a very strong legal case against Galileo. In the first place, he did not remember any personal injunction having been given him by the Commissary-General in 1616. While this does not in any way mean that the injunction was planted in the files or that it was never really given, it does seem to support the position that the injunction had not been served validly. The fact that Galileo repeatedly appealed to Bellarmine's certificate might indicate that Bellarmine's explicit instructions to him were that he had only to refrain from holding or defending the Copernican system, no matter what anyone else, the Commissary-General included, might have said to him.

Secondly, it is true that he violated the intent, at least, of the decree of the Index dated March 5, 1616, which was directed against Copernican writings. Bellarmine's whole purpose in calling Galileo before him had been to make sure that he knew what the decree meant. In the words of the certificate he gave Galileo on May 26, 1616, it meant that the Copernican doctrine was contrary to Holy Scripture and therefore was not to be defended or held. This point must be emphasized, for, although it is true that the decree made a distinction between works which tried to reconcile the new astronomy with Holy Scripture and those which merely taught the system as fact, it is also true that, in silencing attempts to prove the reconcilability of the theory with Scripture, the decree was saying that the system was definitely contrary to the Bible. Therefore, not only the reconcilability, but the system itself, taken as a fact, was not to be defended or held. Galileo understood this. He admitted in his letter to Archduke Leopold of Austria that he held the Copernican system to be true "until it pleased the theologians to suspend the book [the *De revolutionibus*] and to declare the opinion to be false and repugant to Holy Scripture." Even though the Consultors' reports proved beyond doubt that he had violated the decree of the Index, Galileo still had a legal out. The Master, of the Sacred Palace and the Inquisitors who gave him permission to print the *Dialogue* knew about that decree. If they thought that the book was not in accord with it, they should never have granted permission to publish.

What it all came down to was that the Pope, wishing, among other things, to have the name Barberini respected in the world of arts and sciences, had urged Galileo to write. Galileo might well have felt that Urban's support abrogated the instruction from Bellarmine years before, not to hold or defend the Copernican system. But then, in the *Dialogue*, he had ignored the Pope's instructions and gone too far. The Pope, convinced that he had been misused, withdrew his support and had Galileo judged according to the strict prohibitions of the questionable injunction and the decree of the Index. Partially, the conflict was Urban's fault. He did not read the *Dialogue* before publication, nor apparently did he make it clear to the censors exactly what could or could not be said in the book. . . .

Yet there can be no doubt that Galileo took an untenable position when he claimed, as he did throughout the trial, that he had not defended or held the Copernican opinion. Some historians have expressed contempt for Galileo because he did not stand up to the Holy Office and defend his view, whatever the consequences. Such a view is wholly unrealistic. Galileo had no desire to be excommunicated from the Church. Besides, to the very end he kept alive a somewhat sanguine feeling that everything would somehow be all right. The rumors prevalent at the time of his arrival in Rome were that everything was going to be settled quietly. Galileo would be given a severe lecture on authority, and his book would be suspended until he recast it in a more hypothetical mold. Now all that looked like wishful thinking. The repeated questions about an absolute injunction which he did not remember and the lack of impression which his certificate from Bellarmine seemed to make on the authorities left Galileo less than secure at what might happen to him.

Still there was hope. It became evident that he was not without his defenders even on the ten-man board of cardinals assigned to judge the case. Francesco Cardinal Barberini, the Pope's own nephew, had little sympathy with his uncle's anger. When the prohibition had been forced in 1616, the issues had been more doctrinal than personal. But this time it was different. Undoubtedly some Church officials wanted to protect doctrinal authority and others still felt that Copernicanism was heretical. But the men who wanted to see Galileo subjected to the strictest penalties were not so highly motivated as all that. It is hard to say who they were or why they were so anxious to have Galileo grovel in the dust. But that there was a group of clerics bent on humiliating him cannot be denied. Cardinal Barberini, Firenzuola, Riccardi, and Campanella, among others, were pretty sure that this trial was not aimed so much at preserving doctrinal purity as it was at extracting personal revenge. And they wanted no part of it. No doubt they felt that some kind of personal penance was in order. But not complete humiliation.

As a result of what seems to have been a plan discussed by Firenzuola and Cardinal Barberini, a method was devised to spare Galileo as much as possible. Since Galileo had denied what was plainly evident in his book and added evasion to disobedience, the situation did not look hopeful. Firenzuola, with Cardinal Barberini's backing, obtained permission to deal extra-judicially with Galileo: in other words, to make a deal with the accused. The idea was that if Galileo would tell the truth and admit that he had gone too far in his book, he might get off with a private penance and temporary house arrest, the *Dialogue* would be suspended at least until corrections were made, and the matter would end there. "In this way," Firenzuola wrote to Cardinal Barberini on April 28, "the court will maintain its reputation; it will be possible to deal leniently with the accused, and, whatever decision is reached, he will recognize the favor shown him."[3] Firenzuola's letter also describes how he convinced Galileo that accepting the deal was the wise thing to do:

> In order not to lose time, I talked to Galileo yesterday afternoon. After many arguments and counter-arguments, by the grace of God, I attained my objective and brought him to a full understanding of his error so that he clearly realized that he had erred and gone too far in his book. He expressed his deepest feelings with regard to all of this like one who felt great consolation in the recognition of his error. He was also willing to confess it judicially. He asked for a little time in order to consider the most fitting form for his confession, which, I hope, will be substantially as indicated.[4]

Two days later, on April 30, Galileo was called to appear for the second hearing. Asked if he wished to make a statement, he told the court:

> In the course of some days' continuous and intense reflection on the questions asked me on the sixteenth [Galileo is referring to the first hearing which was actually held on April 12] of the present month, and in particular as to whether, sixteen years ago, an injunction was intimated to me by order of the Holy Office, forbidding me to hold, defend, or teach in any way the opinion which had just been condemned . . . it occurred to me to reread my

[3] *Opere*, XV, 107.
[4] *Ibid.*

published *Dialogue,* which I had not seen for three years, in order carefully to ascertain whether, contrary to my most sincere intention, there had inadvertently fallen from my pen anything from which a reader or the authorities might infer not only some sign of disobedience on my part, but also anything else which would induce the belief that I had gone against the orders of the Holy Church.

Being, by the kind permission of the authorities, free to send my servant about, I was able to obtain a copy of my book. And, having obtained it, I applied myself most diligently to studying it and to considering it most carefully. And, because I had not seen it for so long, it seemed to me like a new writing and by another author. I freely confess that it seemed to me composed in such a way that a reader ignorant of my real purpose might have reason to think that the arguments presented for the false side, which I really intended to refute, were expressed in such a way as to be calculated rather to compel conviction by their soundness than to be easily solved.

Two arguments there are in particular—the one taken from the solar spots, the other from the ebb and flow of the tide—which really do strike the reader with a far greater show of force and power than should have been given to them by one who regarded them as inconclusive and who intended to refute them, as indeed I sincerely held and do hold them to be inconclusive and capable of being refuted. And as a personal excuse for having fallen into an error so foreign to my intention, not being content with merely saying that when someone gives the arguments for the opposite side with the object of refuting them, he should (especially if writing in the form of a dialogue) state these arguments in their strictest form and should not cover them over to the disadvantage of his opponents,—not being content, I say, with this excuse, I resorted to that of the natural complacency which every man feels with regard to his own subtleties and in showing himself more skillful than most men in devising, even in favor of false propositions, ingenious and plausible arguments. . . My error then, has been, and I confess it, one of vainglorious ambition and of ignorance and inadvertence. . . .

Having completed his statement, he was dismissed. But he came back and added as an afterthought:

And in confirmation of my assertion that I have not held and do not hold as true the opinion which has been condemned, . . . if there shall be granted to me, as I desire, the means and the time to make a clearer demonstration of this, I am ready to do so; and there is a most favorable opportunity for this, for in the work already published the interlocutors agree to meet again after a certain time to discuss several distinct problems of Nature not connected with the matter already treated. As this affords me the opportunity of adding one or two other "Days" I promise to resume the arguments already brought in favor of the said opinion, which is false and has been condemned, and to refute them in such an effectual way as by the blessing of God may be supplied to me. I pray, therefore, this holy Tribunal to aid me in this good resolution and to enable me to put it in effect.[5]

Galileo admitted that he had gone too far in his book, but he persisted in denying that he had held the new system as true. Now he offered to publish an addition to his work which would not merely water down, but actually contradict his scientific beliefs. Fortunately, even the Holy Office felt no need for that. Koestler believes that

> . . . his fears were exaggerated, and that his self-immolatory offer (which the Inquisition discreetly allowed to drop as if it had never been made) was quite unnecessary, is beside the point. His panic was due to psychological causes: it was the unavoidable reaction of one who thought himself capable of out-witting all and making a fool of the Pope himself, on suddenly discovering that he has been 'found out.' His belief in himself as a superman was shattered, his self-esteem punctured and deflated.[6]

I think that is an overstatement. It had never been his intention to make fun of the Pope. He had been bold, but only because there were reasons which seemed to indicate that he would be allowed some leeway. As Giorgio de Santillana has written:

> He knew, beyond doubt, that he had disregarded the Pope's explicit inten-tions. But he was strong in his certainty that he had not disobeyed the edicts of the Church. He obviously thought—as Ciampoli did for that matter—that he had to contend with the fancies of a vain and headstrong but brilliant personality who was still, for all his pontifical robes, the old Maffeo Barberini whom he had known and loved. There is scarcely an intelligent man who will not believe that people in power cannot take themselves seriously all of the time and who will not naively extend to them his sympathy in the hope of a shade of refreshing complicity in return, of a trace of humor.[7]

Now the law was being applied according to a strict interpretation and Galileo knew he had lost his gamble and that some consequences would be forthcoming. He hid behind the denial that he had held or defended

[5] *Opere*, XIX, 342–344.

[6] Arthur Koestler, *The Sleepwalkers*, p. 489.

[7] G. de Santillana, *Crime of Galileo*, p. 203.

the theory, well aware that there was no way in which he could be forced to tell the whole truth. . . . On May 10, Galileo was summoned before the court and asked if he wished to present a defense. Galileo handed Firenzuola a document which stated his side of the case. It is worth quoting in full:

When asked if I had signified to the Reverend Father, the Master of the Sacred Palace, the injunction privately laid upon me, about sixteen years ago, by order of the Holy Office, not to hold, defend, or in any way teach the doctrine of the motion of the earth and the stability of the sun, I answered that I had not done so. And, not being questioned as to the reason why I had not intimated it, I had no opportunity to add anything further. It now appears to me necessary to state the reason in order to demonstrate the purity of my intention, ever foreign to the employment of simulation or deceit in any operation I engage in. I say, then, that as at that time reports were spread abroad by evil-disposed persons, to the effect that I had been summoned by the Lord Cardinal Bellarmine to abjure certain of my opinions and doctrines, and that I had consented to abjure them, and also to submit to punishment for them, I was thus constrained to apply to His Eminence, and to solicit him to furnish me with an attestation, explaining the cause for which I had been summoned before him: which attestation I obtained, in his own handwriting, and it is the same that I now produce with the present document. From this it clearly appears that it was merely announced to me that the doctrine attributed to Copernicus of the motion of the earth and the stability of the sun must not be held or defended, but that, beyond this general announcement affecting every one, no trace of any other injunction intimated to me appears there. Having, then, as a reminder, this authentic attestation in the handwriting of the very person who intimated the command to me, I made no further application of thought or memory with regard to the words employed in announcing to me the said order not to hold or defend the doctrine in question: so that the two articles of the order—in addition to the injunction not to hold or *'defend'* it—to wit, the words 'nor to teach it in any way whatsoever' —which I hear are contained in the order intimated to me, and registered— struck me as quite novel and as if I had not heard them before: and I do not think I ought to be disbelieved when I urge that in the course of fourteen or sixteen years I had lost all recollection of them, especially as I had no need to give any particular thought to them, having in my possession so authentic a reminder in writing. Now, if the said two articles be left out, and those two only retained which are noted in the accompanying attestation, there is no doubt that the injunction contained in the latter is the same command as that contained in the decree of the Sacred Congregation of the Index. Whence it appears to me that I have a reasonable excuse for not having notified the Master of the Sacred Palace of the command privately imposed upon me, it being the same as that of the Congregation of the Index.

Seeing also that my book was not subject to a stricter censorship than that made binding by the decree of the Index, it will, it appears to me, be sufficiently plain that I adopted the surest and most becoming method of having it guaranteed and purged of all shadow of taint, inasmuch as I handed it to the Supreme Inquisitor at the very time when many books dealing with the same matters were being prohibited solely in virtue of the said decree. After what I have now stated, I would confidently hope that the idea of my having knowingly and deliberately violated the command imposed upon me will henceforth be entirely banished from the minds of my most eminent and wise judges; so that those faults which are seen scattered throughout my book have not been artfully introduced with any concealed or other than sincere intention, but have only inadvertently fallen from my pen owing to a vainglorious ambition and complacency in desiring to appear more subtle than the generality of popular writers, as indeed in my other deposition I have confessed—which fault I shall be ready to correct by writing whenever I may be commanded or permitted by your Eminences.

Lastly, it remains for me to pray you to take into consideration my pitiable state of bodily indisposition, to which, at the age of seventy years, I have been reduced by ten months of constant mental anxiety and the fatigue of a long and toilsome journey at the most inclement season—together with the loss of the greater part of the years of which, from my previous condition of health, I had the prospect. I am persuaded and encouraged to do so by the clemency and goodness of the most eminent lords, my judges; with the hope that they may be pleased, in answer to my prayer, to remit what may appear to their entire justice to be lacking to such sufferings as adequate punishment—out of consideration for my declining age, which too, I humbly commend to them. And I would equally commend to their consideration my honor and reputation, aginst the calumnies of ill-wishers whose persistence in detracting from my good name may be inferred from the necessity which constrained me to procure from the Lord Cardinal Bellarmine the attestation which accompanies this.[8]

It was a strong defense. Since he did not remember any special command "not to teach or discuss in any way" he had not felt it necessary to tell the Master of the Sacred Palace about his audience with Cardinal Bellarmine. Father Riccardi should have known well the limitations which the decree of the Index imposed on astronomical writings. In other words, Galileo is asking why his book was officially approved and is now prohibited. That was a good question. On the other hand, the judges knew that he had knowingly gone against the provisions of Bellarmine's instruction,

[8] Cited by F. S. Taylor, *Galileo and the Freedom of Thought*, pp. 156–159.

the absolute injunction and the decree of the Index, and that he had not been altogether truthful in his answers. He could not be dismissed without some salutary penance. According to the arrangement, all that remained now was to carry out the terms of Firenzuola's compromise and bring the case to a close. . . .

On June 16, the decision of the Pope was entered into the records of the Holy Office. Instead of merely prohibiting the *Dialogue* "until corrected," giving Galileo a private penance and assigning him to house arrest, the scientist was to perform the humiliating act of formal abjuration and his book was to be forbidden:

> His Holiness decreed that the said Galileo is to be interrogated with regard to his intention, even with the threat of torture, and, if he sustains [that is, answers in a satisfactory manner), he is to abjure *de vehementi* (i.e., vehement suspicion of heresy] in a plenary assembly of the Congregation of the Holy Office, then is to be condemned to imprisonment as the Holy Congregation thinks best, and ordered not to treat further, in any way at all, either verbally or in writing, of the mobility of the earth and the stability of the sun; otherwise he will incur the penalties for relapse. The book entitled *Dialogo di Galileo Galilei Linceo* is to be prohibited. Furthermore, that these things may be known by all, he ordered that copies of the sentence be sent to all Apostolic Nuncios, to all Inquisitors against heretical pravity, and especially the Inquisitor in Florence, who shall read publicly the sentence in the presence of as many as possible of those who profess the mathematical art.[9]

Galileo had misused the Pope's friendship, openly disobeyed the express prohibitions against his theory, and plainly failed in his attempt to prove the Copernican astronomy. Still it is hard to see the logic of the sentence. There was no reason to condemn the *Dialogue* outright. It in no way attempted to reconcile the heliocentric system with Holy Scripture as Foscarini's book had done years before. The *Dialogue* defended the new astronomy as true on physical grounds. If this was objectionable, Galileo's book like Copernicus's *De revolutionibus*, should have been suspended until corrected and made more hypothetical. As for Galileo personally, the most that should have been given him was a penance for disobeying Bellarmine's admonition. Condemnation based on the absolute injunction was certainly tenuous, especially in the light of Bellarmine's certificate which was intended to state exactly what had happened to Galileo in 1616 and which made no mention of such an injunction. As for the decree of the Index, it was aimed at books, not authors.

[9] *Opere,* XIX, p. 306–361.

482 CONTESTING PEOPLE, CONTESTED SPACES

The word "torture" in the document cited above has given rise to another legend connected with the name of Galileo, a legend which, until recently, enjoyed wide acceptance. Even today, Bertold Brecht's play on the life of Galileo misrepresents this phase of the famous condemnation. Galileo was not tortured, nor was he shown the instruments of torture. He was verbally threatened with torture. But he knew that the threat carried no weight. It was common knowledge, and canonists and moralists of the period are unanimous in verifying it, that no one of Galileo's age or poor health could be subjected to physical torture.[10] Now there can be no defense of torture, or even threats of torture. But the *territio verbalis* here was a mere formality and Galileo knew it. . . .

The next morning, Wednesday, June 22, 1633, Galileo was escorted to the Dominican convent of Santa Maria Sopra Minerva and the sentence was read to him. It began with a review of the whole case, starting with the first denunciation of his opinion to the Holy Office in 1615, then making public for the first time the verdict of the theological Consultors in 1616, on the two propositions which had been given them to examine, then recalling the audience with Cardinal Bellarmine and the injunction given to Galileo by the Commissary-General in 1616, and the decree of the Index which had declared the opinion to be contrary to Holy Scripture. It cited the fact that Galileo had written the *Dialogue* in support of the forbidden position despite his protestations to the contrary. And even if he did not remember the personal injunctions, he had violated the admonition of Cardinal Bellarmine not to hold or defend the theory. Then it gave the sentence:

> We say, pronounce, sentence, and declare that you, the said Galileo, by reasons of the matters brought forth in trial, and by you confessed as above, have rendered yourself in the judgment of this Holy Office vehemently suspected of heresy, namely, of having believed and held the doctrine which is false and contrary to the Sacred and Divine Scriptures, that the sun is the center of the world and does not move from east to west and that the earth moves and is not the center of the world; and that any opinion may be held and defended as probable after it has been declared and defined contrary to Holy Scripture; and that consequently you have incurred all the censures and penalties imposed and promulgated in the sacred canons and other constitutions, general and

---

[10] "*Dicendum est cum Sanchez, Suarez, Narbona, etc., et Doctoribus in Tribunali Sancti Inquisitionis, diximus senem non esse torquendum esse senem 70 annorum, et etiam 60 si sit infirmae salutis, debilisque complex ionis.*" Antoninus Diana, *Coordinati Resolutionum Moralium*, ed. Martin de Alcolea (Venice, 1728), V, Resol. XXIX, p. 337. This work was first published in 1658, but since Sanchez, Suarez, and Narbona all wrote well before 1633, the citation from Diana confirms that this was the common opinion at the time of the trial of Galileo.

particular, against such delinquents. From which we are content that you be absolved, provided that, first, with a sincere heart and unfeigned faith, you abjure, curse, and detest before us the aforesaid errors and heresies and every other error and heresy contrary to the Catholic and Apostolic Roman Church in the form to be prescribed by us for you.

And, in order that your grave and pernicious error and transgression may not remain altogether unpunished and that you may be more cautious in the future and an example to others that they may abstain from similar delinquencies, we ordain that the book *Dialogue of Galileo Galilei* be prohibited by public edict.

We condemn you to the formal prison of the Holy Office subject to our judgment, and by way of salutary penance we prescribe that for three years to come, you repeat once a week the seven penitential psalms. Reserving to ourselves the right to moderate, commute, or take off, in whole or in part, the aforesaid penalties and penance.

And so we say, pronounce, sentence, declare, ordain, and reserve in this and in any other better way and form which we can and may rightfully employ.[11]

The decree of Sentence was signed by only seven of the ten cardinal-judges of the Holy Office. Conspicuously absent was the signature of Francesco Cardinal Barberini, who had advocated leniency throughout the proceedings and probably considered the decision to be of questionable justice and needless severity. Cardinals Borgia and Zacchia also did not sign the decree, but their motives for abstention are not known.

Galileo, having heard the sentence, expressed a willingness to abjure as required, but asked that two charges be omitted from the formula of abjuration. One was a statement which hinted that he was not a good Catholic; the other was an inference that he had obtained the *Imprimatur* by devious or cunning methods. The officials had no desire to argue the matter and they granted his request. Galileo knelt to recite his formal abjuration:

> I, Galileo, son of the late Vincenzio Galilei, Florentine, aged seventy years, arraigned personally before this tribunal and kneeling before you, Most Eminent and Lord Cardinals Inquisitors-General against heretical pravity throughout the entire Christian Commonwealth, having before my eyes and touching with my hands the Holy Gospels, swear that I have always believed, do believe, and with God's help will in the future believe all that

---

[11] Ibid., 405–406.

is held, preached and taught by the Holy Catholic and Apostolic Church. But, whereas, after an injunction had been lawfully intimated to me by this Holy Office to the effect that I must altogether abandon the false opinion that the sun is the center of the world and immobile, and that the earth is not the center of the world and moves, and that I must not hold, defend, or teach, in any way, verbally or in writing, the said false doctrine, and after it had been notified to me that the said doctrine was contrary to Holy Scripture, I wrote and printed a book in which I treated this new doctrine already condemned and brought forth arguments in its favor without presenting any solution for them, I have been judged to be vehemently suspected of heresy, that is, of having held and believed that the sun is the center of the world and immobile and that the earth is not the center and moves.

Therefore, desiring to remove from the minds of Your Eminences, and of all faithful Christians, this vehement suspicion rightly conceived against me, with sincere heart and unpretended faith I abjure, curse, and detest the aforesaid errors and heresies and also every other error, error and sect whatever, contrary to the Holy Church, and I swear that in the future I will never again say or assert verbally or in writing, anything that might cause a similar suspicion toward me; further, should I know any heretic or person suspected of heresy, I will denounce him to this Holy Office or to the Inquisitor or Ordinary of the place where I may be.

Further, I swear and promise to carry out and observe in their integrity, all penances that have been or shall be imposed upon me by this Holy Office. And if I should violate, which God forbid, any of these my promises and oaths, I submit myself to all the castigations and penalties imposed and promulgated in the sacred canons and other constitutions, general and particular, against such delinquents. So help me God and these Holy Gospels which I touch with my hands.[12]

The condemnation of Galileo was now complete. The scientist had tried to batter down the old view of the universe and the traditional exegesis of Scripture by beating his head against a wall of conservatism and mocking those who felt that it should not be torn down. The wall stood; Galileo's tools had not been the best, nor had he used them effectively. It was his own admirable but imprudent doggedness as much as the strength of the wall that finally drove him to his knees.

---

[12] *Ibid.*, 406. There is a myth that Galileo, upon leaving the Minerva, looked up at the sky and, stamping his foot cried, *"Eppur si muove"*—"Yet it does move!" This particular bit of apocrypha was started by Guiseppe Baretti in 1757 and has been widely repeated in uncritical writings through the years.

∾ **Fastwrite 4**

What is your immediate reaction to Galileo's trial. How do you feel about the outcome? In what ways was the argument predictable? In what ways was it surprising? What might you have said if you were there?

Historical Questions

1. Develop a symptomatic reading of why the church brought Galileo to trial and why the pope gave the sentence he did. Doing a close reading not only of Langford's descriptions, but particularly of the statements from the pope, discuss both the stated reasons for the church's condemnation of Galileo and those that are unstated, but which, from your vantage point today, seem nonetheless significant. In developing your analysis, compare one to two aspects of Galileo's trial to a contemporary situation to help you explore what is unstated but significant in the trial.

2. Like any individual at any historical moment, Galileo occupies a number of different subject positions—scientist, Catholic, private citizen. He stands out, however, because the tensions among his various subject positions are so extreme and because they became so public. Exploring both his own words and his behaviors as described by Langford, discuss how two or three of Galileo's values and beliefs both enabled and constrained certain behaviors in him, given the dominant assumptions of the world he occupied. Why, for example, is Galileo so controlled in his response to his accusers? In what ways might the configuration of his beliefs and his potential actions change if Galileo were living in today's world?

3. Langford questions the sentence Galileo receives. He thinks the church could have narrowed its complaint and punished Galileo without forbidding his book or humiliating him. Do you agree? Why do you think the church acted as it did?

Cultural Questions

1. Describe the dominant perspective on the role of science in Galileo's day. What is the emergent perspective? Analyze two or three of the different assumptions underlying these perspectives. What do you think is the central goal of each perspective?

2. Consider Langford's conclusion: "The wall stood; Galileo's tools had not been the best, nor had he used them effectively. It was his own admirable but imprudent doggedness as much as the strength of the wall that finally drove him to his knees." Langford seems to be blaming Galileo for his own predicament. What assumptions does Langford make about

the relationship of an individual to larger social structures? About the reactions of the dominant within a culture to possible change? About the options available for someone caught between the dominant and a more emergent set of beliefs? Using what you know about the period, what is your position on how and whether Galileo could have avoided censure. What assumptions do you share with Langford? Where do you disagree with him?

ℴ⋟ **Fastwrite 5**

Before reading the following selection, make a list of the institutions to which you have pledged obedience, remembering your rites of passage—for example, confirmations, graduations, and so on. Have you been faithful to your promises? As faithful as Galileo?

GIORGIO DE SANTILLANA

Galileo's Crime (1954)

Giorgio de Santillana (1902-74) taught history and philosophy at the Massachusetts Institute of Technology. Born in Rome, he had a special interest in the science of the Renaissance as evidenced by another of his books, *The Origins of Scientific Thought* (1961). *The Crime of Galileo,* from which the following selection is extracted, was published in 1954.

I

The abjuration itself is not at all the surrender and moral disgrace that self-appointed judges have made it out to be. Galileo knew exactly what he could say and what he could not say without committing the mortal sin of perjury, for he was better trained in moral theology than we are. That was why, as we know from Buonamici, he had stood firm on refusing two points even at the risk of the stake. He was never going to say that he had deceived anyone during the negotiations for the license or that he had ever deviated from Catholic orthodoxy. These would have been acts of the will. The rest was not.

His real statement then amounted to this: "If the Vicar of Christ insists that I must not *affirm* what I happen to *know*, I have to obey. I herewith declare that at no point should my will have consented to my knowledge. Not even God can prevent my reason from seeing what it sees, but by His Vicar's explicit command I can withdraw my public adhesion from it to avoid scandal among the faithful. You most illegally condemn my truth and want submission. I give you submission and keep my truth. As to that matter of a 'judicial injunction,' it is your lie, not mine, that you ask me to recite, and let it be on your own heads. On this I can stand—that my will was not and will never be consciously contrary to that of the Holy Apostolic Church. For the rest, obedience compels me to say publicly whatever you please." . . .

To have recanted was not considered a moral degradation. It was a deliberate *social* degradation, and it was as such that it broke the old man's heart.

II

It did not break his spirit, as time was to show, for, although despairing that he would be allowed to publish, he was to go on from there to his greatest scientific achievement, the *Two New Sciences*.[1] It did not even check the ironic and caustic flashes which broke out at times and drove his enemies to fury, even though they knew he was gagged and helpless in the face of their triumphant refutations. He made no mystery of what he thought of his judges and their judgment, nor did he feel that this scornful appraisal made him insincere in his submission and withdrew him from the communion of the faithful. He went on praying and asking his friends to pray for him. He had even planned a pilgrimage to Our Lady of Loreto to repeat the one he had made after 1616, and only his health prevented him from performing it. But to men like Peiresc he could write:

> I do not hope for any relief, and that is because I have committed no crime. I might hope for and obtain pardon, if I had erred; for it is to faults that the prince can bring indulgence, whereas against one wrongfully sentenced while he was innocent, it is expedient, in order to put up a show of strict lawfulness, to uphold rigor. . . . But my most holy intention, how clearly would it appear if some power would bring to light the slanders, frauds, stratagems, and trickeries that were used eighteen years ago in Rome in order to deceive the authorities! . . . You have read my writings, and from them you have certainly

[1] When the Duke of Noailles, ambassador of the King of France, insisted on visiting Galileo as a prisoner, he could not be refused, and on their meeting he accepted the dedication of the coming work. The manuscript was smuggled out of Italy by Prince Mattia de' Medici and ultimately printed by Elzevir in Holland.

understood which was the true and real motive that caused, under the lying mask of religion, this war against me that continually restrains and undercuts me in all directions, so that neither can help come to me from outside nor can I go forth to defend myself, there having been issued an express order to all Inquisitors that they should not allow any of my works to be reprinted which had been printed many years ago or grant permission to any new work that I would print. . . . a most rigorous and general order, I say, against all my works, *omnia edita et edenda;* so that it is left to me only to succumb in silence under the flood of attacks, exposures, derision, and insult coming from all sides.[2]

This makes his position clear. He had sworn before Christendom that he would never consent to any heresy; but he considered himself in no way bound to recognize as of the faith the arbitrary and wilful decision which broke all Church constitutions. They had forced on him a dishonoring obligation; he was not going to honor the extorted promise. They wanted to destroy him and "extirpate even his memory." He was going to fight back with all the means at his command. Within a month of his leaving Rome, a copy of the *Dialogue* was on its way to Matthias Bernegger in Strasbourg, through trusted intermediaries, so that a Latin translation was ready for the European public in 1637.

There is no clearer sign of the anarchic situation brought about by the authorities through their travesty of legality than the resistance of the public to the prohibition.[3] Pious believers who would never have touched a Protestant tract, priests, monks, prelates even, vied with one another in buying up copies of the *Dialogue* on the black market to keep them from the hands of the Inquisitors. A friend writes scornfully from Padua that

---

[2] Letters to Peiresc, February 22 and March 16, 1635. He had known about the reserved orders to the provincial Inquisitors from Micanzio in Venice. On September 8, 1633, the Pope had further reprimanded the Inquisitor of Florence for giving permission to reprint some past works.

[3] Ascanio Piccolomini must be singled out as a man who was not impressed by pontifical thunderbolts. When Galileo, after his sentence, was intended to spend a long period of penitence in the monastery of Santa Croce in Gerusalemme, Piccolomini, with the help of Cardinal Barberini, obtained custody over him for five months, with strict orders to see no one. As soon as Galileo had arrived in Siena as his guest, he forthwith proceeded to open the archiepiscopal palace to a steady stream of visitors. It was there that the French poet Saint-Amant saw the scientist "dans un logement tapissé de soye et fort richement emmeublé," at work together with Piccolomini on his theory of mechanics, with papers scattered all around the room, "et ne se pouvoit lasser d'admirer cez deux vénérables vieillards, etc." The inevitable informer wrote in anonymously: "The Archbishop has told many that. Galileo was unjustly sentenced by this Holy Congregation, that he is the first man in the world, that he will live forever in his writings, even if they are prohibited, and that he is followed by all the best modern minds. And since such words from a prelate might bring forth pernicious fruit, I herewith report them, etc."

Messer Fortunio Liceti has handed in his copy to the authorities, with the clear implication that he would be the only one to do that. As Micanzio says, most readers would face the "greatest indignations" rather than part with a copy, and the black-market price of the book rises from the original half-scudo to four and six scudi (almost a hundred dollars in our currency) all over Italy.

This degenerates into an undignified chase reminiscent of the Key-stone Cops: as soon as the *Discourses on Two New Sciences* is licensed in Olmütz by the bishop, and then in Vienna, obviously under direct imperial orders, by the Jesuit Father Paullus, the other Jesuits start in hot pursuit after the book. "I have not been able," writes Galileo to Baliani in 1639, "to obtain a single copy of my new dialogue which was published two years ago in Amsterdam [it should have been "Leiden"]. Yet I know that they circulated through all the northern countries. The copies lost must be those which, as soon as they arrived in Prague, were immediately bought up by the Jesuit Fathers, so that not even the Emperor himself was able to get one." The charitable explanation would be that they knew what they were doing. Some one at least may have understood that Galileo's work in dynamics went on quietly establishing the foundations of the system that he had been forbidden to defend. But they were like that gallant man of whom Milton speaks who thought to pound in the crows by shutting the park gate.

There is perforce no longer any question here of spiritual authority or obedience but simply of administrative abuses by a thought police whose decrees are ignored and dodged by each citizen as he can, in a manner that cannot but remind one of the "lawbreaking" under the Volstead Act. We know that Galileo regularly went in for confession and received communion. This shows that he was absolved by his spiritual counselor for ignoring the potential excommunications of Rome. . . .

Thus Galileo's resignation and acceptance could still remain unyielding both in scientific certainty and in what he knew to be the unalterable content of his faith. Although he had been ordered not to write or converse in any manner about cosmology, at the risk of being treated as a relapsed heretic, and the local Inquisitors watched his visitors and correspondence through their informers, he could write in 1641 to Francesco Rinuccini with thinly disguised irony:

> To be sure, the conjectures by which Copernicus maintained that the Earth is not at the center all go to pieces before the fundamental argument of divine omnipotence. For since that latter is able to effect by many, aye, by endless means, what, so far as we can see, only appears practicable in one way, we must not limit the hand of God and persist obstinately in anything in which we may have been mistaken. But, as I hold the Copernican observations and

conjectures to be insufficient, so much more do those of Ptolemy, Aristotle, and their followers appear to me delusive and mistaken, because their falsity can clearly be proved without going beyond the limits of human knowledge.

Historical Questions

1. As we work to understand the past, we are always analyzing it within the context of our present perspectives. From Santillana's perspective, how does Galileo reconcile his obedience to the church with his belief in the truth of his scientific conclusions? Looking as carefully as you can at Galileo's own words in Langford's essay, describe how you think Galileo reconciled his sense of duty to the church with his belief in the truth of his scientific conclusions. Compare and contrast your sense of Galileo's perspective with Santillana's analysis of it. What assumptions are you making? How do they compare with Santillana's and Galileo's?

2. What is your position on obedience to different groups and institutions? What level of submission do you feel that you owe your religion? Your country? Your family? (You may have different ideas about each of these.) Who decides how obedient you should be? Discuss your sense of your appropriate degree of obedience with reference to two to three different contexts or organizations. Compare two to three key aspects of your position on obedience with two to three aspects of Galileo's.

3. Santillana contends that Galileo's recantation was a social degradation not a moral one. What, for Santillana, is the difference between these two? What was their difference for Galileo? Describe a situation today in which you might distinguish between these two positions.

Cultural Questions

1. Pope Urban asked Galileo to recant his belief that the solar system was heliocentric. Why does he ask Galileo to do this? What does the pope hope to accomplish by getting Galileo to abjure his beliefs? What assumptions does Pope Urban have about the nature of change within the individual and within society?

2. How one analyzes the church's position and Galileo's abjuration has much to do with one's assumptions about the nature of change. With specific references to their texts, compare one to two key points of Santillana's analysis of the church's position and Galileo's abjuration with one to two points of Langford's analysis and with your own position, focusing particularly on the assumptions each of you has about the nature of change within the individual and within society.

3. In historical question 2 above you described your position on obedience and compared it to Galileo's; now revisit the question of your obedience from the perspective of the organization in question. For example, if you discussed the obedience you owe your sorority, examine the question from the point of view of the sorority. What sort of loyalty and what level of compliance do they expect? Discuss the expectations of two to three different organizations and explain some of the instances in which you would comply with them and some instances, if at all, in which you would not. What are your reasons?

ॐ   **Fastwrite 6**

In 1992, the Catholic Church issued a statement about the Galileo case that absolved Galileo of his guilt and that was designed to set the record straight once and for all. Imagine that you are assigned to interview the church representative delivering that announcement. Fastwrite three or four questions you would ask.

ᘓᘏᘓᘏᘓ

J A M E S   B .   R E S T O N ,   J R .

Galileo Reconsidered (1994)

James B. Reston, Jr. (b.1941) has been a speech writer for Interior Secretary Morris Udall, a reporter for the *Chicago Daily News,* a lecturer in creative writing at the University of North Carolina, and a sergeant in Army Military Intelligence. He is also a biographer who has written, among others, *The Lone Star: The Life of John Connally* (1989). In "Galileo Reconsidered," extracted from *Galileo: A Life* (1994), he examines the Galileo conflict from the perspective of Pope John Paul II's 1992 absolution of Galileo.

On October 31, 1992, in the ornate royal hall of the Apostolic Palace in the Vatican, Pope John Paul II gathered the Pontifical Academy of Sciences before him to resolve the Galileo affair for the Roman Catholic church once and for all time. It fell to Cardinal Paul Poupard of France, the chairman of Galileo's modern pardon board, to make the initial presentation. Dressed in his floor-length black gown and his red cardinal's hat and speaking in elegant French, the cardinal addressed the assemblage solemnly. The pontiff, a figure of pristine white, slumped in his commodious chair, listened with his chin supported by his fist.

The theologians who attacked Galileo, Poupard declared, failed to understand that the Scripture was not literal when it came to a description of the physical world. Galileo had suffered greatly from their errors of judgment. "These errors must be frankly recognized," the cardinal exclaimed. Then, in his most surprising statement, he accorded Galileo the compliment of being "more perceptive" in his interpretation of Scripture than the theologians who opposed him, even though it had been forbidden by the Council of Trent for any layman to interpret Scripture.

The pope formally received and accepted the findings of his commission, and then he turned to his own formal declaration. Hunching over the sheets without lifting his eyes to his audience, he read without emotion. His discourse was general. He focused on the historic uneasiness between science and the Catholic faith over the years and lamented the "tragic mutual incomprehension" that had marked the relationship. Little was new or specific in his statement; the symbolism of the occasion sufficed. The pope did not mention the eccentricities of his predecessor, Urban VIII, nor did he directly criticize the behavior of the Inquisition. The lessons of the "Galileo affair," he said, remain valid and could be relevant in the future, especially in the area of biogenetics. For technology now made possible morally abhorrent human engineering.

The following morning, the Vatican newspaper, *L'Osservatore Romano,* carried the decision on its front page under the headline FAITH CAN NEVER CONFLICT WITH REASON. Inside, the text of Cardinal Poupard's statement was reprinted with the headline "Galileo Case Is Resolved."

Elsewhere in the world, the headlines were not so dignified. On the front page of *The New York Times,* the headline read: AFTER 350 YEARS, VATICAN SAYS GALILEO WAS RIGHT: IT MOVES. The lead in the *Los Angeles Times* read: "It's Official! The Earth Revolves Around the Sun, Even for the Vatican." Inevitably, the editorial cartoonists feasted. In Milan's national newspaper, *La Repubblica,* under the headline GALILEO, EXCUSE ME, the irrepressible and irreverent cartoonist Fortini depicted the pope opening his papal robes and exposing himself like some dirty old man, as he uttered Galileo's legendary line, *"Eppur si muove."*

Several months later, in April 1993, I went to see Cardinal Poupard. His office is in Trastevere, downstream from the Vatican, in a functional modern complex known as Palazzo San Calisto. His Eminence had invited me to see him in his private apartments on the top floor of the palace. My questions were to be submitted in advance, ostensibly for translation reasons. I conceded the point in return for permission to film the audience.

When the time came, I was ushered into an expansive suite of rooms that had the feel of Park Avenue, full of books from floor to ceiling, oriental rugs, fine paintings and sculpture that the cardinal had collected in his life and travels. From behind the desk of his study, he greeted me sternly, for I was ten minutes late, and I had submitted difficult questions. Why had it taken the church thirteen years to come to grips with the Galileo case? Was the pope's statement of the previous October 31 a formal apology? Was the church embarrassed by the worldwide derision of the pontiff's statement. When I had faxed the questions to the cardinal, the hotel concierge looked at me in astonishment, as if he expected me to be burned at Campo dei Fiori at dusk.

At my request, Cardinal Poupard was dressed in full regalia. Red piping trimmed the borders of his long black robe; red buttons festooned its front, and its waist was cinched with a red silk cummerbund. A heavy silver cross hung around his neck, and his red cap covered the back of his graying head. He cut an imposing figure. About him hung the air of authority.

It was not long before I realized that I was dealing with a politician as much as a priest. Once he arranged himself in his chair, he held up a copy of his own book on Galileo, making sure that the camera zoomed in on the title.

After this moment of ecclesiastical self-promotion, I began softly. Why had the church taken so long to resolve this issue? I asked. An "interdisciplinary" exercise such as theirs took time, he replied, as his translator, a nervous American nun named Sister Anne Clare, read his prepared answer from a printed page on her lap. Was the pontiff's statement of October 31, 1992, a formal apology? Not at all, the cardinal said with a wave of his hand. It was merely a "formal recognition" of error. I did not quite understand the difference but pressed on.

Could he imagine the church ever having to say anything further about the case? Why? he replied rhetorically. It is done. *Finito.* Why, then, did the official statements contain no specific criticism of Urban VIII's bizarre behavior or of the excesses of the inquisitors? Because his commission's study was not about personalities—extraordinary as both Urban VIII and Galileo were—but about events, he replied. Galileo's judges, not the pope himself, were to blame. I thought Urban VIII was one of his judges.

To listen to Cardinal Poupard was to conclude that the church had experienced no anguish whatever in the Galileo reconsideration. The conflict between science and faith was a myth, he said dismissively. Without missing a beat or appreciating the contradiction, he repeated again the standard church line about Galileo that I had heard often in three years of writing: Galileo had been condemned because he insisted on treating his Copernican theory as truth rather than hypothesis, and he could not prove it. This position deflected attention from a simple fact: The Copernican theory *was* true, and the church had used extreme and rigorous methods to crush that truth and protect its falsehood.

The cardinal was talking about the pope as a fancier of science. As a man with a great capacity for trust, John Paul had merely asked toward the end of the commission's work, "At what point are we?"

"I don't think we can take the matter any further," the cardinal had replied.

"Good," the pope said. "Let's get on with it."

But wasn't the church embarrassed at the coverage in the newspapers? *Au contraire.* The coverage was ample, precise, positive, and responsible. To prove it, the cardinal proudly unfolded magazines from France and from Spain with massive and well-illustrated spreads on the Galileo pronouncement, several of which contained pictures of himself. He gave me a copy of his own article on the Galileo resolution that had been printed in the Parisian newspaper *Le Figaro* and which began with a description of how the pope, "*avec une belle intrépidité,*" had instituted this reconsideration.

The cover story of the French monthly *Nostre Histoire* had carried a headline about Galileo as an effort to "purify" Catholic history. And so before I rose to leave his lovely apartment, I asked Cardinal Poupard, "Who is next?" Giordano Bruno?

He smiled indulgently. There are many fascinating personalities, he said, but the case of John Huss, the Bohemian reformer who railed against forged miracles and ecclesiastical greed in the Middle Ages and who burned at the stake in 1415, would be his next "intervention." But, said the cardinal wistfully, his real interest lay with Joan of Arc. She had been condemned by an archbishop and burned, before she was made a saint and became the patron of France.

Historical Questions

1. In your own words, restate Pope John Paul II's reasons for absolving Galileo of his guilt. Then imagine that you are Pope Urban and write a response to Pope John Paul II that justifies your treatment of Galileo, making reference to what you see as the three or four major points of John Paul II.

2. Look back at what you thought were the dominant and emergent perspectives on the role of science in Galileo's time (Langford, cultural question 1). Now look closely at the position of Pope John Paul II, as described in Reston's essay. In what ways has the church's perspective on the role of science changed since Pope Urban tried Galileo? Where might Cardinal Poupard agree with your assessment? Where might he disagree?

3. Langford's and Santillana's essays contain selections of the original transcripts of Galileo's trial. Reread these selections to develop a symptomatic

reading of Cardinal Poupard's interpretation of the trial transcript in which you look at his statements not only as a way to resolve tensions about Galileo, but as a way to resolve tensions between past and contemporary beliefs within organizations today. What are the cardinal's explicit reasons for rethinking Galileo's case? What are his implicit reasons? Why issue a statement about Galileo at all in 1992? Explore two or three explicit connections between the cardinal's statements and the original transcripts as part of your analysis.

Cultural Questions

1. Go to your library and read reports of the pope's October 31, 1992 announcement about Galileo from both a major national paper and from your hometown paper. Compare and contrast the headlines and the tone of the articles. Where in each paper is this story placed? What does this say about the newsworthiness of the Catholic church's admission of an error made over three hundred years ago? What do the similarities and differences in the two articles suggest to you about the spectrum of responses to change within the major institution of the Catholic church today?

2. How do the reports you read for cultural question 1 above differ from Reston's? Does the coverage express a position on the conflict between the church and Galileo? From the articles you read, outline two to three perspectives on the pope's statement and analyze the assumptions underlying them. What trends can you observe?

3. While you are reading the October 31, 1992 papers, look to see if there are any op-ed pieces that express opinions about the announcement. Write a five-hundred-word op-ed piece in which you discuss the pope's statement in light of what you now know about the Galileo affair. Take into account the various perspectives you have encountered.

∾ Fastwrite 7

In the following essay, Edward Cornish presents his best guesses about future developments in technology. He calls his possible future developments *Futuribles*, and when writing, imagines the early decades of the twenty-first century. Before you read his predictions, fastwrite for ten to fifteen minutes on some of your own predictions about the future of technology and on how these developments might change the way you live your life.

ₒₒₒₒₒₒ

EDWARD CORNISH

The Cyber Future (1996)

Edward Seymour Cornish (b.1927) is the founder and president
of the World Future Society, as well as the creator and editor of
The Futurist, a magazine devoted to understanding the future and
from which this article comes. Cornish has written *The Study of
the Future* (1977) and has edited numerous other publications
including *Resources Directory for America's Third Century* (1971),
Communications Tomorrow (1982), and *The Computerized Society*
(1985).

. . . **1. The social and cultural consequences of infotech will be
extremely important but hard to anticipate and often surprising.**   In
1946, only 8,000 homes (all in the United States) had television. By 1994,
some 886 million around the world had television.

And the hours spent watching television are also climbing: The average
American now watches TV four hours a day; the average European, two
hours.

So much time devoted to an activity that did not appear until the mid
twentieth century must be radically changing human life, if only because
it takes people away from other activities.

But it is surely doing much more than that: Some scholars believe the
transistor tape recorder brought about the overthrow of the Shah of Iran
because the tape recorders brought the speeches of the Ayatollah Khomeini
to the people of Iran. Broadcasts and computers also contributed to the
fall of the Soviet Empire. And the fax machine proved invaluable to the
rebels during the 1989 Tienanmen Square face-off in Beijing.

**2. Human activities—both personal and institutional—will be
globalized.**   Cheap, user-friendly telecommunications are dramatically
reducing distance as a barrier to people doing things together. People
thousands of miles apart are now finding ways to work together, buy
things from each other, and form groups for common purposes.

We are moving toward an era when individuals and organizations will
operate almost as if national borders and natural boundaries did not separate them. Japanese and Europeans shop electronically at L.L. Bean's store

in Freeport, Maine. Herdsmen in the remote Russian province of Tuva, bordering Mongolia, now advertise their unique "throat singing" rituals on the Internet.

3. A global culture will develop as infotech ties the world's people together.   The globalization of economic production means that a metal bolt made in Malaysia must precisely fit a nut made in Thailand and hold together parts made in South Africa and Chile. Travelers from Japan, Europe, and the Americas demand the same high standards in McDonald's restaurants whether they are in Paris, Budapest, Moscow, or Beijing.

To meet the demands of the international set, companies everywhere will be under pressure to produce the goods desired by the global traveler, who will be a walking billboard for global lifestyles. A few local variations may be acceptable as curiosities or souvenirs, but most workers will be pushed to make products acceptable to the global market. Locally produced goods will languish along with national customs and languages.

Human models for advertisements may be increasingly chosen for their "generic" appearance. The usual model will not clearly belong to any race or culture or perhaps even age or sex.

4. As the global culture grows, local cultures will decline. Hundreds of languages will disappear.   The world's people now speak several thousand languages, but within the next century, perhaps 90% will disappear. The count will be down to between 250 and 600. Each year now, the state of California loses one of its Native American languages.

Global computer networks and telecommunications systems are reinforcing the status of English as the dominant international language. Speakers of other languages will likely find themselves pushed to learn English if they are going to operate outside their own nations; eventually, many will find it easier to express themselves in English than in their native languages, and their children may grow up speaking English.

Ultimately, English may become the native language of most people around the world.

5. New sorts of culture and language will appear.   The growth of knowledge, stimulated in large part by infotech, is increasing the number of international technical and special-interest groups, which develop complex jargons and customs. Already, many words used in these subcultures are unintelligible to outsiders.

The speedup of social change is also creating more distinctive generational cultures. People born in the 1960s know different words and collectively behave differently from people born in the 1970s.

6. The rate of global change—technical, social, and cultural—will continue to accelerate, creating innumerable surprises and dangers.   In today's world, more change occurs in a decade than occurred in an entire century in times past. And the tempo of change promises to get faster because of the rapid deployment of infotech: Few people write formal letters anymore, preferring phone calls or spur-of-the-moment e-mail messages.

One consequence is that the social order becomes more subject to the butterfly effect, much discussed in chaos theory. Just as a butterfly flapping its wings in Europe might set off a chain of atmospheric events leading to a typhoon in the Pacific, a small event in today's highly networked world may be magnified into big events elsewhere. The growing integration of the world and the rising speed of communications increase the likelihood that small chance events will have major consequences in the future. For this reason, the world may experience more surprises—and have less time to decide how to deal with them.

7. Infotech will reduce the time people devote to local and national affairs simply because it will increase contacts with distant colleagues and friends. Working and chatting over the Internet with very distant colleagues and responding to very distant events, people can easily neglect their local friends and family members. Unless the trend is compensated for, families and neighborhood institutions will suffer.

8. Rural and resort areas may boom as infotech frees people to work at home rather than having to commute to a distant factory or office to work.   Free to live where they choose rather than where their jobs dictate, people will opt for areas with attractive natural and cultural features plus low taxes, little crime, and modest living costs.

9. Communities may be organized increasingly according to lifestyle and ethnicity—another indirect effect of people being less tied to a worksite outside the home.   In the United States, members of each demographic group generally prefer to live with others of their kind. Gay people, artistic people, Koreans, blacks, and other groups often cluster together, and this mutual attraction should grow as infotech permits more freedom from the worksite.

10. The infomedia will tend to desocialize people, making them more prone to antisocial and criminal behavior.   Television is absorbing increasing amounts of people's free time. So is the home computer. Both provide entertainment without any need to associate with other people.

Solitary entertainment deprives people of the social learning acquired during group entertainment. In the days before television and computers, face-to-face conversation was the primary means of entertainment, pursued around the dinner table at home and with the crowd at the local bar. This social entertainment trained people to deal with other people, to respect their interests, and to use them skillfully to meet one's own needs. The rise of electronic entertainment seems to have been accompanied by increasing rudeness, epitomized by drivers shooting each other in traffic incidents.

If electronic entertainment continues to gain, we may become a non-society—a poorly integrated mass of electronic hermits, unable to work well together because we no longer play together.

Institutions such as the family, community, church, and nation will face the challenge of seeking support from people whose loyalty is almost entirely to themselves. . . .

11. New infotech will not just deprive many workers of their jobs; it may leave them stranded in the cyber society.   As computers become faster, cheaper, and easier to use, many businesses find they do not need nearly so many workers as they have. Bank loan officers, insurance clerks, and middle managers fall victim to downsizing.

The results are often tragic, because many individuals find themselves unable to find other jobs offering comparable pay and benefits. Studies indicate that many displaced workers never again reestablish themselves successfully in the work force.

12. Permanent mass unemployment is a serious possibility for the near future. However, it will not arise because the world is running out of work that needs doing.   Some scholars worry that the cyber revolution means there simply will not be enough jobs for all the people who need to earn an income. Already, many countries are finding that a growing number of workers remain unemployed for years and don't know what to do about it.

But the world is NOT running out of work for people to do. There are debilitating diseases that lack health workers and scientific researchers, devastated environments that require remediation, and millions of children who need caretakers and tutors.

Developing programs that will successfully move the unemployed into doing the jobs that need doing is one of the great challenges of the future.

13. In the longer term, robots should be able to perform most necessary services under the guidance of computer networks.   A true age of leisure may be in sight before the end of the twenty-first century. As automated systems churn out goods and services, people could devote themselves entirely to leisure pursuits. They might live like wealthy aristocrats, pleasuring themselves with fine foods, wine, art, sports, and entertainment while letting robots perform the tasks that past generations assigned to slaves and servants.

However, unless human nature changes, some people will not be satisfied with simple pleasures and will seek to outdo their fellows by acquiring ever bigger houses or going on ever longer space voyages to acquire bragging rights. Will such status seeking have to be forbidden? Should nobody be allowed to have more than anyone else?

14. Jobs will become more specialized than ever.   Computer networks should make it easy to locate the exact sort of specialist or product that you want. In the past, poor communications often made it impractical or even impossible for people with highly specialized skills or knowledge to find enough customers to earn a living, but electronic databanks should solve that problem.

The result could be a golden age for highly specialized consultants. People may be able to earn a living by becoming the world's great expert on, say, the Dr. Doolittle books or headgear fashions in medieval Norway. Hiring such an expert for a quick consultation will be easy due to electronic credit systems, which make possible transactions that would have been enormously complicated and costly before the cyber age.

15. Skills and knowledge will become obsolete faster than ever. Employers look for workers with leading-edge skills, but the leading edge can soon become the laggard edge.

The half-life of an engineer's knowledge—as little as three years in some fields—will rapidly shrink. Constant retraining is essential to keep people from becoming increasingly less qualified for their jobs.

16. Infotech will take over far more jobs for which humans were once thought indispensable.   Infotech has made getting an airline seat so simple that members of the public have begun doing it for themselves rather than go through a travel agent or airline reservation clerk.

Often, infotech does not totally eliminate the need for humans but greatly reduces it. In translating documents from one language to another, a computer can provide a rough translation, which a human translator then corrects and polishes. Together, the computer-human team can translate as much text as two human translators without computers.

A Nebraska newspaper has begun using a software program that can write sports stories; once the computer gets a few facts, it can fill in the rest of the words to make a breathless report of a game.

17. The cyber society will put a high premium on entrepreneurship. A fast-changing society poses major dangers for people who have difficulty adjusting to new situations, but it is a wonderland for entrepreneurs— those imaginative and energetic self-starters who can recognize emerging needs and create ways to fill them.

In recent years, entrepreneurs have developed thousands of new occupations. A man in Montana discovered how to build trout streams for people who want to fish on their own property. Result: a new occupation— trout-stream builder. Another business developed when someone recognized that a lot of citizens want to complain to their legislators but don't have time to write a letter. That led to a professional letter-writing firm specializing in legislators.

These new businesses may sound penny-ante, but some of the biggest companies in the world today—Intel and Microsoft, for example—are based on products that could hardly have been imagined a few decades ago. . . .

18. The globalized media will create a world of gods and clods.   The rich and famous who appear in the media will be the new gods, created for our adulation by the media. The rest of us will be the unknown and uninteresting members of the audience. Once, people like us might have earned respect in our communities because people knew our accomplishments and appreciated our qualities. But in the future, we will be increasingly unknown to our neighbors, and this loss of recognition by people around us will probably not be made up by scattered cyber contacts.

As society globalizes, the frustration of people's need for recognition by others may cause them to lose their self-respect: They may come to feel that they count for nothing and their lives are meaningless. Such feelings can move people toward drug abuse, crime, and terrorism.

19. Many people may largely abandon the "real world" in the future, preferring to live in the fictitious worlds created by the entertainment industry.   In the past, highly imaginative people could create dream worlds to which they could retreat. In the future, little imagination will be required, because artists and technologists will shape ultra-realistic simulations of people, places, and events. This fictitious world will be so attractive that most people will want to spend their lives in it.

Already, motion pictures can give us ultra-real representations of everything from dinosaurs to space cities. Future virtual-reality systems will envelop participants with magnificent sensory experiences that almost completely replace those of the real world.

So, in the years ahead, we will live increasingly in fictions: We will turn on our virtual-reality systems and lie back, experiencing heavenly pleasures of sight and sound in a snug electronic nest. The real world will be almost totally blotted out from our experience.

20. Electronic gambling will probably become a major social problem in the years ahead.   In the past, gambling could be largely controlled by rigidly enforced local regulations. But in the future, people may be able to place bets easily and quickly on the Internet. The excitement of casino gambling, which once required a trip to a distant place like Las Vegas, will be easily available in people's homes.

With billions of gambling-susceptible people around the world, the global gaming industry will be able to offer colossal prizes. The day of billion-dollar jackpots is probably not far off. The giant sucking sound of the future may be money disappearing out of homes all over the world when a sweepstakes pot nears bursting.

21. The Internet will allow people easy access to stupendous quantities of information on innumerable subjects, allowing them to become far better informed than in the past.   Most of the information now on the Internet might be obtained free by writing or visiting the provider, but the Internet can make it far easier to obtain. Government agencies and businesses will likely put increasing amounts of information on the Internet because it is cheap to do so. Citizens can get information they want without bothering government workers.

However, most people may continue to make little use of Internet resources, because accessing these sources takes some effort. At present, only a minority of people make much use of libraries or of reference books.

22. Much information on the Internet will remain free or nearly so, but a growing amount of information will carry a charge.   Information providers may spend thousands or even millions of dollars collecting and synthesizing information, so charges will often be levied on people who use them if the information providers lack adequate revenues from advertisers or other sponsors.

23. People's attention may become the world's most precious resource.   With the firmament filled with broadcasts and the ground filled with optical fibers bringing in data, time-starved people will ignore most of the messages sent out by desperate advertisers, publicists, and others. To attract a quick glance from these people, advertisers pay fortunes to celebrities willing to associate their images with the advertisers' products.

24. Intellectual property rights will become a burning issue, perhaps even leading to war.   Copyright protection will be critical if motion picture producers, music composers, artists, and others are to be fairly rewarded for their effort. Even museums like the Louvre in Paris and the National Gallery in Washington, D.C., depend increasingly on payments from those who want to make copies of their paintings.

Unfortunately, copyrighted works are often pirated and sold for profit with nothing given to the creators. Reducing this piracy has already become a focus of international negotiations.

25. Movie fans in the future will have more power to alter films to meet their own specifications.   Suppose you want to see Marilyn Monroe star in *Casablanca* in place of Ingrid Bergman: Your wish may be granted. New technologies can manipulate images of Marilyn and recreate her voice speaking the lines.

Images of Monroe and other popular but dead stars may be used to create new libraries of films so fans can see their idols in new situations.

26. Cybersex systems may become widely available, perhaps early in the twenty-first century.   At least two approaches to cybersex are being discussed: One involves the development of attractive, lifelike robots able to function as lovers. Unlike human lovers, the robots would not be late for dates or throw one over for a younger lover. They could also be traded in for a newer, sexier model without legal proceedings or recriminations.

The second approach, sometimes referred to as teledildonics, is designed for lovers who are separated but connected electronically. Each lover dons a snugly fitting bodysuit containing tiny electronic units woven into its fabric. As the lovers move, the bodysuit conveys appropriate tactile sensations to both parties, so that they feel as if they are actually making love.

The enabling technologies for cybersex appear to be readily available, and prototypes have been created. (The Japanese have built a Marilyn Monroe robot.) Meanwhile, social mores have relaxed. If the AIDS plague continues, health authorities might propose a crash program to develop cybersex as a means of slowing the spread of the disease. Social-welfare advocates might also favor cybersex as a means of reducing illegitimacy, adultery, and sex crimes. Cybersex could become a major growth industry.

27. The new infomedia may make people increasingly egocentric and selfish. Since the infomedia cannot be controlled by any nation, religion, or community, individual consumers will dominate in shaping its content and character because they will choose what to view. To get their attention, content providers will compete in making the audience feel all-important.

Consumers will thus become increasingly narcissistic—infatuated with themselves rather than caring for things beyond themselves.

As television and other electronic entertainments absorb more and more time, people will feel ever less motivated to do things for anyone but themselves.

28. Cyberspace will contain huge "memorial gardens" for the dead. Already, the World Wide Web has a Virtual Memorial Garden where friends and family can display epitaphs and pictures of their loved ones.

In the past, most people departed this life with little or no notice being taken; only exceptional people merited obituaries except in small towns. Now, the most humble may have a home page bearing testimony to their achievements, however modest, and their personalities, however common. Dead pets will also have their home pages, along with defunct houses, cars, and other favored objects.

29. The easy anonymity possible in cyberspace will have surprising results, both good and bad. People can use computer networks to discuss their personal problems anonymously and to summon up information on sex, diseases, and other sensitive topics without anyone knowing. They can also experiment with a new persona, since no one knows who they really are. A man can pretend to be a woman, a child can pretend to be an adult. Thoughts and ideas can be offered for comment before they are advanced in real life.

But the freedom and anonymity of cyberspace also can lead to problems such as "flaming"—angry outbursts that would likely have been curbed in a less anonymous environment where people watch their language more carefully.

30. Privacy will be harder to maintain.   Your life may be an open book to anyone who takes an interest in your personal affairs, such as your lover, your employer, or your nosy neighbor. Already, women are hiring private detectives to check up on their boyfriends, and getting the information is becoming easier thanks to databanks, packed with information about people's personal finances, purchases, employment, medical problems, and more.

Your conversations may increasingly be recorded secretly on film and/ or audio by someone who might later use it against you. People you are talking with may use stress analyzers to determine whether you are telling the truth. To achieve minimum privacy, governments and private firms may feel forced to install specially equipped secure rooms where conversations cannot easily be bugged.

31. People may lose much of their ability to think rationally and make wise decisions.   Channel-surfing—flitting about among all the entertainments available on television at the moment one chooses to watch it—has become one of the most popular leisure time activities. The result is a stream of rapidly changing images, designed to hold the attention of the wandering eye.

The proliferation of information sources—more TV channels, specialized news services, and databanks—has overwhelmed people's ability to focus on particular issues and think logically about them.

So people find it easy to be seduced by superficialities: A handsome, well-built, smooth-talking actor living in a beautiful house attracts out support; the thoughtful political leader with the distinguished record of accomplishment but poor looks is quickly rejected.

32. Awesome possibilities for self-knowledge will open up. Knowing oneself is the true path to wisdom, according to some sages, and to know oneself, one needs to observe oneself in action. The videotape recording makes that possible: At long last, we can see ourselves as others see us.

By observing ourselves interacting with others, we have the possibility of growing in wisdom in a way that people in past ages could not experience. As the technology improves and prices come down, video will likely be used increasingly as a technique for achieving self-knowledge.

Using audiotapes to record one's thoughts and experiences may also prove useful. And both audio and videotapes could be subjected to computer analysis to reveal hidden aspects of our personalities; for instance, word counts might show that a person used the word "father" 400 times and said "mother" only once.

33. Interpersonal relationships will likely be increasingly unstable.
The rapid changes and heightened mobility encouraged by infotech will
tend to break up human groups, not only in the worksite but in the family
and community. Job shifts will separate colleagues and even family members. Whole communities may be disrupted by the outsourcing and emi-
gration of corporations to other nations.

However, it will be possible for people to maintain closer long-term
contact with chosen friends and relatives by means of e-mail, teleconfer-
encing, and other infotech.

So there is at least a possibility that infotech will do as much or more
to bring people together as it does to tear them apart.

**34. Infotech could make everyone reachable 24 hours a day
every-where on earth, but people won't let it happen.**   Individuals are
already developing high barriers to undesired interruptions. They pay for
unlisted telephone numbers or use "bozo filters" to screen out unwanted
e-mail messages. In the future, they will use software programs called intelligent agents to search for things they want to attend to—and reject the rest.

There may also be "personal secretary" systems that will answer tele-
phones and carefully put through calls from friends and colleagues while
warding off telemarketers.

**35. Infotech is encouraging a physically inactive lifestyle that endan-
gers people's health.**   The number of seriously overweight children and
adolescents in the United States has more than doubled over the past three
decades, the National Center for Health Statistics reported in 1995. About
11% of youths aged 6–17 are severely overweight. Back in the 1960s, the
rate was only 5%.

Research by William Dietz of Tufts University and others points the
finger at physical inactivity, induced largely by TV, video games, and PCs,
plus too much munching on high-calorie foods.

Public-health officials fear that today's overweight children will be
tomorrow's overweight adults, at risk for premature heart attacks, strokes,
and diabetes. If the obesity trend continues, college-age youths may start
needing heart transplants and bypass operations.

Health authorities will push research on anti-obesity drugs, which
already look promising, but no real solution for the obesity trend is yet
available. . . .

Conclusion

This compendium of changes likely to result from the cyber revolution
leads to two very broad generalizations. Both seem obvious but quite
important. One gives us reason to be very hopeful about the future; the
other must be a source of enormous concern.

First, we are building up unprecedented power to do whatever we want to do. Infotech is amplifying our ability to produce the material goods of life, to cure diseases, and to expand the human enterprise into the universe. We are becoming godlike in our capabilities.

Second, we do not know how to use our growing power wisely. Rather than growing wiser as our power has increased, we seem actually to be less able to agree on appropriate actions or to delay immediate gratification to achieve long-term goals. Worse, the new supertechnologies can be used in ways that do us tremendous harm.

Our difficulties in using our growing power wisely arise partly from the rapidity of technological growth: Our values developed over thousands of years, during which almost all humans lived as hunter-gatherers and as farmer-pastoralists. Our traditional sacred books were not composed for an industrial age, much less a cybernetic era.

And people around the world will be entering the twenty-first century with the values of cultures that historically have been kept separate—or largely so. Now values are in sharp conflict everywhere as people with very different beliefs and interests strive to dominate the human agenda.

In meeting these challenges, the new resources of the cyber era can be very helpful. The times call for a world future network—a global system that would allow people everywhere to share in sorting out the issues we confront as we struggle to manage the future. How well we respond to the challenges ahead will determine whether the great cybernetic machine will develop into a Moloch or a Messiah.

∽   Fastwrite 8

What was your emotional response to the future Cornish describes? Fastwrite about the one or two changes you liked and the one or two that seemed most threatening.

Historical Questions

1. Compare and contrast two or three assumptions that underlie Cornish's predictions with two or three assumptions on which Galileo rested his conclusions. What similarities and differences do these suggest about the ways in which the two different historical periods deal with change?

2. Describe two to three ways in which electronic networks could damage a long-standing social structure with which you are very familiar, such as the family, neighborhoods, religion, school, or work. Be careful to define and describe the social structure you are examining and to link your predictions to specific technological interventions. What are the social dangers inherent in the new electronic media? Then return to Pope Urban's reaction to Gali-

leo's theories about a heliocentric universe described by Langford and Santillana. With specific reference to the presentation of Pope Urban's position in either of the essays, discuss two ways in which your concerns are similar to his. Discuss two ways in which they are different. What does this comparison suggest to you about past and present reactions to technology?

3. Think about a job that you might realistically have in the future. Describe how that job is performed today. Then imagine that the potential you have glimpsed of electronic networks in Cornish's essay has been fully realized. You have a fast connection, a powerful personal computer, and all the software you need both at work and at home. You can send and receive all kinds of data, including video. You have access to both public and corporate databases. Write a short essay in which you describe how this capacity would affect the way you perform your job. Be as specific as you can.

Cultural Questions

1. Return to fastwrite 8 as well as to any of the historical analyses you have written on Cornish. Explore the various assumptions about change and new technologies that underlie your responses. Point out any contradictions in your responses and, as you did with Galileo, explore some of the larger beliefs, values, and practices that may support these contradictory positions.

2. Which of Cornish's predictions seem the most unlikely to you? Why? In your answer, identify the assumptions you are using to make your argument.

3. Consider which of Cornish's predictions seem the most assured to you. Why? In your answer, identify the assumptions you are using to make your argument.

∾   Fastwrite 9

Before you begin reading Rheingold, fastwrite a short statement in which you describe your current attitude toward the mass media (television, movies, magazines, books, music).

CRCACR

HOWARD E. RHEINGOLD

Will We Live Well and Prosper in the Age of Networks? (1993)

Howard E. Rheingold (b. 1947) is a network enthusiast who has published several books about the history and activities of the electronic world, including *Talking Tech: A Conversational Guide to Science and Technology* (1982), *Virtual Reality* (1991), and *The Virtual Community: Homesteading at the Electronic Frontier* (1993), from which this extract is taken. Rheingold is a long-standing member of WELL, a San Francisco-based network. You can visit his web pages at <http://www.well.com/user/hlr/howard.html>.

Virtual communities could help citizens revitalize democracy, or they could be luring us into an attractively packaged substitute for democratic discourse. A few true believers in electronic democracy have had their say. It's time to hear from the other side. We owe it to ourselves and future generations to look closely at what the enthusiasts fail to tell us, and to listen attentively to what the skeptics fear. . . .

Consider . . . a case history: Prodigy, the service that IBM and Sears spent a reported $1 billion to launch, is advertised on prime-time television as an information-age wonder for the whole family. For a flat monthly fee, Prodigy users can play games, make airplane reservations, send electronic mail to one another (although not to other networks), and discuss issues in public forums. In exchange for the low fees and the wide variety of services, users receive a ribbon of advertising matter at the bottom of their screens. . . .

The idea is that people will pay, and even subject themselves to advertising, in exchange for information presented on a screen that the human viewer can browse by means of a telephone touchpad, keyboard, or other control device. . . .

Prodigy is modeled on the old consumers-as-commodity model that works for mass-market magazines. You use the services and contents of the magazine or television network (or online service) to draw a large population of users, who give you detailed information about their demographics, and then you sell access to those users to advertisers. You tailor the content of the magazine or television program or online service to attract large numbers of consumers with the best demographics, you spend money on polls and focus groups to certify the demographics of your consumers, and then advertising agencies buy access to the attention of those consumers you've "captured." This is the economic arm of the broadcast paradigm, extended to cyberspace. With a reported one million users, and both parent companies in trouble, it is not at all clear whether Prodigy will reach the critical mass of users to repay the investment, but this notion of online subscribers as commodities isn't likely to go away. It's based on one of the most successful money-making schemes in history, the advertising industry.

As a model of a future in which CMC services come to be dominated by a few very large private enterprises, Prodigy previews two key, chilling aspects of online societies that are far from the innocent dreams of the utopians. First there was a wave of paranoia among Prodigy subscribers, much discussed on the Net, regarding the way Prodigy's software works: to use the service, you grant Prodigy's central computers access to a part of your desktop computer (the infamous STAGE.DAT file that shows up on Prodigy users' computer disks) whenever you connect with the service via modem. The idea that Prodigy might be capable of reading private information off your personal computer from a distance, even though there was no proof that Prodigy was actually doing any such thing, stemmed from Prodigy's use of a technology that could, in principle, be used for such a purpose. The prospect of giving up parts of our privacy in exchange for access to information is the foundation of a school of political criticism of communications technologies that I'll come back to.

More chilling is the fact that all public postings on Prodigy are censored; there are actually banks of people sitting in front of monitors somewhere, reading postings from Prodigy subscribers, erasing the ones with offensive content. This measure dealt effectively with the outbreak of racist and anti-Semitic invective. It also dealt effectively with free and open public discussions among Prodigy subscribers of Prodigy's own policies. Prodigy's users sign a contract that gives Prodigy the right to edit all public messages before they are posted, and at the same time the contract absolves Prodigy of responsibility for the content of the messages that are posted by declaring them to be in the public domain. Then Prodigy subscribers used Prodigy's free e-mail feature to create mailing lists to get around Prodigy censorship. Private e-mail is protected by the Electronic Communications Privacy Act of 1986, which requires a court order for any third party to read a private message. So Prodigy management changed the pricing for e-mail, cutting off free messages after thirty per month, surcharging twenty-five cents for each additional message.

Prodigy as a private publisher claims First Amendment protection from government interference, so Prodigy users can't go to court to claim their rights to free speech without stepping on Prodigy's rights. Publishers in the United States have a right to publish what they want to publish; with the exception of libel, the courts have no business restraining editors from using their judgment. If you don't like Prodigy, you can go else-where—as long as there is an elsewhere. The presence of competition is the key. The Prodigy situation might be a preview of what could happen if a small number of large companies manages to dominate a global tele-communications industry that is now a competitive market of small and medium-size businesses that manage to survive and thrive along with the giants.

As long as BBSs remain legal and telephone carriers don't start charging by the amount of data users send and receive (instead of the amount of time they use the telephone connection), there will be a grassroots alter-native to the giant services. But what if some big company comes along in the future and uses its deep pockets, economies of scale, and political power to squeeze out the WELLs and Big Sky Telegraphs and low-cost Internet access providers? Such tactics are not unknown in the history of the telecommunications industry. The telecommunications industry is a business, viewed primarily as an economic player. But telecommunications gives certain people access to means of influencing certain other people's thoughts and perceptions, and that access—who has it and who doesn't have it—is intimately connected with political power. The prospect of the technical capabilities of a near-ubiquitous high-bandwidth Net in the hands of a small number of commercial interests has dire political implications. Whoever gains the political edge on this technology will be able to use the technology to consolidate power.

There might be a fork in the road of technology-dependent civilization, somewhere in the mid- to late 1990s, forced by the technical capabilities of the Net. Two powerful and opposed images of the future characterize the way different observers foresee the future political effects of new com-munications technology. The utopian vision of the electronic agora, an "Athens without slaves" made possible by telecommunications and cheap computers and implemented through decentralized networks like Usenet and FidoNet, has been promoted by enthusiasts, including myself, over the past several years. I have been one of the cheerleaders for people like Dave Hughes and Mitch Kapor as they struggled to use CMC to give citizens some of the same media powers that the political big boys wield. And I admit that I still believe that this technology, if properly understood and defended by enough citizens, does have democratizing potential in the way that alphabets and printing presses had democratizing potential.

The critiques of the cheerleading for unproven technologies such as computer conferencing bear serious attention, and so do the warning signals from Prodigy, and the disturbing privacy issues that are raised by some of the same technologies that promise citizens so many benefits. What if these hopes for a quick technological fix of what is wrong with democracy constitute nothing more than another way to distract the attention of the suckers while the big boys divide up the power and the loot? Those who see electronic democracy advocates as naive or worse point to the way governments and private interests have used the alluring new media of past technological revolutions to turn democratic debate into talk shows and commercials. Why should this new medium be any less corruptible than previous media? Why should contemporary claims for CMC as a democratizing technology be taken any more seriously than the similar-sounding claims that were made for steam, electricity, and television?

Three different kinds of social criticisms of technology are relevant to claims of CMC as a means of enhancing democracy. One school of criticism emerges from the longer-term history of communications media, and focuses on the way electronic communications media already have pre-empted public discussions by turning more and more of the content of the media into advertisements for various commodities—a process these critics call commodification. Even the political process, according to this school of critics, has been turned into a commodity. The formal name for this criticism is "the commodification of the public sphere." The public sphere is what these social critics claim we used to have as citizens of a democracy, but have lost to the tide of commodization. The public sphere is also the focus of the hopes of online activists, who see CMC as a way of revitalizing the open and widespread discussions among citizens that feed the roots of democratic societies.

The second school of criticism focuses on the fact that high-bandwidth interactive networks could be used in conjunction with other technologies as a means of surveillance, control, and disinformation as well as a conduit for useful information. This direct assault on personal liberty is compounded by a more diffuse erosion of old social values due to the capabilities of new technologies; the most problematic example is the way traditional notions of privacy are challenged on several fronts by the case of collecting and disseminating detailed information about individuals via cyberspace technologies. When people use the convenience of electronic communication or transaction, we leave invisible digital trails; now that technologies for tracking those trails are maturing, there is cause to worry. The spreading use of computer matching to piece together the digital trails we all leave in cyberspace is one indication of privacy problems to come.

Along with all the person-to-person communications exchanged on the world's telecommunications networks are vast flows of other kinds of personal information—credit information, transaction processing, health information. Most people take it for granted that no one can search through all the electronic transactions that move through the world's networks in order to pin down an individual for marketing—or political—motives. Remember the "knowbots" that would act as personal servants, swimming in the info-tides, fishing for information to suit your interests? What if people could turn loose knowbots to collect all the information digitally linked to *you*? What if the Net and cheap, powerful computers give that power not only to governments and large corporations but to everyone?

Every time we travel or shop or communicate, citizens of the credit-card society contribute to streams of information that travel between point of purchase, remote credit bureaus, municipal and federal information systems, crime information databases, central transaction databases. And all these other forms of cyberspace interaction take place via the same packet-switched, high-bandwidth network technology—those packets can contain transactions as well as video clips and text files. When these streams of information begin to connect together, the unscrupulous or would-be tyrants can use the Net to catch citizens in a more ominous kind of net.

The same channels of communication that enable citizens around the world to communicate with one another also allow government and private interests to gather information about them. This school of criticism is known as Panoptic in reference to the perfect prison proposed in the eighteenth century by Jeremy Bentham—a theoretical model that happens to fit the real capabilities of today's technologies.

Another category of critical claim deserves mention, despite the rather bizarre and incredible imagery used by its most well known spokesmen—the hyper-realist school. These critics believe that information technologies have already changed what used to pass for reality into a slicked-up electronic simulation. Twenty years before the United States elected a Hollywood actor as president, the first hyper-realists pointed out how politics had become a movie, a spectacle that raised the old Roman tactic of bread and circuses to the level of mass hypnotism. We live in a hyper-reality that was carefully constructed to mimic the real world and extract money from the pockets of consumers: the forests around the Matterhorn might be dying, but the Disneyland version continues to rake in the dollars. The television programs, movie stars, and theme parks work together to create global industry devoted to maintaining a web of illusion that grows more lifelike as more people buy into it and as technologies grow more powerful.

Many other social scientists have intellectual suspicions of the hyper-realist critiques, because so many are abstract and theoretical, based on little or no direct knowledge of technology itself. Nevertheless, this perspective does capture something about the way the effects of communications technologies have changed our modes of thought. One good reason for paying attention to the claims of the hyper-realists is that the society they predicted decades ago bears a disturbingly closer resemblance to real life than do the forecasts of the rosier-visioned technological utopians. While McLuhan's image of the global village has taken on a certain irony in light of what has happened since his predictions of the 1960s, "the society of the spectacle"—another prediction from the 1960s, based on the advent of electronic media—offered a far less rosy and, as events have proved, more realistic portrayal of the way information technologies have changed social customs.

Historical Questions

1. Galileo's theories about a heliocentric solar system threatened the existing world view at his time. Rheingold argues that electronic technologies are rapidly reorganizing our world. How do you think Galileo would respond to a world in which any of us could publish our thoughts without seeking the approval of some central authority? How do you respond to the idea of this kind of world? Or if things turn out a differently, how would Galileo like a world in which our thoughts are monitored by a central authority? How would you respond to such a world? Compare and contrast your own responses and your imagined sense of Galileo's responses to these two different potential worlds. What values and beliefs about change, freedom, and control do you imagine you share with Galileo? On what values do you most differ?

2. Compare and contrast your reactions to emerging science to those of Pope Urban. How did Pope Urban see his role in relation to emerging science? What did he think he was supposed to be doing? Then, using the developments discussed by Rheingold and the possibilities predicted by Cornish, describe your relationship to emerging science. How do you think you are supposed to react to it? How are you currently reacting to it and how do you imagine you will react to it in the future? What is a key similarity and difference you see between your reactions and those of Pope Urban?

3. Pope Urban resisted Galileo's cosmology for a variety of reasons in an attempt to save or conserve the dominant existing values of the time. Rheingold suggests that electronic technologies will change our world, but he is not sure that those changes will be positive. No longer having a Pope Urban to shield us from change, what would you do to conserve the elements of our culture that you value which you feel the new technology might threaten? In other words, what part of the dominant perspective do you find worth preserving, and how can you shape the emerging perspective so that it does not destroy what you value?

Cultural Questions

1. Often an increase in our ability to access information and people comes at the price of reduced privacy; for example, consider the intrusiveness of the telephone. Write a statement in which you spell out the amount of privacy reduction you are willing to tolerate for access to the online world.

2. Rheingold presents three possible anti-utopias: commodification, the Panopticon, and hyper-realism. Discuss one or two examples from the media that support each of these possibilities. Which of them would you advocate for? Which would you argue against? With specific reference to his text, compare and contrast your assumptions with Rheingold's.

3. Choose one of Rheingold's anti-utopias and write an opinion piece arguing that it is already here.

4. With specific reference to both of their texts, compare and contrast two or three of Rheingold's assumptions about the emerging future with Cornish's. (You may want to review what you wrote for Cornish historical question 1.) For each of the points you discuss, describe where you stand and why.

S H E R R Y   T U R K L E

Natural and Artificial Intelligence (1995)

Sherry Turkle (b. 1948) is currently Professor of the Sociology of Science at the Massachusetts Institute of Technology and a licensed clinical psychologist. Named Woman of the Year in 1984 by *Ms.* magazine, her interest in both psychology and computers is evidenced by her books *Psychoanalytic Politics: Freud's French Revolution* (1978; 2nd edition 1992) and *The Second Self: Computers and the Human Spirit* (1984). This selection is from her 1995 book, *Life on the Screen: Identity in the Age of the Internet.*

The field of artificial intelligence has a complex identity. It is an engineering discipline. Its researchers make smart artifacts—industrial robots that assemble cars, expert systems that analyze the stock market, computer agents that sort electronic mail. It also has a theoretical side. AI researchers try to use ideas about computer intelligence to think more generally about human minds. But there is not a clear division between these two sides of AI. Even "engineering AI" is more than a purely technical discipline. Its objects as well as its theories offer themselves as a mirror for contemplating the nature of human identity. Only a few years ago, it was primarily those who inhabited the rather small world of AI researchers who gazed into this mirror. Today, that mirror is starting to turn toward the face of popular culture.

Marvin Minsky, one of AI's founders, once characterized it as "trying to get computers to do things that would be considered intelligent if done by people." Minsky's ironic definition has remained in circulation for nearly a quarter of a century because it captures an enduring tension in the human response to "thinking machines." When confronted by a machine that exhibits some aspect of intelligence, many people both concede the program's competency and insist that their own human intelligence is precisely the kind the computer does not have. Or they insist that the type of intelligence the computer has is not the kind that makes people special. This response to the computer presence is sometimes provoked by an actual program and sometimes by the mere suggestion of one. It occurs not only on the boundary between minds and machines, but on the boundary between ideas about minds and ideas about machines. We have seen that it is not a simple manifestation of resistance to the idea of machine intelligence. It is also a part of how people come to accept the idea. In this complex story, disavowal and appropriation are each tied up with the other.

This chapter traces a pattern of disavowal and appropriation in response to a major change in the philosophy of artificial intelligence research. From the late 1960s to the mid-1980s mainstream AI researchers conceived of computer intelligence as being made up of a complex set of rules programmed in advance. By the late 1980s, the field was more identified with theories of intelligence as emergent. . . . Now the story moves a step further. We will see how emergent AI has recently promoted the idea of a fundamental kinship between human and machine minds.

Information Processing in the Age of Calculation

In the tradition of romantic and magical thought, life is breathed into dead or inanimate matter by a person with special powers. In the early 1950s, there was a growing belief among a diverse group of engineers, mathematicians, and psychologists that this fantasy could be brought down to earth. During those early years, the atmosphere in AI laboratories was heady. Researchers were thinking about the ultimate nature of intelligence, and they were sure it could be captured in machines. The goal, mythic in proportion, was to use computers to generate a fragment of mind. AI researchers combined intellectual fervor with academic imperialism. They aspired to use computational principles to reshape the disciplines of philosophy, psychology, and linguistics.

These early AI researchers divided into two camps, each supporting one of the two primary competing models for how AI should be done. One group considered intelligence entirely formal and logical and pinned its hopes on giving computers detailed rules they could follow. The other envisioned machines whose underling mathematical structures would allow them to learn from experience. The proponents of the second vision imagined a system of independent agents within a computer from whose simultaneous interactions intelligence would emerge. From the perspective of these researchers, a rule was not something you gave to a computer but a pattern you inferred when you observed the machine's behavior.

In the mid-1960s, the early emergent models seemed as promising as the rule-driven, information processing approach. However, by the end of that decade, the emergent models had been largely swept aside. One problem was that the emergent models relied on the results of the simultaneous interactions of multiple independent agents, but the computers of the era could only handle one computation at a time. Additionally, simple emergent systems were shown to have significant theoretical limitations and more sophisticated mathematical techniques for hooking up programs that would operate in parallel were not well developed. Rule-based AI came to dominate the field. It dominated efforts to create general models of intelligence and it dominated the burgeoning subdiscipline of expert systems. Expert systems were literally built out of rules. They were created by debriefing human experts to determine the rules they follow and trying to embody these in a computer.

Douglas Hofstadter, author of *Gödel, Escher, Bach: The Eternal Golden Braid,* called the 1970s the era of AI's Boolean dream. George Boole, the nineteenth-century mathematician, had formalized a set of algebraic rules for the transformation of logical propositions. Apparently not one for understatement, he called these rules the Laws of Thought. Boole's laws were far from an all-inclusive model of mind. For one thing, they needed an external agent to operate them. However, computers were able to breathe life into Boole's equations by placing an operator in the form of a computer program right into the system. Once there, the operator and the laws could be seen as a functioning model, if not of the mind, at least of part of the mind.

Information processing AI gives active shape to formal propositions and creates an embodiment of intelligence as rules and reason. Boole would have felt an intellectual kinship with Allen Newell and Herbert Simon, pioneers of information processing AI, who saw brain and computer as different examples of a single species of information processing device.

In the late 1950s, in the spirit of "The Laws of Thought," Newell and Simon wrote a program called the General Problem Solver (GPS) that attempted to capture human reasoning and recode it as computational rules. Questions about GPS's "reasoning" could be answered by referring to whatever rules it had been given, even though the interaction of the rules might produce unpredictable results.

As the GPS became well known in academic circles, some psychologists began to wonder why it should not be possible to ask similar questions about how *people* solve logical problems. In the intellectual atmosphere of the time, this train of thought was countercultural. American academic psychology was dominated by behaviorism, which rigidly excluded the discussion of internal mental states. Orthodox behaviorists insisted that the study of mind be expressed in terms of stimulus and response. What lay between was a black box that could not be opened. So, for example, behaviorist psychologists would not refer to memory, only to the behavior of remembering.

By the end of the 1960s, however, behaviorism was in retreat. Some psychologists were willing to open the black box of the human mind and talk about the processes taking place inside it. The computer had an important metaphorical role to play in the demise of behaviorism. The very *existence* of the computer and the language surrounding it supported a way of thinking about mind that undermined behaviorism. Computer scientists had of necessity developed a vocabulary for talking about what was happening inside their machines, the internal states of their systems. And AI researchers freely used mentalistic language to refer to their programs—referring to their "thoughts," "intentions," and "goals." If the new machine minds had internal states, common sense suggested that people must have them too. The psychologist George Miller, who was at Harvard during the heyday of behaviorism, has described how psychologists began to feel uneasy about not being allowed to discuss human memory now that computers were said to have one:

> The engineers showed us how to build a machine that has memory, a machine that has purpose, a machine that plays chess, a machine that can detect signals in the presence of noise, and so on. If they can do that, then the kind of things they say about the machines, a psychologist should be permitted to say about a human being.[1]

---

[1]Cited in Jonathan Miller, *States of Mind* (New York: Pantheon, 1983), p. 23.

In this way, the computer presence legitimated the study of memory and inner states within psychology. "Suddenly," said Miller, "engineers were using the mentalistic terms that soft-hearted psychologists had wanted to use but had been told were unscientific." The machines supported an intellectual climate in which it was permissible to talk about aspects of the mind that had been banned by behaviorism.

That these ideas came from a hard-edged engineering discipline raised their status in a community of psychologists that still tended to see science as an objective arbiter of truth. Although information processing ideas challenged behaviorism, their mechanistic qualities also had a certain resonance with it. This shared sensibility eased the way for the appropriation of computational models by psychologists.

This new psychology for describing inner states in terms of logic and rules came to be known as cognitive science and the computer presence served as its sustaining myth. Cognitive science was in harmony with what I have called the modernist intellectual aesthetic of the culture of calculation. Mechanism and at least the fantasy of transparency was at its heart. . . .

During the 1970s to the mid-1980s, many people I interviewed responded to advances in information processing AI by agreeing with the premise that human minds are some kind of computer but then found ways to think of themselves as something more than that. Their sense of personal identity often became focused on whatever they defined as "not cognition" or "beyond information." People commonly referred to spontaneity, feelings, intentionality, and sensuality in describing what made them special. They conceded to the rule-based computer some power of reason and then turned their attention to the soul and spirit in the human machine.

For some, the appropriation and disavowal of computational images of mind took the form of a pendulum swing. In 1982, a thirty-two-year-old nurse said: "I'm programmed to fall for the same kind of man every time. I'm like a damned computer stuck in a loop. . . . I guess my cards are punched out the same way." But a few minutes later, she described her emotional life in terms of what the computer was not: "When people fall in love or their passions for their children, it's like a blinding emotion. Computers don't have anything to do with that." Others split the self. One student spoke of his "technology self" and his "feeling self," another of her "machine part" and her "animal part." When talking about family life, people might insist there was nothing machine-like about their emotions. When talking about business decisions, they thought they might be working like a computer program. Thus, for many people, competing views of the self existed simultaneously. There was no victory of one model over another; there was only ambivalence. . . .

Emergent AI

The renaissance of emergent AI took up a research tradition from the 1960s that was based on a simple emergent system known as the perceptron. A perceptron is a computer program made up of smaller programs called agents, each of which has a narrow set of rules it can follow and a small amount of data on which to base its decisions. All agents "vote" on a question posed to the perceptron, but the system weights their votes differently depending on the individual agent's past record of success. Those agents who guess right more often end up having more of a voice in subsequent decision-making. In this sense, the perceptron learns from its experiences. On a metaphorical level, the perceptron's intelligence is not programmed into it, but grows out of the agents' competing voices.

To get a sense of how this works, imagine trying to design a system for predicting rain. One would begin by accessing the opinions of, say, a thousand simple-minded meteorologists, analogous to the agents of the perceptron, each of whom has a different imperfect method of forecasting rain. Each meteorologist bases his or her judgment on a fragment of evidence that may or may not be related to predicting rain. One possibility would be simply to identify the meteorologist who has the best track record for rain prediction and always go with that meteorologist's vote. Another strategy would be to let the majority of the voting meteorologists decide. The perceptron refines this strategy by weighting each vote according to individual meteorologists' records.

In an information processing model, the concept "rain" would be explicitly represented in the system. In the perceptron, the prediction "it will rain" is born from interactions among agents, none of which has a formal concept of rain. Information processing begins with formal symbols. Perceptrons operate on a subsymbolic and subformal level. The analogy with the neurons in the brain is evident.

If you applied the information processing method to the rain- forecasting example you would have complete breakdown if your chosen meteorologist became incapacitated. But in the brain, damage seldom leads to complete breakdown. More often it produces a gradual degradation of performance. When things go wrong, the system still works, but just not as well as before. Information processing systems lost credibility as models of mind because they lacked this feature. The perceptron showed the gradual degradation of performance that characterizes the brain. Even when injured, with some disabled meteorologists on board, the perceptron still can produce weather forecasts.

This analogy with brain performance was decisive for connectionists, the group of emergent AI researchers who most seriously challenged the information processing approach in the mid-1980s.[2] The connectionists used programs known as learning algorithms that are intellectual cousins to the perceptron. They spoke of artificial neurons and neural nets and claimed that the best way to build intelligent systems was to simulate the natural processes of the brain as closely as possible.[3] A system modeled after the brain would not be guided by top-down procedures. It would make connections from the bottom up, as the brain's neurons are thought to do. So the system could learn by a large number of different connections. In this sense, the system would be unpredictable and nondeterministic. In a manner of speaking, when connectionists spoke of unpredictable and nondeterministic AI, they met the romantic reaction to artificial intelligence with their own romantic machines. . . .

In the mid-1980s, such connectionist images began to capture popular as well as professional attention. The idea that computers would not have to be taught all necessary knowledge in advance but could learn from experience was appealing at a time when it was increasingly clear that it was easier to teach a computer to play chess than to build a mudpie. AI researchers had succeeded in getting computers to play excellent chess but had stumbled on such feats as recognizing human faces. The connectionist models suggested another way to approach the problem. Instead of searching for the rules that would permit a computer to recognize faces, one should "train" a network of artificial neurons. The network could be shown a certain number of faces and be "rewarded" when it recognized one. The network would be woven through with a learning algorithm that could give feedback to the system, establishing the appropriate connections and weights to its elements. Unlike information processing AI, which looked to programs and specific locations for information storage, the connectionists did not see information as being stored anywhere in particular.

---

[2]Connectionism had its origin in work on neural nets as early as the 1940s. Warren McCulloch and Walter Pitts, "A Logical Calculus of the Ideas Immanent in Nervous Activity," *Bulletin of Mathematical Biophysics* 5 (1943): 115–33. There seems to be broad consensus that the term "connectionism" was first coined in 1982 by Jerome Feldman, a computer scientist at Berkeley.

[3]David Rumelhart. one of the most influential connectionist researchers, wrote: "Our strategy has thus become one of offering a general and abstract model of the computational architecture of brains, to develop algorithms and procedures well suited to this architecture, to simulate these procedures and architecture on a computer, and to explore them as hypotheses about the nature of the human information-processing system. We say that such models are *neurally inspired,* and we call computation on such a system, brain-style computation. Our goal in short is to replace the computer metaphor with the brain metaphor." David Rumelhart, "The Architecture of Mind: A Connectionist Approach," in *The Foundations of Cognitive Science,* ed. Michael I. Posner (Cambridge, Mass.: MIT Press. 1989), p. 134.

Rather, it was inherent everywhere. The system's information, like information in the brain, would be evoked rather than found.[4] . . .

The 1980s saw researchers from many different fields writing papers that emphasized both parallel processing and intelligence emerging from the interaction of computational objects. These papers came from engineers enthusiastic about building parallel machines, computer scientists eager to try new mathematical ideas for machine learning, and psychologists looking for computer models with a neurological resonance. As the decade progressed, cognitive psychology, neurobiology, and connectionism developed a sense of themselves as more than sister disciplines; these diverse areas of study were starting to think of themselves as branches of the same discipline, united by the study of emergent, parallel phenomena in the sciences of mind, separated only by the domains in which they looked for them. . . .

With the resurgence of emergent AI, the story of romantic reactions to the computer presence came full circle. In the popular culture, people had been trying to establish human uniqueness in contrast to computers while in the research community the proponents of emergent AI were linking computers to the world of humans through biological and social metaphors. Now both people and computers were said to be "nondeterministic," "spontaneous," and "nonprogrammed." The story of romantic reactions to the computer presence was no longer simply about people responding to their reflection in the mirror of the machine. Now computer designers were explicitly trying to mirror the brain. There had been a passage through the looking glass.

From the beginning, the language of emergent AI borrowed freely from the languages of biology and of parenting. Not only did it refer to associations of networked computational objects as neural nets, but it presented programs as though they were white mice that might or might not learn to run their mazes, or children who might or might not learn their lessons. This way of talking was picked up by the users of the new

---

[4]For example: "In most models, knowledge is stored as a static copy of a pattern. . . . In PDP [connectionist] models, though, this is not the case. In these models, the patterns themselves are not stored. Rather, what is stored is the *strengths* between units that allow these patterns to be recreated. . . . Learning must be a matter of finding the right connection strengths so that the right patterns of activation will be produced under the right circumstances. This is an extremely important property of this class of models, for it opens up the possibility that an information processing mechanism could learn, as a result of tuning its connections, to capture the interdependencies between activations that it is exposed to in the course of processing." David E. Rumelhart, James L. McClelland, and the PDP Research Group, *Parallel Distributed Processing: Explorations in the Microstructure of Cognition,* vol. 1 (Cambridge, Mass.: Bradford Books/MIT Press, 1986), pp. 31-32.

connectionist programs and by the media.[5] Dave, forty years old, a high school English teacher and baseball coach, uses small connectionist programs to help him figure out what team to field. When I talk to him about his work, he speaks about his programs with something akin to fatherly pride. "I love to watch my programs do their thing. They get better right in front of me. When you watch a little creature improve session by session, you think of it as a child even if it is a computer." While developers of information processing AI had been popularly depicted as knowledge engineers, hungry for rules, debriefing human experts so as to embody their methods in theorems and hardware, a computer scientist working in the new tradition of emergent AI was portrayed as a creator of life, "his young features rebelling, slipping into a grin not unlike that of a father watching his child's first performance on the violin," running his computer system overnight so that the agents within the machine would create intelligence by morning.[6]

In the romantic reaction to the computer presence during the late 1970s and early 1980s, it had become commonplace to paraphrase the famous remark of Lady Ada Lovelace, who in 1842 said, "The analytical engine has no pretensions whatever to originate anything. It can do whatever we know how to order it to perform." In other words, computers only do what you tell them to do, nothing more, nothing less, or more colloquially, "garbage in, garbage out." The Lovelace objection to a computer model of mind was essentially that people don't follow rules. People learn and grow. And they make new connections that "mysteriously" emerge. The Lovelace objection worked fairly well for criticizing information processing models of the mind. But emergent AI was characterized by explicitly "anti-Lovelace" representations of the computer. It implied a continuity between computers and people. Connectionism suggested that it was an experimental science and that there was mystery and unpredictably inside its machines. . . .

---

[5]This language was picked up by emergent AI's popularizers, as for example, in this description of how emergent AIs "learn" : "To train NETalk to read aloud. Sejnowski had given his machine a thousand word transcription of a child's conversation to practice on. The machine was reading the text over and over. experimenting with different ways of matching the written text to the sound of spoken word. If it got a syllable right, NETalk would remember that. If it was wrong, NETalk would adjust the connections between its artificial neurons, trying new combinations to make a better fit. . . . NETalk rambles on. talking nonsense. Its voice is still incoherent, but now the rhythm is somewhat familiar: short and long bursts of vowels packed inside consonants. It's not English. but it sounds something like it, a crude version of the nonsense poem "The Jabberwocky." Sejnowski stops the tape. NETalk was a good student. Learning more and more with each pass through the training text. the voice evolved from a wailing banshee to a mechanical Lewis Carroll." William F. Allman. *Apprentices of Wonder: Inside the Neural Network Revolution* (New York: Bantam. 1989) p. 2.

[6]Allman, *Apprentices of Wonder*, p. 1.

The movement from information processing to emergent AI marks a critical change in how AI approaches its central scientific problem. You can't get to connectionism by making incremental improvements to information processing systems. It requires a fundamental change in approach. In the history of science, such changes of approach stir up strong emotion.[7] In the 1980s, the confrontation in the research community between emergent and information processing AI was tense and highly charged. While Douglas Hofstadter tried to capture the spirit of emergent AI in the phrase "waking up from the Boolean dream," the champions of connectionism had found that dream to be more like a nightmare. To them it seemed obvious that since human intelligence was more than a set of rules, the computers that modeled it should not be about rules either. Like nineteenth-century Romantics, connectionists sought to liberate themselves from a rationalism they experienced as constraining and wrong-headed.

In the mid- to late 1980s, the cultural appeal of connectionism was in part that it could describe computers in much the same way that personal computer owners were being encouraged to see them: as opaque systems in which emergent processes occur. There was a certain irony here. A quarter of a century before, the presence of the computer had challenged the behaviorist insistence on the mind as black box, Now, in some ways, emergent AI was closing the box that information processing had opened.

Information processing AI had opened the black box of the mind and filled it with rules. Connectionism replaced the idea that intelligence was based in logical understanding with a new emphasis on experience as the bedrock for learning. It postulated the emergence of intelligence from "fuzzy" processes, so opening up the box did not reveal a crisply defined mechanism that a critic could isolate and ridicule.[8] Information processing had provided an excuse for experimental psychology to return to the consideration of inner process. Now, emergent models invited philosophers, humanists, and a wider range of psychologists to compare machines to humans.

---

[7]Thomas Kuhn, who wrote the classic statement of how paradigm shifts occur within scientific communities, has cited Max Planck's view that a new scientific truth becomes dominant not because it wins converts but because the proponents of the older system gradually die off. Planck remarked that "a new scientific truth does not triumph by convincing its opponents and making them see the light, but rather because its opponents eventually die, and a new generation grows up that is familiar with it." Cited in Thomas Kuhn, *The Structure of Scientific Revolutions,* 2nd rev. ed. (Chicago: The University of Chicago Press, 1972 [1962]), p. 151.

[8]In fact, Searle did try to subject neural net models to a similar treatment in a January 1990 interchange with neurophilosophers Paul and Patricla Churchland. The tactic worked to much less effect. See John R Searle, "Is the Brain's Mind a Computer Program?" *Scientific American,* January 1990: 26-31; and Paul M. Churchland and Patricia Smith Churchland, "Could a Machine Think?" *Scientific American,* January 1990: 32–37.

In the 1980s, connectionism became part of a complex web of intellectual alliances. Its way of talking about opacity made it resonant with the aesthetic of depthlessness that Fredric Jameson had classified as postmodern. Its commitment to neurological metaphors created a link to brain scientists who tried to visualize the mind through sophisticated computer imaging.[9] Its assertion that mind could not be represented as rules made it interesting to humanists and post-positivist philosophers.

Connectionism began to present the computer as though it were an evolving biological organism. The neurons and pathways of connectionism were designed on the template of biology. Connectionism opened the way for new ideas of nature as a computer and of the computer as part of nature. And it thus suggested that traditional distinctions between the natural and artifical, the real and simulated, might dissolve.

Fastwrite 10 ∾

After reading Turkle's piece do a quick fastwrite in which you describe several routine tasks you would like to turn over to an intelligent device and several intellectual tasks you would prefer to do for yourself.

Historical Questions

1. Turkle describes several psychological models for the working of the brain, including behaviorism, which describes the mind as taught by experience, and connectionism, which claims that the mind can learn to respond in new ways. Which of her models might have been most familiar to Galileo? Which might have been most unfamiliar? What does your analysis suggest about the possible continuities and changes that have developed over the last three centuries?

2. Develop a symptomatic reading of your and Turkle's reaction to artificial intelligence by comparing and contrasting Pope Urban's reaction to emerg-

---

[9]Neurobiologists and connectionists could thus begin to share insights about the part that associative networks of neurons play in thinking. In this way, what seemed in some respects to be a black box theory was in others a decidedly nonbehaviorist attempt to unlock the biggest black box of all, the human brain. For a discussion of brain imaging that demonstrates these connectionist affiliations, see Marcus E. Raichle, "Visualizing the Mind," *Scientific American,* April 1994: 58-64. Raichle characterizes brain imaging—including techniques such as positron-emission tomography (PET) and magnetic resonance imaging (MRI)—as seeking to achieve the mapping of thought as it emerges from the activity of networks of neurons (p. 58). In other words, brain imaging spatializes thought and emergent processes in a way that speaks directly to the connectionist hypothesis that thought is accomplished through network associations in a highly parallel system. The author describes "a network of brain areas as a group of individuals in the midst of a conference call," who needed to know "who was speaking" and "who was in charge" in order to organize their conversation (p. 64).

ing science with yours and Turkle's. In Rheingold historical question 2, you described how you thought Pope Urban saw his role regarding emerging science. Describe what his reaction might have been to the idea of artificial intelligence. What might his role have demanded of him? How would he have accomplished it? Describe Turkle's literal reaction to AI and describe your own (these reactions may or may not have significant points of overlap). Then use the comparison with Pope Urban to explore two to three of the larger, unstated assumptions underlying your and Turkle's reactions.

3. Turkle describes how our thinking about computers has influenced our thinking about thinking, and Cornish has stimulated you to imagine the future. Using the contributions of these two writers, describe a future in which we have thinking machines (you can decide which of Turkle's psychological models these machines will employ). Would these machines be conservative (like Pope Urban), conflicted adventurers (like Galileo), or something else entirely? Would they value some of our human contributions? Would they find aspects of us threatening? In other words, what would the dominant perspective of thinking machines be in the future you are describing?

Cultural Questions

1. Write a short review of Turkle's essay in which you argue that she is right about the possibility that machines can replicate human intelligence, that she is wrong, or that it is impossible to know. Draw on what you know about the new technologies and their possible futures from your reading of Cornish and Rheingold.

2. If machines can be built that imitate human thinking, perhaps machines can be built that think better than humans (in the way that telescopes see further than we do). What are the implications of such tools? What would your attitude toward these thinking devices be? (You may want to connect your response here to historical question 3 just above.)

3. Are you curious about just where computers have replaced people? Go to the library and see how many such substitutions you can discover. To narrow your search, you might focus on a single area such as the auto industry or the telephone industry.

∾   Assignment Sequence 1: How Will Technology Affect a Group to Which You Belong?

In this chapter, we have investigated revolutionary ideas and the response they have generated in the culture around them. We examined Galileo's new ideas and the church's response to them. We looked at the rise of computer networks and at new computer developments. We thought hard about the future, and about the ways in which cultural authorities from popes to corporations to consumers react to change.

As a member of our contemporary culture, you belong to a variety of groups: a college, an ethnic background, a neighborhood, and a gender group. You may belong to a church, a sorority, a club, or an athletic team. Each of these groups has expectations of you and you of it. Like Pope Urban, each is always trying to conserve something of value from the past in the face of change.

Essay Question

Develop a position about the possible interactions between some of the new ideas arising from electronic technologies and one established group to which you belong. Use the events from the past you have studied, as well as the various materials you have worked on in relation to recent events, to make your predictions.

Review Questions

A list of suggested questions to review before beginning this essay follows. This list is meant only to suggest review options. You may focus on only a subset of the questions, decide that other questions should be added, or construct your own sequence of questions. We encourage you to choose what you believe is the most appropriate review strategy.

1. Jerome J. Langford, Historical Question 1 (page 485)
2. Fastwrite 4 (page 485)
3. Giorgio de Santillana, Historical Question 2 (page 490)
4. Fastwrite 6 (page 491)
5. Edward Cornish, Cultural Question 1 (page 507)
6. Edward Cornish, Cultural Question 2 (page 507)
7. James Reston, Jr., Historical Question 3 (page 494)

Questions for Further Reflection

1. Now you are ready to write a draft of your essay. New ideas often present a new kind of evidence in support of themselves; they often establish a new kind of authority; and they challenge the culture to find a way to integrate or reject them. Consider the following:

   a. Describe the established group to which you belong and on which you are going to focus this question. Describe how it operates, how it creates membership, how the members interact, how they trust and obey.

    b. How might the new technologies affect the culture of your group? What sorts of changes in behavior can you predict?

    c. How might your group react to the sorts of changes that new technologies will bring? Consider both positive and negative reactions.

2. As you revise your draft, look continually for parallels and points of difference between developments in the group you are writing about and Galileo's situation with the church. Consider the conflicts created in both a group and an individual when confronted with change.

3. You might want to take a look at some of the selections in Further Research.

ॐ   Assignment Sequence 2: How Will Technology Affect the Work You Plan to Do?

Throughout the second half of this chapter, you have read various predictions about future developments in technology. The authors have also offered a number of assessments of these developments. In addition, you have been asked to make a number of your own predictions about technological developments and to explore their implications for a variety of contexts, but especially the workplace, and in particular, a workplace in which you might imagine yourself working someday, or in which you are currently working now.

Essay Question:

Imagine that you have been asked to prepare a report for your boss on the workplace of the future. You will need to do some research on one particular industry; using what you discover and what you have learned about how technology is changing the workplace, write a report that describes the way this job will be performed fifteen years from now. Consider such areas as personnel, tasks, tools, and oversight. Support your predictions with examples from the present.

Review Questions

A list of suggested questions to review before beginning this essay follows. This list is meant only to suggest review options. You may focus on only a subset of the questions, decide that other questions should be added, or construct your own sequence of questions. We encourage you to choose what you believe is the most appropriate review strategy.

1. Sherry Turkle, Cultural Question 3 (page 525)
2. Edward Cornish, Historical Question 3 (page 507)
3. Howard E. Rheingold, Cultural Question 1 (page 514)

4. Fastwrite 10 (page 524)

5. Sherry Turkle, Historical Question 3 (page 525)

Questions for Further Reflection

1. Now you are ready to write a draft of your essay. Remember that you are writing this job description of the future for a corporate boss, so adapt your argument to your audience. Consider the following:

   a. What is the current job like? What does the worker do? What tools are used? What education or training is necessary?

   b. How will the new technologies affect the nature of the work? What sorts of changes in behavior can you predict?

   c. What should this boss do to prepare the company for change? Where will these new workers come from?

2. As you revise your draft, look for opportunities to historicize the changes you are discussing. Remember that your capacity to understand the present can be increased by understanding its similarities and differences from the past.

3. You might want to take a look at some of the selections in Further Research.

For Further Research

Written Texts

Brecht, Bertoldt. *Galileo*. New York: Grove P, 1966.

Bronowski, J., and Bruce Mazlish. *The Western Intellectual Tradition*. New York: Harper, 1960.

Bush, Vannevar. "As We May Think." *The Atlantic Monthly* (July 1945): 101–08.

Gibson, William. *Neuromancer*. New York: Ace, 1984.

Negroponte, Nicholas. *Being digital*. New York: Knopf, 1995.

Roszak, Theodore. *The Cult of Information: A Neo-Luddite Treatise on High-Tech, Artificial Intelligence, and the True Art of Thinking*. 2nd ed. Los Angeles: U of California P, 1994.

Stoll, Clifford. *Silicon Snake Oil*. New York: Doubleday, 1995.

Toffler, Alvin. *Future Shock*. New York: Random House, 1970.

Vallee, Jacques. *The Network Revolution: Confessions of a Computer Scientist*. Berkeley: And/Or P, 1982.

Visual Texts

"Bigger, Better, Faster," program 4. *A Science Odyssey: Tracing the Technological Revolution in the 20th Century*." Narr. Charles Osgood. PBS, WGBH, 1998.

Addresses how technological development has brought significant change to the twentieth century. Information and ordering available from <http.//www.pbs.org/science>.

Life on the Internet. Written and narr. Robert Duncan. Dir. Andrew Cochran. PBS, 1996. Two thirteen-part series featuring such topics as Cyberstudents, Internauts, and Digital Doctors. Information and ordering available from <http.//www.pbs.org/technology>.

"Triumph of the Nerds." narr. Robert X. Cringely. PBS, 1997. Features interviews with Steve Jobs (cofounder, Apple Computers), Steve Wozniak (cofounder, Apple Computers), Bill Gates (cofounder, Microsoft), Steve Ballmer (vice president, Microsoft), and others. Information and ordering available from <http://www.pbs.org/technology>.

PROGRESS OR DESTRUCTION? DEVELOPING THE ENVIRONMENT

Sushil K. Oswal

In these melancholy regions [the deeply forested regions of America], Nature remains concealed under her old garments and never exhibits herself in fresh attire; being neither cherished nor cultivated by man, she never opens her fruitful and beneficent womb.
—COMTE DE BUFFON, 1749

Earth's natural plenty no longer sufficed.
Man tore open the Earth, and rummaged in her bowels.
Precious ores the Creator had concealed
As close to hell as possible
Were dug up . . .

—TED HUGHES, 1997

[W]e are like goldfish who have been living in an aquarium for as long as we can remember; and being clever goldfish, we have discovered how to manipulate the controls . . . Only once we realize we're partly running the aquarium, it scares some of us. What if we make a mistake, and wreck the aquarium entirely? We couldn't live outside it.

—NOEL PERRIN, 1980

[A]t present levels of energy use, every child born in the USA has 72 times the impact on the environment of a baby in India or 200 times that of the hunter/gatherer child.
—SIR RICHARD SOUTHWOOD, 1992

The destruction of our planet is not based on some mythical law of nature but on a conflict, a very human conflict, arising from the domination of some people over other people. But what men and women have done, they can undo or do again differently.
—THIJS DE LA COURT, 1990

530

∾

Introduction: Analyzing our Relationship to the Land

∾ **Fastwrite 1**

Read the quotations at the beginning of this chapter and describe the feelings and thoughts about "earth," "nature," "land," and "America" that these writers arouse in your mind. Whose views come closest to your own on these topics? What values, assumptions, and needs do you share with these authors?

You can't turn on the TV or the radio without coming across a discussion of the environmental problems we confront today: the Chernobyl reactor meltdown taking many lives and injuring thousands of others; the Valdez tanker spilling millions of gallons of oil on the erstwhile scenic Alaskan and Canadian shores and killing uncountable fish and wild life; and the Union Carbide chemical plant in Bhopal blowing up, killing more than six thousand people and disabling another twenty thousand. The list of disasters becomes literally endless if we look around us even with a casual glance—rising mountains of garbage that we call *trash-sites*, thousands of miles of decaying railroad tracks going nowhere and transporting no one, thousands of boarded up apartments and houses awaiting economic regeneration in our inner cities, or the hundreds of vacant shops even in our otherwise well-occupied suburban malls. The dimension of these man-made disasters cannot be measured even in a technologically advanced nation like ours.

We live in an industrial society where a majority of us depends on corporations for employment, consumer goods, services, and even the air we breathe. How should industry respond to this growing environmental crisis? The experts divide their responses into two rough categories—"do nothing" or "do much." Whereas the latter approach adopted by a small minority is in line with the policy of "do well by doing good," the former negative approach of "do nothing" often ignores environmental issues in policy formulation and general decision making. As the public demand for action grows, businesses with the "do nothing" approach react to public criticism with such face-saving tactics as placing the blame on someone else, suppressing information that hurts the company's position, pointing out the economic and social cost of compliance, retorting with a public relations campaign, and employing delay tactics for dealing with the environmental problems to which they are contributing.

Most of us have become all too familiar with such "do nothing" strategies and often feel helpless while our environmental problems continue to mount. At the same time, a cursory review of the international business sections of our own national press suggests that ecologically sound methods of production are gaining ground and may indeed be made compatible with business growth and competition. Many U.S. competitors, particularly in Japan and Europe, have restructured their business policies and decision-making processes and have redefined business strategies more broadly to include aspects of the physical and social environment.

This chapter takes the position that the root cause of our environmental problems is within our culture. Certain economic and cultural values that are dominant in our society and that stand behind our very fundamental motivations guide our day-to-day decisions about the uses and abuses of our land, our natural resources, and our living environment. Beginning with this premise, this chapter moves back into the history of the United States to help understand the causes of our present environmental predicament and to explore the economic and cultural values that have developed our current economic system. It further asks what type of revisioning of these values could develop a new economic system and a new society—one based on the core U.S. democratic values of coexistence, pluralism, and respect for the individual. This new society would serve us without destroying our environment, the environment that is crucial for our very survival.

∾ Fastwrite 2

Review your writing from fastwrite 1. Then, for ten minutes, using one or two specific examples, discuss how you think about your relationship with the earth. How do you perceive yourself when relating to the earth? Do you feel like a stranger or a friend when you focus your thoughts on the earth? Do you feel attached to, estranged, or alienated from the earth? Why do you feel this way? What personal, sociocultural, geographical, historical, or other factors could you hold responsible for evoking these emotions?

Reread what you have written. Then, for another ten minutes, expand on the values that govern your personal relationship with the earth. Familiarize your reader with the assumptions you make, both consciously and not so consciously, about the earth and your relationship to it. You might briefly relate a story about the land that you heard as a child, discuss something on this topic that you have read in the past, or quote from the lyrics of a song that expresses or substantiates your views on the earth and its environment.

∾ Fastwrite 3

Living in the second half of the twentieth century, all of us are familiar with brandnames, visual representations of the products these brandnames stand for, and images of the people who consume them. Equally familiar are the words—*America, land, development, environment, earth, global, nature, progress, science, technology,* and so on—that stream in and out of our ears, sometimes registered consciously by our mind and at other times absorbed by our subconscious, unchecked and unexamined. What effect do these product images and these concepts have on the way we live, shop, and consume? How do these messages shape the way we think about ourselves, about our earth and our relation to it?

Spend ten minutes jotting down your thoughts on the connections you can trace between the messages of the media and your view of the land and your relationship to it. What sort of images do abstract words like *nature* or *progress* evoke when you pause over them? How does the media affect your relationship with the earth and its environment? Go back to the first two fastwrites and see whether you borrowed, consciously or unconsciously, particular metaphors from the media to describe your relationship with the land.

ANNETTE KOLODNY

Surveying the Virgin Land: The Documents of Exploration and Colonization, 1500–1740 (1975)

Annette Kolodny (b. 1941), a literary critic and feminist, is a linguistic consultant to the RAND Corporation, a government think tank. She is currently a professor of cultural and literary studies at the University of Arizona. Her books include *Women: Fantasies of the American Frontiers, 1630–1860* (1983) and *Dancing through the Minefield: Theory, Method, and Politics in Feminist Literary Criticism* (1983). The essay below has been selected from her book *The Lay of the Land: Metaphor as Experience and History in American Life and Letters* (1975).

On the second of July, 1584, two English captains, Philip Amadas and Arthur Barlowe, entered the coastal waters off what is now North Carolina and enjoyed "so sweet and so strong a smell as if we had been in the midst of some delicate garden abounding with all kinds of odoriferous flowers"; from this they determined "that the land could not be far distant." Some days later, landing on a beach "very sandy and low toward the water's side, but . . . full of grapes," they took possession of the land "in the right of the Queen's most excellent majesty" and, "according to her majesty's grant and letters patent," turned it over to the use of "Walter Raleigh, Knight, at whose charge and direction the said voyage was set forth." These ceremonies completed, the two captains proceeded to explore the newly discovered territory and, in their later letter to Raleigh, declared it to be a realm of "wonderful plenty," its rich soil supporting an abundance of game and growing crops "plentiful, sweet, fruitful and wholesome," with "divers other wholesome and medicinable herbs and trees." When the Indians on Roanoke Island greeted the weary explorers "with all love and kindness and with as much bounty (after their manner) as they could possibly devise," the good captains declared them to be "such as live after the manner of the golden age," and left them, after a brief stay, convinced that "a more kind and loving people there cannot be found in the world."[1]

Less than two years later, Master Ralph Lane, the first governor of Raleigh's colonial enterprise in Virginia, averred that his own personal experience in the new colony proved it to have "the goodliest soil under the cope of heaven," with a "climate so wholesome, that we had not one sick since we touched the land here." "So abounding with sweet trees," "so many sorts of apothecary drugs, such several kinds of flax," wheat, corn, and sugar cane, was it, in fact, that he "dar[d] assure [himself], being inhabited with English, no realm in Christendom were comparable to it." "Besides that, it is the goodliest and most pleasing territory of the world; for the continent is of a huge and unknown greatness."[2] Through documents like these, published and circulated widely, England first came to know America. Typical of the "big sell" approach were the enormous Hakluyt collections, comprised of accounts of voyages to the New World—some planned, some already executed, some wholly imaginary, and some a confusing combination of the three; but all cohered to justify John Ribault's assertion that the New World "was the fairest, frutefullest, and pleasauntest of all the worlde, aboundinge" in everything needful and desired by man. Quoting from Ribault in his own 1584 "Discourse of Western Planting," the elder Hakluyt delighted in repeating descriptions of "a place wonderfull fertile and of strong scituation, the grounde fatt, so that it is like that it woulde bringe forthe wheate and all other corne twise a yere"[3] because they implied that here, at last, men might prosper with only minimum effort—an implication designed to spur the

[1] [M. Arthur Barlowe], "The First Voyage Made To The Coasts Of America," in *Explorations of Carolina*, pp. 13-20.

[2] Ralph Lane, "An Extract Of Master Ralph Lane's Letter To M. Richard Hakluyt, Esquire, And Another Gentleman Of The Middle Temple, From Virginia," in *Explorations of Carolina*, p. 33.

[3] Richard Hakluyt, "Discourse of Western Planting," in *Hakluyt Correspondence*, 77:222-23.

kinds of ventures Hakluyt was himself investing in. By the end of the century, private individuals and joint stock companies alike were busy printing, for an avid reading public, the adventures of those who, like Columbus, declared the New World "a land to be desired, and, seen, it is never to be left."[4] Unintentionally, perhaps, their language also reinforced a particular mode of English response, articulated most explicitly by Raleigh himself in 1595 when he described Guiana as a "countrey that hath yet her maydenhead, never sackt, turned, nor wrought."[5] It was an invitation utilized by Robert Johnson in his "Nova Britannia" (1609), when he described not only Virginia's "Valleyes and plaines streaming with sweete Springs, like veynes in a naturall bodie," but also that territory's "hills and mountaines making a sensible proffer of hidden treasure, neuer yet searched"; and again by John Smith, in 1616, when he praised even the rough New England seacoast as a kind of virginal garden, her treasures hauing yet neuer beene opened, nor her originalls wasted, consumed, nor abused.[6] Later documents suggest that these intentionally suggestive invitations had their effect.

If the new American "*Paradise* with all her Virgin Beauties" was, in fact, supposed to provide material ease "from the *spontaneous* Wealth, which overruns the Country," and, by implication, an escape from human labor and grinding poverty, then, declared Thomas Morton in 1632, New England had suffered rude neglect on the part of colonists who had left her

> Like a faire virgin, longing to be sped,
> And meete her lover in a Nuptiall bed.[7]

His "New English Canaan" countered the harsher reports of a cold, barren, and inhospitable New England coast by insisting that any lack of abundance

---

[4] Christopher Columbus, *Select Documents Illustrating the Four Voyages of Columbus*, trans. and ed. Cecil Jane (London: Hakluyt Society, 1930), 1:12. The Spanish and the English are on facing pages.

[5] Quoted from Walter Raleigh's "Discovery of Guiana" (1595), in Howard Mumford Jones, *O Strange New World*, p. 48; Jones's source is Richard Hakluyt, *Principal Navigations* (London, 1598), 10:430. So confused were Europe's ideas of the New World at this time that remarks about any area vaguely in the vicinity of what is now North, South, or Central America were accepted as characteristic of the whole. Jones points out that "by 1607 the New World had stretched to an endless and confusing coastline running from Greenland and Baffin Bay through Gargantuan twistings and turnings to the Strait of Magelland and Tierra del Fuego" (p. 61).

[6] Robert Johnson, "Nova Britannia," p. 11, in *Force's Tracts*, vol. 1; John Smith, "A Description of New England," p. 9, in ibid., vol. 2.

[7] Robert Mountgomry, "A Discourse Concerning the design'd Establishment of a New Colony," pp. 6, 12, in *Force's Tracts*, vol. 1.; Thomas Morton, "New English Canaan; or, New Canaan, Containing An Abstract of New England . . . Written . . . Upon ten Yeers Knowledge and Experiment of the Country" (London, 1632), p. 10, in *Force's Tracts*, vol. 2.

in those colonies was the unfortunate result of the present inhabitants' own reticence. By ignoring "the bewty of the Country with her naturall indowements," the colonists were forcing their potentially fertile Canaan to remain a fruitless "wombe," which

> Not being enjoy'd, is like a glorious tombe,
> Admired things producing which there dye,
> And ly fast bound in darck obscurity.

Cataloging the "temperature of the Climent, sweetnesse of the aire, fertility of the Soile, and small number of the Salvages," he concludes that the land is "not to be paraleld in all Christendome." Its physical layout, promising ease and repose, includes "many goodly groues of trees; dainty fine round rising hillucks: delicate faire large plaines, sweete cristall fountaines, and cleare running streames, that twine in fine meanders through the meads, making so sweete a murmering noise to heare, as would even lull the sences with delight a sleepe." In short, he tells us, "The more I looked, the more I liked it."[8]

Historical Questions

1. In "Surveying the Virgin Land," Kolodny narrates several Euro-American perspectives on the Colonial American land beginning with the accounts of two English explorers in 1584. How do you think these two accounts compare with the comments of the eighteenth-century French writer, Comte de Buffon, quoted at the beginning of this chapter? What personal, economic, or political experiences, purposes and motives might have affected these writers' perspectives on early Colonial America?

2. From your current perspective, what crucial information about early Colonial America do these historical documents leave out? What do these documents imply about Native Americans—the original inhabitants of America—when these explorers first arrived? What do you know today about how Native Americans had viewed this continent up to that time?

Cultural Questions

1. Annette Kolodny, in *The Lay of the Land,* claims that our language not only provides clues to the motivations underlying our actions but also offers clues to our deepest dreams and fantasies. In this piece, the narratives of bounty in early America are not only joyful and optimistic in tone, but also use highly suggestive imagery in which the land is frequently described

[8] Ibid., pp. 41, 10, 14, 41-42.

as a virginal female. Focusing on three to four specific words and phrases used to describe the land in virginal terms, develop a symptomatic reading in which you use the language to speculate about the kind of relationships that might have existed—in reality or fantasy—between men and women, and men and land, in the late sixteenth century.

2. What kinds of language do you think people use today to describe the land? Focusing on two or three specific examples from your own knowledge, from fastwrite 1, or from something you have read, develop a symptomatic reading of this language, exploring what its use can tell us about some of our larger values and practices today.

J O H N   C A R B U T T

Westward the Monarch Capitol Makes Its Way (1866)

John Carbutt (1832–1905) shot more than three-hundred stereoscopic views of the advance of the railroad from the east coast to the western territories, mostly as promotions for railroad companies. These photographs helped the project of westward expansion that Fredrick Jackson Turner later discussed so eloquently in his "frontier thesis" about the pioneers (see p. 541). The 1866 photograph in Figure 9.1 of an unknown location was taken to exhibit the vastness of the land and the enormity of the railroad project to the viewers back east.

Historical Question

In Figure 9.1, we see a vast stretch of railroad ties extending beyond the horizon. The rest of the frame contains equally vast open space with only three men who might be working on this railroad project. What effect do you think this enormous railroad track—a major technological feat of that time—would have had on a viewer at the time? What effect does it have on your mind? How does the empty space further shape your perception of this U.S. landscape? If you photographed this landscape today, on what objects would you focus your camera in this vast space?

Cultural Question

Develop a symptomatic reading of Figure 9.1's photograph's title, "Westward the Monarch Capitol Makes Its Way." How do you think the word choices for this title relate to American history and politics at the time?

Figure 9.1. John Carbutt, "Westward the Monarch Capitol Makes Its Way" (1866)

഻൜൜൜

NATHANIEL CURRIER AND JAMES MERRITT IVES

Across the Continent—Westward the Course of Empire Takes Its Way (1868)

Nathaniel Currier (1813–1888) began his career as a lithographer with the first American company to import the technology shown in Figure 9.2 from Bavaria. James Merritt Ives (1824–1895), a book-keeper by trade with an interest in art, became Currier's partner in 1857. The two complemented each other's artistic abilities and suc-ceeded in producing more than seven thousand prints on a variety of subjects. Whereas most of the prints primarily served a commer-cial purpose in their times, a sizable number have technical merit and historic significance. The print reproduced in Figure 9.2 shows

Figure 9.2 Nathaniel Currier and James Merritt Ives: "Across the Continent— Westward the Course of Empire Takes Its Way" (1868)

the first U.S. transcontinental train. The legend on the train, "Through Line New York to San Francisco," is of particular interest since the print was prepared and published in 1868, a year before the final spike was driven on the rails which connected those two cities!

∞ Fastwrite 4

Colin Simkin, the editor of the collection of nineteenth century prints that contains Figure 9.2, wrote in 1955 that this 1868 Currier and Ives lithograph "contains almost the whole story of the West in one scene." Take about ten minutes to write a reflection on some of the details of this picture. What images of the United States are represented in this scene and what specific meaning might they have had for the viewers of this lithograph at the time it was produced?

Historical Question

How do you "read" the print in Figure 9.2? Why might contemporary viewers see this depiction as ironic? While analyzing, take into consideration twentieth-century economic developments that have taken place since this lithograph was produced.

Cultural Questions

1. What would you guess is the daily routine of this settlement from the various details portrayed in this print?

2. The train is clearly the central image on the canvas and it organizes all other details in the lithograph. Develop a symptomatic reading of this representation of the train for this specific moment in U.S. history. What does it symbolize for the Native Americans? What does it symbolize for the settlers? What does it symbolize for the land? What does it symbolize for the country?

ᏟᏯᏟᏯᏟᏯᏟᏯ

FREDERICK JACKSON TURNER

Pioneer Ideals and the State University (1910)

Frederick Jackson Turner (1861–1932) is best known as the father of the "frontier" thesis. A founding member of the American Historical Association and the winner of the Pulitzer Prize for *The Significance of Sections in American History* (1932), Turner held professorial positions at the University of Wisconsin and Harvard University. He was the first professor to offer a course on the American West. According to Turner, the frontier was the decisive factor in welding together a nation and nationality distinct from other nations and nationalities as well as in producing distinctly American traits. Turner wrote that Westerners felt the natural resources of the nation should be exploited, and therefore, frontiersmen wanted the public lands passed into private ownership as rapidly as possible so that they could be put to productive use. The essay below has been extracted from a commencement address Turner delivered at the University of Indiana in 1910.

The ideals of a people, their aspirations and convictions, their hopes and ambitions, their dreams and determinations, are assets in their civilization as real and important as per capita wealth or industrial skill.

This nation was formed under pioneer ideals. During three centuries after Captain John Smith struck the first blow at the American forest on the eastern edge of the continent, the pioneers were abandoning settled society for the wilderness, seeking, for generation after generation, new frontiers. Their experiences left abiding influences upon the ideas and purposes of the nation. Indeed the older settled regions themselves were shaped profoundly by the very fact that the whole nation was pioneering and that in the development of the West the East had its own part.

The first ideal of the pioneer was that of conquest. It was his task to fight with nature for the chance to exist. Not as in older countries did this contest take place in a mythical past, told in folk lore and epic. It has been continuous to our own day. Facing each generation of pioneers was the unmastered continent. Vast forests blocked the way; mountainous ramparts interposed; desolate, grass-clad prairies, barren oceans of rolling plains, arid deserts, and a fierce race of savages, all had to be met and defeated.

The rifle and the ax are the symbols of the backwoods pioneer. They meant a training in aggressive courage, in domination, in directness of action, in destructiveness.

To the pioneer the forest was no friendly resource for posterity, no object of careful economy. He must wage a hand-to-hand war upon it, cutting and burning a little space to let in the light upon a dozen acres of hard-won soil, and year after year expanding the clearing into new woodlands against the stubborn resistance of primeval trunks and matted roots. He made war against the rank fertility of the soil. While new worlds of virgin land lay ever just beyond, it was idle to expect the pioneer to stay his hand and turn to scientific farming. Indeed, as Secretary Wilson has said, the pioneer would, in that case, have raised wheat that no one wanted to eat, corn to store on the farm, and cotton not worth the picking.

Thus, fired with the ideal of subduing the wilderness, the destroying pioneer fought his way across the continent, masterful and wasteful, preparing the way by seeking the immediate thing, rejoicing in rude strength and wilful achievement.

But even this backwoodsman was more than a mere destroyer. He had visions. He was finder as well as fighter—the trail-maker for civilization, the inventor of new ways. Although Rudyard Kipling's "Foreloper" deals with the English pioneer in lands beneath the Southern Cross, yet the poem portrays American traits as well:

"The gull shall whistle in his wake, the blind wave break in fire,
He shall fulfill God's utmost will, unknowing his desire;
And he shall see old planets pass and alien stars arise,
And give the gale his reckless sail in shadow of new skies.

"Strong lust of gear shall drive him out and hunger arm his hand
To wring food from desert nude, his foothold from the sand.
His neighbors' smoke shall vex his eyes, their voices break his rest;
He shall go forth till south is north, sullen and dispossessed;
He shall desire loneliness and his desire shall bring
Hard on his heels, a thousand wheels, a people and a king.

"He shall come back on his own track, and by his scarce cool camp,
There shall he meet the roaring street, the derrick and the stamp;
For he must blaze a nation's way with hatchet and with brand,
Till on his last won wilderness an empire's bulwarks stand."

This quest after the unknown, this yearning "beyond the sky line, where the strange roads go down," is of the very essence of the backwoods pioneer, even though he was unconscious of its spiritual significance.

The pioneer was taught in the school of experience that the crops of one area would not do for a new frontier; that the scythe of the clearing must be replaced by the reaper of the prairies. He was forced to make old tools serve new uses; to shape former habits, institutions and ideas to changed conditions; and to find new means when the old proved inapplicable. He was building a new society as well as breaking new soil; he had the ideal of nonconformity and of change. He rebelled against the conventional.

Besides the ideals of conquest and of discovery, the pioneer had the ideal of personal development, free from social and governmental constraint. He came from a civilization based on individual competition, and he brought the conception with him to the wilderness where a wealth of resources, and innumerable opportunities gave it a new scope. The prizes were for the keenest and the strongest; for them were the best bottom lands, the finest timber tracts, the best salt-springs, the richest ore beds; and not only these natural gifts, but also the opportunities afforded in the midst of a forming society. Here were mill sites, town sites, transportation lines, banking centers, openings in the law, in politics—all the varied chances for advancement afforded in a rapidly developing society where everything was open to him who knew how to seize the opportunity.

The squatter enforced his claim to lands even against the government's title by the use of extra-legal combinations and force. He appealed to lynch law with little hesitation. He was impatient of any governmental restriction upon his individual right to deal with the wilderness.

∾ **Fastwrite 5**

You have heard stories, read books, or watched movies that historicize the life in Colonial America from the time Columbus landed and began the European colonization process. Many of these stories pertain to the westward expansion by the pioneers. Sketch a word-portrait of a hypothetical pioneer based on your current knowledge of this subject. Use these questions to get started: What picture does the word *pioneer* evoke in your imagination? From what social, economic, and cultural background did this pioneer come? What cultural values did this pioneer bring from Europe that motivated him or her to explore this vast continent? How did this pioneer perceive America—its lands, its flora and fauna, and its people—when newly arrived? As he or she traveled westward?

Historical Questions

1. In the first reading in this chapter, Kolodny offered several explorers' descriptions of the land. How do those descriptions compare with Turner's late nineteenth-century description, particularly in paragraph 4, of the landscape? In what details are these descriptions similar, and in what other

ways are they different? What particular historical factors might have influenced Turner's view of the landscape?

2. In his speech, Turner quotes Rudyard Kipling's poem, "The Foreloper," which has nothing to do with the United States; rather, it deals with the English going from the northern hemisphere to the southern hemisphere to colonize India and Australia approximately fifty years before Turner is writing. From your own contemporary understanding of the American West, develop a symptomatic reading of a passage from Kipling's poem and of Turner's impulse to quote it in its entirety. What attitudes and beliefs does Kipling's poem suggest? How do they relate directly and indirectly to some of the major points of Turner's essay? How do you—from your vantage point, living in a particular region of the United States and from your particular ethnic origin—react to Turner's use of Kipling's poem.

∾ Fastwrite 6

Turner begins his speech, "The ideals of a people, their aspirations and convictions, their hopes and ambitions, their dreams and determinations, are assets in their civilization as real and important as per capita wealth or industrial skill." What specific ideals helped to shape the United States in the eighteenth and nineteenth centuries, according to Turner? Make a list of all the salient characteristics you can find in Turner's description of the pioneers in the first half of this speech. Then analyze this list to see how these characteristics compare with your portrait of the pioneer that you sketched in fastwrite 5. How can you account for the similarities and differences in Turner's and your own beliefs?

Cultural Questions

1. Throughout his lecture, Turner appears to represent the pioneers in an adversarial relationship to nature using such phrases as "unmastered continent," "first blow at the American forest," and "fight with nature for a chance to exist." What other phrases stand out to you in Turner's speech that evoke similar or different images? Focusing on three or four such phrases, determine why the pioneers might have viewed nature as their adversary and why they thought that they had to conquer the U.S. landscape.

2. According to some of Turner's own contemporaries like James Muir and Theodore Roosevelt, what Turner describes as the pioneer "visions" in 1910 had already had devastating implications for the American land, its environment, and its native inhabitants. Why then, do you think, Turner defended these pioneers at that time, particularly when the United States was striving to become an industrial economy? What does this apparent tension suggest about the relationship between the dominant agrarian and emergent industrial values at the time?

3. Focusing on two or three passages in this speech, compare and contrast how you imagine a student at a college graduation in 1910 and a Native American on a reservation in 1910 would have responded to Turner. What might the differences in these responses tell you about dominant values and beliefs at the time?

HENRY ADAMS

From *The Education of Henry Adams* (1907)

Henry Adams (1838–1918), great grandson of the second U.S. president John Adams, grandson of the sixth president John Quincy Adams, editor of the *North American Review,* and a professor at Harvard University, was an influential figure in Washington circles. He endlessly reflected and commented on the social and political life of the country's capital where he maintained an apartment. *The Education of Henry Adams* is a third-person narrative of his life in which he describes, interprets, and reflects on all that was happening around him at the end of the nineteenth century in America. The first excerpt here provides Adams's reflections on a westward trip he took with a geologist friend after he resigned from the editorship of the *North American Review.* The second excerpt provides Adams's commentary on the St. Louis Exposition of 1904, which he attended with then-Secretary of State John Hay.

A year or two of education as editor satiated most of his appetite for that career as a profession. After a very slight experience, he said no more on the subject. He felt willing to let any one edit, if he himself might write. Vulgarly speaking, it was a dog's life when it did not succeed, and little better when it did. A professor had at least the pleasure of associating with his students; an editor lived the life of an owl. A professor commonly became a pedagogue or a pedant; an editor became an authority on advertising. On the whole, Adams preferred his attic in Washington. He was educated enough. Ignorance paid better, for at least it earned fifty dollars a month.

With this result Henry Adams's education, at his entry into life, stopped, and his life began. He had to take that life as he best could, with such accidental education as luck had given him; but he held that it was wrong, and that, if he were to begin again, he would do it on a better system. He thought he knew nearly what system to pursue. At that time Alexander Agassiz had not yet got his head above water so far as to serve for a model, as he did twenty or thirty years afterwards; but the editorship of the *North American Review* had one solitary merit; it made the editor acquainted at a distance with almost every one in the country who could write or who could be the cause of writing. Adams was vastly pleased to be received among these clever people as one of themselves, and felt always a little surprised at their treating him as an equal, for they all had education; but among them, only one stood out in extraordinary prominence as the type and model of what Adams would have liked to be, and of what the American, as he conceived, should have been and was not.

Thanks to the article on Sir Charles Lyell, Adams passed for a friend of geologists, and the extent of his knowledge mattered much less to them than the extent of his friendship, for geologists were as a class not much better off than himself, and friends were sorely few. One of his friends from earliest childhood, and nearest neighbor in Quincy, Frank Emmons, had become a geologist and joined the Fortieth Parallel Survey under Government. At Washington in the winter of 1869–70 Emmons had invited Adams to go out with him on one of the field-parties in summer. Of course when Adams took the *Review* he put it at the service of the Survey, and regretted only that he could not do more. When the first year of professing and editing was at last over, and his July *North American* appeared, he drew a long breath of relief, and took the next train for the West. Of his year's work he was no judge. He had become a small spring in a large mechanism, and his work counted only in the sum; but he had been treated civilly by everybody, and he felt at home even in Boston. Putting in his pocket the July number of the *North American*, with a notice of the Fortieth Parallel Survey by Professor J. D. Whitney, he started for the plains and the Rocky Mountains.

In the year 1871, the West was still fresh, and the Union Pacific was young. Beyond the Missouri River, one felt the atmosphere of Indians and buffaloes. One saw the last vestiges of an old education, worth studying if one would; but it was not that which Adams sought; rather, he came out to spy upon the land of the future. The Survey occasionally borrowed troopers from the nearest station in case of happening on hostile Indians, but otherwise the topographers and geologists thought more about minerals than about Sioux. They held under their hammers a thousand miles of mineral country with all its riddles to solve, and its stores of possible wealth to mark. They felt the future in their hands.

Emmons's party was out of reach in the Uintahs, but Arnold Hague's had come in to Laramie for supplies, and they took charge of Adams for a time. Their wanderings or adventures matter nothing to the story of education. They were all hardened mountaineers and surveyors who took everything for granted, and spared each other the most wearisome bore of English and Scotch life, the stories of the big game they killed. A bear was an occasional amusement; a wapiti was a constant necessity; but the only wild animal dangerous to man was a rattlesnake or a skunk. One shot for amusement, but one had other matters to talk about.

Adams enjoyed killing big game, but loathed the labor of cutting it up; so that he rarely unslung the little carbine he was in a manner required to carry. On the other hand, he liked to wander off alone on his mule, and pass the day fishing a mountain stream or exploring a valley. One morning when the party was camped high above Estes Park, on the flank of Long's Peak, he borrowed a rod, and rode down over a rough trail into Estes Park, for some trout. The day was fine, and hazy with the smoke of forest fires a thousand miles away; the park stretched its English beauties off to the base of its bordering mountains in natural landscape and archaic peace; the stream was just fishy enough to tempt lingering along its banks. Hour after hour the sun moved westward and the fish moved eastward, or disappeared altogether, until at last when the fisherman cinched his mule, sunset was nearer than he thought. Darkness caught him before he could catch his trail. Not caring to tumble into some fifty-foot hole, he "allowed" he was lost, and turned back. In half-an-hour he was out of the hills, and under the stars of Estes Park, but he saw no prospect of supper or of bed.

Estes Park was large enough to serve for a bed on a summer night for an army of professors, but the supper question offered difficulties. There was but one cabin in the Park, near its entrance, and he felt no great confidence in finding it, but he thought his mule cleverer than himself, and the dim lines of mountain crest against the stars fenced his range of error. The patient mule plodded on without other road than the gentle slope of the ground, and some two hours must have passed before a light showed in the distance. As the mule came up to the cabin door, two or three men came out to see the stranger.

One of these men was Clarence King on his way up to the camp. Adams fell into his arms. As with most friendships, it was never a matter of growth or doubt. Friends are born in archaic horizons; they were shaped with the *Pteraspis* in Siluria; they have nothing to do with the accident of space. King had come up that day from Greeley in a light four-wheeled buggy, over a trail hardly fit for a commissariat mule, as Adams had reason to know since he went back in the buggy. In the cabin, luxury provided a room and one bed for guests. They shared the room and the bed, and talked till far towards dawn. . . .

༽

He professed the religion of World's Fairs, without which he held education to be a blind impossibility; and obeyed Mrs. Hay's bidding the more readily because it united his two educations in one; but theory and practice were put to equally severe test at St. Louis. Ten years had passed since he last crossed the Mississippi, and he found everything new. In this great region from Pittsburgh through Ohio and Indiana, agriculture had made way for steam; tall chimneys reeked smoke on every horizon, and dirty suburbs filled with scrap-iron, scrap-paper and cinders, formed the setting of every town. Evidently, cleanliness was not to be the birthmark of the new American, but this matter of discards concerned the measure of force little, while the chimneys and cinders concerned it so much that Adams thought the Secretary of State should have rushed to the platform at every station to ask who were the people; for the American of the prime seemed to be extinct with the Shawnee and the buffalo.

The subject grew quickly delicate. History told little about these millions of Germans and Slavs, or whatever their race-names, who had overflowed these regions as though the Rhine and the Danube had turned their floods into the Ohio. John Hay was as strange to the Mississippi River as though he had not been bred on its shores, and the city of St. Louis had turned its back on the noblest work of nature, leaving it bankrupt between its own banks. The new American showed his parentage proudly; he was the child of steam and the brother of the dynamo, and already, within less than thirty years, this mass of mixed humanities, brought together by steam, was squeezed and welded into approach to shape; a product of so much mechanical power, and bearing no distinctive marks but that of its pressure. The new American, like the new European, was the servant of the powerhouse, as the European of the twelfth century was the servant of the Church, and the features would follow the parentage.

The St. Louis Exposition was its first creation in the twentieth century, and, for that reason, acutely interesting. One saw here a third-rate town of half-a-million people without history, education, unity, or art, and with little capital—without even an element of natural interest except the river which it studiously ignored—but doing what London, Paris, or New York would have shrunk from attempting. This new social conglomerate, with no tie but its steam-power and not much of that, threw away thirty or forty-million dollars on a pageant as ephemeral as a stage flat. The world had never witnessed so marvellous a phantasm; by night Arabia's crimson sands had never returned a glow half so astonishing, as one wandered among long lines of white palaces, exquisitely lighted by thousands on thousands of electric candles, soft, rich, shadowy, palpable in their sensuous depths; all in deep silence, profound solitude, listening for a voice or a foot-fall or the plash of an oar, as though the Emir Mirza were displaying the beauties of this City of Brass, which could show nothing half so beautiful as this illumination, with its vast, white, monumental solitude, bathed in the pure light of setting suns. One enjoyed it with iniquitous rapture, not because of exhibits but rather because of their want. Here was a paradox like the stellar universe that fitted one's mental faults. Had there been no exhibits at all, and no visitors, one would have enjoyed it only the more.

Here education found new forage. That the power was wasted, the art indifferent, the economic failure complete, added just so much to the interest. The chaos of education approached a dream. One asked one's self whether this extravagance reflected the past or imaged the future; whether it was a creation of the old American or a promise of the new one. No prophet could be believed but a pilgrim of power, without constituency to flatter, might allow himself to hope. The prospect from the Exposition was pleasant; one seemed to see almost an adequate motive for power; almost a scheme for progress. In another half-century the people of the central valleys should have hundreds of millions to throw away more easily than in 1900 they could throw away tens; and by that time they might know what they wanted. Possibly they might even have learned how to reach it.

This was an optimist's hope, shared by few except pilgrims of World's Fairs, and frankly dropped by the multitude, for, east of the Mississippi, the St. Louis Exposition met a deliberate conspiracy of silence, discouraging, beyond measure, to an optimistic dream of future strength in American expression.

Historical Questions

1. In his commentary on the St. Louis Exposition, Adams provides us with a flashback of a twelfth-century German exhibition. Why do you think Adams juxtaposes two such dissimilar events as the St. Louis World Trade Fair and a medieval religious festival? Focusing on three or four specific references to the text, explore the information you receive from this flashback about German society and culture at that time. Then, again with specific references, compare and contrast the highlights of the German exhibit and the St. Louis Exposition. What observations might Adams be trying to make about the European culture as it developed from twelfth- century Europe to twentieth-century Euro-America? Speculate about the possible meanings that such an odd juxtaposition might have had for Adams's readers. What meanings do they have for you today?

2. In the second excerpt, Adams comments on his visit to the St. Louis Exposition of 1904. This narrative repeatedly shifts between Europe and St.

Louis, what was then called the *American West*. Pulling together three key points from Adams's description of the fair, explain what the function of these juxtapositions might be. After another century or so of industrial progress in America, describe two or three contemporary juxtapositions that could have an effect similar to those Adams writes about. Describe two or three juxtapositions that might have a different effect from Adams's. Explain and defend your selections.

Cultural Questions

1. Speaking of the geologists surveying the West, Adams states that "they held under their hammer a thousand miles of mineral country with all its riddles to solve, and its stores of possible wealth to mark. They felt the future in their hands." Locate other passages in this excerpt that discuss the activities of the mineral-seeking scientists. Develop a symptomatic reading of the language Adams uses to represent these nineteenth-century U.S. scientists in general and geologists in particular. What does he literally say about them? What does his language also imply about U.S. notions of science at the time? Finally, what does his language suggest about U.S. attitudes towards the exploration for mineral wealth?

2. While describing the palaces and electric lights of the St. Louis World Fair, Adams states that the well-lighted place would have been even more beautiful if it were empty of all commercial exhibits. Likewise, he considers much of the progress exhibited in this fair "extravagant." How would you explain Adams's seemingly contradictory attitude toward commercial and industrial progress? What specific examples can you identify in this excerpt which further underscore this contradictory attitude? Last, how would Adams reconcile his general attitude toward the industrial establishment and his purchase of a state-of-the-art industrial product of 1904, an automobile?

THEODORE ROOSEVELT

Wilderness Reserves: Yellowstone Park (1905)

Theodore Roosevelt (1858–1919), the president of the United States from 1901–1909, a globe trotter, a serviceman and a big-game hunter, was a rather vocal advocate of the preservation movement—a movement for the establishment of public parks to protect game for hunting. He recorded his life-long adventures in such books as *Ranch Life and the Hunting-Trail* (1888), *The Strenuous Life* (1900), *African Game Trails* (1910), and *Through the Brazilian Wilderness* (1914). Roosevelt is a controversial figure in the environmental movement, who, on one hand, preserved such undeveloped lands as Yellowstone Park and, on the other hand, advocated the hunting of wild animals as sport. He propounds his utilitarian philosophy of wildlife in the "wise-use" doctrine. The essay included here further elaborates his views on preservation.

The most striking and melancholy feature in connection with American big game is the rapidity with which it has vanished. When, just before the outbreak of the Revolutionary War, the rifle-bearing hunters of the backwoods first penetrated the great forests west of the Alleghanies, deer, elk, black bear, and even buffalo, swarmed in what are now the States of Kentucky and Tennessee and the country north of the Ohio was a great and almost virgin hunting-ground. From that day to this the shrinkage has gone on, only partially checked here and there, and never arrested as a whole. As a matter of historical accuracy, however, it is well to bear in mind that many writers, in lamenting this extinction of the game, have from time to time anticipated or overstated the facts. Thus as good an author as Colonel Richard Irving Dodge spoke of the buffalo as practically extinct, while the great Northern herd still existed in countless thousands. As early as 1880 sporting authorities spoke not only of the buffalo but of the elk, deer, and antelope as no longer to be found in plenty; and recently one of the greatest of living hunters has stated that it is no longer possible to find any American wapiti bearing heads comparable with the red deer of Hungary. As a matter of fact, in the early eighties there were still large regions where every species of game that had ever been known within historic times on our continent was still to be found as plentifully as ever. In the early nineties there were still big tracts of wilderness in which this was true of all game except the buffalo; for instance, it was true of the elk in portions of northwestern Wyoming, of the blacktail in northwestern Colorado, of the whitetail here and there in the Indian Territory, and of the antelope in parts of New Mexico. Even at the present day there are smaller, but still considerable, regions where these four animals are yet found in abundance; and I have seen antlers of wapiti shot since 1900 far surpassing any of which there is record from Hungary. In New England and New York, as well as New Brunswick and Nova Scotia, the whitetail deer is more plentiful than it was thirty years ago, and in Maine (and to an even greater extent in New Brunswick) the moose, and here and there the caribou, have, on the whole, increased during the same period. There is yet ample opportunity for the big-game hunter in the United States, Canada, and Alaska.

While it is necessary to give this word of warning to those who, in praising time past, always forget the opportunities of the present, it is a thousandfold more necessary to remember that these opportunities are, nevertheless, vanishing; and if we are a sensible people, we will make it our business to see that the process of extinction is arrested. At the present moment the great herds of caribou are being butchered, as in the past the great herds of bison and wapiti have been butchered. Every believer in manliness and therefore in manly sport, and every lover of nature, every man who appreciates the majesty and beauty of the wilderness and of wild life, should strike hands with the farsighted men who wish to preserve our material resources, in the effort to keep our forests and our game beasts, game-birds, and game-fish—indeed, all the living creatures of prairie and woodland and seashore—from wanton destruction.

Above all, we should realize that the effort toward this end is essentially a democratic movement. It is entirely in our power as a nation to preserve large tracts of wilderness, which are valueless for agricultural purposes and unfit for settlement, as playgrounds for rich and poor alike, and to preserve the game so that it shall continue to exist for the benefit of all lovers of nature, and to give reasonable opportunities for the exercise of the skill of the hunter, whether he is or is not a man of means. But this end can only be achieved by wise laws and by a resolute enforcement of the laws. Lack of such legislation and administration will result in harm to all of us, but most of all in harm to the nature-lover who does not possess vast wealth. Already there have sprung up here and there through the country, as in New Hampshire and the Adirondacks, large private preserves. These preserves often serve a useful purpose, and should be encouraged within reasonable limits; but it would be a misfortune if they increased beyond a certain extent or if they took the place of great tracts of wild land, which continue as such either because of their very nature, or because of the protection of the State exerted in the form of making them State or national parks or reserves. It is foolish to regard proper game-laws as undemocratic, unrepublican. On the contrary, they are essentially in the interests of the people as a whole, because it is only through their enactment and enforcement that the people as a whole can preserve the game and can prevent its becoming purely the property of the rich, who are able to create and maintain extensive private preserves. The wealthy man can get hunting anyhow, but the man of small means is dependent solely upon wise and well-executed game-laws for his enjoyment of the sturdy pleasure of the chase. In Maine, in Vermont, in the Adirondacks, even in parts of Massachusetts and on Long Island, people have waked up to this fact, particularly so far as the common whitetail deer is concerned, and in Maine also as regards the moose and caribou. The effect is shown in the increase in these animals. Such game protection results, in the first place, in securing to the people who live in the neighborhood permanent opportunities for hunting; and in the next place, it provides no small source of wealth to the locality because of the visitors which it attracts. A deer wild in the woods is worth to the people of the neighborhood many times the value of its carcass, because of the way it attracts sportsmen, who give employment and leave money behind them.

True sportsmen, worthy of the name, men who shoot only in season and in moderation, do no harm whatever to game. The most objectionable of all game-destroyers is, of course, the kind of game-butcher who simply kills for the sake of the record of slaughter, who leaves deer and ducks and prairie-chickens to rot after he has slain them. Such a man is wholly obnoxious; and, indeed, so is any man who shoots for the purpose of establishing a record of the amount of game killed. To my mind this is one very unfortunate feature of what is otherwise the admirably sportsmanlike English spirit in these matters. The custom of shooting great bags of deer, grouse, partridges, and pheasants, the keen rivalry in making such bags, and their publication in sporting journals, are symptoms of a spirit which is most unhealthy from every standpoint. It is to be earnestly hoped that every American hunting or fishing club will strive to inculcate among its own members, and in the minds of the general public, that anything like an excessive bag, any destruction for the sake of making a record, is to be severely reprobated.

But, after all, this kind of perverted sportsman, unworthy though he be, is not the chief actor in the destruction of our game. The professional skin or market hunter is the real offender. Yet he is of all others the man who would ultimately be most benefited by the preservation of the game. The frontier settler, in a thoroughly wild country, is certain to kill game for his own use. As long as he does no more than this, it is hard to blame him; although if he is awake to his own interests he will soon realize that to him, too, the live deer is worth far more than the dead deer, because of the way in which it brings money into the wilderness. The professional market-hunter who kills game for the hide or for the feathers or for the meat or to sell antlers and other trophies; the marketmen who put game in cold storage; and the rich people, who are content to buy what they have not the skill to get by their own exertions—these are the men who are the real enemies of game. Where there is no law which checks the market-hunters, the inevitable result of their butchery is that the game is completely destroyed, and with it their own means of livelihood. If, on the other hand, they were willing to preserve it, they could make much more money by acting as guides. In northwestern Colorado, at the present moment, there are still blacktail deer in abundance, and some elk are left. Colorado has fairly good game-laws, but they are indifferently enforced. The country in which the game is found can probably never support any but a very sparse population, and a large portion of the summer range is practically useless for settlement. If the people of Colorado generally, and above all the people of the counties in which the game is located, would resolutely co-operate with those of their own number who are already alive to the importance of preserving the game, it could, without difficulty, be kept always as abundant as it now is, and this beautiful region would be a permanent health resort and playground for the people of a large part of the Union. Such action would be a benefit to every one, but it would be a benefit most of all to the people of the immediate locality.

The practical common sense of the American people has been in no way made more evident during the last few years than by the creation and use of a series of large land reserves—situated for the most part on great plains and among the mountains of the West—intended to keep the forests from destruction, and therefore to conserve the water-supply. These reserves are, and should be, created primarily for economic purposes. The semiarid regions can only support a reasonable population under conditions of the strictest economy and wisdom in the use of the water-supply, and in addition to their other economic uses the forests are indispensably necessary for the preservation of the water-supply and for rendering possible its useful distribution throughout the proper seasons. In addition, however, to this economic use of the wilderness, selected portions of it have been kept here and there in a state of nature, not merely for the sake of preserving the forests and the water but for the sake of preserving all its beauties and wonders unspoiled by greedy and short-sighted vandalism. What has been actually accomplished in the Yellowstone Park affords the best possible object-lesson as to the desirability and practicability of establishing such wilderness reserves. This reserve is a natural breeding-ground and nursery for those stately and beautiful haunters of the wilds which have now vanished from so many of the great forests, the vast lonely plains, and the high mountain ranges, where they once abounded.

∽ Fastwrite 7

Fastwrite for about seven to ten minutes elaborating on your views of hunting. What arguments can you present to support or to oppose it?

Historical Questions

1. How do Roosevelt's ideas compare with our dominant views on wildlife today? What particular practical changes have occurred in the past ninety years to raise questions about his perspective? Focusing on three specific passages, explain how you respond to Roosevelt's arguments. How do you think those concerned with animal ethics today might respond to his arguments?

2. What assumptions about nature does Roosevelt evoke when he describes the wilderness as a "playground" for the people? Focusing on three or four specific passages, develop a symptomatic reading of Roosevelt's attitudes toward land and his perception of human beings in relation to land. For example, you might analyze the hierarchies of the hunter and hunted that Roosevelt establishes in his argument. Or you might explore where you think Roosevelt could have found the basic premise for establishing such a hierarchy in which man becomes the center of all that nature is. Citing two or three specific contemporary examples, explore the extent to which dominant values today are the same or different from Roosevelt's.

Cultural Questions

1. Do a symptomatic reading of some of Roosevelt's language to develop a sense of the dominant values about hunting espoused by Roosevelt at the turn of the century. What, for example, does Roosevelt mean by a "manly sport"? What value systems do you think Roosevelt's "true sportsmen" and "perverted sportsmen" held? Analyze the assumptions about masculinity and about hunting that are encoded in the language and tone of Roosevelt's arguments.

2. Although Roosevelt and Turner were writing during the same period in history, there are some significant differences between their views. In what ways does Roosevelt's perspective on the management of wilderness differ from Turner's? How do you think the pioneers would have responded to Roosevelt's conservation policy, which demanded a stop to unchecked destruction of wilderness? Explore what you feel are one or two of the most important cultural factors that account for the differences in these views.

∾ Fastwrite 8

Before you read the next article, fastwrite about when and where you first heard of the term *Greens*? What images does this word evoke in your mind? In the next ten minutes, compose a descriptive portrait of a Green. Include a discussion of the values Greens seem to hold about the environment, natural resources, and consumption of goods. Explain some ways in which Green values might be similar to some of your own values. In what ways might Green values also conflict with some of your values, aspirations, and material desires?

∞∞∞∞

DONELLA MEADOWS

The Limits to Growth (1983)

Donella Meadows (b. 1941) is an environmental activist and systems analyst. She also teaches in the Environmental Studies Program at Dartmouth College and writes a nationally syndicated newspaper column, "The Global Citizen." She is the author of *Beyond the Limits* (1992) and *The Limits to Growth* (1983), both with Dennis L. Meadows and Jorgen Randers. We have chosen an extract from *The Limits to Growth* because historically this book represents one of the first serious acknowledgments by Western powers of the existence of global, not just national, environmental problems.

The following conclusions have emerged from our work so far. We are by no means the first group to have stated them. For the past several decades, people who have looked at the world with a global, long-term perspective have reached similar conclusions. Nevertheless, the vast majority of policy-makers seem to be actively pursuing goals that are inconsistent with these results.

Our conclusions are:

1. If the present growth trends in world population, industrialization, pollution, food production, and resource depletion continue especially unchanged, the limits to growth on this planet will be reached sometime within the next one hundred years. The most probable result will be a rather sudden and uncontrollable decline in both population and industrial capacity.
2. It is possible to alter these growth trends and to establish a condition of ecological and economic stability that is sustainable far into the future. The state of global equilibrium could be designed so that the basic material needs of each person on earth are satisfied and each person has an equal opportunity to realize his individual human potential.
3. If the world's people decide to strive for this second outcome rather than the first, the sooner they begin working to attain it, the greater will be their chances of success.

These conclusions are so far-reaching and raise so many questions for further study that we are quite frankly overwhelmed by the enormity of the job that must be done. We hope that this book will serve to interest other people, in many fields of study and in many countries of the world, to raise the space and time horizons of their concerns and join us in understanding and preparing for a period of great transition—the transition from growth to global equilibrium. . . .

All five elements basic to the study reported here—population, food production, industrialization, pollution, and consumption of nonrenewable natural resources are increasing. The amount of their increase each year follows a pattern that mathematicians call exponential growth. . . .

Most people are accustomed to thinking of growth as a *linear* process. A quantity is growing linearly when it increases by a constant amount in a constant time period. For example, a child who becomes one inch taller each year is growing linearly. If a miser hides $10 each year under his mattress, his horde of money is also increasing in a linear way. The amount of increase each year is obviously not affected by the size of the child nor the amount of money already under the mattress.

A quantity exhibits *exponential* growth when it increases by a constant percentage of the whole in a constant time period. A colony of yeast cells in which each cell divides into two cells every ten minutes is growing exponentially. For each single cell, after ten minutes there will be two cells, an increase of 100 per cent. After the next ten minutes there will be four cells, then eight, then sixteen. If a miser takes $100 from his mattress and invests it at 7 per cent (so that the total amount accumulated increases by 7 per cent each year), the invested money will grow much faster than the linearly increasing stock under the mattress. The amount added each year to a bank account or each ten minutes to a yeast colony is not constant. It continually increases, as the total accumulated amount increases. Such exponential growth is a common process in biological, financial, and many other systems of the world.

Common as it is, exponential growth can yield surprising results—results that have fascinated mankind for centuries. There is an old Persian legend about a clever courtier who presented a beautiful chessboard to his king and requested that the king give him in return one grain of rice for the first square on the board, two grains for the second square, four grains for the third, and so forth. The king readily agreed and ordered rice to be brought from his stores. The fourth square of the chessboard required eight grains, the tenth square took 512 grains, the fifteenth required 16,384, and the twenty-first square gave the courtier more than a million grains of rice. By the fortieth square a million million rice grains had to be brought from the storerooms. The king's entire rice supply was exhausted long before he reached the sixty-fourth square. Exponential increase is deceptive because it generates immense numbers very quickly.

A French riddle for children illustrates another aspect of exponential growth—the apparent suddenness with which it approaches a fixed limit. Suppose you own a pond on which a water lily is growing. The lily plant doubles in size each day. If the lily were allowed to grow unchecked, it would completely cover the pond in thirty days, choking off the other forms of life in the water. For a long time the lily plant seems small, and so you decide not to worry about cutting it back until it covers half the pond. On what day will that be? On the twenty-ninth day, of course. You have one day to save your pond. . . .

The earth's crust contains vast amounts of those raw materials which man has learned to mine and to transform into useful things. However vast those amounts may be, they are not infinite. Now that we have seen how suddenly an exponentially growing quantity approaches a fixed upper limit, the following statement should not come as a surprise. *Given present resource consumption rates and the projected increase in these rates, the great majority of the currently important non-renewable resources will be extremely costly a hundred years from now.* The above statement remains true regardless of the most optimistic assumptions about undiscovered reserves, technological advances, substitution, or recycling, as long as the demand for resources continues to grow exponentially. The prices of those resources with the shortest static reserve indices have already begun to increase. The price of mercury, for example, has gone up 500 per cent in the last twenty years; the price of lead has increased 300 per cent in the last thirty years. . . .

Are there enough resources to allow the economic development of the seven billion people expected by the year 2000 to a reasonably high standard of living? Once again the answer must be a conditional one. It depends on how the major resource-consuming societies handle some important decisions ahead. They might continue to increase resource consumption according to the present pattern. They might learn to reclaim and recycle discarded materials. They might develop new designs to increase the durability of products made from scarce resources. They might encourage social and economic patterns that would satisfy the need of a person while minimizing, rather than maximizing, the irreplaceable substances he possesses and disperses.

All of these possible courses involve trade-offs. The trade-offs are particularly difficult in this case because they involve choosing between present benefits and future benefits. In order to guarantee the availability of adequate resources in the future, policies must be adopted that will decrease resource use in the present. Most of these policies operate by raising resource costs. Recycling and better product design are expensive; in most parts of the world today they are considered 'uneconomic.' Even if they were effectively instituted, however, as long as the driving feedback loops of population and industrial growth continue to generate more people and a higher resource demand per capita, the system is being pushed toward its limit—the depletion of the earth's non-renewable resources.

What happens to the metals and fuels extracted from the earth after they have been used and discarded? In one sense they are never lost. Their constituent atoms are rearranged and eventually dispersed in a diluted and unusable form into the air, the soil, and the waters of our planet. The natural ecological systems can absorb many of the effluents of human activity and reprocess them into substances that are usable by, or at least harmless to, other forms of life. When any effluent is released on a large enough scale, however, the natural absorptive mechanisms can become saturated. The wastes of human civilization can build up in the environment until they become visible, annoying, and even harmful. Mercury in ocean fish, lead particles in city air, mountains of urban trash, oil slicks on beaches—these are the results of the increasing flow of resources into man's hands. It is little wonder, then, that another exponentially increasing quantity in the world system is pollution.

Historical Questions

1. Meadows claims that a basic message of the Club of Rome is that "infinite growth in a finite system is impossible." What does this statement imply about the concept of economic growth? How is this perspective different from Adams's perspective on science and progress in his commentary on the St. Louis Exposition of 1904? What historical and cultural changes of the past seventy-five years might explain Adams's and Meadows's differing perspectives? Explain whose perspective you agree with more and discuss two to three reasons why.

2. Meadows lists five elements of growth—population, food production, industrialization, pollution, and consumption of nonrenewable natural resources—that have increased exponentially in the twentieth century. Compare and contrast these growth rates to what you know of American and European life prior to the industrial revolution. What specific factors in the twentieth century do you think have most contributed to the change in the growth rates of these five elements?

Cultural Questions

1. Focus on one of the five elements of growth Meadows discusses that is most relevant and interesting to you either in terms of your conserving or following the national trend of growth. Discuss one to

two specific examples of the behaviors you engage in that relate to the area of growth—perhaps taking long showers, recycling, growing your own vegetables, buying and discarding many plastic toys for your children. What cultural and economic assumptions do you make when you engage in these behaviors? Be as specific as possible. In what ways might your behaviors be connected to the view that growth is an imperative of twentieth-century economy or that growth is vital to our culture, as described by Meadows? In what ways might your behaviors work against these assumptions?

2. In talking about possible solutions to contemporary environmental problems, Meadows refers to "sticking-plaster" solutions and "root-and-branch change." Compare and contrast these two approaches to change. What U.S. groups today might be more likely to support such changes? Who might be less likely to support them? Which of the groups you have discussed are more dominant in contemporary society? Explore why these groups are dominant, analyzing the values and assumptions behind their perspectives.

~~~~~

CYNTHIA   RIGGS

Access to Public Lands: A National Necessity (1984)

Cynthia Riggs (b. 1931) is a Washington, D.C. based freelance writer who has contributed to a variety of corporate publications and popular magazines. Trained as a geologist, she has written articles, reports, and brochures for the Smithsonian Institution and edited the trade journal *Petroleum Today* for several years. The present excerpt is taken from an article that first appeared in *Exxon USA*, a publication of the Exxon Corporation.

Quick! Name America's largest landowner. No, not the King Ranch. No, not the Bank of America. No, Exxon isn't even in the running. The answer is the federal government. Of America's 2,271 million acres, 720 million belong to Uncle Sam. Add another 966 million underwater acres of the country's continental shelf, and you've got an impressive bit of real estate there.

In terms of the nation's resources, that vast range of public property represents enormous volumes of timber, grass, and minerals. Copper, zinc, gold, vanadium, tantalum, iron, and silver are among dozens of metallic minerals mined on federal lands. In energy minerals alone, government land may contain more than half the nation's remaining resources. According to the Department of Energy, this includes 85 percent of the nation's crude oil, 40 percent of natural gas, 40 percent of uranium, 35 percent of coal, 80 percent of oil shale, 85 percent of tar sands, and 50 percent of geothermal resources.

What does this mean to those of us who don't even own a 50- by 100-foot lot? Like others who visit national parks and camp in national forests and photograph national monuments, we consider these lands our heritage. Divide it among us, and we'd each have something like three acres apiece. Like all landowners, we'd like those three acres cared for, protected, preserved. It's nice to be a landowner. But there's the rub. Each of us also needs farmland for crops, rangeland for grazing, timber for homes, metals for machines, and energy for heat and fuel. For these, we must turn increasingly to those same public lands of ours where such resources are still to be found.

"No one can feel happy about intrusions upon the wilderness," writes Dr. Charles F. Parks, professor of geology at Stanford University, in his book, *Earthbound*. "It is justified only by the urgency of the need."

The need is urgent, and getting more so. Yet tens of millions of acres of public lands have been closed to mineral development by law or administrative actions. As of early 1983, only 162 million acres of federal onshore land and 13 million acres of offshore land were under lease for oil and natural gas exploration and production.

And the trend is away from development and toward preservation. In many cases the economic use of land is prohibited in favor of a single-purpose use, such as preserving an area where a species of bird may nest, setting aside territory for grizzly bears, reestablishing a prairie ecosystem, or saving a historic site. From this clear need to protect a specific site, the drive for preservation has overwhelmed the concept of multiple use until today vast acreages of federal lands are permanently closed without reason or need, often without an evaluation of the land's aesthetic, biological, recreational, and economic resources. Would-be users—miners, skiers, cattle and sheep ranchers, farmers, campers, timber harvesters, energy firms—are affected.

Groups opposed to the multiple use of federal lands defend their stand in strong language: ". . . the industrial juggernaut must not further degrade the environment . . ." says an official of the Wilderness Society. Authors of the original law governing mineral extraction on federal lands are called a "rapacious gaggle of politicos" motivated by "cupidity and corruption."

Under the appealing slogan, "Preserve the Wilderness," the Society fights to keep federal lands out of the hands of the "destroyers."

Who are the destroyers?

"Anyone who uses a sheet of paper, who drives an automobile, who has a telephone, a radio, a refrigerator," Dr. Parks says. "Anyone who owns a television set or uses artificial light. Anyone who heats a home, who applies paint, hammers a nail, or flushes a toilet. Even the staunchest of preservationists is such a destroyer."

Are environmentalists hypocritical, then?

Not really. Most hold their convictions with the best of intentions and genuine good will. They fear that without the strongest of safeguards, all public lands would be subject to indiscriminate development. They see bulldozers coming over every horizon. Yet most federal lands have no potential for mining or oil. Mineral lodes and oil-and-gas-bearing structures are not common. Their very rarity is what gives their development such high priority. The U.S. Geological Survey has identified 260 million of its on-shore acres in the lower 48 states as worth exploring for petroleum, which is a small percentage of the total acreage of federal lands. Of that, oil or gas deposits might lie beneath no more than one out of 10 of those acres. Were oil exploration encouraged to the fullest, few Americans would ever see signs of it. Nor would development, as conducted under today's environmental regulations, result in more than temporary change to the land.

Nonetheless, some environmental professionals continue to insist that more land should be set aside as wilderness. Robert Cahn, Washington editor for *Audubon Magazine*, writing of land within Alaska Wildlife Refuges, says that "the national interest might be served better by wilderness than by development." Cahn praises the Alaska National Interest Lands Conservation Act (which added 10 new national parks, 44 million acres to the National Park, and 56 million acres to the National Wilderness Preservation System) as "the greatest land-protection law in modern history."

And so it is. Yet land withdrawals of such magnitude must inevitably have serious implications for the American economy. "Civilized people want and must have raw materials, especially energy, at moderate prices," emphasizes Dr. Parks. "Nations have gone to the extreme of war to obtain them. For this reason, if for no other, those who advocate the preservation of large wilderness areas known to contain valuable and necessary raw materials are not going to prevail."

Other scientists confirm this view. Dr. William Conway, director of the New York Zoological Society and Bronx Zoo, advises, "It is absolutely impractical to imagine that the human race will not develop the undeveloped lands that remain on this earth." And he calls for a collaborative effort for development and conservation.

Similarly, public officials worried for America's welfare deplore extremes in the name of the environment. John B. Crowell, Jr., Assistant Secretary of Agriculture for Natural Resources and Environment, speaking at an Audubon Society meeting on pressures on the land, told his audience, "We are concerned that additions to the wilderness system be made with careful consideration of the costs . . . of foregoing the long-term availability of resources such as timber, minerals, oil and gas, geothermal power, developed recreation, and forest production."

The wilderness of which he speaks is one of several categories of the federal land system, which includes national parks and national monuments. The former now encompasses 68 million acres of land of exceptional natural, historic, or recreational value; the latter, a much smaller volume, covering the smallest area compatible with proper care or management. National monuments may be single buildings, such as Ford's Theatre in Washington, D.C., or an area of special geologic interest, such as the 211,000-acre Dinosaur National Monument in Utah and Colorado.

Mineral extraction is prohibited in national parks and national monuments.

Wildlife preserves account for almost 90 million acres of federal lands. Almost 54 million acres were added in 1980, all in Alaska. Petroleum exploration and production is permitted by law on wildlife refuges, provided proper environmental precautions are taken. In practice, however, few leases have been granted for such activities in these areas.

Wild and scenic rivers comprise another one million acres in the 49 states other than Alaska, and five million acres in Alaska. This relatively small percentage of federal land has a large impact on energy development because it limits access to other lands. Seismic or exploration crews cannot work across or near scenic rivers, and pipeline rights of way are restricted. Another federal land designation that limits economic use is that of National Grasslands and Wetlands. Petroleum operations are permitted legally, but administrative delays in granting leases drag on for months and even years. Military reservations make up another 30 million acres, and on these lands, public use of all kinds is tightly restricted. Indian lands generally have not presented an access problem, and tribal councils have worked with oil companies to make oil exploration and production compatible with Indian use—and economically desirable.

Two land programs particularly inhibiting to economic development are the Wilderness Preservation System, set up in 1964, and the Endangered Species Act. Together, these programs present a tangle of confusing and sometimes contradictory regulations.

The Wilderness Act defines wilderness as "an area where the earth and its community of life are untrammeled by man, where man himself is a visitor who does not remain." A wilderness area must be at least 5,000 acres in area, roadless, and unimproved. The wilderness program has grown from nine million acres to 80 million acres. If land now under study is added to the system, the wilderness area could be doubled to 167 million acres. The wilderness designation puts land off limits to all but a few users, such as backpackers. Motorized vehicles are prohibited, and road and permanent facilities are not allowed.

Some groups feel this is the way it should be. "Just because (land) is there, it's important, whether you or I or anyone else can get at it or not," says Stephen Chapman, of Minnesota's Clean Air, Clean Water Unlimited. "Perhaps (the land) is even better because we can't get to it."

Of wilderness, an article in *Harper's* magazine explains that "The wilderness concept appears valid if it is recognized for what it is—an attempt to create what are essentially 'ecological museums' in scenic and biologically significant areas of the lands. But 'wilderness' in the hands of environmentalists has become an all-purpose tool for stopping economic activity as well."

Conveniently ignored in all of this is the fact that most government land is not suitable for the "wilderness" category proposed for it. It has little aesthetic or recreational value. It has nothing in common with those spectacular parks such as Yellowstone, Yosemite, the Grand Canyon, or the Grand Teton. When land of scientific and recreational value is subtracted from the total, hundreds of millions of acres remain that can and should contribute to the national welfare through practical use. Its value as a source of raw materials far exceeds its value for recreation or science. Yet these lands, too, are often locked up with the rest.

Ignored, too, is the fact that the environmental impact of such economic activities as oil and gas extraction is slight, temporary, and carried out under strict guidelines that allow the land to revert eventually to its natural state. Yet it continues to be an article of faith among environmental activists that oil and gas activities equate with whole-sale and permanent destruction which can be prevented only by prohibiting access to areas where the presence of hydrocarbons is suspected.

The Endangered Species Act is another law that has been widely used to stop economic activity. The story of the snail darter is well known. This small, minnow-sized fish, found in an area about to be inundated by construction of the Tellico Dam, a part of the TVA system, was pronounced an endangered species. As a result, construction of the multimillion-dollar dam was delayed for years at immense cost while scientists studied the possibility of relocating the fish to a new habitat. Eventually, it was discovered that snail darters are not all that uncommon, and the species was removed from the endangered list. But not until millions of dollars and valuable time had been lost.

Even private land is not exempt from the government's land policies. According to the Chase Manhattan Bank, about 30 percent of private land in the lower 48 states "has been effectively withdrawn by the need to comply with mind-boggling environmental laws and regulations. All this without any explicit analysis of the energy loss associated with alternate land uses."

Should Americans worry about the loss of energy resources? Some say no. We have enough oil and gas now, goes the argument. Let's lock up the land until we need its raw materials.

Yet the argument collapses in the face of the facts:

- America imports one-third of its oil at a cost of $50 billion a year.
- America consumes two barrels of oil from its reserves for each barrel of new oil found.
- On today's oil search, tomorrow's energy security depends.

Oil development is a long-range proposition. From the time a decision is made to prospect for oil, some 10 years may be needed to go through the lengthy process of looking for, finding, testing, developing, and producing oil into the nation's supply system. If the oil search is not pressed today, there won't be enough to go around tomorrow.

This reality lends a sense of urgency to the need to resolve a growing impasse over access to public lands. Arbitrary barriers to exploration and development of minerals on most public lands are neither wise nor necessary. A policy of careful, orderly, and steady development is preferable to one of nothing today followed by a crash program tomorrow when the awful truth sinks in.

Isn't that what you would prefer for your three acres? Should you be among the few to claim three acres in the Grand Canyon, you would certainly vote to protect it. But if you are among the many with three parched acres of sagebrush, tumbleweed, and alkali dust in Nevada's Basin and Range Province, or in the frozen bleak and barren tundra of North Alaska, your decision might well be, "Let's see if there isn't some badly needed oil under that land."

∾ Fastwrite 9

Imagine that you are a descendant of one of the Native American people who inhabited the North American continent for approximately twenty-five thousand years prior to the European invasions. Through a series of one-sided treaties, most of them forced on your people, the U.S. government has reduced your territorial control in North America to random patches of land, known as *reservations*, with very limited power to govern. Most of your people have left these reservations because the interference from the outside world has made it impossible to carry on what was once your way of life. Now imagine that, while reading Riggs's article, you decide to write an essay that explains your position on the public lands controversy.

a. In the next ten minutes, compose a brief sketch of your position on this controversy. Use the following questions to stimulate your thoughts: Do you think that the U.S. government should have the right to control public lands? Should corporations be able to use these lands to access their natural resources? What historical information will you consider while developing your position? What contemporary realities of your ethnic group might affect your attitudes towards the perspectives in this case? What political and cultural conflicts might arise as a result of the position you take?

b. If you are not a Native American, address the same set of questions as in part a. from your particular perspective, taking into account where and how you live, how long your family has lived in the United States, and your family's relationship to the land and to industry. If you are a Native American, now address these questions taking up the perspective that Riggs adopts.

Historical Questions

1. Compare and contrast Riggs's differentiation of "heritage lands" from "less distinguished tracts" of public lands with representations of the land by earlier writers such as Turner or Adams. Focusing on two to three specific points from Riggs's argument about dividing lands, discuss what you feel is a major historical or economic shift between Turner's or Adams's time and the late twentieth century that would encourage Riggs to conceptualize the land as she does. What goals does she want to achieve by dividing these lands, which are ultimately the joint property of the U.S. public? How do you react to her argument? How do you think Turner or Adams would react?

2. Compare Riggs's perspective with Roosevelt's sense of the use of public lands. Discuss two key similarities and two key differences in their arguments. What historical changes and continuities in U.S. values, beliefs, and material realities contribute to these similarities and differences?

Cultural Questions

1. What does it mean to be *civilized*? List specific characteristics that you think are essential for being civilized. Riggs states that "civilized people want and must have raw materials, especially energy, at moderate prices." Paying particular attention to her language and tone, and focusing on two to three specific passages, develop a symptomatic reading of Riggs's notion of civilization. What assumptions about the relationship of the individual

to the land underlie her argument? How do the characteristics you have listed compare with the ones Riggs assumes in her statement? What shared or different values support these definitions of *civilized*?

2. Compare Riggs's definition of *wilderness* with the definition provided by the Wilderness Preservation System and Endangered Species Act of 1964, quoted in her essay. What different value systems operate behind these two definitions? What is your definition of *wilderness*? How does it compare to the two presented in Riggs's essay? (Bear in mind that a spectrum of beliefs exist on any issue, so you do not have to agree with one or the other. Whatever your position is, articulate the values that underlie it and compare them to those presented by Riggs.)

∾ Fastwrite 10

a. Before you read Trainer's "Abandon Affluence!," which argues for an alternative way of life to address our environmental problems, think about the term *alternative*. Briefly sketch out your conception of one aspect of an alternative society? What difficulties or hurdles might you expect to encounter in building such an alternative society? What are the pros and cons of your alternative society, and how would you persuade your detractors of the benefits you see in it?

b. What is your personal definition of *affluence*? Describe what you consider to be an affluent person. What value systems or perspectives do you imagine affluent people hold? What are the dominant ways they receive satisfaction in life? How do *conservers* get satisfaction in life? What values do conservers hold?

TED TRAINER

From *Abandon Affluence!* (1985)

Ted Trainer (b. 1941) is a Green activist, writer, and practitioner of his own philosophy of frugal living. The following excerpt is taken from the conclusion of his book, *Abandon Affluence!* (1985), in which he argues than an affluent society cannot sustain itself without an abnegation of personal responsibility and exploitation of others. Some may think that Trainer is too frank in pointing out the ills that afflict contemporary society, but his critique of our system of mass production and consumerism is difficult to ignore.

The Basic Premise: The Total Rejection of Affluence and Growth

The most obvious requirement is that the alternative society must be one in which per capita rates of consumption of non-renewable resources are *far* lower than they are now in developed countries. The fundamental realization must be that a safe and just society cannot be an affluent society. We have been fooled by decades of cheap resources, principally oil, into believing that Los Angeles provides the appropriate development model for mankind. We have come to assume that the norm for all people can be an expensive house full of electrical gadgets with two cars in the garage, and that it is in order to drive 30 km to work and to jet 3,000 km for a holiday and to eat food produced on the other side of the world. We have seen that a few of us can live like this—but only if the rest do not. . . .

A Materially Frugal Lifestyle

Our alternative society would involve a lifestyle in which a minimum of unnecessary items were produced. It is not easy to say where lines should be drawn, but there are huge numbers of items we could cease producing without significantly affecting anyone's quality of life. We would, in general, have to limit ourselves to acquiring what we needed or could derive a great deal of enjoyment or convenience from, which means we would have to give up the idea of buying things for fun, buying novelties and unnecessary gifts, buying more clothes than we need, buying more expensive and elaborate versions of things that we need, and so on. But would people limit themselves like this? Of course they would not if they continued to hold the values and perspectives most people now hold. The task is to help people to understand the reasons why it is wise to accept a frugal lifestyle and to understand that these reasons include the possibility of achieving a higher quality of life than derives from striving to become materially richer. Acquiring things is important to many of us today because there is not much else that yields interest and a sense of progress and satisfaction in life. In the alternative situation there would be far more important sources of satisfaction available to all.

It goes without saying that it would be a zealously conserving society. People would save, re-cycle, repair, wear out old clothes and look after things. They would be continually concerned to eliminate unnecessary use, to find more efficient ways, and to cut down on resource throughput.

These concerns may strike the conventional housekeeper as inconvenient responsibilities; but in a conserver society they become an important part of the art of living. The conserver derives satisfaction from doing things in resource-efficient ways, in finding uses for things that once were thrown away, in making things last, in caring for tools, in improving designs or procedures. To a conventional outsider it would probably appear to be a somewhat drab and impoverished existence because people would spend much of their times in old and much-repaired clothes and houses, making do with worn and shabby appliances. Things would not gleam with freshly painted and polished surfaces and there would not be a premium on newness and fashion. But to the conserver, worn or makeshift or patched- up appearances are sources of considerable satisfaction since they represent important achievements. When one understands the shortage of resources in the world, making an old jumper last two more years through darning and careful use becomes a valuable and satisfying contribution. . . .

As Much Self-Sufficiency as Possible

Our high per capita resource-use rates are due in large part to the fact that households and neighbourhoods produce for themselves so few of the goods and services they consume. Commercially produced food not only requires a lot of energy to produce, but perhaps ten times as much energy has to be spent getting it from the farm gate to the kitchen. On the other hand, food grown in the backyard may not involve any cost in non-renewable resources. Our alternative society will achieve much of its saving through producing many goods and services at home and in the neighbourhood. We can make most of our own clothing and footwear, we can grow much of our own food, we can make most of our own furniture, solar panels and indeed our own housing. We can also provide many of the services we need, such as care of convalescents, handicapped and old people, and toddlers, using the non-professional human resources within our neighbourhood. Surpluses from one household could be exchanged for those from others nearby, through co-operatives or weekend bazaars, or simply by being left at the drop-in centre for others to take as they wish.

A high degree of self-sufficiency will require neighbourhoods to be permeated by small-scale productive devices, most obviously gardens, workshops, craft centres, animal pens, ponds for fish and ducks, re-cycling systems, storage sheds, greenhouses, and solar and wind systems. For many purposes, the block with its ten to twenty houses would be the appropriate unit for organization and interaction. These houses might all flush their wastes into the one garbage gas unit, which would also produce high quality garden fertilizer (at more than half a tonne per person per year, when kitchen scraps are included). They might all draw from the one windmill and heat storage tank, and make most use of the house on the block which has been converted to a group workshop, craft centre, library, computer terminal, store, drop-in centre and focal point for meetings, hobbies, leisure activities and entertainment. Where the back fences used to meet there might be a compact collection of jointly operated fowl pens, fish ponds, fruit trees and greenhouses. . . .

But would it not be far less efficient to produce things in back-yards than in factories? We would retain many large factories with sophisticated plants, and much more production would be carried out in the many small decentralized firms. But perhaps most of the important things we now consume could be produced by households. In many cases that efficiency would rival that of our present large-scale producers. This is especially so in primary industry. The peasant and the home gardener are usually much more efficient producers than agribusiness when energy and other non-labour inputs are considered. McRobie discusses small brickworks operating in the Third World producing bricks at half the unit price typical of normal plants with a hundred times the output. Nevertheless many of the things produced at home certainly would be much more costly in terms of labour time than factory produced items. A homemade chair may well be ten times as 'expensive'; but this might not matter at all if its home production is experienced as a satisfying activity. If our concern is simply to maximize the efficiency of production, where this is defined solely in dollar terms, then we should allow the transnational corporation to set up one or two super-technology factories in Taiwan to supply all the world's chairs; but along with the efficiency we will get non-repairable throwaway chairs, no control over the industry, and loss of jobs, and all chair-making labour will have been turned into a boring process of watching computerized machinery. . . .

Alternative Technology

It should not need to be pointed out that a low resource-use society would make extensive use of alternative technologies. These are generally simple, exciting, ecologically sensible and in need of little or no research and development. There are many well-understood and widely practised alternative procedures for the production of food, clothing, housing, water and energy. Our houses and backyards could contain solar panels, ponds, re-cycling systems, compost heaps, windmills, and greenhouses. We would make maximum use of passive solar housing design. Above all we would convert to the use of the best, cheapest and most abundant building material known, namely, earth. Rammed earth or mud-brick technologies are ideal for house construction. These houses can be superior to conventional houses in durability, insulation capacity, fire resistance and especially in dollar and non-renewable resource costs. A family could build its own basic dwelling in a few months, gaining exercise and satisfaction in the process and incurring little or no debt. . . .

All wastes from the block would go into a garbage gas digester or compost heaps, and then into ponds and gardens, eliminating all need for sewage treatment works, mains, pumping for domestic wastes. All space heat would come from solar panels via the underground hot water storage tanks which double as the source of domestic water. Most of the water would be collected from roofs, eliminating the need for most water supply mains. Some fraction of electricity could come from windmills and photo-electric cells. On the national level, biomass could become the main source of liquid fuels. Some of these alternatives involve high capital costs, but they will not be needed in the quantities required to sustain an industrialized society and it is therefore probable that we will be able to afford sufficient capacity.

It is not necessary to devote much space here to outlining the technologies available since most of them are common knowledge. Some reference, however, should be made to permaculture. Even densely populated suburban areas could be planted with shrubs and herbs that in time form a largely self-maintaining permanent ecosystem supplying many food items and materials with little cost in labour or resource inputs. Whereas a great deal of energy is needed to sow and harvest a wheat field, a permaculture forest will look after itself year after year and provide fruits and materials that can be taken when needed. The many niches in the ecosystem can be filled with plants and animals which meet each other's needs and therefore do much of the 'work' required to maintain the system. Worms do most of the digging, fowls can feed themselves on fallen fruit, large trees can shelter herbs from the sun, fowls can cultivate shrubs while foraging for soil organisms. . . .

The decentralization of much production into backyards and factories within easy cycling distance of home will cut down the high distribution costs we now incur. We will cease to transport most food over large distances. We will reduce travel to centralized work places. We will make huge savings by dealing with sewage on the block rather than pumping it tens of kilometres to be thrown away through resource and energy-intensive treatment works. Some of the most spectacular savings will derive from the local production of energy. Electricity generated in a conventional power station represents only about one third of the energy in the power station fuel, but one sixth of the electricity is then lost in transit to your house and in running the Electricity Commission's workshops and offices. There will be hardly any losses of this sort when the energy comes from the solar panels and windmill on the block, which we can maintain without the need for an electricity bureaucracy or expert technicians.

A Shift to More Communal and Co-operative Ways

Some of the most valuable and generally unrecognized benefits of de-development would occur in the realm of community relations. Here we would become richer in 'spiritual ways' precisely because we had become poorer in material ways. De-development would force people together, it would require them to co-operate on important common goals, to share, to get to know each other, to depend on and to help each other and therefore to build the social relations that are so impoverished in affluent society.

The neighbourhood would have to take on the organization and running of many services now provided by centralized and resource-expensive agencies, notably councils and corporations. Because councils and central authorities would be much less extensive, small local groups would have to organize themselves to deal with many problems like maintenance of libraries and public parks. Rosters and responsibilities would have to be arranged for the care of small children, maintenance of the windmill, care of the old and of convalescents. There would have to be committees and meetings although most things might be attended to through informal and spontaneous discussion and co-operation. Neighbours would have to talk to each other about important things. After the roads had been dug up more communal property would exist so communal decisions would have to be made about the best uses to which it is to be put. Communities would have to take responsibility for themselves. . . .

A Place for High Technology

The tight energy budget underlying this discussion should permit all important high technology to continue. There is no reason why medical research, for instance, should be curtailed. Remember that perhaps half the world's scientists and technologists are now working on arms production and many of the remainder are working directly or indirectly on the production of unnecessary gadgets. When we cut back on the production of non-necessities we should be able greatly to increase research on projects that contribute to the quality of life.

Reducing resource consumption need not require much change in the availability of electronic media, computerized information services or the use of microprocessors, as these are not very expensive in terms of energy and resource use. The media would take on a significant responsibility in substituting for travel to different lands and to events such as theatre performances, and in keeping a less mobile population informed about what was happening in other places.

Historical Questions

1. Compare Trainer's concept of de-development with the concept of progress discussed in Adams's autobiography. Discuss two to three key historical changes in the United States since Adams's times that could have affected Trainer's construction of the term *de-development*? Why de-development instead of progress?

2. Trainer insists on reducing personal possessions and he encourages communal ownership of facilities and lands. Using specific examples from Trainer's essay as well as passages from Turner or Roosevelt, discuss the relationship of Trainer's views on property rights to those that have been dominant historically in the United States Then, explore what your own position is and the values that underlie it. For example, are there particular aspects of the dominant that you embrace as well as particular aspects of Trainer's emergent perspective? Be as specific as you can be in relating your perspective to the historically dominant position and the emergent position Trainer offers.

Cultural Questions

1. Analyze Trainer's concept of de-development by applying it to one specific example in your family or your community. Describe exactly how de-development could (or does) work. Who in your family or community might support it? What values and assumptions would underlie a positive family or community reaction to this idea? Explain the advantages of de-development in your family or community.

2. What arguments could you develop against de-development? Why might you argue that it doesn't, or wouldn't work? How many hurdles do you see? What values or beliefs lie behind these hurdles? What might it take to surmount them?

∿∿∿

AL GORE

Environmentalism of the Spirit (1992)

Al Gore (b. 1948), U.S. representative, senator, and environmental activist, who first became famous in the environmental movement by championing the Superfund Act of 1980, comes from a prominent political family in Tennessee. Elected to the office of vice president of the United States in 1992 and 1996, Gore has continued to support the environmental cause. This essay is from his book, *Earth in the Balance* (1992). Gore believes that our current environmental crises are as much spiritual as economic and that the solution to these problems lies in striking a balance between individual spirituality and the civilization to which we aspire.

Twenty years ago, E. F. Schumacher defined an important new issue arising from the relationship between a technology and the context— social, cultural, political, and ecological—in which it is used. For example, a nuclear power plant can certainly generate a lot of electricity, but it may not be an "appropriate" technology for an underdeveloped nation with an unstable government, a shortage of trained engineers, an absence of any power grid to distribute the electricity generated, and a megalomaniacal ruler anxious to acquire fissionable material with which to construct nuclear weapons. The appropriateness of a technology becomes increasingly important as its power grows and its potential for destroying the environment expands.

It is time we asked a similar question about ourselves and our relationship to the global environment: When giving us dominion over the earth, did God choose an appropriate technology?

Knowing what we do about our new power as a species to interfere with and even overwhelm the earth's natural systems and recognizing that we are now doing so with reckless abandon, one is tempted to answer, the jury is still out.

Whether we believe that our dominion derives from God or from our own ambition, there is little doubt that the way we currently relate to the environment is wildly inappropriate. But in order to change, we have to address some fundamental questions about our purpose in life, our capacity to direct the powerful inner forces that have created this crisis, and who we are. These questions go beyond any discussion of whether the human species is an appropriate technology; these questions are not for the mind or the body but the spirit.

A change in our essential character is not possible without a realistic hope that we can make change happen. But hope itself is threatened by the realization that we are now capable of destroying ourselves and the earth's environment. Moreover, the stress of coping with the complicated artificial patterns of our lives and the flood of manufactured information creates a pervasive feeling of exhaustion just when we have an urgent need for creativity. Our economy is described as post-industrial; our architecture is called post-modern; our geopolitics are labeled post–Cold War. We know what we are not, but we don't seem to know what we are. The forces that shape and reshape our lives seem to have an immutable logic of their own; they seem so powerful that any effort to define ourselves creatively will probably be wasted, its results quickly erased by successive tidal waves of change. Inevitably, we resign ourselves to whatever fate these powerful forces are propelling us toward, a fate we have little role in choosing.

Perhaps because it is unprecedented, the environmental crisis seems completely beyond our understanding and outside of what we call common sense. We consign it to some seldom visited attic in our minds where we place ideas that we vaguely understand but rarely explore. We tag it with the same mental labels we might use for Antarctica: remote, alien, hopelessly distorted by the maps of the world we inhabit, too hard to get to and too unforgiving to stay very long. When we do visit this attic, when we learn about how intricately the causes of the crisis are woven into the fabric of industrial civilization, our hope of solving it seems chimerical. It seems so forbidding that we resist taking even the first steps toward positive change.

We turn by default to an imprudent hope that we can adapt to whatever changes are in store. We have grown accustomed to adapting; we are good at it. After all, we have long since adapted, with the help of technology, to every climate extreme on the surface of the earth, at the bottom of the sea and even in the vacuum of space. It is by adapting, in fact, that we have extended our dominion into every corner of the earth. And so it is tempting to conclude that this familiar strategy is the obvious response to our rapidly emerging dilemma.

But the magnitude of the change to which we must now consider adapting is so large that the proposals quickly tend toward the absurd. A study sponsored by the National Academy of Sciences, for example, suggested that as the earth warms, we might create huge corridors of wilderness as pathways to accommodate all of the species trying to migrate from south to north in search of a familiar climate. (Meanwhile, of course, we are laying siege to many of the wilderness areas that already exist—in the

Pacific Northwest, for example—in search of timber and other resources.) Some even imagine that genetic engineering will soon magnify our power to adapt even our physical form. We might decide to extend our dominion of nature into the human gene pool, not just to cure terrible diseases, but to take from God and nature the selection of genetic variety and robustness that gives our species its resilience and aligns us with the natural rhythms in the web of life. Once again, we might dare to exercise godlike powers unaccompanied by godlike wisdom.

But our willingness to adapt is an important part of the underlying problem. Do we have so much faith in our own adaptability that we will risk destroying the integrity of the entire global ecological system? If we try to adapt to the changes we are causing rather than prevent them in the first place, have we made an appropriate choice? Can we understand how much destruction this choice might finally cause?

Believing that we can adapt to just about anything is ultimately a kind of laziness, an arrogant faith in our ability to react in time to save our skin. But in my view this confidence in our quick reflexes is badly misplaced; indeed, a laziness in our spirit has estranged us from our true selves and from the quickness and vitality of the world at large. We have been so seduced by industrial civilization's promise to make our lives comfortable that we allow the synthetic routines of modern life to soothe us in an inauthentic world of our own making. Life can be easy, we assure ourselves. We need not suffer the heat or the cold; we need not sow or reap or hunt and gather. We can heal the sick, fly through the air, light up the darkness, and be entertained in our living rooms by orchestras and clowns whenever we like. And as our needs and whims are sated, we watch electronic images of nature's destruction, distant famine, and apocalyptic warnings, all with the bone-weariness of the damned. "What can we do?" we ask ourselves, already convinced that the realistic answer is nothing.

With the future so open to doubt, we routinely choose to indulge our own generation at the expense of all who will follow. We enshrine the self as the unit of ethical account, separate and distinct not just from the natural world but even from a sense of obligation to others—not just others in future generations, but increasingly even to others in the same generation; and not just those in distant lands, but increasingly even in our own communities. We do this not because we don't care but because we don't really live in our lives. We are monumentally distracted by a pervasive technological culture that appears to have a life of its own, one that insists on our full attention, continually seducing us and pulling us away from the opportunity to experience directly the true meaning of our own lives.

How can we shake loose this distraction? How can we direct our attention to more important matters when our attention has become a commodity to be bought and sold? Whenever a new source of human interest and desire is found, prospectors flock to stake their claim. Using every available tool—newspapers, movies, television, magazines, billboards, blimps, buttons, designer labels, junk faxes—they assault our attention from every side. Advertisers strip-mine it; politicians covet it; pollsters measure it; terrorists steal it as a weapon of war. As the amounts close to the surface are exhausted, the search for fresh supplies leads onto primal paths that run deep into our being, back through our evolutionary heritage, past thought and beyond emotion, to instinct—and a rich vein of primal fears and passions that are also now exploited as raw material in the colossal enterprise of mass distraction. The prospectors of attention fragment our experience of the world, carry away the spoils, and then, in an ultimate irony, accuse us of having short attention spans.

The way we experience the world is governed by a kind of inner ecology that relates perception, emotions, thinking, and choices to forces outside ourselves. We interpret our experience through multiple lenses that focus— and distort—the information we receive through our senses. But this ecology now threatens to fall badly out of balance because the cumulative impact of the changes brought by the scientific and technological revolution are potentially devastating to our sense of who we are and what our purpose in life might be. Indeed, it may now be necessary to foster a new "environmentalism of the spirit." How do we, for example, conserve hope and minimize the quantity of corrosive fear we spill into our lives? How do we recycle the sense of wonder we felt as children, when the world was new? How do we use the power of technology without adapting to it so completely that we ourselves behave like machines, lost in the levers and cogs, lonesome for the love of life, hungry for the thrill of directly experiencing the vivid intensity of the ever-changing moment?

No wonder we have become disconnected from the natural world— indeed, it's remarkable we feel any connection to ourselves. And no wonder we have become resigned to the idea of a world without a future. The engines of distraction are gradually destroying the inner ecology of the human experience. Essential to that ecology is the balance between respect for the past and faith in the future, between a belief in the individual and a commitment to the community, between our love for the world and our fear of losing it—the balance, in other words, on which an environmentalism of the spirit depends.

To some, the global environmental crisis is primarily a crisis of values. In this view, the basic cause of the problem is that we as a civilization base our decisions about how to relate to the environment on premises that are fundamentally unethical. And since religion has traditionally been the most powerful source of ethical guidance for our civilization, the search for villains has led to the doorstep of the major religious systems.

Here in the West, some have charged—inaccurately, I believe—that the Judeo-Christian tradition chartered the relentless march of civilization to dominate nature, beginning with the creation story of Genesis, in which humankind is granted "dominion" over the earth. In its basic form, the charge is that our tradition assigns divine purpose to our exercise of virtually complete power to work our will over nature. It is alleged that by endowing human beings with a completely unique relationship to God and then delegating God's authority over nature to human beings, the tradition sanctions as ethical all choices that put a higher priority on human needs and desires than on the rest of nature. Simply put, according to this view, it is "ethical" to make sure that whenever nature gets in the way of what we want, nature loses.

But this is a cartoon version of the Judeo-Christian tradition, one that bears little resemblance to the reality. Critics attack religion for inspiring an arrogant and reckless attitude toward nature, but they have not always read the relevant texts carefully enough. Although it is certainly true that our civilization is built on the premise that we can use nature for our own ends without regard to the impact we have on it, it is not fair to charge any of the major world religions with promoting this dangerous attitude. Indeed, all of them mandate an ethical responsibility to protect and care for the well-being of the natural world.

In the Judeo-Christian tradition, the biblical concept of dominion is quite different from the concept of domination, and the difference is crucial. Specifically, followers of this tradition are charged with the duty of stewardship, because the same biblical passage that grants them "dominion" also requires them to "care for" the earth even as they "work" it. The requirement of stewardship and its grant of dominion are not in conflict; in recognizing the sacredness of creation, believers are called upon to remember that even as they "till" the earth they must also "keep" it.

This has long been clear to those who have dedicated their lives to these duties. Richard Cartwright Austin, for example, a Presbyterian minister working among the poor in Appalachia, reports on his experience in trying to stop irresponsible strip mining: "I learned early on from my years as a pastor in Appalachia and from the days when I started fighting strip mining in southwest Virginia that the only defense those mountains have from exploitation by the energy conglomerates' bulldozers is the poor, isolated people who live in those hollows, who care so deeply that they would fight for that land. Take those people away and the mountains are totally defenseless. . . . From the biblical point of view, nature is only safe from pollution and brought into a secure moral relationship when it is united with people who love it and care for it."

All around the world, the efforts to stop the destruction of the environment have come mainly from people who recognize the damage being done in that part of the world in which they themselves have "dominion." Lois Gibbs and the other homeowners at Love Canal, Christine and Woodrow Sterling and their family, whose well water was poisoned in West Tennessee, "Harrison" Gnau and the indigenous peoples of the Sarawak rain forest in East Malaysia, Chico Mendes and his rubber tappers in the Amazon, the unemployed fishermen of the Aral Sea—all began their battles to save the environment because of the marriage of dominion and stewardship in their hearts. This is precisely the relationship between humankind and the earth called for in the Judeo-Christian ethic.

In my own religious experience and training—I am a Baptist—the duty to care for the earth is rooted in the fundamental relationship between God, creation, and humankind. In the Book of Genesis, Judaism first taught that after God created the earth, He "saw that it was good." In the Twenty-fourth Psalm, we learn "that the earth is the Lord's and the fullness thereof." In other words, God is pleased with his creation, and "dominion" does not mean that the earth belongs to humankind; on the contrary, whatever is done to the earth must be done with an awareness that it belongs to God.

My tradition also teaches that the purpose of life is "to glorify God." And there is a shared conviction within the Judeo-Christian tradition that believers are expected to "do justice, love mercy, and walk humbly with your God." But whatever verses are selected in an effort to lend precision to the Judeo-Christian definition of life's purpose, that purpose is clearly inconsistent with the reckless destruction of that which belongs to God and which God has seen as "good." How can one glorify the Creator while heaping contempt on the creation? How can one walk humbly with nature's God while wreaking havoc on nature?

The story of Noah and the ark offers further evidence of Judaism's concern for stewardship. Noah is commanded by God to take into his ark at least two of every living species in order to save them from the Flood—a commandment that might appear in modern form as: Thou shalt preserve biodiversity. Indeed, does God's instruction have new relevance for those who share Noah's faith in this time of another worldwide catastrophe, this time one of our own creation? Noah heeded this commandment, and after he and his family and a remnant of every living species on earth survived the Flood, God made a new covenant with him which affirmed His commitment to humankind. Often overlooked, however, is the second half of God's covenant, made not only with Noah but with "all living creatures," again affirming the sacredness of creation, which He pledged to safeguard in "seed time and harvest, cold and heat, summer and winter." It was the promise never again to destroy the earth by floods, which, according to Genesis, is the symbolic message of every rainbow. . . .

The richness and diversity of our religious tradition throughout history is a spiritual resource long ignored by people of faith, who are often afraid to open their minds to teachings first offered outside their own system of belief. But the emergence of a civilization in which knowledge moves freely and almost instantaneously throughout the world has led to an intense new interest in the different perspectives on life in other cultures and has spurred a renewed investigation of the wisdom distilled by all faiths. This panreligious perspective may prove especially important where our global civilization's responsibility for the earth is concerned.

Native American religions, for instance, offer a rich tapestry of ideas about our relationship to the earth. One of the most moving and frequently quoted explanations was attributed to Chief Seattle in 1855, when President Franklin Pierce stated that he would buy the land of Chief Seattle's tribe. The power of his response has survived numerous translations and retellings:

> How can you buy or sell the sky? The land? The idea is strange to us. If we do not own the freshness of the air and the sparkle of the water, how can you buy them? Every part of this earth is sacred to my people. Every shining pine needle, every sandy shore, every mist in the dark woods, every meadow, every humming insect. All are holy in the memory and experience of my people. . . .
>
> If we sell you our land, remember that the air is precious to us, that the air shares its spirit with all the life it supports. The wind that gave our grandfather his first breath also received his last sigh. The wind also gives our children the spirit of life. So if we sell you our land, you must keep it apart and sacred, a place where man can go to taste the wind that is sweetened by the meadow flowers.
>
> Will you teach your children what we have taught our children? That the earth is our mother? What befalls the earth befalls all the sons of the earth.
>
> This we know: the earth does not belong to man, man belongs to the earth. All things are connected like the blood that unites us all. Man did not weave the web of life, he is merely a strand in it. Whatever he does to the web, he does to himself.
>
> One thing we know: Our God is also your God. The earth is precious to Him and to harm the earth is to heap contempt on its Creator.

A modern prayer of the Onondaga tribe in upstate New York offers another beautiful expression of our essential connection to the earth:

> O Great Spirit, whose breath gives life to the world and whose voice is heard in the soft breeze . . . make us wise so that we may understand what you have taught us, help us learn the lessons you have hidden in every leaf and rock, make us always ready to come to you with clean hands and straight eyes, so when life fades, as the fading sunset, our spirits may come to you without shame.

The spiritual sense of our place in nature predates Native American cultures; increasingly it can be traced to the origins of human civilization. A growing number of anthropologists and archaeomythologists, such as Marija Gimbutas and Riane Eisler, argue that the prevailing ideology of belief in prehistoric Europe and much of the world was based on the worship of a single earth goddess, who was assumed to be the fount of all life and who radiated harmony among all living things. Much of the evidence for the existence of this primitive religion comes from the many thousands of artifacts uncovered in ceremonial sites. These sites are so widespread that they seem to confirm the notion that a goddess religion was ubiquitous throughout much of the world until the antecedents of today's religions—most of which still have a distinctly masculine orientation—swept out of India and the Near East, almost obliterating belief in the goddess. The last vestige of organized goddess worship was eliminated by Christianity as late as the fifteenth century in Lithuania.

Historical Questions

1. Gore quotes from a speech delivered by Chief Seattle to the representatives of the U.S. government in 1855. Seattle gave this speech when his tribe was forced onto a reservation from the lands that we today call the state of Washington. Chief Seattle raises several questions about the well-being of the land, even though he no longer had political jurisdiction over it. In this excerpt, both Gore (1992) and Chief Seattle (1855) discuss the relationship between the human spirit and ecology, yet they express what they mean quite differently. Develop a symptomatic reading of the cultural and historical differences between Gore and Seattle by focusing on their language and tone as well as the different ways they have of approaching the issue. How do their differing styles affect the way you respond to their ideas?

2. Gore questions the power of genetic engineering to adapt our physical form. He also questions our contemporary scientific belief system that he calls an "arrogant faith." Focusing on specific passages from the text, compare and contrast Gore's sense of science in the later part of the twentieth century with Adams's sense of science at the beginning of the century. What aspects of each of their arguments do you most agree with? Most disagree with? What values underlie their and your positions?

Cultural Questions

1. Chief Seattle delivered his speech not much more than a decade before Carbutt's (1866) and Currier and Ives's (1868) visual representations of

westward expansion were published. Juxtaposing specific passages from Chief Seattle with particular aspects of the photograph and the lithograph in Figures 9.1 and 9.2, discuss and analyze what you feel to be three or four key perspectives about the individual's relationship to the land during the period. What underlying values helped to create the tension among these perspectives? If you had lived then, what perspectives do you think you would have taken up? Why?

2. What similarities and differences can you identify between contemporary Native American and Euro-American attitudes toward nature and science? How, for example, does Gore's understanding of dominion or stewardship differ from Onondaga attitudes toward nature that are reflected in such phrases as *make us, help us,* and *come to you* in their prayer?

3. Gore suggests that the contemporary advertising media, which he calls "engines of distraction," are in part responsible for our "global environmental crisis." Focusing on his language and tone, as well as on the specifics of his argument, develop a symptomatic reading of Gore's discussion of the relationship of the media to our behavior toward the land. What does he literally say is their connection? What does he suggest are their larger connections? Develop a specific example of how the media might affect an aspect of your living habits and day-to-day interaction with the earth's environment. If you were to accept Gore's position, how might this affect your reactions to the contemporary advertising media?

∾ Fastwrite 11

Think again about Chief Seattle's words to President Franklin Pierce in 1855, when he asked if the United States would teach her children what he had taught his children: "The earth is our mother and what befalls the earth befalls all the sons of the earth." Write freely about this statement as you explore the following questions: How do you explain what has happened to U.S. land since 1855? In what specific ways has Chief Seattle's advice been heeded? In what specific ways has it been ignored?

∽∽∽∽

DENIS SMITH

Business and the Environment: Towards a Paradigm Shift? (1993)

Denis Smith (b. 1956) is professor of management and the head of the Centre for Risk and Crisis Management at Liverpool University. He coedited *Waste Location: Spatial Aspects of Waste Management, Hazards and Disposal* with M. Clark and A. Blowers (1992). His research interests include corporate management, risk assessment, and crisis management. This excerpt is from his anthology, *Business and the Environment: Implications of the New Environmentalism* (1993).

The 1980s saw the emergence of environmental issues on to both corporate and political agendas throughout the western nations. In the UK the government proposed new legislation in order to arrest our continued slide towards widespread environmental damage. At the international level there were also a series of treaties put into place in an attempt to control the problem of environmental degradation. The political and corporate development of environmental issues seems destined to remain a major agenda item during the 1990s. As corporate groups struggle to maintain their legitimacy in the face of more stringent public demands, there is a growing need for business educators to give the next generation of managers the skills to cope with the demands of this new environmentalism. The present curricula for most management courses give little time to the question of 'green issues' and it comes as little surprise, therefore, to find that a number of managers find some difficulty in dealing with such problems. For many, the question is one of perspective: they argue that all human activities result in environmental degradation of some form and, consequently, society has to strike a balance between its material desires and the requirement for a cleaner environment. The convenience afforded by the motor vehicle, for example, has been a principal factor in the increase of NO_x pollution, the increase in tetraethyl and tetramethyl lead deposits and the problem of waste materials arising from the consumption of oils and component parts. Similarly, the pollution of rivers and watercourses by sewage, generated within urban conurbations, has long been a problem.

The growth in CFC pollution, the presence of dioxins in the food chain and the increasing burden of hazardous waste deposits are all testimony to the effects of unfettered economic growth. The desires of the consumer society have been allowed to encourage the increase in levels of such pollutants within the context of relatively weak international regulatory regimes. Consequently, the notion of sustainable growth necessitates changes being made in the core beliefs of society as well as those of industry. In order to sustain ourselves as a 'post-industrial' society we have to recognize that only through a process of 'green' development will it be possible to arrest the decline in environmental quality at the local, regional and global levels.

Throughout the latter part of the 1980s business became more actively aware of the growth in public concern over environmental issues. This concern was heightened by two of the biggest industrial accidents of all time. The first of these involved the release of methyl-isocyanate from the Union Carbide plant at Bhopal, India, which killed some 3,000 people and committed many thousands more to progressive debilitation and premature death. The accident sent waves of panic through the chemical industry, particularly in the USA, as it shattered the belief that such accidents were beyond the limits of credibility. Whilst the long-term impact of the accident in many western countries was somewhat muted through physical separation, it nevertheless pointed to the fallibility of expert judgements and undermined the power of the technocratic elite. The second accident also had a major impact on societal views regarding the acceptability of its host activity. In 1986 the nuclear power plant at Chernobyl in the USSR came close to a core meltdown—the oft-quoted 'China Syndrome'—and resulted in the release of large quantities of radioactive material into the environment. This 'radioactive' cloud drifted over most of western Europe, caused some 10,000 'immediate' deaths in the USSR and may have contributed significantly to many more early deaths by cancer across Europe. In addition to such acute systems failures, there was also considerable concern expressed over so-called 'leper ships' which epitomized the problems associated with the international trade in hazardous waste. The problem stems from the potentially exploitable nature of poorly regulated industrial activity, as wastes from western countries were dumped in the developing world. The range and scale of incidents such as these undermined public confidence in certain sectors of industry and combined with concern over low-level pollution and product quality to put industry under severe pressure to literally 'clean up its act.'

One of the main problems associated with the whole issue of environmental pollution relates to source determination and the associated evaluation of causality. There is a view expressed within certain sectors of industry that the public does not understand the source of much of our pollution and that in relative terms the impact of industrial production on the environment is not as great as often perceived (see Figure 9.3). However, the data in this table is far from complete and fails to detail a range of heavy metals, chlorinated hydrocarbons and other 'specific' substances and consequently the data needs to be treated accordingly. For substances such as SO_2 we find that power stations contribute the bulk of the problem with road transport being the prime source of CO pollution. In addition, it should be remembered that certain pollutants have a greater toxicity and longevity than others and many arise at point sources rather than from the more diffuse sources that are associated with urban areas. It is the large polluting point sources that often capture public attention and concerns because the damage caused is often 'easier' to detect.

Given the complexity that surrounds environmental impacts, there is a need for business and public groups to engage in more open discourse about the nature of both acute and chronic pollution episodes. If industrial groups are concerned about public perceptions of their activities then they should be prepared to provide more information about their activities. In this context the UK badly needs a Freedom of Information Act that would remove the secrecy that has surrounded pollution regulation in the past. The difficulty in obtaining accurate information often fuels public con-

Figure 9.3 Pollution Sources and Composition (Selected) in the UK

Source/ pollutant	Sulphur Dioxide	Nitrogen Oxides	Carbon Dioxide	Carbon Monoxide	Methane and Volatile Organic Compounds	Smoke
Power Stations	71%	32%	33%	1%	–	5%
Industry	17%	13%	24%	6%	37%	17%
Agriculture	–	–	–	–	18%	–
Road transport	1%	45%	18%	85%	9%	34%
Domestic	4%	3%	15%	7%	–	42%
Commercial	3%	2%	6%	–	–	–
Refineries	3%	1%	3%	–	–	–

Sources: 1. Warren Spring/DTI data for 1988. 2. Howarth, J.H., derived from *Digest of Environmental Protection and Water Protection* (1989) no. 12, p. 30.

cerns, and this is illustrated by the case of water quality data, with six years separating the release of government reports in 1985 and 1991.

In terms of pollution to watercourses, 23 per cent of all incidents arise from oil operations, 15 per cent from chemical (and other) industrial sources, with 17 per cent arising from farming and 19 per cent resulting from sewage discharges. In a report leaked to the UK media in October 1991, it was claimed that rivers in England and Wales had shown a considerable decrease in water quality since 1985 (nett 6 per cent with a maximum of 39 per cent in certain regions). However, these statistics need to be qualified by noting that 11 per cent of the country's waterways, which were seen as being the most polluted in 1985, have shown an improvement in water quality. The implication here is that the largest point source polluters have improved their practices but that the overall trend is continuing downwards, with perhaps the greatest contribution to this trend arising because of government cuts in spending for sewage treatment programmes. The point that needs to be reinforced here is that pollution is a complex multi-faceted problem which covers a range of industrial and business activities, from agriculture to power generation, and is heavily influenced by societal and consumer demands.

Pollution as a Political Issue

Political and corporate concern for environmental quality is not a new concept. Indeed, some of the earliest concern can be traced back to the industrial revolution when a number of writers voiced an awareness of environmental degradation. Within the last forty years there have been numerous expressions of concern over the international dynamics of continued pollution. Whilst many of these objections have been likened to Malthusian fears over population growth, their significance has taken on a new dynamic with the scientific controversy over global warming and ozone depletion. The concerns expressed during the 1960s, represented through the publication of *Limits to Growth*, culminated in the now seminal conference on the environment held in Stockholm in 1972. For many, the Stockholm conference established the legitimacy of environmentalism as a political movement. Despite this early concern about the environment, however, the issue slipped down the political agenda during the 1980s only to re-emerge during the 1990s through the Bergen Conference (1990), the Second World Industry and Environmental Management Conference in Rotterdam (1991) and the 1992 UN Conference on Environment and Development. The obvious question that one needs to address at this juncture is 'Why, after twenty years, has the environmental question not been fully addressed?' The answer lies, in part, in the cyclical nature of policy issues. The oil crises of 1974 and 1979 combined with the onset of a world recession to submerge environmental issues within the international political agenda. It is only with the recognition of the scale, complexity and severity of the issues that public environmental concerns have again emerged as a potent political force. Within this context there has also been a major shift in the driving forces for greater environmental safeguards. Whilst industry has long been seen as the root cause by many environmental groups, there is now a growing recognition that it also has the resources and expertise necessary to solve many of the environmental problems that currently beset our society. The issue has now emerged on to the policy agenda at public, governmental and corporate levels and there is a need for a partnership approach between these groups in order to ensure that the best policy options are followed to ensure environmental improvements.

The treatment of the environment within the academic literature has, in part, reflected the wider subjugation of environmental issues in world politics. Political scientists and international relations academics, for example, were preoccupied with super-power rivalry, Third World issues and domestic political upheaval throughout the 1970s and mid-1980s. The visibility and urgency of these issues served to overshadow the environment as a topic for academic discourse. Consequently, some writers have suggested that the issue has lain dormant at both the local and global levels whilst others have suggested that the complexity and multidisciplinary nature of the problems have conspired to encourage their relative neglect by some academic disciplines. This is not to say that the issues have not been addressed and a quick glance at the literature would suggest that the academic coverage of environmental impacts has been wide and varied. However, almost certainly the more obvious environmentally concerned disciplines, such as geography and business studies, have been notable by their lack of fully fledged involvement. The academic business community in particular has, until very recently, been loath to take the matter seriously. Such neglect of an issue which is central to business is surprising at one level and yet understandable at another. Environmental concerns, like the vexed issue of corporate responsibility, run counter to the dominant, finance-based, business paradigm. As a consequence, we should not be too surprised that business practitioners and academics have shown a certain reluctance to fully address the challenges that these issues present. However, the corollary to this view is that the relationship between business and the environment lies at the heart of the wider environmental problem and that a feeling of being uncomfortable with the issues should not be a sufficient justification for their neglect. In its broadest sense, it is 'business,' through the extraction, production and consumption process, which is responsible for a considerable amount of environmental degradation and any attempts at changing the behaviour of corporations will require a fundamental shift in the values and behaviour of managers. However, the caveat here is that society must also change its buying behaviour to accommodate the demands of the new environmentalism. It would seem churlish of society to demand that industry cleans up its act without making corresponding shifts in its own behaviour. Whilst the impact of individual behavioural change may seem trivial compared to that of a corporate body, the collective impact of such changes can be considerable in terms of environmental quality. The success of the Body Shop has illustrated that there is a demand from society for environmentally friendly products and, if the constituency of the green consumer can be widened, then more companies will see the market opportunities of being green and will shift the focus of their manufacturing accordingly. However, in the short term, by far the greatest improvements in environmental quality can undoubtedly be achieved by changing the behaviour of those corporations who are large point-source polluters.

Historical Questions

1. Meadows' *Limits to Growth*, published after the Stockholm Conference of 1972, is considered to be the first charter of environmental issues in the history of Western industrialism. Smith's essay, written two decades later, is a new landmark in environmental discourse because he argues that environmental issues must become an integral part of business strategy to respond to what he calls "the New Environmentalism" of the 1980s. What new audiences does Smith engage in his discussion that Meadows does not? What might be some of the implications of bringing in these new audiences to a discussion of environmental issues? In what ways does Smith make a different argument to these audiences for the protection of the environment than Meadows? With close reference to both of their texts, explore whose argument you respond to more and give two or three reasons why.

2. Carefully review the information in Smith's essay about the key historical events of the 1980s. Try to determine how these events might have shaped his position about the roles that industry and consumers must play to address the environmental problems beyond 1993. What additional information can you provide about the social and economic atmosphere of the 1980s that Smith does not include in his essay but that might have further affected his position in the 1990s?

Cultural Questions

1. Both Riggs and Smith regard consumers and industry to be an integral part in the study of the environment, yet their positions differ quite significantly. Develop a symptomatic reading of their differences first by comparing and

contrasting the literal differences between Smith's concept of sustainable growth and Riggs's imperative of economic growth and development. Then, focusing on their language and tone as well as some of their unstated assumptions, explore the underlying reasons why these two industry-oriented writers assign somewhat different responsibilities to the consumer for protecting the environment.

2. Representing the perspective of business managers in the first half of this piece, Smith states that "all human activity results in environmental degradation of some form and, consequently, society has to strike a balance between its material desires and the requirement for a cleaner environment." How might you react if a person in a business that produces consumer goods suggested to members of society who purchase those goods that they curb their desires for material products? With specific reference to his text, explore the assumptions Smith makes both about business and about his audience. Explain whether you feel his position is more dominant or more emergent. Explain why. Do you find his position persuasive?

∽ Assignment Sequence 1: On Changing Perspectives of the Land

The readings in this chapter represent perspectives on early Colonial American land and the process of its colonization since the arrival of European explorers. Whereas the early narratives compiled by Kolodny comment in general terms on the richness and bounty of the early American land, the later works from nineteenth- and twentieth-century writers represent American perspectives and attitudes on the appropriation and use of land just before, during, and after the industrial revolution.

Essay Question

Examine the changes in perspectives on the land in the United States over time. What key issues concerning the land have evolved? What position on the land do you now support? In your view, what goals should Americans now have concerning the land?

∽ Fastwrite 12

Consider how you will organize the various historical perspectives, which can be roughly categorized into three periods: those of the nineteenth century, those at the turn of the twentieth century, and contemporary perspectives. Fastwrite briefly on each of them exploring some of the following questions: What major events occurred? What is the dominant attitude toward the land in each period? How is it linked to the material day-to-day existence of people living in the United States at that time? What attitudes do you consider more emergent in each period? What particular beliefs, assumptions, and physical realities guide them?

Review Questions

A list of suggested questions to review before beginning this essay follows. This list is meant only to suggest review options. You may focus on only a subset of the questions, decide that other questions should be added, or construct your own sequence of questions. We encourage you to choose what you believe is the most appropriate review strategy.

1. Annette Kolodny, Historical Question 1 (page 536)
2. Annette Kolodny, Cultural Question 1 (page 536)
3. John Carbutt, Cultural Question 1 (page 538)
4. Frederick Jackson Turner, Cultural Question (page 544)
5. Theodore Roosevelt, Historical Question 2 (page 555)
6. Cynthia Riggs, Historical Question 1 (page 566)
7. Al Gore, Historical Question 1 (page 581)

You might also review whatever fastwrites you composed while analyzing the individual readings in this chapter. Highlight the key factors—perhaps categorizing them according to economic, political, and social/cultural issues—that contributed to the transformation of the U.S. landscape. Once you have created a systematic account of these factors, analyze your findings to determine your own position among the claims that various of the authors make about the causes of our contemporary environmental problems.

Questions for Further Reflection

1. What economic, social, and natural forces, have shaped the changing U.S. view of the land?

2. What views about land and nature in general seemed dominant among the early European explorers? What other responses and attitudes might these explorers have had from their first experience with a land and society so unlike their own? How did these explorers and their descendants handle this difference as they move across time and space in North America?

3. Which aspects of our contemporary views on land are indicative of an emergent U.S. perspective? Which other aspects are residues of the dominant Euro-American perspectives of the earlier times? Still, what other historically dominant U.S. attitudes of the past remain equally dominant in our contemporary view on land and nature?

∞   Assignment Sequence 2: On the Meanings of Progress and Development

Is it progress to have an oil pipeline in Alaska that funnels oil to the lower forty-eight states? Is it progress to vote against such a project? Is landing on Mars an example of progress? The writers in this chapter use terms such as *progress* and *development* to represent their specific notions of economic growth. To debate what progress and development mean today, how many different perspectives would you need to identify? Which particular perspectives would you include in such a debate? This assignment sequence asks you to grapple with the meanings of these words.

Essay Question

As individuals and as a nation, we can progress in many ways—socially, economically, politically—that affect our environment directly and indirectly. What does progress and development mean in contemporary U.S. culture?

∞   Fastwrite 13

Fastwrite to develop your own definition of *progress*. Describe your concept of progress in detail. For example, what does a progressive community look like? Defend the appropriateness of your definition against some of the other definitions of progress implied in the readings in this chapter. Which of the authors come closest to your concept of a progressive society? How are they similar? Why are their perspectives more valuable than others to you?

Review Questions

A list of suggested questions to review before beginning this essay follows. This list is meant only to suggest review options. You may focus on only a subset of the questions, decide that other questions should be added, or construct your own sequence of questions. We encourage you to choose what you believe is the most appropriate review strategy.

1. Nathanial Currier and James Merritt Ives, Historical Question (page 540)
2. Henry Adams, Historical Question 2 (page 549)
3. Donella Meadows, Historical Question 1 (page 559)
4. Donella Meadows, Cultural Question 1 (page 559)
5. Cynthia Riggs, Cultural Question 1 (page 566)
6. Ted Trainer, Historical Question 1 (page 573)
7. Denis Smith, Cultural Question 1 (page 588)

Questions for Further Reflection

1. How would you categorize the developments that modern science and technology have made possible?

2. How can scientific progress sometimes conflict with human progress? What examples can you list of such conflicts?

3. What notions of progress appeal to you in the futuristic films and readings you are familiar with? Are these notions of progress more or less appealing to you than the current state of progress? Why?

ᗡ

For Further Research

Writen Texts

Baer-Brown, Leslie, and Bob Rhein, ed. *Earth Keepers: A Sourcebook for Environmental Issues and Action.* San Francisco: Mercury, 1995.

Brown, Lester R., Christopher Flavin, and Sandra Postel. *Saving the Planet: How to Shape an Environmentally Sustainable Global Economy.* New York: Norton, 1991.

Brown, Michael H. *The Toxic Cloud: The Poisoning of America's Air.* New York: Harper, 1987.

Byrd, William. "A Journey to the Land of Eden in the Year 1733." *The Prose Works of William Byrd of Westover; Narratives of a Colonial Virginian.* Cambridge: Harvard UP, 1966.

Carson, Rachel. *Silent Spring.* New York: Fawcett, 1962.

Clark, Mary E. *Ariadne's Thread: The Search for New Modes of Thinking.* New York: St. Martin's, 1989.

Columbus, Christopher. *Select Documents Illustrating the Four Voyages of Columbus.* Trans. Cecil Jane. London: Hakluyt Society, 1930.

Dobson, Andrew, ed. *The Green Reader: Essays Toward a Sustainable Society.* San Francisco: Mercury, 1991.

Durning, Alan Thein. *How Much Is Enough?: The Consumer Society and the Future of the Earth.* New York: Norton, 1992.

Kempton, Willett, James S. Boster, and Jennifer A. Hartley. *Environmental Values in American Culture.* Cambridge: MIT P, 1995.

Manes, Christopher. *Green Rage: Radical Environmentalism and the Unmaking of Civilization.* New York: Little Brown, 1990.

McKibben, Bill. *The End of Nature.* New York: Random House, 1989.

Naar, Jon. *Design for a Livable Planet: How You Can Help Clean up the Environment.* New York: Harper, 1990.

Orr, David W. *Ecological Literacy: Education and the Transition to a Postmodern World.* Albany: SUNY P, 1992.

Piacentini, Pablo, ed. *Story Earth: Native Voices on the Environment.* San Francisco: Mercury, 1993.

Saign, Geoffrey C. *Green Essentials: What You Need to Know about the Environment.* San Francisco: Mercury, 1994.

Schumacher, E. F. *Small Is Beautiful: A Study of Economics as if People Mattered.* London: Blond, 1973.

Sharp, Bill, et al. *The New Complete Guide to Environmental Careers.* Washington, DC: Island, 1993.

Shiva, *Staying Alive: Women, Ecology and Development.* London: Zed, 1989.

Turner, Frederick Jackson. *The Frontier in American History.* New York: Holt, 1920.

Videos

All of the following videos are by the Foundation for Global Community, 222 High St., Palo Alto, CA 94301, phone 650-328-7756, fax 650-328-7785.

Art of the Wild. Fourteen writers of prose and poetry discuss how they became interested in the natural world. Baylands Productions, 1996.

Children and Nature: Awakening a Sense of Wonder. Narr. Peter Coyote, incl. Jane Goodall, marine biologist Dr. Sylvia Earle, naturalist and children's guide Lee Cole. Baylands Productions, 1997. Focus is on how children can make meangful connections with the natural world.

Ecopsychology—Restoring the Earth, Healing the Self. Incl. historian Theodore Roszak, clinical psychologist Sarah Conn, and Carl Anthony, president of Earth Island Institute. Baylands Productions, 1995. Ecopsychology is a new science linking psychology and ecology, drawing connections between the state of nature and human consciousness, our mental health, and the health of the planet.

A Sense of Place. Narr. Susan Sarandon, incl. author and bioregionalist Kirkpatrick Sale, biologist John Todd, editor Nancy Jack Todd, Grammy Award-winning musician Paul Winter, and community innovator, Jeff Bercuvitz. Baylands Productions, 1994. Focus is our relationship with the whole living system.

The Unfolding Story. Narr. Mike Farrell., incl. storytellers Thomas Berry, Elisabet Sahtouris, Davis Sizuki, Miriam MacGillis, Audery Shenandoah, E. O. Wilson, and others. Baylands Productions, 1993. Focuses on an interconnected, interdependent universe. Winner of the Silver Award at the Worldfest Houston International Film Festival.

Voices of Change. Vol. I. Incl. educator and artist Miriam MacGillis, bioregionalist and author Kirkpatrick Sale, Director of Schumacker College, England, Satish Kumar. Baylands Productions, 1996.

Voices of Change. Vol II. Incl. evolution biologist E. Sahtouris, cultural historican T. Roszak, author C. Spretnak. Baylands Productions, 1996.

Voices of Change. Vol III. Incl. Pulitzer Prize-winning author Gary Snyder, author and naturalist Terry Tempest Williams, ethnobotanist and natural history writer, Gary Paul Nabhan. Baylands Productions, 1996.

CREDITS

Maya Angelou, "Gi' Me a Penny" (editor's title) from *Singin' and Swingin' and Gettin' Merry Like Christmas* by Maya Angelou. Copyright © 1976 by Maya Angelou. Reprinted by permission of Random House, Inc.

Lucius Apuleius, "Cupid and Psyche" from *Mythology* by Edith Hamilton. Copyright 1942 by Edith Hamilton; Copyright © renewed 1969 by Dorian Fielding Reid and Doris Fielding Reid. By permission of Little, Brown and Company Inc.

Bruno Bettelheim, "Resolution and Restoration in *Beauty and the Beast*" (editors' title) from *The Uses of Enchantment* by Bruno Bettelheim. Copyright © 1975, 1976 by Bruno Bettelheim. Reprinted by permission of Alfred A. Knopf, Inc.

Stanley Booth, "Situation Report: Elvis in Mephis; 1967" from *Rhythm Oil* by Stanley Booth. Copyright © 1991 by Stanley Booth. Reprinted by permission of Pantheon Books, a division of Random House, Inc.

Angela Carter "The Tiger's Bride" from *The Bloody Chamber* by Angela Carter. Copyright © Angela Carter 1979. Reproduced by permission of the Estate of Angela Carter c/o Rogers, Coleridge & White Ltd., 20 Powis Mews, London W11 1JN.

Chellis Clendinning, "What's Good About San Francisco. . . ?" from *Utne Reader* (September/October 1994, no. 65) Reprinted with permission of author.

Edward Cornish, "The Cyber Future." Originally appeared in the January/February 1996 issue of *The Futurist*. Used with permission from the World Future Society, 7910 Woodmont Avenue, Suite 450, Bethesda, Maryland 20814. 301/656-8274; fax 301/951-0394; http://www.wfs.org/wfs.

Richard Dahl, "What's Good About Boston. . . ?" from *Utne Reader* (September/October 1994, no. 65) Reprinted with permission of author.

John Darnton, "Skeletal Models Create Furor over British *Vogue*" from *The New York Times* (June 3, 1996). Copyright © 1996 by the New York Times Company. Reprinted by permission.

Giorgio De Santillana, "Galileo's Crime" (editors' title) excerpts from *The Crime of Galileo* by Giorgio De Santillana. Used with permission from The University of Chicago Press.

John Dewey, "Between Traditional and Progressive Education" (editors' title) from *Experience and Education* by John Dewey. Copyright © 1938. Kappa Delta Pi, an International Honor Society in Education.

J. C. Flugel, "The Great Masculine Renunciation" (editor's title, originally from *The Psychology of Clothes)* Copyright © 1930. Reprinted with permission from the Estate of J. C. Flugel and Hogarth Press.

Jonathan Franzen, "Why We Need Cities" (editors' title, original title "First City: Why America Should Have More New Yorks"). Copyright © 1996 by Jonathan Frazen, originally published in the *New Yorker.*

Marjorie Garber, "Pushing Borderlines: Gender Crossover" (editors' title, excerpted from *Vice Versa: Bisexuality and the Eroticism of Everyday Life).* Reprinted with the permission of Simon & Schuster from *Vice Versa* by Marjorie Garber. Copyright © 1995 by Marjorie Garber.

Richard Goldstein, "The Gay Family." Excerpted from an article that originally ran in the *Village Voice* (July 1, 1986). Reprinted with permission.

Ellen Ryan. "What's Good About St. Paul. . . ?" from *Utne Reader* (September/October 1994, no. 65) Reprinted with permission of author.

Myra Sadker and David Sadker, "Missing in Interaction." Reprinted with the permission of Scribner, a Division of Simon & Schuster from *Failing at Fairness: How America's Schools Cheat Girls* by Myra and David Sadker. Copyright © 1994 by Myra Sadker and David Sadker.

Theodore R. Sizer, "What High School is" from *Horace's Compromise* by Theodore R. Sizer. Copyright © 1984 by Theodore R. Sizer. Reprinted by permission of Houghton Mifflin Co. All rights reserved.

Peter Stearns, "Reinventing the Family" (editors' title) from *Be A Man! Males In Modern Society* second edition by Peter N. Stearns (New York: Holmes & Meier, 1979). Copyright © 1990 by Holmes & Meier Publishers, Inc. Reproduced with the permission of the publisher.

Denis Smith, "Business and the Environment" from *Business and the Environment: Implications of the New Environmentalism* by Denis Smith. Copyright © 1993 by Denis Smith. Reprinted with permission of St. Martin's Press, Incorporated.

Ted Trainer, "From Abandon Affluence!" Copyright © 1985 by Zed Books Ltd. Reprinted with permission by Zed Books Ltd.

Sherry Turkle, "Natural and Artificial Intelligence." (editors' title) Reprinted with the permission of Simon & Schuster from *Life on the Screen* by Sherry Turkle. Copyright © 1995 by Sherry Turkle.

Adam Walinsky, "Cities Under Assault" Copyright © 1995 by Adam Walinsky, first published in the *Atlantic Monthly*.

Marina Warner, "Go! Be a Beast" excerpt from "Go! Be a Beast" from *From the Beast to the Blonde* by Marina Warner. Copyright © 1994 by Marina Warner. Reprinted by permission of Farrar, Straus & Giroux, Inc.

Cornel West, "Waiting" (editors' title) from *Race Matters* by Cornel West. Copyright © 1993 by Cornel West. Reprinted by permission of Beacon Press, Boston.

Kalamu ya Salaam, "What's Good About New Orleans. . . ?" from *Utne Reader* (September/October 1994, no. 65) Reprinted with permission of author.

Jack Zipes, "*Beauty and the Beast*: A Lesson in Submission" (editors' title). Copyright © 1994, from *Fairy Tale As Myth/Myth As Fairy Tale* by Jack Zipes. Reprinted with permission of the University Press of Kentucky.

Photo Credits

Figure 2.1: Andrew Waller; Figure 2.2: Corbis-Bettmann; Figure 2.3: Corbis-Bettmann; Figure 2.5: The Granger Collection, New York; Figure 2.6: Corbis-Bettmann; Figure 2.7: Regan Cameron © British Vogue/The Condé Nast Publications Ltd.; Figure 2.8: J. Kirk Condyles/Impact Visuals; Figure 3.1: © Art Rogers/Pt. Reyes; Figure 3.2: Corbis-Bettmann; Figure 3.3: Tom McKitterick/Impact Visuals; Figure 4.1: © Walt Disney Co./Photofest; Figure 4.2: Courtesy of Special Collections and Rare Book Department, University of Minnesota Libraries; Figure 4.3: The Arthur Rackham illustration has been reproduced with kind permission of his family; Figure 4.4: Illustration by Diane Goode; Figure 4.5: Photofest; Figure 5.1: Will Faller; Figure 5.2: Will Hart; Figure 6.1: Hatch Show Print/Country Music Foundation; Figure 6.2: MICHAEL OCHS ARCHIVES/Venice, CA; Figure 6.3: Chuck Fishman/Woodfin Camp & Associates; Figure 6.4: Mark Humphrey/AP/Wide World Photos; Figure 6.5: Copyright, 1997, *The Commercial Appeal*, Memphis, TN; Figure 7.1: North Wind Picture Archives; Figure 7.2: The Granger Collection, New York; Figure 7.3: © 1999 Artist Rights Society (ARS), New York / ADAGP, Paris / FLC; Figure 9.1: Corbis-Bettmann; Figure 9.2: The Granger Collection, New York.

INDEX

599